OF COURTIERS & KINGS

CONSTITUTIONALISM AND DEMOCRACY

Gregg Ivers and Kevin T. McGuire, Editors

OF
COURTIERS
& KINGS

*More Stories of Supreme Court
Law Clerks and Their Justices*

Edited by Todd C. Peppers and Clare Cushman

University of Virginia Press | Charlottesville and London

University of Virginia Press

© 2015 by the Rector and Visitors of the University of Virginia

All rights reserved

Printed in the United States of America on acid-free paper

First published 2015

9 8 7 6 5 4 3 2 1

Library of Congress Cataloging-in-Publication Data

Of courtiers and kings : more stories of Supreme Court law clerks and their justices /
edited by Todd C. Peppers and Clare Cushman.

pages cm. — (Constitutionalism and Democracy)

Includes bibliographical references and index.

ISBN 978-0-8139-3726-7 (cloth : alk. paper) — ISBN 978-0-8139-3727-4 (ebook)

1. United States. Supreme Court—History—20th century. 2. Law clerks—United
States—Biography. I. Peppers, Todd C., editor. II. Cushman, Clare, editor.

KF8742.O34 2015

347.73'26—dc23

2015017198

CONTENTS

Illustrations follow page 134

JUSTICE JOHN PAUL STEVENS (RET.)

Foreword

The essays in this volume contain a wealth of information about changes in two important institutions—the Supreme Court and the role of law clerks in its work. Having participated in that work both as a clerk and later as a justice, I particularly enjoyed the additional insights provided by these essays. They tell us more about what has happened in the past than about the present Court, but are nonetheless of great interest. They illuminate both important changes that have occurred over the years and important aspects of the work of a justice that have not really changed at all since the Court began its work.

Before there were any clerks, the justices made their decisions on the basis of the arguments advanced by the parties, their study of the facts of the case, their own research and deliberation, and their discussions among themselves. That remains true today, even though clerks now provide important help with research, have an opportunity to discuss the merits of cases with their bosses, and play an increasingly important role in the process of explaining those decisions after they have been made. The fact that clerks now provide important assistance to their justices really has little impact on the most important work that justices do—deciding cases. It has, however, made it more difficult for litigants to persuade the Court to grant certiorari, and it has made many opinions longer than necessary. They sometimes read more like law review essays than attempts to explain the Court's reasons for making a particular decision.

The two most notable changes that occurred during the interval between my clerkship and my job as the employer of clerks are the increase in the number of clerks and the increase in their postclerkship compensation. Instead of one or two clerks in each associate justice's chambers as in October term 1947, four clerks now handle the increased mountain of cert petitions and the decreased volume of argued cases. And instead of taking a pay cut when clerks enter private practice—as my colleagues and I did when we left government employment at the end of June 1948—I understand that signing bonuses that exceed a justice's salary are now common.

While we may have been underpaid, I still remember my clerkship as by far the best job available to a law school graduate, not merely because of the privilege of working at the Court under the supervision of a lovable and inspiring boss but also because of the friendship of a remarkable bunch of co-clerks. I remember liking and admiring every one of them. I was particularly fortunate to share Justice Rutledge's chambers with Stan Temko, who had by far the best sense of humor in the group as well as an extraordinary ability to translate complexity into simplicity.

Stan and I both particularly enjoyed our friendship with Jim Marsh, the Jackson clerk described in John Barrett's essay. I am still indebted to Jim for providing me with a treasured souvenir that is still on display in my chambers. He was an avid baseball fan who filled in scorecards for World Series games as he listened to them on the radio. When he learned that I had witnessed Babe Ruth's famous "called shot" home run in Wrigley Field in 1932, he gave me his treasured copy of the scorecard that he had prepared at the time. Before framing and hanging the card on my wall, I corrected his misidentification of the Cubs' starting pitcher, but I continue to admire the accuracy of his record of a historic occasion.

Readers of these essays will, I trust, gain some insights into why a clerkship at the Court is such a fabulous job.

OF COURTIERS & KINGS

Introduction

In the popular imagination of law students, being hired to clerk at the Supreme Court is something like winning Willy Wonka's golden ticket. In exchange for working round-the-clock hours for one year, young clerks get to help the justices select which cases to take up for review, research important issues of constitutional law, prepare the first draft of opinions, act as sounding boards, and serve as ambassadors to clerks in other chambers. From their vantage point inside the walls of the Marble Palace, these young men and woman have the rare opportunity to observe the personalities who occupy the Supreme Court bench as well as to actively participate in the resolution of critical questions of constitutional law and social policy. And if learning at the proverbial knee of our country's most prominent jurists is not a sufficient incentive to seek a clerkship, the clerks become part of a lifetime network that coalesces around their individual justice. After a year of exhausting work, clerks leave the Supreme Court faced with a glittering array of professional opportunities and financial windfalls from which to select. Indeed, the salaries and signing bonuses awaiting them at top law firms outweigh those earned by the justices themselves.

The "golden age" of the law clerk, however, did not always exist. The men who clerked in the last decades of the nineteenth century and the first decades of the twentieth were usually either older professional stenographers who served for years or decades at the Court, or younger men who juggled their clerkship duties with law school studies at night (the law clerks to Horace Gray and Oliver Wendell Holmes Jr. were the exceptions to this rule). They worked long hours for low pay and assumed tedious duties that were mainly secretarial in nature—including taking dictation, typing up opinions, cutting and pasting revisions, and performing nonjudicial tasks (such as paying bills and balancing checkbooks) for their justices. None of these law clerks felt as if they had grabbed the proverbial brass ring; they were simply working at a job that most of the clerks hoped would lead to a job as an attorney in the private or public sector as soon as possible. As late as 1952, Abner Mikva (then clerking for Sherman Minton) found that while a Supreme Court clerkship may have been an excellent credential in Washington, D.C., job offers in his hometown of Chicago were not plentiful, and he was often asked why he had "wasted" a year at the Supreme Court.

How a Supreme Court clerkship has evolved in terms of professional status is one of several themes running through the essays. In selecting articles for this project, we had two goals in mind. First, we wanted the authors to take the reader inside the judicial chambers for a peek at specific justices, their personalities and work habits, and their professional and personal relationships with their clerks. Our second goal was to arrange the essays in chronological order so that the reader could see how the customs and norms that compose the "clerkship institution" have changed over time. Such changes include the demographic and educational backgrounds of the clerks, the methods of selecting law clerks (with the attendant concerns about the diversity of the law clerk corps), the rise of the "feeder court" judge in the selection process, the length of their service as law clerks, the number of justices for whom they work, the change from working inside a justice's home to his or her chambers in the Supreme Court, the number of clerks and other staff allocated to each justice, their working hours, the job duties assigned to the clerks, the creation of a law clerk code of confidentiality, the strengthening and then weakening of the social bonds between the justices and their clerks, the interaction of clerks with other chambers, the increasing concerns about law clerk influence, and the perceived prestige of the financial and professional rewards of clerking at the Court.

First and foremost, the essays contained in *Courtiers and Kings* introduce us to some of the more fascinating men and women who have sat on the Supreme Court. They include such legendary figures as the jovial William Howard Taft, who achieved his lifelong dream of sitting on the Supreme Court; James Clark McReynolds, the most dyspeptic of all justices to sit on the bench; and Robert H. Jackson, who took a leap of faith on a law clerk who did not have a college diploma. We will learn that the tennis-playing Hugo Black adopted the role of surrogate parent to his law clerks, lecturing them on their personal habits and meddling in their romantic affairs; that Sherman Minton was the last justice to use a spittoon; and that Harold Burton did not smoke, drink, or swear. We will be introduced to the genial "Uncle" Stanley Reed, the Stetson-wearing Tom Clark, the poker-playing Chief Justice Fred Vinson, the courtly John Marshall Harlan II, the White House–insider Abe Fortas, the imperious Warren Burger, and the soft-spoken Lewis F. Powell. We will have a front-row seat to the deft coalition building of the master politician Earl Warren, the cooking skills of Chief Justice Burger, and future chief justice William H. Rehnquist's love of meteorology, low-stakes betting, and charades. And, finally, we will see the modern Supreme Court at work through essays on the trailblazing Sandra Day

O'Connor, who took her clerks fishing and white-water rafting, the bow-tie wearing John Paul Stevens, and the reclusive and independent David Souter.

During our insider tour of the hallways and chambers of the Supreme Court, we also meet other legendary staffers who helped build the institution. They include Supreme Court messengers, such as Harry Parker, the long-suffering aide to Justice McReynolds who helped a generation of law clerks survive clerking for the irascible justice, and Gerald Ross, who donned a white jacket while serving Justice Reed's lunch but passed out copies of *The Autobiography of Malcolm X* to the justice's law clerks. In the home office of Chief Justice Taft, we will encounter William Mischler—whose tenure as Taft's private secretary stretched from the War Department to the White House to the Supreme Court. A short, timid man who sought the spotlight, Mischler made sure that the rotating elite law clerks appreciated his insider status with the chief justice. As we move forward in time, we will meet other formidable secretaries—including Margaret McHugh, secretary to both Chief Justices Vinson and Warren who was given the nickname "Chief Justice McHugh" by the clerks, and the redoubtable Ethel McCall, who once refused to type an opinion drafted by Justice John Marshall Harlan because she believed it to be chauvinistic.

Besides exposing the working life inside chambers, the essays reveal the changing selection and hiring practices at the Supreme Court. During the early decades of the clerkship institution, prospective law clerks simply mailed their résumés to specific justices, or directly to the clerk of court to see if there was a vacancy with any of the nine. As more and more law clerks were drawn from elite law schools, the justices began relying on a handful of trusted law school professors to recruit their best students (who often did not meet their individual justices until after the start of the term). Today, thousands of clerkship applications pour into the Supreme Court—and it is considered bad form not to apply to all nine justices. Some of the applications are vetted by committees made up of former clerks, others by the justices and their staffs. While there are no formal, written requirements to be a law clerk, we see in the essays that de facto norms have slowly emerged: attendance at a top-ten law school, an editorial position on the law review, letters of recommendation from esteemed law professors (often themselves former clerks), and a clerkship with a prominent federal appeals court judge. Prior clerkship experience with a lower court judge was rare in the 1960s, but had become de rigueur by the 1980s. And, finally, in the last few years more and more law clerks are working at top law firms before clerking at the Court.

Court observers have suggested that a law clerk's political ideology has become an unspoken but important factor in the selection process.[1] At least one current member of the Supreme Court confirms that he does consider an applicant's policy positions. "I won't hire clerks who have profound disagreements with me," Justice Clarence Thomas once publicly observed. "It's like trying to train a pig. It wastes your time, and it aggravates the pig."[2] Some social scientists confirm that the justices employ ideological litmus tests when picking clerks.[3] Yet none of the former law clerks who have contributed essays in this book assert that their political ideology was relevant to the selection process. In fact, essayist Craig Bradley writes that he was not asked about his views when interviewing with then–associate justice William H. Rehnquist (although the justice did ask him "if I was aware of his political beliefs and felt that I could work with him") in 1975. Similarly, Rebecca Hurley notes that Chief Justice Warren Burger imposed no "litmus test" upon candidates for positions as his law clerk, and hired many "who considered themselves more 'liberal' than he."

Academic, racial, and social diversity is one aspect of the hiring process that has been slow to change over time. It is rare that the justices look beyond a handful of law schools, although Mimi Clark Gronlund, daughter of former justice Clark, writes that her father purposely looked to law schools traditionally not represented in the hiring process in order to give their students the opportunity to clerk at the Supreme Court. While the first female law clerk— Lucile Lomen—and the first black law clerk—William T. Coleman Jr.—were both hired in the 1940s, in subsequent decades the Supreme Court was slow to embrace racial and gender diversity in the law clerk corps. It would not be until the 1960s that the Supreme Court would see another female law clerk (Margaret Corcoran) or another black law clerk (Tyrone Brown) work at the Court, and the female and minority clerks to follow were conscious of the pressure to prove that they belonged. Essayist Mary Mikva, former law clerk to William J. Brennan, writes that, as the justice's second female law clerk, she "felt a burden to perform well so as to open the door for more female clerks."

The evolving hiring and employment practices are also reflected in the number of clerks the justices hire as well as the tenure of the clerkships. As essayists Barry Cushman and Clare Cushman reveal, many justices in the early decades of the twentieth century only hired a single clerk (even when they had authorization to hire both a law clerk and a "stenographic clerk") and expected that clerk to stay in the position for years—if not decades. And some of these clerks from this time period, such as John E. Hoover and S. Edward Widdifield, worked for as many as five justices, often being inherited by an incoming justice when an older one retired. By the 1940s, the practice of clerking for multiple years had mostly been replaced with a one-year, rotating clerkship model, with the stenographic clerk position having become a permanent secretarial job staffed by a woman. But as late as the 1950s, some justices were still keeping a clerk on for more than one term. In the 1970s, Potter Stewart took his clerks for two-year staggered terms, hiring only one new clerk per year to ensure continuity.

Until the 1940s, each justice had huge discretion in hiring practices, including setting each clerk's salary within the budgeted range (and sometimes supplementing with pay out of his own pocket to sweeten the deal). They also determined the exact beginning and ending clerkship dates, down to the day and month. Moreover, the line between leaving the clerkship and starting a new job was fuzzier, as we will learn when we meet former Taft law clerk Leighton Homer Surbeck and former McReynolds law clerk Milton S. Musser—both of whom completed their clerkships while simultaneously working in their new law firms. By the 1940s, the clerkship job became regularized, and clerks were systematically kept on for a whole year—August to August—and given a month of accrued leave.

The number of law clerks allocated to the chief justice and the associate justices has grown over time to accommodate a rising workload. While once a single clerk (sometimes plus a stenographic clerk) worked for a single justice, the associate justices were routinely hiring two law clerks per chamber by 1947, three per chamber by 1970, and four per chamber by 1974.[4] The chief justices have often carried additional law clerks, either through formal authorization or by availing themselves of the underutilized talents of clerks working for retired justices (and in at least one instance, a sitting one—George Sutherland). Arguably, the increasing number of clerks has impacted the clerkship institution in a number of different ways. A complete reading of the essays raises the question of whether it is possible for a justice to have the same close professional and personal relationship with a chamber full of law clerks, and, more important, whether the number of law clerks is responsible for the increased delegation of job duties. For example, Victor Brudney reveals that when Wiley Rutledge only had one clerk, "he was at liberty, one half hour before a decision was to be announced, to go into the justice's office and plead again that he change his vote." But Brudney notes that when a second clerk was added, the relationship changed and became more hierarchical, and Rutledge did not ask for clerks' input on draft opinions.[5] While the number of cases adjudicated each term rose steadily until the 1980s (roughly 150) and then receded significantly (now roughly 75), the number of appeals filed with the Court, as well as the number of working hours for the law clerks, has continued its upward trajectory. Abner Mikva reports that Sherman Minton's clerks came in a half an hour before he did (10:00 a.m.) and left a half an hour after the justice did (5:00 p.m.), and seldom worked Saturdays or evenings. They even managed a few rounds of morning golf before arriving in chambers. While clerks in his era saw their clerkship as "a break before they started their legal careers in earnest," by the

1980s the expectation was for clerks to work seven days a week and twelve- to fifteen-hour days. Mary Mikva and her co-clerks were thankful that the Court's computer system shut down on Sunday evening, forcing them to take a break.

The increasing responsibilities of law clerks is another theme running through the essays. While historically job duties varied across chambers, the modern law clerk is involved in all aspects of chamber life. One of the justices' main duties is disposing of the thousands of discretionary appeals (called "petitions for writ of certiorari") filed before the Supreme Court. It was not until the 1940s that clerks were routinely tasked with summarizing cert petitions. Louis D. Brandeis believed that law clerks should not be involved in the review of these appeals (former Brandeis law clerk Dean Acheson explained that the justice wanted to read the appeals "with a judicial mind unscratched by the scribbling of clerks"[6]), but even in his time he was an anomaly. Today all Supreme Court justices require their clerks to write "cert memos" summarizing the issues on appeal as well as recommending whether the justices should grant or deny the cert petition. For eight of the nine justices on the current Supreme Court, the cert petitions are divided among their law clerks, and the written memos are combined into a "pool" for the eight justices to review; Justice Alito's chambers is not part of this pool, and his clerks prepare cert memos for all pending appeals.[7] These essays give several valuable perspectives on the rationale for the introduction of the cert pool in 1973, and the reasons why certain justices have declined to participate in it.

The essays also demonstrate that by the 1970s many justices began asking their clerks to prepare them for oral argument through the drafting of a bench memorandum, a document that summarizes the salient case facts, the dispositive legal issues, the arguments contained in the parties' briefs as well as the amicus curiae briefs filed by nonparties, and also provides questions to ask during oral argument and a suggested disposition of the case. Writing about his clerkship with Chief Justice Earl Warren, essayist Earl Dudley Jr. notes that "a bench memo in a case where cert had been granted was a much more elaborate affair [than a cert memo]. We would outline the parties' arguments in considerable detail and offer our own analysis of those arguments and of the Court's precedents in the area. It was harder here to separate our legal analysis from our opinions, but we tried to confine the latter to a section at the end, longer than the final section of a cert memo, where we would spell out our views in somewhat greater detail." Rebecca Hurley's essay reveals that when Chief Justice Burger assigned a clerk to write a bench memo, the clerk was expected to stay with that particular case until the end.

The justices have followed a similar pattern in regard to the delegation of opinion writing. Before 1940, no justice even considered allowing a clerk to draft an opinion, except as a purely academic exercise—as a way of teaching his clerk the law. Justices like Robert H. Jackson or Sherman Minton continued to prepare the first drafts of opinions, but others began assigning clerks to work on first drafts, often based on the bench memos they prepared to brief the justice on a case before oral argument. Stanley F. Reed initially wrote his own first drafts, but as workload pressures increased the justices delegated more to their clerks. Conversely, Tom C. Clark started off delegating, but then took over the drafting of opinions and would have his clerks critique his drafts. But even justices who completely delegated drafting opinions to their clerks kept control of the decision-making process. For example, Earl Dudley explains that "the fact that [Warren] did not put the words on paper, however, did not mean that the opinions were not ultimately the Chief's product. Before a law clerk began work on an opinion draft, the chief justice would have a lengthy conversation with the clerk, in which he made clear what he wanted the opinion to say and what arguments he found persuasive. Once the law clerk had produced a draft with which he was happy and that had passed the inspection of the other clerks in chambers, it would be submitted to the chief justice. After he had read it carefully, the Chief would call the law clerk into his office and go over the opinion literally word by word, reading it aloud to the clerk, including the footnotes."

By the time of the Warren Court era, most justices were having their clerks write preliminary drafts, or would ask them to research and draft a particular aspect of the opinion. One clerk notes that Potter Stewart "would sometimes write a draft and ask for checking and editing; or he would give detailed guidance orally and ask for a clerk draft based on his guidance; or he would give pretty free rein for the clerk to do a first draft, which he would review carefully and thoughtfully." Craig Bradley, William H. Rehnquist's first clerk, writes that clerks in his chambers wrote the initial draft of opinions and "used an 'NFL draft' system choosing the most desirable cases first and the less desirable (for example, tax cases) last." The only justice who has continued to consistently write his own opinion drafts in the last four decades is the recently retired justice John Paul Stevens. In her essay, Nancy Marder explains that the justice "wrote his own first drafts because he believed that the writing process helped him to understand the case. If an opinion was proving difficult to write, it might signal that he should reexamine his view of the case." In writing his own first drafts, Stevens has said that he was emulating Justice Rutledge, whom he clerked for in October term 1947.

Related to the question of law clerks drafting opinions is the question of influence, a broad term that can encompass various types of stylistic (word choice, sentence structure, grammar) and substantive (serving as a sounding board, helping the justice craft an opinion, assisting in the decision of how to vote) influence. The most prevalent type of influence discussed is the role of law clerk as a sounding board or intellectual sparring partner, practices followed by such justices as Harold Burton, John Marshall Harlan, William H. Rehnquist, David Souter, and Potter Stewart (whose debating sessions with his law clerks prior to conference were nicknamed "Thursday Night Fights"). Interestingly, while Abe Fortas had his clerks write drafts of opinions, he did not use his clerks as sounding boards.

Clerks in all eras and for all justices are careful to point out that the justices do not delegate the decision-making process to their law clerks, although the media perennially likes to question whether too much responsibility is being placed on the shoulders of recently graduated law students. Almost all authors in this book, however, dismiss the idea that they wielded substantive influence. Former law clerk Dudley writes that "I was never really sure that the chief justice paid much attention to the recommendations that we made in either our cert memos or bench memos," a sentiment echoed by former Souter law clerk Kermit Roosevelt III: "I have no doubt that Justice Souter would have changed his position had a clerk convinced him that his initial views were wrong, but I am also quite sure that such a thing never happened." And contributor Mimi Clark Gronlund recounts a revealing episode where Justice Clark's law clerks tried, but failed, to get the justice to vote to overturn an obscenity conviction, further evidence that the justice kept his own counsel.

However, these pages do contain three examples of significant clerk influence—probably exceptions that prove the rule. In his essay on Justice John Marshall Harlan, former Harlan law clerk Norman Dorsen writes that "Harlan was famously open-minded and was willing to listen to his clerks' views even when he began with a pretty fixed opinion." As evidence of this open-mindedness, Dorsen recalls the time that an influential memorandum drafted by Harlan clerk Thomas Krattenmaker caused the justice to change his vote in the famous First Amendment case *Cohen v. California*. This episode was at the core of HBO's 2013 movie *Muhammad Ali's Greatest Fight*, which, while excellent, may unwittingly give a wide television audience the wrong impression that clerk influence is widespread. Finally, Craig Bradley recounts a single instance when he convinced then-justice Rehnquist to switch from joining a concurring opinion written by Justice Powell to a majority opinion written by Justice Brennan.

Of more significance, former Vinson law clerk Arthur Seder shares a story in which he convinced not only Chief Justice Vinson but also the justices who had joined Vinson that they needed to change their votes in what Seder characterizes as a "commercial case of limited importance." However, scholars have pointed to Chief Justice Vinson as an example of a justice who overly relied on his law clerks, adding that Vinson wrote opinions "with his hands in his pockets."[8] In short, we must be very cautious in drawing conclusions about influence based on the practices of one justice.

Another theme explored in these essays is how much clerks from different chambers communicate with each other. Since the 1940s, clerks have eaten lunch together in a private room (or, since 1986, a soundproof glass room in the cafeteria), and have discussed cases among themselves in confidentiality. Indeed, John D. Fassett recalls that he knew where all eighteen clerks in October term 1953 stood ideologically on all the major issues. This deep level of familiarity diminished as the clerks corps grew, but clerks continued to make an effort to forge a strong social bond each term. Indeed, Renée Lettow Lerner (Kennedy, October term 1996) and Kristen Silverberg (Thomas, October term 1999) report that in the late 1990s, "Chambers took turns hosting happy hour in the courtyards for the other clerks, and several generous clerks organized parties for all clerks, at their respective homes" and that "relations among the clerks . . . were good, with little friction and plenty of fellowship."

The question of whether clerks were encouraged to network for their respective justices, serving as ambassadors to clerks in other chambers, is another theme. Hurley reports that under Burger, "the Chief's clerks worked most closely with the law clerks of justices who were joining the Chief in an opinion or hoping to secure his joinder in one of theirs, as the language of such opinions was carefully crafted and refined to accommodate the nuances of each of their views. For that reason, we naturally saw a great deal of our colleagues in the chambers of Justices O'Connor, Powell, and Rehnquist." However, Kermit Roosevelt III writes that David Souter "placed no restrictions on our contacts with other chambers, knowing, I expect, that talking about cases with fellow clerks was one of the most fun parts of the job and also one of the parts least likely to have any effect on the Court's actual decisions."

Finally, we encourage readers to pay attention to how the personal bonds between justices and their clerks have changed as the number of law clerks has grown, the job duties assigned to those clerks have increased, and the rules surrounding the clerkship institution have become more formalized across chambers. To that end, these essays track the various social rituals between justices and their clerks—be it an annual cocktail party or formal dinner, casual dinners at the justice's home, an invitation to Thanksgiving dinner (Tom C. Clark), brown-bag lunches or tea parties in chambers, or social engagements with justices in other chambers. Postclerkship relationships and the reunion rituals that are unique to each justice are also featured. While modern Supreme Court justices continue to socialize with their clerks and serve as mentors, it is clear that the intimate and lifelong bonds that were once a hallmark of the clerkship institution are diminishing as the nature of the job evolves.

Some Court-watchers fret that the dizzyingly high status of a Supreme Court clerkship, and the ensuing lucrative earning power, has changed the nature of the job and altered the relationship between justice and clerk. In these pages

Porter Wilkinson, an October term 2008 clerk to Chief Justice John Roberts, worries that "the lionizing of contemporary law clerks can make them forget they are serving the institution." It is indeed much harder for clerks nowadays to be humble, particularly in comparison to the Fuller and White Court "private secretaries" or to the clerks who were demeaned by the irascible Justice McReynolds. But the ideal of a Supreme Court clerkship as purely public service never existed. In its first half-century, the clerkship was seen as a way for young law students or law graduates to gain a toehold on the bottom rung of the legal employment ladder, be it in a law firm or in a government agency. Now it has become a way for them to vault to the top of that ladder. It has always been about professional advancement, but with a side element of public service and a heaping dose of respect for the Supreme Court and the men and women who have served on it.

Of greater concern is the length of the résumés of clerks at the time of hiring. Experience as a clerk to a lower court judge became the norm in the 1970s, but now some clerks are being hired who have already worked as an attorney in private practice or for the government, or have served in the military. While some practical knowledge may be beneficial, we wonder if the relationship between clerk and justice will change if it is no longer the clerk's first significant professional work experience. As Porter Wilkinson puts it: "The intergenerational exchange between those near the end of a long and distinguished career and those at the very beginning of a promising path in law is a special thing. It is true that this traditional model requires the justices to educate clerks for legal practice rather than vice versa. But the distinctive value of a clerkship is that of an apprenticeship. And if we clerks arrive at the Court in a pristine state, that only enhances our eagerness to perform at the highest level and it only deepens our affections for our first mentors over the years." Looking back at the changing ways that the justices have staffed their chambers in the last century and a quarter, however, we have faith that the justices know best how to operate in the most efficient and effective manner. As Court-watchers, we can merely observe as institutional norms change and the clerkship function at the Supreme Court continues to evolve.

Notes

1. Adam Liptak, "A Sign of Court's Polarization: Choice of Clerks," *New York Times*, September 6, 2010.

2. David G. Savage, "Clarence Thomas Is His Own Man," *Los Angeles Times*, July 3, 2011.

3. Corey Ditslear and Lawrence Baum, "Selection of Law Clerks and Polarization in the U.S. Supreme Court," *Journal of Politics* 63, no. 3 (August 2001): 869–85.

4. Artemus Ward and David Weiden, *Sorcerers' Apprentices: 100 Years of Law Clerks at the United States Supreme Court* (New York: University of New York Press, 2006), 36–45.

5. Victor Brudney and Richard F. Wolfson, "Mr. Justice Rutledge—Law Clerks' Reflections," *Indiana Law Journal* 25, no. 4 (1950): 456.

6. Todd C. Peppers, "Isaiah and His Young Disciples: Justice Louis Brandeis and His Law Clerks," in *In Chambers: Stories of Supreme Court Law Clerks and Their Justices,* edited by Todd C. Peppers and Artemus Ward (Charlottesville: University of Virginia Press, 2012), 73.

7. Adam Liptak, "A Second Justice Opts Out of a Long-Time Custom: The 'Cert. Pool,'" *New York Times,* September 25, 2008.

8. Kermit Hall, ed., *The Oxford Companion to the Supreme Court of the United States,* 2nd ed. (New York: Oxford University Press, 2005), 708.

I The Early Days of the Clerkship Institution

CLARE CUSHMAN

The "Lost" Clerks of the White Court Era

In 1912, Justice Willis Van Devanter received a letter from a former student seeking employment. Like other justices, he regularly fielded queries from applicants asking to be his "private secretary":

> I am a competent stenographer and typewriter; have had five years experience in active practice, largely before local courts and the Interstate Commerce Commission. In addition I have lectured and taught constitutional, corporation, and railroad law in a local law school for the same length of time. My degrees are L.L.B., L.L.M., M. Dip., and D.C.L.—all conferred by the George Washington University.... When a student in the undergraduate department of the law school of the University (then Columbian) I sat under you in Equity Jurisprudence, and hence, am taking the liberty of addressing this letter to you.[1]

As impressive as these credentials were, Van Devanter turned him down. He had already hired another former student, Frederick H. Barclay, who had the advantage of being from the justice's home state of Wyoming.

Why would someone with several advanced degrees and experience both teaching and practicing law want to apply to be a stenographic clerk, albeit for a Supreme Court justice? After all, in that era the job entailed taking dictation in shorthand and then transcribing the words on a typewriter, cutting and pasting revisions, rushing finished opinions to the printing house downtown, performing personal errands, and paying bills. "Most of the Justices had secretaries who were lawyers," wrote Justice Charles Evans Hughes of his time on the White Court, "but these spent the greater part of their time on stenographic work and typewriting correspondence, memoranda and opinions."[2] One Court-watcher said their purpose was "to relieve their superiors of much of the drudgery that is involved in conning over the briefs and records that are submitted in every case."[3] Perhaps most degrading was Justice David J. Brewer's characterization of a Supreme Court stenographer in 1905 as "simply a typewriter, a fountain pen, used by the judge to facilitate his work."[4] Moreover, each clerk toiled alone in his justice's home and did not benefit from the camaraderie and excitement of being part of the Supreme Court as an institution.

This query letter thus highlights the paradox of the early clerkship experience. While these clerks were highly educated, hardworking, and ambitious, their jobs were clerical, were dull, and required little brainwork. In terms of substance, they contributed little to the business of the Court. They are variously referred to as "career stenographers" or "private secretaries," and historians have expressed little interest in them. Except for those who clerked for justices who have been the subject of exhaustive biographies, or those who left behind letters or memoirs about their clerkships, we know almost nothing about them. Yet the competitive nature of the selection process hints that these men were accomplished and considered a stint as a legal secretary to a justice, however menial, a stepping-stone to advance their careers. And the clerical and quotidian support they gave to their justices—working closely with them in their homes and allowing them to function at the highest level—deserves recognition.

While articles have been written about clerks to some of the more influential, scholarly, or long-serving justices on the White Court (1910–1921), such as Van Devanter, Hughes,[5] Oliver Wendell Holmes Jr., Louis D. Brandeis, James C. McReynolds, and William R. Day,[6] this essay considers the unknown clerks of the underexamined associate justices who served under Chief Justice Edward Douglass White—John H. Clarke, Horace H. Lurton, Joseph Rucker Lamar, Joseph McKenna, Mahlon Pitney, Owen J. Roberts, and Edward T. Sanford—as well as those employed by White himself.

To rescue these clerks from obscurity, it is necessary to piece together basic biographical information and accurate clerkship dates so each clerk's life and service to the Court may be documented. Who were they? Did they have law degrees? How were they selected? Where did they end up in their postclerkship careers? Descriptions of the relationship between clerk and justice and the nature of a clerk's duties will also be examined whenever possible, but information on that topic is scarce.

Edward D. White, 1894–1921

When Edward D. White was elevated to chief justice in December 1910, the genial, warm-hearted Louisianan had already been on the Court for sixteen years and had employed three clerks. White inherited his first stenographer, William H. Dennis, from his predecessor, Justice Samuel Blatchford, for whom he had clerked for five years.[7] Dennis was a graduate of Georgetown University, having received his L.L.B. in 1876 and his M.A. in 1883, and had served concurrently as deputy register of wills in D.C. from 1876 to 1886.[8] Dennis was also author of *The Probate Law of the District of Columbia* (1883), and served as a U.S. commissioner for the District of Columbia in 1889.[9] When Blatchford

died in July 1893 following a short illness, Dennis was kept on the payroll awaiting his successor. That was the custom in those days, so that a new justice could
benefit from an experienced clerk and be given the choice of whether to retain
him for a new term.

Dennis ultimately waited more than seven months for a new boss. Grover
Cleveland's first two choices did not pass muster with Congress, and so the
frustrated president decided to appoint White, who was serving as a U.S. senator, on the assumption that senators would easily approve their popular colleague from Louisiana. Indeed, Senator White was both nominated and confirmed as an associate justice on February 19, 1894. But White chose not to be
sworn in until March 12 in order to lead the Senate battle against the president's
tariff reform legislation. And when White finally took his seat, he brought along
his private secretary from the Senate. Dennis probably showed them both the
ropes before stepping down at the end of the term.[10] After leaving the Court,
he went on to be a highly respected D.C. lawyer, serving as chairman of the
committee on bar admissions for the District of Columbia Bar Association.[11]

White's private secretary was his cousin James T. Ringgold, a native Wash-
ingtonian.[12] A cousin on his mother's side, he was the grandson of Tench Ringgold, a U.S. marshal who owned the famous Georgetown mansion where Chief
Justice John Marshall and the associate justices boarded in 1831–33 when they
were in town for the Supreme Court term. Young Ringgold graduated from
Maryland University School of Law in 1874, and then practiced law in Baltimore for several years, teaching at the Baltimore University School of Law.[13]
He wrote and published *Ringgold's Digest of the Decisions of the Court of Appeals
of Maryland*. Like Dennis, he served as a U.S. commissioner in the 1880s, acting
as a sort of magistrate in the District of Columbia circuit court.[14] Ringgold
was counsel to the Seventh Day Adventist Church and in 1894 wrote *Sunday,
Legal Aspects of the First Day of the Week*, a seminal book on laws involving Sunday closings, which is still in print today.[15] When the Louisiana state senate
appointed White to fill a vacancy in the U.S. Senate in 1891, he had naturally
hired his accomplished cousin to be his aide. Age forty, Ringgold knew his way
around the nation's capitol.

Sadly, Ringgold developed a debilitating mental illness that dramatically cut
short his Supreme Court clerkship and his life. He was sent to an asylum in
1896 after falling apart upon the death of his beloved wife. Ringgold died two
years later, at age forty-five, from abusing alcohol and opiates.[16] He had probably only clerked for a few months before White had to replace him.

William H. Pope officially succeeded Ringgold on December 6, 1895, and
stayed with White as his private secretary for nearly two decades—through
October term 1913.[17] Born in England in 1857, he had immigrated to Ohio as a
boy and graduated from Tennessee's Cumberland Law School in 1893. Pope had

been clerking in the Office of the Attorney General when White hired him.[18] Like all White's clerks, he worked out of the justice's massive stone house at 1721 Rhode Island Avenue. Pope died in his late fifties while faithfully serving White as a career secretary.[19]

In hiring Pope away from the attorney general's office, Justice White probably offered to supplement his income out of his own salary (associate justices then earned $13,000 a year, raised to $15,000 in 1911), to avoid Pope having to take a $200 pay cut. According to Charles Evans Hughes, who served with White from 1910 to 1916, the chief justice "hired a law clerk and paid him out of his own pocket."[20] All the justices had paid their clerks directly until 1886, when Congress, recognizing they were overburdened, first appropriated funds to pay for secretarial help. A Supreme Court clerk's yearly salary rose from $1,000 to $1,600 in 1895 (but Pope was earning $1,800 at the Justice Department) and continued at that level until 1911.[21] Other justices with long-serving personal secretaries—notably William R. Day and William H. Taft—privately supplemented their clerks' incomes as well.[22]

After Pope's death, White hired a Columbia Law School graduate, Bertram F. Shipman, on July 1, 1914, who clerked for four terms.[23] Born in Leon, Iowa, Shipman had attended Simpson College, a small Methodist school in Indianola, Iowa, and earned his law degree from Columbia in 1913.[24] (It is interesting to note that White never sought a clerk from his alma mater, Tulane University Law School.) Whether Shipman, with a law degree from an elite school, provided more substantive legal assistance than Pope, a career secretary, is unknown. After his clerkship, Shipman entered private practice in 1918 with the New York law firm Rushmore, Bisbee & Stern, which eventually became Mudge, Stern, Baldwin & Todd.[25] He specialized in corporate law. Shipman returned to the Supreme Court to argue a case in 1926, after White had died; his client was a New York corporation in bankruptcy.[26]

For October term 1918, Chief Justice White briefly engaged Leonard Bloomfield Zeisler, of Chicago. His illustrious father, Sigmund Zeisler, had famously defended two prominent anarchists in 1886–87 in what became known as the Haymarket cases, and his mother was the celebrated pianist Fanny Bloomfield Zeisler.[27] Leonard received an L.L.B. in 1910 from the University of Chicago with highest honors, and was admitted to the New York and Illinois bars.[28] He spent six years in private practice at his father's firm of Zeisler & Friedman in Chicago before moving to Washington, D.C., in January 1918 to join the Justice Department as an assistant attorney general in the Public Lands Division. His salary was $2,400, which means that he took a $400 pay cut to work for the chief justice (unless White supplemented his income).[29]

After hiring Zeisler on August 1, Chief Justice White decided he "could not use" him because of "his lack of stenographic knowledge."[30] It is unlikely that

White had problems with him other than his inability to take dictation, since he was welcomed back to his previous job, where he quickly excelled. Zeisler returned to work for Assistant Attorney General Thomas J. Spellacy, who was in charge of the seizure and administration of enemy property in the United States, and Zeisler received a salary promotion ($3,250) in early December. On December 22, Spellacy successfully argued that Zeisler's salary should again be raised (to $4,000) because he "has proved himself to be a very valuable man to both my predecessor and me," and has "been engaged largely in brief and opinion writing."[31]

Indeed, Zeisler was on the brief for the U.S. government in *Seufert Bros. Co. v. U.S.*, which was argued before the Court in January 1919.[32] He faced the chief justice again in the courtroom in October 1920, when he sat as co-counsel with Spellacy, who argued a pair of cases involving contractors who defaulted on loans to the United States on account of bankruptcy.[33] Zeisler moved to New York in 1922, where he practiced law before becoming a Wall Street stockbroker.[34] He returned to Washington in 1939 to be assistant attorney general at the Federal Security Agency, which Franklin D. Roosevelt created to administer the Social Security pension plan, public health programs, and education funding, and to oversee food and drug safety.[35]

In order to reinstate Zeisler in his old position, Chief Justice White engaged John J. Byrne, who had succeeded him in his job in the Public Lands Division at the Justice Department on August 1. The swap was conducted "with the understanding that if Mr. Byrne failed to satisfy the chief justice the position should be given up by Mr. Zeisler and that Mr. Byrne should have it."[36] In other words, Byrne, who started working for White on October 14, had a guaranteed reentry.

A native of Boston, Byrne had clerked for Edwin W. Sims, the U.S. Attorney for the Northern District of Illinois in 1906.[37] He then received his L.L.B. (1909) and L.L.M. (1910) degrees from Georgetown Law School, winning a prize for writing the best law thesis in his class.[38] Like Zeisler, Byrne may have accepted a $400 pay cut in coming to work for White. Byrne was promoted to "law clerk" for October term 1921, when Congress provided funds for the justices to hire legal assistants in addition to (or instead of) stenographic clerks, and his salary jumped to $3,600.

Byrne served the chief justice for three terms, staying with White until the chief justice's death in May 1921. Byrne then wrote to his successor, Chief Justice William H. Taft, asking to be kept on: "I have acquired a familiarity with the duties of [the] position which I believe you will find of vast service were I permitted the high honor of serving you in a similar capacity."[39] Taft agreed to engage him as his law clerk to supplement his longtime personal secretary, Wendell W. Mischler, who would be hired at the stenographer's salary.[40] Taft explained to Byrne, however, that because "[t]he compensation for a stenographic clerk is quite inadequate," to avoid envy on the part of Mischler, "I must make up to [him] out of my own income, so that his compensation will be equal to yours."[41]

Byrne clerked for the new chief justice until the end of the 1923 term, returning to his native Boston when Attorney General Harlan Fiske Stone appointed him to head up efforts to prosecute bootleggers in the New England area. By 1925, he had returned to the Justice Department, eventually becoming a special assistant attorney general.[42] Byrne served under Assistant Attorney General Mabel Willebrandt as co-counsel in several Prohibition cases that the government argued before the Supreme Court.[43]

During his last two terms on the Court, Chief Justice White, despite being "dreadfully hampered" by failing health,[44] did not take advantage of the funds Congress provided to employ a second assistant. This seems surprising because White suffered from cataracts and could have benefited from having a second clerk to read briefs to him (he was also going deaf). He probably also needed extra help with the administrative matters he was tasked with as chief justice. Yet White was not alone in keeping to one clerk; indeed, the transition from lone stenographer to stenographer plus law clerk was not made uniformly from chambers to chambers. This is partly because Congress had been both proactive and unclear about offering the justices new salaries for law clerks. In March 1919, the Supreme Court had requested the usual appropriation for nine "stenographic clerks," but in July Congress appropriated money "[f]or nine law clerks, one for the chief justice and one for each associate justice, at not exceeding $3,600 each, $32,400."[45] This cannot have been a complete surprise, for as Charles Evans Hughes recalled in his memoir, the need for law clerks had been discussed, if passively, when he was an associate justice (1910–1916): "Occasionally, the question of providing law clerks in addition to secretaries would be raised but nothing was done. Some suggested that if we had experienced law clerks, it might be thought that they were writing our opinions."[46]

But when the justices heard the news that funds were appropriated for law clerks, they were puzzled as to whether these new assistants were meant to replace or supplement the stenographic clerks. Justice Willis Van Devanter went so far as to query members of Congress, relaying their position back to the clerk of the Court for clarification:

> I had a short conference before leaving with the chairman of the Appropriations in the Senate and the chairman of the like committee in the House and it was then their purpose, as plainly expressed, to give each member one clerk or secretary who should be known as a law clerk and receive compensation larger than heretofore allowed.[47]

The matter was clearly resolved by a May 20, 1920, statute from Congress providing for one law clerk ($3,600) and one stenographic clerk ($2,000) for each justice.[48]

Despite this new law, many justices, including Chief Justice White and Justices Holmes, Brandeis, McKenna, Day, Pitney, Clarke, Sanford, and Sutherland, continued to employ just one assistant.[49] Brandeis did not hire a stenographic clerk in addition to a law clerk because he relied on the Court's printer to type up his drafts, which were carried back and forth by his messenger (the other justices only sent opinions to the printer when their clerks had typed and readied them for circulation). Indeed, Brandeis may have arranged for the money budgeted for his stenographer to be diverted directly to the printer. Another reason Brandeis did not think he needed a second clerk was that he continued to review all incoming petitions for certiorari himself—a task that the other justices, particularly those employing two clerks, were now routinely delegating to their clerks, who were asked to write brief summaries of the petitions.

Joseph McKenna, 1898–1925

Joseph McKenna had been on the Court for nearly twelve years when his bench-mate and close friend Edward Douglass White became chief. Two months after McKenna took his seat in January 1898, he hired James Cecil Hooe—the first of only three clerks whom he would employ during his entire twenty-six-year tenure. McKenna engaged Hooe as a stenographer from March 1, 1898, until December 1910,[50] just before the White Court era commenced. Descended from an illustrious Virginia family, Hooe had moved to Washington in 1891 to work for Elisha Edward Meredith, a U.S. representative from Virginia, and had earned his law degree in 1892 and his L.L.M. the following year, both from Columbian College (later renamed the George Washington University).[51]

Hooe served as a clerk in the Department of Agriculture in 1895 before becoming private secretary to Pheobe Hearst, wife of Senator George Hearst, of California.[52] A philanthropist with a strong interest in education, she was active in founding the National Congress of Mothers (precursor to the Parent-Teacher Association) during the time Hooe worked for her. It is not known how much Hearst paid Hooe as her secretary, but he had previously been earning $1,800 at the Department of Agriculture—$200 more than a Supreme Court clerk. Popular in Washington social circles, Hooe married Edith Dingley, the daughter of Representative Nelson Dingley, of Maine, in 1897. Tragically, in 1910 his life was cut short by tuberculosis. Hooe was forty. The justice attended his funeral, along with other prominent Washington dignitaries.[53]

Justice McKenna's next stenographer was Ashton F. Embry, who clerked from January 6, 1911, until his abrupt and suspicious resignation on December 16, 1919.[54] Born in Hopkinsville, Kentucky, in 1883, Embry had moved to Washington in 1905 and found a job as a copyist in the Justice Department at the tender age of sixteen.[55] He quickly moved up the ranks: from clerk to stenographer, to confidential clerk. Embry was hired in June 1908 as a law secretary to future Supreme Court justice Edward T. Sanford, who had just been appointed a district court judge for middle and eastern Tennessee. Embry returned to Washington in October 1909 to work as a stenographer for Solicitor General Frederick W. Lehmann.

Three years later, Embry, now twenty-seven, was hired by Justice McKenna. He attended National University School of Law at night and graduated in 1912, at the end of his first term as McKenna's clerk.[56] When Congress appropriated funding for law clerks in 1919, Embry resigned his $2,000-a-year-post, and McKenna promoted him to the new position at the higher salary of $3,600.[57] He also found time to develop a bakery business with his brother, Barton Stone Embry, and with James Harwood Graves, a Justice Department stenographer he knew from his time working there.

In a stunning turn of events, Embry resigned abruptly from his clerkship after nine years. His resignation letter to McKenna offered an apparent explanation: "[M]y bakery business having expanded to such an extent as to require practically all my time, I feel that in justice to your work and my health, I ought not to try to continue as your secretary—for it seems impossible for me to do my full duty to both places."[58] But the real reason, as the justice no doubt knew, was that Embry was under investigation by the Justice Department for conspiring with several Wall Street speculators to leak them inside knowledge of an upcoming Supreme Court decision in a railroad case, *United States v. Southern Pacific*.[59] Embry was indicted by a grand jury several months later but pleaded innocent. He petitioned the Supreme Court for certiorari, but it was denied in 1921. Eventually, the Justice Department realized that it lacked reliable witnesses and dropped the case quietly in 1929. Embry and his brother would develop a very successful bakery business that expanded to seven locations by the time of his retirement in 1950.[60]

An interesting detail of the leak case involves Embry's social friendship with one of Justice Willis Van Devanter's clerks, Mahlon D. Kiefer,[61] who had graduated a few years before Embry from National University School of Law. During the investigation, when Embry was asked about his actions on November 16, 1919 (the day before the Supreme Court handed down its *Southern Pacific* decision), Embry said he went to his bakery with his wife, Grace, and with Kiefer and his wife, and that the two couples then had Sunday dinner at the Kiefers' apartment. Embry admitted he stayed behind at the bakery before joining them at dinner to give a "loan" of $6,000 to Graves, his bakery partner. Graves promptly took the overnight train to New York and shorted the stock, returning Embry's money plus $600 a few days later. He also conveyed Embry's insider information to two Wall Street speculators with whom he was in cahoots.

As clerks, Embry and Kiefer both would have known the result of the Saturday conferences, the votes having been recorded in their justices' docket books. Dean Acheson, who clerked for Justice Brandeis during the leak scandal, wrote in his autobiography: "One of the joys of being a law clerk was to open the book on Saturday afternoon and learn weeks ahead of the country what our masters had done."[62] But Kiefer was not involved in the leak scheme, and he testified against his friend and fellow clerk at the grand jury hearing.

Kiefer left Van Devanter's employ in 1926 to join the Prohibition and Taxation Department at the Department of Justice.[63] He met up again there with John J. Byrne, Chief Justice White's former clerk, who would have known both Kiefer and Embry during his clerkship at the Supreme Court. At the Justice Department, Byrne and Kiefer went on to brief two Supreme Court cases (in 1931 and 1932) involving illegal searches of liquor under the Prohibition Act.[64]

Not surprisingly, when Justice McKenna hired a replacement for Embry—Robert F. Cogswell—he made sure to lecture him on the importance of clerk secrecy.[65] Born in Washington, D.C., in 1890, Cogswell earned a stenography and typing diploma from Business High School and graduated in 1913 from Georgetown Law School.[66] He worked for five years as an assistant clerk in the Clerk's Office at the Supreme Court while attending night school. With the advent of World War I, Cogswell enlisted, serving overseas for eight months with the Eightieth Division as an artillery lieutenant.[67] James D. Maher, the clerk of the Court, wrote a farewell letter asking him to carry with him "the assurance of my hearty appreciation of your work in this Office, and my sincere regret that a more imperative duty compels you to give up your position here."[68] Upon his return from France, Cogswell applied unsuccessfully to be a stenographer for Justice Day, and briefly became assistant clerk to the House of Representatives' Committee on Post Office and Post Roads.[69] Finally, McKenna hired Cogswell, age thirty, as his law clerk on April 1, 1920, more than three months after Embry's abrupt resignation.[70]

During Cogswell's tenure, Justice McKenna's mind was slipping. While formerly kind, gentlemanly, and shy, McKenna became prone to angry outbursts. Chief Justice Taft eventually stopped assigning McKenna all but the easiest opinions, and the other justices shouldered his work. They also secretly agreed that because of his senility they would not allow McKenna's vote to be decisive when decisions were close. As his sole clerk, this situation must have affected Cogswell, who worked in the somewhat reclusive justice's apartment at 1150 Connecticut Avenue. Unfortunately, he did not leave an account of his clerkship. In a 1959 interview, he did say that the justice "disliked having so much as a sentence of his opinions changed by a clerk, although he permitted suggestions for changes."[71] Cogswell also told another interviewer that although McKenna "possessed a good library, the justice was not an omnivorous reader."[72]

When Chief Justice Taft finally persuaded McKenna to step down in January 1925, McKenna's successor, Associate Justice Harlan Fiske Stone, inherited Cogswell. Stone took his seat in March, and kept Cogswell on to the end of the term.[73] In 1926, Cogswell entered private practice in D.C., specializing in estate and probate law and negotiating landlord-tenant cases. He argued a case before the Supreme Court in 1928.[74] When housing shortages as a result of World War II caused rents to skyrocket in D.C., Congress passed a law freezing rents. Cogswell was appointed in 1941 to run the Office of Administrator of Rent Control, a powerful job that oversaw 150,000 dwelling units in D.C. Congress repealed the rent control law in 1953, and Cogswell moved on to oversee the Department of Occupations and Professions, the D.C. agency that licenses professionals and technicians.[75]

Horace Lurton, 1910–1914

Horace Lurton was the first justice appointed to the White Court, taking his oath of office two weeks after White was elevated to chief justice. Having attended law school in Nashville, Tennessee, and having served on the Tennessee Supreme Court for nearly eight years, it is no surprise that Lurton chose a fellow Tennessean, Harvey D. Jacob, as his law clerk. Lurton (like Pitney, Sanford, and Roberts) would only employ one clerk during his years on the Supreme Court. Born in 1886, in Wheeling, Alabama, Jacob began his career at age thirteen as a messenger in a Nashville law firm. He married at seventeen, earned an undergraduate degree at Vanderbilt University, and worked his way up to stenographer.[76] In 1906, at age twenty, Jacob found himself widowed with two young children.[77]

Horace Lurton was appointed to the U.S. Court of Appeals for the Sixth Circuit in Cincinnati in 1893, and he hired Jacob to serve as his private secretary toward the end of his tenure.[78] During that time, Lurton was also teaching at Vanderbilt Law School, serving as its dean from 1904 to 1910. When President Taft appointed him to the Supreme Court, Lurton brought Jacob with him to Washington, arriving in January 1910.

Jacob enrolled in evening law school at Georgetown, became a founding member of the *Georgetown Law Journal,* and was voted "Most Popular Man in His Class" and "Man Who Has Done the Most for the Class." Jacob graduated in the same 1913 class as Justice McKenna's clerk Robert F. Cogswell and as Justice James C. McReynolds's clerk Leroy A. Reed;[79] he socialized with Reed, but his service at the Court did not overlap with Cogswell's. While it may seem overly burdensome to be a Supreme Court clerk during the day and attend law school in the evening (Jacob was also yearbook editor and chancellor of *The Tredecium*, a student group), this was actually a common paradigm for ambitious young men. Still others held stenographer or messenger jobs in various government branches while attending evening law school at Georgetown, National, or George Washington and then became clerks to Supreme Court justices *after* graduation.

Before taking his seat, Lurton had written to his friend and former benchmate from the Sixth Circuit Court of Appeals, William R. Day, now sitting on the Supreme Court, for advice about staffing. He explained that he was reluctant to bring his messenger with him because, despite him being "an absolutely sober and honest man," Lurton's "only reason" for continuing to employ him would be that "somebody has got to take care of him." In contrast, he told Day he was confident about his choice of stenographer: "My purpose is to keep Mr. Jacob, who is now my stenographer, as he desires to go with me to Washington. I suppose there is no difficulty about this, but to whom shall I report his selection[?]"[80]

During his four-year tenure, Lurton used Jacob as a private secretary, not as a legal assistant. Jacob later told an interviewer that he "had practically nothing to do with the opinions until they reached the proofreading stage," and admitted he "also did little with the certiorari petitions." His duties were "confined largely to typing, proofreading, checking citations, and handling personal matters for the justice."[81] Some sources suggest that Jacob lived with Lurton in his apartment at 2129 Florida Avenue, but this scenario is unlikely given that he had two children and married his second wife, Camille, in 1913. Jacob would name one of their sons Horace Lurton Jacob.[82]

When Lurton died suddenly of a heart attack on vacation in Atlantic City on July 12, 1914, Jacob accompanied the body back by special train to Clarksville, Tennessee, along with the justice's widow, Fanny, and Lurton's married children. He was then involved in probating the justice's handwritten will.[83] Ten days after Lurton's death, Jacob was hired as an assistant attorney at the Justice Department.[84] He was promoted to attorney in the Court of Claims Division in January 1916, earning an salary of $3,000—at least $1,000 more than what he received as a stenographer for Lurton. Jacob continued his career there until 1920, when he became general counsel to the National Press Club building, the National Building Corporation, and the Home Owners Loan Corporation for D.C.[85]

Joseph Rucker Lamar, 1911–1916

When Joseph R. Lamar joined the Court in January 1911, he did not bring his secretary with him from his native Georgia. Instead, he inherited a seasoned clerk, S. Edward Widdifield, who is more obscure than he should be given his long service to the Court. Born in Canada in 1875 into a Quaker family, Widdifield immigrated at age six to Traverse City, Michigan. He graduated from Detroit College of Law in 1898, and then became an attorney in Traverse City.[86] Widdifield moved to Pittsfield, Massachusetts, to work as a "stenographic secretary" at the Stanley Electrical Company,[87] and then, when he was more than thirty years old, to Washington, D.C., where Justice Rufus Peckham hired him as his stenographer. He stayed in Peckham's employ from February 6, 1905, until the justice died on October 24, 1909, only a few weeks into that term.[88] In a reply to a query from a researcher in 1944 about his service to Peckham, Widdifield yielded little: "It is true that I was his secretary for over four years but that was a business relationship. . . . He had a well trained legal mind, and when he dictated a rough draft of an opinion, very few changes in it were necessary, the facts and the law stated lucidly and briefly."[89]

Widdifield was kept on until mid-December,[90] when it became clear that Peckham's successor, Horace Lurton, appointed December 13, would bring his own clerk with him from Tennessee. When Lamar joined the Court in January 1911 he rehired Widdifield, who clerked for him for six months in his stately house at 1751 New Hampshire Avenue. Still single at age thirty-six, Widdifield was living with his mother, a widow, but the following year he returned to Traverse City to marry Maud Huntingdon, thirteen years his junior.[91] From 1913 to 1916, he worked as a messenger for the Senate Committee on Congress, earning $1,444 a year, slightly less than the $1,600 Justice Lamar had paid him.[92] The Widdifields had two children.

For the 1912 term, Justice Lamar replaced Widdifield with another experienced secretary: John E. Hoover. Born in 1879, Hoover was a sixth-generation native of Washington, D.C., whose father was in the "shoe business."[93] From about age fourteen he worked as a "stenographer, typewriter, and general law clerk" to Nathaniel Wilson and J. Hubley Ashton, Washington lawyers with an "active practice" before the Supreme Court. Hoover gave William R. Stansbury, then deputy clerk at the Supreme Court, as a reference as to his "ability, integrity and steadfastness to [his] work," when he applied for a stenographer position with newly appointed Justice Day in 1903.[94] While Day did not hire him, Justice Peckham did, but only for three months. Hoover clerked for Peckham from October 24, 1904, to February 1905, when Widdifield replaced him as his third and final stenographer.[95] Where Hoover attended law school is unclear.[96]

On July 1, 1906, a year and a half after leaving Peckham's employ, Hoover returned to the Court to clerk for Justice John Marshall Harlan. During that interim, Hoover worked for James S. Harlan, a Chicago lawyer who had clerked for Chief Justice Melville Fuller in the 1888 term and presumably was keen to engage a Supreme Court stenographer for his law practice. James must have introduced Hoover to his father, Justice Harlan, when he was looking for a new clerk toward the end of his thirty-four-year tenure.[97] Hoover became the justice's last private secretary and developed a close relationship with him during their five terms together. He spent summers with Harlan at his home in Murray Bay, Canada, and reportedly met his wife there "while watching Secretary of War Taft and Justice Harlan engaged in a game of golf."[98] Harlan became so dependent on Hoover that he requested that Congress continue to provide him with a secretary after he stepped down from the bench because his was "almost indispensable."[99]

Harlan never did retire; he died in November 1910. Hoover was so close to the justice's family that he took it upon himself to write to Harlan's eldest son, Richard, to describe his father's last day on the Court.[100] He also named his son, born in 1910, Warren Harlan Hoover, in honor of the justice.[101] Hoover stayed on briefly with Harlan's successor, Mahlon Pitney, when he took his seat on March 18, 1911, seeing him through the term, but Pitney then chose to bring his private secretary from home.

When Hoover signed on with Lamar for the 1912 term to replace the justice's first stenographer, Widdifield, he again found himself managing a sitting justice's demise. On September 1915, after five years on the Court, Lamar suffered a paralytic stroke. He never recovered enough to resume his role as a justice and died on January 2, 1916. Hoover helped manage this tragic situation, and was kept on the payroll for the rest of the 1915 term to clerk for Associate Justice Charles Evans Hughes, who then stepped down to run for president.[102] Hoover's obituary characterized his duties during his twelve-term stint clerking for five different justices as purely secretarial: "During that time he prepared memorandums on motions for rehearings, took down opinions stenographically, transcribed them and reviewed them for errors before they were circulated among the justices for comment and approval."[103]

Hoover moved on to work at the Justice Department in August 1916.[104] Like Lurton's former clerk, Harvey Jacob, he was hired by the Court of Claims Division. Hoover's salary—$2,500 as an assistant attorney—was $700 more than his stenographer's pay. Much to his annoyance, however, Hoover's younger cousin, who bore the same name, joined him a year later at the Justice Department as an attorney in the Department of National Security and Defense.[105] His niece says Hoover forced his cousin to change his name: "Apparently . . . their memos, papers, mail, et al, were getting mixed up. So Uncle John (in his own usual gruff manner) called his cousin into his office saying something must be done about their names. So J. Edgar walked away forever after known as J. Edgar."[106]

Hoover no doubt continued to be irritated when J. Edgar Hoover, who was hired at an inferior salary of $1,800, began making the same salary as his uncle in 1920—$3,000—and quickly surpassed him on his way to becoming director of the Federal Bureau of Investigation (FBI).

John E. Hoover spent his entire career in government. Promoted to attorney in the Court of Claims Division in 1920, he defended suits against the government.[107] He argued the government's side in a hearing at the Department of Labor that resulted in the deportation of Ludwig A. C. Martens, the head of the Russian Soviet Government Bureau, which had been established during the Russian Civil War as a stopgap trade and information agency and which the U.S. government suspected of subversion.[108] In 1922, Hoover defended his own Justice Department against charges that liquor seized in Prohibition raids had been diverted to members of its staff.[109] From 1931 to 1933, he worked for the general counsel of the General Accounting Office, moving to the Credit Administration for nine more years as special assistant. Hoover retired in 1942 upon reaching mandatory retirement age at sixty-four.[110]

Mahlon Pitney, 1912–1922

When he joined the Supreme Court in March 1912, Mahlon Pitney briefly inherited Hoover from his predecessor, John Marshall Harlan. But Pitney quickly arranged to bring his private secretary from his home state of New Jersey for October term 1913. Horatio Stonier Jr. was born in Staffordshire, England, in 1878, and his family immigrated to Jersey City when he was ten. His law school affiliation, if any, is unknown. Pitney probably hired Stonier as his secretary in his law firm in Morristown, New Jersey, and brought him with him when he was appointed justice on the New Jersey Supreme Court in 1901.[111] Stonier's official job title was "stenographic clerk typewriting opinions on the New Jersey Court of Errors and Appeals,"[112] a court that then consisted of the chancellor, the justices of the supreme court (one of whom was Pitney), and six part-time judges. In 1908, when Pitney was appointed chancellor of New Jersey, the highest position in the New Jersey court system, he retained Stonier as his private secretary.

Chancellor Pitney brought Stonier with him to the Supreme Court four years later. When William Howard Taft selected Pitney to fill a Supreme Court vacancy in February 1912, it was his secretary who tracked him down on the golf course in Atlantic City to give him the good news (Pitney finished playing the round.)[113] In announcing Stonier's appointment on April 1, the *Trenton Evening News* said his salary was "$3,000 a year," which may mean that Pitney was supplementing the $1,600 salary out of his own pocket.[114] Justice Pitney asked for "a private office in the Capitol," because he "found the books to which he so constantly referred could not be housed at home."[115] Accordingly, Stonier may have worked in the Capitol building as well as in the justice's home—a Federalist-style row house located at 1763 R Street.

After Congress approved salaries for law clerks in addition to stenographers, Pitney engaged a second assistant, William A. D. Dyke, for October term 1922, at the higher law clerk compensation. Dyke had been serving as an assistant clerk in the U.S. Senate, earning a salary of $1,600.[116] He had also been attending Georgetown Law School, receiving an L.L.B. and an M.P.L. in 1921. Dyke was class poet and a classmate of John T. Fowler, whom Justice McReynolds hired as a clerk for the 1922–26 terms.[117] Sadly, Pitney suffered a debilitating stroke in August (retiring officially on December 31, 1922), so it is doubtful that Dyke performed much work for him. He stayed on to clerk for Justice Pierce Butler, who took his seat in January 1923.

The law apparently did not appeal to Dyke, who dropped his legal career after seeing out one term with Butler. He switched to medicine, earning his M.D. at Georgetown in 1929, and pursuing his medical internship the following year.[118] Dr. Dyke died tragically at age forty-two, in a car accident.[119]

When Pitney retired, Stonier stayed on at the Court, but not as a clerk to a justice. Like Widdifield, he was hired to work in the Office of the Clerk of Court to assist Deputy Clerk Charles Elmore Cropley. His starting salary as assistant clerk in 1923 was $4,000 a year.[120] Stonier was promoted to deputy clerk in 1928 when Cropley became clerk of the Court, earning $4,583.[121] He retired in 1929. Like Pitney, he excelled at playing golf.[122]

John H. Clarke, 1916–1922

S. Edward Widdifield was enticed back to the Supreme Court from his Senate messenger job to clerk for John H. Clarke, the last justice appointed to the White Court, whom he served for Clarke's full six-year tenure. While Widdifield began his service on October 1, 1916, as a stenographic clerk, he "resigned" on August 1, 1919, so he could be reappointed the next day as a law clerk at the higher salary.[123] When interviewed by Clarke's biographer, Widdifield told him the justice liked to write out a rough draft of his opinion in longhand and then revise it while dictating a second draft to his clerk.[124] He worked out of Clarke's apartment at 2400 Sixteenth Street, in the same building where the justice's nemesis on the Court, James C. McReynolds, lived. Widdifield lived with his family about ten blocks away.

When Clarke's surprise departure from the Court at the end of the 1921 term left Widdifield at loose ends, the experienced clerk was snapped up by newly appointed George Sutherland for the 1922 and 1923 terms. All told, Widdifield and John E. Hoover both deserve veteran clerk awards. Widdifield served four different justices (Peckham, Lamar, Clarke, Sutherland) for twelve terms; Hoover served five justices (Peckham, Harlan, Lamar, Pitney, Hughes) during eleven terms (some terms were only partial).

Widdifield left the Court to work for the Mixed Claims Commission between the United States and Germany, which had been established in the aftermath of the war to settle property claims between the United States, its citizens, and Germany. He was also developing a robust real estate business in the resort town of North Beach, Maryland, where he served as mayor for many years.[125] After serving from 1924 to 1929 as a clerk on the Mixed Claims Commission, he became an assistant clerk for the House Judiciary Committee.[126]

Widdifield returned to the Supreme Court in 1931, at age fifty-six, when he was hired to work in the Office of the Clerk of Court. Yet the new position was less remunerative than his clerkship to Sutherland had been a decade earlier. In 1936, he only earned $1,800 as an assistant clerk, a figure that rose to $2,000 in 1940, and to $2,650 in 1946.[127] Perhaps the realities of the Depression persuaded him to take the less prestigious job, or maybe it was a love for the Court. Seeking to regain the higher salary, he tried to leave the Clerk's Office in 1937 and go back to chambers as a law clerk. Indeed, fourteen years after his last clerkship term with Justice Sutherland, Widdifield, age sixty-two, applied to clerk for newly appointed Justice Hugo L. Black.[128] "I am a stenographer, typewriter and lawyer—and member of the bar of the above [Supreme] Court—[and] familiar with the duties of the position," he wrote. Black did not hire him, but instead chose a newly minted graduate of Harvard Law School. Widdifield retired in the summer of 1949, at age seventy-three, having worked for the clerk of the Court for eighteen years.[129]

Two Post-White Court Stenographers

EDWARD SANFORD, 1923–1930

The death of Chief Justice White in 1921, after serving on the Court since 1894, made way for a new era. White's style had been firmly old fashioned: indeed Clarinda Lamar, the wife of Justice Lamar, once remarked that he was "quite early Victorian in his courtesies."[130] Fewer justices used stenographic clerks, preferring to engage only a law clerk and, increasingly, a female secretary. On May 25, Chief Justice William Howard Taft wrote a letter to the associate justices informing them that Congress had changed the way it appropriated funding for stenographic clerks:

> The Court is advised that Mr. Justice Holmes, Mr. Justice Brandeis, Mr. Justice Sutherland and Mr. Justice Sanford do not desire the assignment to them of clerical assistants. They prefer to do their work through their Law Clerks. The Court authorizes the fixing of salaries of stenographic

clerks to Mr. Justice Van Devanter, Mr. Justice McReynolds, Mr. Justice Butler and Mr. Justice Stone as the names and amounts shall be certified to you by these Justices. The total sum of course will be within the amount appropriated by law for clerical assistants.[131]

In other words, the four associate justices using stenographers (plus Chief Justice Taft, who used his nonlawyer private secretary for the stenographer position) would have to figure out how to divide the $20,160 Congress had appropriated as a lump sum for all the stenographic clerks. (Law clerks' salaries were fixed at a maximum of $3,600, but a justice could offer less.) The following year, Congress did away completely with the distinction between law clerks and clerical assistants by granting a lump sum "for all officers and employees" of the Court.[132] This salary allocation method has continued to this day.

Most justices serving on the Court in the 1920s and 1930s—Holmes, Brandeis, Sutherland, Stone, Cardozo, and Black—would subscribe to the modern clerkship model, with single-term clerks given substantive legal research duties, thus allowing the justices to recruit from the best students at elite law schools. But the stenographer/private secretary model did not arbitrarily end with the White Court. Of the justices appointed after 1921, two conformed to the "stenographic era" clerkship model: Justices Edward Sanford and Owen J. Roberts. At first glance, Pierce Butler (1923–1939) might be considered a third because he hired John F. Cotter, a twenty-three-year-old D.C. native who had graduated from a local law school, The Catholic University of America, and whom Butler kept employed for his entire sixteen-year tenure on the Court. Butler, however, always employed a second law clerk and gave both Cotter and his co-clerk substantive legal duties.[133]

Justice Sanford hired only one clerk during his seven-year tenure, William R. Loney. A native of Baltimore, Loney clerked in the Office of the Attorney General from 1898 to 1906, when he was promoted to stenographer to Solicitor General Henry M. Hoyt.[134] He attended National University School of Law at night, graduating in 1907.[135] By the time he was hired by Sanford in 1923, Loney was fifty-four years old and had spent his entire career as a stenographer/law clerk for the federal government, most recently in the Office of the Assistant Attorney General for the Enforcement of Antitrust Laws.[136] More research in Sanford's papers might reveal what kinds of duties he delegated to Loney, but he probably had him summarizing petitions for certiorari.

Sanford died suddenly on March 8, 1930, and Loney obtained a thirty-day temporary appointment with Justice Sutherland while waiting either for the arrival of Sanford's successor or a transfer to a clerk job at the Justice Department. Desperate for work during the Depression with one son "about to enter his senior year in college,"[137] Loney, age sixty-one, begged Chief Justice Hughes for help finding new employment. "Having been so long with the Court," he wrote,

I have become interested in its work ... [and] in view of the urgent necessity for obtaining continuous appointment, [I suggest] that the Court consider appointing me to a position, under the Marshal's appropriation, as an assistant in the library, available for such work as may be required, and in anticipation of extra help being needed for the new building when completed (the Marshal's office being one short of what it used to be).[138]

Sutherland obtained a second thirty-day extension for Loney while waiting vainly for Sanford's successor, Judge John J. Parker, of North Carolina, nominated on March 20, to be confirmed. Sutherland also "kindly telephoned" Charles P. Sisson, the assistant attorney general in charge of administrative matters, to lobby for a job at the Justice Department for his late colleague's clerk. Judge Parker's nomination was rejected by the Senate on May 7, and a frantic Loney again pressed Chief Justice Hughes for a job in the library.[139] The chief promptly replied that "no further assistance" was needed in the library or the marshal's office and that he "was very sorry" that Loney had "not yet found a permanent place," and trusted he would "find one at the Justice Department."[140] Having a break in government service would harm Loney's benefits and pension, so he persuaded Van Devanter to help him obtain a third one-month extension. It was granted on May 9. When Philadelphia lawyer Owen J. Roberts was confirmed to fill Sanford's seat on May 20, he kept Loney on in June, but only until the end of the summer. Finally, like so many clerks before him, Loney was offered a position at the Justice Department. He retired eight years later, in 1938.[141]

OWEN J. ROBERTS, 1930–1945

Justice Roberts brought his private secretary, Albert J. Schneider, from his law practice in Philadelphia—Roberts, Montgomery & McKeehan—for October term 1930. In many ways Schneider can be considered the last of the Supreme Court stenographers (even though he was hired as a law clerk). Indeed, he was the last private secretary to be brought by a justice from his hometown and who worked without benefit of a co-clerk.

Schneider was also a whiz at taking dictation. In 1921, at the World's Championship Contest of the National Shorthand Reporters' Association, Schneider won first place by transcribing 280-words-a-minute dictation (with a 69.84 percent accuracy rate).[142] Like so many Supreme Court clerks before him but few after, Schneider attended law school at night (George Washington University), graduating in 1934. A loyal private secretary, he stayed with Roberts throughout the justice's entire fifteen-year tenure, until 1945.

Because Roberts was the first justice to work full time in the new Supreme Court building, which opened in 1935, Schneider was also part of a new era. By

1941, clerks no longer spent their days at their justice's dwelling, only coming to the Court to use its private library on the ground floor of the Capitol or, if time permitted, to hear an argument, and rarely interacting with other clerks or justices.

In another modern twist, Schneider came to work at the Court every day with his wife, Bertha, whom Justice Roberts had engaged as his secretary.[143] As such, Bertha Schneider was one of the earliest women to work as a secretary directly for a justice. Gertrude Jenkins, who served Harlan Fiske Stone throughout his tenure on the Court from 1925 to 1946, was another. One of Stone's clerks described Jenkins's duties as stenographic: "[Stone's] draft was written in pencil on yellow sheets of paper, in a scrawl notorious for illegibility. After he wrote two or three pages, he would summon Miss Jenkins and immediately dictate what he had written."[144]

Jenkins worked in a partitioned section of Stone's huge home library, where the justice sat at his large desk; his law clerks, who changed every year and were recruited from Columbia Law School, had a desk on the balcony above. In short, Jenkins filled the increasingly archaic position of male stenographic clerk or career private secretary. One wonders if Bertha Schneider did the same for Justice Roberts even though her husband had not graduated from an elite law school and was a loyal private secretary who presumably was more amenable to performing clerical work.

After Justice Roberts stepped down in 1945, his longtime clerk, Schneider, was hired as a reporter at the U.S. House of Representatives. As such he was "[c]harged with jotting down every word of parliamentary prose on the House floor" as "part of a seven-man team that record[ed] debate in five-minute takes for almost split-second transcription and printing." He stayed in the job for thirty-three years. As the last quintessential stenographer to work for a justice, Schneider was likely the best, at least at shorthand.[145]

Due to increasing demands of the workload, Congress authorized the justices to hire two law clerks in 1947. But the advent of World War II had already marked the end of the male stenographer, as young men were needed for the war effort and female secretaries had become the norm.[146] By then, it had come to seem degrading for a man to turn speech into shorthand or to type out a draft of an opinion. While performing the same clerical work, female secretaries in the 1930s and 1940s were not lawyers and did not see the job as a stepping-stone to a legal career. In fact, one woman who wrote to ask Justice William R. Day as early as 1906 for evening stenography work reassured the justice that although she had just graduated from night law school: "I have no intention of attempting to practice law, but I am hoping my bit of legal training may be of assistance in obtaining legal dictation [work]."[147] Eventually, some female secretaries did pursue law studies. Most notably, Alice O'Donnell, career secretary to Justice Tom C. Clark (1949–1967), graduated from night law school at the George Washington University in 1954 and expanded the boundaries of her job beyond clerical support. She supervised Clark's chambers and became a liaison between the justice and his clerks.[148]

Conclusion

So what picture emerges of the "lost" law clerks of the White Court? First of all, these early clerks all had law degrees or were attending law school at night (with the possible exception of Horatio Stonier). This finding runs contrary to the common belief that many of these early judicial assistants were not attorneys. In addition, they learned shorthand at local D.C. trade schools, a skill that was a prerequisite for gaining a toehold on the first rung of the employment ladder. Many attended Strayer's Business College or Business High School, both of which opened their doors in 1904 to accommodate a growing demand for (white) clerical workers in the federal government. As seen in the case of Leonard B. Zeisler, graduating from an elite law school *did not* compensate for a deficit in stenography skills.

Curiously, none of the justices examined above hired clerks from their law school alma maters. This is probably because most of these private secretaries were selected from local law schools: National (2), Columbian/George Washington (2), Maryland (1), and Georgetown (5). As noted above, many law clerks had attended—or were still attending—law school at night, working day jobs to support themselves. Columbian University, which became the George Washington University in 1906, offered evening law classes that met "for an hour three times a week."[149] Georgetown Law School, situated only a few blocks from the Supreme Court, was founded as an evening program in 1870—announcing at its founding that "[t]he exercises will be held in the evening in order to facilitate the attendance of gentlemen who are engaged in the service of the Government." Georgetown finally introduced morning classes in 1921, but the following year it enrolled only 193 in its morning class compared to 1,012 students in its "late afternoon" class.[150]

If there were law faculty members actively recommending promising students to the White Court justices, I have found no evidence of it. Students simply wrote query letters and then supplied letters of recommendation from professors, friends, and previous employers. And it does not appear that openings at the Court were actively advertised—many of the clerks had been working in government agencies and learned about openings at the Court through the grapevine. Because justices hired their clerks themselves, and then later informed the clerk of the Court of their selection, there was no central recruitment process. But the clerk of the Court did forward query letters from potential candidates to new justices seeking clerks or tried to find new employment for a clerk whose justice was stepping down.[151] The Clerk's Office was also the contact point for the funds coming from Treasury to pay the clerks' salaries (prior to 1888, positions at the Court—like the stenographic clerks—were paid out of the marshal's office funds).

Was there a clerk network through which the justices indirectly communicated to each other about circulating opinions and other Court business? Many Supreme Court clerks knew each other from law school. Some clerks did socialize together, but they were all working out of the justices' homes, so it is unclear how much they saw of each other. Most of the dwellings of the justices did, however, tend to be clustered northeast of Dupont Circle, within easy walking distance. Clerks may have interacted dropping off opinions at the printer's shop, attending oral arguments, or retrieving books from the law library. There is no evidence of the Court organizing a social gathering at the beginning of term for clerks, as is the practice today. Since many former clerks went on to work at the Justice Department, one wonders if a former Supreme Court clerk network developed there.

Most of these clerks were married with families. Many of them were already in their thirties when they were hired and, as heads of established households, had mouths to feed. There is no evidence that any of them actually lived with their justice.

For the modern Supreme Court justice, experience clerking for a lower court judge is an informal requirement to be hired as a clerk—but only a few of these "lost" clerks had previous experience clerking for a sitting judge. Ashton Embry clerked for Edward Sanford while he was a district court judge in Tennessee, Harvey D. Jacob for Horace Lurton when he was a judge there on the court of appeals, and Horatio Stonier for Mahlon Pitney when he was chancellor of New Jersey courts. Several had previous experience clerking for a justice on the Supreme Court (Dennis, Byrne, Widdifield, Hoover, Dyke, Loney) and were inherited by the justice's successor when he stepped down.

While current law clerks remain with a justice for a single term and receive the same salary as clerks in other chambers, it is clear that wide variations in tenure, promotion, and remuneration existed for the White Court clerks. It is difficult to gather information about this subject because there is not much of a paper trail: appointment commissions were specified only for a single year and were renewed annually without new forms being processed (unless there was a change in salary). Nearly all of these clerks served their justices for multiple terms. It would be interesting to know whether the justices retained good clerks by giving verbal commitments of long-term employment.

In piecing together their exact dates of service, it becomes apparent that not all term dates are equal and that some clerks only worked a partial term for a particular justice. This scenario usually occurred when a justice retired due to illness and his clerk stayed on to help his successor for a few months until the end of the term. Being inherited by a new justice is very different from being interviewed and selected, and Supreme Court clerk databases should reflect this nuance. Moreover, it is possible that some of these clerks who were inherited at the end of a term by new justices did not actually perform work for them but were merely kept on the payroll. Keeping clerks employed had its obvious advantages. It allowed a clerk to fill out his commission, gave him time to find a new job, and afforded the new justice the opportunity to try out the veteran clerk and see if he wanted to retain him the following term.

While many were kept on, there was, however, no guarantee that a clerk would be paid through the term and the summer after his justice's tenure ended. This uncertainty may be tied to the fact that there was not a consistent employment policy about start and end dates in clerks' commissions: some clerks began their term as early as July, others not until the Court opened in October. A striking example of this irregularity was the case of William Loney, who was not automatically kept on until Justice Sanford's successor took his seat. Indeed, Justice Sutherland had to petition twice for thirty-day temporary appointments to keep Loney employed, and Justice Van Devanter hired him for a third month to tide him over until Sanford's seat was finally filled by Owen J. Roberts. But Roberts, who intended to bring his clerk from home, only kept Loney on the payroll through the summer. It is not even clear whether Loney should be counted as a clerk to Sutherland, Van Devanter, and Roberts, as we do not know if he was tasked with any work by those justices during his brief stints with them or if they hired him out of pity until he could find another government job.

Another example of end-date uncertainty occurred when Justice Henry B. Brown retired on May 28, 1906. His clerk, Charles F. Wilson, said he had been told that he "was to be paid during the summer months, or until [a] successor was appointed." However, he complained to Justice William R. Day that the disbursing clerk of the Department of Justice "holds that I ceased to hold the office the day that Mr. Justice Brown retired, and would not even pay me for the month of June, although I worked for the Judge up until the day he left town, June 23rd.... It has left me in an embarrassing position, as there is very little business in Washington in the summer time."[152] Justice Day, who was in need of a clerk, did not hire Wilson. Instead, Wilson was engaged by Justice Brown's successor, William H. Moody, when he was confirmed in December.

During those six months of waiting, however, Wilson was anxious about his lack of income. In July, he wrote Day that if he was not interested in hiring him Wilson would be "very glad to hold the position until you shall have appointed some one else."[153] After Moody retired, Wilson clerked for Secretary of State Philander Knox, but apparently continued to miss the Court. When Justice

Day had a vacant clerk position in 1914, Wilson applied for it—again unsuccessfully.[154] Wilson's salary as Knox's private secretary was $1,000, so he had other reasons for wanting to clerk for Day—a $700 promotion.[155]

Finally, salaries varied significantly among the White Court clerks. Several justices supplemented their clerks' income out of their own pocket; it would be interesting to know if the others did as well. Before 1921, some justices probably found it necessary to offer premiums to hire clerks away from other branches of government so they would not face a pay cut. But the discretion justices had over clerks' salaries went the other direction as well: they could make low-ball offers well below the salary ceiling. Such was the case with the notoriously stingy Justice James C. McReynolds, who offered his clerks a salary that was below the normal rate and liked to discharge them before the end of the term so he would not have to pay them during the summer recess when the workload was reduced.[156]

Discounting the aberrations (medical school, bakery business, death), these early clerks mostly went on to government service, not private practice, after leaving the Court. While today there is no question that a Supreme Court clerkship is a springboard to financial success, during the White Court era this was not necessarily so. A few clerks took modest pay cuts when they moved on to the Justice Department or other government agencies. They did, however, go on to respectable careers with steady paychecks, which was no small feat during the Depression.

None of these early clerks left memoirs, and few were interviewed about their clerking experiences. Being a stenographer, even to a justice, was not considered prestigious enough to attract the attention of judicial biographers or historians in their lifetimes. And those who were interviewed did not reveal much about the clerking function and how the workload was managed in chambers. Thus, many of their stories are lost to history.

Finally, these clerks' loyalty is noteworthy. Despite their modest salaries and financial struggles, none of these law secretaries—with the unfortunate exception of Ashton Embry—sold valuable information about impending Court decisions. Many devoted years to their justices, often working long hours. Mahlon Kiefer, who clerked for Willis Van Devanter from 1914 to 1923, described his work life in terms that underscores why these clerks' service to the Supreme Court should neither be underestimated nor forgotten: "I worked with him many a night all night long when he was trying to finish an opinion. While the hours were long and the work with the Justice was hard—hard because of the responsibility he put on his clerk and the fact that with him there was simply no excuse for a mistake—there was not that strain on the nervous energy which results from working under high pressure, confusion and excitement; there was always that calm, judicial atmosphere and agreeable surroundings."[157]

Notes

1. Pascal Oberlin to Willis Van Devanter, October 5, 1912, Willis Van Devanter Papers, Library of Congress.

2. David J. Danelski and Joseph S. Tulchin, eds., *The Autobiographical Notes of Charles Evans Hughes* (Cambridge, Mass: Harvard University Press, 1973), 163.

3. Edward G. Lowry, "The Men of the Supreme Court," in *The World's Work: A History of Our Time* (Garden City, N.J.: Doubleday, 1914), 27:637.

4. David J. Brewer to William Rufus Day, August 13, 1905, Box 20, File A–C, William R. Day Papers, Library of Congress (hereafter cited as Day Papers).

5. There is as yet no scholarly examination of Hughes's clerks, but the chief justice described their function in his own writings. See Danelski and Tulchin, *Autobiographical Notes,* 323, in which Chief Justice Hughes wrote: "I had highly competent law clerks." He emphasized, however, that while they "did the preliminary work in examining records and briefs and preparing copious memoranda" for each of the cert petitions, Hughes "made it a practice to check them by [his] own examination of the records and briefs."

6. See, for example, I. Scott Messinger, "The Judge as Mentor: Oliver Wendell Holmes Jr. and His Law Clerks," in *In Chambers: Stories of Supreme Court Law Clerks and Their Justices,* edited by Todd C. Peppers and Artemus Ward (Charlottesville: University of Virginia Press, 2012), 24; Todd C. Peppers, "Isaiah and His Young Disciples: Justice Louis Brandeis and His Law Clerks," in Peppers and Ward, *In Chambers,* 67; Barry Cushman, "The Clerks to Justices George Sutherland and Pierce Butler," this volume; Clare Cushman, "Beyond Knox: James C. McReynolds's Other Law Clerks, 1914–1941," this volume; Clare Cushman, "Sons of Ohio: William R. Day and His Clerks," *Journal of Supreme Court History,* forthcoming. John Marshall Harlan is not featured in this essay because his thirty-four years of service to the Court included only one year on the White Court.

7. Dennis was appointed July 1, 1888, to work for Blatchford. Correspondence on Appointment of Stenographic Clerks, 1881–1931 and 1939–40, RG 267, Stack Area 17E4, Row 8, Compartment 23, Shelf 1, Box 1, National Archives, Washington, D.C. William H. Dennis has been confused with William Cullen Dennis because of a June 5, 1929, article in the *Washington Post,* "William C. Dennis Named President of Alma Mater," which erroneously mentions that "he was secretary to Justice White."

8. *Georgetown Alumni Directory,* 1947. He also received his A.B. from Georgetown in 1874 and founded and edited the *Georgetown College Journal.* Dennis was born in Philadelphia in 1856 and raised by his mother, a widow. See generally John Paul Earnest, "In Memoriam, William Henry Dennis Esq.," *Columbia Historical Society Journal* 22 (January 1, 1919): 244–45; "W. H. Dennis, 65, Bar Leader, Dies," *Washington Post,* March 24, 1919. Earnest's memorial tribute notes that Dennis was "for a time private secretary of Justice Blatchford of the Supreme Court of the United States," but does not mention White.

9. Commissioners made their money from court fees, not from a government salary, and were allowed to maintain their private law practices on the side.

10. Dennis's clerkship dates were provided by the Supreme Court of the United States Library in correspondence in April, May, and July 2013 (hereafter cited as Supreme Court Library). While there is no complete list of all Supreme Court law clerks, the Supreme Court Library maintains unofficial internal files relating to clerks' service at the Court, which it recognizes may contain incomplete and unverified information. Note also that from 1890 to 1895, Dennis is classified as an "assistant" and "general secretary" in the Washington, D.C., *City Directory*.

11. See generally *Washington Law Reporter* (Washington, D.C.: Law Reporter, 1895), 12:407, which reports that Dennis and Enoch Totten argued a case, *Ferguson v. Railroad Company*, in the Court of Appeals for the District of Columbia; "The Legal Record," *Washington Post*, January 1, 1899; "Berret Residence Sold," *Washington Post*, June 5, 1903; "Dennis's Bitter Complaint," *Washington Post*, September 11, 1903; "Official Admitted to Bar," *Washington Post*, November 3, 1908; "Fight for Life Insurance," *Washington Post*, March 17, 1911; "Funeral for R. R. Perry," *Washington Post*, July 20, 1913; "H. T. Taggert Eulogized," *Washington Post*, December 16, 1914; "W. H. Dennis, 65, Bar Leader, Dies," *Washington Post*, March 24, 1919.

12. Correspondence on Appointment of Stenographic Clerks, 1881–1931 and 1939–40, RG 267, Stack Area 17E4, Row 8, Compartment 23, Shelf 1, Box 1, National Archives. The Supreme Court Library misspells his name as James T. Ruiggold and lists him only for the 1893 term. But Ringgold is listed as a Supreme Court clerk in 1895 in the *Official Register of the United States, U.S. Civil Service Commission, United States Bureau of the Census* (Washington, D.C.: Government Printing Office, 1895), 971.

13. 1874 Catalog of the University of Maryland School of Law, http://www.law.umaryland.edu/marshall/schoolarchives/documents/Catalog1874.pdf. He is listed as being on the faculty in 1892 at the Baltimore University School of Law, which merged in 1911 with the Baltimore Law School (neither exists today). See http://archive.org/details/baltimoreuniver00balt.

14. *Official Register of the United States, U.S. Civil Service Commission, United States Bureau of the Census* (Washington, D.C.: Government Printing Office, 1883), 677; *Official Register of the United States, U.S. Civil Service Commission, United States Bureau of the Census* (Washington, D.C.: Government Printing Office, 1889), 808; *Official Register of the United States, U.S. Civil Service Commission, United States Bureau of the Census* (Washington, D.C.: Government Printing Office, 1890), 988.

15. James T. Ringgold, *Sunday; Legal Aspects of the First Day of the Week* (Jersey City, N.J.: Frederick D. Linn, 1891; reprint, Clark, N.J.: Lawbook Exchange, 2003). In the 1881 Washington, D.C., *City Directory*, Ringgold calls himself a "journalist."

16. "James T. Ringgold Found Dead, Heart Disease Aggravated by Dissipation Ends the Life of a Well Known Lawyer," *Baltimore Sun*, January 18, 1898; "Death of Mrs. Ringgold; She Was the Wife of Jas. T. Ringgold, Who Was Sent to Spring Grove Asylum," *Baltimore Sun*, April 3, 1896; "James T. Ringgold's Death," *Washington Post*, January 18, 1898.

17. Correspondence on Appointment of Stenographic Clerks, 1881–1931 and 1939–40, RG 267, Stack Area 17E4, Row 8, Compartment 23, Shelf 1, Box 1, National Archives. I have been unable to confirm either a date of death or an end-of-service date, but Pope

is listed as a stenographer in 1911, the last year that Supreme Court clerks are reported by name in the *Official Register* of the federal government. See *Official Register, Persons in the Civil, Military, and Naval Service to the United States, Directory, Bureau of the Census* (Washington, D.C.: Government Printing Office, 1911), 1:95.

18. *Official Register of the United States* (1895), 800.

19. Supreme Court Office of the Curator Research Files.

20. Danelski and Tulchin, *Autobiographical Notes,* 163.

21. See *Official Register of the United States* for the years 1895, 1897, 1900, 1903, 1905, 1907, 1911. Stenographer salaries are recorded under "Supreme Court" at the top of the Judiciary section.

22. See, for example, William H. Taft to William M. Mischler, July 12, 1921, and William H. Taft to John J. Byrne, July 17, 1921, both in Personal Papers of William Howard Taft, Library of Congress (hereafter cited as Taft Papers); William R. Day to James G. Bachman, June 28, 1917, Box 32, Letter B, Day Papers.

23. Correspondence on Appointment of Stenographic Clerks, 1881–1931 and 1939–40, RG 267, Stack Area 17E4, Row 8, Compartment 23, Shelf 1, Box 1, National Archives. The Supreme Court Library research files only list Shipman for the 1914 term, but the list often gives the date of only the first term that an early clerk began his service. "Bertram Shipman, A Lawyer Here," *New York Times,* November 23, 1963, notes that he clerked for four years, and it is logical that he stayed until his successor, Leonard B. Zeisler, was appointed for the 1918 term.

24. *Catalogue of the Officers and Graduates of Columbia University, 1916.* Shipman is listed as a graduate of the law school class of 1913 and living in Washington, D.C.

25. *The Lawyer's List* (New York: Hubert Rutherford Brown, 1922), 240.

26. *United States v. Buttersworth-Judson Corporation,* 269 U.S. 504 (1926). Shipman was also of counsel for the appellant in a Fourteenth Amendment Supreme Court case, *Consolidated Textile Corp. v. Gregory,* 289 U.S. 85 (1933), and was one of eleven counsel for the petitioners, a railroad company, in *Continental Illinois Nat. Bank & Trust Co. of Chicago v. Chicago, R.I. & P. RY. Co. et al.,* 294 U.S. 648 (1935).

27. "Sigmund Zeisler, Noted Lawyer, Dies," *New York Times,* June 5, 1931.

28. *Alumni Directory of the University of Chicago, 1910. Yearbook of New York County Lawyer's Association 1921,* 14:59, notes he had received an A.B. from the University of Wisconsin in 1907.

29. Sigmund Zeisler to U.S. Senator Medill McCormick, February 21, 1921, Justice Department File on Leonard B. Zeisler, National Archives and Records Administration, St. Louis (hereafter cited as Zeisler Personnel File); *Register of the Department of Justice* (Washington, D.C.: Government Printing Office, 1919), 23.

30. Memorandum from Francis J. Kearful to the Appointment Clerk, Department of Justice, October 16, 1918, Zeisler Personnel File.

31. Memorandum from Thomas J. Spellacy to the Attorney General, December 22, 1919, Zeisler Personnel File. Zeisler was promoted to special assistant attorney general on January 1, 1920, at a salary of $4,000.

32. 249 U.S. 194.

33. *United States v. National Surety Co.* (two cases) 254 U.S. 73 (1920).

34. See, for example, *New York Tribune,* January 13, 1922, 19, reporting that Zeisler was appointed receiver by the U.S. District Court in a bankruptcy case involving women's wear; *New York Tribune,* September 7, 1922, 17, reporting that Zeisler was appointed receiver in a bankruptcy case involving a button company; *New York Tribune,* September 19, 1922, 18, reporting that Zeisler was appointed receiver in a bankruptcy case involving woodworkers. The New York *City Directory* lists Zeisler as a lawyer in New York from 1922 to 1928. The 1930 Census lists his profession to be a broker on Wall Street.

35. Zeisler's name is on the briefs as an attorney with the Federal Security Administration in *Beers v. Federal Security Administrator,* 172 F.2d 34 (2nd Cir. 1949); *Ewing v. Gardner,* 185 F.2d 781 (6th Cir. 1950); *Ewing v. McLean* 189 F.2d 887 (9th Cir. 1951); *Stull v. Ewing,* 194 F.2d 707 (2nd Cir. 1952); *Jennie Stull v. Oscar R. Ewing, Federal Security Administrator,* 194 F.2d 707 (2nd Cir. 1952).

36. Memorandum from Francis J. Kearful to the Appointment Clerk, Department of Justice, October 16, 1918, Zeisler Personnel File.

37. *Register of the Department of Justice* (Washington, D.C.: Government Printing Office, 1928), 5.

38. *Georgetown Alumni Directory,* 1947.

39. John J. Byrne to William H. Taft, July 6, 1921, Taft Papers.

40. See Todd C. Peppers, "Summer Vacation with Will and Misch: Chief Justice William Howard Taft and His Law Clerks," this volume; "Boston Man Named by Taft," *Boston Daily Globe,* July 31, 1921.

41. William H. Taft to John J. Byrne, July 17, 1921, Taft Papers.

42. "Liquor Prosecution to Be Decentralized: Stone Appoints Regional Prosecutor for New England," *Washington Post,* July 30, 1924; *Register of the Department of Justice* (1928), 72.

43. *United States v. Zerbey* 271 U.S. 332 (1926); *Lederer v. McGarvey* 271 U.S. 342 (1926); *Shields v. United States* 273 U.S. 583 (1927).

44. Oliver Wendell Holmes Jr. to Felix Frankfurter, June 22, 1920, quoted in Robert M. Mennel and Christine L. Compston, *Holmes and Frankfurter: Their Correspondence, 1912–1934* (Hanover, N.H.: University Press of New England, 1996), 94.

45. 41 Stat. 209 (July 19, 1919).

46. Danelski and Tulchin, *Autobiographical Notes,* 163.

47. Willis Van Devanter to James D. Maher, Clerk of Court, July 5, 1919, quoted in Chester A. Newland, "Personal Assistants to Supreme Court Justices: The Law Clerks," *Oregon Law Review* 40 (June 1961): 302.

48. 41 Stat. 686–87 (May 29, 1920). The stenographic clerk salary was raised to $2,240 in 1924.

49. Newland, "Personal Assistants," 302. The author has added McKenna and Day to Newland's list.

50. Correspondence on Appointment of Stenographic Clerks, 1881–1931 and 1939–40, RG 267, Stack Area 17E4, Row 8, Compartment 23, Shelf 1, Box 1, National Archives.

51. *Catalogue of the Columbian College in the District of Columbia,* 1893, 131. Hooe earned his L.L.B. from Columbian College in 1892, winning the "First Essay Prize."

52. *Official Register of the United States* (1895), 809; "James Cecil Hooe a Colonel,"

Washington Post, November 27, 1898. See also "Architects to Meet Sept. 1," *New York Times,* August 17, 1899, in which Hooe is mentioned as Pheobe Hearst's "representative in Washington" who will accompany by train a group of architects from New York to San Francisco, where they will serve as the jury for the design of the new University of California building that Hearst is sponsoring.

53. "James Cecil Hooe Is Dead," *Washington Post,* December 29, 1910; "Dies After Long Illness, James Cecil Hooe," *Washington Herald,* December 29, 1910 (which notes that he had been ill since the summer); "Funeral of James C. Hooe," *Washington Herald,* January 1, 1911, 1. McKenna attended, along with the current senators from Montana, Indiana, and California; former senators from New Hampshire and Louisiana; and former postmaster general Robert J. Wynne.

54. Correspondence on Appointment of Stenographic Clerks, 1881–1931 and 1939–40, RG 267, Stack Area 17E4, Row 8, Compartment 23, Shelf 1, Box 1, National Archives.

55. See generally John B. Owens, "The Clerk, the Thief, His Life as a Baker: Ashton Embry and the Supreme Court Leak Scandal," *Journal of Supreme Court History* 27, no. 1 (2002): 14–44. Owens persuasively establishes that Embry was guilty of leaking information to Wall Street speculators.

56. "Obituary, Ashton F. Embry, Lawyer, Former Government Aide," *Washington Evening Star,* November 8, 1965, C5, says Embry got his law degree from Georgetown University, but the school has no record of him having attended. Karen Wahl, archivist at the George Washington University Law School, confirms Embry's 1912 graduation date from National University School of Law. (National University and the George Washington University merged in 1954, and the latter maintains the former's archives.)

57. Ashton Embry to Clerk of Court James Maher, July 29, 1919, Correspondence on Appointment of Stenographic Clerks, 1881–1931 and 1939–40, RG 267, Stack Area 17E4, Row 8, Compartment 23, Shelf 1, Box 1, National Archives.

58. Ashton Embry to Joseph McKenna, December 16, 1919, Correspondence on Appointment of Stenographic Clerks, 1881–1931 and 1939–40, RG 267, Stack Area 17E4, Row 8, Compartment 23, Shelf 1, Box 1, National Archives.

59. 251 U.S. 1 (1919).

60. Owens, "Clerk," 35–36.

61. Kiefer served as a clerk for the solicitor of the treasury in the Office of the Attorney General beginning in 1904, and was promoted to a second-class clerk in 1907. *Register of the Office of the Attorney General,* no. 2 (1911): 17. Kiefer graduated from National University School of Law in 1907 and continued at the Office of the Attorney General until Van Devanter hired him as a stenographic clerk from June 29, 1914, to July 18, 1919, and then promoted him to law clerk from July 19, 1919, to September 25, 1923. Supreme Court Office of the Curator Research Files.

62. Dean Acheson, *Morning and Noon, A Memoir* (Boston: Houghton Mifflin, 1965), 85.

63. Kiefer was hired September 1, 1926. *Register of the Department of Justice* (Washington, D.C.: Government Printing Office, 1927), 4.

64. *United States v. Sprague,* 282 U.S. 716 (1931); *Colorado v. Symes,* 286 U.S. 510 (1932).

65. Robert F. Cogswell, interview by Chester Newland, January 29, 1959, quoted in Newland, "Personal Assistants," 310.

66. *Georgetown Alumni Directory*, 1947.

67. "Robert Cogswell, District Aide, Dies," *Washington Post*, October 20, 1971, B10.

68. James D. Maher to Robert F. Cogswell, July 1, 1919, Box 23, Letter M, Day Papers.

69. *Annual Report of the House of Representatives* (Washington, D.C.: Government Printing Office, 1920), 55.

70. Correspondence on Appointment of Stenographic Clerks, 1881–1931 and 1939–40, RG 267, Stack Area 17E4, Row 8, Compartment 23, Shelf 1, Box 1, National Archives.

71. Cogswell interview, quoted in Newland, "Personal Assistants," 312.

72. Robert F. Cogswell, interview, n.d., quoted in Brother Matthew McDevitt, *Joseph McKenna, Associate Justice of the United States* (Cambridge, Mass.: Da Capo Press, 1974), 227.

73. "Robert Cogswell, District Aide, Dies." His obituary says that he clerked for Taft as well, and it is possible that he did work for the chief justice from January to March 1925.

74. *Dugan v. Ohio*, 277 U.S. 61 (1928).

75. "New District Job Goes to R. F. Cogswell," *Washington Post*, September 17, 1953.

76. *Who's Who in the Nation's Capital* (Washington, D.C.: Consolidated Publishing, 1921–22), 201. The Nashville *City Directory* lists Jacob as a stenographer in the years 1906, 1907, and 1908.

77. He married Cecelia Fenstel in 1903.

78. "Harvey Jacob, Lawyer, Legal Aide to Justice," *Washington Post*, April 17, 1970.

79. *Ye Domesday Booke*, 1913 (Georgetown University yearbook); "Musicale and 500 Party," *Washington Herald*, December 21, 1913. Mrs. Harvey Jacob's sister gave a party for members of Delta Theta Pi Law Fraternity of Georgetown Law School in honor of Leroy A. Reed, which the Jacobs attended.

80. Horace H. Lurton to William R. Day, December 21, 1909, Box 26, Letter L, Day Papers.

81. Harvey D. Jacob, interview by Chester Newland, January 14, 1959, quoted in Newland, "Personal Assistants," 312.

82. "Miss Galloway Is Affianced," *Herald Statesman, Yonkers, New York*, July 28, 1949.

83. "Will of Mrs. Helen M. Schweitzer Offered for Probate," *Washington Post*, August 23, 1914, reported that "Justice Lurton's son, Horace H. Lurton, Jr., and Attorneys William Henry White and Harry D. Jacobs [*sic*] applied to Justice Stafford yesterday" to admit the testamentary paper drawn by Lurton on June 5, 1896, in Nashville. Affidavits were submitted proving that it was in Justice Lurton's handwriting.

84. *Register of the Department of Justice* (Washington, D.C.: Government Printing Office, 1918), 19. Jacob was hired July 22, 1914.

85. "Harvey Jacob, Lawyer."

86. He was born in 1875 in the province of Uxbridge. "Former Aid of Supreme Court Dies," *Washington Post*, October 2, 1960, lists Widdifield as a graduate of Detroit College of Law. However, the registrar of Michigan State University College of Law (which

has been affiliated with the Detroit College of Law since 1997) has no record of Widdifield attending or graduating from the school. Polk's *Traverse City and Grand Traverse County Directory, 1901–1902* (Detroit: R. L. Polk, 1902), 206, gives Gilbert & Widdifield as the name of his law firm.

87. Application for Memberships, Massachusetts Society of Sons of the American Revolution, Boston, 1905.

88. Correspondence on Appointment of Stenographic Clerks, 1881–1931 and 1939–40, RG 267, Stack Area 17E4, Row 8, Compartment 23, Shelf 1, Box 1, National Archives.

89. Edward S. Widdifield to Paul Mandelstam, January 25, 1944, on file with author. Mandelstam received his A.B. in 1944, his A.M. in 1946, and his M.D. in 1950 from Harvard University.

90. According a handwritten note in the Supreme Court Office of the Curator Research Files.

91. 1910 Census; 1920 Census.

92. *Official Congressional Directory* (Washington, D.C.: Government Printing Office, 1914), 218; *Official Congressional Directory* (Washington, D.C.: Government Printing Office, 1915), 42; *Official Congressional Directory* (Washington, D.C.: Government Printing Office, 1916), 44.

93. "Aged Resident of Washington Dead," *Washington Times,* June 8, 1917, 4.

94. J. E. Hoover to William R. Day, March 5, 1903, Box 18, Letter H, Day Papers.

95. Correspondence on Appointment of Stenographic Clerks, 1881–1931 and 1939–40, RG 267, Stack Area 17E4, Row 8, Compartment 23, Shelf 1, Box 1, National Archives.

96. Hoover identified himself as a "clerk/lawyer" in the 1900 Census, when he was twenty-one. His obituary says he attended Georgetown Law School ("John E. Hoover, 76, Dies," *Washington Star,* May 3, 1954), but he is not on record there. His brother, William H. Hoover, graduated from Georgetown Law School in 1916. A student named John E. Hoover graduated from George Washington Law School, earning an L.L.B. degree in 1916 and an L.L.M. in 1917. But this is a younger cousin—the future FBI director J. Edgar Hoover—who famously worked as a clerk and cataloger at the Library of Congress from 1913 to 1917 while attending evening law school. "Young Lawyers Join Local Bar," *Washington Herald,* October 14, 1913, 10, records a John E. Hoover passing the D.C. bar.

97. Harlan's biographer characterizes Hoover as James's secretary at the Interstate Commerce Commission, but James was appointed to that entity in August 1906, after Hoover began clerking for his father. See Loren P. Beth, *John Marshall Harlan, The Last Whig Justice* (Louisville: University Press of Kentucky, 1992), 189.

98. *Evening Star,* October 6, 1907, 2. Laura Delina Warren was Canadian.

99. "Harlan May Retire," *Washington Post,* March 26, 1908.

100. John E. Hoover to Richard D. Harlan, October 11, 1911, John Marshall Harlan Papers, University of Louisiana, quoted in Beth, *John Marshall Harlan,* 189–90. Harlan had fallen ill on the bench and was taken home in a taxicab by Justice McKenna, dying three days later.

101. "John E. Hoover, 76, Dies"; 1920 Census.

102. Hoover's obituary says he clerked for Chief Justice Charles Evans Hughes, but

the Supreme Court Library research files do not list him as either a Pitney or a Hughes clerk.

103. "John E. Hoover, 76, Dies."

104. *Register of the Department of Justice* (1919), 20.

105. J. Edgar Hoover was hired on July 26, 1917. *Register of the Department of Justice* (1918), 24.

106. Ann Hoover Holcombe posted a note dated October 22, 2000, at http://wc.rootsweb.ancestry.com/cgi-bin/igm.cgi?op=GET&db=jdamewood&id=I4295.

107. During World War I, Hoover (age forty) did not leave Washington, but served as a draft board member. *Register of the Department of Justice* (Washington, D.C.: Government Printing Office, 1920), 78.

108. "Martens Deportation Hearings Scheduled for December 7," *New York Tribune,* November 13, 1920, 7.

109. "Hints Lawmaker Got Liquor Seized by Government," *Washington Herald,* May 28, 1922, 8.

110. "J. E. Hoover Rites to Be Here Today," *Washington Post,* May 4, 1954.

111. Stonier is first listed in the city directory for Trenton as a stenographer in 1901. His father is listed as an engineer.

112. See *Treasurer's Report, New Jersey* (Trenton, N.J.: Treasury Department, 1907), 325–28; *Treasurer's Report, New Jersey* (Trenton, N.J.: Treasury Department, 1908), 380–93.

113. Alan B. Reed, "Mahlon Pitney" (senior thesis, Princeton University, 1932), 29.

114. "Justice Pitney Names Secretary," *Trenton (N.J.) Evening News,* April 1, 1912.

115. Reed, "Mahlon Pitney," 156.

116. *Report of the Secretary of the Senate* (Washington, D.C.: Government Printing Office, 1920), 41; *Report of the Secretary of the Senate* (Washington, D.C.: Government Printing Office, 1922), 24.

117. *Georgetown Alumni Directory,* 1947; "Tablet Unveiled for Hilltop Boys Who Died in the War," *Washington Herald,* June 15, 1921, 2.

118. The 1930 Census lists him as an intern in a hospital and his wife, Cuba A. Dyke, as a milliner in a department store. The Washington, D.C., *City Directory,* 1933, lists him as a physician.

119. "Deaths," *Southern Medical Journal* (December 1941): 1294. There is no obituary for Dyke in the Washington, D.C., newspapers.

120. Records of the Office of the Marshal 1864–1940, General Correspondence of Clerk's Accounts, RG No. 267, Entry 71, National Archives, see "Disbursements by Charles Elmore Cropley, Clerk of United States Supreme Court," for Horatio Stonier.

121. "United States Supreme Court," *New York Times,* February 21, 1928. "W. R. Stansbury, 71, 45 Years Supreme Court Officer, Dies," *Washington Post,* June 6, 1927, notes that "active pallbearers" were Deputy Clerk C. Elmore Cropley and Assistant Clerks Reginald C. Dilli, Horatio Stonier, Reynolds Robertson, Harold Wiley, and Rodolph Waggaman.

122. See, for example, "Henry-Williams Cup to Horatio Stonier," *Washington Post,* August 15, 1921.

123. Supreme Court Office of the Curator Research Files.

124. S. Edward Widdifield interview, n.d., in Hoyt Landon Warner, *The Life of Mr. Justice Clarke* (Cleveland: Western Reserve University Press, 1950), 76.

125. "Chosen North Beach Mayor: E. Widdifield Returned at Town Election—People's Ticket," *Washington Post*, June 27, 1922.

126. *Official Register of the United States, U.S. Civil Service Commission, United States Bureau of the Census* (Washington, D.C.: Government Printing Office, 1929), 78.

127. Records of the Office of the Marshal 1864–1940, General Correspondence of Clerk's Accounts, RG No. 267, Entry 71, National Archives.

128. S. Edward Widdifield to Hugo L. Black, August 12, 1937, Box 442, Hugo L. Black Papers, Library of Congress.

129. "Former Aid of Supreme Court Dies," *Washington Post*, October 2, 1960. See also "Widdifield, 74, Retires as Supreme Court Aide," *Washington Post*, February 1, 1949.

130. Clarinda Pendleton Lamar, *The Life of Joseph Rucker Lamar* (New York: G. P. Putnam's Sons, 1929), 180.

131. William Howard Taft to the Justices, May 25, 1925, Willis Van Devanter Papers, Library of Congress.

132. 44 Stat. 344 (April 25, 1926).

133. Newland, "Personal Assistants," 312. Newland interviewed Cotter on February 5, 1959.

134. *Register of the Office of the Attorney General* (Washington, D.C.: Government Printing Office, 1911), 9. His salary was $1,600.

135. "William Loney Dead," *Washington Post and Times Herald*, December 11, 1956, sec. B.

136. *Official Register of the United States, U.S. Civil Service Commission, United States Bureau of the Census* (Washington, D.C.: Government Printing Office, 1921), 64.

137. William R. Loney to Charles Evans Hughes, May 7, 1930, MSS 19, 201, Charles Evans Hughes Papers, Library of Congress (hereafter cited as Hughes Papers).

138. William R. Loney to Charles Evans Hughes, April 15, 1930, MSS 19, 201, Hughes Papers.

139. William R. Loney to Charles Evans Hughes, May 7, 1930, MSS 19, 201, Hughes Papers.

140. Charles Evans Hughes to William H. Loney, May 7, 1930, MSS 19, 201, Hughes Papers.

141. "William Loney Dead." In the 1930 Census, Loney reported that he was a "lawyer for the U.S. government."

142. http://gregg.angelfishy.net/anaboutg.shtml.

143. The 1940 Census reveals that Albert was born in 1897 and Bertha in 1893, both in Pennsylvania. He is listed as "law clerk, supreme court," and she as "secretary, supreme court." See also Supreme Court Staff Directory, 1936 term (on file with the author), which lists "A. J. Schneider" and "Mrs. A. J. Schneider" as Roberts's staff, as well as a messenger, W. Harold Joice.

144. Milton C. Handler, "Clerking for Justice Harlan Fiske Stone," *Journal of Supreme Court History* (1995): 116. In the 1930 Census, Jenkins, age thirty-three, lists her occupation as "stenographer."

145. "2 Men Conclude 74 Years as Official Reporters for House," *Washington Post,* October 24, 1965, sec. A.

146. See Cushman, "Beyond Knox."

147. Mrs. Gertrude Ballard Fowler to William R. Day, November 23, 1906, Box 21, Letter F, Day Papers. She explained that her day job was "Assistant Examiner in the Legal Division of the U.S. Reclamation Service," and her typing speed was 150 words per minute.

148. See "She's More Than Just a Secretary: Legal Knowledge Needed—So She Passed the Bar," *Washington Post,* September 7, 1966, sec. C-6; http://www.c-span.org/video/?125827-1/women-working-supreme-court-.

149. http://encyclopedia.gwu.edu/index.php?title=Law__School.

150. Alfred Findlay Mason and Samuel Epes Turner, eds., *American Law School Review* 5 (1922): 29. In comparison, National College enrolled 650; George Washington, 925; Catholic University, 71; and the University of Maryland, 557. Georgetown continues to be ranked the best law school in the United States for part-time students taking classes at night while working for "the government, non-profits, lobby groups, the courts, or other agencies." See http://www.law.georgetown.edu/academics/academic-programs/jd-program/part-time-program/.

151. See, for example, Charles F. Wilson to William R. Day, July 9, 1906, Box 21, Letter W, Day Papers.

152. Ibid.

153. Ibid.

154. James D. Maher to William R. Day, September 21, 1914, Box 29, Letter M, Day Papers.

155. *Official Congressional Directory* (1913), 9.

156. See Cushman, "Beyond Knox."

157. Mahlon D. Kiefer, "Memorandum for Mr. Wendell Berge, Assistant Attorney General, Re: Mr. Justice Van Devanter," February 24, 1942, Collection on Justice Van Devanter, Box 1, Folder 6, Office of the Curator, Supreme Court of the United States.

TODD C. PEPPERS

Summer Vacation with Will and Misch

Chief Justice William Howard Taft and His Law Clerks

Throughout my fifteen years of research on Supreme Court law clerks, I have discovered that historical data on clerks and their experiences at the Court can be found in the strangest of places. A silver loving cup slumbering away in a dark safety deposit box in Boston, given to Justice Horace Gray upon his retirement from the Court, bears the once-missing names of the first law clerks to work at the Supreme Court. Forgotten letters related to a former clerk's time at the Court molder in attics. An old videotape in the Lewis Powell Archives at the Washington and Lee School of Law provides a front-row seat to a raucous law clerks' reunion. A rambling, unpublished book manuscript bares the personal and professional agonies of a law clerk from the 1930s. Dusty appointment records at the National Archives contain the precise dates of service of a neglected generation of early law clerks.

In the case of Chief Justice William Howard Taft, the relationship between Taft and his clerks is revealed in countless letters contained in Taft's personal papers at the Library of Congress. While the Library of Congress cannot be considered an unusual place to find judicial papers, the fact that the letters exist is not due to the chief justice's desire to memorialize his clerkship practices. In point of fact, many of these letters were written because Taft spent his summers vacationing in Murray Bay, Canada, but expected his law clerks to work throughout the summer in the steamy conference room of the old Supreme Court and produce a steady stream of memoranda discussing the pending appeals before the Supreme Court. Thus, throughout the summer months a constant flow of letters between Taft and his clerks passed from Washington, D.C., to Murray Bay. While many of the letters between Taft and his law clerks are perfunctory, the occasional aside or personal observation gives us a heretofore undiscovered window into the world of a Taft law clerk.

The Culmination of a Dream: Taft Becomes Chief Justice

William Howard Taft achieved a lifelong goal on July 11, 1921, when he became chief justice of the U.S. Supreme Court. It was an open secret that Taft had longed to occupy the center chair at the Supreme Court, and he had steadily maneuvered himself into position to be the nominee in the years after his presidency. "I love judges, and I love courts," Taft once said. "They are my ideals, that typify on earth what we shall meet hereafter in heaven under a just God."[1] Taft had watched his dream almost slip from his fingers, undercut by the personal aspirations of his wife as well as the treacherous tides of Washington politics, but once on the Supreme Court, he embraced his new position with newfound energy and joy.

Taft did not come to the Court alone. At his side was his longtime stenographer, personal secretary, and aide, Wendell W. Mischler. A native of Ripley, Ohio, Mischler was originally hired by Taft to serve as his assistant private secretary in the War Department. Mischler's duties at the War Department were primarily stenographic in nature. Mischler worked for Taft during the 1908 presidential campaign, and he was awarded the position of assistant private secretary at the White House. While the position of private secretary was the equivalent of the modern White House chief of staff, Mischler's assistant private secretary position again drew primarily upon his skills as a stenographer.

When Taft left the White House and became president of Yale University, Mischler remained at his side. At Yale, Mischler evolved from a stenographer to a full-fledged personal assistant. Taft biographer Henry F. Pringle writes that Mischler single-handedly took on the responsibilities of press agent, scheduling the speaking engagements that proved to be a financial windfall for Taft.[2]

Described by a Taft biographer as a "mousy but loyal" man who was frightened of First Lady Nellie Taft,[3] Mischler appears to have craved a small measure of the limelight. A review of national and state newspapers from the early twentieth century reveals an unexpected number of articles about the diminutive stenographer and his travels.[4] The August 18, 1906, edition of the *Daily Public Ledger* (Maysville, Kentucky) proudly noted that "old Ripley O[hio] boy Wendell Mischler had been summoned to Taft's summer home to assist the Secretary of War" (the implication being that Mischler was simply indispensable), and the *Georgetown Gazette* trumpeted his appointment as assistant secretary to the president.[5] Not to be outdone, the May 12, 1909, *Ripley Bee* declared that Mischler was "the best stenographer in the world."

> And those who saw Mr. Mischler work on the eight months' [*sic*] Taft Trip, during the campaign and afterward, have no difficulty in believing him. Mr. Mischler was always "there," no matter what the crush, and he

would have the speeches that "the Chief" made in typewriting almost before Mr. Taft returned to the train. The only delay in getting the speech on the wire was caused by Mr. Taft himself.[6]

Assuming that Mischler himself was the source of this information, it is odd that the loyal "Misch" (as Taft nicknamed him) would throw his boss under the proverbial train by blaming *him* for delaying wire releases of his own speeches.

After Taft's defeat in the 1912 presidential election, newspaper articles discussed Mischler's future plans as well as the former president's. The *Washington Herald* reassured its readers that the team of Taft and Mischler was not breaking up, and that Mischler—who "can write more than 200 words a minute shorthand, and typewrite from printed matter more than 200 words per minute, keeping this up for hours"—would serve as Taft's personal secretary at Yale.[7] The *Washington Post* also reported on Mischler's new position, describing him as "one of the ablest and most reliable aids [*sic*] the President has ever had. . . . [I]t is because of his rare talents that Mr. Taft requested that Mr. Mischler accompany him to Yale."[8]

When Taft was elevated to the Supreme Court, the press again singled out the former president's personal secretary. The *Sandusky Star Journal* reported that Mischler—"a self-made man, having had no college training, but is considered one of the most efficient secretaries in the country"—would be returning to Washington with the new chief justice.[9] Not to be outdone in the lavish praise of Mischler, the *Wichita Daily Times* chimed in:

> "Misch" is forever busy at the typewriter, the Dictaphone, the telephone, or what not, making Mr. Taft's engagements, keeping up with his correspondence, and performing all manners of service. "Misch" is no union man, for he works very often from sunrise until 10 and 11 o'clock at night. . . . You could not pry "Misch" away from Taft. They are inseparable. "Misch" loves his job, and he loves Mr. Taft, and they will be faithful until death, for the reason that "Misch" believes in Mr. Taft, and believes also his own job as secretary is the most important job in all the world.[10]

Undoubtedly, Mischler was the unidentified source for these breathless recitations of his stenographic prowess and insider status. While one can be amused at Mischler's clumsy public relations campaign, it is clear that Taft himself appreciated Mischler's stenographic skills. An autographed picture that Taft gave Mischler bore the following inscription—"To my dear friend and indispensable co-worker, Wendell W. Mischler, a model in accuracy, foresight, intelligence, and loyalty, without whose aid I could not do half the work I do"[11]—and Taft himself marveled at Mischler's stenographic skills, writing to Nellie Taft that "I cannot write on the [train] cars and how Mischler is able to do so I don't understand."[12]

Mischler is important to an understanding of the Taft clerkship practices because the loyal stenographer and personal assistant often served as a stern and prickly gatekeeper between Taft and his law clerks. Taft's awareness of Mischler's territorial nature is reflected in an early letter to his first law clerk, John J. Byrne (October terms 1921–23), in which Taft carefully delineates the titles to be held by Mischler and Byrne:

I write in order that there be no misunderstanding between you and Mr. Mischler, who has been with me for seventeen years, and who has been Secretary for the past eight years, and whom I expect to continue as my Secretary. The compensation for a stenographic clerk is quite inadequate [justices were permitted to appoint both a law clerk ($3,600) and a stenographer ($2,000)], and I must make up to him out of my own income, so that his compensation will be equal to yours. But what I want to have understood is that he is to have the title of Secretary to the Chief Justice—a title which goes by courtesy, for the law does not create the office in that name. I must ask you, therefore, if you use any title on your cards to make it "Law Clerk to the Chief Justice" ["law" was penciled in after the letter was typed]. It is quite possible that the office of Secretary to the Chief Justice may be created under a new bill which is in process of being drafted, and in that case I shall expect to put Mr. Mischler in the place; but meantime, in order to avoid misunderstanding, please observe what I have written.[13]

A graduate of Georgetown Law School, Byrne had already spent three years clerking for Chief Justice Edward D. White.[14] Perhaps Byrne was offended by the letter, and the lecture about his "proper" position and title, but he did not show it. "Your statement as to the respective official designations of Mr. Mischler's and myself," Byrne responded, "coincides perfectly with what has been my understanding from the beginning and is perfectly satisfactory to me. In accordance with your instructions, should I find it necessary to have any more cards engraved, I shall use the 'law clerk' title."[15]

Byrne clerked for Taft for three years, and the letters contained in Taft's personal papers indicate that the law clerk enjoyed a good professional working relationship with both Taft and, more important, Mischler. Byrne was the only law clerk permitted to call the private secretary "Misch," and Byrne and his wife socialized with Mischler and his wife, Mary. From time to time, Mischler would discuss his various ailments and dissatisfactions in letters to Byrne, complaining about the Washington heat, the substandard food and lodging in Murray Bay, and the "roaring in his ears" that plagued him.

The other Taft law clerks did not become close friends with Mischler. Taft's second law clerk, C. Dickerman Williams (October term 1924), later confessed that "Misch and I did not hit it off; I think that he resented me, but we never had any open quarrel and, of course, I spent a good deal of time in the Supreme Court Library."[16] And in a letter to incoming law clerk John E. Parsons (October term 1928), current clerk Leighton Homer Surbeck (October term 1927) reassures Parsons, "you made a very good impression on the Chief"—adding that "Mr. Mischler himself thinks he is going to like you!"[17]

Taft's Selection Practices

In the spring of 1924, Byrne resigned and took a position in the Prohibition division of the Department of Justice.[18] Following the lead of such justices as Oliver Wendell Holmes Jr. and Louis Brandeis, Taft decided to look to an elite law school for a new clerk; unlike Holmes and Brandeis, however, Taft decided to look to Yale rather than Harvard. In a May 17, 1924, letter to Yale Law School dean Thomas W. Swan, Taft sketches out the demands of the job:

> The pay is $3600 a year, and I desire his entire time. I should wish to know him and talk . . . with him while I am at Commencement. The work which I would expect him to do would be to prepare for me a succinct statement of the briefs and record in every application for a certiorari, and to prepare, under my direction of course, the per curiams, which include nothing but references to authorities upon which the case is disposed of. There will be of course other things I shall need him for in the running down of lists of authorities and the finding of authorities where the briefs are insufficient in this regard. Then I would wish him to correct the proofs of my opinions and to keep track of my docket and keep it up to date. I should not insist of course on his staying longer than a year, but I would be glad if he could stay longer.[19]

In a subsequent letter to Swan, the chief justice expanded on what qualities he sought in a clerk. "It isn't exactly mental brilliancy that I need. What I need is plodding, thoroughness and somewhat meticulous attention to details in the matter of jurisdiction."[20]

Dean Swan wasted no time in replying to Taft's inquiry, writing that he was "delighted" by the opportunity to place a Yale Law School graduate in the chief justice's chambers—especially when it came at the expense of Harvard Law School. "It has been a fine thing for the Harvard Law School to have one or two of their brilliant men go down to Washington each year to serve under Justice Holmes and Justice Brandeis," he writes. "I feel confident we can supply you with men who will measure up to the standard of these Harvard graduates." Swan closes his letter with the promise that he would not "recommend anyone on whom I am not willing to stake the reputation of the school."[21]

Three days later, Dean Swan drafted a letter in which he submitted the names of three young men whom he considered to be Yale's best and brightest. After summarizing their intellectual strengths and weaknesses, as well as their respective personalities, Swan raised an additional question about a skill that was rapidly becoming important in government service. "Your letter says nothing with reference to the necessity of your law clerk being able to use a typewriter. I should suppose the ability to do so would be a decided advantage." Taft clearly agreed, later referring to a clerkship candidate as possessing the "very useful power of typewriting."[22]

Taft did not always follow the recommendation of Dean Swan. In the spring of 1924, Yale Law School student William Douglas Arant, a young man of "fine character and agreeable personality," was the first choice of Swan and the Yale faculty. While Taft initially extended a job offer to the young man from Alabama, he subsequently withdrew it.

> I have seen Arant and talked with him. I find he is very well pleased with his position in Birmingham, where he tries a good many cases and is in the full blush of successful work due to the absence of some members of his firm, which throws on him a valuable responsibility. He receives $1800, which is only half of what I could offer him. On thinking it over, I am going to withdraw that offer. From my conversation with him I am quite sure that he would not enjoy this place, and I don't wish a man who will become dissatisfied to come.[23]

Taft later made a clerkship offer to C. Dickerman Williams, who became his first Yale law clerk.

For the next four years, Chief Justice Taft would turn to Dean Swan for clerkship recommendations. Swan's responses, containing detailed information on the nominees, provide a fascinating glimpse into what data the dean considered to be relevant to Taft's decision. Regarding the nomination of Hayden Newhall Smith as a law clerk for October term 1925, Swan writes:

> He does not take a very active part in classroom discussion, but he evidently thinks about the discussion which goes on and does extraordinarily well on examinations. He is a tall, good[-]looking chap, very quiet in manner and emulates the honored President of the United States in not wasting words. Apparently, however, he knows how to speak when the occasion arises for he has just become engaged to Miss Esther Butterworth, a daughter of Frank Butterworth of New Haven, whom you probably know. I believe you will find him capable and will like him.[24]

I can find only one instance in which a law clerk did not immediately "snap to attention" upon receiving a clerkship offer. In December 1925, Dean Thomas Swan offered the chief justice his annual list of clerkship nominees. At the top of the list was William Winslow Crosskey, whom Swan described as possessing the "best mind of any man in the School" but lacking in "social polish" and as a "little obstinate" but "perfectly presentable and does not appear crude."[25] Dean Swan may have been mincing his words about Crosskey, who was a legend among his Yale Law School peers as "[t]he student who sat in the front row, scowling at everything said, his arms obdurately folded as he conspicuously declined ever to take a note and who as legend must have it went on to lead his class."[26] Crosskey's classmates were also in awe of the fact that Crosskey balanced his studies with a job as an aluminum siding salesmen to pay for law school.

Despite this mixed recommendation, Taft extended a clerkship offer—only to find that Crosskey was reluctant to move to Washington by the August 1 deadline proposed by Taft. While Crosskey quickly wrote the chief justice "to express my pleasure and satisfaction" with the job offer,[27] by the spring he claimed to be confused by the start date ("my original understanding had been that you did not want me until August 15") and suggested that "I suppose it will be possible for me to get away from Washington for a few days at several odd times during the summer at which times it is almost necessary for me to be elsewhere."[28] While the chief justice was amenable to this schedule, reminding Crosskey that he could periodically leave Washington "provided you can keep me supplied from time to time during the summer with the certioraris,"[29] less than a month later Crosskey requested that the chief justice allow him to work in Minneapolis for the summer. A distressed Taft immediately responded, writing that "I don't want to interfere with your plans, but I do think it would be well if I could see you . . . and I could then tell you what I wish to say."[30] Even then, Taft indicated his willingness to permit Crosskey to work in Minneapolis— and even suggested that the clerk of the Court could send Crosskey the court records and legal briefs necessary to prepare the cert petitions. The chief justice's response was not sufficiently swift, and before his response could arrive Crosskey was telegraphing Mischler and requesting that Mischler promptly send a return telegraph with Taft's decision.[31]

The Taft papers do not contain a copy of any such telegraph, but one wonders how the prickly Mischler responded to Crosskey's impatient inquires. Although the system of mailing legal materials to Minneapolis, having Crosskey return the materials and his digests to Washington (presumably at taxpayer expense), and then having the digests sent to Murray Bay, Canada, appears to have worked, Crosskey did not always promptly complete his assignments. In an August 22, 1926, letter to the chief justice, Crosskey apologizes for a tardy set of digests—but offers a good excuse. "I am sorry to have been so slow with these last cases, but there have been several patent cases [among the cert petitions] and they mean next to nothing to me."[32] Crosskey himself did not arrive in Washington until the first week of September, shortly before the chief justice returned for the start of October term 1926.

In December 1927, Chief Justice Taft deviated slightly from his selection practices by asking acting Yale Law School dean Robert M. Hutchins to assess the qualifications of Yale Law student John Edward Parsons, son of the late congressman Herbert Parsons. It is clear from Dean Hutchins's response that Parsons was not among the faculty's top choices; while Hutchins writes that Parsons "will unquestionably be a very successful lawyer," he adds that he is a "brilliant student when he wishes to work" and has not "shown here the capacity for industry" demonstrated by the other candidates.[33]

Undeterred by the lukewarm recommendation, Taft wrote to Parsons's mother—the famed anthropologist Elsie Clews Parsons.[34] "What I want to know is whether your boy will be interested in the work he will have to do for me and will do it," wrote Taft. "It is not very heavy or absorbing work but when occasions call it must be done. Now if your boy says he will do it, I know he will." Taft reassured Parsons that he had faith in her son's abilities, adding that his low grades at Yale Law School were easily explained away. "It was to be expected that the interruption of the marriage should take off the fine edge of the application to the course and affect the marks."[35] At the end of the letter, Taft reveals his motivation for reaching out to the young Parsons and offering him a clerkship: "My relation to you and to his father, my love and admiration for Herbert, and my conception of your boy's capacity derived as I have said from Dean Hutchins' letter and from other sources, all lead me to do this if he and you wish it. I am quite sure I would like association with him."[36]

Having not heard back from Elsie Parsons by the end of January (she was traveling overseas), Taft reached out to John Parsons regarding the clerkship offer. The young man immediately responded, gratefully accepting the offer. "I know that I should find it [the clerkship] both interesting and profitable. The appointment has always seemed to me the best opportunity that [is] offered at the close of law school. . . . If you do me the honor of appointing me, I feel that I can do the job."[37] In subsequent correspondence, Parsons referred to the clerkship as his "great wish since I entered law school" and pledged to "justify your choice."[38]

Once Taft extended the offer to Parsons, he felt compelled to write Dean Hutchins and explain his decision. Noting his close friendship with the late congressman Parsons and his wife, and once again explaining away the young Parson's grades as the result of the "interference" of marriage, Taft gently apologized for overlooking the recommendations of the Yale faculty. "I like to appoint men from your Law School, and I like generally to take the man that the

Faculty recommends, because I believe in marks, and I believe in the reward of hard work. But I think I may venture this year to make such an exception to my rule as this may involve."[39]

By all accounts, Parsons was a successful law clerk with whom Taft enjoyed a warm relationship (Parsons was the only clerk whom Taft referred to by his first name in his correspondence). In an August 17, 1928, letter, Taft writes Parsons to tell him that his digests are "very well done and quite satisfactory to me. I like your method of presenting them, and I like your judgment also."[40] At the end of his clerkship, Parsons wrote Taft that "I shall never forget my year in Washington and do not expect to have as pleasant and interesting a job for a long time. I cannot begin to thank you for the opportunity and your interest."[41] In response, Taft wrote: "It has been a very great pleasure to have you with me in this matter, John. You have done well, and I hope that you found something which will prove to be useful in your future professional experience. I shall always look back with pleasure upon our association."[42]

The chief justice's practice of hiring Yale Law School graduates, however, ended with John Parsons. Nothing in the Taft papers specifically explains why Taft stopped hiring Yale men, although the chief justice's rapidly declining health may have spurred him to look for a clerk who would not need extensive training. In a newspaper article on law clerks that appeared in the *Appleton (Wis.) Post-Crescent*, the reporter offered the following explanation for the break from tradition: "Taft wearied of breaking in a new man every year or so and having him leave just as he became familiar with the work. So he picked a young man who worked in the office of the clerk of the court as his assistant, with the understanding that he would remain as long as he held his position on the bench."[43]

The young man in question was John Reynolds Robertson (October term 1929), who became Taft's final law clerk. By the time Taft selected Robertson as his law clerk, Robertson had worked from 1922 to 1929 as an assistant clerk in the Supreme Court clerk's office and had written a book on Supreme Court procedure.[44] During his clerkship, he would coauthor a widely used book with fellow Hughes law clerk Francis R. Kirkham on Supreme Court jurisdiction.[45] After Taft's death in February 1930, Robertson would clerk for Chief Justice Charles Evans Hughes.

Robertson remained with Hughes until the fall of 1934, when he was fired because of alcoholism. Seeking a fresh start, Robertson passed the New York bar exam and found a job with the prestigious law firm of Cravath, deGersdorff, Swaine & Wood, where he worked as one of the lead attorneys representing the Schechter Poultry Company in its efforts to have the National Recovery Act declared unconstitutional.[46] Robertson performed well on the case, and received a one-month vacation in Bermuda in recognition of his hard work.[47]

Robertson's life continued to unravel because of his drinking, however, and by January 1940 he found himself standing in a New York state court, pleading guilty to passing bad checks at the Waldorf-Astoria Hotel. Evidence introduced at the hearing demonstrated that this was not a onetime occurrence and that Robertson had been forging checks for the last five years. Telling the weeping Robertson that "[i]t is too bad you find yourself in a court over which you should be presiding," trial court judge John J. Freschi took notice of the fact that he had received letters from "many of the most prominent men in the country asking for leniency in your behalf"—including Chief Justice Hughes. Before receiving a suspended sentence (Robertson had already been in jail for six months awaiting trial), the trial court judge warned Robertson "to save yourself before you fall into the gutter and become a derelict" and elicited Robertson's promise that—"with the help of God"—he would avoid drink.[48]

Five months later, Robertson voluntarily returned to court. While he claimed that he had not resumed drinking, he stood before the same trial court judge and requested that he be committed. Having received testimony from Bellevue Hospital doctors that Robertson was delusional, Judge Freschi ordered him committed to the Rockland State Hospital for the Insane—where Robertson remained until his death in 1966. During the twenty-six years that Robertson was committed to the hospital, he had no visitors. Of his former colleague and coauthor, Francis R. Kirkham would write: "[w]ithout any qualification I still say, after half a lifetime of practice . . . that I have never met anyone with a finer legal mind [than Robertson]. Even at his early age in the 1930s, he was one of the great figures of the American bar."[49]

Life as a Taft Clerk

Thanks to the stream of letters between Taft and his law clerks, we have a fairly accurate picture of the clerks' activities (Taft referred to the clerkship in general as "the school house"[50]). Taft encouraged his outgoing clerks to correspond with the incoming clerks and educate them as to the duties and expectations of their position. The clerkship typically started in early August, and the clerks worked on reviewing cert petitions and preparing "digests" at the dining table in the Supreme Court's stifling hot conference room at the U.S. Capitol. All completed cert memoranda (or digests) included a recommendation as to the disposition of the appeal, and they were subsequently mailed by the clerk to Chief Justice Taft's summer home in Murray Bay, Canada; the clerk of the Court separately mailed the cert petitions themselves, the parties' briefs, and other related materials.

In later years, Taft permitted a few of his law clerks to work on the cert petitions in other cities if the locations had an adequate law library (Crosskey worked in Minneapolis, while Parsons worked in North Haven, Maine). Occasionally this system hit snags, such as the time that the post office refused to mail a package of Parson's cert memoranda and related material because it weighed in at fourteen pounds.[51] Taft himself did not arrive in Washington, D.C., until early September.

The correspondence between Taft and his law clerks indicates that the clerks initially struggled to strike the right balance in their cert memos. In one of his first letters to Taft, Williams announces that he is digging through the stack of fifty-seven cert petitions awaiting him in the conference room. "The only digest I have as yet completed is of the case of Bower v. United States. Although I made no recommendation I am afraid I may have indicated my own views too strongly and devoted too much energy to comments on the petitioner's argument rather than to an exposition of it."[52]

Responding to the clerk's concerns, Taft advised him to not be "too elaborate" in summarizing the cert petitions, adding that "[t]he question of the correctness of the ruling below is not the one you know which turns our granting a certiorari—it is the character of the question of the existence of a conflict on the point between two Circuit Courts of Appeal which determine our action." Taft also requested that Williams "send me the certioraris as you dispose of them—perhaps two or three at [a] time—but don't let me accumulate. It is easier for me to get rid of them as they come in that way."[53]

For his part, Williams now worried that he gone too far in the other extreme.

> As you probably have noticed I have cut down considerably on my later digests the length that I reached in my earlier efforts. This I did on the advice of Mr. Byrne and the suggestion in your first letter not to be too "elaborate." I am now afraid that perhaps I have been overdoing it, particularly since receiving your letter commending me on the initial two [digests] which were, I think, my most extensive. I have been aiming to present the facts necessary to an adequate comprehension of the issues, without necessarily commenting on the various points made nor giving any pretentious resumé of the arguments. Please let me know if I have [been] going too far in my search for bare simplicity. If any of the digests leave you in doubt on any point, I can make a supplement if you will ask the questions you want answered.[54]

Taft, however, seemed pleased with the work product. In an August 29, 1924, letter, he acknowledged the arrival of the first wave of cert memoranda, and he urged Williams to "[l]et the good work go on."[55] Taft would subsequently reassure Williams that he had read the young man's first thirty-five memos and that "them [sic] seem to me to be all right. I can make some suggestions to you when I return to Washington, but for the present I have none to make."[56]

Once Taft returned to Washington, the law clerks worked in a small office in the attic of Taft's home located at 2215 Wyoming Avenue. The law clerks initially shared the office space with Mischler, who was characteristically displeased with the situation. Perhaps sensing the tension between Mischler and his clerks, Taft divided the attic space into two offices. The chief justice explained the new renovations in a letter to incoming clerk Smith:

> I am going to give you a new room in my house. It is on the third floor just next to Mr. Mischler's. I have directed the Marshal to fit it up with book cases like the ones in Mr. Mischler's room, so that we may transfer from the crowded shelves in that room books and records enough to give him room and to give you room. You can have your desk in the new room. The only difficulty about it is that while there is a furnace pipe leading to the room, the furnace does not work very well on that side of the house, and when it is cold you may find it necessary to transfer your desk temporarily to be with Mr. Mischler. Heretofore my Law Clerk has had to be in Mr. Mischler's room, and there was evidently great inconvenience for both, but with the increased shelf space and desk room, I think you can be very much more comfortable. I think perhaps we ought to put in your room a telephone instrument, a branch of the one from my room to Mr. Mischler's, but we can settle that when I come back.[57]

Taft himself worked on the home's third floor, in a spacious, airy office that had formerly been a sleeping porch.[58] In later years, an elevator would be installed at the Taft residence so the chief justice would not have to negotiate the stairs.

Besides working on petitions for certiorari, the law clerks periodically reviewed drafts of Taft's opinions, conducted legal research, and performed minor clerical work related to the annual judicial conference of judges. Taft discussed the merits of pending cases with his law clerks,[59] and occasionally the clerks assisted in the editing and reviewing of opinions. Regarding one of Chief Justice Taft's more well known opinions—*Myers v. United States*[60]—Taft sent former clerk Smith a copy of the opinion and wrote: "I don't insist that you read it to your wife, but you can tell her that you contributed a number of telling quotations in the majority opinion."[61]

At least in one instance, the job duties of a Taft law clerk extended beyond the formal end of the clerkship. In 1924, Taft was actively lobbying for Congress to pass legislation to give the Supreme Court new discretionary power to review cert petitions. As a law clerk, Byrne had worked on the legislative language of the bill, and in November 1924 Taft called upon his former clerk to draft a memorandum that would address new attacks raised against the legislation.[62] Within days, Byrne had responded with a five-page typed, single-spaced letter,[63] which Taft praised as "valuable."[64]

In summing up his clerkship experience, outgoing law clerk Homer Surbeck explains to incoming clerk John E. Parsons that "[t]he association with the Chief Justice is very pleasant and enjoyable—in fact quite inspirational. That alone will make your year in Washington well worthwhile. In addition, there is no question but that one can, and does, learn quite a bit." After summarizing the various job duties of the law clerks, Surbeck closes with this reassurance: "I think I should add that you will not find the work unduly burdensome."[65] After a review of the Taft papers, it is safe to say that the other Taft law clerks would likely have agreed with Surbeck's assessment of the clerkship.

The Personal Bonds between Chief Justice and Clerk

Many historians speak of Taft's genial personality, so it is not surprising that Taft took an interest in the personal as well as professional lives in his law clerks. Whether it was sharing a Thanksgiving turkey, commiserating with a clerk over the removal of his tonsils ("they are nothing but sponges to take up and cultivate noxious germs"[66]) or his preparations for the New York bar exam ("I am sure you knew more about the Federal questions put to you than the examiners"[67]), giving the law clerks career advice, or writing letters of character and fitness for the state bar examiners, Taft proved to be a mentor to his law clerks. Surbeck recalls an occasion when, in a moment of existential crisis, he asked the chief justice if it was possible to both practice law and be honest. An amused Taft laughed and responded:

> There is more opportunity for chicanery in the practice of law than in any other profession. That is why there are so many undesirables in it. But at the top of the profession the ethics and standards are higher than in any other profession.... Give law a trial. Get a job as a law clerk in a prestigious Wall Street law firm where the standards are high, and the opportunity is great. You will have no regrets.[68]

Surbeck followed the chief justice's advice and joined the New York law firm of Hughes, Schurman & Dwight, of which future chief justice Charles Evans Hughes was a founding partner.

Before Surbeck left for New York, however, Taft warned him against the dangers of limiting himself to an appellate practice. Upon learning that Surbeck's first assignment would be working on a federal antitrust appeal, Taft reminded him that "I strongly advised you against limiting your activities to brief making in [the] New York office.... However, you must work out your own salvation according to your own judgment and it may be that you will demonstrate that I am wrong. I hope you may."[69] Surbeck began work for Hughes, Schurman & Dwight in July 1928, while simultaneously completing his clerkship with Taft, an unheard-of practice for today's modern clerkship. Surbeck continued reviewing cert petitions after he joined the law firm, and he even recused himself from one case because his firm had filed a brief on behalf of one of the parties.[70] Apparently a bit of a renaissance man, Surbeck took time from his legal work to invent—and obtain a patent for—a self-threading sewing needle[71] as well as to write a self-help book with a foreword written by Norman Vincent Peale.[72]

An example of the high esteem in which Taft held his former clerks can be found in the flowery letters of recommendation that the chief justice wrote in support of their bar applications. Regarding former clerk Smith, Taft wrote:

> The Faculty of the Law School recommended him to me as my Law Clerk to aid me in my work in the Supreme Court of the United States. He served for a year and I found him in every way worthy. He is a gentleman, of education and of refinement, an admirably equipped lawyer and of high character. He married the daughter of Frank Butterworth, whom I have known for years, and the granddaughter of Hon. Benjamin Butterworth who was one of my best friends and a distinguished member of Congress of his day. Mr. Smith's environment, therefore, is of the best. I am sure that he will make an admirable member of the Bar and that his character and his principles of action are in entire accord with the best morality and ethics of his profession.[73]

In turn, the former law clerks kept the chief justice up to date on their own professional successes and failures and visited their former employer when in Washington. Upon learning that former clerk Williams had lost a federal appeal, Taft wrote to console him. "It won't hurt you to lose your first case in the Court of Appeals. It is well to get used to that experience, then when you win you will feel happier."[74] And the clerks themselves were not reticent in sharing with the chief justice their gratitude for the experience of clerking on the Supreme Court. Writing to Taft shortly after the end of his clerkship, Hayden Smith penned the following words: "I shall always look back upon my year with you as one of the best possible in every way, and I want you to know how very much I appreciate having had the privilege of working for you, your kindness, and the constant pleasure I had in that work."[75] These letters from the former clerks to the chief justice are more than perfunctory thank-you notes; the Taft clerks had genuine affection for Taft and were grateful for the opportunity to work with him.

Taft at the End

Taft biographer Alpheus Thomas Mason writes that by the start of October term 1929, Taft was dramatically declining physically and mentally. Yet the chief justice was determined to stay in the center chair "in order to prevent the Bolsheviki from getting control."[76] Mischler would remain by the chief justice's side until the very end. As Taft lay slowly dying in his Washington home in February 1930, Mischler wrote a member of the Taft family about his own grief at watching Taft slowly slip away:

> The Chief Justice arrived at 7 o'clock this morning from Asheville, and he was in a very weakened condition.... [He] could not walk, and it took four men to bring him out of his drawing room and get him off the train on to a rolling chair. It took them a long time to get him off the car, but he was perfectly helpless. He was in a dazed condition and spoke very little, but occasionally he would say "Darling" to Mrs. Taft.
>
> It is difficult for me to have to write you these truths about his condition. I have been with the Chief Justice 26 years this 4th day of February.... Mrs. Mischler and I grieved over the situation last night and could not sleep. It would indeed be hard to sever a relationship that has existed for so many years. I had to force back the tears this morning when I saw him so helpless.[77]

For Mischler, the sight of the failing Taft was akin to watching "some sturdy oak tottering."[78]

On February 11, 1930, Mischler stood by the former chief justice's bedside and helped him sign a letter of farewell and thanks to his fellow justices.[79] It was likely the last official function that he performed for the dying former chief. Taft would be dead within a month, leaving in his will a behest of $5,000 to his loyal assistant.

Mischler remained at the Supreme Court, becoming Chief Justice Charles Evans Hughes's private secretary. Hughes, like Taft, found Mischler to be an invaluable assistant, commenting that Mischler was a man of "tact and discretion" and provided "meticulous attention to every detail ... and never-failing devotion to duty."[80] In fact, Hughes found Mischler's services to be so invaluable that he requested that President Roosevelt exempt Mischler from a law dictating a mandatory retirement age of seventy for federal employees.[81] After the retirement of Chief Justice Hughes, Mischler and his wife lived out their days as permanent residents in the Hotel Roosevelt in Washington, D.C.

Taft's law clerks enjoyed a large measure of professional success. John J. Byrne remained at the Department of Justice, while C. Williams Dickerman balanced his corporate law practice with a fierce devotion to free speech cases. Hayden Newhall Smith spent his career at the New York law firm of Winthrop, Stimson, Putnam and Roberts, with a brief interruption by military service in World War II. After working in private practice, William Winslow Crosskey became a well-known and controversial professor at the University of Chicago Law School. As discussed above, Leighton Homer Surbeck spent his career as a corporate lawyer. John Edward Parsons also practiced in New York (like Smith, he started his legal career at Winthrop, Stimson, Putnam, and Roberts), but also pursued his interest in firearms by writing several books on the topic.[82] Only the disgraced Robertson saw his legal career cut short, and this tragic figure may have surpassed all the Taft clerks had he defeated his demons.

Conclusion

Chief Justice William Howard Taft's eight law clerks worked during a time in which the rules and norms surrounding the hiring and utilization of law clerks were changing. The model of the professional "private secretary" and stenographer who worked for years at the Court was fading away, replaced by a system in which young men from prominent law schools were hired to assist with substantive legal work—at first the review of cert petitions, later the drafting and editing of legal opinions. And the environment in which these assistants worked was also changing; while once the clerks worked in the homes of their justices, subsequent generations of law clerks would work in the new Supreme Court envisioned by William Howard Taft.

As a group, the Taft law clerks were relatively silent about clerking for Chief Justice Taft. The tradition of law clerks writing "in memoriam" pieces in law reviews had not been established, and the clerks did not contribute to the biographies written on Taft. Only former clerk Williams spoke publicly about his clerkship, writing a wonderful piece for the *Supreme Court Historical Society Yearbook*.[83] Yet because of the chief justice's habit of escaping the Washington heat every summer, the Taft personal papers, and its letters between the chief justice and his clerks, help give us a glimpse into clerking at the Supreme Court in the 1920s.

Notes

1. Alpheus Thomas Mason, *William Howard Taft: Chief Justice* (New York: Simon and Schuster, 1964), 19 (internal quotations removed).

2. Henry F. Pringle, *The Life and Times of William Howard Taft: A Biography* (New York: Farrar & Rinehart, 1939), 2:856.

3. Carl Sferrazza Anthony, *Nellie Taft: The Unconventional First Lady of the Ragtime Era* (New York: Harper & Row, 2005), 288.

4. "A Ripley Boy Assistant Secretary to President Taft," *Daily Public Ledger* (Maysville, Ky.), March 6, 1909.

5. "Brown County Boy to the Front: Wendell Mischler, A Ripley Boy, Made Assistant Secretary to the President," *Georgetown (Ohio) Gazette*, March 10, 1909. See also "Mischler Named as Taft's Assistant: Former Ripley Boy Named Under Secretary for the New President," *Ripley Bee*, March 10, 1909.

6. "Best Stenographer in the World," *Ripley Bee*, May 12, 1907.

7. "Private Stenographer to Stay with Taft: Wendell W. Mischler to Go to New Haven with President after Inauguration," *Washington Herald,* February 11, 1913.

8. *Washington Post,* February 11, 1913.

9. *Sandusky Star Journal,* July 23, 1921.

10. *Wichita Daily Times,* July 17, 1921. See also "Taft Secretary: Chief Justice Appoints Cincinnatian Who Aided Him in War Post," *New York Times,* July 22, 1921.

11. *Marion Star,* June 6, 1941.

12. William Howard Taft to Nellie Taft, August 9, 1912, quoted in Lewis L. Gould, ed., *My Dearest Nellie: The Letters of William Howard Taft to Helen Herron Taft, 1909–1912* (Lawrence: University Press of Kansas, 2011): 253.

13. William Howard Taft to John J. Byrne, July 17, 1921, Personal Papers of William Howard Taft, Library of Congress (hereafter cited as Taft Papers).

14. "Boston Man Named by Taft," *Boston Daily Globe,* July 31, 1921.

15. John J. Byrne to William Howard Taft, July 25, 1921, Taft Papers.

16. C. Dickerman Williams, "The 1924 Term: Recollections of Chief Justice Taft's Law Clerk," *Supreme Court History Society Yearbook* (1989): 43.

17. L. Homer Surbeck to John E. Parsons, June 4, 1928, Rye Historical Society, New York.

18. "Byrne Named as Dry Prosecutor," *Boston Daily Globe,* July 30, 1924.

19. William Howard Taft to Thomas W. Swan, May 17, 1924, Taft Papers. In a July 7, 1927, article in the *New York Times,* Taft provided a similar description of a clerk's responsibilities: "I have a law clerk who goes over the records and briefs. He makes a statement for me of what is in each, and then with that statement before me I read the briefs and make such references to the records as seem necessary. But I always read the briefs so as to know what the claim on both sides is, and then I read the opinions of the courts below so I become familiar with the case and know what the issues are. When these petitions for review come before us we know what the cases are about, and whether they present questions we should pass upon" (Allen E. Ragan, *Chief Justice Taft* [Columbus: Ohio State Archaeological and Historical Society, 1938], 112).

20. William Howard Taft to Thomas W. Swan, May 30, 1924, Taft Papers.

21. Thomas W. Swan to William Howard Taft, May 21, 1924, Taft Papers.

22. William Howard Taft to Charles D. Hilles, May 28, 1924, Taft Papers.

23. William Howard Taft to Thomas W. Swan, May 31, 1924, Taft Papers.

24. Thomas W. Swan to William Howard Taft, February 17, 1925, Taft Papers.

25. Thomas W. Swan to William Howard Taft, December 4, 1925, Taft Papers.

26. Harry Kalven Jr., "Our Man from Wall Street," *University of Chicago Law Review* 35 (Winter 1968): 229.

27. William W. Crosskey to William Howard Taft, January 17, 1926, Taft Papers.

28. William W. Crosskey to William Howard Taft, May 5, 1926, Taft Papers.

29. William Howard Taft to William W. Crosskey, May 7, 1926, Taft Papers.

30. William Howard Taft to William W. Crosskey, June 22, 1926, Taft Papers.

31. Western Union telegram from William W. Crosskey to Wendell Mischler, June 25, 1926, Taft Papers.

32. William W. Crosskey to William Howard Taft, August 22, 1926, Taft Papers.

33. Robert M. Hutchins to William Howard Taft, December 20, 1927, Taft Papers.

34. "Dr. Elsie Parsons, Ethnologist, Dies," *New York Times,* December 20, 1941.

35. William Howard Taft to Elsie Parsons, January 8, 1928, Taft Papers.

36. Ibid.

37. John E. Parsons to William Howard Taft, January 25, 1928, Taft Papers.

38. John E. Parsons to William Howard Taft, February 7, 1928, Taft Papers.

39. William Howard Taft to Robert M. Hutchins, January 27, 1928, Taft Papers.

40. William Howard Taft to John E. Parsons, August 17, 1928, Taft Papers.

41. John E. Parsons to William Howard Taft, July 3, 1929, Taft Papers.

42. William Howard Taft to John E. Parsons, July 9, 1928, Taft Papers.

43. Herbert Plummer, "A Bystander in Washington," *Appleton (Wis.) Post-Crescent,* December 27, 1930.

44. Reynolds Robertson, *Appellate Practice and Procedure in the Supreme Court of the United States* (New York: Prentice-Hall, 1928).

45. Reynolds Robertson and Francis R. Kirkham, *Jurisdiction of the Supreme Court of the United States* (St. Paul, Minn.: West Publishing, 1936).

46. *A.L.A. Schechter Poultry Corp. v. United States,* 295 U.S. 495 (1935).

47. Author's 2012 correspondence with John Reynolds Robertson Jr.

48. "Brilliant Lawyer, Once Clerk for Chief Justices, Admits Forgery," *Daily Boston Globe,* January 5, 1940; "Ex-High Court Aide Put on Probation," *New York Times,* January 5, 1940; "Lawyer Freed by Court: 2 Check Charges against John R. Robertson Dropped," *New York Times,* January 9, 1940.

49. Francis R. Kirkham to John Reynolds Robertson Jr., March 18, 1952 (in author's possession).

50. William Howard Taft to John E. Parsons, February 10, 1928, Taft Papers.

51. John E. Parsons to William Howard Taft, July 6, 1929, Taft Papers.

52. C. Dickerman Williams to William Howard Taft, August 16, 1924, Taft Papers.

53. William Howard Taft to C. Dickerman Williams, August 20, 1924, Taft Papers.

54. C. Dickerman Williams to William Howard Taft, September 5, 1924, Taft Papers.

55. William Howard Taft to C. Dickerman Williams, August 29, 1924, Taft Papers.

56. William Howard Taft to C. Dickerman Williams, September 9, 1924, Taft Papers.

57. William Howard Taft to Hayden Newhall Smith, August 30, 1925, Taft Papers.

58. Ragan, *Chief Justice Taft,* 112.

59. Homer Surbeck explains to incoming clerk John E. Parsons that "the Chief Justice enjoys discussing cases and is considerate enough to explain the grounds of decisions." Homer Surbeck to John E. Parsons, February 21, 1928, Rye Historical Society.

60. 272 U.S. 52 (1926).

61. William Howard Taft to Hayden Newhall Smith, November 3, 1926, Taft Papers.

62. William Howard Taft to John J. Byrne, November 28, 1924, Taft Papers.

63. John J. Byrne to William Howard Taft, December 2, 1924, Taft Papers.

64. William Howard Taft to John J. Byrne, December 10, 1924, Taft Papers.

65. Homer Surbeck to John E. Parsons, February 21, 1928, Rye Historical Society.

66. William Howard Taft to C. Dickerman Williams, July 12, 1925, Taft Papers.

67. Ibid.

68. Homer Surbeck, *The Success Formula That Really Works* (Pawling, N.Y.: Foundation for Christian Living, 1986), 26.

69. William Howard Taft to L. Homer Surbeck, July 14, 1928, Taft Papers.

70. Homer Surbeck to William Howard Taft, July 12, 1928; Taft to Surbeck, July 14, 1928; Taft to Surbeck, July 21, 1928, all in Taft Papers. The case that Surbeck "recused" himself from was *Green v. Victor Talking Machine*, 278 U.S. 602 (1928).

71. Stacy V. Jones, "Wall Streeter Assists Housewife; Puts Needle-Threading in Groove," *New York Times*, May 8, 1954.

72. Surbeck, *Success Formula*.

73. William Howard Taft to the Committee on Character and Fitness, June 3, 1927, Taft Papers.

74. William Howard Taft to C. Dickerman Williams, January 9, 1926, Taft Papers.

75. Hayden Newhall Smith to William Howard Taft, October 3, 1926, Taft Papers.

76. Alpheus Thomas Mason, *William Howard Taft: Chief Justice* (New York: Simon and Schuster, 1964), 294 (quotation from November 14, 1929, letter written by William Howard Taft to Horace D. Taft).

77. Wendell W. Mischler to Mr. Taft, February 4, 1930, Taft Papers.

78. Pringle, *Life and Times of William Howard Taft*, 2:1079.

79. Ibid.

80. Merlo J. Pusey, *Charles Evans Hughes* (New York: Macmillan, 1952), 2:667.

81. "Roosevelt Waives 70-Year Act, Hold Hughes Aid on Job," *Washington Post*, November 24, 1937.

82. John Edward Parsons's books include *The Peace-maker and Its Rivals* (New York: William Morrow, 1953); *Smith & Wesson Revolvers: The Pioneer Single Action Models* (New York: William Morrow, 1957); *The Peacemaker and Its Rivals: An Account of the Single Action Colt* (New York: William Morrow, 1965); and *The First Winchester: The Story of the 1866 Repeating Rifle* (New York: Winchester Press, 1969).

83. C. Dickerman Williams, "The 1924 Term: Recollections of Chief Justice Taft's Law Clerk," *Supreme Court Historical Society Yearbook* (1989).

CLARE CUSHMAN

Beyond Knox

James C. McReynolds's Other Law Clerks, 1914–1941

One of the more poignant scenes in John Knox's memoir of clerking for James C. McReynolds during October term 1936 is when one of the justice's former clerks pays a call at his apartment during lunchtime. Having been told that Maurice J. Mahoney was McReynolds's "most successful" clerk and had stayed with him for many years, Knox, new to the clerkship and still starry eyed, was curious to meet him. Spying on the clerk-justice reunion in the dining room, however, Knox sees to his dismay that his new boss does not even invite Mahoney to sit, let alone dine, and that the justice "maintained a cool, detached formality toward his caller and scarcely gave any indication that he had ever seen the young man before." "If he is as formal and cold as that with a Southerner who was the most successful secretary he ever had," Knox worries, "then there is absolutely no hope that I can be a success in this position."[1] Poor Knox's prediction ended up coming true, as his compelling chronicle of his abysmal experience clerking for McReynolds reveals.

Thanks to Knox's extraordinary document, a great deal about how McReynolds mistreated his private secretary in the 1936 term is known. But what about the other seventeen clerks McReynolds engaged during his lengthy Court tenure (1914–41)? In his recent work examining the clerks of the "Four Horsemen," Barry Cushman has helpfully rescued these men from obscurity and given them their due alongside Knox.[2] We now know who they were, where they came from, when they clerked, and what they did after their clerkship. We can also conclude that Knox was an anomaly in that his postclerkship career never took off and he had to cobble together various low-level legal jobs to remain solvent. By contrast, McReynolds's other clerks went on to solid, even stellar, careers in government, law, the military, and business.[3] But the question that remains unanswered is, was Knox's experience *during* his clerkship typical? While Knox alone recorded an account of his clerkship for posterity, there are enough clues from other clerks to provide a framework in which to place Knox's experience, especially letters written home by Milton S. Musser, the justice's penultimate clerk.

Clerk Overview

With the exception of Knox, a Northwestern Law School and Harvard Law School graduate, and Blaine Mallan, a University of Virginia Law School alumnus, McReynolds did not recruit clerks from national law schools. In fact, Mallan was the only clerk the justice selected from his alma mater, probably after meeting him when Mallan organized a University of Virginia alumni banquet in D.C. shortly after graduating in 1916.[4] Like most of his brethren, McReynolds mainly hired from area law schools, particularly Georgetown University, which offered evening classes for students who needed to support themselves with day jobs in nearby government agencies.[5] Some of McReynolds's clerks had already finished law school, but others undertook the exhausting challenge of working as a stenographer during the day while pursuing their law studies in the evening. For example, T. Ellis Allison graduated from Georgetown Law School in 1918, halfway through his two-year tenure with McReynolds. His classmates viewed his clerkship as difficult, writing on his yearbook page: "Ellis admits that he likes the ladies but his social functions do not keep him from doing his arduous duties as Secretary to Supreme Court Justice James C. McReynolds." Norman Frost also finished his legal studies during his clerkship, double-duty, which his yearbook entry said took its toll: "Due to his rather strenuous life as Secretary to one of the U.S. Supreme Court Justices, Norman has not been as active in school affairs as some of his 'buddies.'"[6]

Hiring men from modest backgrounds with non-elite legal training was common in the 1910s because Supreme Court clerkship duties were mostly clerical. "Stenographic clerks," as they were then called, performed such humble tasks as taking dictation in shorthand and then transcribing the words on a typewriter, carrying written opinions to the printer, running personal errands, answering social invitations, and paying bills for the justices. In 1920, Congress began providing salaries for law clerks ($3,600) in addition to stenographic clerks ($2,000, raised to $2,240 in 1924), and some justices began engaging two assistants.[7] Although the justices now had the opportunity to hire a second clerk who would also be tasked with performing substantive legal research, not many immediately took advantage of the offer.[8] McReynolds only employed both a stenographic clerk and a law clerk for two months in the 1921 term, and one month in the 1925 term, and then reverted back to one clerk.[9] McReynolds tended to write terse opinions that were less about scholarship than showing an unwavering faith in his conclusions, so he may not have thought he needed a second clerk's help with legal research.

Aside from Knox, the best source for understanding how McReynolds generally treated his clerks is the political scientist Chester Newland, who conducted interviews with seven unnamed clerks in 1959 (his notes were since destroyed in a flood). He concluded from these interviews that the notoriously irascible McReynolds demeaned them: "McReynolds was plagued with troubles in locating and retaining clerks. Especially in his early years he insisted that his clerks remain single and refrain from the use of tobacco. Because of his strong language and asperity toward his subordinates, the atmosphere was too demeaning for some of his assistants. And, as his reputation spread, the Justice Department and acquaintances of the justice apparently found it difficult to locate clerks for him."[10]

Newland's contention is supported by McReynolds's high turnover rate: he employed eighteen clerks in his twenty-seven years on the Court. In comparison, most of his contemporaries kept their clerks for multiple terms: Joseph McKenna, three clerks in twenty-two years; William R. Day, five in nineteen years; Willis Van Devanter, five in twenty-six years; Joseph Lamar, one in five years; Mahlon Pitney, two in ten years; John H. Clarke, one in six years; George Sutherland, four in fifteen years; Pierce Butler, six in seventeen years; Edward Sanford, one in seven years; and Owen J. Roberts, one in fifteen years. The others—Oliver Wendell Holmes Jr., Charles Evans Hughes, Louis Brandeis, Harlan Fiske Stone, and Benjamin Cardozo—rotated their clerks frequently, but with good reason. They ascribed to the modern clerkship model whereby they recruited top students from elite law schools, gave them both clerical and substantive legal duties, and then mentored them on to successful careers after a single term. McReynolds also rotated his clerks, but did not consider it his job to mentor them or interest himself in their welfare.[11]

Despite this high turnover, there is evidence that McReynolds did value continuity and sought to retain satisfactory clerks who were able to tolerate his behavior. Breaking in a new clerk had its downside. According to his longtime clerk Mahlon Kiefer, Justice Willis Van Devanter believed "that a clerk, no matter how able, was of little real value to him until he had been on the work a year or more."[12] Accordingly, McReynolds rehired eight of his clerks.[13] As his first two clerks, he chose men who had been "confidential clerks" in the Office of the Attorney General during the year and a half McReynolds served as attorney general: Leroy E. Reed (October term 1914) and S. Milton Simpson (October term 1915).[14] Justice McReynolds recruited Simpson back into service for a third time to serve in October term 1919, hiring him away from his position as special assistant to U.S. Attorney for the Southern District of New York.[15] Similarly, Harold Lee George, who clerked for the last few months of October term 1918, was rehired at the higher law clerk position from April 12 to June 27, 1920 (to replace Simpson). Other stalwarts were T. Ellis Alison, who began clerking on March 1, 1917, and resigned April 20, 1919—his tenure stretching across three terms[16]—and Norman B. Frost, who was McReynolds's clerk for October term 1920, but who filled in on two other occasions when the justice needed him

(April 9 to April 11, 1920, and January 19 to March 1, 1922).[17] More steadfastly, McReynolds retained John T. Fowler for five continuous terms and Maurice J. Mahoney for seven. Chester Newland has noted that the "former clerks interviewed varied sharply in their attitudes toward Justice McReynolds," which allows that some were content enough with their clerkship to agree to stay longer with McReynolds.[18]

McReynolds may also have been forced to press back into service former clerks when others did not work out. Indeed, Newland's assertion that the justice had trouble retaining clerks is supported by their start and end employment dates, which are curiously irregular. Six of McReynolds's clerks did not even serve a full term, including Knox, who was fired in June, thirteen days before the end of the 1936 term.[19] The 1921 term was particularly disjointed: McReynolds employed four clerks, but only two overlapped (for three months).[20] In those days, clerks were hired directly by their justices, who decided their salary (within a range) and their exact employment dates. According to Knox's diary, all it took to dismiss a clerk was a phone call from the justice to the clerk of the Court, and a man's salary was suspended.

We can only guess whether clerks quit or were fired, because it is difficult to extrapolate from clerkship dates without knowing the full story. But in one respect that distinction matters little. All clerks were in a vulnerable situation because leaving a justice's employ without a reference could lead to unemployment in an era when legal jobs were scarce. As Newland observed: "A challenging reality for a clerk in a dreadfully demeaning position was that, following acceptance of an appointment, early voluntary departure could result in an appearance of having been fired—and joblessness. Yet, clearly some had the luck and/or wisdom to quit or be fired early, preserving a modicum of human dignity."[21] Because of the job's low pay, low status, and tedium, most Supreme Court clerks in McReynolds's era hoped to move on to become practicing attorneys as soon as a position became available to them, but they all needed to stay long enough to ensure a good reference.

McReynolds, whom Knox characterized as "unbelievably stingy,"[22] may have had an ulterior motive for wanting to dispense with a clerk before the term was over. When Milton S. Musser signed on for October term 1938, he repeated gossip he had learned about the justice's modus operandi in a letter home: "[McReynolds] gives his law clerk the minimum and fires him every summer at the end of term and then hires a new one in the fall term so he won't have to pay a clerk over the summer months."[23] The justice's parsimony may indeed explain why his clerks' employment end dates did not always extend into August or September: he did not see the need to keep them on the Court's payroll when the workload diminished at the end of the term. (Ideally, a clerk wanted to be engaged for twelve months and then earn a month of accrued leave.) Although this seems harsh, it was not without precedent. In the nineteenth century, some low-level Court employees did not earn wages during the summer recess when the justices were away.

Mahoney: The Southern Clerk

Maurice J. Mahoney, the "successful" clerk Knox dishearteningly witnessed the justice treat so diffidently, stayed with McReynolds from October term 1927 through October term 1933. In return for providing the justice with continuity, Mahoney had a positive experience. "Father spoke about the clerkship with respect and with happiness that he had done it," his son recalls. "Father didn't say anything negative about McReynolds."[24] Born in the small town of Blythe, Georgia, Mahoney's southern upbringing helped him get along with the Kentucky-born justice. His son speculates that McReynolds kept him on "probably because my father was 'genial,' liked by all, and a Southerner." Harry Parker, the justice's African American messenger and general factotum, told Knox that Mahoney was "real nice," was "real polite," and that even though he was from the Deep South, Mahoney was not "like some secretaries . . . who never paid . . . attention to me at all."[25] Having trained as a stenographer and a bookkeeper in Georgia, Mahoney came to D.C. to work as an accountant while attending evening classes at Georgetown Law School. His class of 1925 yearbook page calls him a "Southern Gentleman" who "has retained the goodwill and respect of the class." His classmates also noted that he "divide[d] his time equally between the ladies and the law," and predicted "much success for him in these fields."[26]

Mahoney was a relatively mature twenty-eight years old when he began his clerkship, and his success with women translated quickly into marriage. He wed Julia Johnson in June 1929—the end of his second term—and left McReynolds to take a job in the Admiralty Division at the Department of Justice. Within a month, however, he resigned and "returned to Justice McReynolds at his urgent request."[27] Although McReynolds, a bachelor, firmly preferred unmarried clerks, Mahoney's son reports that while his father knew "that marriage and children were frowned upon," the justice "didn't get upset" when he wed. (Mahoney did, however, wait until two years after his clerkship before he and his wife had children.) McReynolds's tolerance is surprising given that in 1936 Parker would warn Knox that if he wanted to survive the term, he could not have "dates with girlfriends during the year. If anybody is going to do any dating, it will be the Justice and nobody else."[28] To be fair, McReynolds was by no means the only justice who favored unmarried, childless clerks. Oliver Wendell Holmes Jr. adamantly enforced the "no-marriage rule" with his clerks, and Louis D. Brandeis firmly implied it.[29]

While they all wanted their clerks' undivided attention and unfettered energy, McReynolds may have had another reason for preferring his clerks be unencumbered by family obligations. If indeed McReynolds liked to dismiss clerks before the end of the term, their lost summer wages would have affected wives and children, a heartless situation McReynolds likely wanted to avoid. He had a soft spot for children. The justice financially supported the local D.C. children's hospital, left part of his estate to children's charities, and was generous to the teenage pages at the Court, who were all sons of widows.

McReynolds found himself in precisely the merciless situation he hoped to avoid when he felt compelled to fire a clerk whose wife was pregnant after the clerk failed to correct a small error in an opinion. In his diary, Knox recounted Harry Parker's version of the episode:

> I asked [Parker] if he thought I should ever "talk back" when McReynolds proved unreasonable, but Harry cautioned me not to do that. "He'll tell you to leave if you do!" said Harry. "And after you're fired he'll say there are plenty of other fish in the sea—meaning plenty of other secretaries available." Why Harry said that the Justice once discharged a secretary for just overlooking one error in the final proof of an opinion. The Circuit from which a case had originated was referred to incorrectly—such as the "Third Circuit" instead of the "Second Circuit." McReynolds was reading the opinion during a session of Court when the Chief Justice suddenly noticed the mistake. Either at that moment or later in the day Hughes brought the error to McReynolds' attention. Despite the fact that all the other Justices had failed to catch the same mistake when the proofs of the opinion were first circulated to them for comments, McReynolds rushed back to the apartment and immediately fired his secretary. "You have embarrassed me before the Chief Justice!" he declared in anger. . . . The secretary then pleaded for a second chance as it was in the middle of the term, his wife was going to have a baby, and he didn't have any other source of income. But the Justice was adamant, and since then he has insisted that his secretaries not only be infallible proof readers but also bachelors.[30]

Who was the poor clerk? The most likely candidate is Chester Gray, who left McReynolds's employ on March 23, 1926—one month after he had started his clerkship. Gray's wife, Ruth, was four months pregnant with their daughter, Jane, at the time of the firing. Moreover, Gray had learned stenography at age sixteen to support himself, and definitely "didn't have any other source of income." But Taft was chief justice in 1926, so for it to be Gray, Knox must have misidentified the chief justice as Hughes.

While this episode may have reinforced McReynolds's desire to hire only bachelors, among his subsequent clerks only Knox and Raymond W. Radcliffe (his last clerk, October term 1940) were unmarried: Mahoney and Musser were hired as bachelors but wed during their clerkships—reportedly without ruffling the justice's feathers. Newland gleaned from clerk interviews that McReynolds insisted on bachelors "especially in his early years," so the justice may have relaxed the no-marriage rule. Musser was particularly nervous about announcing to McReynolds his impending nuptials in 1939 because he had heard that "in the past he ha[d] fired two excellent secretaries for just such an offense."[31] He did not identify the two clerks, but one was probably McReynolds's first clerk, Leroy E. Reed, who came with him from the Office of the Attorney General. Reed served a full term, but then was replaced on November 4, 1915, by S. Milton Simpson, his law school classmate who had also worked for McReynolds in the Office of the Attorney General. Reed married Helena Doocy, a Washington College of Law graduate, on November 3.[32]

Knox's Unforgettable Diary

The hiring of John Knox in 1936 came about in an unusual manner. A Supreme Court "groupie," in college and law school he had corresponded with Justices Holmes, Van Devanter, and Cardozo, and invited himself to Washington to meet them. His letters to Van Devanter, which asked for career advice, led to the kindly justice arranging for his friend McReynolds to hire him. With mediocre grades at Harvard Law School, Knox was not protégé material for Professor Felix Frankfurter, who fed his best students to Holmes, Brandeis, and Cardozo.[33]

When he summoned Knox to Washington for an interview, McReynolds warned that he wanted "an all round man who can & will do everything possible to help me." While some justices by then were employing both a law clerk and a female secretary, McReynolds insisted he "had no use for women secretaries and always prefer[red] my law clerk to do secretarial work, too." He asked Knox if he smoked (not allowed), took dictation, and typed, and for a handwriting sample. McReynolds gave Knox six weeks of unpaid time to get up to speed on shorthand and offered him a salary of $2,400 a year. Neither McReynolds nor Van Devanter asked him about his politics, but "just assumed [he] was a staunch Republican, or at least anti–New Deal." McReynolds did, however, ask which church he attended.[34]

Knox was hired on condition he rent an apartment in McReynolds's elegant building on Sixteenth Street, which was expensive. On Knox's first day of work, McReynolds announced he was bumping up his salary (at the urging of his messenger, Harry Parker) to $2,750, but considering the government allotted each justice between $2,400 and $3,750 per clerk, and most other clerks were earning $3,000, this was not generous.[35] Like all the clerks before him, Knox worked in the library of the justice's apartment even though McReynolds now had the option of moving his staff into the spacious new chambers awaiting him in the newly opened Court building. (The other justices were equally ret-icent to move their offices out of their homes, and Brandeis, like McReynolds, never moved into his Supreme Court chambers.) McReynolds required Knox to stay in the apartment all day in case there were phone calls to answer and to "be available at all times in case I need you."[36] Isolated, it was a lonely year for Knox. Clerks for other justices also complained about the isolation of working in an individual justice's home and rarely being permitted to attend oral argu-ments at the Court.[37]

Initially, the most time-consuming task that McReynolds assigned Knox was digesting and summarizing the hundreds of petitions for certiorari that had poured in over the summer. Since Knox did not start until August, there was a huge backlog, and he threw himself "into the task with a fervor."[38] At the bottom of each typed summary Knox would write his own "recommendation as to whether the petition should be allowed or denied." "I gradually became almost like an automaton," he wrote in his diary, "I read a certain number of petitions each day. . . . The pile of typed sheets grew ever higher."[39] While labo-rious, the continual cert work pleased Knox, as he believed he was contributing substantive legal work. Indeed, not every clerk was tasked with summarizing petitions; Brandeis, for example, allowed his clerks to perform legal research, but insisted on reading all the cert petitions himself.

Knox soon realized, however, that McReynolds did not rely on his summa-ries in discussing cert petitions with the other justices in conference. As the second most senior justice, McReynolds could listen to the chief justice frame the debate and then the more junior justices discuss the petition before it was his turn to vote on whether to take up the case, at which point he had a good handle on the issue. "Therefore," Knox concluded, "any recommendations which I might make in my digests of the petitions for certiorari were more or less superfluous." "Even if I had not read and briefed a single petition, it would not have been too much of a loss for the Justice," he theorized. After seeing the justice blithely throw the summarized petitions in the wastebasket after an October conference, Knox suspected that McReynolds "regarded [his] work on these petitions as little more than a mental exercise to keep [him] busy and out of mischief."[40]

The justice did once assign his clerk an opinion to draft, much to Knox's delight. "Like a fire horse waiting to run to the nearest conflagration,"[41] Knox sweated over four drafts of the opinion while the justice was out of town for a few days. Upon his return, McReynolds called Knox to his office to "start writ-ing the opinion as it should be written!" and "quietly reached across the desk and silently, almost gently" let Knox's work "glide downward into his waste-basket." Harry Parker had warned Knox that the assigning of a draft opinion was just a "trick" to keep Knox busy while the justice was away. "He's done the same with other secretaries, too," he cautioned.[42] While McReynolds's behavior seems disingenuous, it could also be seen as hearkening back to the apprenticeship model, when justices had their clerks study and brief petitions, not to help the justice with his work, but so the clerk could learn the law.[43] When a bitter Knox eventually read McReynolds's own draft opinion in the same case, he criticized the justice's extensive quoting from the briefs and found overall that "it did not live up to [his] expectation of what a Supreme Court Justice should be able to write."[44]

Knox chafed at being treated as a mere stenographer, calling himself "little more than a machine and an efficient one at that." When McReynolds was preparing an important dissent later in the term, Knox grumbled that he "merely typed his dictation and contributed nothing to the substance of the opinion." By March, Knox complained in his diary that his duties "had now become so routine that [he] almost never made an error either in taking dictation or in transcribing [his] shorthand notes."[45]

Despite Knox's proficiency, McReynolds mercilessly fired Knox on June 17, thirteen days before the term ended. When he returned from a trip, the justice found that instead of being in the apartment all day as required, Knox has been at the Court in the air conditioning studying for his upcoming bar exam. As there was no Court business left to deal with except for a few incoming cert petitions, Knox was understandably furious. On hearing the news, Clerk of the Court Charles Elmore Cropley was also dismayed because clerks were usually paid for a whole year's worth of work, and Knox had been expecting his summer wages. Indeed, Knox's premature termination on a flimsy pretext gives credence to McReynolds's reputation for being averse to keeping clerks on the payroll when the workload was diminishing.

Cropley tried to comfort Knox by telling him that working for McReynolds was "too strenuous for a man just out of law school" (Knox was thirty), and should go to a man "over forty," such as his successor, John T. McHale, who was forty-seven with four teenage children.[46] McHale had been Van Devanter's clerk for eight terms when the justice announced he would be stepping down and asked his friend McReynolds to hire his trusted clerk. Although in his diary Knox never expressed interest in staying on for a second term, one wonders if McHale had not been "given" to him whether McReynolds would have pressed Knox into staying another term instead of abruptly firing him. Before he left, Knox spent a day with McHale at the Court instructing him on "how to avoid various pitfalls during the coming year" and "bringing all of McReynolds' accounts for May up to date." He predicted that "the change from

Justice Van Devanter to Justice McReynolds would be a very difficult one for [McHale] to make."[47]

Despite his aloofness and bursts of anger, Knox recorded in his diary that on occasion McReynolds "exhibited unexpected friendliness" or spoke "in a very pleasant and friendly tone of voice." But by the end of his clerkship he concluded that McReynolds was an unreconstructed curmudgeon. Nevertheless, Knox returned to Washington in July 1938 and paid a visit to his former employer. The justice received him "with a cool and detached formality that almost made [him] believe that [McReynolds] had never seen him before." This led Knox to recall the interview he had witnessed between the justice and Mahoney at the start of his clerkship, and to note that "the wheel of fate had now come full circle." Knox's last impression of the justice was that he was "attempting to break through some invisible wall that surrounded him, and to communicate with [his clerk] somehow, but this attempt was doomed to failure."[48]

As Knox predicted, McHale disliked clerking for McReynolds. In a letter to Knox, Harry Parker painted a miserable picture of life with the justice the following term:

> [McReynolds] gets worse. Mr. McHale is having a hard time. I am sure he would not stay if he could get anything else to do. While writing this letter I had a run in with the Judge. You are lucky that you got out and don't have to go through what we have to it is next to hell.[49]

McHale took a job regulating motor carrier registrations at the Interstate Commerce Commission and left in May.[50]

Milton S. Musser's Letters to His Family

McReynolds's penultimate clerk, a twenty-seven-year-old Utahan named Milton S. Musser, committed to two terms and stoically managed to stick through them. Letters he wrote home during his clerkship—May 1938 to October 1940—provide a valuable comparison to Knox's writings and corroborate Knox's characterization of McReynolds as being extremely difficult to work for.

Musser was born in 1911 into a well-known Utah family that continued to openly practice polygamy after the Church of Jesus Christ of Latter-day Saints (LDS Church) renounced the practice in 1890. His family's papers are archived at the Utah Historical Society, but the biographical profile accompanying Milton's papers curiously fails to mention his clerkship at the U.S. Supreme Court.[51] It does, however, give a useful account of his formative years: "He graduated from Latter-day Saints High School and also attended LDS Junior College and LDS Business College, where he learned shorthand and business fundamentals. In 1930, he was called on a mission in the British Isles by the

Church of Jesus Christ of Latter-day Saints. During his final missionary year he worked in the European Mission Office at Liverpool under its president, John A. Widtsoe."

Musser's papers include correspondence with his mother, Ellis Shipp Musser, who received a B.A. in 1907 from the University of Utah and was working part-time as an insurance agent. Her husband, Joseph White Musser, spent his time shuttling between four wives, publishing pro-polygamy tracts, and trying to earn a living in the oil and gas business, leaving Ellis to struggle financially and to care for Milton and his four siblings. Joseph would be jailed in 1944 for openly practicing plural marriage, and he died in 1954. Ellis renounced polygamy in later life after being excommunicated from the LDS Church; her children did not follow their father in the practice of plural marriage.[52]

Musser's letters also include correspondence with his younger brother, Samuel; with his older sister, Ellis; and with her husband, Francis R. Kirkham, whom she married in 1928. Kirkham had also grown up in Salt Lake City, where he earned the nickname "Czar" because of his strong leadership qualities. The couple moved to Washington, D.C., to attend the George Washington University. Ellis earned a B.A. in 1931; Francis received his B.A. in 1930 and his J.D. in 1931, graduating first in his law school class. While still in school, he was hired by Supreme Court justice George Sutherland, a fellow Utahan, and clerked for him for the 1930–33 terms.[53] Remarkably brilliant, Kirkham was asked to stay on for October term 1934 by Chief Justice Charles Evans Hughes, who needed help with administrative matters at the Court.[54]

Milton Musser followed his brother-in-law's lead in moving to Washington in 1932 to enroll at the George Washington University, first as an undergraduate and then for law school. Czar and Ellis looked out for him as he studied law at night and worked by day as a legislative researcher on the staff of Senator William H. King, of Utah (1932–34), and then as a law clerk to Nathan Cayton, municipal court judge of the District of Columbia (1934–38). As such, Musser became the only McReynolds clerk other than McHale and Allison (who was secretary to the chief judge of the U.S. Court of Appeals for the District of Columbia Circuit) to have had previous clerkship experience with a judge.

When Musser decided to leave Judge Cayton and the municipal court for greener pastures, he was fortunate that his brother-in-law was a veteran Court insider who could help him navigate the ways of attaining a Supreme Court clerkship. In December 1935, Kirkham had decided to move to San Francisco to join the law firm of Pillsbury, Madison & Sutro, but his work for Hughes continued. He coauthored a much-needed handbook for lawyers about Supreme Court practice,[55] and drafted a report for the chief justice suggesting revisions to the way people filed for bankruptcy, a crucial subject in the wake of the Great Depression.[56]

Kirkham no doubt would have liked to secure his brother-in-law a position with his former boss, Justice Sutherland, but John W. Cragun, whom both Kirkham and Musser knew from growing up in Salt Lake City, had already succeeded him. Like his fellow Utahans, Cragun had studied law at the George Washington University while working by day as a stenographer.[57] While a law clerk to Sutherland in the 1934–37 terms, Cragun, like Kirkham, was also assigned to work on special projects for Chief Justice Hughes. As Musser would later brag to Justice McReynolds in his job interview, he helped both Kirkham and Cragun with these extracurricular assignments.

When Sutherland announced he was retiring from the Court on January 17, 1938, Musser saw his opportunity and enlisted Kirkham to campaign for him. In the short time before Sutherland's successor, Solicitor General Stanley F. Reed, took his seat on January 31, Musser strategized that Cragun would be kept on as Justice Reed's new law clerk and that Reed would also hire him as his stenographic clerk (the term Musser used was "secretary"). The plan was for Cragun to stay until summer and for Musser "to take over [as law clerk] without breaking the routine of the office."[58] Kirkham obligingly lobbied Cragun, Reed, Sutherland, and Clerk of the Court Cropley to press his brother-in-law's case.[59]

Disappointingly, Cragun decided to go directly into private practice, having been counseled by Sutherland to move on. Reed brought Harold Leventhal, who was clerking for him in the Office of the Solicitor General, to his chambers at the Court to serve out the term. A Columbia Law School graduate, Leventhal was already experienced in the ways of the Court because he had clerked for Justice Harlan Fiske Stone the previous term. Reed also decided to retain his secretary, Helen Gaylord, who had assisted him since his days as general counsel of the Reconstruction Finance Corporation, effectively hiring her for the position that Musser was gunning for.

Thus it was not, as Musser feared, the lack of a completed law degree that hurt him, but changing employment norms whereby the practice of hiring a law clerk and a stenographic clerk, followed by only some of the justices since its inception in 1920, was becoming obsolete. When Musser relayed the disappointing news to Kirkham, he said he supposed Justice Reed hired Gaylord "so she could help Mrs. Reed," revealing that Musser did not realize that female secretaries were replacing male stenographic clerks.[60]

Shifting gears, Musser turned his focus to Justice McReynolds, but not without trepidation. He asked Kirkham whether he should take the McReynolds position being vacated early by McHale or wait for another opening at the Court:

> Both [Richard Hogue, Chief Justice Hughes's clerk] and Cragun told me McReynolds is looking for a law clerk. He now has Van Devanter's old law

clerk. They both tell me not to apply. What do you think? I would only consider it as an "in" to the court. I should like to have your advice on this matter. . . . Hogue and Cragun were very nice to me—Hogue especially. There is talk of both McReynolds and Brandeis retiring this spring. Also, the feeling is that Cardozo will not be back. Maybe other chances will come my way. Damn! I knew I should have been attending Church more regularly.[61]

Musser quickly realized, however, that a clerkship with McReynolds was his only viable option. Accordingly, he lobbied John T. Suter, a reporter who covered the Supreme Court for the Associated Press and whom McReynolds had hired as his private secretary when he was appointed attorney general twenty-five years earlier:[62]

> This morning I immediately arranged for an appointment with Suter and saw him. He was very nice—took down information about me relative to church affiliation, age, habits, experience as social secretary and otherwise, etc. etc. He told me he was of the impression that McReynolds might resign at the end of this term. He was very cordial and I think I quite beneficially put over the impresario act. He said that if the Justice is in town he will see him tomorrow morning and try and arrange for an appointment.[63]

Musser was fully aware of the difficulties of working for McReynolds. "You, of course, know about McReynolds," he wrote his mother. "He is supposed to be a ? X ! X X = !"[64] But, he bravely asserted, the justice's "apparent idiosyncrasies do not frighten me. They present a real challenge." His level of knowledge about the justice's habits is telling. "I certainly can handle those Sunday morning teas [McReynolds] gives the fairer sex,"[65] Musser assured Kirkham, indicating that he had been apprised of the justice's custom of hosting Sunday brunches and inviting his many female society friends. It would be interesting to know if Musser, Cragun, or Sutherland had spoken directly with Sherier, Knox, or McHale about their clerkship experiences with McReynolds or if the justice's habits were common knowledge in Washington.

In any case, Musser was determined to "land the position": "If I get the interview I shall pull the poisonality [sic] out of the bag and try my best—holding out for the $3600 [top of the clerk salary range], being careful to become not too disappointed no matter how the outcome is. Here is one question. I don't think I made it too clear to Suter that I am still in school. I understand that this might be a very great drawback to my landing the position."[66]

Musser wired Kirkham to ask him to arrange a recommendation from Sutherland:

McReynolds impressed by my conference with him. Left impression will be available if he makes immediate change but prefer to remain with Cayton until small claims court established.[67] Loyalty demands this. He agreed. Sutherland's immediate recommendation vital. Please arrange this. Will count on it. Letter follows. Affectionately. Milt.[68]

Kirkham duly wrote the retired justice, reminding him that he had met his brother-in-law several times in Washington and had been acquainted with his grandfather in Utah. Not wanting to "impose," Kirkham only asked that he be willing to "speak favorably of Milton" should McReynolds inquire about him. Tellingly, Kirkham praised not only Musser's legal and clerical qualifications but also his "qualities," which "will please" McReynolds: "his personality is unusually pleasant; he is unmarried; he does not smoke; and he is an exceedingly conscientious worker."[69] Whether McReynolds asked Sutherland for his input on Musser is unknown.

Musser's mid-April interview with McReynolds went well, and he followed it up with a letter touting the research support he had provided his brother-in-law and Cragun on their special assignments for Chief Justice Hughes:

> Frequent assistance which I have rendered members of the United States Supreme Court staff has made me familiar with the duties of a secretary to a Justice of that Court. Frequently during the past four years, Mr. Francis R. Kirkham and Mr. John W. Cragun (formerly law clerks to the Chief Justice and Mr. Justice Sutherland respectively) sought and obtained my help in the work of revising the Rules, research work on the Bankruptcy Act, and on petitions for certiorari.[70]

Given that he was clerking for a judge and in law school classes at night, one wonders how Musser had found time to help them. Was Musser paid by the Court, or paid directly by Kirkham and Cragun, or did he work pro bono? In any case, he went on to summarize for the justice his other experience:

> I am twenty-six years of age and unmarried. Recently I passed the District of Columbia Bar examination and was admitted to the practice of the law on April 12, 1938. I have the degree of Bachelor of Arts from The George Washington University and will be awarded the degree of Bachelor of Laws at the next term. For the past year I have been a member of the Board of Editors of *The George Washington Law Review*.
>
> During my study of the law I have been law clerk and secretary to Honorable Nathan Cayton, Judge of the Municipal Court of the District of Columbia. This has involved extensive research and secretarial work in all its phases, both legal and personal. During the past two years I have been in complete charge of formulating and putting into effect, the plan

for the organization of a Small Claims and Conciliation Branch in the Municipal Court. This plan was first proposed to be introduced by rule of court and later was enacted into law by the Congress. My duties consisted in supervising all the paper, drafting, and proof-reading work connected with this proposal. With Judge Cayton I drafted the rules, the Act itself, the committee reports, and the great mass of paper work pertaining to this novel and widely discussed proposal.

Prior to my service with Judge Cayton I had served for several months in a secretarial capacity with Senator William H. King of Utah, handling practically all of his personal correspondence and speeches. In that position I became thoroughly familiar with the routine of legislative and governmental procedure.[71]

Musser included a list of references, divided in two categories. He listed Senator King and Judge Cayton as references for "stenographic and secretarial ability," and for "personal references" he gave the names of Cropley, Kirkham, Cragun, Richard Hogue (Hughes's clerk), and John A. McIntire, faculty editor in chief of *The George Washington Law Review*.

One unanswered question is whether McReynolds considered Musser's religion before extending a job offer. The justice asked Knox his religious affiliation in his interview, and Suter queried Musser on his "church affiliation," so McReynolds knew that Musser was Mormon. Although Musser's father openly advocated plural marriage, it seems doubtful that McReynolds would have heard about his activities in Utah. In those days the justices did not perform background security checks on potential clerks; they used letters of recommendation to screen candidates. One does wonder what McReynolds, intolerant of Jews, blacks, working women, and smokers, would have thought about hiring the son of a famous polygamist.

Musser promptly received an offer from McReynolds, but checked with Kirkham before accepting it. His brother-in-law's reply was encouraging but clear-eyed. He held out hope that McReynolds would retire and that Musser would be inherited by a new justice:

[I]t is my opinion that you should accept the job which is certain to be difficult and is unlikely to be pleasant. The consideration which would incline me to accept the place is that you have reached a point now where just a good job is not enough and you must plan on the future. If you expect to practice law you should begin immediately, now that you have passed the Bar, rather than stay in a related field in a good job. And I do think that work with McReynolds will be a better stepping off place into the practice. . . .

I do not see how accepting the job with McReynolds will prevent your taking a law class this summer; in fact, I should think it would be easier to do so with him than with Cayton. It will, of course, mean much harder work but your hours will be pretty much your own and you ought to be able to get some help on the certiorari from Dick Hogue.

McReynolds' proposed retirement may, of course, work out more favorably than if he remains, since you may continue through the term with whomever is appointed. I hate to give an opinion on a question so important to you and in the end you, of course, must use your own judgment. I would not, however, let the amount of the salary be a determinative factor. If you make yourself indispensable he will increase your salary in order to keep you.[72]

Musser accepted the offer and then persuaded Judge Cayton to hire Kirkham's younger brother. He wrote to his mother: "I have been able to work Grant Kirkham into my old job. I owed this much to Czar who has done so much for me in shaping my legal career. I would have been unable to get with McReynolds without his help and past record at the Court." He also told her that he could "hardly wait to take over [his] new duties." While he had heard enough stories about the justice to be nervous, he was determined to succeed: "Mother dear, . . . I must be successful in this position. This will require the exclusion of *everything* which does not fit in absolutely with McReynolds plans. He is that way."[73] He was also optimistic that McReynolds had been unfairly characterized and was hiding "a heart of gold": "I now start on something much more difficult—working for a man who is known to never have a kind word for anyone. Yet, from a few sources I have heard that he has a heart of gold. I am going on the assumption that he is greatly misunderstood. I shall do my best for him. I hope that will be sufficient. I do think the old codger likes me."[74]

Once in McReynolds's employ, his letters to his mother, to Kirkham, and to his younger brother, Samuel, echo some of Knox's complaints and reveal that Musser's optimism about the justice was misplaced. Like Knox, Musser worked out of the justice's apartment instead of in his chambers at the Court, where most of the other justices were now ensconced. If he had been allowed to work inside the Court building, Musser, like Knox, might not have been so much at the mercy of McReynolds's behavior. "His demands on my time are paramount to the last iota. That was the agreement and with that I must abide," he wrote his mother.[75] At least Musser was never required to rent a room in the same building, as Knox had been told to do for McReynolds's convenience.[76]

Musser took up his duties in May, and McHale, McReynolds's outgoing clerk, turned over the new cert work to him. At first Musser's clerkship went reasonably well despite his "shaking knees." He wrote updates to Kirkham about his breaking-in period:

My somewhat shaking knees have come to an abrupt though probably temporary stop. The Justice has just left for conferences with thirty-three of my briefs tucked away in an envelope. I had just four days in which to do them and during that time, was also busily engaged in performing my various and multifarious secretarial duties. You can well imagine that I have had little time in which to prepare for two [law school] examinations which I have taken this week. . . .

Of course, you know what it is like. I haven't seen McHale and other boys have been so busy that I did not have the heart to ask them any questions. Consequently, I have had to barge right in and make the best of this last Hell week. I should tell you that the Justice did compliment me this morning after he had gone over my briefs. He said, "They are done very well indeed." Don't you think that is quite a compliment to receive?

The Justice is leaving tonight for the South. He will probably be gone a week. That will give me a breathing spell and an opportunity to associate myself with the office and all that is contained therein. It would be wonderful if he went to Europe thereafter.

However, Musser added an ominous last line to the letter: "Professional integrity will not allow me to tell you many of the really hard things about the position. Anyway, why talk about them. I certainly knew, or should have known, what I was getting into."[77] Kirkham's reply was encouraging, recalling his own clerkship days:

Thirty-three briefs to begin with! I certainly sympathize with you. It so happened that I started with Sutherland in the middle of the Term and, as luck would have it, the first week I had the fewest number of certs that I had in any one week while I was with the Court. I believe there were three. I also remember distinctly that I worked all week on the three of them. For you to have done thirty-three, and, quite evidently to have done them well, is a real achievement. I suppose you are willing to agree with me that there is no better way to learn a lot of law in a short time than to work on the certs.

I hope the Justice goes to Europe so that your time will be your own while you are working in this summer. I hope the "really hard things" you mention are smoothing out and that the job will become enjoyable as well as profitable.[78]

Musser's complaints about the onerous workload particularly concerned his law studies. This additional burden was one with which Knox did not have to contend. Musser was anxious about the difficulty of both fulfilling the justice's "every whim and wish" and completing his law school requirements over the summer, and desperately hoped McReynolds would travel to Europe with friends, as usual, despite war looming. He wrote Kirkham:

I am not certain that the Justice is going abroad this summer. My position with him is quite unique. Confidentially, he is slowing down somewhat and has reached the stage in life where he desires and expects his secretary to be on hand all the time in order that he may satisfy his every whim and wish. It is needless to say that this, therefore, is my first duty. As I informed you, the Justice had told me before I accepted the position with him that I would be unable to attend summer school. Supposedly, the reason for this is that he may want me to drive with him down to Virginia and other nearby states for a few days at a stretch.

Nevertheless, I must complete one more course at school if I die in the attempt. Therefore, I am registering for Government Corporations this evening. The course lasts six weeks. I understand the final examination is on or about July 25. If I am unable to make enough of these classes to pass the course I shall try again the second summer session.

I, also, am more than anxious to vacation with you this summer. I would give almost anything to have that opportunity.... You may well understand that because of the definite characteristics of the man for whom I work, I shall do nothing to incur his disfavor if such is within my power, but I do hope we can get together if only for a short time.[79]

Musser's vacation with Kirkham never happened. "Certs, are now coming in at the rate of 25 a week. Who mentioned my taking a couple of weeks off," he wrote on June 30.[80] In the end, though, the justice did go to Europe, and Musser managed to complete his law course in late July. Musser wrote to his mother triumphantly:

Have been working very hard recently on my "certs." Have 85 of them to do but they are coming easier. Justice has been very nice to me. Has even told me to quit work early the last three days because of the heat. I took my *final* law exam last Monday. If I pass it, I am through. Do you realize what that means to me? Six years work has culminated in reaching one of my goals. I probably won't receive my LLB until next February but I am all through and can give my time to my work.[81]

Musser's letters during his clerkship capture the complexity of McReynolds's nature by showing that, while the justice often behaved decently as an employer, his personality was repellant. And the justice had such power over him that Musser, like Knox, continually walked on eggshells for fear of displeasing him, triggering his wrath, and getting fired. For example, after a week in the hospital because of food poisoning, he wrote: "Had to get back to the office today or the Justice might have fired me. He's funny that way. He just *can't* be inconvenienced."[82] He also worried about the quality of his cert petition summaries, praying that McReynolds would find "nothing fundamentally wrong with my briefs" while in conference at the Court.[83] Musser was keenly aware that McReynolds had once fired a clerk for a small error in an opinion.[84]

Yet McReynolds did not always prove to be as vindictive as feared. On February 18, 1939, Musser married his girlfriend, LaVeda Westover, who worked as a secretary for FBI director J. Edgar Hoover.[85] LaVeda was raised in a Mormon family in Arizona and had attended Brigham Young University from 1933 to 1935. Musser told his mother about his impending nuptials to his "beautiful and intelligent" fiancée, but expressed his fear about informing the justice, knowing he did not want his clerks to marry and start families: "I may not tell McReynolds. In the past he has fired two excellent secretaries for just such an offense. I just don't feel like letting him hold back my happiness to that extent."[86] "I have no fear of getting another job," he reassured her, "but there is always that contingency."[87] Perhaps because he did not want to search for a new clerk, the justice took the news with equanimity: "Finally told the Justice last night I intended to go ahead and get married. He was very nice about it. Said 'I'm sorry Musser—think your making a mistake—but I suppose I can't stop you.' So I guess I did not get fired, at least not right away—and I am happy I decided to go ahead."[88]

As the end of 1938 term neared, Musser weighed the merits of a second term for his postclerkship job prospects. Like Knox, the longer Musser worked for McReynolds, the worse his opinion of him as a person became:

> I have been illthinking [*sic*] quite seriously about my position with the Justice. Day by day it becomes more repulsive. He treats me splendidly as far as the work is concerned and I really think I have proved satisfactory to him. It is just that I hesitate to be around a man so small that no matter how hard he tries, will never become as big as his position.... Certainly, association with him for another year, will not help to improve my own chances of getting another position.... Well, life goes on and is never *too* hard to bear.[89]

But Musser did fulfill his promise to stay on for a second term, reporting a week later that the justice "is just as cantankerous as ever but treats me well."[90]

Finances, more than his lack of respect for the justice, were compelling Musser to consider seeking better employment. He regularly sent money to his mother to supplement her small commissions from writing insurance policies. In August 1939, LaVeda gave birth to a daughter, Marcia, and Musser began worrying increasingly about supporting a family on his clerk's income. "The baby's early arrival has caught me with a flattened purse," he wrote. "Boy, I'll be glad when I am out of debt."[91] With his growing family, Musser had to put down a deposit for a larger rental apartment, but he still had debts from law school.

In his second term, Musser became increasingly exhausted by his duties and fed up with the justice. "I am up to my neck in work," he complained. "Don't have time for anything."[92] "I shall be so happy when June comes," he wrote in November. "My work with McR. altho invaluable and constructive has been a sore trial."[93] In February, Musser let off steam to his mother: "If I had to stay with him another year I would probably hit him in the face. Not that he is so terrible—he is not, in his way—but only that I can't take it much longer. It will be so pleasant to kiss him goodbye."[94] Come April, he was determined to move on: "Working for McReynolds is like being in prison—maybe worse—and I certainly must leave him soon or go batty. Johnny Cragun who took Czar's place with Justice Sutherland told me some time ago I should stay with Mac no longer than one year, and in any event no longer than two. . . . Well my two years are up and I intend to leave. Don't know yet what my next step will be."[95]

As usual, the end of the term was particularly onerous. Musser dutifully continued to work on petitions for certiorari, which, as with Knox, the justice had been asking him to read and summarize throughout his service. "During the last week of court I had fifty-seven petitions for certiorari to review compared with a general weekly average of perhaps fifteen," he wrote his mother. "Other work increased proportionately and altogether the place was quite a madhouse."[96] Unlike Knox, however, Musser made no mention of how little he believed McReynolds actually relied on his summaries. If he thought the justice was not reading his work on the cert petitions, Musser might be expected to complain about it in his letters.

The justice must have been satisfied with Musser's performance because he saw fit to give him a raise. Stunned, Musser wrote his brother: "Instead of following his usual (too usual) custom of firing me at the end of term, the justice has seen fit to give me a 300 buck raise. Nice of him eh what? I was really startled not to say surprised because it was so voluntary on his part. I didn't even have to ask for it."[97]

With the outbreak of war in Europe, Musser had been hatching plans to join the army reserves. In September 1939, he had written his mother: "Did I tell you I am taking courses of instruction preparatory to receiving a commission in the Army? I think it is a smart idea would much rather be behind a desk in War Dept than cleaning mud off the captain's shoes when the deluge comes."[98] And in a letter to his brother, probably written in June 1940, he crowed: "Which reminds me that I'm already for war now. Received my Second Lieutenant papers a few weeks ago and mobilization. I am assigned to Camp Lee, Virginia where a training camp will be established. Quite exciting, n'est ce pas?"[99]

Musser delayed tendering his resignation for fear the justice would avoid paying his summer salary, the way he had reportedly done to Knox and other clerks. He decided not to inform the justice he was leaving until after he attended a two-week training camp in July. "I may not tell the Justice until the last day [of camp],"[100] he wrote his mother, noting that he had a commission in "the Quartermaster Reserves and that all Arm[y] and Service Assignment Officers are expected to attend Camp Holabird July 7–20." Musser worried that McReynolds "might say, 'I'm sorry to see you go but if you are going you might as well quit now.'" He would then have no income between July and the start of the new law firm job he had signed on to start in September. He complained to his mother:

[I]f the Justice were only half a man he would give me my accrued leave to which I am entitled as a matter of right. I would then be on his payroll (without actually Working for him) at least until October 1st. . . . I'll have to work everything just exactly right, and then rely primarily on luck, or I'm bound to be out on a limb. The Justice will kick like a mule before he will give me a day's leave, especially if I resign.

The whole thing is about as ticklish a proposition as telling him I was contemplating marriage. I will keep you informed, of course, and at the same time must ask for your good wishes when I approach the lion in his den.[101]

As with the marriage, McReynolds took the news of his military training better than expected:

Concerning my own plans—Yesterday I told the Justice I had been ordered on a weekend trip to Southern Virginia by the Army, to familiarize myself with a location for one of the largest contemplated training and replacement centers in the United States. I also suggested that within the near future I expect to be ordered to camp for two weeks. Contrary to expectation the Justice did not grumble. He simply asked for notice a day or two in advance. What I now plan to do is wait until after camp (July 20th) and then inform the Justice I wish to terminate my services on September first. His reaction to my quitting will determine whether we can go out West this summer. If the Justice insists that I stay with him a month, I shall, of course, do so.[102]

To Musser's relief, when he returned from training camp and informed McReynolds on July 25 that he was resigning as of September 1, the justice was "very nice" and even took an interest in his professional welfare. A surprised Musser reported home:

I told the Justice I am planning to resign. Contrary to expectations he was very nice, said he wanted to do nothing to interfere with my future, his own plans were uncertain, etc. etc. He then quizzed me on the steps I wish to take, told me to consider everything very carefully before making a move, and suggested a complete investigation of the firm's possibilities before definitely making up my mind. I informed the Justice the firm wanted me as of Sept. 1st. Have, as yet, said nothing about annual leave from this job, but will approach him on that subject in 2 or 3 days. It is a grand relief to have informed the Justice of my contemplated resignation.[103]

Throughout August, Musser straddled two jobs: working for the law firm and "clearing up all the loose ends with McReynolds." He hoped to get paid for thirty days of accrued annual leave by working as McReynolds's clerk for the full year. (The propriety of performing overlapping duties to a law firm and the Supreme Court went unquestioned.) Musser complained about the situation to his mother:

> So a week ago I started my new labors (having *not* completed my job with the Justice who has been out of the city the past 3 weeks). I work at my law office in the daytime and at court at night. It's a real bad job, this clearing up all the loose ends with McReynolds. . . .
> My name is already on the door of the law firm and I have a dozen cases on my desk—as a mere starter. The new activities are extremely interesting. If I can only finish my work with the Justice by September first I'll be happy, at least won't be quite so busy.[104]

A week later he wrote: "The Justice is still out of town—expected home this coming Saturday. I have just completed reviewing more than two hundred petitions for certiorari in my spare moments. During the day while I have been working at the law firm."[105]

In the end, McReynolds and Musser parted on cordial terms. And Musser did manage to receive a salary from the Court (approved by McReynolds) until October 1. He wrote home triumphantly: "The Justice returned last Friday and I had my last innings with him. I came out of the melee with never a feather ruffled. He even gave me a month's leave. That means that I get double pay for September, I hope. And will it be appreciated. The Justice was very nice to me, and asked me to keep in touch with him."[106]

The war, however, quickly interfered with Musser's career plans, and by April he was on active duty with the army. His description of his duties at the firm of Roberts & McGinnis, however brief his stay there, is worth relaying because it reveals how stimulating it was to work as an attorney compared to being a law clerk, which he had found "dishearteningly monotonous":[107]

"My new work is very exciting. Already I have been assigned cases involving dissolution of a corporation, auto collision, divorce, reorganization of RR, appeal and circuit court in Cleveland Ohio, Interstate Commerce Commission case, Supreme Court application for certiorari and others. In other words, it has proved to be an excellent step into the actual practice of the law."[108] The financial arrangement the firm offered him was also a step up: "Roberts specializes in utilities. The first year they *grossed* $55,000, the second year $75,000. My arrangements will be $3,000 per year plus 33⅓ of all business I originate, plus an annual bonus undetermined. I think it is grand to be onto something more than a mere salary."[109] Yet he also found that the job was "twice as time consuming" as his clerkship with McReynolds.[110]

Musser stayed with the army until November 1945, attaining the rank of lieutenant colonel. He started with the Corps of Engineers, supervising internal security at construction sites, but then transferred to the Office of the Inspector General in 1943, where he investigated alleged fraud in the building of the Pan American Highway. After his military service, he made his way to Los Angeles and cofounded the law firm of Musser & Wilson, where he spent the rest of his career.[111] He was, however, called back to active duty by the army to work again as an investigator with the inspector general for most of the 1950s. He traveled and worked all over the world, and for a time Musser was headquartered in Panama, conducting investigations throughout Central and South America.

Conclusion

Of McReynolds's eighteen clerks, apparently only Knox took the trouble to keep a diary of his clerkship experience. Nor did they later write reminiscences of their Supreme Court clerkship. This is perhaps because none of McReynolds's clerks went on to academia, where memoirs of clerkship experiences are encouraged and valued. They may also have been eager to downplay their clerkship—both because of the justice's cantankerous behavior and because their secretarial duties were lowly and not worth touting once they had moved up in their careers. Thus information about McReynolds's clerks is scarcer than with some of his contemporaries.

Little is known, for example, about how McReynolds recruited his clerks, except in the case of Knox, who was recommended by Justice Van Devanter, and Musser, who was backed by Kirkham, Cragun, and Cropley. In those days, candidates were encouraged by friends and associates of the justice, or personnel officers at the Justice Department, to apply directly to the justice by letter. Clerk of the Court Cropley also fielded letters from prospective candidates and passed them on to justices in need of a clerk, which, according to Newland, McReynolds frequently was. Musser also reports that McReynolds used

John T. Suter, a reporter for the Associated Press who covered the Supreme Court in the 1930s, to perform preliminary vetting. A longtime Washington correspondent for the *Chicago Record-Herald,* Suter had cut short his presidency of the National Press Club when McReynolds was appointed attorney general in 1913 and hired him to be his private secretary. It seems unimaginable today that a member of the Supreme Court press corps would be asked to vet clerkship applicants for a justice. There is no evidence of particular law school professors scouting clerks for McReynolds, or that he was screening for a particular ideological bent, although Musser being recommended by Sutherland's clerks may perhaps be considered ideological vetting. Knox reported that he was never asked about his politics by either Van Devanter or McReynolds, probably because the job was considered clerical.

McReynolds did not have a clear plan for breaking in new clerks. While Knox spent a day "training" McHale to succeed him, he himself was not indoctrinated by Sherier, whose last day was July 1, and Knox started in August. Musser was hired in April and overlapped with McHale in May, but complained, "I haven't seen McHale and other boys have been so busy that I did not have the heart to ask them any questions." Musser does not report breaking in his successor, Raymond Radcliffe, or even meeting him. McReynolds's longtime messenger, Harry Parker, apparently provided much of the training and continuity.

Musser's letters support his predecessor's portrait of McReynolds as a self-centered employer and an extremely dislikeable person. McReynolds's preference for unmarried clerks stemmed from this self-centeredness, but also reveals that he wanted his clerks to be expendable at a moment's notice. If they displeased him or did not have enough work to do, he needed to be able to fire them without having to think about the financial impact on a wife or child. As cold-blooded as his behavior was, Musser and Knox do point out that McReynolds was mostly polite in their daily working relations. Moreover, they both clerked for him toward the end of his tenure, and it is likely that McReynolds, who suffered from hearing loss and painful bouts of gout, became more ornery as he aged.

Knox's and Musser's frustration with their justice may have stemmed from a deeper issue. In his third decade on the Court, McReynolds continued to treat them as old-fashioned private secretaries when the Supreme Court clerkship was evolving into a different model, whereby clerks were not personal servants but legal assistants. Moreover, he may not have relied upon the only substantive legal work (summarizing cert petitions) that he asked his clerks to perform. He assigned Knox to write a draft opinion he clearly never intended to read, using it as an exercise to keep him busy and perhaps to learn how to write an opinion—at best an archaic "teaching" model harkening back to Horace Gray, the first justice to employ a clerk. Musser never mentions being assigned an opinion to draft, but Parker told Knox that McReynolds had "done the same with other secretaries, too" (we have to take Knox's word for what Parker said). His bench-mate, Justice John H. Clarke, criticized McReynolds for being "lazy" and not keeping up with the times, saying he "continued to the end living by the legal standards of his law school days."[112] While Clarke clearly was referring to his jurisprudence, with which Clarke disagreed, McReynolds's reactionary views also spilled over into the way he treated his staff.

Moreover, the grim job prospects of the Depression probably allowed McReynolds to continue to recruit highly intelligent lawyers and treat them as secretaries longer than he might have if the economy had given these young men better choices. And his clerks were willing to take a gamble working for him even though they knew they risked being fired, and that even if he was satisfied with their work, the justice would not help them find better employment (in contrast, for instance, to McReynolds's friend Van Devanter).[113] A gadfly like Knox, and Musser with his family connections, must have been aware that other justices were giving their clerks more substantive duties and helping them with their careers. As for Mahoney, he probably put up with McReynolds more cheerfully than did Knox, who had already tasted Harvard elitism, both because he came from a tiny town in the Deep South and because he served in an earlier time period of lower clerkship expectations.

Yet McReynolds did not behave like "the lion in the den" to Musser and Mahoney the way he did to Knox. Mahoney had a positive experience with McReynolds and remembered his seven years of service fondly to his son. And although he admonished his clerks not to start families during the clerkship, McReynolds surprisingly took the weddings of both Mahoney and Musser in stride. Moreover, McReynolds clearly appreciated Musser more than Knox. While Musser admitted that McReynolds "treats me nicely," "he treats me splendidly," Knox only conceded that the justice could be "unexpectedly friendly." The justice was accommodating of Musser's need to go to training camp, but not to Knox's need to prepare for the bar exam. He gave Musser a raise, allowed him to receive his summer salary while he was in army training, and gave him a month of accrued annual leave when he resigned. In contrast, McReynolds fired poor Knox abruptly when he had no more use for him, depriving him of the wages he expected to receive for the end of June and the summer.

These discrepancies raise the question of whether McReynolds's mistreatment of Knox may have been more egregious than with other clerks. They are perhaps why, despite at times wanting to "hit him in the face," Musser's overall portrait of McReynolds seems more balanced. Musser and Mahoney were clearly more grounded and appealing people than Knox and thus better able to absorb the indignities of their clerkships. Indeed, in the stellar recommendation letter Judge Cayton wrote to McReynolds about Musser's three years of service to him, he praised not only his clerk's "mechanical excellence as a secretary and stenographer," but his "innate tact and wisdom" and his "outstanding . . . ready personal adaptability."[114] Kirkham similarly touted his brother-in-law as "unusually pleasant." As for Mahoney, his son calls him "genial," and Parker praised the southerner's kindness.

It is tempting to think that if Knox's personality had been different he might have had an easier time with McReynolds. He was a lonely, unconnected man who came to the Supreme Court through an unorthodox route. Perhaps if Knox had enjoyed a supportive family network like Musser, he would not have been so put out that he did not develop a social relationship with McReynolds, the way he managed to with Justices Van Devanter, Brandeis, and Cardozo. After his clerkship, Knox struggled to pass the bar and then drifted through a series of low-paying legal jobs, dying alone and broke.[115] In contrast, Mahoney would go on to steady employment at the Justice Department and a steel company, and Musser would develop a successful law practice in addition to his impressive career in the army. However, despite the striking differences in their career outcomes, Musser's negative clerkship experiences are similar enough to Knox's to confirm that the trouble in the relationship lay largely with the justice.

Notes

I wish to thank Karen Arthur for her invaluable research assistance in the Utah State Historical Society archives. Barry Cushman provided generous editorial help and advice both about McReynolds's clerks and the Milton Musser Papers.

1. Dennis J. Hutchinson and David J. Garrow, eds., *The Forgotten Memoir of John Knox: A Year in the Life of a Supreme Court Law Clerk in FDR's Washington* (Chicago: University of Chicago Press, 2002), 52 (hereafter cited as *Knox Memoir*). Harry Parker, the justice's messenger, tells Knox that the clerk is from Georgia, which confirms that it is Maurice J. Mahoney. Parker served McReynolds from 1919 until the justice's retirement in 1941 as messenger, chauffeur, butler, and confidant.

2. Barry Cushman, "Clerks to the Four Horsemen," *Journal of Supreme Court History* 39 (Part I) (2014): 386–424, and 40 (Part II) (2015): 55–78.

3. See ibid. for an in-depth examination of McReynolds's clerks' careers. See also "Reed Secretary to McReynolds," *Washington Post*, October 24, 1914; "S. Milton Simpson, Lawyer Here, Dies," *Washington Post*, May 30, 1965; "Mallan Rites to Be Held on Monday," *Washington Post*, July 16, 1955; "T. E. Allison, Retired U.S. Attorney," *Washington Post*, October 31, 1974; "Harold L. George, Ex–Beverly Hills Mayor, Dies at 93," *Los Angeles Times*, March 30, 1986; "Carlyle Baer Dies Ex-Justice Lawyer," *Washington Post*, November 28, 1969; "Norman B. Frost, Lawyer in D.C. since 1923, Dies," *Washington*

Post, August 23, 1973; "Tench Marye, Wife, Killed in Car Accident," *Washington Post,* December 16, 1971; "Andrew Federline," *Washington Post,* May 6, 1977; "James Fowler, Justice Dept Aide, Dies," *Washington Post,* July 30, 1953; "Chester H. Gray Dead, Chief D.C. Legal Officer," *Washington Post,* November 28, 1965; "Maurice Mahoney, Steel Firm Official," *Washington Post,* March 8, 1978; Ward Elgin Lattin Obituary, *Washington Post,* March 30 1985; "J. Allan Sherier, 52, Government Attorney," *Washington Post,* December 29, 1965; "R. W. Radcliffe, 67," *Washington Post,* September 24, 1982.

4. "College Men to Feast," *Washington Post,* April 9, 1916. McReynolds had whizzed through University of Virginia Law School in fourteen months, graduating in 1884.

5. McReynolds's clerks who attended Georgetown Law School are Tench T. Marye (1911), Leroy E. Reed (1913), S. Milton Simpson (1913), T. Ellis Allison (1918), Norman Burke Frost (1920), John T. Fowler Jr. (1921), Maurice J. Mahoney (1925), and Ward E. Lattin (L.L.B. 1932, J.D. 1937, S.J.D. 1938). John T. McHale attended Georgetown but did not graduate (class of 1914). *Georgetown Alumni Directory,* 1947.

6. *Ye Domesday Booke,* 1918 (Georgetown University yearbook); *Ye Domesday Booke,* 1920 (Georgetown University yearbook).

7. 41 Stat. 686–87 (May 29, 1920).

8. See Clare Cushman, "The 'Lost' Clerks of the White Court Era," this volume.

9. In October term 1921, McReynolds employed Carlyle Solomon Baer, Norman B. Frost, and Tench T. Marye for the newly created law clerk position: Baer served from November 15, 1921, to January 18, 1922; Frost from January 19 until February 28; and Marye from March 1 to May 31. Frost and Marye must have become acquainted as they argued a case together before the D.C. Court of Appeals in August 1922, representing the Episcopal Diocese in a real estate case. *Washington Law Reporter* (Washington, D.C.: Law Reporter Printing, 1922), 557. A fourth clerk, Andrew P. Federline, was brought in at the end of that term as a stenographic clerk at the lower salary, serving from March 1 to June 30, 1922. In October term 1925, Chester Gray was hired as a stenographic clerk to supplement John T. Fowler, but he only served from February 25 to March 23, 1926. Supreme Court Office of the Curator Research Files. General clerkship dates are also provided by the Supreme Court of the United States Library in correspondence in April, May, and July 2013 (hereafter cited as Supreme Court Library). While there is no complete list of all Supreme Court law clerks, the library maintains unofficial internal files relating to clerks' service at the Court, which it recognizes may contain incomplete and unverified information.

10. Chester A. Newland, "Personal Assistants to Supreme Court Justices: The Law Clerks," *Oregon Law Review* 40 (June 1961): 306–7. Note, however, that Newland incorrectly states that "for three months in 1922 Justice McReynolds employed three assistants instead of his usual one" (ibid., 303).

11. Some accounts express surprise that McReynolds did not have better relationships with his clerks because he himself had served for two years as a secretary to Justice Howell E. Jackson. But he clerked for Jackson when Jackson was a senator (D-TN), not a judge. One of McReynolds's first assignments for Senator Jackson was to help draft the legislation authorizing stenographers for the Supreme Court justices, a bill that was passed in 1886.

12. Mahlon D. Kiefer, "Memorandum for Mr. Wendell Berge, Assistant Attorney General, Re: Mr. Justice Van Devanter," February 24, 1942, Collection on Justice Van Devanter, Box 1, Folder 6, Supreme Court Office of the Curator Research Files.

13. Leroy E. Reed, S. Milton Simpson, T. Ellis Allison, Norman B. Frost, Harold Lee George, John T. Fowler, Maurice J. Mahoney, and Milton S. Musser were all rehired.

14. See B. Cushman, "Clerks to the Four Horsemen."

15. Justice McReynolds engaged Simpson as a stenographic clerk from November 4, 1915, to August 25, 1916, and then rehired him as a law clerk at the higher salary from October 1, 1919, to April 3, 1920. Supreme Court Office of the Curator Research Files. Simpson had previously served as a confidential clerk to Attorney General McReynolds from January to March 1914.

16. Allison served as a stenographic clerk from March 1, 1917 (replacing Blaine Mallan, who enrolled in the navy as an assistant paymaster lieutenant [j.g.]), to August 25, 1917. Allison went to work at the Justice Department, but after ten days was recalled by McReynolds when his replacement backed out. Allison was reappointed on September 11, 1917, and served October terms 1917 and 1918, resigning on April 20, 1919.

17. Clerking dates are from the Supreme Court Library and the Supreme Court Office of the Curator Research Files.

18. Newland, "Personal Assistants," 307n23.

19. George, Baer, Marye, Federline, Gray, and Knox did not serve full terms. I am not counting Mallan because he was recruited to join the World War I effort, or Raymond Radcliffe, because his term ended when McReynolds retired in January 1941. A possible explanation for why George (April 23 to August 13, 1919, as stenographic clerk, and April 12 to June 27, 1920, as law clerk) quit early was his eagerness to return to flying, having seen action as a bombardier pilot in World War I. In 1920, he said he "threw his law books in an attic trunk and entered the Regular Army from the Reserve," embarking on what would become an illustrious military career. "Man of War: Harold Lee George," *Washington Post*, November 12, 1942.

20. See note 9.

21. E-mail to author from Chester A. Newland, Emeritus Professor of Public Administration, University of Southern California, August 15, 2013.

22. *Knox Memoir*, 246.

23. Milton S. Musser to Ellis Shipp Musser, n.d., [probably April 1938], Box 22, Folder 2, Musser Family Papers, 1852 to 1967, Utah State Historical Society.

24. Maurice J. Mahoney Jr., interview by Todd C. Peppers, May 30, 2012.

25. *Knox Memoir*, 52.

26. *Ye Domesday Booke*, 1925 (Georgetown University yearbook).

27. "Mahoney-Johnson Wedding an Event of Great Interest," *Washington Post*, June 30, 1929. For Mahoney's employment record, see B. Cushman, "Clerks to the Four Horsemen."

28. *Knox Memoir*, 13.

29. See, for example, I. Scott Messenger, "Oliver Wendell Holmes, Jr., and His Law Clerks," in *In Chambers: Stories of Supreme Court Law Clerks and Their Justices*, edited by Todd C. Peppers and Artemus Ward (Charlottesville: University of Virginia Press,

2011), 46–47. Todd C. Peppers quotes law clerk Adrian S. Fisher saying, "[I]t was also implied that you should not be married. Nothing explicit, but it seemed clear," in "Justice Brandeis and His Law Clerks," in Peppers and Ward, *In Chambers*, 79.

30. John Knox, "Experiences as Law Clerk to Mr. Justice James C. McReynolds of the Supreme Court of the United States during the Year that President Franklin D. Roosevelt Attempted to 'Pack' the Court (October Term 1936)," Box 10240-W, Knox MSS, Special Collections, Alderman Library, University of Virginia.

31. Milton Musser to Ellis Shipp Musser, January 2, 1939, Box 22, Folder 2, Musser Family Papers.

32. "Washington Woman Named an Assistant U.S. Attorney," *Washington Post*, March 17, 1943. Who was the second clerk fired for getting married? Simpson, Mallan, Marye, Federline, and Radcliffe all married *after* their clerkship with McReynolds. George, Frost, Fowler, Gray, Ward E. Lattin, J. Allen Sherier, and John T. McHale were married *before* they were hired. Baer and Knox never married. Mahoney and Musser wed during their clerkships, but McReynolds did not dismiss them. That only leaves Allison, who married Minnie Esther Gorman in October of the 1918 term but did not resign until April 20, 1919 (although he began applying for a job at the Bureau of Internal Revenue several months earlier, which may indicate he felt compelled to leave). See note 16.

33. Knox received his L.L.M. at Harvard in 1936, having earned an L.L.B. from Northwestern University Law School in 1934.

34. *Knox Memoir*, 7, 17, 10, 110n10.

35. Ibid., 16. Parker told Knox that was the salary range. Clerk of the Court Charles Elmore Cropley revealed to Knox this $3,000 figure after he was fired at the end of the term. Ibid., 256.

36. Ibid., 10.

37. See, for example, "it was a lonesome job" quote by J. Willard Hurst, in Peppers, "Justice Brandeis and His Law Clerks," 75.

38. *Knox Memoir*, 29.

39. Ibid., 23.

40. Ibid., 30, 29, 85–86.

41. Ibid., 132.

42. Ibid., 133–34.

43. Samuel Williston, clerk to Horace Gray in 1888, wrote: "Often he would ask his secretary to write opinions in these cases, *and though the ultimate destiny of such opinions was the waste-basket*, the chance that some suggestion in them might be approved by the master and adopted by him, was sufficient to incite the secretary to his best endeavor." Quoted in Todd C. Peppers, "Horace Gray and the Lost Law Clerks," in Peppers and Ward, *In Chambers*, 21 (emphasis added).

44. *Knox Memoir*, 134.

45. Ibid., 192–93.

46. Ibid., 256.

47. Ibid., 259.

48. Ibid., 38, 113, 261.

49. Harry Parker to John Knox, January 20, 1938, Knox MSS, Box 10240-A, Special Collections, University of Virginia.

50. For McHale's biography, see B. Cushman, "Clerks to the Four Horsemen."

51. Musser Family Papers.

52. Her finding aid in the Musser Family Papers provides a poignant description of her life: "There is evidence that her excommunication from the Mormon Church in 1944 embittered her against polygamy and against what she felt was hypocrisy on the part of some officials who had, she said, accepted her tithes and the missionary labors of her sons knowing that she was a plural wife, but never rallied to her support. Despite profound shock at her excommunication, she remained firmly committed to the church of her birth. She took great pleasure and pride in the accomplishments of her children and in those of her mother, the well-known Dr. Ellis Reynolds Shipp. Yet, her own life and achievements were quite remarkable. She received her bachelor of arts degree from the University of Utah in 1907. In later life, she took courses at the University of California, Berkeley, and at age seventy she was the oldest student at the University of Utah. At a time when few women entered business, she achieved notable success in the insurance field."

53. Supreme Court Library; "Death: Francis R. Kirkham," *Deseret News,* October 27, 1996.

54. Mark Cannon, interview by author, July 22, 2013. In 1972, Congress appointed Cannon to be the first administrative assistant to the chief justice of the United States.

55. *Jurisdiction of the Supreme Court of the United States; A Treatise Concerning the Appellate Jurisdiction of the Supreme Court of the United States, Including a Treatment of the Principles and Precedents Governing the Exercise of the Discretionary Jurisdiction on Certiorari* (St. Paul, Minn.: West Publishing, 1936).

56. This well-regarded report, "Suggested Revisions to the General Orders and Forms of Bankruptcy," was published in 1939. Material relating to this report can be found in the Francis R. Kirkham Law Clerk Papers, circa 1935–38, Biddle Law Library, National Bankruptcy Archives, University of Pennsylvania. Francis R. Kirkham was issued checks by Clerk of the Court Charles Elmore Cropley "to cover certain expenses incident to certain specified work for this Court undertaken and performed by direction of the Chief Justice." Written orders from Chief Justice Hughes to Cropley are filed with the check receipts: March 3, 1936, $535; May 26, 1936, $250; November 14, 1938, $167.50; December 17, 1938, $400; January 4, 1939, $250; January 16, 1939, $505. Records of the Supreme Court of the United States, Records for the Office of the Clerk, Entry 46, Box 1, National Archives.

57. Francis R. Kirkham graduated from the George Washington Law School in 1931, Cragun in 1934, and Musser in 1938. Unlike Kirkham and Musser, Cragun was not a member of the LDS Church.

58. Francis R. Kirkham to Milton Musser, January 20, 1938, Box 24, Folder 3, Musser Family Papers.

59. See, for example, Francis R. Kirkham to Milton Musser, January 20, 1938, Box 24, Folder 3; Francis R. Kirkham to Milton Musser, January 27, 1938, Box 24, Folder 3; and Charles Elmore Cropley to Francis Kirkham, January 21, 1938, Box 25, Folder 1, all in Musser Family Papers.

60. See C. Cushman, "'Lost' Clerks of the White Court Era," for a discussion of the advent of female secretaries at the Supreme Court. According to a Reed clerk, Gaylord would provide the justice with clerical support formerly performed by male stenographic clerks, as well as new duties: "While denominated a secretary, as with the administrative assistants to other justices, [Gaylord's] functions were far broader. In addition to typing memos, communications, and opinions, she maintained Reed's docket books and his financial records, followed the status of activities of the Court, often communicated with other justices or their staffs with respect to Court matters, and, though not a lawyer, often acted as an additional law clerk, seeking requested information or research materials for Reed. She ... worked the same long hours as did Reed and his law clerks" (John D. Fassett, *New Deal Justice: The Life of Stanley Reed of Kentucky* [New York: Vantage Press, 1994], 210).

61. Milton Musser to Francis R. Kirkham, February 2, 1938, Box 23, Folder 1, Musser Family Papers.

62. "Secretary to McReynolds," *San Francisco Call*, August 23, 1913; *Congressional Directory*, 2nd ed., 1913, 1914; "Suter, Reporter of Supreme Court Scoop, Ends Long Career," *Palm Beach Post*, December 1, 1941.

63. Milton Musser to Francis R. Kirkham, February 21, 1938, Box 23, Folder 1, Musser Family Papers.

64. Milton Musser to Ellis Shipp Musser, n.d. [probably April 1938], Box 22, Folder 2, Musser Family Papers.

65. Milton Musser to Francis R. Kirkham, February 21, 1938, Box 23, Folder 1, Musser Family Papers.

66. Ibid.

67. Musser gives details of this effort in a letter to Ellis Shipp Musser, August 5, 1938, Box 21, Folder 2, Musser Family Papers: "For the last two years I have been working my head off trying to assist the Judge [Cayton] in organizing the Small Claims Court. When we finally got the President's signature on the bill and it became law, we set up the court which has grown so much in the last three months that it is handling about 24,000 cases a year. Not only did the Judge give me all the credit but I was made the first Clerk of the Court. My dear, certainly I haven't taken that job. I GAVE IT UP TO GO WITH THE JUSTICE! [McReynolds]."

68. Milton Musser to Francis R. Kirkham, March 24, 1938, Box 23, Folder 1, Musser Family Papers.

69. Francis Kirkham to George Sutherland, March 28, 1938, on letterhead from Pillsbury, Madison & Sutro in San Francisco, Box 25, Folder 1, Musser Family Papers.

70. Milton Musser to James C. McReynolds, April 16, 1938, Box 23, Folder 1, Musser Family Papers.

71. Ibid.

72. Francis R. Kirkham to Milton Musser, April 27, 1938, Box 24, Folder 3, Musser Family Papers.

73. Milton Musser to Ellis Shipp Musser, May 11, 1938, Box 21, Folder 2, Musser Family Papers. "In the classroom" is handwritten at the top.

74. Milton Musser to Ellis Shipp Musser, May 1, 1938, Box 21, Folder 2, Musser Family Papers.

75. Milton Musser to Ellis Shipp Musser, June 2, 1938, Box 21, Folder 2, Musser Family Papers.

76. Milton Musser to Ellis Shipp Musser, October 3, 1938, Box 21, Folder 2, Musser Family Papers: "Please note that I have moved to Apt. 203, The Heatherington, 1421 Massachusetts Avenue, N.W. It is a delightful apartment. . . . Court convenes at noon today and everything is under control."

77. Milton Musser to Francis R. Kirkham, May 28, 1938, Box 23, Folder 1, Musser Family Papers.

78. Francis R. Kirkham to Milton Musser, June 10, 1938, Box 24, Folder 3, Musser Family Papers.

79. Milton Musser to Francis R. Kirkham, June 13, 1938, Box 23, Folder 1, Musser Family Papers.

80. Milton Musser to Francis R. Kirkham, June 30, 1938, Box 23, Folder 1, Musser Family Papers.

81. Milton Musser to Ellis Shipp Musser, July 30, 1938, Box 21, Folder 5, Musser Family Papers. The George Washington University Law School records Musser as having earned his L.L.B. in 1938.

82. Milton Musser to Ellis Shipp Musser, October 24, 1938, Box 21, Folder 5, Musser Family Papers. He was absent for a week with food poisoning.

83. Milton Musser to Ellis Shipp Musser, October 15, 1938, Box 21, Folder 5, Musser Family Papers.

84. Milton Musser to Ellis Shipp Musser, n.d. [probably April 1938], Box 22, Folder 2, Musser Family Papers.

85. Marcia Musser, interview by Todd C. Peppers, September 2013.

86. Milton Musser to Ellis Shipp Musser, January 2, 1939, Box 22, Folder 2, Musser Family Papers. The identities of the two clerks allegedly fired for getting married are not identified.

87. Milton Musser to Ellis Shipp Musser, January 10, 1939, Box 21, Folder 4, Musser Family Papers.

88. Milton Musser to Ellis Shipp Musser, January 29, 1939, Box 21, Folder 5, Musser Family Papers.

89. Milton Musser to Ellis Shipp Musser, March 23, 1939, Box 21, Folder 5, Musser Family Papers.

90. Milton Musser to Ellis Shipp Musser, March 31, 1939, Box 21, Folder 5, Musser Family Papers.

91. Milton Musser to Ellis Shipp Musser, August 31, 1939, Box 21, Folder 5, Musser Family Papers.

92. Milton Musser to Ellis Shipp Musser, October 31, 1939, Box 21, Folder 4, Musser Family Papers.

93. Milton Musser to Ellis Shipp Musser, November 28, 1939, Box 22, Folder 1, Musser Family Papers.

94. Milton Musser to Ellis Shipp Musser, February 24, 1940, Box 21, Folder 5, Musser Family Papers.

95. Milton Musser to Ellis Shipp Musser, April 8, [1940] (the year is omitted on letter), Box 21, Folder 5, Musser Family Papers.

96. Milton Musser to Ellis Shipp Musser, June 4, 1940, Box 21, Folder 4, Musser Family Papers.

97. Milton Musser to Samuel Musser, n.d., Box 22, Folder 7, Musser Family Papers.

98. Milton Musser to Ellis Shipp Musser, September 16, 1939, Box 21, Folder 5, Musser Family Papers.

99. Milton Musser to Samuel Musser, n.d., Box 22, Folder 7, Musser Family Papers.

100. Milton Musser to Ellis Shipp Musser, May 4, 1940, Box 21, Folder 5, Musser Family Papers.

101. Milton Musser to Ellis Shipp Musser, June 4, 1940, Box 21, Folder 4, Musser Family Papers.

102. Milton Musser to Ellis Shipp Musser, June 26, 1940, Box 21, Folder 2, Musser Family Papers.

103. Milton Musser to Ellis Shipp Musser, July 25, 1940, Box 21, Folder 2, Musser Family Papers.

104. Milton Musser to Ellis Shipp Musser, August 28, 1940, Box 21, Folder 5, Musser Family Papers.

105. Milton Musser to Ellis Shipp Musser, September 4, 1940, Box 21, Folder 4, Musser Family Papers.

106. Milton Musser to Ellis Shipp Musser, September 11, 1940, Box 21, Folder 2, Musser Family Papers. See also Milton Musser to Charles Elmore Cropley, October 1, 1940, Box 23, Folder 1, Musser Family Papers.

107. Milton Musser to Ellis Shipp Musser, n.d. [probably Spring 1939], Box 22, Folder 2, Musser Family Papers.

108. Milton Musser to Ellis Shipp Musser, September 16, 1940, Box 21, Folder 5, Musser Family Papers. Letterhead with "Supreme Court of the United States Washington DC" has title scratched out and replaced with 4015 Benton St. NW.

109. Milton Musser to Ellis Shipp Musser, May 4, 1940, Box 21, Folder 5, Musser Family Papers.

110. Milton Musser to Ellis Shipp Musser, October 11, 1940, Box 21, Folder 5, Musser Family Papers.

111. "Obituary: Woodrow S. Wilson," *Deseret News,* January 13, 2005. Musser and his partner's clients included Lawrence Welk, Liberace, and Betty White.

112. John H. Clarke to Josephus Daniels, September 5, 1941, quoted in Carl Wittke, "Mr. Justice Clarke in Retirement," *Western Law Review* 1 (June 1949): 34.

113. See, for example, a letter from R. V. Fletcher, General Counsel of Illinois Central Railroad System, to Willis Van Devanter, June 18, 1929, which thanks the justice for his letter inquiring about a position for Arthur J. Mattson, who clerked for him for four years and is now seeking legal work. Willis Van Devanter Papers, Library of Congress.

114. Nathan Cayton to Stanley F. Reed, January 31, 1936, Box 25, Folder 1, Musser Family Papers.

115. See generally "Afterword" by Hutchinson and Garrow in *Knox Memoir,* 269–75.

BARRY CUSHMAN

The Clerks to Justices
George Sutherland and Pierce Butler

ecent years have witnessed a flowering of scholarship concerning the
Supreme Court clerkship. Yet most of this literature focuses on the
more modern justices. And for the justices who served in the years
between Justice Horace Gray's appointment in 1882, when the Supreme Court
clerkship was created, and Franklin D. Roosevelt's appointment of Hugo Black
in 1937, the literature leans heavily toward those generally thought to be "liberal": Oliver Wendell Holmes Jr., Louis D. Brandeis, Harlan Fiske Stone, and
Benjamin N. Cardozo.

This tendency is not surprising, for several reasons. First, Holmes, Brandeis,
Stone, and Cardozo are of particular interest, as they are typically regarded as
among the greatest justices of the twentieth century. Second, the extensive biographical literature on each of them, as well as the large collection of private
papers left by all but Cardozo, gives the researcher ample material with which
to work. And third, there is a substantial remembrance literature generated by
their former clerks.

Law clerks to the early-twentieth-century justices known collectively as the
"Four Horsemen"—Willis Van Devanter, James Clark McReynolds, George
Sutherland, and Pierce Butler—thus have received little attention. With the
exception of Sutherland, these more "conservative" contemporaries of Holmes
and Brandeis are typically rated as judicial "failures." The biographical literature on each of them is not nearly as thick, and the remaining private papers
are neither as extensive nor as revealing.[1] And only two of the thirty-five young
men who clerked for these justices ever published a recollection of his time
served in chambers.

The more notable and extensive of these remembrances was that of John
Knox,[2] who clerked for Justice McReynolds during the 1936 term, and whose
diary was annotated by Dennis Hutchinson and David Garrow in a splendid
edition published by the University of Chicago Press. Thanks to this volume,
Knox's exposé of McReynolds's tempestuous and cruel mistreatment of his
messenger, Harry Parker; of his maid and cook, Mary Diggs; and, of course, of
Knox himself is now well known to scholars of the Court. Knox reported that

all of the employees of the "sadistically inclined" McReynolds "lived in a reign of terror and were crushed under foot without any hesitation on his part." By the end of his clerkship, Knox had concluded that McReynolds was "the most contemptible and mediocre man I ever came into contact with," "unbelievably stingy," and "gravely unbalanced." His "selfishness and vindictiveness" were "unbelievable."[3]

There is good reason to believe that Knox's unpleasant tour of duty clerking for McReynolds was representative of the justice's treatment of his other clerks.[4] On the other hand, we can be reasonably confident that Knox's experience was not representative of the experiences of those who clerked for Van Devanter, Sutherland, and Butler. For example, when Arthur Mattson, who clerked for Van Devanter for five years, was preparing to leave his post to pursue a legal career in New York, he wrote to his boss:

> You have been so good to me during the nearly five years I have been in your employment, and my association with you has been such a fine thing in my life, that I would be ungrateful not to tell you of my deep appreciation. Your uniform kindness, consideration, and patience is something I shall never forget. You have been at once a kind and just employer and a good father to me. Perhaps I can best show my appreciation by striving always in the years to come to reflect your kind manner and sweet disposition, your noble character and your profound knowledge of law and men. They will be treasured memories of mine always.[5]

Three of Van Devanter's other clerks remained with him for stretches of three, nine, and eleven years, which suggests that they, too, found the association agreeable. Like Van Devanter,[6] Sutherland was uniformly regarded as a nice fellow,[7] and the fact that each of his four clerks remained with him for multiple terms similarly suggests that they also found the experience personally rewarding. Butler, who employed two law clerks in his chambers at all times, retained one of them during his entire tenure at the Court, and another for nine terms.[8] Here again, the likelihood of job satisfaction seems high.

Knox's duties while working for McReynolds also were not typical of the duties of all of the Four Horsemen's clerks. The tasks that McReynolds expected Knox to perform were more secretarial than legal. They included typing, taking dictation, responding to social invitations, and answering the telephone. The only lawyerly duties that Knox undertook throughout the year were the preparation of summaries of petitions for certiorari and some occasional legal research.

By contrast, Butler's long-term clerk John F. Cotter "wrote first drafts of many opinions, expressing the justice's views so accurately that the drafts often required few changes." Butler's clerks also summarized petitions for certiorari, and the justice encouraged his clerks to offer criticism and suggestions

as they assisted him in the research and writing of opinions.[9] William D. Donnelly, who served as a Butler clerk for nine years, described his duties as also
including "the preparation of notes . . . on some of the argued cases prior to
the conferences of the Court," and assistance "in the writing of opinions in assigned cases," including "[p]reparation of detailed statements of fact from the
records," "analysis of briefs," and "research on points not briefed by the parties."[10] Not much is known about the duties of clerks for Justices Van Devanter
and Sutherland, but it does appear that the clerks of at least one of the Four
Horsemen were not simply legally trained stenographers, but instead shouldered substantial lawyerly responsibility.

There is an additional respect in which the Knox story was not representative, and it is to the illumination of that dimension that the balance of this
essay is devoted. One reason for the greater interest in the men who clerked for
Holmes, Brandeis, Stone, and Cardozo concerns the highly successful careers
they pursued following their clerkships. Many of these alumni clerks rose to
positions of great distinction in law practice, business, law teaching, or government service.

Consider, by contrast, the postclerkship career of John Knox. After leaving
McReynolds, he failed the bar examination three times before finally passing
the Illinois exam in March 1939. Following his second failure, he was fired from
Mayer, Meyer, Austrian, & Platt after less than a year of employment. He then
parlayed a family friendship into a job with the Chicago firm of Loesch, Sco-
field, Loesch, & Burke. When that firm began to crumble in 1942, Knox began a
two-year stint at the War Production Board before being dismissed in late 1944.
By early 1945, he was in New York working in the war-depleted ranks of Cravath, Swaine, & Moore, but was let go in less than two years. For most of 1947
he negotiated and drafted theatrical contracts for the Marquis Georges de Cue-
vas, the grandson-in-law of John D. Rockefeller Sr. When that work dried up
in November, Knox returned to Chicago and spent the next nine years trying
unsuccessfully to save his family's mail-order business selling self-help books
to salesmen. In 1956, he took a job as a claims adjuster for the Allstate Insurance Company, and remained in that firm's employ until his retirement in 1973.
For the remainder of his life he lived in poor health and straitened financial
circumstances. He died in 1997 at the age of eighty-nine, a lonely and childless
bachelor. In 1962, at the age of fifty-five, Knox wrote in his diary, "[i]n many
ways I am a pathetic failure." The following year he complained that he had "no
money, am thousands of dollars in debt and just hanging on to the status quo
by a thread." As Hutchinson and Garrow put it, Knox "had become a pudgy,
sour, and chronically ill middle-aged man with no career accomplishments and
bitter recriminations, mostly directed at himself."[11]

How representative was Knox's postclerkship career? Until recently, it was not easy to know. But the proliferation of online sources now has made it possible to reconstruct at least the outlines of the lives of the men who clerked for the Four Horsemen. For reasons of space, this essay discusses the lives and careers of the clerks to only two of the Four Horsemen, Justices Sutherland and Butler. From the available biographical data, one can discern that their clerks typically went on to enjoy successful careers, apparently happy family and social lives, and active participation in the affairs of their communities. To be sure, none of them became attorney general of the United States or secretary of state. But one is nevertheless impressed by how entirely uncharacteristic was the life of John Knox.

The Sutherland Clerks

Justice Sutherland served from 1922 to 1938, but during that time he had only four clerks. The first, whom he inherited from his predecessor in office, was a career civil servant. The others were all graduates of the George Washington University's law school, and went on to enjoy interesting and highly successful careers in private practice.

Samuel Edward Widdifield was an 1898 graduate of the Detroit College of Law who clerked for Sutherland during the 1922 and 1923 terms.[12] Widdifield might be characterized as a career or serial clerk: he clerked for four different justices. Born in Uxbridge, Ontario, Widdifield moved to Michigan as a young boy in 1880 and was naturalized in Detroit in 1896. He was admitted to practice in Michigan in 1898, and in Massachusetts in 1904. Early in his career, Widdifield handled collections in the office of a Detroit lawyer and practiced with the Traverse City, Michigan, firm of Gilbert & Widdifield. He then moved to Pittsfield, Massachusetts, where he was secretary and law assistant to the president of the Stanley Electrical Company.[13] He first came to the Court in 1904 at the age of twenty-nine to clerk for Justice Rufus Peckham. After Peckham's death in 1909, Widdifield clerked for Justice Joseph Rucker Lamar during the 1910 and 1911 terms.[14] Following his clerkship with Justice Lamar, Widdifield engaged briefly in private practice in Lansing, Michigan, before returning to Washington to serve as a secretary to Senator James P. Clarke, of Arkansas, and as a messenger to the Senate Commerce Committee from 1913 to 1916.[15]

Widdifield then returned to the Court to clerk for Justice John Hessin Clarke, and upon Clarke's resignation in 1922, Widdifield moved to the chambers of Clarke's successor, Justice Sutherland. After two years with Sutherland, Widdifield left to serve for more than five years as assistant counsel to the German Mixed Claims Commission in the State Department. In 1930, he operated his own real estate business in North Beach, Maryland, where he served as mayor. From December 1930 to August 1931 he worked as an assistant clerk to the House Judiciary Committee. Widdifield then returned to the Court as assistant clerk, a position that he held for eighteen years until his retirement in 1949.[16] In 1937, he sought to return to the position of law clerk, unsuccessfully applying for a position with the incoming Justice Hugo Black.[17] He died in 1960 at the age of eighty-five, a widower survived by two children, six grand-children, and one great-grandchild.[18]

Alan E. Gray clerked for Sutherland from the 1924 term through the 1930 term.[19] Gray may have been the most colorful of the Sutherland clerks. His father was a Scottish immigrant who came to Minnesota at a young age and settled in Grafton, North Dakota, in 1891.[20] Alan was born in 1899, took his B.A. from the University of North Dakota in 1921, and received his law degree from the George Washington University in 1924.[21] That year he married fel-low Graftonite, Grace Lunding Hope, and the couple moved to Chevy Chase, Maryland.[22] Following his clerkship with Sutherland, Gray remained for sev-eral years in Washington,[23] where he engaged in a law practice focused on tax matters.[24] By 1938, the Grays had moved to Southern California, where they divorced by 1948. Gray quickly married Joan Kettering in 1949, but was as quickly divorced from her the following year. He then married Jan Hanson Fisher, who left him a widower. In 1967, he married his old Grafton schoolmate Helen Tombs, to whom he remained married until his death in 1984.[25]

Gray practiced in Southern California for the balance of his career.[26] He continued to specialize in the tax area,[27] and was recognized as an "income tax expert."[28] This expertise brought him into contact with a number of celebrities in the entertainment industry. He represented George Burns and Gracie Allen in their 1938 claim for a refund on their 1935 state income taxes.[29] From 1937 to 1941, he prepared the income tax returns of W. C. Fields, and was called as a witness in the sensational 1949 trial over the comedian's estate.[30] And in 1951 he represented actor Charles Coburn and four of his poker buddies charged with flouting the gambling ordinance of Beverly Hills.[31] He kept an office in Los Angeles until 1984, when he died at the age of eighty-four.[32] His estate plan cre-ated an endowment with the University of North Dakota Foundation, which the university has used to establish a law professorship in his name.[33]

Justice Sutherland's most distinguished alumnus was Francis Robison Kirk-ham, who clerked for the justice during part of the 1930 term and for the 1931, 1932, and 1933 terms.[34] Kirkham was born in Fillmore, Utah, in 1904. His grand-parents were among the earliest Mormon pioneers to settle in the Salt Lake Valley, and his mother and father met at Brigham Young University (BYU). His father went on to take a bachelor's degree at the University of Michigan, a law degree from the University of Utah, and a Ph.D. in education from the Uni-versity of California at Berkeley. The senior Kirkham taught at BYU, served as Utah's director of education, and was the superintendent of the largest school district in the state. The Kirkham parents emphasized the importance of education: each of their six children graduated from college, and each of the three sons obtained an advanced degree. Francis's brother Don became a distinguished physicist.[35]

Kirkham was admitted to the Naval Academy at Annapolis for college, but, at his father's insistence, remained in Utah, studying for two years at the University of Utah and then at the Utah Agricultural College. As a young man he served in the National Guard, did a two-year mission for the Church of Jesus Christ of Latter-day Saints in England, and spent six adventure-filled months backpacking around Europe and the Middle East with a friend. For a time he worked some of the farms his father owned, but regional droughts drove the father to New York to serve as the director of the National Child Welfare Association, and the son in 1927 to the George Washington University to complete his undergraduate degree and to study law.[36]

Kirkham received his A.B. from the George Washington University in 1930, and graduated first in his law school class the following year. To pay his way through school, he worked part-time at the Interstate Commerce Commission and later in the Washington office of the Cravath firm. During Kirkham's final year of law school, a chance conversation between Justice Sutherland and Bill Allison, a Kirkham friend who was deputy clerk of the Supreme Court, resulted in Kirkham being invited to interview with the justice. Sutherland winnowed the field to two candidates, Kirkham and a graduate of Columbia University Law School. Sutherland then arranged a competition for the finalists. He gave each of them several sets of the briefs and records of cases in the Supreme Court, and asked them to prepare memoranda for him. Kirkham labored all night in the law school library on the assignment, and Sutherland selected him for the position. Kirkham worked part-time for Sutherland alongside Alan Gray while he was completing his studies and taking the D.C. bar examination, on which Sutherland informed him that he received the highest score among the 480 students sitting for that administration. He began clerking for Sutherland full time at the outset of the 1931 term.[37]

As Sutherland's law clerk, Kirkham prepared statements analyzing petitions for certiorari and making recommendations concerning whether the writs should be granted. He also conducted research for the opinions that Sutherland wrote. Among his more notable contributions were the historical research appearing in Sutherland's 1932 majority opinion in Powell v. Alabama,[38] the decision holding that the Due Process Clause entitled the "Scottsboro Boys" to competent defense counsel in a capital case, and the historical research appearing in Sutherland's dissent in Home Building & Loan Association v. Blaisdell,[39] the 1934 decision upholding the Minnesota Mortgage Moratorium.

Kirkham described the working atmosphere with Sutherland as "a very close personal relationship.... [H]e was an extraordinarily wonderful person to be with and work with. A warm nature, very brilliant scholar, extremely appreciative.... [Y]ou'd just do anything and he'd overpraise you for it and that'd make you work your tail off to do something better." Kirkham recalled an occasion on which Sutherland asked him to see whether he could find some authority in support of a particular statement contained in one of his draft opinions. Kirkham searched diligently, but came up empty. He went to Sutherland and said to him, "Mr. Justice, I just can't find anything. Your statement is right, it should be the law, I just can't find the case that says that it is." Sutherland "looked up and smiled, picked up his pen, signed his opinion and said, 'Well, it is now.'"[40] At the conclusion of his clerkship with Sutherland in the summer of 1934, Kirkham stayed on to clerk with the "indefatigable" Chief Justice Hughes until December 1935.[41]

In 1929, Kirkham married Ellis Musser, whom he had known from his youth in Utah. Ellis, who had studied at the University of Utah and Mills College before marrying Francis, moved to Washington and completed her undergraduate studies at the George Washington University in 1931. While Francis was working day and night clerking for Sutherland and Hughes, Ellis worked for the National Academy of Sciences, spent six months traveling in Europe and the Middle East, and completed her first year of medical school. Together, the couple would have four children.[42] Ellis was the older sister of Milton Musser, and Kirkham played a role in facilitating Milton's clerkship with Justice McReynolds during the Court's 1938 and 1939 terms.[43]

Ellis's medical studies were cut short when Francis concluded his clerkship with Hughes in December 1935. Though Francis had accepted an offer to join the Cravath firm, the Kirkhams were apprehensive about living in New York. Judge Harold Stephens, of the U.S. Circuit Court of Appeals for the District of Columbia Circuit, who was an old family friend, intervened and persuaded Francis to consider opportunities in other cities. On his own initiative, Stephens wrote letters of introduction for Kirkham to numerous firms around the country. Cravath gracefully released Kirkham from his acceptance, and after interviewing in several cities, the Kirkhams decided to move to San Francisco in 1936 to join the firm of Pillsbury, Madison & Sutro. As his partner James O'Brien relates, "His talents and skill were so quickly recognized that even senior partners soon vied for his help in major cases making their way to the Supreme Court." Kirkham became a partner at Pillsbury in 1940, and remained with the firm until 1960, when he left to serve as general counsel to Standard Oil. He returned to Pillsbury in 1970, retiring as senior partner in 1991.[44]

During his career, Kirkham represented many of his clients before the Supreme Court of the United States.[45] He became a Fellow of the American College of Trial Lawyers, a member of the American Law Institute, the chairman of the American Bar Association's Section on Antitrust Law, and a member of two important national commissions on law reform: the Attorney General's National Committee to Study the Antitrust Laws (1953–55) and the National Commission on the Revision of the Federal Appellate System (1973). He was also the author of two highly regarded works, *The Jurisdiction of the Supreme Court of the United States* and *General Orders and Forms in Bankruptcy*.[46] He was a member of the American Judicature Society, the American Society of International Law, the Order of the Coif, and several clubs. He received the George Washington University Alumni Achievement Award in 1970 and the University of Utah Alumni Merit Honor Award in 1976. The law school at Brigham Young University, on whose Board of Visitors he served, established a professorship in his name in 1989. He also served on the Board of Visitors of the University of Chicago Law School. He died in 1996 at the age of ninety-two.[47]

At Pillsbury, Kirkham always wore a dark blue suit, a white shirt, black shoes, and a black tie.[48] His partners spoke of him with unreserved admiration. Turner H. McBaine described him as "an absolutely outstanding man: superb intellect, marvelous personality, ability to get along with people, and a man full of enthusiasm for what he was doing." "His legal writing was excellent," and his briefs were "a pleasure to read," "not only technically outstanding, but artistically outstanding, as a matter of the English language." Kirkham's "habits were not always regular, in the sense that no matter what time he started working in the morning, if he got into something, he might well be there at three the next morning. And he produced, time after time, legal miracles."[49]

Wallace Kaapcke similarly portrays Kirkham as "a wonderful fellow," "the most welcoming and warm, friendly person," a "kind, accomplished gentleman."[50] Kaapcke marveled at the way in which Kirkham "accomplished the brilliant results that he often did" in difficult cases, achieving "the impossible."[51] For example, explains James O'Brien, "Against all odds, he persuaded the antitrust division to permit the merger of Standard Oil Company of Kentucky and Standard Oil of California."[52] John Bates notes that Kirkham "was always looked upon as being the most powerful legal intellect in the firm. I mean he was the bright star; he was the real genius. He took on all the complicated antitrust cases." Kirkham "had a really powerful reputation in the legal community, and he deserved every bit of it. And yet he was and is a very humble, likeable, politic person."[53] Yet Kirkham was not a retiring bookworm. Even as he got older, "[h]e'd still go any anyplace, anytime."[54] As James O'Brien put it, "Kirkham is the kind of lawyer . . . that was prepared to take off his coat and get down and wrestle on the barroom floor."[55]

O'Brien, who wrote the introduction to the interview that Kirkham provided for the Pillsbury, Madison & Sutro Oral History Series, was particularly effusive in his praise. "Few men have come to the profession of law with greater gifts of mind, spirit, and will," O'Brien wrote. "None has used those exceptional gifts and experiences with greater skill in achieving a national reputation as a superb advocate" and "a devoted and compassionate friend." Kirkham had "a rare combination of qualities: a strong constitution, boundless energy and vitality, resourcefulness, the will and tenacity to master his profession," and "confidence in his capacity to deal with any issue that involved the law." "His pioneer background" had given him "a sturdy independence, a sense of responsibility," and "individual initiative." "Few lawyers" could "match the quality of his writing: clear and simple, plain and compelling, seemingly effortless." Kirkham was a "tall, handsome figure, dignified, courteous, with a warm, confident personality, a quick and easy smile, a resonant voice." He was "a formidable courtroom adversary" who had "made friends of his adversaries." O'Brien described Kirkham as a gentle, compassionate, modest person who loved "life," "nature," "song and laughter," "his myriad friends," and "his beautiful family." He was "a great lawyer" who "fashioned a memorable career at the Bar." It was, O'Brien concluded, "difficult to conceive that a single lawyer [could] have achieved so much in one lifetime."[56]

John Wiley Cragun was Sutherland's final clerk, serving from the 1934 term through the justice's retirement during the 1937 term.[57] Cragun was born in Ogden, Utah, in 1906. He arrived in Washington in 1924, and worked as a clerk, typist, and stenographer in the Department of the Interior for several years before receiving his A.B. from the George Washington University in 1932.[58] He then attended the George Washington University's law school while working simultaneously as a legal stenographer in the Washington office of Cravath, Swaine, & Moore. He compiled "an excellent academic record," graduated in 1934, and was promptly admitted to the D.C. bar.[59] During his clerkship with Sutherland, Cragun occasionally took on special assignments for Chief Justice Hughes, and "established among the justices and the employees of the Court a reputation for excellence, which was later to play an important role in his professional practice."[60]

For the rest of his life, Cragun engaged in an active Washington practice. Following his clerkship, Cragun entered a successful association and later partnership with what would become the firm of Wilkinson, Cragun & Barker.[61] He went out on his own for five years beginning in 1945, and in 1950 and 1951 was associated with the specialized tax practice of D.C. lawyer Robert Ash.[62] In 1951, he returned to the Wilkinson firm as a partner, and remained there until his death at the age of sixty-two in 1969.[63] His clients included the National Grange and a large number of Native American tribes.[64] He was remembered as "an unusually expert brief writer" who "was often employed to prepare petitions for writs of certiorari to the Supreme Court of the United States." Indeed, a midcentury survey indicated that "he had achieved a higher degree of success in obtaining grants of certiorari than any other private practitioner."[65]

Cragun was a lawyer of national prominence. He served on a wide variety of professional committees, including as chairman of the American Bar Association's Section of Administrative Law and chairman of the American Bar Association's Special Committee on the Code of Administrative Procedure.[66] In the late 1940s, Cragun lectured on civil procedure at his alma mater. He was a member of numerous clubs, and was the founder and recording secretary of the Society for Appropriate Recognition of Elegant Mixed Metaphors. Cragun married three times. His first marriage, to Hazel Gabbard in 1931, produced three children before ending in divorce. He remarried to Hilda Henderson in 1957, but she left him widowed seven years later. His third and final marriage, to Priscilla A. Martin in 1965, endured until complications from emphysema brought about his untimely demise nearly four years later.[67]

The Butler Clerks

Although Congress had appropriated funds in 1919 so that the justices could hire a law clerk and a stenographer, Justice Sutherland managed with just one clerk. Justice Butler, by contrast, employed two. One, John Francis Cotter, remained in Butler's employ for the justice's entire tenure on the Court. Others joined Cotter for shorter stints of service.[68]

Cotter was born in 1900 in the District of Columbia, and graduated from its Central High School. As a young man he worked as a messenger in the Treasury Department, as a stenographer for the Interstate Commerce Commission, and as a clerk for the U.S. Shipping Board and the Census Bureau. He also served briefly in the army during World War I.[69] He received his law degree from Catholic University in 1921,[70] and was admitted to the District of Columbia bar in September of that year.[71] After serving as a stenographer and law clerk to a local attorney for a little over a year, the young bachelor went to work for Butler in February 1923, shortly after the justice took his seat. He was hired as a "stenographic clerk" at a salary of $2,000, but was promoted to law clerk at a salary of $3,600 for the 1925 term.[72]

At Butler's death, it was Cotter who carried out Butler's instructions that his Court papers be destroyed.[73] Cotter also served as the administrator of Butler's estate, and prepared his estate tax returns.[74] Thereafter he embarked upon a successful career as an attorney in the Public Lands Division of the Justice Department, for which he is listed as counsel in a series of appeals before the federal courts between 1940 and 1956.[75] In 1942, the now-confirmed bachelor enlisted in the army, and within fewer than four years he had risen to the rank of major. He served as an officer in the JAG Corps and as a member of the Claims Commission sitting in France, Belgium, and the United Kingdom.[76] After his return from military leave, he resumed his duties in the Public

Lands Division, from which he retired in the latter part of 1955.[77] From 1957, Martindale-Hubbell lists him as a lawyer in private, perhaps solo, practice, in Washington, D.C.,[78] though his absence from other public records during this period suggests that he may have been in semiretirement. He died in November 1978.[79]

William A. D. Dyke, who clerked for Justice Mahlon Pitney for the portion of the 1922 term preceding the justice's stroke and retirement in December of that year, spent only the remainder of that term in Butler's chambers.[80] Before clerking for Pitney, Dyke worked as an assistant clerk in the U.S. Senate from 1918 to 1921[81] and was initiated into the Order of the Elks.[82] In 1921, he received an L.L.B. and an M.P.L. from Georgetown University, where he was the class poet. After leaving Butler, Dyke returned to Georgetown to earn an M.D. in 1929, and went on to pursue a medical career.[83] He is listed as a first lieutenant serving in the Medical Corps of the U.S. Army Reserve at a Pennsylvania Civilian Conservation Corps camp in 1933.[84] Dr. Dyke died in an automobile accident in 1941 at the young age of forty-two, leaving a widow, Cuba A. Dyke. Seven years later, she met a dramatic end, collapsing and dying immediately following Christmas dinner. The couple, who are buried side by side at Arlington National Cemetery, apparently had no children.[85]

Norris Darrell joined Cotter in Butler's chambers as a law clerk for the 1923 and 1924 terms.[86] Darrell was born on St. Kitts in 1899, was brought by his parents to the United States the following year, and was naturalized in 1910. The son of a "modestly paid clergyman," as he would later describe his father, he served in the infantry during World War I. In 1923, he received his L.L.B. from the University of Minnesota, where he was elected to the Order of the Coif. The summer following his graduation from law school, Darrell was traveling on the West Coast and contemplating a career practicing in that region when he received a telephone call from the dean of his alma mater. Dean Everett Fraser informed Darrell that Justice Butler had asked him to recommend a member of the graduating class to serve as a law clerk, and that Fraser had recommended Darrell. Fraser asked Darrell to cut his western trip short and to return to Minneapolis so that he might meet with Justice Butler to discuss the possibility. The conversation must have gone well, as Darrell soon found himself at Butler's elbow in Washington.[87]

The clerkship with Butler changed the course of Darrell's professional career. The justice urged him to return to Minneapolis to practice, insisting that he would enjoy a fuller and happier life there.[88] But Noel Dowling, who had taught Darrell at Minnesota and recently moved to Columbia, encouraged the young lawyer to consider practicing in New York. Dowling enlisted former Columbia dean Justice Harlan Fiske Stone in his campaign of persuasion, and it was at Stone's urging that Darrell interviewed with Sullivan & Cromwell. Darrell was offered a position with Sullivan and two other Wall Street firms, and his future path was set during a consultation with Dean Fraser on a return trip to Minneapolis. Darrell held his breath as Fraser examined the letterhead of each of the firms listing their partners. Then, Darrell later reported,

> he suddenly threw down one of them, pointed to the name of a partner far down the list who was unknown to me and said that I should by all means go there because he had taught that man when he was teaching Property-Future Interests at a law school in Washington, D.C., that the man never kept notes in class as expected—his notebook being usually blank except for doodles—but that he regularly had the highest marks in his class.

The firm was Sullivan & Cromwell; the doodling student was John Foster Dulles. Near the end of his career Darrell wrote that following Fraser's advice was a decision that he never regretted.

In his conversation with Darrell about his future, Butler told him about two of his former associates from Minnesota who had pursued divergent professional paths. One accepted an offer with a New York firm and "worked hard in his practice, made a lot of money and gave a lot to charity but he never married. He rode the subways, was little known in his community and played no part in community affairs." The other lawyer declined a New York firm's offer and instead remained in St. Paul. He "lived very comfortably with his wife and family on his income of a hundred thousand to one hundred fifty thousand dollars a year, was widely known and greatly and admired in his community in which nothing of great importance happened without his participation." Years later, Butler and Darrell "had a good laugh" over the story and the subsequent history of its protagonists. The man who went to New York was Carl Taylor. The man who stayed in St. Paul was William D. Mitchell, who went on to become attorney general of the United States. After concluding his service in Washington, however, Mitchell did not return to St. Paul. Instead, he moved to New York and joined Taylor's firm.[89]

Darrell went on to enjoy a distinguished career with Sullivan & Cromwell in New York, Paris, and Berlin. He was made a partner in 1934, eventually becoming both head of the tax group and vice-chairman of the firm, and remained with Sullivan & Cromwell as counsel following his retirement from the partnership in 1976. He served on the boards of numerous corporations and professional organizations, including the American Law Institute, of which he was president for fifteen years and chairman of the council thereafter. He was also the chairman of the Supervisory Committee of the American Law Institute Tax Project that culminated in the Internal Revenue Code of 1954.

Darrell received several awards recognizing his professional achievements, including the University of Minnesota's Outstanding Achievement Award in 1965, the Marshall-Wythe Medallion from the College of William and Mary in 1967, and the New York Bar Association's Gold Medal Award for Distinguished Service in the Law in 1978. In 1953, the Eisenhower administration approached Darrell about taking the position of undersecretary of the Treasury. Darrell did not want the job and did not want to leave New York, but also did not believe that he could say no. Fortuitously, his senior partner, John Foster Dulles, who did not know of Darrell's preferences, inadvertently helped Darrell to wriggle off the hook. Dulles had been named secretary of state, and his brother Allen, also a Sullivan & Cromwell partner, had been tapped to head the Central Intelligence Agency (CIA). As John Foster Dulles and Eisenhower were returning from a trip to Hawaii, Dulles talked the president out of the Darrell appointment, suggesting that it would be unfair to ask three senior partners from the same firm to serve the administration at the same time. Dulles wrote to Leonard Hall, the head of the Eisenhower transition team, that were the administration to appoint three Sullivan & Cromwell partners to such important posts, "a rather frightening picture could be drawn by unfriendly persons." A relieved Darrell thus was able to remain in his beloved New York.[90]

Darrell married Doris Clare Williams in 1925, and together they had two sons. Doris died in 1943, and in 1945 Darrell married Mary Hand Churchill, the divorced daughter of Judge Learned Hand, the liberal icon who had derided Butler as one of the "mastiffs" back in the 1920s and 1930s.[91] It was Darrell who, as literary executor of Hand's estate, persuaded Gerald Gunther to write Hand's biography.[92] In 1966, Darrell joined Warren Christopher, Lloyd Cutler, Erwin Griswold, Burke Marshall, Louis Pollak, Eugene Rostow, and ten other leading lawyers in a letter to Congress supporting the constitutionality of the proposed Civil Rights Act of 1966.[93] Darrell died in Manhattan in 1989 at the age of ninety, survived by Mary, the two sons from his first marriage, a stepson, and two grandchildren.[94]

After Darrell left Butler's employ, Cotter was promoted to law clerk and served alone during the 1925 and 1926 terms. Butler hired Richard L. Sullivan to work alongside Cotter during the 1927 term at the "stenographic clerk" salary.[95] Sullivan was born in 1901, and by 1926 had graduated from both college and law school at the University of Minnesota.[96] By the early 1930s, Sullivan had been admitted to the Supreme Court bar and become associated with the Manhattan firm of Kirlin, Campbell, Hickox, Keating, & McGrann.[97] He was a member of the Maritime Law Association of the United States, and his practice focused an admiralty matters.[98] In 1933, he became a member of the Aeronautics Committee of the Bar of the City of New York, on which he served until at least 1937.[99] He practiced with the Kirlin firm until 1953.[100] He died in 1970 in Oakland, California.[101]

William Devereaux Donnelly served as Cotter's co-clerk from the 1928 term through the 1936 term.[102] He earned the lower "stenographer" salary, but performed all the duties of a law clerk. Donnelly was born in Cass Lake, Minnesota, in 1905, and graduated from Central High School in Minneapolis. He came to Washington in 1928 after taking his law degree from the University of Minnesota, where he also received his bachelor's degree. He married Patricia Arnold in 1932. After clerking for Butler, he worked as an attorney in the Public Lands Division of the Justice Department from 1937 to 1940, serving as special assistant to the attorney general in 1939 and 1940.[103] In 1940, he went to work for the newly formed Washington, D.C., firm of Cummings & Stanley (later Cummings, Stanley, Truitt & Cross).[104] The Cummings in question was of course Homer Cummings, Franklin D. Roosevelt's former attorney general and the author of the infamous Court-packing plan introduced during Donnelly's final year of service with Butler.[105] Donnelly engaged in a widely varied practice with the Cummings firm, ranging from civil and criminal litigation to estate planning.[106] Shortly after joining the firm, for instance, Donnelly assisted Cummings in representing the notorious Chicago gambler William R. Johnson on charges of tax evasion. In 1946, Donnelly was called before a special federal grand jury looking into how Johnson had managed to stay out of prison for five-and-a-half years following his conviction.[107]

Donnelly was admitted to the Supreme Court bar in 1939,[108] and periodically briefed and argued cases before the Court.[109] The capstone of his career as a Supreme Court advocate came with his successful representation of the petitioner in the landmark Free Exercise case of *Sherbert v. Verner.*[110] Like Adell Sherbert, Donnelly was a Seventh-Day Adventist, and he represented the Bethesda community in the Church's General Conference.[111] Donnelly represented his church in other legal proceedings as well,[112] and in 1955 testified on its behalf at hearings on proposed amendments to the Fair Labor Standards Act held before the Senate Committee on Labor and Public Welfare.[113] In 1964, he joined 227 other constitutional scholars and lawyers in signing a letter to the House Judiciary Committee coauthored by Brandeis clerk Paul Freund in opposition to the proposed Becker Amendment to the Constitution, which would have overruled the recent school-prayer and devotional Bible-reading decisions of *Engel v. Vitale* and *Abington School District v. Schempp.*[114]

Donnelly was a partner in the Cummings firm by 1945,[115] and remained with the firm until 1956,[116] when he established his own solo practice.[117] A decade later he formed a partnership with a young lawyer named Gerald Golin,[118] and he continued to practice with Donnelly & Golin until his death in 1975.[119] He was an active member of the District of Columbia Bar Association,[120] where he served on committees with John Cragun.[121] He also belonged to the University Club and the Congressional Country Club. A widower, he died of a stroke at the age of sixty-nine, leaving four children.[122]

Irving Clark joined Butler for the 1937 term,[123] immediately following his graduation from Harvard Law School. A native of Duluth, Minnesota, Clark received his bachelor's degree in literature and philosophy from the University of Minnesota in 1934. In 1938, the justice's son Francis met Clark while visiting the elder Butler in Washington, D.C., and he asked Clark to join his St. Paul firm upon the completion of his clerkship. Excepting his service in the army during the Second World War, Clark remained with Doherty, Rumble & Butler from 1938 until his retirement in 1985, acting as the firm's managing partner from 1953 to 1975.[124] His practice was varied,[125] but it centered on agricultural cooperatives and nonprofit organizations.[126] He served on the boards of many charitable foundations,[127] and he was the board chairman of the Twin Cities' antipoverty agency in the 1960s.[128] He died at the age of eighty-four in January 1997, leaving a widow, three children, and three grandchildren.[129]

Luther E. "L.E." Jones Jr. was the last clerk to team up with Cotter, working for Butler during the 1938 term and until the justice's death in November 1939.[130] Jones was in some ways Butler's most interesting case, in part because he was a protégé of Lyndon Baines Johnson. Jones was the son of an impoverished druggist, and grew up in a Houston slum from which he was desperate to escape.[131] As a student at Sam Houston High School working part-time as a delivery boy, Jones was remembered as "tall, handsome, brilliant, but stiff and aloof—'smart as hell, but cold as hell.'"[132] In Jones's senior year of 1930–31, Johnson came to teach at Sam Houston, and under the tutelage of his new public-speaking instructor and debate coach Jones progressed to the finals of the Texas State Debate Championship. His loss by a narrow vote of 3–2 actually prompted his deeply disappointed and notoriously uncouth coach to vomit on the spot.[133] After his graduation in 1931, Jones worked his way through two years at Rice University (then Rice Institute), but he feared that he would be unable to secure employment upon graduation. Johnson had in the meantime left teaching to become secretary to Congressman Richard M. Kleberg, and asked Jones to come to Washington to serve on Kleberg's staff at a salary of $1,100 a year. Johnson wrote to him, "I know you are going places and I'm going to help you get there," urging him that the place to begin was in a government position in Washington.[134] Jones insisted that he needed a salary of $1,200, and Johnson cut his own salary in order to provide the extra $100.[135] Jones worked out of the Corpus Christi office from August to December 1933, when he went to Washington.[136] There he shared a small basement room in the Dodge Hotel with Johnson and Gene Latimer, Jones's high school debate partner who had come to Washington to work for Johnson the preceding summer. Each of the three roommates paid rent of $15 per month, and shared a bathroom with the adjoining room.[137]

Jones's clerkship with Butler must have seemed like a stroll in the park after working for Lyndon Johnson. Johnson "drove himself and his staff relentlessly."[138] "They worked phenomenally hard—fourteen-, sixteen-, often eighteen-hour days," frequently seven days a week.[139] Jones reported for work at 7:30 a.m. and often could be found at his desk at midnight.[140] Johnson forbade them to take a break to drink a cup of coffee, smoke a cigarette, or receive a personal telephone call.[141] "Even going to the bathroom was frowned upon."[142] Johnson "insisted on perfection," Jones recalled, and when he first started made him rewrite and retype hundreds of letters, no matter how long it took.[143] Johnson would compare members of his staff unfavorably in order to instill competition among them.[144] LBJ reserved his greatest abuse for the scholarly Jones, who was the best educated and most independent and self-contained member of his staff.[145] "He would publicly ridicule any error he found in one of his letters, belittling his style of writing, his spelling, his typing, or any failing that put him in a subordinate position."[146] The "stiff" and "prim" Jones was also the first victim of what became Johnson's lifelong, revolting practice of insisting that subordinates come into the bathroom with him to receive instructions or take dictation while he sat on the toilet defecating.[147] Jones "would stand with his head and nose averted, and take dictation," Latimer later told Robert Caro.[148] For Jones, "it was a source of humiliation and a means by which Johnson dominated him or exercised control."[149] Jones was understating the matter when he later reflected that "Lyndon Johnson was a hard man to work for."[150]

"At times, Latimer and Jones found it nearly impossible to keep working" for Johnson. "He was so demanding and occasionally so overbearing and abusive that they periodically wanted to quit."[151] But other considerations led Jones to persevere. First, this child of the Houston slums was very ambitious, and LBJ cultivated that ambition, telling him, "You work hard for me, and I'll help you." Later in life Jones would recall, "I always had the feeling that if I worked for Lyndon Johnson, goodies would come to me. . . . I was on the make, too. . . . I wanted to improve myself."[152] Second, Jones was personally drawn to Johnson's own talent, energy, and ambition. Years later, Jones would report that "[m]ost people who had anything to do with Lyndon Johnson loved him. . . . [T]he people who worked for him liked him. He had some faults, but most people were willing to overlook them because the guy was obviously a genius in politics."[153] "I always felt like we were making history," Jones added.[154] "The atmosphere was full of challenge, and this guy's enthusiasm was just absolutely contagious." Even then, Jones and his coworkers thought it was likely that Johnson would one day be president. They were convinced that he was "going to be a man of destiny."[155] Johnson, whom Jones later remembered as "a steam engine in pants,"[156] drove himself as hard as he drove his staff, and his fierce loyalty to his subordinates inspired reciprocal loyalty from them. "Both Jones and Latimer recall that when all was said and done, they liked, even loved Lyndon Johnson."[157]

One illustration of Johnson's concern for his staff occurred when Jones and Latimer decided to enroll in evening classes at Georgetown's law school in the fall of 1934. Johnson gave each of them a raise—for Jones, it was an additional $150 per year—and made sure that they had two to three hours free each day to study.[158] (Jones turned out to be a diligent student, completing his first year of law school at Georgetown; but Johnson, who briefly enrolled along with them, never studied, did not enjoy the experience, and soon dropped out with what he called a "B.A.—Barely Attended.")[159] During the fall of 1934, Johnson and Jones also worked together on liberal firebrand Maury Maverick's successful congressional campaign.[160] But soon Jones had saved enough money to pay tuition at the University of Texas Law School, and in the late spring of 1935 he returned to Austin to complete his legal studies. He told Maverick's son that he "had to get away" from Johnson, or he would "be devoured."[161]

As it would happen, Johnson also returned to Texas in the summer of 1935 to head the Texas chapter of the National Youth Administration (NYA). That summer, Jones worked as a part-time administrative assistant for Johnson at the NYA in Austin, and he continued to do so briefly after beginning his studies in the fall. For a time he lived with Johnson and his wife, Lady Bird, in an upstairs room of their Austin duplex, and during this period he looked on Lyndon as an older brother with whom he was proud and excited to be associated.[162] In his third year of law school Jones worked as an apprentice for the firm of Johnson's patron and mentor, Texas state senator Alvin J. Wirtz, and he was present in Wirtz's office for the conference between Johnson and Wirtz during which Johnson decided to run for Congress.[163] Jones worked as an advance man for Johnson's successful 1937 congressional campaign, driving a sound truck announcing Johnson's imminent appearance through small towns in Texas.[164] Jones graduated from the University of Texas Law School in June 1937, and then moved to Washington to work as a temporary secretary in the offices of Kleberg and Johnson until the new congressman helped him to secure a job as a briefing attorney in the Public Lands Division of the Justice Department that December.[165] During his stint at the Justice Department, Jones continued to lend a hand in Johnson's office in the evenings and on the weekends.[166]

Jones went to work for Butler in October 1938, and remained with the justice until Butler's death in November 1939. Like Donnelly, he earned the lower "stenographic clerk" wage, but he worked alongside Cotter preparing critical analyses of certiorari petitions and researching opinions for the justice. Jones then worked on a temporary basis in LBJ's congressional office while he looked for another full-time position.[167] There he encountered the young John Connally, who had joined Johnson's staff earlier in the year. Randall Wood reports that "[a]mong his fellow roomers at the Dodge, Connally quickly gained a reputation for vanity. Luther Jones remembered him standing in front of the mirror by the hour brushing his lustrous, wavy hair."[168] Jones soon found steadier work back at the Public Lands Division, but in January 1940 Wirtz became undersecretary of the Department of the Interior, and he hired Jones to serve as his executive assistant. After a year of service at Interior, Jones returned to the Public Lands Division offices in Houston and Corpus Christi to work on federal condemnation cases for land for the Naval Air Station. He took an indefinite leave from the Justice Department in December 1942 to enlist in the army.[169]

During his time with Wirtz, Jones still periodically performed services for Johnson. One Sunday morning at Johnson's Dodge Hotel apartment, Jones had the honor of introducing Johnson to Jake Pickle.[170] Jones and Pickle had been Delta Theta Phi fraternity brothers at the University of Texas, and Pickle was then a young member of the Texas NYA who had been summoned to Washington to discuss a proposed highway project with Johnson. Little did they know at the time that Pickle would later become Johnson's successor to the congressional seat, which Pickle would hold for thirty-one years.[171] As Pickle relates the story, "As I prepared myself for the big meeting, Luther kept telling me how important LBJ was, how the Congressman was going places, and how, if I played my cards right, I could go places, too. We all could. 'You should watch him, Pickle!,' Luther said. 'He's amazing. He'll have you doing things you never thought possible. Big things! Important things!'"[172]

They entered the apartment to find Johnson seated "on the throne," as Pickle put it. Pickle ducked back behind a door, but Johnson insisted that Luther join him in the bathroom. After a few minutes, Pickle relates, Johnson said, "'Luther, hand me some more paper!' And Luther did."[173] After Johnson had concluded his "business" in the *salle de bain*, the three men had a meeting about the proposed highway project. Pickle reports that "[n]othing was settled, but the meeting gave Johnson the chance to observe me, and vice versa. Of course, I had already observed more of Johnson that day than I had anticipated! . . . [I]f I had looked forward to a personal meeting, I sure got one!"[174] "That day, as we left Johnson's room," Pickle concludes the story, "I couldn't resist sticking it to Luther. 'You're right,' I said. 'Johnson *does* have you doing things you never thought possible. Important things! For instance, I notice you did a fine job handing him that paper!'" "Luther," Pickles adds, "took it good-naturedly."[175]

Jones was destined to go on to even bigger and more important things. After serving as a second lieutenant in the army during the war, he returned to Corpus Christi, this time as a full-time assistant to City Attorney Oliver Cox.[176] In 1947, he entered a successful solo practice specializing in criminal law and oil and gas law.[177] The following year Johnson called on him in a moment of crisis, asking Jones to join the legal team representing Johnson in the controversy arising out of the disputed Texas Democratic Party U.S. senatorial primary election of 1948. Jones answered the call of duty, and Johnson went on to win a seat in the Senate, but this marked the end of their professional association.[178] In 1958, Jones was elected to serve as a member of the Board of Directors of the National Association of Criminal Defense Lawyers.[179] In 1965, President Johnson had his old debate student and other honored guests bussed from Corpus Christi to the little one-room schoolhouse just down the road from the LBJ Ranch to witness the signing of the historic Elementary and Secondary Education Act.[180] That same year, Jones was honored by the Texas State Bar for his distinguished service. A magazine profile published in 1968 characterized Jones as a "lawyer's lawyer," the "finest appellate lawyer" in Texas, and "the man with probably the finest technical legal knowledge in the state." "As a money earner," the article proclaimed, "he is probably in the top five percent of Texas lawyers; as a legal scholar he is second to none. Many colleagues consider him the finest appellate lawyer in the country."[181] That year Jones was among 250 honored guests at a White House reunion of longtime friends of Lyndon and Lady Bird Johnson.[182] In 1968, he also sat on the state bar's committee charged with revising the Texas Code of Criminal Procedure, and was made first assistant district attorney for Nueces County.[183] He retired from that position in 1970 in order to spend time with his family and to pursue his interests in philosophy, literature, travel, and dancing,[184] but he continued to publish law review articles and to engage in occasional private practice into the 1980s.[185]

Throughout his professional career, Jones retained his fierce independence. He "would never join a law firm, because he did not want partners." Even "at the peak of his career, when he was earning impressive legal fees, he worked alone in a converted, book-lined garage behind his house in Corpus Christi."[186] Luther Jones died at the age of eighty-five in September 1999, survived by his wife, four children, and nine grandchildren.[187]

Conclusion

The careers of some of the clerks for these "conservative" justices may seem at first blush counterintuitive, but only because of the power of such reductive political taxonomy to mislead. It may seem odd that Luther Jones became one of the nation's leading criminal defense attorneys, until we recall that Chief Justice Hughes regarded Butler as a stickler for the protection of the rights of the accused,[188] so much so that his colleague Justice Stone thought that Butler was soft on crime.[189] It may seem strange that John Cragun became one of his generation's leading lawyers for Native American tribes, until we are reminded that Justice Van Devanter was an Indian law expert whose colleagues regarded him as "the Indians' best pal" on the Court.[190] Upon closer inspection, these ostensible ironies dissipate.

Some of the personal and professional relationships of these clerks might also seem at first glance surprising: Luther Jones's secretarial post with the young Lyndon Johnson; Norris Darrell's marriage to Learned Hand's daughter; William Donnelly's partnership with Homer Cummings. The last of these, which notably did not occur until after Justice Butler's death, may remain puzzling even upon reflection. But at least some of these pairings seem less startling when we recall that Butler's first law partner was Stan Donnelly, the son of Butler's friend, the Populist leader Ignatius Donnelly,[191] and that regular Republicans Van Devanter and Sutherland reportedly got along very well with their more liberal colleagues.[192] These justices could disagree without being disagreeable.

A review of the careers of the clerks of the Four Horsemen also serves to highlight the anomalous character of the case of John Knox, the only clerk of the Four Horsemen about whom much has been written previously. To be sure, only a few of these men rose to what might be regarded as the heights of their professions. But a great many of them had interesting and varied careers, achieving admirable success in business, private practice, government service, or some combination of these. Moreover, unlike the unfortunate, isolated John Knox, most of them seem to have been blessed with fulfilling family and social lives, and were actively engaged in the affairs of their communities. This may help to explain why these other clerks did not write comparable remembrances of their service in chambers. Unlike Knox, who was lonely and often at loose ends, they had busy lives and other things to do.

Despite all of the interesting variation in the careers of the clerks of the Four Horsemen, however, they share one common similarity: unlike the clerks for Holmes, Brandeis, and Stone, and their many successor justices, not a single one of them developed a career as a law professor. This, too, may help to account for the absence of a clerkship remembrance literature, which has been generated predominantly by academics. And relatedly, I would suggest that this fact has had a powerful effect on the ways in which these justices have been perceived by the academy, and by the legal profession at large. But that is a story for another day.[193]

Notes

Thanks to Patty Cushman, Clare Cushman, Joel Goldstein, Dennis Hutchison, and the participants in a faculty workshop at St. Louis University School of Law for helpful comments, and to Patrick Bottini, Carli Conklin, Anna Crandall, Trez Drake, Jessica Ettinger, Samantha Glass, Dwight King, Beth Klein, Lisa Meissner, and Chris O'Byrne for indispensable research assistance. I am grateful to the Bancroft Library of the University of California at Berkeley for permission to quote from the Pillsbury, Madison & Sutro Oral History Series.

1. For a survey of the literature on the Four Horsemen, see Barry Cushman, "The Clerks of the Four Horsemen," *Journal of Supreme Court History* 39, no. 3 (Part I) (2014): xx.

2. The other is a slim and not particularly revealing essay by Norris Darrell, who clerked for Justice Butler during the 1923 and 1924 terms. See Norris Darrell, "Some Personal Reminiscences," in "Reminiscences by Alumni Who Graduated Fifty Years or More Ago from the University of Minnesota Law School," unpublished manuscript on file with the University of Minnesota Law School, 1976. For an abridged version of this essay, see "Appendix: Reminiscences of Two University of Minnesota Law Graduates: Norris Darrell," in Robert A. Stein, "In Pursuit of Excellence: A History of the University of Minnesota Law School, Part III: The Fraser Years—A Time of Excellence and Innovation," *Minnesota Law Review* 62 (1978): 1161, 1202–4. See also Robert T. Swaine, *The Cravath Firm and Its Predecessors 1819–1948* (New York: Ad Press, 1948), 3:175.

3. Dennis J. Hutchinson and David J. Garrow, eds., *The Forgotten Memoir of John Knox* (Chicago: University of Chicago Press, 2002), vii–ix, xv–xviii, 5–8, 246; John Knox, "John Knox Diary" (January 22, 1941), unpublished manuscript, Folder 10240-g, Knox MSS, Special Collections, University of Virginia.

4. See Clare Cushman, "Beyond Knox: James C. McReynolds's Other Clerks, 1914–1941" this volume, which concludes that McReynolds's mistreatment of Knox may have been only slightly more egregious than that of his other clerks.

5. Arthur Mattson to Willis Van Devanter, July 25, 1929, Files M–S, Van Devanter MSS, Library of Congress, quoted in Todd C. Peppers, *Courtiers of the Marble Palace: The Rise and Influence of the Supreme Court Law Clerk* (Stanford, Calif.: Stanford University Press, 2006), 69.

6. See David Schroeder, "More Than a Fraction: The Life and Work of Justice Pierce Butler" (Ph.D. diss., Marquette University, 2009), 79, 128, 150, 153, 180, 234; Hutchinson and Garrow, *Forgotten Memoir of John Knox*, 58. Even those who were critical of Van Devanter's jurisprudence conceded that he was "courteous" and "likeable." See Drew Pearson and Robert S. Allen, *The Nine Old Men* (New York: Doubleday, 1936), 198.

7. See Joel Francis Paschal, *Mr. Justice Sutherland: A Man Against the State* (Princeton, N.J.: Princeton University Press, 1951), 115–17, 233; Jay S. Bybee, "George Sutherland," in *The Supreme Court Justices: Illustrated Biographies 1789–2012*, 32nd ed., edited by Clare Cushman (Washington, D.C.: CQ Press, 2012), 316–17; Schroeder, "More Than a Fraction," 150–51; Timothy Hall, *Supreme Court Justices: A Biographical Dictionary* (New York: Facts on File Library of American History, 2001), 281. Pearson and Allen were even more lavish in their assessment of Sutherland's temperament, characterizing the justice as "suave" and "gentle," blessed with "amiability," an "inoffensive good nature," an "agreeable manner," and a "sweetness of disposition." Pearson and Allen, *Nine Old Men*, 159, 200, 201, 199.

8. Butler clearly was liked and admired by many, including his longtime clerk John F.

Cotter. See Schroeder, "More Than a Fraction," 21–22, 38–40, 50n112, 55–56, 79, 82, 90n220, 150–54, 167–68, 180–81, 228–29, 233–35, 237–38, 240; Richard J. Purcell, "Mr. Justice Pierce Butler (1866–1939)," *Recorder* 10 (May 1, 1940): 33, 36–37; Richard J. Purcell, "Mr. Justice Pierce Butler," *Catholic Educational Review* (September 1944): 426–31; David J. Danelski, *A Supreme Court Justice Is Appointed* (New York: Random House, 1964), 9, 11.

9. Chester A. Newland, "Personal Assistants to Supreme Court Justices: The Law Clerks," *Oregon Law Review* 40 (June 1961): 312; see also Employment Record of John Francis Cotter, National Personnel Records Center, Valmeyer, Illinois (in author's possession) (hereafter cited as Cotter Employment Record).

10. William D. Donnelly to Hugo L. Black, August 27, 1937, Box 442, Hugo Black MSS, Library of Congress, quoted in Peppers, *Courtiers of the Marble Palace,* 93.

11. Hutchinson and Garrow, *Forgotten Memoir of John Knox,* 272–77; Swaine, *Cravath Firm,* 175; "John Knox," *Chicago Tribune,* March 3, 1997, 5; Knox Diary, December 28, 1962, and June 18, 1963, Box 20, Knox Papers, Georgetown University Library, quoted in Hutchinson and Garrow, *Forgotten Memoir of John Knox,* 272.

12. Employment Record of Edward S. Widdifield, National Personnel Records Center, National Archives at St. Louis (in author's possession) (hereafter cited as Widdifield Employment Record). George Sutherland's clerks' dates of service were provided by the Supreme Court of the United States Library in correspondence dated June 26, 2002 (hereafter cited as Supreme Court Library Correspondence). While there is no complete list of all Supreme Court law clerks, the library maintains unofficial internal files relating to clerks' service at the Court, which it recognizes may contain incomplete and unverified information.

13. Widdifield Employment Record; *Polk's Traverse City and Grand Traverse County Directory: 1901–1902* (1902), 2:106.

14. Widdifield Employment Record; Artemus Ward and David L. Weiden, *Sorcerer's Apprentices: 100 Years of Law Clerks at the United States Supreme Court* (New York: New York University Press, 2006), 32; "Former Aide of Supreme Court Dies," *Washington Post,* October 2, 1960, B6; "Widdifield, 74, Retires as Supreme Court Aide," *Washington Post,* February 1, 1949, 13.

15. Widdifield Employment Record; *Official Congressional Directory,* 2nd ed. (Washington, D.C.: Government Printing Office, 1914), 218; *Official Congressional Directory,* 1st ed. (Washington, D.C.: Government Printing Office, 1915), 190; S. Doc. No. 627 (1914), 18 (Report of the Secretary); S. Doc. No. 1 (1915), 11 (Report of the Secretary); S. Doc. No. 556 (1916), 11, 21 (Report of the Secretary); *Official Congressional Directory,* 1st ed. (Washington, D.C.: Government Printing Office, 1916), 215; Christopher J. Doby, Financial Clerk, U.S. Senate, to the author, March 20, 2014 (in author's possession).

16. Widdifield Employment Record; "Former Aide of Supreme Court Dies"; "Widdifield, 74, Retires as Supreme Court Aide"; *Official Congressional Directory,* 2nd ed. (Washington, D.C.: Government Printing Office, 1931), 257; "Miss Widdifield Will Be Bride of E. H. Fraser," *Washington Post,* June 2, 1935, S2; e-mail from Katherine Logan, CPP, Director of the Office of Payroll and Benefits, U.S. House of Representatives, to the author, April 29, 2014.

17. Widdifield to Black, August 12, 1937, Box 442, Hugo L. Black Papers, Library of Congress, quoted in Peppers, *Courtiers of the Marble Palace*, 61.

18. "Former Aide of Supreme Court Dies."

19. Francis R. Kirkham, "Sixty Rewarding Years in the Practice of Law: 1930–1990," an oral history conducted 1985–90 by Sarah Sharp and Carole Hicke, Regional Oral History Office, Bancroft Library, University of California at Berkeley (1994), 11–12 (hereafter cited as Kirkham Oral History). See also Supreme Court Library Correspondence.

20. "James E. Gray," *North Dakota Bar Briefs* 21 (1944): 125.

21. *The Martindale-Hubbell Law Directory*, 73rd Annual Edition (New York: Martindale-Hubbell, 1941), 1:1308 (microformed on LLMC Martindale-Hubbell, Directories No. 92-001A F5); "Area Briefs: UND's Zierdt Gets Law Professorship," *Grand Forks (N.D.) Herald*, November 28, 2001, 2001 Westlaw NewsRoom 2295318.

22. http://www.walshhistory.org/publications/walsh-heritage/Walsh-Heritage-Volume-1/files/assets/basic-html/page164.html, 169.

23. See, for example, "$461,650 in Sales, Recently Effected, Reported by Firm," *Washington Post*, November 6, 1927, R5 (Gray purchase of home in Chevy Chase, Maryland); "Legal Notices," *Washington Post*, October 7, 1933, 21 (Gray publication of legal notice stating his occupation and office address in the Old Shoreham Building).

24. See, for example, *Jewel Tea Co., Inc. v. United States*, 90 F.2d 451 (2d Cir. 1937); *Keener Oil & Gas Co. v. Commissioner*, 32 B.T.A. 186 (1935); *Anderson v. P. W. Madsen Inv. Co.*, 72 F.2d 768 (10th Cir. 1934); *Severs Hotel Co. v. Commissioner of Internal Revenue*, 62 F.2d 1080 (10th Cir. 1932).

25. http://www.walshhistory.org/publications/walsh-heritage/Walsh-Heritage-Volume-1/files/assets/basic-html/page164.html, 169; Charles Curtis, "Jack Gage Wrecks Par," *Los Angeles Times*, June 3, 1939, 10 (listing Gray as a resident of the San Diego suburb of Lakeside).

26. See, for example, *The Martindale-Hubbell Law Directory*, 70th Annual Edition (New York: Martindale-Hubbell, 1938), 1:1348 (microformed on LLMC Martindale-Hubbell, Directories No. 92-001A F5); *The Martindale-Hubbell Law Directory*, 87th Annual Edition (New York: Martindale-Hubbell, 1955), 1:119 (microformed on LLMC Martindale-Hubbell, Directories No. 92-001A F7); *The Martindale-Hubbell Law Directory*, 177th Annual Edition (New York: Martindale-Hubbell, 1975), 1:343 (microformed on LLMC Martindale-Hubbell, Directories No. 92-001A F14).

27. See, for example, *Wilson v. Commissioner of Internal Revenue*, 14 T.C.M. (CCH) 299 (1955); *Cole v. Internal Revenue Service*, 13 T.C.M. (CCH) 1135 (1954); *Hutchins v. Commissioner of Internal Revenue*, 8 T.C.M. (CCH) 809 (1949); *Dean v. Davis*, 166 P.2d 15 (Cal. Dist. Ct. App. 1946).

28. "Mrs. Fields Called 'Vulture' in Letter," *Los Angeles Times*, May 6, 1949, 2.

29. "Burns-Allen Tax Plea Filed," *Los Angeles Times*, December 15, 1938, 1.

30. "Mrs. Fields Called 'Vulture' in Letter."

31. "Coburn and His Poker-Playing Friends Fined," *Los Angeles Times*, June 14, 1951, A1.

32. *The Martindale-Hubbell Law Directory*, 116th Annual Edition (New York: Martindale-Hubbell, 1984), 1:385 (microformed on LLMC Martindale-Hubbell, Directories

No. 92-001A F7); Social Security Death Index (Lexis Advance, Public Records, Death Records).

33. "Area Briefs."

34. Kirkham Oral History, 11–12. See also "Francis Robison Kirkham," *The Complete Marquis Who's Who* (2001), reproduced in *Biography Resource Center* (Farmington Hills, Mich.: Gale Group 2002), http://www.galenet.com/servlet/BioRC (Document Number: K2021035780); Supreme Court Library Correspondence.

35. Kirkham Oral History, viii, 1–2, 98–101; "Francis Robison Kirkham"; "Francis R. Kirkham," *San Francisco Chronicle,* October 26, 1996, A20; "Death: Francis R. Kirkham," *Deseret News,* October 27, 1996, 11.

36. Kirkham Oral History, 3–7.

37. Ibid., iii, 11–12; "Francis Robison Kirkham"; "Francis R. Kirkham"; "Death: Francis R. Kirkham."

38. 287 U.S. 45 (1932).

39. 290 U.S. 398 (1934).

40. Kirkham Oral History, 12–14.

41. Ibid., 14–16, 23.

42. Ibid., 7–9; "Francis Robison Kirkham"; "Francis R. Kirkham"; "Death: Francis R. Kirkham."

43. After his interview with McReynolds, Musser wrote to Kirkham: "Sutherland's immediate recommendation vital. Please arrange this. Will count on it." Telegram from Milton S. Musser to Francis R. Kirkham, March 24, 1938, Box 23, Folder 1, Milton Shipp Musser MSS, Utah State Historical Society. Musser also listed Kirkham as a reference on the résumé he submitted to McReynolds following the interview. See Musser to McReynolds, April 16, 1938, Box 23, Folder 1, Musser MSS. For more details on Kirkham's role in the events leading up to McReynolds's hiring of Musser, see Clare Cushman, "Beyond Knox: James C. McReynolds's Other Clerks, 1914–1941," this volume.

44. Kirkham Oral History, vi, 16–19, 23; "Francis Robison Kirkham"; "Francis R. Kirkham"; "Death: Francis R. Kirkham"; *Hearings Before the Subcommittee on Multinational Corporations of the Committee on Foreign Relations,* 93rd Cong. (1974), 405 (statements by Francis R. Kirkham, cited as General Counsel to Standard Oil Co. of California).

45. See, for example, *Western Union Tel. Co. v. Nester,* 309 U.S. 582 (1940); *Leh v. General Petroleum Corp.,* 382 U.S. 54 (1965); *United States v. Leiter Minerals, Inc.,* 381 U.S. 413 (1965); *City of San Francisco v. Skelly Oil Co.,* 389 U.S. 817 (1967); *Perkins v. Standard Oil Co. of California,* 393 U.S. 1013 (1969); *Hawaii v. Standard Oil Co. of California,* 405 U.S. 251 (1972).

46. Kirkham Oral History, v–vi, 16, 23–24, 122–24; "Francis Robison Kirkham"; "Francis R. Kirkham"; "Death: Francis R. Kirkham." See also Francis R. Kirkham et al., "Colloquy on Complex Litigation," *Brigham Young University Law Review* (1981): 741; Francis R. Kirkham, "Problems of Complex Civil Litigation," *Federal Rules Decisions* 83 (1979): 497; Francis R. Kirkham, "Complex Civil Litigation—Have Good Intentions Gone Awry?," *Federal Rules Decisions* 70 (1976): 199; Reuben G. Hunt, "Arrangements

Under Chapter XI of Bankruptcy Act, 1939," *American Bar Association Section of Commercial Law Report of Proceedings* (1939): 21, 22.

47. Kirkham Oral History, 125; "Francis Robison Kirkham"; "Francis R. Kirkham"; "Death: Francis R. Kirkham."

48. Wallace Kaapcke, "General Civil Practice: A Varied and Exciting Life at Pillsbury, Madison and Sutro," an oral history conducted 1986–87 by Carole Hicke, Regional Oral History Office, Bancroft Library, University of California at Berkeley (1990), 21, 310, http://archive.org/stream/generalcivilpracticeookaaprich/generalcivilpracticeooka aprich_djvu.txt.

49. "I had a long association with him and I enjoyed every bit of it. I enjoyed it intellectually and enjoyed it personally. And I stress both, because sometimes you can enjoy people personally that maybe you don't enjoy intellectually and vice versa, but Mr. Kirkham is one of the outstanding lawyers that I've ever had any contact with in combining those two qualities." Turner H. McBaine, "A Career in the Law at Home and Abroad," an oral history conducted 1986 by Carole Hicke, Regional Oral History Office, Bancroft Library, University of California at Berkeley (1989), 69–70, http://www .archive.org/stream/careerlawathomeoomcbarich#page/n9/mode/2up.

50. Kaapcke, "General Civil Practice," 21.

51. Ibid., 248.

52. Kirkham Oral History, vii.

53. John Bates, "Litigation and Law Firm Management at Pillsbury, Madison and Sutro," an oral history conducted in 1986 by Carol Hicke, Regional Oral History Office, Bancroft Library, University of California at Berkeley (1988), 202–3. Explaining why Kirkham did not serve on the firm's management committee, Bates stated, "I think the senior partners felt that Francis Kirkham was so valuable to the total profession, really a genius in the practice of law, that they didn't want to impose on him to bother with the management of the affairs of the firm. They were quite happy to give him top recognition and distributions and all that sort of thing, but they didn't want to burden him with the day-to-day management of the affairs of the firm." Ibid., 204, http:// archive.org/stream/litigationlawfirmoobaterich/litigationlawfirmoobaterich_djvu.txt. See also Charles F. Prael, "Litigation and the Practice of Labor Law at Pillsbury, Madison and Sutro, 1934–1977," an oral history conducted in 1985 by Carol Hicke, Regional Oral History Office, Bancroft Library, University of California at Berkeley (1986), 26, http://archive.org/stream/litigationpracoopraerich/litigationpracoopraerich_djvu .txt (Kirkham "contributed tremendously to the standing of the firm").

54. McBaine, "Career in the Law," 77.

55. James O'Brien, "Odyssey of a Journeyman Lawyer," an oral history conducted in 1987–89 by Carole Hicke, Regional Oral History Office, Bancroft Library, University of California at Berkeley (1991), 210, http://archive.org/stream/odysseylawyer ooobririch/odysseylawyerooobririch_djvu.txt. See also ibid., 194–96, on Kirkham's talents as a lawyer.

56. Kirkham Oral History, ii–viii.

57. Supreme Court Library Correspondence.

58. Employment Record of John W. Cragun, National Personnel Records Center,

National Archives at St. Louis (in author's possession); *Who Was Who in America* (Chicago: Marquis Who's Who, 1973), 5:156; "Indian Claims Commission Files of Wilkinson, Cragun, & Barker, ca. 1950–1982," Brigham Young University, http://files.lib.byu.edu/ead/XML/MSS2291.xml.

59. *Who Was Who in America*; Robert W. Barker, "Memorial to John Wiley Cragun Presented to the United States Court of Claims, May 6, 1969," *Administrative Law Review* 21 (1969): xvii.

60. Barker, "Memorial," xvii.

61. *Who Was Who in America.*

62. "Indian Claims Commission Files of Wilkinson, Cragun, & Barker." See, for example, *Pierce Estates, Inc. v. Commissioner*, 16 T.C. 1020 (1951); Barker, "Memorial," xvii.

63. *Who Was Who in America*; "Indian Claims Commission Files of Wilkinson, Cragun, & Barker"; Barker, "Memorial," xvii.

64. *Who Was Who in America*; Barker, "Memorial," xviii, xix. See, for example, *Federal Power Commission v. Southern California Edison Co.*, 376 U.S. 205 (1964); *Menominee Tribe v. United States*, 391 U.S. 404 (1968); *Kake Village v. Egan*, 369 U.S. 60 (1962); *Squire v. Capoeman*, 351 U.S. 1 (1956); *Dodge, Superintendent of the Osage Indian Agency v. United States*, 362 F.2d 810 (Ct. Cl. 1966); *Big Eagle v. United States*, 300 F.2d 765 (Ct. Cl. 1962); *Upper Skagit Tribe of Indians v. United States*, Indian Claims Commission 381 (1969) 20:381, http://digital.library.okstate.edu/icc/v20/iccv20p381.pdf; *Northern Cheyenne Indians of the Tongue River, Montana v. United States*, Indian Claims Commission 13 (1963): 1, http://digital.library.okstate.edu/icc/v13/iccv13p001.pdf. See generally "Indian Claims Commission Files of Wilkinson, Cragun, & Barker."

65. Barker, "Memorial," xviii.

66. *Who Was Who in America*; Barker, "Memorial," xvii–xviii; Robert M. Benjamin, "A Lawyer's View of Administrative Procedure—The American Bar Association Program," *Law & Contemporary Problems* 26 (1961): 203, 206n14; John W. Cragun, "Who Is the Judge, Agency or Court?" *Wyoming Law Journal* 13 (1958): 111; John W. Cragun, "Admission to Practice: Present Regulation by Federal Agencies," *American Bar Association Journal* 34 (1948): 111.

67. *Who Was Who in America*; Barker, "Memorial," xx.

68. Chester A. Newland, "Personal Assistants to Supreme Court Justices: The Law Clerks," *Oregon Law Review* 40 (June 1961): 303, 307, 308, 312; Norman Dorsen, "Law Clerks in Appellate Courts in the United States," *Modern Law Review* 26 (1963): 265; Schroeder, "More Than a Fraction," 166–67; John G. Kester, "The Law Clerk Explosion," *Litigation* 9 (1983): 20, 22; Supreme Court Library Correspondence.

69. Cotter Employment Record.

70. *The Martindale-Hubbell Law Directory*, 88th Annual Edition (New York: Martindale-Hubbell, 1956), 1:403 (microformed on LLMC Martindale-Hubbell, Directories No. 92-001A F20). See also Supreme Court Library Correspondence; Schroeder, "More Than a Fraction," 166.

71. Schroeder, "More Than a Fraction," 166–67.

72. Ibid., 166; Cotter Employment Record.

73. Schroeder, "More Than a Fraction," 4, 82n197, 167.

74. Cotter Employment Record.

75. See, for example, *U.S. v. Fixico*, 115 F.2d 389 (10th Cir. 1940); *U.S. v. Tilley*, 124 F.2d 850 (8th Cir. 1941); *U.S. v. Foster*, 131 F.2d 3 (8th Cir. 1942); *U.S. v. Waterhouse*, 132 F.2d 699 (9th Cir. 1943); *Sioux Tribe of Indians v. United States*, 329 U.S. 684 (1946); *Arenas v. U.S.*, 331 U.S. 842 (1947); *U.S. v. Woodworth*, 170 F.2d 1019 (2d Cir. 1948); *U.S. v. Hayes*, 172 F.2d 677 (9th Cir. 1949); *City of Fort Worth v. U.S.*, 185 F.2d 397 (5th Cir. 1950); *U.S. v. Marks*, 187 F.2d 784 (9th Cir. 1951); *Title Ins. & Guar. Co. v. United States*, 194 F.2d 916 (9th Cir. 1952); *United States v. Catlin*, 204 F.2d 661, 662 (7th Cir. 1953); *United States v. South Dakota*, 212 F.2d 14 (8th Cir. 1954); *Werner v. United States*, 233 F.2d 52, 53 (9th Cir. 1956).

76. AncestryLibrary.com, U.S. World War II Army Enlistment Records, 1938–1946; Cotter Employment Record.

77. Cotter Employment Record.

78. See, for example, *The Martindale-Hubbell Law Directory*, 89th Annual Edition (New York: Martindale-Hubbell, 1957), 1:365 (microformed on LLMC Martindale-Hubbell, Directories No. 92-001A F7); *The Martindale-Hubbell Law Directory*, 97th Annual Edition (New York: Martindale-Hubbell, 1965), 1:592 (microformed on LLMC Martindale-Hubbell, Directories No. 92-001A F27); *The Martindale-Hubbell Law Directory*, 107th Annual Edition (New York: Martindale-Hubbell, 1975), 1:945 (microformed on LLMC Martindale-Hubbell, Directories No. 92-001A F47).

79. Ancestry.com, U.S. Social Security Death Index, 1935–Current.

80. Supreme Court Library Correspondence.

81. Christopher J. Doby, Financial Clerk, United States Senate, to the author, March 20, 2014 (in author's possession); S. Doc. No. 158 (1919), 14 (Report of the Secretary).

82. "What the Big Fraternal Orders Are Doing," *Washington Post*," March 21, 1920, 57.

83. *Georgetown Alumni Directory*, 1947; "Tablet Unveiled for Hilltop Boys Who Died in the War," *Washington Herald*, June 15, 1921, 2.

84. "Names Asked of Reservists for Schooling: Infantry and Engineer Courses," *Washington Post*, October 15, 1933, 16.

85. "Mrs. C. A. Dyke Dies Following Holiday Feast," *Washington Post*, December 26, 1948, M12; "Deaths," *Southern Medical Journal*, December 1941, 1294.

86. Supreme Court Library Correspondence.

87. See "Norris Darrell, Lawyer and Tax Expert, 90," *New York Times*, August 15, 1989, B5; "Norris Darrell," *Newsday*, August 16, 1989, 45; *Who's Who in American Law*, 2nd ed. (Chicago: Marquis Who's Who, 1979), 198; Darrell, "Some Personal Reminiscences," 4.

88. Darrell, "Some Personal Reminiscences."

89. Ibid., 5–6.

90. See "Norris Darrell, Lawyer and Tax Expert," B5; "Norris Darrell," 45; *Who's Who in American Law*, 198; Nancy Lisagor and Frank Lipsius, eds., *A Law Unto Itself: The Untold Story of the Law Firm Sullivan & Cromwell* (New York: Paragon House 1988), 100, 119–20, 130, 203–4; Sullivan & Cromwell, *Sullivan & Cromwell, 1879–1979: A Century at Law* (New York: William Morrow, Sullivan & Cromwell, 1979), 39, 58–60, 64; "Reminiscences of Norris Darrell," in *Lamplighters: The Sullivan and Cromwell Lawyers April 2, 1879 to April 2, 1979*, edited by William Piel Jr. et al. (New York: Sullivan & Cromwell,

1981), 110–17. Darrell published widely on issues of federal taxation and professional responsibility. See, for example, Norris Darrell and Paul A. Wolkin, "The American Law Institute," *New York State Bar Journal* 52 (1980): 99; Norris Darrell, "Conscience and Propriety in Tax Practice," in *The Lawyer in Modern Society*, 2nd ed., edited by Vern Countryman et al. (Boston: Little, Brown, 1976), 361, 363; Norris Darrell, "Reflections on the Federal Income Tax," *The Record, New York City Bar Association* 28 (1973): 412; Norris Darrell, "The Role of Universities in Continuing Professional Education," *Ohio State Law Journal* 32 (1971): 312; Norris Darrell, "Responsibilities of the Lawyer in Tax Practice," in *Professional Responsibility in Federal Tax Practice*, edited by Boris I. Bittker (Branford, Conn.: Federal Tax Press, 1970), 87; Norris Darrell, "The Tax Lawyer's Duty to His Client and to His Government," *Practical Lawyer* 7 (1961): 3; Norris Darrell, "Some Challenges of the Legal Profession," *Brief* 57 (1961): 8; Norris Darrell, "The Use of Reorganization Techniques in Corporate Acquisitions," *Harvard Law Review* 70 (1957): 1183; Norris Darrell, "Responsibilities of the Lawyer in Tax Practice," in *Materials on the Lawyer's Professional Responsibility*, edited by William M. Trumbull (Boston: Little Brown, 1957), 291; Norris Darrell, "Internal Revenue Code of 1954—A Striking Example of the Legislative Process in Action," *1955 S. Cal. Tax. Inst.* 1 (1955); Norris Darrell, "The 1954 Internal Revenue Code—One Year Later: A General Review," *Tax Executive* 8 (1955): 23; Norris Darrell, "The Tax Treatment of Payments Under Section 16(B) of the Securities Exchange Act of 1934," *Harvard Law Review* 64 (1950): 80; Norris Darrell, "Recent Developments in Nontaxable Reorganizations and Stock Dividends," *Harvard Law Review* 61 (1948): 958; Norris Darrell, "The Scope of Commissioner," *Taxes* 24 (1946): 266; Norris Darrell, "Creditors' Reorganizations and the Federal Income Tax," *Harvard Law Review* 57 (1944): 1009; Norris Darrell, "Corporation Liquidations and the Federal Income Tax," *University of Pennsylvania Law Review* 89 (1941): 907; Norris Darrell, "Discharge of Indebtedness and the Federal Income Tax," *Harvard Law Review* 53 (1940): 977. He was also a frequent public speaker on these issues: see, for example, "Further Revisions Seen in U.S. Income Tax Laws," *Los Angeles Times*, October 21, 1954, 36; "Douglas, Bradford Listed as Speakers in Harvard Law Series," *Daily Boston Globe*, December 9, 1951, C24; "Display Ad 190—No Title," *New York Times*, October 7, 1946, 35; "Events Today," *New York Times*, April 27, 1944, 21.

91. See "Norris Darrell, Lawyer and Tax Expert," B5; "Norris Darrell," 45; "Norris Darrell Takes Bride," *Washington Post*, June 29, 1945, 12; "Reminiscences of Norris Darrell," 116–17. Hand had kinder things to say about Butler at the justice's death. See Purcell, "Mr. Justice Pierce Butler (1866–1939)," 33, 36.

92. "Reminiscences of Norris Darrell," 116–17; Gerald Gunther, "'Contracted' Biographies and Other Obstacles to 'Truth,'" *New York University Law Review* 70 (1995): 697; Gerald Gunther, *Learned Hand: The Man and the Judge* (New York: Knopf, 1994), xix; David Margolick, "In the Mentor's Steps: Law Professor Tries to Capture Professional, Personal Aspects of Jurist Learned Hand," *Dallas Morning News*, May 8, 1994, 8a.

93. "17 Leading Lawyers Call Civil Rights Bill Constitutional," *New York Times*, September 19, 1966, 37.

94. See Norris Darrell, "Lawyer and Tax Expert, 90," *New York Times*, August 15, 1989, B5; "Norris Darrell," 45.

95. Supreme Court Library Correspondence.

96. *The Martindale-Hubbell Law Directory,* 67th Annual Edition (New York: Martin-dale-Hubbell, 1935), 1:11406 (microformed on LLMC Martindale-Hubbell, Directories No. 92-001A F4).

97. *Journal of the Supreme Court of the United States* (1932); *U.S. v. Stephanidis,* 47 F.2d 554 (2d Cir. 1931).

98. Annual Meeting, The Maritime Law Association of the United States, April 26, 1935 (Document No. 207, April, 1935), 2135; *The Santa Lucia,* 44 F. Supp. 793 (D.C.N.Y. 1942); *Public Warehouses of Matanzas, Inc. v. Fidelity & Deposit Co. of Maryland,* 77 F.2d 831 (2d Cir. 1935); *Lloyd Royal Belge Societe Anonyme v. Elting,* 289 U.S. 730 (1933); *St. Paul Fire & Marine Ins. Co. v. Pure Oil Co.,* 63 F.2d 771 (2d Cir. 1933); *Insurance Law Journal* 81 (1933): 315; *Earl & Stoddart, Inc. v. Elderman's Wilson Line, Ltd.,* 287 U.S. 420, 423 (1932); *Prince Line v. American Paper Exports, Inc.,* 55 F.2d 1053 (2d Cir. 1932); *The Pasadena,* 55 F.2d 51 (4th Cir. 1932).

99. "Bar Adds Notables to Its Committees," *New York Times,* July 12, 1933, 34; "Bar Committees Chosen for Year," *New York Times,* July 10, 1936, 10.

100. See, for example, *Martindale-Hubbell Law Directory,* 67th Annual Edition, 1:11406; *The Martindale-Hubbell Law Directory,* 77th Annual Edition (New York: Martindale-Hubbell, 1945), 1:1452 (microformed on LLMC Martindale-Hubbell, Directories No. 92-001A F49); *The Martindale-Hubbell Law Directory,* 85th Annual Edition (New York: Martindale-Hubbell, 1953), 2:1530 (microformed on LLMC Martindale-Hubbell, Directories No. 92-001A F67).

101. Richard L. Sullivan, AncestryLibrary.com.

102. Peppers, *Courtiers of the Marble Palace,* 93.

103. Employment Record of William D. Donnelly, National Personnel Records Center, National Archives at St. Louis (in author's possession); "William D. Donnelly, Former D.C. Lawyer," *Washington Post,* March 12, 1975, C6. See, for example, *U.S. v. Price,* 111 F.2d 206 (10th Cir. 1940); *U.S. v. Harris,* 103 F.2d 1020 (9th Cir. 1939); *City of Springfield v. U.S.,* 99 F.2d 860 (1st Cir. 1938). In August 1937, Donnelly applied to serve as Justice Black's clerk. Peppers, *Courtiers of the Marble Palace,* 93.

104. "William D. Donnelly, Former D.C. Lawyer." See, for example, *Decker v. U.S.,* 140 F.2d 375 (4th Cir. 1944); *Douglas Aircraft Co. v. U.S.,* 95 Ct. Cl. 140 (1941).

105. See Homer Stille Cummings Papers, Special Collections, University of Virginia, Series III, V, and VI.

106. See Boxes 323, 325, and 327, Cummings Papers.

107. "Attorney Ends Testimony in Johnson Probe," *Chicago Tribune,* April 24, 1946, 8; "Johnson Legal Aid Denounces U.S. Jury's Quiz," *Chicago Tribune,* April 23, 1946, 20.

108. *Journal of the Supreme Court of the United States* 1938 (1939): 127.

109. See, for example, *Girouard v. U.S.,* 328 U.S. 61 (1946); *Herget v. Central Nat. Bank & Trust Co. of Peoria,* 324 U.S. 4 (1945); *Chrysler Corp. v. U.S.,* 316 U.S. 556 (1942); *Glasser v. U.S.,* 315 U.S. 60 (1942). See also, for example, *Diaz v. Southeastern Drilling Corp. of Argentina, S.A.,* 449 F.2d 258 (5th Cir. 1971); *Cap Santa Vue, Inc. v. NLRB,* 424 F.2d 883 (D.C. Cir. 1970); *Rossi v. Fletcher,* 418 F.2d 1169 (D.C. Cir. 1969); *Schleit v. British Overseas Airways Corp.,* 410 F.2d 261 (D.C. Cir. 1969); *Vinson v. Rexrode,* 404 F.2d 830

(D.C. Cir. 1968); *Wheaton Triangle Lanes, Inc. v. Rinaldi*, 236 Md. 525 (1964); *Trent Trust Co. v. Kennedy*, 307 F.2d 174 (D.C. Cir. 1962).

110. 374 U.S. 398 (1963); *American Bar Association Journal* 50 (1964): 82.

111. "Solicitors' Ordinance Draws Fire," *Washington Post*, October 28, 1953, 32. Donnelly also represented the Seventh-Day Adventist Welfare Service, Inc. in *Orient Mid-East Lines, Inc. v. Cooperative for Am. Relief Everywhere, Inc.*, 410 F.2d 1006 (D.C. Cir. 1969), and the General Conference in *Town of Green River v. Martin*, 71 Wyo. 81 (1953).

112. See, for example, *Orient Mid-East Lines, Inc. v. Cooperative for Am. Relief Everywhere, Inc.*, 410 F.2d 1006 (D.C. Cir. 1969); *Gallagher v. Crown Kosher Market*, 366 U.S. 617, 618 (1961); *Town of Green River v. Martin*, 71 Wyo. 81 (1953). Donnelly also filed an amicus brief on behalf of his church in *McCullom v. Board of Education*, 333 U.S. 203 (1948). The Church had the firm on retainer, and also asked Donnelly and Cummings to file an amicus brief in *Everson v. Board of Education*, 330 U.S. 1 (1947). Before this request was made, however, Cummings was approached about the matter by an acquaintance taking the opposing position. Cummings was embarrassed by the conflict, and asked both parties to seek other representation. William H. Speer to Homer Cummings, June 10, 1946; Homer Cummings to William D. Donnelly, June 12, 1946; William D. Donnelly to Homer Cummings, June 20, 1946; Homer Cummings to William H. Speer, June 21, 1946; William D. Donnelly to Homer Cummings, August 10, 1946; Homer Cummings to William H. Speer, August 16, 1946; William H. Speer to Homer Cummings, August 22, 1946, all in Box 323, Cummings Papers.

113. *Congressional Record* 101 (1955): D271; *Hearing on S. 18, S. 57, 274, S. 662, S. 1288, S. 1437 and S. 1447 Before the Senate Subcommittee on Labor of the Committee on Labor and Public Welfare*, 84th Cong. 1156 (1955) (hearings on proposed minimum wage legislation, testimony of William D. Donnelly).

114. *Hearing on H.R.J. Res. 693 Before the H. Comm. on the Judiciary*, 88th Cong. 2483–85 (1964).

115. Cummings & Stanley Partnership Agreement, January 1, 1945, Box 258, Cummings Papers.

116. See, for example, *The Martindale-Hubbell Law Directory*, 82nd Annual Edition (New York: Martindale-Hubbell, 1950), 1:348 (microformed on LLMC Martindale-Hubbell, Directories No. 92-001A F19); *Martindale-Hubbell Law Directory*, 87th Annual Edition, 1:219.

117. *Martindale-Hubbell Law Directory*, 88th Annual Edition, 1:219.

118. *Martindale-Hubbell Law Directory*, 98th Annual Edition (New York: Martindale-Hubbell, 1966), 1:630 (microformed on LLMC Martindale-Hubbell, Directories No. 92-001A F29).

119. *Martindale-Hubbell Law Directory*, 177th Annual Edition, 1:343.

120. See *Journal of the Bar Association of D.C.* (hereafter cited as *J. B. ASSN. D.C.*) 29 (1962): 544; *J. B. ASSN. D.C.* 28 (1961): 528; *J. B. ASSN. D.C.* 26 (1959): 399; *J. B. ASSN. D.C.* 25 (1958): 487; *J. B. ASSN. D.C.* 23 (1956): 558; *J. B. ASSN. D.C.* 22 (1955): 483; *J. B. ASSN. D.C.* 21 (1954): 415, 536; "District Barristers Hear about Flotsam, Jetsam and Ligan at 70th Annual Dinner," *Washington Post*, December 7, 1941, 14.

121. *J. B. ASSN. D.C.* 27 (1960): 483; *J. B. ASSN. D.C.* 26 (1959): 399; *J. B. ASSN. D.C.* 23 (1956): 557–58; *J. B. ASSN. D.C.* 21 (1954): 536; *J. B. ASSN. D.C.* 16 (1949): 231, 582.

122. "William D. Donnelly, Former D.C. Lawyer."

123. Supreme Court Library Correspondence.

124. "Civic Leader Irving Clark Dies at 84; Was St. Paul Law Firm Partner," *Minneapolis Star Tribune*, January 21, 1997, 7B.

125. See, for example, *Matter of Schroll*, 297 N.W.2d 282 (Minn. 1980); *Walgreen Co. v. Commissioner of Taxation*, 252 Minn. 522 (1960); *Cut Price Supermarkets v. Kingpin Foods, Inc.*, 256 Minn. 339 (1959); *U.S. v. Goodson*, 253 F.2d 900 (8th Cir. 1958); *Gilfillan v. Kelm*, 128 F. Supp. 291 (D.C. Minn. 1955); *Reynolds v. Hill*, 184 F.2d 294 (8th Cir. 1950); *Myers Motors v. Kaiser-Frazer Sales Corp.*, 178 F.2d 291 (8th Cir. 1950); *State v. Peery*, 224 Minn. 346 (1947); *U.S. v. Northwest Airlines*, 69 F. Supp. 482 (D.C. Minn. 1946). See also Irving Clark and Eugene M. Warlich, "Taxation of Cooperatives: A Problem Solved?," *Minnesota Law Review* 47 (1963): 997.

126. "Civic Leader Irving Clark Dies at 84." See, for example, *Land O'Lakes Co. v. U.S.*, 675 F.2d 988 (8th Cir. 1982); *Associated Milk Producers, Inc. v. Commissioner*, 68 T.C. 729 (1977); *Louis W. and Maud Hill Family Foundation v. U.S.*, 347 F. Supp. 1225 (D.C. Minn. 1972); *Farmers Union Co-op Oil Assn. of South St. Paul v. Commissioner of Taxation*, 1968 WL 20 (Minn. Tax. Ct. 1968).

127. "Civic Leader Irving Clark Dies at 84"; "Funeral Notices," *St. Paul Pioneer Press*, January 18, 1997, B5; "Hill Family and Foundation Squabble over Charity's Future," *Minneapolis Star Tribune*, January 31, 1994, 1a; "Minnesota Foundations Keep Family Connections," *Minneapolis Star Tribune*, January 31, 1994, 6a.

128. "Antipoverty Pioneers Defend Legacy of {ap}6os," *Minneapolis Star Tribune*, May 24, 1992, 1A.

129. "Civic Leader Irving Clark Dies at 84"; "Funeral Notices."

130. Supreme Court Library Correspondence; Employment Record of Luther E. Jones, Jr., National Personnel Records Center, National Archives at St. Louis (hereafter cited as Jones Employment Record) (in author's possession).

131. Robert A. Caro, *The Years of Lyndon Johnson: The Path to Power* (New York: Knopf, 1982), 230.

132. Ibid., 207–8.

133. Luther E. Jones Jr., interview by David McComb, June 13, 1969, Lyndon Baines Johnson Library, 1, 2–4, http://millercenter.org/scripps/archive/oralhistories/detail/ 2638; Caro, *Years of Lyndon Johnson*, 207–11; Merle Miller, *Lyndon: An Oral Biography* (New York: Putnam, 1980), 35.

134. McComb interview, 1–2, 5; Caro, *Years of Lyndon Johnson*, 229–30; Robert Dallek, *Lone Star Rising: Lyndon Johnson and His Times, 1908–1960* (New York: Oxford University Press, 1991), 100; Alfred Steinberg, *Sam Johnson's Boy: A Close-Up of the President from Texas* (New York: Macmillan, 1968), 59; Jones Employment Record.

135. Randall B. Wood, *LBJ: Architect of American Ambition* (Cambridge, Mass.: Harvard University Press, 2006), 78; Dallek, *Lone Star Rising*, 100.

136. Dallek, *Lone Star Rising*, 100.

137. McComb interview, 8; Wood, *LBJ*, 78; Dallek, *Lone Star Rising*, 100; Caro, *Years*

of Lyndon Johnson, 231; Ronnie Dugger, *The Politician: The Life and Times of Lyndon Johnson: The Drive for Power, From the Frontier to Master of the Senate* (New York: W. W. Norton, 1982), 166.

138. Wood, *LBJ,* 79.

139. Dallek, *Lone Star Rising,* 100; Wood, *LBJ,* 79; Steinberg, *Sam Johnson's Boy,* 77; Miller, *Lyndon,* 41.

140. McComb interview, 9; Dallek, *Lone Star Rising,* 100.

141. Wood, *LBJ,* 79; Dallek, *Lone Star Rising,* 101; Caro, *Years of Lyndon Johnson,* 232.

142. Dallek, *Lone Star Rising,* 101.

143. McComb interview, 6; Dallek, *Lone Star Rising,* 101; Miller, *Lyndon,* 41; Steinberg, *Sam Johnson's Boy,* 77.

144. Wood, *LBJ,* 79; Caro, *Years of Lyndon Johnson,* 232.

145. Caro, *Years of Lyndon Johnson,* 339; Dallek, *Lone Star Rising,* 101; Wood, *LBJ,* 79.

146. Dallek, *Lone Star Rising,* 101. See also Wood, *LBJ,* 79.

147. Caro, *Years of Lyndon Johnson,* 238–39; Dallek, *Lone Star Rising,* 101–2; Wood, *LBJ,* 79; Irwin Unger and Debi Unger, *LBJ: A Life* (New York: John Wiley and Sons, 1999), 371.

148. Caro, *Years of Lyndon Johnson,* 239.

149. Dallek, *Lone Star Rising,* 102. See also Caro, *Years of Lyndon Johnson,* 239; Unger and Unger, *LBJ,* 371.

150. McComb interview, 6; Wood, *LBJ,* 79; Dallek, *Lone Star Rising,* 101; Miller, *Lyndon,* 41.

151. Dallek, *Lone Star Rising,* 101. See also Wood, *LBJ,* 79.

152. Caro, *Years of Lyndon Johnson,* 238.

153. Luther E. Jones Jr., interview by Michael L. Gillette, October 14, 1977, Lyndon Baines Johnson Library, 15, http://Millercenter.Org/Scripps/Archive/Oralhistories/Detail/2639. See also McComb interview, 29.

154. Dugger, *Politician,* 187.

155. McComb interview, 9; Miller, *Lyndon,* 41.

156. McComb interview, 23; Dugger, *Politician,* 125.

157. Wood, *LBJ,* 79–80.

158. Ibid.; Dallek, *Lone Star Rising,* 102; Unger and Unger, *LBJ,* 44; Steinberg, *Sam Johnson's Boy,* 77. Johnson also frequently wrote to each of the young men's parents to report on their progress. Wood, *LBJ,* 80.

159. McComb interview, 2; Gillette interview, 18–20; Wood, *LBJ,* 90; Dugger, *Politician,* 179; Caro, *Years of Lyndon Johnson,* 338; Unger and Unger, *LBJ,* 44–45.

160. Gillette interview, 23–24; Hal K. Rothman, *LBJ's Texas White House* (College Station: Texas A&M University, 2001), 28; Dugger, *Politician,* 174–75; Caro, *Years of Lyndon Johnson,* 276–77.

161. Dugger, *Politician,* 217; Caro, *Years of Lyndon Johnson,* 239.

162. McComb interview, 2; Gillette interview, 26, 28; Caro, *Years of Lyndon Johnson,* 340–48; Paul K. Conkin, *Big Daddy from the Pedernales: Lyndon Baines Johnson* (Boston: Twayne, 1986), 75; Wood, *LBJ,* 114; Dugger, *Politician,* 186–87; Jones Employment Record.

163. McComb interview, 16, 20; Gillette interview, 13–15; Jones Employment Record; Caro, *Years of Lyndon Johnson*, 396; Conkin, *Big Daddy*, 80; Dugger, *Politician*, 190. Jones reported that it was also decided at that meeting that Johnson would support the Court-packing plan, to which Wirtz was opposed and about which Johnson simply did not care. The men agreed that Johnson could not win without the Roosevelt vote. Dugger, *Politician*; Caro, *Years of Lyndon Johnson*, 396.

164. McComb interview, 2–3, 19–20; Gillette interview, 35; Caro, *Years of Lyndon Johnson*, 443–44.

165. McComb interview, 22; Gillette interview, 37–38; "Former Assistant District Attorney Jones Dead at 85; Luther E. Jones Jr. Served Corpus Christi in Various Areas of Legal Practice, Served as Assistant to Federal Agencies," *Corpus Christi Caller-Times*, September 9, 1999, F6; e-mail from Katherine Logan, CPP, Director of the Office of Payroll and Benefits, U.S. House of Representatives, to the author, April 29, 2014 (in author's possession); Dallek, *Lone Star Rising*, 102. When Jones had left Washington to attend law school in Austin, Johnson had promised him that he would help Jones find a Washington job upon his graduation. Dallek, *Lone Star Rising*; Caro, *Years of Lyndon Johnson*, 239.

166. McComb interview, 23; Dallek, *Lone Star Rising*, 186.

167. Wood, *LBJ*, 131; Jones Employment Record. See also Gillette interview, 20–21; McComb interview, 23 ("I became clerk to Justice Butler on the Supreme Court for about thirteen months"). This is the only mention of the Butler clerkship in the Jones oral history. The interviewer made no further inquiry about the clerkship.

168. Wood, *LBJ*, 133. For Jones's more discursive report of Connally's love affair with his own locks, see Miller, *Lyndon*, 40.

169. Jones Employment Record; McComb interview, 23; Gillette interview, 13; "Former Assistant District Attorney Jones Dead at 85." See, for example, *U.S. v. 2,049.85 Acres of Land, More or Less, in Nueces County, Texas*, 49 F. Supp. 20 (S.D. Tex. 1943); *U.S. v. 250 Acres of Land, More or Less, in Nueces County, Texas*, 43 F. Supp. 937 (S.D. Tex. 1942); *U.S. v. 16,572 Acres of Land, More or Less*, 45 F. Supp. 23 (S.D. Tex. 1942).

170. Jake Pickle and Peggy Pickle, *Jake* (Austin: University of Texas Press, 1997), 37–38.

171. Ibid.; Lynwood Abram, "Congressman Shares Storied Tenure," *Houston Chronicle*, June 1, 1997, 1997 Westlaw Newsroom 6609922.

172. Pickle and Pickle, *Jake*, 38.

173. Ibid.

174. Ibid., 38–39.

175. Ibid., 39.

176. McComb interview, 23; "Former Assistant District Attorney Jones Dead at 85"; "Local History: Mayor Makes Hires," *Corpus Christi Caller-Times*, April 9, 2003, B1, 2003 Westlaw Newsroom 13171034.

177. "Former Assistant District Attorney Jones Dead at 85." See, for example, *Ex Parte Flores*, 452 S.W.2d 443 (Tex. Crim. App. 1970); *Gonzalez v. State*, 397 S.W.2d 440 (Tex. Crim. App. 1965); *Huffmeister v. State*, 170 Tex. Crim. 460 (1960); *Adame v. State*, 162 Tex. Crim. 78 (1955); *Niemann v. Zarsky*, 233 S.W.2d 930 (Tex. Civ. App. 1950); *Wingo v.*

Seale, 212 S.W.2d 968 (Tex. Civ. App. 1948); "Corpus Christi Insurance Man Surrenders on Charge of Selling Note Illegally by Mail," *Wall Street Journal,* January 13, 1964, 6.

178. McComb interview, 22, 24–27; Caro, *Years of Lyndon Johnson,* 239; Dallek, *Lone Star Rising,* 337; Josiah M. Daniel, "LBJ v. Coke Stevenson: Lawyering for Control of the Disputed Texas Democratic Party Senatorial Primary Election of 1948," *Review of Litigation* 31 (2012): 1, 42; *Johnson v. Stevenson,* 170 F.2d 108 (5th Cir. 1948); *Johnson v. Stevenson,* 335 U.S. 801 (1948).

179. Norman L. Reimer, "2008: NACDL's Year of Celebration, Transition—and Hope (Inside NACDL)," *Champion* 32 (2008): 39.

180. Wood, *LBJ,* 567; Rothman, *LBJ's Texas White House,* 186.

181. Bowmer, "Texas Parade," May 1968, 45, quoted in Caro, *Years of Lyndon Johnson,* 237–38, 807.

182. McComb interview, 27; "Johnsons Are Hosts at Reunion," *Washington Post,* September 14, 1968, E1.

183. "Former Assistant District Attorney Jones Dead at 85." See, for example, *Buntion v. State,* 444 S.W.2d 304 (Tex. Crim. App. 1969).

184. "Former Assistant District Attorney Jones Dead at 85"; "Funerals, Obituaries, Deaths: Jones," *Corpus Christi Caller-Times,* September 8, 1999, http://Www.Caller2 .Com/1999/September/08/Funeralstext.Html.

185. See, for example, *Moser v. U.S. Steel Corp.,* 676 S.W.2d 99 (Texas 1984); *Hart v. Sims,* 702 F.2d 574 (5th Cir. 1983); *Atchley v. Greenhill,* 517 F.2d 692 (5th Cir. 1975); *Hoover v. Beeto,* 439 F.2d 913 (5th Cir. 1971); Jim D. Bowmer, Bob Burleson, and Luther E. Jones Jr., "Aggravated Robbery: Texas Style," *Baylor Law Review* 33 (1981): 947; Percy Foreman and Luther E. Jones Jr., "Submitting the Law of Parties in a Texas Prosecution," *Baylor Law Review* 33 (1981): 267; Luther E. Jones Jr., "Theft: Texas Style," *Texas Bar Journal* 33 (1978): 1062; Percy Foreman and Luther E. Jones Jr., "Indictments Under the New Texas Penal Code," *Houston Law Review* 15 (1977): 1; Luther E. Jones Jr., "Admissibility of Confessions in a State Prosecution," *Baylor Law Review* 29 (1977): 1; Luther E. Jones Jr., "Criminal Law and Procedure," *Southwestern Law Journal* 27 (1973): 227; Luther E. Jones Jr., "Translating Recent Supreme Court Decisions into Courtroom Reality," *Baylor Law Review* 19 (1967): 391; Luther E. Jones Jr., "Fruit of the Poisonous Tree," *South Texas Law Review* 9 (1967): 17; Luther E. Jones Jr. and Warren Burnett, "The New Texas Code of Criminal Procedure," *South Texas Law Review* 8 (1966): 16; Jim D. Bowmer, Bob Burleson, and Luther E. Jones Jr., "Peace Officers and Texas: New Code of Criminal Procedure," *Baylor Law Review* 17 (1965): 268; Jim D. Bowmer, Luther E. Jones Jr., and John H. Miller, "The Charge in Criminal Cases," *Baylor Law Review* 12 (1960): 261.

186. Caro, *Years of Lyndon Johnson,* 238.

187. "Former Assistant District Attorney Jones Dead at 85."

188. Francis J. Brown, *The Social and Economic Philosophy of Pierce Butler* (Washington, D.C.: The Catholic University of America Press, 1945), 92. See also Danelski, *Supreme Court Justice Is Appointed,* 181–82; Barry Cushman, "The Secret Lives of the Four Horsemen," *Virginia Law Review* 83 (1997): 559, 571–79, 639–42.

189. Recollection of Herbert Wechsler, in Katie Louchheim, *The Making of the New*

Deal: The Insiders Speak (Cambridge, Mass.: Harvard University Press, 1983), 53 (Stone "thought Butler was too soft in dealing with criminal matters").

190. "The Honorable Supreme Court," *Fortune,* May 1936, 79, 180, 182. See also John E. Semonche, *Charting the Future: The Supreme Court Responds to a Changing Society, 1890–1920* (Westport, Conn.: Greenwood Press, 1978), 249.

191. Richard J. Purcell, "Mr. Justice Pierce Butler," *Catholic Educational Review* (April 1944): 192; Danelski, *Supreme Court Justice Is Appointed,* 8.

192. See Paschal, *Mr. Justice Sutherland,* 115–17, 233; Jay S. Bybee, "George Sutherland," in *The Supreme Court Justices: Illustrated Biographies 1789–2012,* 3rd ed., edited by Clare Cushman (Washington, D.C.: CQ Press, 2012), 316–17; Schroeder, "More Than a Fraction," 79, 128, 150–51, 153, 180, 234; Pearson and Allen, *Nine Old Men,* 41, 159, 198–201.

193. See Barry Cushman, *The Four Horsemen in Historical Memory* (forthcoming).

S. Edward Widdifield came to Washington in 1905 to work as Justice Rufus Peckham's stenographer. After Peckham died in 1909, Widdifield would clerk for three more justices: Joseph R. Lamar, John H. Clarke, and George Sutherland. Widdifield returned to the Supreme Court in 1931 when he was hired to work in the office of the clerk of Court, where he would spend eighteen years before retiring at age seventy-three. (Courtesy of the family of S. Edward Widdifield)

Another veteran, John E. Hoover, clerked for five Justices (Peckham, John Marshall Harlan, Lamar, Mahlon Pitney, and Charles Evans Hughes) during eleven terms (some of which were only partial ones), ending his Supreme Court clerkship tenure in 1916. Like other clerks of his era, he then signed on as an assistant attorney at the Justice Department. (Courtesy of the family of John E. Hoover)

ABOVE: William Howard Taft with his loyal private secretary, Wendell W. Mischler. Having served as Taft's secretary at the War Department, the White House, and Yale University, Mischler was territorial when it came to his relationship with the chief justice and made sure that the Taft law clerks knew their place. (Personal Papers of William Howard Taft, Library of Congress)

RIGHT: The irascible Justice James C. McReynolds had a reputation for lowballing his clerks' salaries, and then firing them at the end of the term so he wouldn't have to pay them during the summer months while he was on vacation. (Harris and Ewing Collection, Prints and Photographs Division, Library of Congress)

LEFT: Milton S. Musser, who clerked for Justice McReynolds from May 1938 to October 1940, complained to his mother: "Working for McReynolds is like being in prison—maybe worse—and I certainly must leave him soon or go batty." (Used by permission, Utah State Historical Society)

RIGHT: Justice Hugo Black playing tennis at the St. Petersburg Tennis Club in 1948. Marathon tennis matches on the clay court behind the justice's Alexandria townhouse were a staple of a Black clerkship. (AP Images)

Justice Stanley F. Reed and his law clerks at a reunion dinner. Bennett Boskey later said of these occasions: "His remarks at our dinners would always give us far more credit than was our due, and in our hearts each of us knew how much we owed him." (Photography by Joseph Tenschert, Tenschert Photo Studio)

Justice Robert H. Jackson with then–law clerk James Marsh at the Supreme Court in the spring of 1949. In applying for a clerkship with the justice, Marsh had to overcome Jackson's concerns about hiring a law clerk who, like himself, did not graduate from college. (Courtesy of the family of James M. Marsh)

Justice Harold H. Burton (*seated*) was photographed in chambers with his October term 1954 clerks Raymond S. Troubh (*second from right*) and James R. Ryan (*right*), along with his messenger Charles H. Mitchell and secretary Tess H. Cheatham. Congress had authorized the associate justices to hire two law clerks per chamber in 1947. (Courtesy of Raymond S. Troubh)

Mimi Clark with her father, Associate Justice Tom Clark, at her wedding in 1953. Her family hosted her father's clerks for Thanksgiving annually throughout his eighteen years as an active justice and ten years of retirement. (Courtesy of Mimi Clark Gronlund)

The gentlemanly Justice John Marshall Harlan kept his hat and bowtie on when he joined his clerks to pitch against Covington & Burling in a 1958 softball game. (Supreme Court Historical Society)

Justice Abe Fortas meeting with his law clerks in 1967. Unlike other modern justices, Fortas kept his law clerks at arm's length and did not serve as a mentor or teacher. (George Tames/ The New York Times/Redux)

Justice John Paul Stevens with law clerks Ronald D. Lee (*left*) and Lawrence C. Marshall (*right*) during October term 1986. Stevens's experience of clerking for Supreme Court Justice Wiley Rutledge during October term 1947 shaped how he utilized his own law clerks. (Lynn Johnson/National Geographic Creative)

Chief Justice William H. Rehnquist conferring with law clerk David G. Leitch during October term 1986. Essayist and former clerk Craig Bradley writes that Rehnquist enjoyed having law clerks with differing political ideologies because the justice "liked having someone to argue with." (Lynn Johnson/National Geographic Creative)

Justice Sandra Day O'Connor encouraged her female law clerks to attend the weekday morning aerobics class she inaugurated. This took place in the "highest court in the land," the basketball gym on the top floor of the Court building, and its slogan was "Justice Never Rests." (Joel W. Benjamin)

II The Rise of Clerks

TODD C. PEPPERS

Justice Hugo Black and His Law Clerks
Matchmaking and Match Point

Changes in the rules surrounding the hiring and employment of law clerks is one thread that ties together the essays in this book. Since Justice Horace Gray hired the first Supreme Court law clerk in 1882, the justices have slowly adopted new guidelines and norms regarding how they select their clerks, the schools to which they look for law clerks, the tenure of the clerkships, and the responsibilities given to the clerks. While clerkship practices are specific to the individual justices, much of the change has been driven by the Court's rising workload and the number of law clerks assigned to the justices.

The most dramatic evolution in the clerkship institution is found in the personal relationships that form between the justice and his or her clerks. Certainly modern law clerks enjoy a positive mentoring relationship with their justices, and many of the clerks stay in touch with their former employers after the clerkship ends. My research and writing, however, have led me to conclude that the personal bonds between justices and clerks have weakened over time. The result is that a Supreme Court clerkship is not as unique and memorable as it once was.

In support of this argument, I submit the case study of Hugo Black and his clerks. After reviewing the law clerk files in the personal papers of Justice Hugo Black, as well as talking with his children and his former law clerks, it became apparent to me that scholars have not fully appreciated the extraordinary experience it was to clerk for Justice Black. In this essay, I highlight two distinctive aspects of the Black clerkship—the justice's role as guardian and matchmaker to a generation of young clerks as well as the central place that tennis occupied in the clerkship experience.

Justice Black and His Clerks

Like other justices on the Supreme Court, Justice Black hired law clerks to assist with the work of the Court. Each year, his law clerks assisted in reviewing cert petitions, edited opinion drafts, and performed related legal research. These job duties, however, were only one dimension of the Black clerkship. As the justice himself once remarked to a law clerk applicant, "I don't pick my law clerks for what they can do for me, I pick my law clerks for what I can do for them."[1] And what the justice could "do for them" extended beyond legal training. Hugo Black Jr. explains that his father took a personal interest in all of his young clerks and "attempted to change their lives."[2] "He was truly interested and concerned about the way they conducted their private lives as well as the way they performed in their professional lives," adds Josephine Black Pesaresi, Justice Black's daughter.[3] Referring to her father as a "natural born teacher," Pesaresi explains that the justice "always looked at the whole person and felt that strength of character, including most predominately kindness, integrity, and humility, must be part of every aspect of anyone's life." For Justice Black, the worst transgression a law clerk could commit was being "puffed up" with self-importance.

The law clerks themselves were well aware of the justice's interest in their professional skills and personal failings. "The Judge was a delightful teacher and friend, and became almost a second father," writes former law clerk J. Vernon Patrick (October term 1955). "He quickly noted my deficiencies and set about to improve me."[4] Over the years, the justice gave his law clerks unsolicited advice on their personal appearance and habits (such as not turning off the electricity when they left a room, talking on the telephone too long, or the pretentious practice of using a first initial in their name), their driving skills, their social graces, and even their weight. In a letter to former law clerk C. Samuel Daniels (the father of mystery writer Patricia Cornwell), Justice Black praises his former law clerk for resuming recreational tennis. "This is not only a good game at which you are excellent, but from what the grapevine has told me I am inclined to think that you might stand the loss of a few pounds. I cannot imagine the trim, handsome Sam Daniels remaining corpulent."[5]

The advice, however, went beyond the superficial. When interviewing future law clerk Larry Hammond (October term 1971), Justice Black startled the young applicant by announcing that he decided to meet with Hammond because he knew that the young man stuttered. Black proceeded to show Hammond several books on stuttering and hypothesized it was a psychological condition. Hammond later humorously recalled that he was literally "tongue-tied" during the interview, since he hadn't dreamed that his stuttering would be a topic of conversation.[6]

Justice Black also took a great interest in the intellectual development of his clerks, sharing his love of reading with them. Writes former law clerk Daniel J. Meador (October term 1954):

Have you read these books? This question from Justice Black was heard by many a new law clerk shortly after coming on the job. "These books" usually referred to some of his volumes of Tacitus, Thucydides, Plutarch, or Livy, or to *The Greek Way* [by Edith Hamilton], or to some other historical work he might happen to be reading at the moment. On getting a negative response, as he did all too often, Black would say something like: "Well, they're your first assignment. What they have to say about human nature and history is more relevant than anything I can think of to the issues now before the Court."[7]

According to Meador, Justice Black believed that the lessons to be gleaned from these authors served two purposes—not only were the writings relevant in understanding the complex issues facing the Supreme Court, but they would also make his clerks better members of society. "He would rather have had his clerk spend his reading time on literature of that sort than on a book on federal jurisdiction. He seemed to think that his clerks had had enough technical indoctrination in law school."[8] Echoing Meador, former law clerk Guido Calabresi (October term 1958) recalls the justice telling his clerks that "you cannot be a lawyer if you haven't read Tacitus."[9]

Even illness could not stop the justice from assigning books to his law clerks to read. During the year that Melford O. Cleveland clerked for Justice Black, the justice was suffering from an extraordinarily painful bout of shingles. Despite illness, the education of his law clerks continued. "I remember one night in particular when your foot was in such pain that you had to hold it high off the floor," writes Cleveland. "Yet you kept searching for a book for me to read, not for your work but for my education."[10]

As a side note, it should be pointed out that the justice's reading assignments were not limited to his law clerks. Josephine Black Pesaresi recalls that the family milkman had shared his tales of domestic disharmony with the justice, prompting her father to give him a copy of *The Greek Way*. And when the justice was hospitalized at the Bethesda Naval Hospital for prostate problems, Pesaresi was amused to discover that her father—who was reading the collected works of Bertrand Russell—had assigned his doctors and nurses reading from the British philosopher (and was threatening to give reading quizzes to the medical staff).

Occasionally, Justice Black used the law clerks themselves to make what the justice deemed necessary changes in their personal habits. After selecting George C. Freeman Jr. (October term 1956) to be his clerk, Justice Black told him that he had picked Freeman and his co-clerk (Robert A. Girard) with a dual motive in mind:

He told me later on in the year, "You know, I picked you and Bob . . . because you are opposites and I thought that the two of you had something to teach each other. Bob's a very intense, hard-driving, ambitious fellow who married young and has stayed in the books. He's the kind of fellow who just works all the time. Your problem is you've never worked hard in your life. And I figured if I put the two of you together, he'd speed you up and you'd slow him down. And that would be good for both of you."[11]

Freeman responded: "Well, I said 'Judge, it's like putting the hare and the tortoise in yoke together. But in this case the hare didn't go to sleep. And my little legs are mighty worn.'" It might have been this fatigue that once caused Freeman to take an ill-advised nap on a couch in the justice's chambers. "I will never forget waking up from an after-lunch nap on the sofa in the clerks' office just in time to see the Judge tiptoeing in to close the connecting door to his chambers." Rather than admonishing the mortified Freeman, the justice quietly said, "Go right ahead, George. The only reason I am closing the door is that the Chief and I can't hear each other over your snoring."[12]

Justice Black's Pygmalion-like efforts extended to the romantic lives of his clerks. He once explained to a former law clerk that he could not comprehend why men and women permitted so much time to pass between engagement and marriage. "Many things can happen during that period of time, but the main thing that can happen . . . is that you and the young lady will lose the pleasure of each other's association during that time."[13] Accordingly, Justice Black pushed his law clerks to get married. Former Black law clerk Marx Leva (October term 1940) writes that the justice was "the man who made me get married—which is a function usually reserved, I believe, for shot-gun carrying 'father-in-laws.'"[14] According to Leva, shortly after his clerkship ended, "it came to the Judge's attention that I had (in a rash moment, no doubt) expressed the intention of getting married after the war, when I would (so I hoped) be back from sea duty." Leva soon received "an irate longhand letter from the Judge, advising me that under no circumstances would such conduct by tolerated by him." Concludes Leva: "Being a compliant fellow (and being under some pressure to the same effect from Shirley), I was married on October 31, 1942, under the watchful eye of the Judge."

Yet the justice had not finished giving Leva advice on love and marriage. "A short time after my marriage, while my LST [landing ship, tank] was still based in Norfolk, I received a second irate longhand letter from the Judge," writes Leva.

[T]he Judge had heard . . . that it was my then intention not to have any children until after my return from sea duty. According to the Judge's letter, this plan of action (or, perhaps, inaction) was even worse, if possible, than my previous plan of not getting married until after my return from sea duty. In his letter, the Judge waxed eloquently on the prospect of my early demise as a result of German submarine warfare or otherwise, and expressed grave doubts, also on my chances of having children, at my advanced age, after the war. All in all, he felt that the facts of the situation— as in any Hugo Black decision—permitted only one outcome—namely, children before sea duty, rather than after.

This time, however, Justice Black failed to persuade his former clerk and his bride. Concludes Leva: "To sum up . . . my one victory over the Judge—other than my numerous victories on the tennis course, of course—consisted in the postwar arrival of Leo Marx Leva (1946) and Lloyd Rose Leva (1947)."

Leva was not the only clerk for whom the justice played cupid, as former law clerks Drayton Nabers Jr. (October term 1965) and George Freeman can attest. Regarding Nabers—Justice Black served as a self-appointed godfather to Fairfax Virginia Smothers, the daughter of former U.S. senator William Howell Smothers, of New Jersey. Both Black and Smothers served together in the U.S. Senate, and the justice's first wife, Josephine Black, was Fairfax Smother's godmother. Nabers started his clerkship on July 1, 1965, and by August 9 he found himself on a date with Faixfax Smothers—courtesy of Hugo Black. Nabers met with the justice shortly before the date, and he recalls the justice giving him the following advice. "Let me tell you something. Fairfax is a lovely lady. And young women come to Washington to find husbands. She has been here for over two years now—if she wants you, she is going to get you."[15] Adds Nabers: "as predicted by the Judge, we were married in December of 1965."

The justice also worked his matchmaking magic with George Freeman, who writes that "the Judge picked out my wife for me before he or I ever knew she existed."[16]

When I left the Judge to go to Richmond he suggested that I ought to find there an attractive cousin of Graham's [wife of Hugo Black Jr.] for a wife. The first cousin I brought back to Washington for the Judge's inspection was pronounced deficient in only one respect—she had not gone to Bryn Mawr like Graham. Subsequently that cousin decided on another young man and to ease my rejection introduced me to another cousin! Fortunately Cousin Anne had gone to Bryn Mawr. That settled it.

Like many justices in the 1950s and 1960s, Black also came to the rescue of law clerks whose clerkships were in jeopardy because of their draft status. After having his request for an occupational deferment for law clerk Stephen J. Schulhofer denied by two local draft boards, Justice Black wrote a lengthy letter to the Presidential Appeal Board of the Selective Service System that laid out in great detail the "vital assistance" provided to him by law clerks such as Schulhofer. In the letter, the justice sharply concludes: "I cannot believe it is more important to the Government to have Mr. Schulhofer in the Army than it is for me to continue in his work with me."[17] Schulhofer received his deferment.

In return for the life lessons imparted by the justice, the law clerks gave the justice their undivided loyalty. They defended Black's reputation from the slings and arrows of biographers and critics, and, in the case of former law clerk Neal P. Rutledge (October term 1951), literally almost took a bullet for the justice. Rutledge has humorously noted that he "may be the only person who was shot at in the Supreme Court." One night Rutledge found himself working late in Justice Black's chambers at the Supreme Court. During his late-night session, Rutledge discovered that he needed some files from the secretary's office. Because of the lateness of the hour, and the fact that Justice Black was at home, Rutledge decided to save time by cutting through the justice's personal office. Entering the office, he flipped on a light. As he crossed the room, a rifle shot came crashing through the justice's window. Rutledge's marine training kicked in, and he fell to the floor to avoid the unfriendly fire before crawling to a telephone. "Of course, I got on the telephone immediately because it looked like it was an attempt to assassinate the Justice, and I called the Justice at home to warn him," recalls Rutledge. "This was when his first wife, Josephine Black, was in her final stage of illness. The justice was not worried about himself, but was worried that the news would disturb his wife. So we were all sworn to secrecy." In hindsight, Rutledge does not believe it was an assassination attempt. "I really think—in light of the fact that no other attempt was made on his life—that someone just saw the light come on and started to shoot away." Nevertheless, Rutledge has the dubious honor of being the only Black law clerk to come under hostile fire during his clerkship.

On the rare occasions when the justice was low, it was the law clerks who came to his rescue. This was never more evident in the months and years following the death of Josephine Black, when his daughter proposed that the clerks live with her father. "My father was lonely, depressed and grieving after my mother's death," recalls Pesaresi. "And he was in terrible pain from shingles. I knew my father enough to know that he was the happiest when he was teaching other people. By having the clerks living with him, he could talk about his books and his philosophy."[18] Clerks who lived with the justice included C. Sam Daniels (October term 1951), Melford O. "Buddy" Cleveland (October term 1952), and Charles A. Reich and David J. Vann (October term 1953). While, by all accounts, the living arrangements were harmonious, former clerk Melford "Buddy" Cleveland learned the importance of keeping track of his house key: "One night I tried to sneak into his house through a window because I had left my key inside. My friend, Jiggar [*sic*], the dog, attacked me like a lion, and the Judge boomed out from his bedroom window with the voice of ten men, 'Who is trying to break into my house?'" The clerks themselves realized the toll that Josephine Black's death had taken on the justice. "I do not know whether I have ever sufficiently expressed to you my admiration for the great courage which you showed during the term I worked for you," writes Cleveland. "You never wavered through illness and numerous defeats."[19]

It is evident that Justice Black's attempts to teach and educate his law clerks was sparked by the open affection that he felt for "his boys," and evidence of his love is found in the law clerk files in Justice Black's personal papers. Justice Black once wrote that "my clerks stand almost in the relationship of my family to me,"[20] and a wonderful example is contained in a letter written by Justice Black to Mrs. George Brussel Jr., the mother of law clerk Charles Reich. The justice writes: "Each of my clerks has a secure place in his affections. I think my affection for your Charles began the first time he came to see me, when he smiled. There is something peculiarly warm and appealing in his smile. And he has the kind of integrity and humanity about him that I like. . . . My prediction is that many people will live happier and better lives because of Charlie."[21]

Justice Black's law clerks were equally open in their affection for their mentor. "Your influence, as much as that of any man, has made me whatever it is I am," writes former law clerk Nicholas Johnson.[22] In a letter to Black, former law clerk Charles F. Luce writes:

> During the year that I was privileged to work with you I learned more about many things than in any other comparable period of my life. Your devotion to mankind and to a legal system which will serve mankind has been a constant inspiration in the nineteen years since I was in your office. In making major decisions I have frequently found great help by asking the question: "What would the Judge think I should do?" I know that the other men who were lucky enough to be associated with you feel the same way as I do.[23]

And in discussing their affection for the justice, more than one former clerk lamented the loss of the rare gift of their clerkship. "Though it [private practice] is interesting, that rewarding feeling of 'laboring in the cause of righteousness' is somehow missing," writes George Freeman. "I miss it; even though I realize that I could not continue to dwell forever on Olympus."[24]

As more tangible signs of their devotion, former clerks showered the justice with gifts on birthdays and holidays. Through the years the mail carrier delivered a steady stream of hams, avocados, pears, oranges, Wisconsin cheese, peanuts, smoked fish, jam, English walnuts, chestnuts, grapefruit, sorghum, and pickles to the justice's residence. Former law clerk Sidney M. Davis (October term 1944) set the standard for gift giving, and for twenty-five years Davis presented Justice Black with expensive ties on his birthday and on Christmas. "It is bad to have to repeat the same thing," Black wrote in a January 1957 letter to Davis, "but there is no one who is a better tie picker than you."[25] Thirteen years later Black continued to praise Davis for his fashion sense. "I can't cease to admire your taste in the selection of ties," admitted Black. "I never buy ties that expensive myself and so that may be responsible for the fact that the ones I buy are not equal to yours."[26]

Justice Black, His Law Clerks, and Tennis

If improving the lives of his law clerks was one constant element of Justice Black's clerkship practices, the second was sharing his love of tennis with his clerks. "The most important things in my father's life were Alabama, the Constitution, his books, and the tennis court—and not necessarily in that order," explains Josephine Black Pesaresi. "A choice between the tennis court and the Supreme Court was a hard choice to make for Daddy." She adds that her father used to say that he could retire from the Supreme Court as long as he had tennis.

Justice Black did not start playing tennis until he was a middle-aged man. Biographer Roger Newman writes that "[t]he Senate doctor had told him that no man in his forties should play singles, he liked to say, so he waited until he was fifty."[27] Tennis satisfied the justice's need for both exercise and competition. "My father was ahead of his time in understanding the importance of exercise. He did floor exercises every day of his life," explains Pesaresi. "Things like walking and golf bored him, but he loved tennis because it involved competition." Hugo Black Jr. recalls that the Black children nicknamed their father "the Great Competitor," noting that the justice "never liked to lose at anything." While Justice Black loved tennis, and practiced endlessly, his children offer different assessments of his skills. While Pesaresi describes her father as a "fair, very consistent," and "accurate" player, Hugo Black Jr. describes him as "mediocre." "He just hit the ball over the net and figured that most people couldn't hit it back; he didn't hit the ball to a spot, he hit it straight."

Regardless of his skill, his devotion to the game was unquestioned; when the justice suffered an injury to his right elbow, he taught himself to play tennis left-handed. "Maybe I shall be able to play tennis with your 'left-handed' son when he gets a little older," writes Justice Black to former law clerk (and frequent tennis partner) C. Samuel Daniels. "Due to a strained right wrist I have been playing with my left hand for the last month."[28]

The key to Justice Black's game was endurance, and, in his sixties and seventies, he played tennis four to six hours a day. "He played tennis every day in the summer, and he could outlast anybody," recalls Pesaresi. Hugo Black Jr. echoes this sentiment. "Although he had played some real experts, he would never accept defeat after losing a match but would always insist on playing again until the other guy either quit from sheer exhaustion or was beaten."[29]

The law clerks were aware of the justice's strategy of outlasting his opponents. "The Judge never succeeded in defeating his first law clerk on the tennis court in any set," brags Jerome "Buddy" Cooper (October terms 1937–39). "Oh, to be sure, an occasional game was dropped to him, and at the end of every losing set, while the clerk gasped, the Judge always inquired 'Why don't we play just one more set? I believe I could beat you.'"[30] Adds former law clerk George M. Treister (October term 1950), himself an excellent tennis player and a past captain of the UCLA tennis team:

> The Judge is the only man I've ever known who made me feel a coward when I wanted to quit playing tennis after four or five sets. It mattered not that my hand was blistered through the heavy tape; in such cases he never permitted a graceful way out. He held that snow and darkness were the only valid excuses. And these he surely would have enjoyed if he could have established jurisdiction over the weather and the rotation of the earth.[31]

When it came to competing with his children, however, Justice Black had his limits. Once his children were able to defeat their father on the tennis court, they never again faced him in singles competition.

Occasionally, Justice Black would show a flash of anger over his own tennis game. "He was then, as now, an even-tempered man, but I learned in time to recognize the days when he had had a bad day on the court—the tennis court," writes former law clerk Sidney M. Davis (October term 1944). "Such occasions came to be known by me as 'Tennis the Menace' days."[32]

The justice's tenacity and competitiveness meant that he fought for every point. Hugo Black Jr. recalls a match between his father and Treister. Having grown tired of the justice's competitiveness, Treister hit a slice shot in such a manner that the only way it could be returned was for the justice to run into the garden wall (the assumption being that Black would let the shot go). The justice chased the ball into the wall. Treister hit the shot again. Black again pursued it. An astonished Treister watched as Black crashed into the wall again and again, forcing the young man to abandon the strategy before the justice gravely injured himself.[33] On the tennis court, even Justice Black's famous sense of courtliness toward women was eclipsed by his competitive nature. Former clerk John W. Vardaman Jr. (October term 1965) recalls playing mixed doubles with the justice against Elizabeth Black (the justice's second wife) and fellow law clerk Drayton Nabers Jr. Concerned about the skill of his younger opponent, and the lack of skill evidenced by Vardaman, the justice gave his law clerk the following advice: "when the ball comes to you, hit it to Elizabeth."[34]

Justice Black built his clay tennis court in the backyard of his Alexandria townhouse. The justice selected a clay court because it was "the only acceptable style of court, in his view."[35] The court shared the large backyard with a rose and vegetable gardens, a grape arbor, and a small fish pond, and a table and chairs were placed in the shade of cherry, black walnut, and pecan trees for post-tennis conversation and relaxation. For at least one law clerk, the most memorable part of the tennis matches was the fellowship that followed the marathon sessions. "It wasn't the tennis per se [that enriched the clerkship experience]," explains John Vardaman. "It was the opportunity to go out to the house, play tennis, and then socialize with the Judge and Elizabeth. It turned the relationship from professional to personal." Vardaman remembers that tennis would be followed by wide-ranging conversations between the justice and his clerks on such topics as the war in Vietnam, politics, constitutional history, the Court, and famous personalities that the justice had known. "He provided us with a fascinating view of history . . . it made for such a rich experience to sit with the Judge and have so much fun."[36]

The justice and his law clerks maintained the tennis court, which Drayton Nabers Jr. nicknamed "the hottest court in the land." "Weather permitting, and sometimes when it didn't, the Judge would role and line the tennis court," recalls George Treister. "His displays of energy were overwhelming. I gained the impression that I was of little real help in this technical task." Not surprisingly, the justice would not bow to Mother Nature. "On occasion there was not much incentive [in rolling and lining the court] since it obviously was going to rain before the court could be readied, yet he insisted on the gamble. On these days he seemed to take rain as a personal insult."[37]

According to former law clerk Frank M. Wozencraft (October term 1949), Justice Black created a second, temporary tennis court during October term 1949. Wozencraft writes that the tennis court was located in "the attic" of the Supreme Court, and that the justice and his clerk played with tennis balls that Supreme Court marshal Thomas E. Waggaman had "dyed orange in a fruitless effort to improve the visibility."[38] Thus, at least for one term of court, Hugo Black presided over the highest court in the land.

Justice Black politely suffered through matches with those clerks whose tennis skills were suspect, although he did take precautions to minimize the loss of new tennis balls. Early into his clerkship, John Vardaman was invited to play tennis with Justice Black. Vardaman had never played tennis, and he accepted the justice's invitation with "considerable apprehension." Prior to the match, Vardaman decided to warm up by hitting some practice balls—and immediately missed the first ball lobbed to him. "The Judge did not miss the significance of this inauspicious beginning for he immediately announced that we would play with old balls that day lest one of my errant shots send a new ball over the fence into the neighboring yard."[39]

The frugal Justice Black was not deterred when a wild tennis shot resulted in a lost ball. Drayton Nabers Jr. writes of playing a doubles match with outgoing law clerk James L. North (October term 1964) and the Blacks. During the practice session prior to the game, a tennis ball disappeared into the thick foliage that grew along a brick wall adjacent to the court. "Because the ball was of an older vintage," explains Nabers, "it was, without much ado, replaced by another ball from the Judge's basket." After a three-hour match, the exhausted law clerks and Elizabeth Black sat down to rest in the shade—only to notice that Justice Black had disappeared.

> Shortly thereafter Jim and I pushed ourselves from our chairs and began looking for the mysteriously absent Judge to see if we could be of any help. We found him in [an] Atlas-like posture with a ten foot aluminum ladder hoisted on his back. Since I smelt no fires, saw no treed cat, and knew that his peaches were not yet ripe, I was rather baffled. "I'd better get that ball down out of the vines before it slips my mind," he explained. At once I understood more clearly the work that would be expected of me this year.[40]

Perhaps aware of the justice's thriftiness, former clerks used the holidays to make gifts of tennis balls to the justice. In a letter to former law clerk George Treister, Justice Black thanks him for the box of tennis balls, writing "you know where my heart is." The justice muses in the letter that he does not know if he has ever played with "nylon and Dacron balls," but assures his former clerk that "I know I shall enjoy these."[41]

Even when faced with the most dismal of tennis partners, Justice Black remained undaunted. When George Freeman confessed to the justice that he did not know how to play tennis, the justice accused him of being "modest" and demanded to see the evidence for himself. "It soon became clear that I was a disaster," recalls Freeman. "The following Friday, the Judge came into my office and said, 'George, I have made an appointment for you with the tennis pro at the Army Navy Country Club tomorrow at ten o'clock. Listen carefully and follow his instructions. This will take a number of Saturdays for you to come up to speed.'" The justice's prediction proved to be overly optimistic, as Freeman struggled to master the basics. "Thereafter I slowly started getting a few backhands, but my serves remained almost unattainable," writes Freeman. "Fortunately, in the Fall our work on cases began to pick up, and I came to look forward to having to work in the office on Saturdays as a 'God Send.'"[42]

A few clerks, however, were judged to be beyond the help of a good tennis pro (former law clerk Guido Calabresi, for one, recalls Justice Black's "total disdain—expressed as politely as possible—of playing tennis with so puny a player as I"[43]) and instead satisfied the justice's competitive nature by serving as a fourth for bridge. "We would often play after the Friday conference, and the Judge was often tired because he was losing 5 to 4 on civil liberty cases," recounts Calabresi. "A good clerk would have loved to help him win [to cheer him up], but he was so competitive that he would not be happy if he knew that you were helping him win." So Calabresi came up with an ingenious solution that involved former law clerk Charles A. Reich.

> During my clerkship, we routinely played with Charlie Reich and another individual. What we decided to do—and I don't know if Charlie realized this—is to arrange so that Charlie would never be the Judge's partner. We told the Judge that we made this arrangement because Charlie loved the Judge too much, and was too emotional, to be the Justice's partner, but it was really because Charlie—who is brilliant—is too quixotic for bridge. Thus, by putting Charlie on the other team we made sure that the Judge would always win.[44]

If Justice Black became wise to his law clerks' affectionate duplicity, he never mentioned it to them.

Conclusion

Today the justices' chambers are commonly referred to as "nine little law firms." This description is particularly apt when it comes to the law clerks, whose ranks have swelled to four law clerks per associate justice (the chief justice can hire five law clerks). The role of these modern clerks has also changed and evolved. While clerks were once legal assistants and social companions, today they more closely resemble law firm associates who are called upon to master complex areas of the law, counsel the senior partner/justice as to the best method of resolving tricky legal issues, and draft complex legal documents.[45]

The justices still have cordial relationships with their law clerks, and they socialize with them outside of the Court. And even the practice of playing sports with law clerks continues. Justice Byron White was known for his fierce competitive streak, battling his law clerks on the basketball court as well as challenging them to putting and Ping Pong contests.[46] Justice Clarence Thomas also played basketball with law clerks until tearing his Achilles' tendon during a pickup basketball game in 1993.[47] And while aerobics may not be considered a sport, generations of Sandra Day O'Connor's law clerks sweated away pounds in the justice's morning exercise class.

As for tennis, at least two recent justices took tennis into account when selecting their clerks; Supreme Court lore asserts that Justice O'Connor selected one tennis-playing law clerk each term, and that Chief Justice Rehnquist hired three—rather than four—clerks so he and his young charges could play doubles tennis on Thursday mornings.[48] While the chief justice arguably cared more about getting the requisite number of players than either beating his clerks or picking clerks with basic tennis skills (letting the chief justice win was not a requirement of the clerkship, nor was hitting him with a serve a fireable offense),[49] Justice John Paul Stevens, an avid tennis player, did not view his law clerks as suitable opponents. "I and some other former clerks were planning a clerks' reunion with Justice Stevens, and one suggested a tennis tournament," writes former Stevens law clerk Cliff Sloan. "Justice Stevens didn't approve. 'Why not?' asked the organizer. 'Most of the clerks aren't very good,' he [Stevens] responded. He didn't want to waste his time playing with hackers. He was 85 at the time."[50]

Despite the fact that some law clerks and their justices continue to engage in athletic competitions, the clerkship model of Hugo Black is essentially a relic of the past; no longer do the justices play school master, matchmaker, and surrogate parent to their clerks. Perhaps this is why former Black law clerks speak so glowingly of their clerkship experiences—because they were the beneficiaries of a rare and fleeting opportunity to become the students and tennis partners of one of the most unique individuals to sit on the U.S. Supreme Court. As a testament to their lasting devotion, in the decades after the justice's death the remaining Black law clerks, joined by Hugo Black Jr., held regular reunions at the Supreme Court where they reminisced about their days with "the Judge" and raised a glass in his honor.

Notes

1. Shelley Rolfe, "Justice Hugo Black: Two Former Law Clerks Recall One of the Court's Towering Figures," *Richmond Times-Dispatch*, December 12, 1971.

2. Hugo Black Jr., interview by author, 2004.

3. Josephine Black Pesaresi, interview by author, 2010.

4. J. Vernon Patrick, "Confessions of the Law Clerks: Extracted for the 80th Birthday of Mr. Justice Black," February 27, 1966 (in author's possession).

5. Hugo Black to C. Samuel Daniels, October 18, 1960, Box 459, Daniels File, Personal Papers of Hugo Black, Library of Congress (hereafter cited as Black Papers).

6. Larry Hammond, interview by author, 2000.

7. Daniel J. Meador, *Mr. Justice Black and His Books* (Charlottesville: University of Virginia Press, 1974), 30.

8. Ibid., 31.

9. Guido Calabresi, interview by author, 2010.

10. Melford O. "Buddy" Cleveland to Hugo Black, June 28, 1962, Box 459, Cleveland File, Black Papers.

11. George C. Freeman Jr., "Confessions of the Law Clerks: Extracted for the 80th Birthday of Mr. Justice Black," February 27, 1966 (in author's possession).

12. Ibid.

13. Hugo Black to Guido "Guy" Calabresi, November 4, 1960, Box 459, Calabresi File, Black Papers.

14. Max Leva, "Confessions of the Law Clerks: Extracted for the 80th Birthday of Mr. Justice Black," February 27, 1966 (in author's possession).

15. Drayton Nabers Jr., interview by author, 2010.

16. Freeman, "Confessions of the Law Clerks."

17. Hugo Black to Presidential Appeal Board, January 26, 1968, Black Papers.

18. Pesaresi interview.

19. Melford O. "Buddy" Cleveland to Hugo Black, June 28, 1962, Box 459, Cleveland File, Black Papers.

20. Hugo Black to John K. McNulty, February 14, 1971, Box 465, McNulty File, Black Papers.

21. Hugo Black to Mrs. George Brussel Jr., March 12, 1963, Box 466, Reich File, Black Papers.

22. Nicholas Johnson to Hugo Black, January 23, 1970, Box 464, Johnson File, Black Papers.

23. Charles F. Luce to Hugo Black, October 4, 1962, Box 465, Luce File, Black Papers.

24. George C. Freeman Jr. to Hugo Black, November 6, 1957, Box 462, Freeman File, Black Papers.

25. Hugo Black to Sidney M. Davis, January 10, 1957, Box 460, Davis File, Black Papers.

26. Hugo Black to Sidney M. Davis, March 2, 1970, Box 460, Davis File, Black Papers.

27. Roger K. Newman, *Hugo Black: A Biography* (New York: Fordham University Press, 1997), 302.

28. Hugo Black to C. Samuel Daniels, October 24, 1957, Box 459, Daniels File, Black Papers.

29. Hugo Black Jr., *My Father: A Remembrance* (New York: Random House, 1975), 110.

30. Jerome A. Cooper, "Confessions of the Law Clerks: Extracted for the 80th Birthday of Mr. Justice Black," February 27, 1966 (in author's possession).

31. George M. Treister, "Confessions of the Law Clerks: Extracted for the 80th Birthday of Mr. Justice Black," February 27, 1966 (in author's possession).

32. Sidney M. Davis, "Confessions of the Law Clerks: Extracted for the 80th Birthday of Mr. Justice Black," February 27, 1966 (in author's possession).

33. Ibid.

34. John W. Vardaman Jr., interview by author, 2010.

35. Daniel J. Meador, "Hugo Black and Thomas Jefferson," *Virginia Quarterly Review* (Summer 2003): 459–68.

36. Vardaman interview.

37. Treister, "Confessions of the Law Clerks."

38. Frank M. Wozencraft, "Confessions of the Law Clerks: Extracted for the 80th Birthday of Mr. Justice Black," February 27, 1966 (in author's possession).

39. Vardaman, "Confessions of the Law Clerks."

40. Drayton Nabers Jr., "Confessions of the Law Clerks: Extracted for the 80th Birthday of Mr. Justice Black," February 27, 1966 (in author's possession).

41. Hugo Black to George Treister, January 14, 1957, Box 467, Black Papers.

42. Author's 2010 correspondence with George C. Freeman Jr.

43. Guido Calabresi, "Confessions of the Law Clerks: Extracted for the 80th Birthday of Mr. Justice Black," February 27, 1966 (in author's possession).

44. Calabresi interview.

45. Mark Tushnet was the first to suggest that the modern court could be thought of as individual law firms, with the justices holding the position of senior partners and the law clerks as junior associates. See Mark Tushnet, "Thurgood Marshall and the Brethren," *Georgetown Law Journal* 80 (August): 2109–30, 2110–11.

46. David M. Ebel, "Law and Character: Byron White—A Justice Shaped by the West," *University of Colorado Law Review* 71 (2000): 1421–26; Kevin J. Worthen, "Shirt-Tales: Clerking for Byron White," *Brigham Young University Law Review* (1994): 349–61.

47. Kevin Merida and Michael A. Fletcher, *Supreme Discomfort: The Divided Soul of Clarence Thomas* (New York: Doubleday, 2007), 287.

48. David G. Savage, "Former Rehnquist Clerks Recall His Warmth, Wit," *Los Angeles Times*, September 7, 2005; Todd C. Peppers, *Courtiers of the Marble Palace: The Rise and Influence of the Supreme Court Law Clerk* (Palo Alto, Calif.: Stanford University Press, 2006), 197.

49. Savage, "Former Rehnquist Clerks"; Brad Nelson, "In His Own Words: Neil Richards Recounts His Time as a Clerk for Chief Justice Rehnquist," *Student Life: The Independent Newspaper of Washington University in St. Louis since Eighteen Seventy-Eight*, September 9, 2005.

50. Cliff Sloan, "My Boss, Justice Stevens," *New York Times*, April 9, 2010.

JOHN D. FASSETT

Clerking for Stanley F. Reed

The October 1953 term of the U.S. Supreme Court was an unusually interesting term to be a law clerk to Justice Stanley F. Reed. The unexpected death of Chief Justice Fred Vinson, which was followed by the appointment by President Dwight Eisenhower of Earl Warren as Vinson's successor, created a new and unknown atmosphere. This was particularly true in view of the scheduled arguments early in the term of the several cases involving the constitutionality of racial segregation in public schools, which had originally been argued during the prior term.

The result was the momentous unanimous decisions in those cases on May 17, 1954. For Justice Reed, who had assumed his seat as associate justice on January 31, 1938, October term 1953 was his sixteenth on the Court, and he was looking forward to his seventieth birthday at the end of 1954. During my retirement, I have written both a biography of Justice Reed and several published articles about his role in the school segregation cases as well as other aspects of his career. While this essay draws upon those writings, it will be confined to my knowledge regarding the selection and experiences of the justice's forty-seven law clerks.

How Reed Selected Clerks

Stanley F. Reed's first clerk was Harold Leventhal, who was working with him in the Office of the Solicitor General at the time President Franklin D. Roosevelt sent Reed's nomination to the Senate in January 1938. Leventhal agreed to accompany his boss to the Supreme Court and serve as his clerk for the remainder of the term. Having Leventhal as his first law clerk afforded Justice Reed a significant advantage over most new justices since Leventhal, a Columbia Law School graduate and a former editor in chief of the *Columbia Law Review,* had recently completed a term as law clerk to Justice Harlan Fiske Stone and thus was well acquainted with both the work and the personnel of the Court.

Leventhal and subsequent clerks were ably supported by Justice Reed's secretary, Helen Gaylord. A former upstate New Yorker who had worked for the justice since his days as general counsel of the Reconstruction Finance Commission (RFC), Gaylord had been a real insider to the events of the early New Deal administration and could relate intriguing tales of the activities of Thomas Corcoran, Ben Cohen, and Jesse Jones at the RFC. While denominated a secretary, as with the administrative assistants to other justices, her functions were far broader. In addition to typing memos, communications, and opinions, she maintained Justice Reed's docket books and his financial records, followed the status of activities of the Court, often communicated with other justices or their staffs with respect to Court matters, and, though not a lawyer, often acted as an additional law clerk, seeking requested information or research materials for Justice Reed. She resided with her sister, also a government employee, in a Washington suburb and worked the same long hours as did Justice Reed and his law clerks.

On the recommendations of Harvard Law School professors Felix Frankfurter and Erwin Griswold, and with the endorsements of Harold Leventhal and Paul Freund, Justice Reed selected another Harvard Law School graduate, John Sapienza, to be his law clerk for October term 1938. Since Sapienza was currently clerking for Judge Augustus Hand on the Court of Appeals for the Second Circuit, and would not be able to start his new position until August 15, Leventhal, although now back in the solicitor general's office after completing his work for Justice Reed and enjoying a vacation in Europe, received permission from Solicitor General Robert H. Jackson to volunteer to review and write memos with respect to some of the deluge of petitions for certiorari that arrive each summer.

On August 1, Leventhal wrote to the justice to advise him that, in addition to over 100 petitions for certiorari that the justice had already received in Nantucket, another 150 probably would be distributed during the month. He suggested that he and Sapienza "split up the rest of the certs, in some equitable fashion, and send them on to you with memoranda," commenting that "I had rather expected that we would do all of the certs, and hope that your vacation has not been rendered less enjoyable because of them."[1] He noted that it had always been the custom of Justice Stone's new and departing clerks to share the job of doing the summer certs. Justice Reed replied, accepting Leventhal's suggestion, and thereafter the chore of reviewing and writing memoranda on all certs was a prime duty of Reed's law clerks.

As his law clerk for his third term on the Court, Justice Reed again selected a Harvard graduate, based on the recommendations of Frankfurter and of his former associates in the solicitor general's office who were now on the faculty at Harvard Law School. However, unlike his predecessors, Philip T. Graham, who had been president of the *Harvard Law Review* in his senior year, came directly from law school rather than first clerking for a judge on a lower federal court.

With the precedent of the prior summer established, Sapienza completed and sent to Justice Reed several batches of certs before Phil Graham took over in mid-July. Graham sent his first batch to Justice Reed on July 26 with a cover letter noting that Frankfurter had stopped by "to make sure that John and I were properly serving you." Justice Frankfurter obviously thought so highly of Graham that, upon completion of his term with Justice Reed, he was selected to serve the following term with his former Harvard professor who had since been appointed to the Supreme Court.

Justice Reed's fourth law clerk, Bennett Boskey, was also a Harvard Law School graduate who had clerked for a year for Judge Augustus Hand on the Court of Appeals for the Second Circuit. Boskey had the unique experience of being requested to clerk an additional two years for the new chief justice. After being elevated to the center chair by Franklin D. Roosevelt, Chief Justice Harlan Fiske Stone concluded that, with his new administrative responsibilities, it would be appropriate to have two law clerks, the senior of whom would be familiar with Court procedures.

John H. Maclay Jr., the fifth clerk, was once again a Harvard Law School graduate who had been an editor of the *Harvard Law Review* and had clerked for a year for Judge Hand. His successor, David Schwartz, was similarly recommended to Justice Reed by his former Harvard Law School professor, Felix Frankfurter. Schwartz was also backed by a colleague of Reed's from the Office of the Solicitor General, Edward J. Ennis, who was Schwartz's boss at the Alien Enemy Control Unit (this was shortly after Pearl Harbor). L. Earle Birdzell Jr., hired in 1943, was the sixth in Reed's succession of clerks exclusively from Harvard Law School. The engagement of Byron E. Kabot, who came to him from the University of Chicago Law School in 1944, broke the streak, and of Reed's subsequent twenty-one hires, only seven were from Harvard (the rest were from Yale, Virginia, Columbia, Chicago, and Georgetown; see the list in the appendix to this essay).

Several factors appear to have significantly influenced Justice Reed's deviation from hiring clerks exclusively from Harvard Law School. The first, which was a common problem for judges and justices during World War II, was that there was no exemption for military service for attendance at law school or for a clerkship—which resulted in a greatly reduced pool of candidates. Second, some friction had development between Justices Reed and Frankfurter, who was the primary proponent of selecting law clerks from Harvard. Third, Justice Reed's experience with law clerk Byron Kabot was particularly satisfying (Helen Gaylord told me that Kabot was among the justice's favorite clerks), thus encouraging the justice to abandon his reticence regarding non-Harvard candidates. Finally, in 1946 Wesley Sturges became dean of Yale Law School (Reed had an undergraduate degree from Yale) and became a strong annual promoter of Yale candidates.

Hiring and Training of New Clerks

Departing at the end of October term 1944, Byron E. Kabot wrote to the justice at the end of July to assure Reed that he had managed to get the certiorari petitions under control before his successor, Emmanuel G. Weiss, started work. He also assured him that he would have a sufficient supply of golf balls:

> Prior to the receipt of your letter I had mentioned to Manny the confidential nature of the work at the Court. . . . With respect to certs, we are sending you a bag containing 30 or 40 with memos, today. This bag contains all certs received so far except for those which were just delivered this afternoon. . . . Thus, when I leave, Manny will have a clean slate and no backlog to harass him during the coming months.
>
> Miss Gaylord suggested before she left that we keep a look out for golf balls for you. The Sports Center procured her some and called the other day to say that they had put two aside for you. They allow only two to a customer.[2]

When Fred Vinson became chief justice in 1946, one of his first administrative decisions was to increase his own authorization of law clerks to three. The chief justice relied so heavily on his two clerks to draft opinions and to perform administrative chores that one commentator opined that the new chief justice had "turned the once lonely job of Chief Justice of the United States into a staff operation."[3] Following the precedent established by the chief justice, it was decided that commencing with October term 1947, each justice would be authorized to employ two law clerks. Thus, when F. Aley Allen completed his term with Justice Reed, he was succeeded by both John Spitzer and Robert von Mehren. Spitzer was a Yale Law School graduate (and veteran of four years of military service) heartily recommended by Judge Charles Clark, of the Second Circuit. Von Mehren came from Justice Reed's traditional feeders, having attended Harvard Law School and clerked for Judge Learned Hand. The relative luxury of having two law clerks to prepare memos and assist in the drafting of opinions significantly eased the pressure on the justice, but the fact that he produced only eleven majority opinions during October term 1947 also contributed to it being a less hectic period.

Justice Reed's practice was to select his two law clerks for each ensuing term about February 1. Besides annual recommendations from his contacts at law schools, the justice often received recommendations regarding possible candidates from other sources. For example, during 1949 one of Reed's old friends endorsed the candidacy of Lewis C. Green, who was due to graduate from Harvard Law School in 1950. While he did not select Green for the October 1950 term, Justice Reed was favorably impressed by his personality and record and suggested that if the candidate would acquire further experience by clerking for a court of appeals judge, he would consider him for the position during October term 1951. Accordingly, Green accepted a clerkship with Judge William Orr, of the Ninth Circuit, and, having received that judge's enthusiastic endorsement, was selected by Justice Reed to join John D. Calhoun, a Yale Law School graduate who had been employed for two years at the Wall Street law firm of Cravath, Swaine & Moore, as his other clerk.

Unlike some of the other justices, Justice Reed did not have any rigid geographical or other selection criteria for clerks. However, it is apparent that there were several types of experiences that were deemed by Justice Reed to provide advantages in the selection process. In addition to a prior federal clerkship, prior military experience was considered advantageous by the justice, who himself had seen military service during World War I. Of course, strong support from an old Reed professional associate was the critical factor in many cases. A history of having served as a law review editor, and particularly of having produced a legal note, comment, or article, was clearly very persuasive. Justice Reed made no effort to encourage applicants from Kentucky, but in a few cases such a background influenced the selection process.

On June 1, 1951, shortly before departing for an extended visit to Maysville, Kentucky, plus a stay of a couple of weeks in Durham, North Carolina, to undergo his annual checkup at the Duke Medical Center, Justice Reed wrote to Green and Calhoun:

> This letter is addressed to both of you so that if there are any rough spots as between the two new clerks, they can be promptly adjusted. . . . The first new clerk should report here July 16. . . . Mr. Zimmerman will be here and work closely with the new clerk until Mr. Zimmerman leaves on July 24th. This gives opportunity for Mr. Zimmerman to familiarize him with the work of his office. So far as the second clerk is concerned, he should report on August 24th. . . . While he will not have the benefit of the experience of Mr. Zimmerman, the first new clerk can pass along his instruction. As Mr. Green has had experience as a court law clerk, I think it better for Mr. Calhoun to come first. . . . If this arrangement is undesirable . . . discuss the matter between [yourselves] and I am agreeable to whatever arrangement is made.[4]

The October term 1951 clerks commenced work as suggested and, prior to the justice's return to Washington in September, prepared several hundred memoranda on appeals and petitions for certiorari, which Gaylord forwarded to the justice either in Kentucky or North Carolina. After arriving in Washington in September, Justice Reed commenced his habitual schedule of extended hours in his chambers at the Court. Lew Green commented that "the justice was in the habit of working 9 a.m. to 7 p.m., six days a week, and enjoying every minute."[5]

Reed's Work Habits

As he had from the outset of his tenure on the Court, Justice Reed relied heavily on the work of his law clerks throughout his Court career. One of his early clerks commented:

> The careful analysis and dissection of cases in his chambers was something the justice genuinely enjoyed and took to be an essential part of his obligation. Over the long years of his judicial experience this process continued. He would plough through the statute books and the judicial precedents himself, just as he expected his law clerks to do. He would look to his clerks for ideas and suggestions, sometimes for memoranda on a troublesome point, and above all for candid discussion. At the opinion-writing stage he would often—though by no means always—accept drafting suggestions.[6]

Several clerks have noted that Justice Reed struggled with his writing. Bennett Boskey recalls: "He did not have the laconic eloquence that enriches Douglas' better opinions. But he put high value on clarity; he knew how to achieve it; and sometimes he would struggle to find what he felt was exactly the right word to convey a proper meaning or avoid an ambiguity. (Justice Reed was very pleased when, at one of our annual gatherings, the law clerks presented him with a set of the unabridged *Oxford English Dictionary*)."[7]

David O'Brien, an illustrious observer of the Supreme Court, has written with considerable accuracy about Justice Reed's use of law clerks in his book *Storm Center*: "Reed, for one, struggled to write what he wanted to say. 'Wouldn't it be nice if we could write the way we think,' he once lamented. Like many of his successors, Reed for the most part relied on his clerks for first drafts—the clerk had the first word and he had the last word."[8] O'Brien went on to compare Justice Reed's method to those of other justices:

> Even though they delegate the preliminary opinion writing, justices differ in their approach when revising first drafts. If a clerk's draft is "in the ballpark," they often edit rather than rewrite. But some, like Burton, virtually rewrite their clerk's drafts, while others, like Reed, tend to insert paragraphs in the draft opinions prepared by their clerks. As one former clerk recalled, Reed simply "didn't like to start from the beginning and go to the ending." Consequently, his opinions tend to read like a dialogue with "a change of voice from paragraph to paragraph." Reed's patchwork opinions did not stem from excessive delegation of responsibility or lack of dedication. At least in his early years on the Court, he took opinion writing seriously but found the words did not flow easily for him. . . . In time, as Reed grew older and the pressures of the workload increased, he,

like others on the Court, found it necessary to delegate more and more opinion writing to law clerks.[9]

Just as the extent to which justices relied on their law clerks varied among the justices, so quite clearly did the degree to which Justice Reed gave assignments to his law clerks vary depending on the rapport he had established with them and his evaluation of their work.

My Clerking Experience

My personal experience as a Reed clerk during October term 1953 was of a close working relationship in which he relied heavily on me and my co-clerk. During the term, the relationship developed into a much more personal one. From the day of my arrival, the justice evidenced genuine interest regarding my wife (also a World War II veteran) and our children (a clerk with two children was obviously unique to his experience), in my two tours of military duty, and in my work at Yale Law School with Professor Ralph S. Brown—which had resulted in my being listed as a coauthor of two articles in law journals. But my experience was probably atypical, because the school segregation cases occupied so much of his time and energy that year. I recount my story here knowing that it is merely one of the voices of Justice Reed's forty-seven clerks.

Toward the end of the first semester of my third year at Yale Law School, Dean Sturges advised me one day after class that he proposed to recommend me to Justice Reed for a clerkship for the next term of the Supreme Court. He said that he was also recommending the current editor in chief of the *Yale Law Journal*, Ernie Rubenstein, to Associate Justice Tom C. Clark, and that the odds of success on that recommendation were probably better, since Justice Clark seemed to be partial to candidates with that credential. He added, however, that while Reed in the past had chosen his clerks mostly from Harvard, he had also had a few from Columbia and Yale, including Bayless Manning from Yale's class of 1949.

Having heard nothing further about the clerkship, in January 1953 my wife and I completed our house hunting in the Hartford, Connecticut, area (where I expected to begin my legal career) by making a deposit on a home. Only a few days later I was jubilant and surprised when the mail delivery brought a letter from Justice Reed offering me the clerkship for October term 1953. Apparently based on Dean Sturges's letter, Justice Reed had decided to forego any preselection interview. Incidentally, I discovered the original of the dean's letter in the justice's papers in the archives at the University of Kentucky forty years later while I was doing research for my biography of the justice. The letter was a three-page masterpiece composed, I suspect, by Clare Campbell, who had interviewed me when I applied to Yale and had subsequently become the dean's wife. Justice Reed's letter merely suggested that I work a trip to Washington into my schedule as soon as feasible so that we could discuss the details of the position. Needless to say, I responded immediately, accepting the justice's offer and canceling our plans for Hartford.

I had known virtually nothing regarding Stanley F. Reed at the time the dean advised me of his proposed action. Anticipating a possible interview and hoping for a stroke of lightning, I attempted to increase my knowledge in the law library, but discovered that, although he had been on the Supreme Court since being appointed by President Roosevelt in 1938, not a single biography or critique solely of his work had been written. Accordingly, I was forced to resort to scanning several recently published commentaries about the entire Court for mentions of Justice Reed. During my quick trip to Washington in response to the justice's letter, I had a very pleasant, very general, discussion with the justice, and met his secretary, Helen Gaylord, and his messenger, Gerald Ross, who had been a caddy for Justice Reed in Kentucky and now served as the justice's chauffeur, bartender, and general factotum. I also spent a short period with his two current law clerks.

Justice Reed asked me to begin work after graduation and take the bar exam as soon as possible, since he wanted me to be senior clerk. As such, it was necessary that I arrive in time to work with my predecessors, and then to orient my fellow clerk, who would not arrive until mid-August. While the basic salary for clerks was the same as I had been offered for work for the Department of Justice, Justice Reed had decided that my military and other experience qualified me for the next higher salary level. I was pleasantly surprised when presented the official appointment signed by Chief Justice Fred Vinson to see that my rate would be only a few dollars less than the $5,200 offer I had received from the Cleveland law firm of Jones Day. Since I served somewhat longer than a year, my total Supreme Court salary was $5,594.

Promptly after my wife, Betty, and I arrived in Washington, I went to the Supreme Court to be sworn in as a clerk and to assume my duties. The swearing-in plus a lot of paperwork was accomplished in the office of the clerk of the Court. After that, I proceeded to Justice Reed's chambers, and, to my surprise, he was ready to depart for Durham for his annual medical examination at the Duke University Medical Center. As a result, I had only a relatively brief meeting with the justice. He had been on the Duke rice diet program for a number of years, and had been making a return pilgrimage to see the same doctors and have a review of his diet shortly after the Court recessed every year. One reason the justice was very anxious to get away was that the Court had just concluded a very contentious series of conferences during which the majority, including Justice Reed, had declined to stay the executions of Ethel and Julius Rosenberg, who had been convicted of atomic espionage.

Helen Gaylord was left with the responsibility of performing the balance of my orientation. She shepherded me to the security office, where I was assigned a parking spot in the carefully guarded basement of the building, and introduced me to the personnel at the Court's large law library. It was not just justices who were fast departing with the completion of October term 1952. One of Justice Reed's clerks had already left for a vacation before commencing work at a Washington firm, and the other, who was charged with indoctrinating me with respect to the role of a Reed clerk, was obviously champing at the bit to get away. He had recently been married and was anxious for a delayed honeymoon before beginning his position with another Washington firm.

The chambers of the justices were all on the ground floor at the rear of the Supreme Court building, guarded by heavy brass gates. Justice Reed's office was in the southern corner, and it could be entered only through the office that housed his secretary and messenger on one side, or the office shared by his two law clerks on the other. Both of those offices had doors opening on the corridor surrounding the courtroom. There was very little traffic in the corridor, so I generally kept the door to the clerks' office open, in order to be aware of anything taking place outside.

I was most pleased when, in the latter part of July, George Mickum, Reed's other clerk, showed up and stated he was available to commence work. I had already begun to feel swamped with work, since the justice was sending requests for research projects in connection with the rearguments of the school segregation cases. I was also trying to perform reviews of files being delivered daily by the clerk's office covering petitions for certiorari. The practice in Reed's chambers and in most of the other chambers was for law clerks to read and analyze each petition and write a one- or two-page memorandum recommending that the petition be granted or denied. Since each clerk had his own typewriter for producing these memos, as well as other memos and drafts of opinions, I was glad I had taken a typing course in high school.

George Mickum and I worked closely together during the term and became fast friends. He had graduated from Georgetown Law School and clerked for Judge Charles H. Fahy on the Court of Appeals for the D.C. Circuit for a year. Justice Frankfurter's clerks always were Harvard graduates with prior clerkship experience, and a number of the other clerks also had that qualification. An amazing statistic during the 1953 term was that five clerks were Yale Law School graduates. In addition to myself and two of my Yale classmates who were clerking for Justices Tom C. Clark and Sherman Minton, two members of a prior Yale class who had each clerked for a year for a federal appeals court judge were clerking for Justices Hugo Black and Harold Burton.

A private dining room exclusively for law clerks was provided near the public cafeteria in the Supreme Court building. It was imperative that this room be secure because much of the subject matter of discussion, sometimes heated, among the clerks was pending applications for certiorari, argued cases, or Court politics. With occasional exceptions, all of the clerks brought their trays of food from the cafeteria to the private dining room every day at noon. Within a short time after all the eighteen clerks had reported for October term 1953, I had a pretty good idea of where each of them stood ideologically in the liberal to conservative spectrum on criminal law issues, federal government regulatory power issues, and civil rights issues. There were eighteen clerks because during the term, Chief Justice Vinson had retained a third clerk to work primarily on in forma pauperis petitions to the Court. They were applications, primarily by prisoners in state or federal prisons, seeking reviews of their situations without the benefit of legal representation. Justice William O. Douglas employed only one clerk, but had two secretaries, one of whom was assisting him in completing his most recent tome regarding his world travels.

A highlight of our sessions in the clerks' dining room was our occasional luncheon guest. At a point during the term when they were not hearing oral arguments, each of the associate justices accepted our invitation to join us, and a couple of those sessions were quite stimulating. I recall Douglas regaling us about his travels in Asia and the United States. And Felix Frankfurter was in his glory—lecturing to us like a Harvard Law School class about past justices and chief justices he had known. His ideals, of course, were Justices Holmes and Brandeis. He parried questions from intrigued clerks well into the afternoon. In later life I often recalled one of his parting admonitions: "Do not aspire to be a Supreme Court Justice unless you want to be constantly frustrated, since appointment to the Court is based 99% on luck and 1% on ability."[10] We had a number of other luncheon visitors during the term, but the ones I still recall were Attorney General Herb Brownell and maverick Washington senator Wayne Morse.

I met Justice Felix Frankfurter only a few days after my arrival at the Court when he burst into my office and introduced himself, a most unnecessary gesture. The introduction was superfluous since no one could have mistaken the amazingly short, pudgy, but vivacious person who appeared. I had been forewarned by Justice Reed that such an event would occur since Frankfurter was notorious for attempting to "seduce" the clerks of certain other justices as a possible route to influencing votes supporting his always infallible views on pending applications or decisions. Frankfurter gave up on me, or more accurately on Justice Reed, a couple of months into the term, probably because he was then directing his undivided energies toward "educating" the new chief justice.

Justice Frankfurter and I had one major confrontation before he gave up. During October term 1953, the justices still assembled at 10 a.m. each Saturday morning to discuss and act on pending matters. At five minutes before ten,

Reed's messenger (Gerald Ross) would wheel the justice's portable bookshelf containing sets of briefs and records on applications and arguments, plus often treatises or other materials he wished to have at hand, to the conference room. Then, promptly at ten, the justice would head down the corridor after meeting Justices Douglas, Minton, or Clark en route. He would carry his black, locked, so-called docket book under his arm. During the first few weeks before the formal commencement of the term, when there were many petitions to be considered, or during the later weeks when there had been oral arguments, the Saturday conferences often would continue until 6 or 7 p.m. with only a brief intermission for lunch. Except on very special occasions, Justice Reed restricted his lunch, whether in his chambers or in the justices' dining room, to what was prescribed by his Duke diet: a platter of cooked rice and fresh fruit.

Justice Reed had returned from the conference one Saturday near 6 p.m. and was hurriedly going through his notes in his docket book and summarizing for George and me the developments during the session. Casually dressed in a bright orange-colored sweater, Justice Frankfurter walked into the room wishing to debate further the outcome of a procedural case in which Frankfurter had been on the losing side. As soon as the former professor began, Justice Reed responded that he had followed my advice on that vote, and he had to leave, since he and Mrs. Reed were due at a reception. He packed his briefcase and, with Ross, departed, but Frankfurter remained and proceeded to debate the issue with me. Helen stood in one doorway of the justice's chambers and George in the other, but were having trouble containing their mirth because the louder Frankfurter got, the louder I responded. The "discussion" went on for some time before Justice Frankfurter apparently concluded I was hopeless.

As for social life, my wife, Betty, and I had few occasions to engage with the justices. It was, however, the first year of President Eisenhower's first term, and he and Mamie decided to reinstate some of the traditional White House entertainments that had been abandoned during the war, and not hosted by the Trumans. One of these was the annual reception for the justices of the Supreme Court and their wives. Betty and I, as well as all the other law clerks and the wives of the half that were married, were most pleasantly surprised in mid-November when we all received engraved invitations in the mail: "The President and Mrs. Eisenhower request the pleasure of the Company of Mr. and Mrs. Fassett at a reception to be held at the White House Tuesday evening, December the first nineteen hundred and fifty-three at nine o'clock."

All of the clerks had to rent formal outfits, and most of the wives required new finery for the occasion. One of the highlights of the reception occurred in the receiving line. President's Eisenhower's military aide discovered that Betty had served as an army nurse in Europe during the Second World War, and the president actually momentarily delayed the line while he discussed this fact with Betty.

Justice and Mrs. Reed did invite George and me and our wives once to their apartment in the Mayflower Hotel for cocktails and dinner. The Reeds had resided in that hotel since coming to the city for an ostensibly temporary stay as general counsel to the Federal Farm Board during the Hoover administration. We arrived with my co-clerk and his wife at the Reed apartment and were warmly greeted by the justice. I accepted an offering of Kentucky bourbon and water, which was prepared and served by Gerald Ross. He also served the nice dinner, which had been prepared by the hotel staff. Mrs. Reed and our wives conversed about children and other matters while the justice, George, and I talked—but without mentioning pending cases or other justices.

From the time I arrived as a clerk until the day I left, I was too busy and preoccupied with my job to have any desire to engage in any other activity. Six days a week and often on Sunday, I would drive into the Court garage before 8:00 a.m. In accordance with tradition, both George and I always arrived before the justice, and, except on rare special occasions, neither of us left until the justice was on his way to the Mayflower. The justice invariably loaded one of his leather briefcases with cert memos or other study materials when he departed each night, including Saturday, and he usually had questions for George and me regarding the matters the following morning. The justice's two briefcases each bore the inscription "Stanley F. Reed, Solicitor General," and he once told me they were the only items he ever took away from any of his government positions.

Cases Decided during October Term 1953

Aside from my work with the justice on the school segregation cases,[11] my most challenging project during the year was preparing a draft opinion for the justice in *Radio Officers' Union vs. NLRB*.[12] The case primarily presented for interpretation the scope of a provision of the National Labor Relations Act that declared it to be an unfair labor practice for an employer to discriminate among employees "to encourage or discourage membership in any labor organization." Conflicting interpretations had been rendered by several courts of appeals, and the three cases being reviewed had been reargued during October term 1953 since the Court had been unable to resolve the issues following argument in 1952. A number of additional cases presenting related issues under the same act also sought review by the Court, and decisions on whether to grant review of them were being deferred, pending resolution of the argued cases.

When Justice Reed received the assignment from the chief justice to write majority opinions in the three cases, we discussed the feasibility of resolving all of the issues presented in a single opinion. He then asked me to prepare a draft of such an opinion. For several weeks, including most of the Christmas and New Year's holidays, I labored to produce a draft, which I gave to Helen

Gaylord. She made a clean typed copy, which came to thirty-six pages of text and sixty-one footnotes. I had intended to review and edit Helen's product, but before she could deliver it to me, the justice claimed it and took it home in his briefcase. When I inquired the following day regarding the whereabouts of my draft, I was informed that it had been delivered to the printing office for printing. There is a print shop in the basement of the Supreme Court that, subject to strict security controls, produced all of the Court's products. Accordingly, the draft was already a thirty-four-page printed document before I got a chance again to review it, discuss it with the justice, and have George check all of my citations for accuracy. Those three steps were accomplished in a couple of days, and copies of a new printing with a few minor changes were distributed to the other justices on January 7.

Within a few days Justice Reed received notes from the chief justice and Justices Jackson, Minton, Clark, and Burton, joining the opinion. Justice Burton wrote: "This was a big and difficult job. I am glad you handled the cases together, and spelled out the reasoning. I agree." In my youthful enthusiasm, I had commenced the legal analysis portion of the opinion by asserting that the statutory provision in contention was "not ambiguous." Shortly after the circulation of Reed's opinion, Justice Frankfurter, who obviously knew my role with respect to the opinion, accosted me and stated, "you don't really intend to retain in the opinion the claim that the provision is not ambiguous, do you?" Somewhat concerned, I raised the issue with Justice Reed, and he quickly responded that we had six votes, and the language would remain.

Justice Black filed a dissent. Justice Frankfurter filed an opinion concurring in the result, but primarily attempting to demonstrate that the contested provision was, in fact, ambiguous. Justice Reed was somewhat annoyed, but he brightened when columnist Arthur Krock, of the *New York Times,* devoted his next column to a lengthy and laudatory review of Reed's opinion.

I produced the first drafts of three of Justice Reed's other opinions during the term, and George did the other three. Mine involved state taxation of interstate airlines, the availability of the common law writ of *coram nobis* in federal courts, and the applicability of the doctrine of collateral estopped as a defense to an antitrust claim in a federal court civil action. George's involved the imposition by a state of a sales tax on sales of equipment to the navy, the validity of a design copyright on a figurine lamp base, and a technical issue under the Securities Act of 1933. All Supreme Court decisions are significant, but none of these was momentous.

The collateral estopped case was the catalyst for another interesting interlude with another justice, however. On a morning shortly after Reed's proposed opinion was circulated, I arrived at the garage simultaneously with Justice Black. When we entered the elevator, he put it on hold and good-naturedly challenged one of the key bases for the holding—that, if a party did not challenge a crucial finding in a prior case in which it was a party, it was bound by that finding during subsequent litigation. Hugo Black's point was that no lawyer would ever appeal a case decided in his favor, even if the decision included some findings that were unfavorable. Needless to say, Justice Black dissented from Reed's majority opinion, but the majority held fast.

One question on the final exam in Eugene Rostow's course my last term at Yale had been to write a hypothetical opinion for the Supreme Court either affirming or reversing Judge Wyzanski's trial court opinion in the government's antitrust suit against United Shoe Machinery Company.[13] Wyzanski's opinion was a recent, very long opinion we had been assigned to read, but had never discussed in class. What I wrote must have been reasonable because Rostow gave me a grade of "excellent" in the course. During October term 1953, the direct appeal to the Supreme Court of Wyzanski's decision came before the justices for review. There was much discussion about the desirability of scheduling oral argument and a full review, but, instead, an order was issued without argument, affirming the decision on the basis of the trial court opinion. The day the order was announced, I dispatched a copy to my former professor with the notation, "I'll bet you would have flunked me if I had answered the exam in this way." His prompt reply challenged my suggestion!

While there was not much opportunity for frivolity at the Court, there were some lighter moments. Although Justice Reed was normally quite serious and staid, he did appreciate a little humor. Justices Douglas and Minton each stopped by the chambers on a couple of occasions to relay jokes, and, on occasion, while they were on the bench Justice Jackson would pass a note with some humorous comment to Reed. On the day following the Monday when Justice Reed delivered his opinion in the airline taxation case, which upheld Nebraska's right to tax Braniff Airways,[14] Justice Jackson sent to our chambers a black-bordered sheet of paper carrying a newspaper report of the demise of Paul Braniff. It contained the notation: "Stanley—See what you did yesterday. The shock was more than he could take. Aren't you sorry. Bob."

Departure and Reunions

After Fred Vinson's death on September 7, and until President Eisenhower announced the appointment of Earl Warren to be chief justice, virtually the only subject of conversation around the Court was the vacancy. Among the names mentioned in Washington papers as Vinson's successor was Justice Reed, but he was already sixty-eight years old, and indicated to me he no longer had any aspiration to the center seat on the Court. Upon Warren's appointment, Reed commented that he thought Warren would be a good man for the job. While Warren was sworn in during the opening session of the term on October 5, he obviously was a reticent participant in Court procedures at the outset. He retained the three law clerks Vinson had hired for the term, but it was fairly clear that their early contacts with their new boss were limited and not relaxed. During the first few conferences of the justices, Warren accepted Hugo Black's offer to preside in order to enable the newcomer to "learn the ropes." Warren did not begin to make visits to any of the brethren down the corridors until several months of the term had gone by. Thus, while we had been introduced shortly after his arrival, and he somehow remembered my first name the few times we thereafter crossed paths, I did not really become acquainted with the chief justice until after the summer adjournment of the Court on June 7.

As usual, Justice Reed departed from Washington promptly after the summer adjournment. Before he left, he told me that the chief justice was aware of the collection of materials we had assembled regarding school segregation. Justice Reed added that the chief had indicated that he would like to talk to me regarding the materials, but I was skeptical that I would be contacted. George left to begin work at a large Washington law firm shortly after the adjournment, and both Helen and I were trying to clean up all the loose ends that accumulate at the end of a term. She was looking forward to departing by July 1 for her annual visit to Cape Cod, and I was awaiting the arrival of the first of the justice's clerks for October term 1954, who was scheduled to arrive after July 4.

Initially after the Court adjourned, Chief Justice Warren wandered down the virtually deserted corridor from his chambers to my office and borrowed some of the segregation materials. Then, before he took some time away from the Court, he invited me to his chambers for a couple of discussions. The last of these was a very long, completely informal, extremely relaxed chat. He put his feet up and we discussed many things, including our respective high school careers and our first experience with having friends who were black. He was a big bear of a man, and I could easily discern why he had been a successful politician. I liked him a lot.

By the time my successor, Gordon Davidson, who had the credentials of being both from Kentucky (Louisville Law School) and Yale Law School, arrived, I was also anxious to depart the Court. I spent a couple of relaxed weeks showing Gordon the routines and explaining the challenges. Since each justice was allowed a budget for only two annual salaries for clerks, and the justice's second clerk was scheduled to arrive on August 16, I had to complete both my tenure and any paid vacation by that date in order for him to go on the payroll.

I completed my clerkship days in unique style. After packing up our apartment, I drove Betty and the children to Connecticut to visit my parents. For the ensuing days after I returned to D.C., until I said good-bye to the Marble Palace, I actually lived in that impressive building. Justice Reed's chambers contained a large couch on which he took afternoon naps on many days when the Court was not in session. It was a very comfortable bed. His office also contained a fireplace that was actually lit on a few occasions during the winter and a large lavatory with a walk-in shower. The fireplace was purely decorative in July, but the lavatory made the chambers a comfortable abode. Most important, the chambers were efficiently air-conditioned, which is very important along the Potomac in July. Security personnel at the Court had been advised of my so-journ there, so they were not surprised to find me there at odd hours.

On June 4, before he left Washington, Justice Reed had presented me a framed copy of his official Court portrait autographed "with real appreciation for your assistance in the work of the Court." Shortly after I commenced work at the Connecticut law firm Wiggin and Dana, I received a different photo-graph from Justice Reed, bearing the inscription "To a law clerk who was will-ing to forgo Washington and New York for the satisfactions of life under the Elms. All good wishes." Both photographs are valued mementos of an exciting and incomparable year.

I attended a Reed clerk reunion during my clerkship year, and two more after moving to Connecticut (I had to miss one reunion because of my teach-ing schedule at Yale). On each occasion, one of the D.C.-area law clerks held a cocktail party for the clerks and their wives on the day after the formal dinner (which was held in either a dining room at a local hotel or, on one occasion, at the Army-Navy Club dining room). After a brief time for assembling and hav-ing a drink, the group of clerks sat down with the justice for dinner at a large table with the justice in the middle and with Harold Leventhal opposite him and acting as emcee. After the justice made his always warm and genial open-ing remarks, the clerks were invited to inform the group regarding any new or interesting activities. At one of the dinners I attended, the justice accepted a few questions about his career on the Court—including his feelings about the school segregation cases. He responded that they were among the most important cases the Court had ever decided and that it was critical that the decisions be unanimous.

Perhaps Bennett Boskey has captured the flavor of these occasions best: "In our annual gatherings with the justice he overflowed with generosity toward his law clerks. In this he never wavered. His remarks at our dinners would al-ways give us far more credit than was our due, and in our hearts each of us knew how much we owed him."[15] A note that the justice sent to us on January 31, 1955, just after a dinner to celebrate his seventeenth anniversary on the Court, is typical. He wrote:

> It is a fine group of men when one sees the old law clerks grouped around the table, young, poised, intelligent and prepossessing. I am proud that it has been my good fortune to work with them over the years.
>
> As long as Fate leaves me on this good though troubled world, I hope that those who have done so much for me will let me be helpful toward them in any way that will advance their careers.[16]

Again, when he retired from the Court early in 1957, he wrote to his law clerks: "Our group has reached its allotted number. You have steered me safely through the rapids and guarded my steps. I am grateful to each one for his able assistance and loyalty. Your help enabled me to accomplish my tasks."

Besides the clerk dinners, I had a number of written and personal contacts with the justice after I completed my clerkship. I saved a few notes from the justice, and they are among my clerkship materials donated to North Carolina Central University Law School Library and are nicely displayed there.

I had two significant personal visits with the justice subsequent to his retirement from the Court. The first was the result of a telephone request from Helen Gaylord, stating that the justice would like to converse with me. I promptly went to Washington, where we discussed at length the new Civil Rights Commission and whether I would be interested in joining him if he accepted the appointment.[17] The second visit in 1964 was far less controversial since it was a social visit and my teen-age daughter accompanied me on my lengthy visit with the justice and Helen Gaylord. I was at the Court for the purpose of being admitted to the bar, and my daughter has a strong recollection of sitting with Helen and listening intently as the justice and I reminisced.

I never visited the justice after he and Mrs. Reed moved to a nursing home on Long Island in 1974, and I did not attend his funeral in Kentucky after his death on April 2, 1980, at age ninety-six. The law clerks had no role in the funeral, and the Court was represented by only Justice Potter Stewart.

Appendix: Justice Reed's Clerks, January 31, 1939, to February 25, 1957

Term	Clerk	Law School
1937	Harold Leventhal	Columbia
1938	John T. Sapienza	Harvard
1939	Philip A. Graham	Harvard
1940	Bennett Boskey	Harvard
1941	John H. Maclay	Harvard
1942	David Schwartz	Harvard
1943	L. Earle Birdzell Jr.	Harvard
1944	Byron E. Kabot	Chicago
1945	Emanuel G. Weiss	Harvard
1946	F. Aley Allen	Yale
1947	John B. Spitzer	Yale
1947	Robert von Mehren	Harvard
1948	Mac Asbill Jr.	Harvard
1948	William W. Koontz	Virginia
1949	Joseph Barbash	Harvard
1949	Bayless Manning	Yale

1950	Edwin M. Zimmerman	Columbia
1950	Adam Yarmolinsky	Yale
1951	Lewis C. Green	Harvard
1951	John D. Calhoun	Yale
1952	Robert L. Randall	Chicago
1952	William D. Rogers	Yale
1953	John D. Fassett	Yale
1953	George B. Mickum	Georgetown
1954	Gordon B. Davidson	Louisville and Yale
1954	Joel A. Kozol	Harvard
1955	Julian Burke	Georgetown
1955–56	Roderick M. Hills	Stanford
1956	Manley O. Hudson Jr.	Harvard

Notes

1. John D. Fassett, *New Deal Justice, The Life Of Stanley Reed of Kentucky* (New York: Vantage Press, 1994), 237.

2. Ibid., 390

3. John P. Frank, "Fred Vinson and the Chief Justiceship," *University of Chicago Law Review* 21 (1954): 246–46.

4. Fassett, *New Deal Justice*, 504.

5. Ibid.

6. Ibid.

7. Bennett Boskey, "Justice Reed and His Family of Law Clerks," *Kentucky Law Journal* 69 (1980–81): 869–76.

8. David O'Brien, *Storm Center: The Supreme Court in American Politics* (New York: W. W. Norton, 1986), 128–29.

9. Ibid.

10. Jack Fassett, *The Shaping Years: A Memoir of My Youth and Education* (Ex Libiris, 2001), 137.

11. For an account of my firsthand observation of Reed's evolving stance in the school segregation cases, see my article in the *Yearbook of the Supreme Court Historical Society* (1986): 48–63. That terrain has been amply covered, and I choose to focus on Reed's more typical workload in this essay.

12. 347 U.S. 17 (1954).

13. *United States v. United Shoe Machinery Corporation*, 89 F. Supp. 349 (D. Mass. 1950).

14. *Braniff Airways v. Nebraska Board*, 347 U.S. 590 (1954); Boskey, "Justice Reed and His Family of Law Clerks," 869–76.

15. Boskey, "Justice Reed and His Family of Law Clerks," 869–76.

16. Ibid.

17. Reed declined the appointment.

No College, No Prior Clerkship

How Jim Marsh Became Justice Jackson's Law Clerk

In his first four years on the Supreme Court, Justice Robert H. Jackson employed, in sequence, three young attorneys as his law clerks. The first, John F. Costelloe, was a Harvard Law School graduate and former *Harvard Law Review* editor who until summer 1941 was, like then attorney general Jackson, working at the U.S. Department of Justice. Costelloe became Justice Jackson's first law clerk shortly after his July 1941 appointment to the Court and stayed for a little over two years. Jackson's next law clerk, Phil C. Neal, came to Jackson in 1943 after graduating from Harvard Law School, where he had served as president of the *Harvard Law Review*. Jackson's third law clerk, Murray Gartner, arrived in spring 1945, also having graduated from Harvard Law School and serving as *Harvard Law Review* president.

At one level, the Harvard, Harvard, Harvard, star, star, star pattern of Justice Jackson's early law clerk hiring is no surprise. Supreme Court clerkships were then, as they are now, demanding jobs for very bright, very well trained, very skillful young lawyers. Costelloe, Neal, and Gartner were all of that, both naturally and thanks to the Harvard Law School. They also came to Jackson highly recommended by his son William E. Jackson, who himself became a Harvard Law School student in fall 1941, just a few weeks before his father first sat on the Supreme Court bench. During the next two years, Bill Jackson served with Phil Neal and Murray Gartner on the *Harvard Law Review* and was influential at recommending that his father hire them as law clerks.

At another level, Justice Jackson's early law clerk hiring pattern is surprising. Jackson was no snob, and, more to the point, he was no Harvard man. Robert Jackson graduated from public schools in western New York State and never attended college. Indeed, he barely attended law school—he attended Albany Law School in 1911–12 for only the "senior" year of its two-year program. Jackson studied to become a lawyer, albeit an excellent and in time a prominent one, mostly by serving as an apprentice to two lawyers in Jamestown, New York. Thirty years later, Jackson had risen through private practice and notable public service, including as solicitor general of the United States and then as attorney general of the United States, to become a Supreme Court justice who hired as his law clerks some of the top graduates of Harvard Law School. He was happy with their work and fond of them personally.

In 1947, Justice Jackson tried something different. Following the three Harvard Law School men, Jackson hired a Temple Law School graduate to be his next law clerk. This man had been a successful law student, but in a non-elite law school and, indeed, in its night school division. His name was James Milton Marsh, and this is the story of how he became, improbably, a Supreme Court law clerk.

Justice Jackson in the World Spotlight

In spring 1945, while that year's Supreme Court term was still ongoing, Justice Jackson lost his law clerk, Phil Neal. This "loss" was consensual. It began when State Department official Alger Hiss, acting on the recommendation of Justice Felix Frankfurter, a great networker and talent scout, contacted Jackson's second-year law clerk, Phil Neal, about joining the State Department staff at the San Francisco conference that would produce the United Nations. Neal was interested and discussed this opportunity with Jackson, who was supportive and authorized Neal's departure. This did not, however, leave Jackson clerkless. Neal arranged for his good friend Murray Gartner, who had graduated earlier that winter from Harvard Law School and had already been hired to begin clerking for Jackson in summer 1945 (when Neal originally was planning to depart), to start "early," upon Neal's departure.

Shortly after Murray Gartner's arrival at the Supreme Court, still prior to the justices concluding their 1944 term and beginning their summer recess, Justice Jackson himself embarked on something similar to Neal—albeit at a higher level: he left the Court to serve in the executive branch. In late April 1945, President Harry S. Truman recruited Jackson to serve as U.S. representative and chief of counsel to prepare and prosecute before an international tribunal the European Axis leaders and others who had committed atrocities and war crimes.

President Truman announced Jackson's appointment on May 2, 1945, attracting significant attention and press coverage in the United States and internationally. Jackson continued, but with much more prominence and at an accelerating pace, to perform the war crimes prosecutor work he had been doing privately since Truman had recruited him a few weeks earlier. Jackson built his staff. He began to master new legal and factual material. He worked with officials across the U.S. government and with other relevant parties. He also juggled, and he somewhat neglected, Supreme Court work in the final weeks of its term.

On May 8, Nazi Germany surrendered unconditionally to the Allies. Germany thus ceased to exist. The Allies, still fighting Japan in the Pacific Theater, assumed the European Theater responsibilities of victory and military occupation. They began to deal with the devastated continent, which was covered with myriad survivors, displaced persons, defeated soldiers, and prisoners. The Allies increasingly discovered and struggled to comprehend evidence of enormous Nazi atrocities. The Allies, especially Justice Jackson, began to implement their leaders' clear but undeveloped wartime commitments to, after defeating the Nazis militarily, prosecute them as international criminals.

In mid-May, Justice Jackson made his initial trip to Europe, to consult military and civilian leaders and to survey the situation. Due to the trip, Jackson missed some Supreme Court sessions late in the term, and of course he was not present to work with his new law clerk, Murray Gartner.

On June 6, Jackson delivered to President Truman a formal report on his early progress and his plans. The president immediately released the report to the public, resulting in its widespread publication and its extensive discussion in the press and among the public.[1] Jackson's report stated, in detail and with eloquence, his commitments to law, fairness, expedition, and accountability in prosecuting leading Nazis.

The Supreme Court began its summer recess on June 18. Justice Jackson and his core staff left Washington for Europe that same afternoon. After a summer working in London and on the European continent, Jackson returned briefly to Washington that September to consult with President Truman and others. Later that month, Jackson relocated to Nuremberg in the U.S. zone of occupation in the former Nazi Germany. In November, Jackson began trial work there as U.S. chief prosecutor. The Nuremberg trial ran from November 1945 until October 1, 1946. Jackson's service there caused him to miss the full 1945–46 term of the Supreme Court.

James M. Marsh, Jackson-Watcher and Prospective Publisher

Among the millions who read or heard of Justice Jackson's May appointment to prosecute Nazi war criminals and his June report to President Truman was James M. Marsh, a thirty-one-year-old chief warrant officer in the U.S. Army Signal Corps. Since late 1944, he had been serving in Italy on the staff of U.S. Army brigadier general George Irving Back, chief signal officer of the Mediterranean Theater. Marsh's tasks there included working on office reorganization, preparing reports, selling fixed wire communication facilities that were located around the Mediterranean, appraising army signal facilities in Italy and France, and, following the surrender of Axis forces, transferring those facilities to the postwar Italian and French governments.

"Jim" Marsh had many accomplishments and a range of work experiences that predated his military experience. He was born and raised in Brookville, a county seat city in western Pennsylvania. (Brookville is located, coincidentally, about seventy miles south of Spring Creek, Pennsylvania, where Justice Jackson was born, twenty-one years before Marsh, on his family's farm.) In 1931, Marsh graduated from Brookville's high school. He then went to work as clerk and stenographer to a local attorney (who also was a relative).

In early 1934, Marsh became his county's manager of the Home Owners Loan Corporation (HOLC), a program that helped people in economic distress during the Great Depression to refinance their home mortgages. After a year, Marsh was promoted to the HOLC district office in Johnstown, Pennsylvania, where he worked as an administrative assistant in the accounting and legal departments.

In 1936, Marsh returned to Brookville. He worked for the next three-plus years selling cars and managing a local Oldsmobile dealership. In January 1940, he moved to Bradford, Pennsylvania, where he worked for the *Bradford News* as an office manager, handling wholesale distribution of the newspaper and other publications.

Nine months later, following the fall of France to Nazi Germany and the start of its blitz against Great Britain, Marsh enlisted in the army.

In early 1941, the army, which had trained Marsh for infantry service, assigned him to work in Pennsylvania at a major troop induction center. He handled property accounting and supervised office and warehouse personnel.

In June 1942, the army assigned Marsh to the Signal Corps in Philadelphia. His work there included designing and maintaining procurement records, setting office procedures, supervising personnel, and reviewing and analyzing contractor financial statements and accountants' reports.

In spring 1943, Marsh became, de facto, an army lawyer. He became assistant officer in charge of the legal division at the Signal Corps' Philadelphia Field Office. In that position, Marsh conducted legal research and wrote legal opinions on procurement and pricing matters. He also served as his commanding officer's executive officer, editing and approving legal opinions drafted by civilian staff, and as that chief's administrative officer, supervising a staff of thirty people.

In June of that year, Chief Warrant Officer Marsh also became a law student. At the urging of his commander, who recognized his aptitude for legal work, Marsh began to attend the Temple University School of Law. It was located on the ninth floor of Gimbel's Department Store on Ninth Street, just south of Market Street, in downtown Philadelphia.

Because Marsh had only a high school diploma and no college degree—indeed, he had no college experience at all, although he did take, at some point, a correspondence course in accounting—Pennsylvania rules decreed that he could not become a law student. Marsh was determined to get a law school education, and, working in tandem with Temple and state authorities, he obtained an exemption from the college degree requirement. He first persuaded Temple to admit him on the condition that the state grant him an exemption from the college-degree requirement. He then petitioned the Pennsylvania State Board of Law Examiners to exempt him based on his employment and military experiences and letters of recommendation. The State Board granted Marsh's petition, and soon he was a student in Temple law school's evening program. He continued to work as a Signal Corps officer on active duty by day and attended his law classes at night.

Marsh took a leave from law school to serve in Italy. By fall 1945, he was back in Philadelphia, still in the Signal Corps and again attending Temple Law School as an evening student. Marsh earned strong grades and, in time, a position on the staff of the *Temple Law Quarterly*, the school's law review.

By his "junior" (third) year, Marsh was the *Temple Law Quarterly's* legislation editor. In that capacity, he decided—no doubt with agreement and support from his colleagues on the *Quarterly*—that Justice Jackson's prosecutorial assignment was so significant and so underreported in legal periodicals that they should, in effect, cover it.[2]

The First Publication

Marsh's immediate objective was to republish Justice Jackson's April 13, 1945, speech at the American Society of International Law (ASIL) annual meeting dinner. Jackson delivered this speech the day after the death of President Franklin D. Roosevelt, on the Friday evening that began the weekend of his funeral and burial. Jackson's speech thus received little notice at that time. Indeed, the speech was unknown to President Truman and his aides when they, two weeks later, recruited Jackson to serve as U.S. chief of counsel to prosecute Nazi leaders as international criminals. But Jackson's ASIL speech belatedly drew prominent notice in the general press.[3] Marsh had read about Justice Jackson's assignment from President Truman and knew of Jackson's early pronouncements about how he was pursuing his task. In Marsh's view, Jackson's ASIL speech and all of his early work toward international prosecutions of Nazis for specific crimes, while covered well in the general press, were being insufficiently publicized and explicated for more sophisticated legal audiences.

So Marsh, in September or October 1945, telephoned Justice Jackson's Supreme Court chambers. By that time, Jackson was working in Europe, but Marsh succeeded in speaking to Jackson's law clerk, Murray Gartner. (Jackson left Gartner working in Washington, justice-less, for all of the 1945–46 Supreme Court term that Jackson missed while he was prosecuting in Nuremberg. Jackson made this up to Gartner by keeping him on as law clerk for an additional year—they worked together at the Court during the 1946–47 term.)

In their initial telephone conversation, Marsh asked Gartner if the *Temple Law Quarterly* could publish Justice Jackson's ASIL speech. Gartner, who himself recently had been a law student publishing a law review at Harvard, said that Jackson would have no objection to that—indeed, he would be pleased.[4] Gartner told Marsh that he would mail Marsh a copy of the speech.[5] A few weeks later, after Marsh had not received it, he wrote to Gartner to remind him to send it.[6] On October 29, Gartner sent the speech to Marsh.[7]

While Marsh was waiting to receive the speech, Jackson and his allied prosecutor counterparts signed and filed the Nuremberg indictment on October 18, 1945. On November 20, the International Military Tribunal (IMT) commenced trial proceedings in Nuremberg. The next day, Justice Jackson, chief prosecutor for the United States, delivered his opening statement to the tribunal.

Law student Marsh, following these developments, expanded the scope of his project. In its January 1946 issue, the *Temple Law Quarterly* published— as no other law review had or did—seven major documents. It captioned this collection "The Legal Basis for Trial of War Criminals." Its contents: Justice Jackson's April 13 speech to the ASIL,[8] his June 6 public report to President Truman,[9] a Walter Lippmann column regarding that historic Jackson report,[10] the August 8 London Agreement creating the IMT,[11] the IMT Charter that accompanied the London Agreement,[12] Jackson's statement on the signing of the London Agreement and IMT Charter,[13] and the October 18 indictment of the accused Nazi international criminals.[14]

At the end of February 1946, Chief Warrant Officer and *Temple Law Quarterly* legislation editor James Marsh sent a copy of the issue to Justice Jackson in Nuremberg. The trial there had just reached the end of the prosecution cases. Marsh, in a thorough cover letter written on "Army Service Forces, Office of Chief Signal Officer, Philadelphia Field Office of the Legal Division" stationery, apologized for printing difficulties that had delayed publication a bit. Looking ahead to the trial's conclusion, he asked Jackson to send the prosecutors' summations and the IMT's decision for publication. Marsh also expressed interest in publishing any article that Jackson might write about the trial after its conclusion. And Marsh noted, in closing, that Jackson's

> various treatises outlining the legal and moral necessity for the Nuremberg trial, and particularly your opening address, have been most inspiring to me as a law student and . . . , from discussions with many people, it has been made clear to me that they have a widespread salutary effect upon American thought.[15]

Marsh's letter reached Justice Jackson. After reading it, he wrote a note on it to his son, a young lawyer and U.S. Navy officer who was serving at Nuremberg as his father's executive assistant: "Bill please answer[.] I cant give them an article but we can give them stuff ie organization arguments now for example[.]"[16]

The Second Publication

Bill Jackson, following his father's instruction, wrote back to Marsh in March 1946. Jackson enclosed a copy of the justice's February 28 Nuremberg trial argument regarding the criminality of the Nazi organizations that the Allies were prosecuting, along with twenty-one individual defendants, "for whatever use you wish to make of it.... The problem of these organizations as well as what the prosecution proposes to do about them has generally been misunderstood and perhaps the Justice's statement may help in dispelling the confusion."[17]

In April, Marsh, now editor in chief of the *Temple Law Quarterly,* wrote to thank Bill Jackson.[18] Marsh later informed him that the *Quarterly* would be publishing, in its April 1946 issue, Justice Jackson's "organizations" argument almost in its entirety.[19]

In May, Bill Jackson advised Marsh that because Justice Jackson would not be returning to the United States "for a month or so," Marsh should send the April issue of the *Quarterly* to Jackson's Nuremberg office.[20] In June, Marsh did so.[21] The issue contains, as its second piece, a nearly complete text of Justice Jackson's February 28, 1946, Nuremberg courtroom argument on the criminality of Nazi organizations.[22]

The Third Publication

In late July 1946, while Justice Jackson was completing his prosecuting work at Nuremberg, Marsh obtained from Jackson's Pentagon office the text of his July 26 closing argument. On July 31, Marsh wrote to Jackson at the Supreme Court (to which he returned to work on August 3, for an interim period before he returned to Nuremberg to hear the international court there render its judgment). Marsh reported that he had arranged, despite the impending next issue of the *Temple Law Quarterly* already being at the printer, to publish in that issue a somewhat condensed version of Jackson's Nuremberg closing.[23] It soon appeared in the July 1946 (cover date) issue.[24]

The First Meeting

On November 1, 1946, Jim Marsh finally met Justice Jackson in person. Following the advice of his former army chief, Philadelphia attorney J. Harry LaBrum,

Marsh had told Jackson's office that he (Marsh) had plans to be in Washington soon and would like to stop at the Supreme Court to say hello to the justice. This was untrue—and the gambit worked. As LaBrum had predicted, Marsh was invited to Jackson's chambers on that Friday afternoon.

Marsh, accompanied by fellow Temple law student William Heefner, met with Justice Jackson for about an hour.[25] They discussed many topics, including the late president Franklin Roosevelt and the New Deal (in which both Jackson and Marsh had served, albeit in positions at somewhat differing levels). They discussed Jackson's recently completed prosecutorial work at Nuremberg. Jackson was, throughout their discussion, very careful. Marsh told Jackson that the *Temple Law Quarterly* planned to publish the full text of the Nuremberg tribunal's judgment and Jackson's final report to President Truman. Marsh asked Jackson to write a foreword to that issue, and he agreed to do so. (Following this midday Friday meeting, Jackson promptly dictated and edited into final form a four-paragraph essay, which his secretary typed up, marked with Jackson's final edits, and mailed to Marsh on the following Monday.[26])

As their meeting was winding down, Marsh followed advice that he had received from his wife and from LaBrum. Confessing that he had come to the meeting with an "ulterior motive," Marsh asked Jackson to consider hiring him as his law clerk.[27] Knowing that Supreme Court law clerks generally held college degrees and he had none, Marsh told Jackson of his (Marsh's) special admission to Temple Law School following the Pennsylvania State Board of Law Examiners' decision to grant Marsh's petition for permission despite lacking a college degree.

Jackson replied that he would think about it. He told Marsh that he (Jackson) had already talked to some people about possibly becoming his next law clerk. Indeed, he said he had made "a tentative commitment to one of the present Circuit Court clerks." But he advised Marsh "to file an application and letters of recommendation, on the chance that a vacancy might materialize with him or with one of the other Justices."[28]

Following this Washington meeting, Marsh returned to Philadelphia. Although he was a final semester law student, he spent a significant amount of time during the next two months working on matters relating to Justice Jackson.

During the week following their Washington meeting, Marsh wrote to Jackson. Marsh thanked the justice for his "courtesy" and "kindness" during Marsh's visit. He reported the sequence in which the *Temple Law Quarterly* would publish, beneath Jackson's foreword, final Nuremberg-related documents. Marsh stated his plan to prepare and publish an index to those and all Jackson and Nuremberg material published in the *Quarterly*. Marsh also promised that he and his law school dean would not give the printer who produced the *Quarterly* "any rest until this issue is in the mails."[29]

Marsh also wrote, simultaneously, to Jackson's secretary, Mrs. Elsie L. Douglas. He thanked her for sending Jackson's foreword, noting that he "was pleasantly surprised to receive it so promptly." He added, for himself and Heefner, that her "friendly hospitality was certainly a big factor in our enjoyment of the visit."[30]

Applying for the Clerkship

In the final weeks of 1946, Marsh avidly commenced his campaign to persuade Jackson to hire him as a law clerk. Marsh identified and wrote to at least ten attorneys whom he knew to some degree, telling them of his possible clerkship opportunity with Justice Jackson and asking them to write letters of recommendation to him. They included four of his former Signal Corps supervising officers (including one, Boston lawyer Leonard ["Andy"] Wheeler Jr., who had gone on to work for Jackson at Nuremberg during fall 1945), five friends or former employers from western Pennsylvania, and a Temple Law School dean.

Then, in early January 1947, Marsh wrote to Justice Jackson. Marsh reiterated his "hope," first voiced in their meeting two months earlier, to "be[] considered for a clerkship."[31] In his cover letter, carefully composed and thorough but confined to one page, Marsh summarized his "short on formal education and long on practical experience" background, including a year working in the Signal Corps Legal Division. He attached a comprehensive two-page summary of his life, education, and work experiences, reminding Jackson that the Pennsylvania State Board of Law Examiners had acted on this record plus letters of recommendation when they had granted Marsh's petition to attend law school despite not having a college degree. At the end of this summary, Marsh listed— not alphabetically; he listed Wheeler first—ten men who would be writing to Jackson on Marsh's behalf.[32]

Days later, Justice Jackson began to receive recommendation letters regarding Marsh. (As they arrived, Jackson had Elsie Douglas write Marsh to acknowledge receipt of his letter of application, and to inform Marsh that Jackson would keep it "on file until a later date when he will make his appointment."[33]) Jackson received two strong, succinct recommendation letters from Brookville, Pennsylvania, Marsh's hometown. Raymond Brown, an attorney, wrote that he had known Marsh from his childhood, that his reputation was excellent, and that he and another had been the first men in the county to volunteer for military service "at the [1940] outbreak of the late hostilities."[34] The presiding judge of Pennsylvania's Fifty-Fourth Judicial District, sitting in Brookville, wrote that he had known Marsh well for fifteen years, and that he was "able, affable, careful, fair, honest and reliable. He has demonstrated that hard work pays and everything accomplished by him to date has been through his own efforts while acting in the most painstaking manner."³⁵

Justice Jackson also received a longer, also glowing, letter from attorney Leonard Wheeler, formerly a prosecutor on Jackson's Nuremberg staff. Wheeler reported his perspective as one of Marsh's former senior officers:

> Although Marsh served abroad during the time I was Officer in Charge of the Signal Corps Legal Office in Philadelphia, I had an opportunity to see a good deal of him, and of his work, when I was Executive Officer and Assistant to the Legal Director in Washington. He [Marsh] is a man of great energy and ability, with a very quick and discerning mind and excellent judgment. When I first became associated with him I was frankly surprised to learn he was not already a member of the Bar, but was still studying law, as his work bore all the earmarks of a good lawyer. He was very quick to get at the heart of a problem, and very resourceful in its solution. He occupied a somewhat delicate position as assistant and close friend of my predecessor as Officer in Charge, but in spite of not being a member of the Bar, and in spite of his somewhat anomalous rank of Warrant Officer, he was able to keep the staff pulling together, to resolve disagreements soundly and tactfully, and to carry a great deal of the load of his chief. He is persistent and fearless, but he makes friends easily, and keeps them, and should go a long way in his profession.³⁶

Jackson next received a letter from the predecessor whom Wheeler had referenced, Philadelphia lawyer and former Signal Corps lieutenant colonel J. Harry LaBrum. He described supervising Marsh in the army as he performed administrative duties; making him, "although he was junior in rank to many other officers under my command," LaBrum's administrative officer; bringing Marsh along when LaBrum took charge of the Signal Corps' Field Division Legal Office (where Marsh supervised ten full-time lawyers, "did research and wrote legal opinions, and his work in all instances compared favorably with that done by our top lawyers"); and having Marsh as his (LaBrum's) executive officer during a tour in Italy. LaBrum also wrote of Marsh's successes in law school and described him as, overall, "a young man of sound judgment, tact, and good common sense. . . . My belief in his diligence, integrity and ability have [sic] been born of my long association with him, and substantiated by his accomplishments in spite of numerous obstacles."³⁷

The onslaught continued. By the end of January, Jackson had also received four more letters: from Temple Law School's administrative dean;³⁸ from a Philadelphia attorney who had, as Home Owners Loan Corporation (HOLC) district counsel in Johnstown, Pennsylvania, during 1935–36, supervised Marsh's work there;[39] from a western Pennsylvania attorney who did HOLC legal work with Marsh in his home county in 1933–35;[40] and from Marsh's former commanding officer, Brigadier General Back.[41] In varying words and based on differing experiences, each described Marsh's excellence and urged Jackson to hire him.

The Fourth Publication

Marsh himself added to what had become, in effect, a pile of material supporting his clerkship application. In its December 1946 issue, the *Temple Law Quarterly* published, beneath Jackson's foreword,[42] the IMT's (the Nuremberg international criminal court) final judgment,[43] the dissenting opinion of its Soviet member,[44] and Jackson's final report to President Truman.[45] The *Temple Law Quarterly* had indeed, and uniquely, under Marsh's leadership, brought fundamental Nuremberg trial and related documents to the attention of the U.S. legal academy and legal profession.

Jackson Interviews Marsh

Justice Jackson reacted positively to Marsh's publication efforts, to meeting him, to his clerkship application, and to the letters recommending his hiring. During the winter, Jackson invited Marsh, who that February received his Temple law degree, to come back to Washington, this time for a formal clerkship interview.

On the morning of March 4, 1947, they met in Justice Jackson's chambers at the Court. At some point during this meeting, Marsh asked Jackson to inscribe for Temple Law School's dean and its administrator two issues of the December 1946 *Temple Law Quarterly*, and Jackson did so graciously.

The core of this meeting, however, was a simple challenge from Jackson to Marsh. As Marsh recalled it, Jackson said the following:

> You give me a problem. I have no doubt that you can handle the job. But if I hire you as my law clerk we will be operating these chambers without even one college degree. I do not have a degree; my secretary [Elsie Douglas] does not have a degree; and you do not have a degree. I have always felt that my writing has suffered because of my lack of formal education. So I would be compounding a weakness. What do you have to say about that?[46]

Marsh also recalled his quick response:

> Mr. Justice, every lawyer and every judge in the country knows that you are the best writer on this Court, college degree or not. And if there is

anything that I can do well, it is write, rewrite and edit. I am sure you can find lots of lawyers who know more about the law than I do, but I don't think any of them could do the writing and critiquing part of the job as well as I can. So if you want someone with that kind of talent, and a flair for ideas and people and politics, who would be fiercely loyal to you, I'm your man.[47]

After the interview, Marsh returned to Philadelphia. The next day, he wrote to Elsie Douglas that Jackson's inscriptions in the copies of the December issue of the *Temple Law Quarterly* had created a "tremendous stir" at the school, and that his "exulta[nt]" fellow law students were each "most anxious to receive an inscribed copy." Marsh enclosed the names of ten students he said were "equally deserving," explained that he had arranged for ten additional copies of the December issue to be sent to her, and said that he would "be most grateful if [Justice Jackson] could take the time to inscribe copies to those students."[48]

These books soon arrived, and Douglas presented them, with Marsh's letter, to Justice Jackson. He inscribed them as Marsh had requested—on the letter, Jackson noted "Done" and wrote his initials.[49]

Jackson's Hiring Decision

In March 1947, Justice Jackson reached the point of deciding which of five prospects who had come to his attention in varying ways—Stafford R. Grady, D. Bret Carlson, Arlin M. Adams, Robert B. von Mehren, and James M. Marsh—would become his next law clerk. To focus his thinking, Jackson drew by hand, on a page of yellow legal paper turned sideways, a simple chart comparing the qualifications of each candidate. The categories of comparison were "Prior [Law Clerk] Service," "College [and/or law school]," "Relig[ion] etc," "Experience," and an unlabeled column for other relevant information.

Jackson noted, in this order, some of the qualifications and characteristics of each candidate. Stafford Grady was clerking for Jackson's friend Justice Harold M. Stephens of the D.C. Court of Appeals, had earned his law degree at the George Washington University, was a product of Catholic schools, and had administrative work experience.[50] Bret Carlson had not yet served as a law clerk, but he was from Jackson's adult hometown of Jamestown, had served in the U.S. Navy during World War II, and was about to graduate from Harvard Law School, where he was a "high scholar." Arlin Adams also had navy service and was about to graduate from the University of Pennsylvania Law School, where he ranked second in his class and was editor in chief of the *Pennsylvania Law Review*. Robert von Mehren was clerking for Judge Learned Hand on the U.S. Court of Appeals for the Second Circuit, had attended Harvard Law School (where he had been president of the *Harvard Law Review*), and was of German descent. Jim Marsh had no prior clerkship and nothing else that Jackson noted as relevant personal background or experience. Indeed, Jackson's only note regarding Marsh was his college: "None."

Justice Jackson then noted his decisions, in a series of circled numbers. Bret Carlson was his third choice. Robert von Mehren was his second. James Marsh was his first.[51]

Offer and Acceptance

On April 9, Jackson wrote to Marsh, at the Temple Law School office of the *Temple Law Quarterly,* to offer him a one-year clerkship starting July 1 at an annual salary of $4,288.68. (Jackson later requested, and the chief justice approved, paying Marsh the senior law clerk salary, $5,116.32 per year, based on Marsh's military service and work experiences.[52]) Jackson's letter covered numerous job details. Marsh's clerkship actually could begin, Jackson explained, with a couple of vacation weeks. Then Marsh's first task would be to deal with petitions for writs of certiorari, jurisdictional statements and briefs that would accumulate during the summer. Jackson explained that he would want Marsh to prepare and type up, for each of these, memoranda stating case history, facts, issues, and his recommendation. Jackson here indicated some of what had impressed him in Marsh's background: "There is in this work a good deal of typing of cert notes and memoranda, but I gather you are well qualified to run a typewriter. There is also research—no novelty to you."[53]

Jackson also explained that, later in the term, the clerkship would involve work on opinions. "I usually prepare a draft opinion. You will prepare and type a memo of criticisms, suggestions and substitutions. These we will discuss and work out together. I want from a clerk the most severe criticism of both form and substance." Jackson, again alluding to Marsh's work experiences, noted that "there is proofreading and editing of opinions for printing. That, too, is not new to you." With commendable candor, Jackson also described what many law clerks have experienced (and treasured): "Of course, a score of chores and incidentals are thrown in just to keep you out of mischief."

Justice Jackson, perhaps thinking that Marsh would come to the clerkship with less elite legal education than would his clerk peers, also included some reading recommendations for his "spare time." Jackson recommended articles that then Harvard Law School professor Felix Frankfurter had published in the *Harvard Law Review* "on the work of the Court from year to year, and also his book on the Federal Courts. . . . Also, of course, any reading on constitutional subjects, particularly the Commerce Clause and Due Process Clause, will prove useful."

Jackson closed by acknowledging that Marsh would probably find it difficult to find satisfactory housing for his family in overcrowded postwar Washington. "There is not much that one can do to assist another in this," Jackson wrote, "but if there is anything I will be glad to be of help."[54]

Nothing in Jackson's letter caused Marsh to have second thoughts about clerking. He received the offer letter on April 10 and immediately wrote back his grateful acceptance.[55] In a subsequent letter to Jackson's secretary, Elsie Douglas, who was trying to help the Marshes—they had been married since 1942 and had two young daughters—find an acceptable apartment, he added that his clerkship "appointment was most gratifying to the Law School as well as to me."[56]

Clerkship, Success, Gratitude

In Philadelphia, Chief Justice George W. Maxey, of the Pennsylvania Supreme Court, administered the oath of office to Marsh as a new law clerk to Justice Robert H. Jackson on June 30, 1947.[57]

Thereafter, Marsh moved with his family to Washington. Justice Jackson sent his messenger, Harry Parker, to pick them up when they arrived by train at Union Station.

Marsh soon reported to work. He was Jackson's sole law clerk during the Court's October term 1947. That winter, Jackson asked Marsh to stay on for a second year, and he accepted. He thus clerked for Jackson from summer 1947 until summer 1949.

Justice Jackson regarded Jim Marsh as one of his finest law clerks and remained close to him and his family, who returned to Philadelphia following Jim's clerkship, for the rest of Jackson's life. They exchanged letters, telephone calls, and gifts; saw each other regularly when Marsh visited Washington; and saw each other on occasion when Jackson visited Philadelphia (including the Marshes' home). Justice Jackson liked everything about Jim Marsh, and that warm feeling was entirely reciprocated—Marsh, for all of his long life, was filled with admiring memories of Jackson and deep gratitude for the life-shaping clerkship opportunity he gave to Marsh.[58]

That Justice Jackson turned out to be right—entirely right—about Jim Marsh does not, however, explain why Jackson made the unorthodox decision in 1947 to hire Marsh. That had many parts. One part was Jackson's open mind—he was receptive, as few other justices were then (or since), to a clerkship applicant who was not the usual. Marsh and Jackson also had a Nuremberg link, which mattered deeply to Jackson—Marsh's *Temple Law Quarterly* Nuremberg publications impressed Jackson and gave Marsh a connection to what Jackson regarded as the most important work of his life. Marsh's work history, military service, and work ethic also impressed Jackson very much.

Obviously Jackson liked Marsh when they met. Elsie Douglas liked him too—as Marsh came to learn, she urged Jackson to hire Marsh, and that mattered. And Marsh's letters of recommendation, in their quantity, coming from many impressive quarters, each filled with detail and enthusiasm, helped his cause.

Another factor, maybe the central one, was the matter of pure resemblance. When he looked at Jim Marsh—western Pennsylvania; little higher education; New Deal service; war-related service; ambition; writing skill; love of language; call to the law; earning his rise by succeeding again and again ahead of his peers, precociously; attracting admirers, believers, and mentors at each step—Robert Jackson saw a version of himself.

Notes

I thank Judge Arlin M. Adams, the late D. Bret Carlson, Jeffrey M. Flannery and his Library of Congress Manuscript Division colleagues, the late Murray Gartner, the late Stafford R. Grady, Dr. Stafford R. Grady Jr., the late William F. Heefner, the late Judge Cornelia G. Kennedy, the late Antoinette M. (Ferraro) Marsh, the late James M. Marsh, Phil C. Neal, Gregory L. Peterson, Janis Carlson Ruslink, Arthur R. Seder, Justice John Paul Stevens, and Robert B. von Mehren for their generous assistance; former St. John's law students Lecia M. Griepp and Andrew G. Lipton for excellent research; and Todd Peppers and Clare Cushman for their friendship, scholarship, and invitation to write this essay.

Jim Marsh, age ninety-two, died on June 25, 2006. Toni Marsh, his hometown sweetheart who became his wife and partner of sixty-four years, died that December. I had the great fortune to become their friend. I dedicate this essay to their dear memories and thank their children for their friendship and assistance.

1. See, for example, Robert C. Nixon (International News Service), "Jackson Urges Trial of All German Nazis," *Baltimore News-Post*, June 7, 1945, 1; Lewis Wood, "Punishing of War Criminals by U.S. Pledged by Jackson," *New York Times*, June 8, 1945, 1, 5; "The Text of Justice Jackson's Report to the President on Trials for War Criminals," *New York Times*, June 8, 1945, 4; George Connery, "No Hampering in War Trials, Jackson Says," *Washington Post*, June 8, 1945, 1, 2.

2. See James M. Marsh '47, "Law Quarterly Printed Nazi War Crimes Proceedings," *Temple Esquire* (Spring 1989): 2.

3. See, for example, Arthur Krock, "Justice Jackson's 'Honorable' Substitute for War," *New York Times*, April 27, 1945, 18 (summarizing Jackson's April 13 ASIL speech); "World Law," *Washington Post*, May 4, 1945, 6 (editorial summarizing and praising the speech).

4. Gartner might have checked, at least after the fact, that his permission to Marsh had Justice Jackson's approval. See William E. Jackson note, October 2, 1945 ("Marsh") (written in London) (in author's possession).

5. Murray Gartner to Mr. James M. Marsh, October 29, 1945, Box 43, Robert H. Jack-

son Papers, Manuscript Division, Library of Congress, Washington, D.C. (hereafter cited as RHJL).

6. James M. Marsh to Murray Gartner, Esq., October 22, 1945, RHJL, Box 43.

7. Murray Gartner to James M. Marsh, October 29, 1945, RHJL, Box 43.

8. Honorable Robert H. Jackson, "The Rule of Law Among Nations," *Temple Law Quarterly* 19 (1946): 135–43.

9. Honorable Robert H. Jackson, "Justice Jackson's Report to President Truman on the Legal Basis for Trial of War Criminals," *Temple Law Quarterly* 19 (1946): 144–56.

10. Walter Lippmann, "An Historic State Paper," *Temple Law Quarterly* 19 (1946): 157–59 (reprinting a June 1945 Lippmann newspaper column).

11. "Agreement for the Establishment of an International Military Tribunal," *Temple Law Quarterly* 19 (1946): 160–61.

12. "Charter of the International Military Tribunal," *Temple Law Quarterly* 19 (1946): 162–68.

13. Honorable Robert H. Jackson, "Statement of Chief U.S. Counsel Upon Signing of the Agreement," *Temple Law Quarterly* 19 (1946): 169–71.

14. "Indictment against Major Nazi War Criminals," *Temple Law Quarterly* 19 (1946): 172–235. The *Quarterly* also published, in the back half of this issue, collected materials concerning the new International Court of Justice (ICJ). The U.S. Senate had, on July 28, 1945, ratified the Charter of the United Nations (UN) and, annexed thereto, the statute of the ICJ. This court, known informally as the World Court, supplanted the Permanent Court of International Justice (PCIJ) that had existed under the League of Nations to resolve disputes among member states in accordance with international law. The Temple journal published, as an assembled set of ICJ materials, a background report by Judge Manley O. Hudson, U.S. representative to the PCIJ and instrumental supporter of the World Court, plus the UN Charter, the ICJ statute, and a Hudson essay on the World Court's future. See Hon. Manley O. Hudson, "Report of the Honorable Manley O. Hudson," *Temple Law Quarterly* 18 (1946): 236–46; "Charter of The United Nations," ibid., 247–75; "Statute of the International Court of Justice," ibid., 275–89; Hon. Manley O. Hudson, "World Court—The Next Step," ibid., 290–95.

15. James M. Marsh to Honorable Robert H. Jackson, February 28, 1946, 1–2, RHJL, Box 108.

16. Note from Robert H. Jackson to William E. Jackson, on letter from James M. Marsh to Honorable Robert H. Jackson, February 28, 1946, ibid., 1. Bill Jackson added on this letter his note that Marsh's letter should be filed in Justice Jackson's office files under "Misc[ellaneous]. Coresp[ondence]. M.," and presumably it was. Bill Jackson also, until his death in 1999, kept the January 1946 issue of the *Temple Law Quarterly* in his personal papers regarding Nuremberg.

17. Lieutenant (jg) William E. Jackson to James M. Marsh, March 21, 1946, RHJL, Box 108.

18. James M. Marsh to Lieutenant (jg) William E. Jackson, April 11, 1946, RHJL, Box 108.

19. James M. Marsh to Lieutenant (jg) William E. Jackson, April 26, 1946, RHJL, Box 108.

20. Lieutenant (jg) William E. Jackson to Mr. James M. Marsh, May 13, 1946, RHJL, Box 108.

21. James M. Marsh to Honorable Robert H. Jackson, June 20, 1946, RHJL, Box 108.

22. See Robert H. Jackson, "The Law Under Which Nazi Organizations Are Accused of Being Criminal," *Temple Law Quarterly* 19 (1946): 371–89. The opening article in the issue is William O. Douglas, "The Lasting Influence of Justice Brandeis," 361–70.

23. James M. Marsh to Honorable Robert H. Jackson, July 31, 1946, RHJL, Box 108.

24. See Robert H. Jackson, "Closing Arguments for Conviction of Nazi War Criminals," *Temple Law Quarterly* 20 (1946): 85–107.

25. William F. Heefner, telephone interview with author, August 29, 2006. Much of my account of this meeting is based on Heefner's recollection.

26. See Elsie L. Douglas to Mr. James M. Marsh, November 4, 1946 (with typed and marked foreword), RHJL, Box 108. Jackson's foreword, as published as the opening page of the *Quarterly*'s December 1946 issue, is dated November 5, 1946. See Robert H. Jackson, "Foreword: The Nürnberg Trial Becomes an Historic Precedent," *Temple Law Quarterly* 20 (1946): 167.

27. James M. Marsh and Antoinette M. Marsh, interview by Gregory L. Peterson and John Q. Barrett, Chautauqua Institution, Chautauqua, New York, October 24, 2003. Antoinette Marsh believed, with an understandable Depression mentality, that one should not hesitate to ask another, more powerful person for a job, because a job is "your first line of defense" in life. Ibid.

28. James M. Marsh to Dr. Elden S. Magaw, January 10, 1947. Jackson was referring to Stafford R. Grady, law clerk to Justice Harold M. Stephens of the District of Columbia Court of Appeals. See note 51.

29. James M. Marsh to Honorable Robert H. Jackson, November 7, 1946, RHJL, Box 108. In this letter, Marsh proposed a title for Jackson's foreword. Elsie Douglas promptly wrote back, relaying Jackson's answer "that he will rely on your good judgment to choose an appropriate title for the foreword." Elsie L. Douglas to Mr. James M. Marsh, November 9, 1946, RHJL, Box 108. As the opening page of its December 1946 issue, the *Quarterly* published Jackson's foreword with the title that Marsh had proposed. See note 26.

30. James M. Marsh to Mrs. Elsie L. Douglas, November 7, 1946, RHJL, Box 108. A few weeks later, Marsh wrote again to Douglas, "to let [her] and Justice Jackson know that the material for the special issue is now being worked on by the printer and he has promised to have it out by late December without fail." James M. Marsh to Mrs. Elsie L. Douglas, November 24, 1946, RHJL, Box 108.

31. James M. Marsh to Honorable Robert H. Jackson, January 7, 1947, RHJL, Box 135, Folder 12.

32. Jackson's office files, as archived at the Library of Congress, seem to contain letters from only nine of the ten.

33. Elsie L. Douglas to Mr. James M. Marsh, January 15, 1947, RHJL, Box 135, Folder 12.

34. Raymond E. Brown to Honorable Robert H. Jackson, January 14, 1947, RHJL, Box 135, Folder 12.

35. Jesse C. Long to Honorable Robert H. Jackson, January 14, 1947, RHJL, Box 135, Folder 12.

36. Leonard Wheeler Jr. to Mr. Justice Robert H. Jackson, January 14, 1947, at 1, RHJL, Box 135, Folder 12.

37. Letter from J. Harry LaBrum to Hon. Robert H. Jackson, January 15, 1947, at 1–2, RHJL, Box 135, Folder 12.

38. Elden S. Magaw to Honorable Robert H. Jackson, January 20, 1947, RHJL, Box 135, Folder 12.

39. J. Charles Short to Mr. Justice Jackson, January 21, 1947, RHJL, Box 135, Folder 12.

40. Merritt H. Davis to Honorable Robert H. Jackson, January 27, 1947, RHJL, Box 135, Folder 12.

41. George I. Back to Honorable Robert H. Jackson, February 3, 1947, RHJL, Box 135, Folder 12.

42. Jackson, "Foreword," 167.

43. "Judgment of the International Military Tribunal against Major Nazi War Criminals and Criminal Organizations," *Temple Law Quarterly* 20 (1946): 168–317.

44. I. T. Nikitchenko, "Dissenting Opinion of the Soviet Member of the International Military Tribunal," *Temple Law Quarterly* 20 (1946): 318–37.

45. Robert H. Jackson, "Justice Jackson's Final Report to the President Concerning the Nürnberg War Crimes Trial," *Temple Law Quarterly* 20 (1946): 338–44.

46. James M. Marsh, "Supreme Court Justice without a College Degree," *Supreme Court Historical Society Quarterly* 21 (2000): 19.

47. Ibid.

48. James M. Marsh to Mrs. Elsie L. Douglas, March 5, 1947, RHJL, Box 108.

49. Note by Robert H. Jackson on letter from James M. Marsh to Mrs. Elsie L. Douglas, March 5, 1947, ibid. Jackson also received belatedly, after he had interviewed Marsh on March 4, one more letter from a Marsh recommender. Brigadier General Conrad Snow, who during the war had served as counsel and legal division director under the army's chief signal officer, wrote that Marsh's service in the Philadelphia Field Office had been "of the highest efficiency." General Snow noted that Marsh had borne "a very large share of the administrative burden of the office," described him as "assiduous, intelligent and cooperative to a high degree," and gave him a "hearty recommendation." General Snow also reminded Jackson that they had known each other when they served together in the American Bar Association's House of Delegates, probably in the late 1920s or early 1930s. And General Snow noted, in closing, that it was his legal office that had sent then colonel Leonard Wheeler from Washington to join Jackson's staff at Nuremberg. See Brigadier General Conrad E. Snow to Mr. Justice Jackson, March 6, 1947, RHJL, Box 135, Folder 12.

50. Stafford Grady served as a deputy clerk of court at the U.S. District Court for the District of Columbia for his final twenty months as a student at the George Washington Law School. He then, in July 1945, began to clerk for Justice Stephens at the D.C. Court of Appeals. In that approximate time period, Justice Jackson interviewed Grady and offered him a clerkship for the following Supreme Court term, 1946–47. Jackson later pushed that offer back because, after his year away at Nuremberg, he be-

lieved that he owed Murray Gartner a full clerkship year and kept him on instead. In November 1946, Jackson believed that he still had a tentative commitment to employ Grady during the following Supreme Court term, 1947–48. See note 28 and accompanying text. In the end, that changed. Jackson hired Marsh to clerk during 1947–48, and Grady, after clerking for Justice Stephens until November 1947, became an assistant U.S. attorney in the District of Columbia. See generally Justice Harold M. Stephens to Stafford Grady, September 9, 1946, at 1 ("I assume you have heard nothing from Mr. Justice Jackson, otherwise you would have mentioned it."), in Box 15, Papers of Harold M. Stephens, Manuscript Division, Library of Congress, Washington, D.C.; "Stafford Grady Takes Oath," *Washington Times-Herald,* November 11, 1947, 5; Stafford R. Grady, telephone interview by author, September 6, 2006.

51. Jackson's chart ranking the candidates is in RHJL, Box 135, Folder 12. Although the chart is undated, it seems that Jackson decided in March 1947, probably very shortly after their March 4 meeting, to hire Marsh as his next law clerk. See Robert H. Jackson to Dr. Charles T. McCormick, March 31, 1947, 1 ("I have made a commitment as to a law clerk for the coming year so that it will not [be] possible to consider a University of Texas man this time."), RHJL, Box 135, Folder 12.

52. See Robert H. Jackson to The Chief Justice [Fred M. Vinson], June 18, 1947, RHJL, Box 135, Folder 12.

53. Robert H. Jackson to Mr. James M. Marsh, April 9, 1947, 1, RHJL, Box 135, Folder 12.

54. Ibid., 1–2.

55. See James M. Marsh to Honorable Robert H. Jackson, April 10, 1947, RHJL, Box 135, Folder 12.

56. James M. Marsh to Mrs. Elsie L. Douglas, April 12, 1947, RHJL, Box 135, Folder 12.

57. See "Oath," *Philadelphia Inquirer,* July 1, 1947, 16 (publishing a photograph of the event).

58. See generally James M. Marsh, "The Genial Justice: Robert H. Jackson," *American Bar Association Journal* 60 (1974): 306–9, reprinted in *Albany Law Review* 68 (2005): 41–49; James M. Marsh, "Affirm, If Possible," *Supreme Court Historical Society Quarterly* 18 (1997): 4–5.

RAYMOND S. TROUBH

A Great American

Tribute to Mr. Justice Burton

The first part of this essay consists of my remarks at a convocation of the Bar of the U.S. Supreme Court on May 24, 1965, honoring, in a memorial service, the life and career of Mr. Justice Harold Hitz Burton, who died on October 28, 1964. The second part features additional reflections of my experiences as a law clerk. I was the only former law clerk who was privileged to speak about Mr. Justice Burton at the proceedings, which included the reminiscences of congressional colleagues and political and judicial figures who were important in Burton's life. Former president Harry S. Truman was originally listed among the speakers, but the illness of his wife, Bess, caused him to cancel his appearance. His telegram (no e-mail in those days) stated: "I HAVE BEEN HOPING AGAINST HOPE THAT MRS. TRUMAN AND I COULD AT-TEND THE SERVICES IN HONOR OF THE LATE JUSTICE BURTON. IT NOW APPEARS THAT IT WILL NOT BE POSSIBLE FOR US TO BE PRESENT. THIS IS THE CIRCUMSTANCE THAT I DEEPLY REGRET, FOR I HAD EXPECTED TO EXPRESS ON THIS OCCASION MY HIGH REGARD AND DEEP RESPECT FOR HIS MAGNIFICANT SERVICE TO THE NATION AND IN A PERSONAL WAY MY WARM FRIENDSHIP FOR HIM. HARRY S. TRUMAN"

Truman was a hero of mine for his strength, basic unvarnished honesty, and solid common sense, and I was looking forward to meeting him. He was the first presidential candidate for whom I voted. I also thought Truman, basically a political unknown from the Tom Prendergast Democrat machine in Kansas City, who had the guts to make Burton his first appointee to the U.S. Supreme Court, had made a remarkable and courageous choice. Think of it—Burton, a conservative Republican from Ohio is the first Supreme Court appointment by Truman, a conventional machine Democrat from Missouri. Among the reasons, apparently, was that the two men had served together on the Truman Senatorial War Preparedness Committee investigating corruption in supplying U.S. arms and matériel during World War II. Truman admired the then-senator

Burton's integrity, coolness, and fairness, and these qualities reportedly inspired him to ignore the pressure from his party-line cronies in nominating Burton instead of a Democratic ally.

This is really the point of my apparent and youthful innocence, guilessness, naïveté, and unsophistication in the remarks appearing below—that is, the proof that some good guys indeed do finish first. I felt then (in 1965) and, upon reflection, feel today that Harold H. Burton was an outstanding example of humanity at its best—fair, honest, loyal, reasonable, generous, and courageous. At the time of his retirement from the Supreme Court, his colleagues said of him—"Without exception, we believe that of all the Justices who have sat on this Bench, not one has adhered more closely than you to the ideal for which we all strive—'Equal Justice Under Law.'"

I believed that every word of this praise then was accurate and sincere, and I believe now that every word of it was genuinely felt, and I believe each of the justices who signed this paean of tribute believed it also. One should contrast this picture of this decent man with the Supreme Court jungle populated by some conflicted personalities as depicted in the riveting tales told by Noah Feldman in a book called *Scorpions,* describing the enmities, jealousies, envies, and disappointments among Franklin D. Roosevelt's four powerful appointments to the Supreme Court: Justices Black, Douglas, Frankfurter, and Jackson.[1] I was a law clerk to Burton then and witnessed these gentlemen in action, and I can concur in much of what Feldman says of these giant personalities and their peccadilloes.

1965 Memorial Service Remarks

Mr. Chairman, Mrs. Burton, and Friends:[2]

The Chairman has not indicated why I am here today to offer my tribute to Mr. Justice Burton. Partly I think it is because I was his only law clerk from Bowdoin College. I was born a New Englander as he was. Bowdoin is a small college in Maine, and its graduates tend to stick together. They are proud of each other's achievements. I think Justice Burton was just a little pleased by the fact that one of his many law clerks was graduated from the same school as he, just as he was proud of the fact that Melville Weston Fuller, the Chief Justice of the United States for 22 years, was also a Bowdoin graduate. Justice Burton used to introduce me as his Bowdoin clerk or his "Bowdoin boy" even though he frequently forgot my name. Justice Burton was very close to Bowdoin; he spent many years on its Governing Boards, and he was dedicated to preserving its traditions and promoting its well-being. When he was awarded an honorary degree there in 1937 he was described by President Kenneth C. M. Sills in down east style as "honest as the sunlight and brave as they make them."

I want to tell you about working with Justice Burton in a close personal relationship and speak of him as a human being occupying a high place—not as a Senator, not as a mayor of a great city, not as a Justice of the United States Supreme Court, not as a public figure. It's a refreshing and a proud job that I have to perform here because Harold Burton was such a totally decent man. He was without guile and without deceit. When you use words to describe him as courageous, sincere, democratic, just, honorable, you say them without fear of contradiction—because no one knew him otherwise. He dignified and enriched everything and everybody around him. He treated all men alike. He had a reverence for this Court unmatched by anyone—he never entered this building without first removing his hat. When one works closely with a man for a year as his law clerk nothing really can be hidden. After a short time you know whether you're dealing with the genuine article or whether there are some artificialities to be suffered. From the day that Harold Burton greeted us as his new law clerks to the day we left we experienced a full term of yearning with him for fairness and truth in all matters that he was called upon to give judgment.

The imposing quality was that of total conscientiousness—absolute dedication. He refused to follow blindly the fashion of the day and cared not because one group of commentators thought he was too liberal on occasion and others thought he was too conservative. He was as free of prejudice as any human being could be.

As qualified and as salty an observer as Felix Frankfurter has said of Harold Burton that "No member of the Supreme Court deserves admiration more than you for exercising with exquisite and unqualified fidelity the judicial powers entrusted to members of the Court." Mr. Justice Frankfurter also said that Harold Burton "never consciously or unconsciously relied on any consideration except the traditional basis on which the Anglo-American courts adjudicate cases before them." I could go on and on but the point, I think, is made.

While he was a saintly man, he was no saint. I remember that he could show a bit of temper on occasion—one of which was always on our late Friday night sessions at the Court when he felt that one or the other law clerk had not done as much homework on the cases and petitions to be discussed as Justice Burton himself had done. The penalty for this lapse was to have the Justice wheel around to the bookshelf of bound volumes behind him and read the precedent aloud and in full. We were fortunate indeed when these precedents were written by men of brevity. The other occasion for temper that I recall vividly was when a fellow Justice who sat to his left—the only Justice in recent years to use the spittoon—missed. Now Justice Burton never spat, never smoked, never swore, and never drank. I wrote that recently, but I have since been corrected by Mrs. Cheatham, his secretary of 18 years. She told me that some years ago she once heard him say "damn."

Most of you will recall that until only a few years ago the Justices met on Saturday mornings privately, where they discussed the petitions for certiorari, and voted on cases.

Mr. Justice Burton had a tradition of meeting with his law clerks on Friday nights to review every item of Saturday's agenda. We worked very hard and very late on those Fridays, and I can assure you our lights burnt far into the night. I suppose under the current edict banning excessive use of electricity in government we would have had to hold our night meetings under streetlights—which, I may add, would not have daunted Justice Burton in the slightest. He approved of frugality in high places. He is reported to have come to Washington to take his place as a United States Senator in an upper berth.

Justice Burton gave his clerks complete freedom of expression during those nightly sessions. We were encouraged to suggest how we would vote. We could criticize his views—we were equals in shirtsleeves on those nights. I remember one well-known case of that term where a California gambler claimed he had been denied due process of law when the police had a key made to his house and planted a microphone in various rooms, including the bedroom. We spent hours until early in the morning going over the enormous record in that case and practically reconstructed to the minutest detail the police activity claimed to be illegal. We carefully reviewed constitutional cases on point and relevant cases in which Mr. Justice Burton had written a majority or dissenting opinion. It wasn't until late the next afternoon as we waited in our office for the Saturday conference to end that we knew how the Justice voted. But the one clear thing was that he alone voted—he had the responsibility and exercised it only after the most painstaking analysis and research. The passage of time meant nothing—the objective was to arrive at the right, the truth, justice if you will. I believe that he was the best prepared of all the Justices both for the Saturday conference and for the cases to be heard the following week. Even though he was so well prepared, while on the bench he didn't press counsel merely to bait him or ask questions to show off his knowledge of the case or his legal background. Personal glory was not his goal. Justice Burton was a gentleman on and off the bench.

I must tell you about some of the important cases in which he wrote majority decisions or wrote a dissenting opinion.

It was quite clear from the beginning he was going to be independent. His votes were never automatically conditioned by the nature of the parties to the case. For example, he voted against the President of the United States, in 1952, in the *Steel Seizure* case.[3] He frequently was the lone dissenter. In those days of identities and labels it was good to work for a man who could be typed neither as a "judicial activist" nor one preaching restraints; neither as a "liberal" nor a "conservative"; neither for widows and orphans nor against them. If we must have a label he may be called a "swing man." No one could depend with certainty that he would vote either with one group or another merely by looking at his prior affiliations. His opinions are marked by reliance on legislative history and by prodigious research—and, although he always had two willing and eager law clerks—he himself took a most active role in this research.

He had a well-defined judicial philosophy, and his concept of the role of the Supreme Court in the American system is best illustrated by the story he loved to tell of the young boy on the sand lot who told him, "Well, when we want to last a full nine inning ball game, then we have an umpire." The essence of Justice Burton's judicial philosophy appears in this explanation of the "umpire" story. He said, "The fact is that our Constitution has established a governmental system in which the umpires, although not infallible, are expected to be impartial, to know the rules, and to apply them promptly and courteously to the best of their ability."

He had a habit which endeared him to the newspaper reporters covering the Court, of expressing clearly in the opening paragraphs both the questions raised by the case and the Court's disposition of them. You had to read no further than the second paragraph to know the answer. And while he frequently was assigned difficult cases of interpretation of congressional intent because of his experience as an administrative and political official—many of which decisions never appeared in the headlines of the day—he wrote some important decisions. His opinion in the *Henderson* case[4] in a way anticipated the 1954 school segregation decision. He held there, for a unanimous Court, that the Interstate Commerce Act was violated by separation of races on dining cars in trains traveling in interstate commerce. His decision in the *Laburnum*[5] case, which has found its way into the casebooks, held that a union could be sued in a state court for damages arising from conduct which also constituted an unfair labor practice under the Taft-Hartley Act. During his first term on the Court, he wrote the important *American Tobacco*[6] decision, which attracted widespread attention as a significant application of the "conspiracy" language of the Sherman Act to participants in an oligopoly market structure.

Perhaps even as noteworthy were his very strong dissents both in the *DuPont*[7] case, where he felt that a 40-year period was too long for the government to wait before applying the Clayton Act to the DuPont company's earlier acquisition of General Motors stock; and in the baseball[8] antitrust case where he showed to the satisfaction of many—although not a majority of the Court—that baseball was really a big business and should be subject to the application of the antitrust laws. I want to remind you that Justice Burton was not anti-baseball. He was in fact an avid sports fan. I have it on good authority that he was a brilliant quarterback for the Bowdoin team in the seasons 1908–1909. I assure you from my own knowledge that he thought the Cleveland Indians were the ball players of the century. I shouldn't publicly acknowledge this but he was even willing to wager a dime or two on their chances in the World Series.

The conscientiousness of which I spoke earlier is perhaps best illustrated by a wonderful anecdote which was repeated often after his death: "One Sunday just before the opening of the baseball season, the Mayor of Cleveland stood in the ball park, pegging fast balls to his secretary. This was because the year before, throwing the first ball for the Indians' opening game, he had been a bit wild. Harold Hitz Burton, who was to become a United States Senator and Associate Justice of the United States Supreme Court, was not wild again."[9]

Now even a man of conscience needs to relax on occasion. As an ex-Senator he had privileges in the Senate Pool, and he used to sneak away on an afternoon for a dip with his former colleagues. His other relaxing moments came when he could mingle with crowds visiting the Court. He loved to answer the questions of visitors standing on the other side of the gates. He gave guided tours of the Court, and he was good at it because the history of the Court was his hobby—he was once offered a tip by a visitor who didn't recognize him as a Justice but who recognized that he'd been a peach of a guide. His most publicized tour of the Court was the one he gave to the nation on Ed Murrow's *Person to Person* television show. There he and Mrs. Burton gave a gracious, informative, and lively tour.

Mrs. Burton merits a full share of this tribute. She was more than a right arm. She contributed immensely to his successes. She drove him all over the state of Ohio in an old car while he campaigned for Senator. She worked with him for hours and hours while he mastered public speaking and helped him overcome a difficult stutter. She helped the incoming law clerks overcome their own nervousness too. She arranged lively birthday parties for each law clerk in Chambers. She supplied the ice cream, cake, favors, and surprises. She brought in mince pie on Thanksgiving Day, cherry pie on Washington's birthday, and there were gifts from summer trips to Switzerland, and theatre parties and other happy occasions.

Earlier I spoke of Justice Burton's rare qualities—of his many virtues—and I am going to close on that note for that is his legacy to us. He was a man of the old-fashioned virtues—a man of integrity. As Justice Frankfurter has said, a fitting title for a biography of Justice Burton would be "A Triumph of Character."[10] From his early days he picked out five great men from whom he sought to learn: Washington, Marshall, Lincoln, Edison, and Theodore Roosevelt. We here can learn from Justice Burton's life that the old-fashioned virtues remain triumphant; that they still merit rewards of leadership and honor. We can learn from his life that decency and faith and fairness should govern us in our transactions with other men.

Additional Recollections

Nearly fifty years after giving that memorial address, I call upon my memory to provide some additional details about my experiences as a law clerk. I also discuss my experiences as a law clerk to Chief Judge Thomas W. Swan, who, when I graduated in 1952 from Yale Law School, was the presiding judge of the Second Circuit Court of Appeals. The reason is that one of Burton's unbending rules was that every one of his newly appointed law clerks must have seen prior duty as a law clerk in another court. My serving Chief Judge Swan certainly qualified me, but the strong differences in the two judge's personalities and the strong differences in my relationships with each was so striking that I believe they are worth some discussion in this essay.

After my graduation from Yale Law School in June 1952, I went immediately to work for Chief Judge Thomas W. Swan of the Second Circuit Court of Appeals in New York City. As he also lived and had offices in Connecticut and the court convened in New York only one week a month, most of my work was done near home. I had been recommended to Judge Swan by his law clerk, Ed Snyder, and although my record really did not overwhelmingly qualify me for the job, Judge Swan was near retirement and wanted a low-key, hardworking, nonconfrontational law clerk, which he decided I could become.

Judge Swan and I did not see things from the same point of view. Previously dean of the Yale Law School, he was an ultraconservative, brilliant, cautious New Englander who married a wealthy woman (Mabel Dick Swan was an heiress to the great Dictaphone Company in Chicago) and had, as I recall, no children. I was a knee-jerk liberal Jewish law clerk, and I wanted to find a way to decide nearly every case in favor of the defendants and against the government or against the railroad, as it were. Our biggest personal battle came during the appeal of the alleged Rosenberg spies; Judge Irving Kaufman, at the federal district court level, had sentenced them to death for spying on behalf of the Soviet government during a period of atom bomb hysteria. I sided with Judge Jerome Frank, who was on the Second Circuit panel that heard the appeal. Judge Frank was, like me, Jewish and a knee-jerk liberal, but he was also a man of considerable achievement who had been a Securities and Exchange Commission (SEC) commissioner and had taught at Yale Law School. I wrote Judge Swan memo after memo pointing out what I thought to be inadequacies and prejudices in the trial and inadequacies in the rulings of Judge Kaufman, but to no avail: the Rosenbergs' lost their appeals, and they were each executed, after some last-minute legal maneuvering at the U.S. Supreme Court level. I am not saying I thought they were innocent, but I believed a new trial under more balanced media conditions was required. I also thought Ethel Rosenberg, at least, would have received a less severe sentence from a temperate judge who did not need to go to a synagogue for religious guidance on sentencing convicted felons, as Judge Kaufman had.

Lawyers then widely considered the Second Circuit Court of Appeals the most important federal circuit court. It had always had prominent judges who had been well-known lawyers and educators. Foremost among them was the great Learned Hand, a powerful and brilliant man before whom even the most astute and successful lawyers quailed. If he thought a lawyer was dumb or his argument weak, Judge Hand would turn his chair so only the back showed to the appellant. He loved singing in his chambers old sea-dog chanteys, many with dirty lyrics, and he vilified several sitting federal judges in legal memos intended for internal use only. His cousin, Gus Hand, served with him and was equally brainy but not as troublesome. Other august judges on this court then were Jerome Frank, Charles Clark, and Harrie B. Chase, of Vermont. Judge Swan, as chief judge, had to keep these prima donnas productive yet in check. It was a tough job, given their huge egos and lifetime appointments, but because of their respect for Swan's evenhandedness and basic honesty, they toed the line.

My first wife, Betty, and I lived downstairs in a nice two-family home on Bradley Street in New Haven from June 1952 until June 1953. We had the usual good life of a young, ambitious working couple there. We ate in wonderful, inexpensive Italian restaurants; we saw pre-Broadway tryouts; we went to the beaches around Madison, Connecticut, where Judge Swan lived. Judge Swan's only real indulgences, so far as I could tell, were taking a hot bath while smoking cigarettes and drinking martinis after a round of golf with his cronies. In the evenings a little bridge was permitted.

We were proud of my position. This was a great job, being a law clerk to the chief judge of one of the great courts in the United States. I even became a little cocky. My relationship, however, with the judge stayed ragged, largely because of our political differences. It turned out, however, that the then-president of Bowdoin College, Kenneth "Casey" Sills, had, without telling me, mentioned to the only living Bowdoin College graduate on the U.S. Supreme Court that I was a law clerk to Judge Swan and that perhaps Mr. Justice Harold H. Burton, Bowdoin 1906, might consider me as a law clerk to him. To my amazement, Burton brought me down to Washington, interviewed me, and after checking with Swan—who gave me a decent but not great letter of recommendation—named me as one of his two law clerks for the 1954 term of the Supreme Court.

I was a hero to my classmates at Yale Law School, to my family, and to myself. A Supreme Court clerkship in those days, and even today, was something for which every law student from every American law school would kill. Each justice then had two law clerks, with the exception of the chief justice, who took three, and Mr. Justice William O. Douglas, who only took one. I arrived in

Washington to assume my clerkship on nearly the very day that former governor Earl Warren, of California, arrived to take up his seat as chief justice, having been appointed by President Dwight D. Eisenhower to replace Fred Vinson, who had died suddenly. (As life would have it, Earl Warren's mentor and sponsor in California was Jesse Steinhardt, who was the father of my future wife's mother.)

This was the time of *Brown v. Board of Education*, which had been argued in the 1953 term but had not been decided. Being around the Court at that time with great and overpowering judges such as Felix Frankfurter, Hugo L. Black, Robert H. Jackson, and William O. Douglas—brilliant, imposing men—is a memory that I cherish. The bench also included Justice Sherman Minton, who, during oral arguments before the Court, chewed and spat tobacco juice, which, when it missed the spittoon, often stained Burton's pants and shoes. Burton, being a peace-loving, nonconfrontational man, ignored the stains and juices.

Burton was not considered a legal giant, but he was, I believe, the most prejudice-free person I ever encountered. He was a naturally conservative, parsimonious New Englander, but I don't believe he ever decided anything in a biased way based on race, color, or creed or even because of the inability of some attorneys to argue well or properly.

My fellow law clerk at that time was a very bright and convivial University of Pennsylvania law graduate named Jim Ryan. Burton believed his law clerks were part of his family. We celebrated everyone's birthday in his chambers; his wife, Selma, would bring the cakes and presents, and we all participated.

Burton was the hardest-working judge on that Court. We worked every single Saturday when the Court was in session. Jim Ryan and I would come in and type away during the morning while Justice Burton met with his colleagues to vote on cases from about eight to noon. Then he would be assigned to write a case, and we would spend the Saturday afternoon until around six discussing how it should be analyzed and approached. We wrote for the justice what we called "bench memos" in which we in effect wrote an entire opinion. He didn't use our opinions as his own. He looked at them, he was guided by them (and sometimes quoted them) in some way, but he frequently ignored our essays; he wrote every single published opinion by himself. He was not a great writer, but to this day I consider him a great human being, and I think most of his colleagues did as well. I revere his memory and his humanity.

Being a law clerk had trappings of power (we even had parking spaces in the Supreme Court basement), though the power varied from law clerk to law clerk and from justice to justice. Even if you weren't powerful, you were perceived to be by your friends, and that was more than enough for my ego. Justice Frankfurter thought or pretended to think that law clerks exercised great influence on some justices, and he would visit us frequently to talk shop and to try to seduce us into adopting his reasoning and opinions. He always referred to us clerks as "the College of Cardinals," adding much to our self-esteem, which already was high. He invited some of us to his home for Sunday afternoon events. This was a calculated exercise, and it had some success. I had to endure recitals chez Frankfurter by some of the great musical artists of our time, including one appearance by Wanda Landowska, the renowned harpsichordist. (I would have preferred to watch the Washington Redskins.) While some of the other justices were sociable sometimes, Frankfurter was the only one who aggressively pursued our influence and our votes.

Frankfurter was perhaps the best known of the justices, partly because he knew how to manipulate the media and spoke out frequently. My own opinion was that Justice Jackson excelled at the craft of writing opinions and Justice Douglas had the greater cerebral capacity, although he was not perceived to be a nice man. Jackson had been the chief U.S. prosecutor at the Nuremberg trials of the Nazi leadership and had always harbored a desire to be the chief justice as well as, it was said, to be president of the United States.

In those days my first wife, Betty, and I lived in Alexandria, Virginia, at a housing complex called Park Fairfax, which was typical of the clean, pleasant, well-run developments created by the Metropolitan Life Insurance Company; but Alexandria being a small southern town in the 1950s, Park Fairfax apparently had white residents only. We paid about $80 a month for a two-bedroom, two-bathroom apartment, and we commuted every day to Washington, where I enjoyed my private parking spot at the Court and Betty worked for one of the trade associations, the Machine Tool Manufacturers Association. We had a good life. I recall that most of the law clerks were married, and we were a proud, compatible group. We played softball and touch football in the shadows of the Washington Monument; we partied, had dinner together frequently, and were very, very cocky. We argued passionately every day about the wisdom and creativity of our justices against the others. One circulating joke was that the writing style of one or two of the justices changed every year; meaning, of course, each year their law clerks wrote their opinions.

Nearly every law clerk's career contains a story about an invitation extended to his justice and wife to a dinner at the clerk's modest abode. Nearly every justice accepted (at least once), and, in similar fashion, something went wrong—either someone was late, lost his way, was ill, or had experienced some similar mishap. Ours involved the roast beef being overcooked because we fell asleep while the beef roasting was going on. The Burtons took it all in stride (probably experiencing similar discomforts with every clerk and his wife every year). We still reminisce about this embarrassing incident.

Every single day, Monday through Friday, the law clerks met at three o'clock in the afternoon in the cafeteria of the Supreme Court, and I ate a huge brownie covered with vanilla ice cream with a glass of milk. I put on about ten pounds over what would have been my fighting weight in Portland, Maine (my hometown). (Though I avoided the bouts there, I always dreamed of being the middleweight boxing champion, or at least a contender.) I did get some exercise. There was a basketball court above the main courtroom—naturally dubbed "the highest court in the land"—where we played frequently, often with the law clerks (all of whom were male and white) opposing the messengers (all of whom were male and black). The messengers always won, big time. Poker, not bridge, was the evening card game of choice among the law clerks.

My most memorable moment at the Court was one of the most historic moments of the Court itself—the decision on May 17, 1954, in *Brown v. Board of Education*.[11] Since this was near the end of my term, I invited my sister, Charlotte, down to Washington to spend a few days with us. The family always assumed I knew when the decision was coming, but I didn't. Fortunately, she was in the courtroom for the historic moment when Chief Justice Warren announced the unanimous opinion that the doctrine of separate but equal, which had stood since the *Plessy v. Ferguson* decision of 1896,[12] was unconstitutional and therefore unlawful. The Court later, in its decree, ordered that the nation's schools must begin "with all deliberate speed" to desegregate and offer equal educational opportunities to blacks and whites at the same time and in the same schoolrooms. We law clerks sat together in a specially reserved box to the left of the bench, and it had to be the greatest moment in each clerk's life to that time. The attendees seemed stunned but satisfied. Most realized they were listening to history being made, and they were part of it. It was a never-to-be-forgotten moment, renewed for some of us fifty years later when Yale Law School invited all seven of the Yale Law clerks involved in the decision to a seminar expressing their reminiscences, some sad, some happy.

Nearing the end of my Supreme Court clerkship, I had lots of opportunities for employment; law firms sought to interview me, rather than the other way around. Law firms and governmental agencies wanted Supreme Court law clerks because of their experience and their supposed intelligence and legal savvy. I could have had almost any type of law job in the United States. Betty wanted me to stay in Washington because she liked the life and the liberal views of our friends there. She was delighted when I was offered the opportunity to work at $4,000 a year for the solicitor general's office, where I ultimately might be arguing cases before the Supreme Court on behalf of the U.S. government, a highly prestigious role. I, on the other hand, had lots of long-standing educational debts to repay, and I believed the greatest opportunity for economic and career achievement was only in New York City. If you were smart enough, and industrious enough, and tough enough, you could make it there, as the song goes.

Notes

1. Noah Feldman, *Scorpions: The Battles and Triumphs of FDR's Great Supreme Court Justices* (New York: Twelve, 2010).

2. Proceedings of the Bar and Officers of the Supreme Court of the United States, May 24, 1965, Proceedings Before the Supreme Court of the United States, May 24, 1965, In Memory of Harold H. Burton, Washington 1965, Remarks of Mr. Troubh.

3. *Youngstown Sheet & Tube Co. v. Sawyer,* 343 U.S. 579 (1952).

4. *Henderson v. United States,* 339 U.S. 816 (1950).

5. *United Const. Workers v. Laburnum Const. Corp.,* 347 U.S. 656 (1954).

6. *American Tobacco Co. v. United States,* 328 U.S. 781 (1946).

7. *United States v. E. I. du Pont de Nemours & Co.,* 353 U.S. 586, 608 (1957).

8. *Toolson v. New York Yankees, Inc.,* 346 U.S. 356, 357 (1953).

9. Ray Troubh, *Bowdoin Alumni Magazine* 39, no. 2 (January 1965): 2 (quoting from the *New York Herald Tribune*).

10. "In Memoriam: Harold Hitz Burton," *Harvard Law Review* 78 (1964–65): 799.

11. 347 U.S. 483.

12. 163 U.S. 537.

ARTHUR R. SEDER JR.

Law Clerk for Chief Justice Vinson

Anumber of years after my retirement from a career in law and business, I wrote a memoir for my family that included a chapter on my two years as a law clerk for Chief Justice Fred M. Vinson. While it was written for nonlawyers and is necessarily a personal account, what follows in this essay is largely that memoir plus additional comments on some of the matters that came before the Court while I was there. I have exchanged recollections with the two Vinson clerks who succeeded me, Howard J. Trienens and Newton W. Minow, but the opinions here expressed are my own and do not necessarily reflect the views of others.

How I Came to Clerk for the Chief Justice

I entered Northwestern University Law School in September 1945, only a few weeks after my relief from duty with the U.S. Army Air Corps at the end of World War II. I found the study of law greatly to my liking. With a wife and child waiting at home, I had every incentive to study hard and seek to excel.

Very early in the term I found that one of my classmates, who had served as a naval officer, was equally determined to succeed in law school and was exceptionally well qualified. His name was John Paul Stevens, and he later served thirty-five years as a Supreme Court justice. We quickly became close friends and, because of comparable academic records, were chosen coeditors of the *Illinois Law Review* (now the *Northwestern University Law School Journal*).

As graduation approached in the spring of 1947, we were told that a member of the Northwestern faculty, Willard Wertz, had been given the opportunity to nominate a student to serve as a law clerk for Justice Wiley Rutledge in the coming term of Court. I do not know what conversations took place among the faculty members, but in the end John and I were asked to toss a coin to determine whose name would be submitted to Justice Rutledge. We both agreed, and the coin was duly tossed. Murphy's Law was working splendidly; John won the toss and went on to serve as clerk to Justice Rutledge for October term 1947.

I was disappointed to say the least. I knew, however, that another member of the Northwestern faculty, Willard Pedrick, had a long and close relationship with Chief Justice Vinson and would probably have the opportunity to recommend a candidate for a clerkship for October term 1948. In fact, one of the Chief's then current clerks, Francis Allen, had been recommended by Pedrick and was about to serve a second year. To make it possible for me to wait the intervening year, I was granted a fellowship at the law school and given the opportunity to teach a class in contract law. I gratefully accepted this offer.

In the spring of 1948, I received word that, upon Pedrick's recommendation, the chief justice would meet with me to discuss a clerkship for the following two terms. As I was still in the Army Air Force Reserve, I was able to commandeer a training plane for the flight to Washington. There, I met with the chief justice for a brief but cordial interview and, within a few days, was advised that I had been accepted and should report for duty as soon as possible after my teaching assignment was finished. While John Stevens has told me that his year with Justice Rutledge was very rewarding, in retrospect I have never regretted losing the coin toss and gaining the opportunity to spend two years as a law clerk to Chief Justice Vinson.

Learning on the Job

When I reported for work my first day as a law clerk to the chief justice, I was shown to my office, a large room adjoining the conference room where the justices met each week to discuss and vote on decisions and petitions for certiorari. The office is lined with bookcases full of Supreme Court opinions and other legal aids and included desks for two law clerks, a couch, and miscellaneous other furniture.

I was directed to my desk and introduced to one of the Chief's law clerks from the preceding year, Lawrence F. Ebb, who left later in the summer. My course of instruction was brief. My new acquaintance handed me a pile of petitions for certiorari (always referred to as "cert petitions") and told me my job for the summer was to read, analyze, and prepare a memorandum for the chief justice on each petition. They would be acted upon at the end of summer, prior to the opening of October term 1948.

The end product of this analysis was a three- or four-page memorandum briefly stating the facts and arguments made by the parties and a recommendation to the chief justice as to whether he should vote to grant or deny the petition. The analysis necessarily required reading the lower courts' decisions, other materials cited by the parties, and portions of the record of proceedings in the lower court. No one gave me any guidance as to how to prepare these memoranda. However, I immediately went to work and tackled the pile of cert petitions. My ability to type immediately became important as we had very little secretarial assistance. At first the process went very slowly, but as the summer progressed I began to develop a "feel" for the more important cases. One problem was that the chief justice was absent most of the summer, so I lacked any guidance concerning the kinds of cases he might consider worthy of review.

At this point I wish to make two comments with regard to the experience I just described. First, I concluded later that it is unwise for a justice to hire a clerk who has not had at least a year's experience clerking for an appellate judge, preferably a member of a U.S. Court of Appeals. Learning on the job at the Supreme Court level is a significant leap for even the best law school graduates. Second, the Supreme Court clerk would do well to keep a copy of Eugene Gressman's *Supreme Court Practice* on his or her desk at all times. It was several months before I became aware of its usefulness and importance.

At the time, each associate justice was authorized to have two law clerks (although Justice William O. Douglas hired only one each year). However, the chief justice was authorized to have three clerks because, in those days, the hundreds of in forma pauperis petitions for certiorari filed by prison inmates raising postconviction constitutional issues arrived in single typewritten copies. Rather than making copies for circulation to the other justices (remember, this was over sixty years ago when the mimeograph was the latest technology), these petitions were reviewed by the Chief's law clerks and their memoranda circulated to all the members of the Court. One former Vinson law clerk has expressed his concern at being given sole responsibility for advising the entire Court as to whether a prisoner should be given a hearing concerning denial of his constitutional rights.

As the summer progressed and law clerks assembled in each of the justices' chambers, we became acquainted and established good personal and professional relationships. The clerks usually had lunch together and occasionally found time to visit each other's chambers to discuss current cases and the national issues of the time. I soon met the other two law clerks that the chief justice had selected for the coming year. David Feller, a holdover from the previous term, was a Harvard Law School graduate, and Isaac Groner was a graduate of Yale Law School. Both quickly became friends and valued associates. Among the clerks for other justices I made a number of lifelong friends, most of whom enjoyed exceptional careers in law and public service.

In October term 1948, the members of the Supreme Court, in addition to the chief justice, included Justices Hugo L. Black, William O. Douglas, Felix Frankfurter, Stanley F. Reed, Frank Murphy, Harold H. Burton, Robert H. Jackson, and Wiley Rutledge.

Justice Black, the senior member and former senator, was the leader of the liberal/activist faction on the Court. He had a razor-sharp mind and an instinct for the jugular. He asked few questions from the bench, but when he leaned forward to interrogate a lawyer you could be sure it went to the heart of that lawyer's argument.

Justice Douglas, formerly dean of the Yale Law School and chairman of the Securities and Exchange Commission (SEC), was another member of the activist wing of the Court. I thought him aloof and inconsiderate of the law clerks, including his own. While he was the darling of left-wing legal scholars, he was not a favorite of the law clerks.

Justice Murphy, a politician who had been elected mayor of Detroit and governor of Michigan during the Depression, almost invariably followed the lead of Black and Douglas. He became ill during the term and died the following summer. Justice Rutledge, a former law professor, was an earnest and sincere judge who regularly turned up on the liberal side as well. Justice Jackson, who had prosecuted the Nazi war criminals at Nuremberg, was the best opinion-writer on the Court and usually sided with Justice Frankfurter. Justices Reed and Burton also usually turned up on the conservative side of divided decisions. Justice Frankfurter, formerly a professor at Harvard Law School and an adviser to presidents, became increasingly conservative as the years passed (although he would probably have denied that characterization). He was an adherent of Justice Oliver Wendell Holmes Jr. and believed, with Holmes, that the Court should leave policy decisions to the legislative branch.

My most notable contacts with an associate justice were with Justice Frankfurter. Virtually all such occasions were chance encounters in the hallway. But Frankfurter, still very much the professor, would immediately launch into a discussion of some legal issue that interested him, hoping for—and sometimes getting—an argumentative response. A year or two after leaving the Court I returned on a visit and happened to see Justice Frankfurter in the hall. He recognized me and immediately began to discuss some legal question as if only two minutes, rather than two years, had gone by. He also urged me a number of times to teach law, and I nearly did so, having received an invitation to join the faculty of the University of Pennsylvania Law School.

Justice Frankfurter was sometimes accused of proselytizing other justices' law clerks, but in my case he never tried and, in any event, would not have succeeded. However, I did enjoy talking with him. So I was surprised and pleased when, before leaving Washington at the end of my second year at the Court, Justice Frankfurter invited me, together with his own law clerks, to dinner at his house in Georgetown. That evening was one of the most stimulating and engrossing of my life. Justice Frankfurter's wife, Marion, greeted us as we arrived and joined in our conversation before dinner, adding greatly to our comfort level. However, when dinner arrived, she excused herself, and we were alone with the justice.

Before, during, and after dinner the conversation flowed like wine. Well, that flowed too! We talked of the Court, of the law, of law schools, of politics, of domestic policy, of foreign policy, of presidents and judges—there were no boundaries to our discussion. Justice Frankfurter was the perfect host, leading the discussions but not dominating them, arguing good-naturedly with his young guests and chiding them for views with which he disagreed. As we left his house about midnight, I walked on air.

The Term Begins

The Supreme Court term begins on the first Monday in October, and as that date approached, the pace of work quickened.[1] The justices returned from their summer vacations, and there was little time for chit-chat among the law clerks. The big event prior to the beginning of the term was a conference of the justices that took place over a two- or three-day period. At that conference, the Court decided which petitions for certiorari filed during the summer should be granted review. Of course we clerks were never permitted to enter the conference room while the justices were there, but we felt "close to the action" as only a single door separated our office from the conference room.

With the beginning of the term I had my first exposure to actual practice before the Supreme Court. Law clerks attended sessions of the Court as their work permitted and were allotted several alcoves at one side of the courtroom near the bench. I remember well the court bailiff's cry, "Oyez, oyez, all those who have business before the honorable, the Supreme Court of the United States, draw near, for the Court is now in session." As the cry rang out, everyone in the courtroom stood, the nine black-robed justices appeared from behind the drapery, assembled behind their chairs, and remained standing until the bailiff had completed his cry. Very impressive!

After admission of new lawyers to practice before the Court, the clerk called the first case, and the lawyers involved moved to their seats at the counsel table. The term had begun. I listened, fascinated, while the arguments proceeded, noting how each justice reacted to the arguments. I would have enjoyed spending all my time listening to arguments, but since I had much work to do, that was impossible. However, throughout my two years at the Supreme Court I frequently attended Court sessions, particularly when important cases were being heard or notably accomplished lawyers were engaged.

During the term, the cert petitions continued to flood in. Each of the Chief's clerks took one-third of the petitions without any particular allocation procedure. In some offices the law clerks prepared supplemental memoranda on the basis of the briefs on the merits of the case to be argued orally. The chief justice seldom asked us to prepare additional memoranda, however, preferring to rely on our earlier cert memos and his own reading of the briefs. Occasionally, one of us would prepare a memorandum suggesting particular lines of questions the chief justice might ask at oral argument. Occasionally, he asked questions we had suggested; more often he did not.

The Court's procedure was to hear oral argument each day for two weeks and then recess for the next two weeks. After each week of oral argument, the Court met in conference on Saturday to discuss and vote on the cases heard during the week. At the end of the conference, the Chief called the clerk of the Court, Harold B. Willey, into his office to provide him with the list of orders to be issued the following Monday. The Chief also invited his three law clerks to attend these sessions, which we were glad to do because we were naturally eager to hear the results of the voting.

The most interesting part of our jobs was what followed after Willey had left the room. At that point the chief justice, noticeably relaxed and with considerable flare, rehashed the substance of the discussions that had taken place at the conference. As far as I know, no other justices followed that practice. We were, therefore, given insights into the inner workings of the Court provided to few other law clerks.

These sessions often went on for over an hour, and, while they made for late hours on Saturday afternoons, they were the high point of the week for the Chief's clerks. In that respect we were the envy of our colleagues. While the Chief's comments necessarily referred to the positions taken by other justices with whom he disagreed, he was careful not to impugn either their attitudes or arguments except to complain at times about the length of discussion on the part of some justices.

During my time at the Court, the result in many controversial cases was a four-to-four split. Chief Justice Vinson therefore often found himself in the middle. Although he was a lifelong Democrat, more often than not he voted with the conservative wing when the Court split along philosophical lines.

Within a few days after the Court had voted on the argued cases, the chief justice, when he was in the majority, assigned the cases to individual justices for the preparation of opinions. When the Chief was in the minority, the assignment was made by the senior associate justice in the majority. We were always interested in these assignments, but were never consulted. In fact, I was never able to tell what criteria the Chief employed in making his assignments, other than taking into account individual case loads as the end of the term approached.

My two associates and I were somewhat disappointed in the Chief's selection of the cases he chose to keep for himself. We believed that he assigned the more interesting civil rights and constitutional law cases to other justices and was more likely to write opinions in cases involving taxes, government regulation, or statutory interpretation. The Chief, however, did write the opinions of the Court in three important cases that laid the basis for the unanimous ruling in *Brown v. Board of Education*,[2] which overturned the "separate but equal" rubric. These cases included *Shelley v. Kramer*,[3] (outlawing state court enforcement of racially restrictive covenants), *Sweatt v. Painter*,[4] and *McLau-*

rin v. Oklahoma State Regents[5] (holding that state efforts to exclude or isolate racial minority students from graduate schools violated the Equal Protection Clause of the Fourteenth Amendment). I have little doubt that, had he lived to participate in *Brown*, he would have written the opinion of the Court in that case as well.

When the chief justice assigned an opinion to himself, the law clerk who had prepared the original memorandum on the petition for certiorari was expected to prepare a draft opinion for the Chief's consideration. While he seldom gave us specific instructions as to how the opinion should be structured, we knew his position on the issues because of our Saturday postconference sessions and other discussions.

I prepared my first draft of opinion in what I thought might pass as Supreme Court style and, with considerable trepidation, sent it in to the chief justice. I had, of course, thoroughly analyzed the briefs submitted by the parties, familiarized myself with the record in the case, and done original research into the law on the subject. Several days later I was summoned into the Chief's office, where we went over my draft of opinion in considerable detail. While the Chief directed me to rewrite certain parts of the opinion to reflect his views more accurately, on the whole he accepted what I had written without major change. I quickly rewrote parts of the opinion to reflect the changes he had directed, and, after another session or two in his office, the Chief had the opinion printed by the Court's printing office and circulated to the other justices. The same procedure was followed in subsequent cases.

My two fellow law clerks did not fare as well in preparing drafts of opinion for the chief justice. It certainly was not because of a lack of intellectual capacity or writing skill. However, as I suggested earlier, the Chief was relatively conservative or middle-of-the road in his judicial leanings, whereas my fellow clerks were inclined toward more liberal or activist positions. Their drafts of opinions, therefore, sometimes required extensive rewriting to reflect the Chief's views.

While we law clerks had definite opinions as to whether cert petitions should be granted and how cases should be decided, our opinions had little effect on the chief justice's votes. I can only recall one instance where I had a decisive role in the result of a case. In that instance, which was a commercial case of limited importance, the chief justice assigned the preparation of an opinion to himself and directed me to prepare a draft. As I delved into the issues, however, I became convinced that the majority, including the chief justice, were wrong in their conclusion. I therefore took the bold, and perhaps inappropriate, step of preparing a memorandum, couched in the form of an opinion, deciding the case contrary to the majority vote.

I submitted my memorandum to the chief justice with some trepidation, explaining my reasons for doing so and suggesting that, if he agreed, the memorandum could be circulated to the other justices for comment. After much discussion he agreed, and the memorandum was printed and sent to the other justices. Those who had been in the minority approved the changed result and, with the Chief's vote, formed a new majority. My memorandum was therefore recast as the opinion of the Court and adopted, while members of the erstwhile majority dissented.

I found being at the center of one of the three branches of our national government to be exciting and rewarding beyond measure. We were provided with every facility to assist us in our work. Law books from the Supreme Court library and texts from the Library of Congress were delivered to our offices promptly upon call; the complete legislative history of any statute could be provided in a few minutes; we were assigned parking spaces in the basement of the Supreme Court building; the Court cafeteria served fine meals at low cost; and our office accommodations were splendid. The only convenience lacking was secretarial help. But I found, as in law school, that I could "think on the typewriter" so the work got done. I must say in retrospect, however, that it would have been incomparably more efficient if word processors had been available rather than old-fashioned mechanical typewriters.

For October term 1949, the chief justice selected a University of Pennsylvania Law School graduate, Murray Schwartz, to replace Dave Feller, while Ike Groner and I stayed on for a second term in accordance with our understanding with the Chief. Some notable additions among clerks in other offices included Warren Christopher (Douglas), who later enjoyed a distinguished career as a lawyer in Los Angeles and as secretary of state in the Clinton administration; Philip Tone (Rutledge), who served on the Court of Appeals for the Seventh Circuit; Albert Sacks (Frankfurter), who became dean of Harvard Law School; and Bayless Manning (Burton), who went on to serve as dean of Stanford Law School.

Toward the close of my first term the chief justice told me that he had selected me to be the chief law clerk for the coming term. The only real consequence of this designation was a slightly higher salary than the other clerks and assignment to a personal office in a front corner of the Supreme Court building. And what an office! It was about thirty feet square, with twelve-foot-high ceilings, floor-to-ceiling bookcases, a large desk, a couch, and several chairs. It was the equal of most cabinet offices and commanded a superb view of the capitol dome. It was much too grand for a law clerk, and not many years later it was appropriated to another use. (By coincidence, "my" office was occupied by Justice John Paul Stevens during the last years of his service on the Court!)

While my designation as chief clerk had little importance as such, I was gratified by this expression of approval. However, I believe it reflected mainly the Chief's greater comfort level with clerks whose backgrounds were more like his own and who held what he regarded as more balanced views than recent graduates of some eastern law schools. While this is pure supposition on my part, the fact is that, in subsequent years, the Chief chose most of his law clerks from Northwestern University Law School, including all three of his clerks during one term.

Law Clerk Activities

The law clerks saw a great deal of each other on a daily basis and enjoyed cordial relationships despite whatever animosities there may have been among their employers. The Court's business was a continual subject of discussion, but all of the clerks were very circumspect with regards to the inner workings of their respective offices. We clerks usually lunched together at a table in the Supreme Court cafeteria. (It was not until a year or two later that the clerks began gathering monthly for lunch in a private room, with one of the justices as a guest.) I have been told by one clerk who attended those luncheons that Justices Stanley F. Reed, Sherman Minton, and Harold H. Burton were especially cordial and that "Douglas came and tried to be." Justice Robert H. Jackson went even further, holding an annual cocktail party in his chambers for all the clerks. Unfortunately, there were no such occasions while I was a clerk, and our social gatherings were limited to a single family picnic at the end of my second term—without the justices.

One interesting event that occurred during my first term was a tribute by the law clerks to the memory of Justice Oliver Wendell Holmes Jr. This tribute to the great justice was occasioned by the closing of the Gaiety Theater in Washington, D.C., the capital's only remaining burlesque theater. Tradition has it that Justice Holmes had enjoyed burlesque shows and regularly attended that theater. Believing that so important a tradition should not go unobserved, a delegation of law clerks attended the last night's performance at the Gaiety (I believe in Holmes-era costume of some kind), which certainly would have pleased the great justice.

Personal Relations with the Chief Justice

Chief Justice Vinson's relations with his law clerks were uniformly proper and respectful. However, those relationships were limited to the work of the Court and lacked any personal component. My wife and I were never invited to his apartment or to a social engagement. In fact, my wife never met the chief justice, and I never met his wife. This probably reflects the fact that for many years as a member of Congress and as a high-level Executive Department official and cabinet officer he had necessarily given up much of his personal life to the demands of his positions.

That continued to be the case after he became chief justice. He was on intimate terms with President Truman, with whom he spoke regularly and enjoyed evenings around a poker table. (While I was aware that the proper address to the chief executive was "Mr. President," it still came as a surprise, given their close personal friendship, that the chief justice, even while talking with Truman on the telephone, always addressed him as "Mr. President.") An effort was made by the Democratic leadership to persuade him to run against General Eisenhower for the presidency in 1952, which he wisely declined. (He was also a good friend of Eisenhower, with whom he enjoyed playing bridge.) And he was approached about the possibility of becoming commissioner of Major League Baseball in 1951, which he also declined—although it would have meant a tripling of his salary and very agreeable duties.

In 1953, some of the Chief's former law clerks arranged a reunion dinner with the Chief in Washington, which I attended. But apart from that, I had little communication with him after leaving the Court. I never lost my liking or respect for the Chief, and I could not have asked for a more friendly or cordial boss in the office. Still, having some kind of relationship that went beyond the four corners of the Supreme Court building would have been gratifying.

One final anecdote concerning Chief Justice Vinson deserves repeating, as several of the clerks who succeeded me had the same experience. On days when the chief justice had detailed his own car and driver for his wife's use, he regularly asked me to drive him to his home at the Wardman Park Hotel after work. I was glad to do so, but the doorman at the Wardman Park always had a horrified look on his face as my battered old 1938 Ford drew up to the imposing hotel entrance. I have no doubt he would have ordered us peremptorily off the premises if he had not spotted the stately figure of the chief justice of the United States emerging from the front seat. That is how I prefer to remember the Chief.

Notes

1. One cause for excitement as the Court's term was about to begin was the report that President Harry S. Truman was considering sending Chief Justice Vinson to Moscow for personal discussions of U.S.-Russian relations with Joseph Stalin. The Chief's clerks naturally wondered what effect this would have on their jobs—even the possibility of accompanying the chief justice. The Chief never spoke to us about the suggestion, and it was soon laid to rest.

2. 347 U.S. 483 (1954).

3. 334 U.S. 1 (1948).

4. 339 U.S. 629 (1950).

5. 339 U.S. 637 (1950).

Tom Clark and His Law Clerks

My father, Tom Clark, had been a U.S. attorney general for four years when, in 1949, President Truman appointed him to the Supreme Court following the sudden death of Justice Frank Murphy.[1] The switch to the Supreme Court was comparable to entering a new world. At forty-nine, he was young and vigorous—an action-oriented, gregarious man. The Supreme Court's quiet, scholarly, and somewhat isolated environment was a stark contrast to the hectic, crisis-ridden Office of the Attorney General. His adjustment to the Court was difficult, and it was at least three years before he began to feel totally comfortable and to truly love his work as associate justice.

Despite his initial reaction to his new position—a common one among newly appointed justices[2]—he immediately enjoyed working with the talented and dedicated young men who became his law clerks. I am certain that none of those who served during my father's early years suspected that he was dissatisfied in any way with his position, for my father, in all his relationships, rarely expressed unhappiness, and his warm personality and informal manner created a collegial atmosphere marked by mutual respect and genuine affection. Bill Powell (October term 1957) described himself as "amazed at how [Justice Clark] treated inexperienced law clerks, fresh out of law school, with respect, courtesy and importance."[3] John Nolan (October term 1955) viewed him as "understanding and sympathetic to any personal need of his staff no matter how far removed from the work of the Court."[4] "Let me know if there is anything you need," my father would offer as they began the year—and he meant it!

The office atmosphere was that of a family, and a number of his law clerks considered him a surrogate father during their year of service. His staff, consisting of his secretary, Alice O'Donnell (Miss Alice), and messenger, Oscar Bethea, both of whom came with him from the Department of Justice, were also part of the family. They were devoted to my father, and Miss Alice, as gracious as she was efficient, contributed to the general warmth and congeniality of the office.

My father established the tradition of inviting his law clerks to our family's

Thanksgiving dinner each year when he first went on the Court and continued the tradition throughout his eighteen years as an active justice and ten years of retirement. Miss Alice was also invited and usually a friend or two who would otherwise be alone. For many of the law clerks it was a highlight of their year. Mother, a charming southern lady, was as welcoming and warm a host as my father; both my parents treated them as guests in their home. On one occasion, Ellis McKay (October term 1953) was accompanied by his wife and three-year-old son. The little boy was going through a very shy stage and stayed under the dining room table for most of the meal, much to his parents' embarrassment. After dinner, my father managed to coax the little boy out from under the table and persuaded him to sit next to him on the couch, where my father began to tell tall tales of lions and tigers. The child's shyness evaporated.

My father extended his hospitality to family members of law clerks as well. When parents visited, he and mother often took them out to dinner. If any family member visited a session of the Court, my father always sent them a note from the bench—a courtesy he extended to his own friends and family.

When my father served on the Supreme Court, associate justices had two law clerks and retired justices had one. His method for selecting his law clerks changed during the course of the years. Initially he followed a traditional process similar to that of other justices. He considered each application, interviewed the applicants he determined were most appropriate, and made his decision for the following term soon after the first of the year. During his first years on the Court, all of his law clerks were from well-known, prestigious law schools.

In the mid-1950s, he decided that the pool of law schools should be expanded so that lesser-known law schools would have the opportunity to send a student to serve at the Court. During the next twenty years, he hired law clerks from fourteen law schools that had previously never had a graduate serve as a law clerk: New York University, Southern Methodist University, Notre Dame University, University of Southern California, Fordham University, Drake University, University of Mississippi, University of Indiana, Villanova University, South Texas College (Houston), St. Mary's University (San Antonio), University of Houston, Loyola University (New Orleans), and Washburn University. In the early 1960s, another element was added to the selection process. The Phi Alpha Delta law fraternity began a nationwide competition for the purpose of identifying candidates for Tom Clark's law clerks. The winners' names were sent to him with the fraternity's recommendation. My father, however, kept the prerogative of making his own selection and did not always choose the Phi Alpha Delta candidate.

He also chose a small number of law clerks who were sons of friends. All but two of those were from well-known law schools. The two exceptions were Marshall Groce (October term 1966), a graduate of St. Mary's University School of Law in San Antonio, and Tom Marten (October term 1976), a graduate of Washburn University School of Law and now a U.S. District Court judge for the district of Kansas. These choices helped my father fulfill his goal of selecting clerks from previously unrepresented law schools.

While his treatment of and personal relationship with his clerks was consistent throughout the years, his work assignments evolved and varied at times. Clerks who served during the early years typically wrote the first drafts of opinions. By the mid-1950s, my father was more likely to write the first drafts in longhand on yellow legal pads and have Alice O'Donnell type them. He might ask a law clerk to review certain points within the opinion. According to John Nolan (October term 1955), each law clerk was responsible for following a specific case from its beginning (cert memo) to its final form. Then they would work together with the justice on editing, revising, and so forth. Both clerks would often work on "big" cases—those that were controversial or unusually complex. My father's law clerks especially appreciated his openness with them. They were allowed to see the Conference Book where he recorded discussions and made notes, so they knew which cases had been decided and which would be handed down the following Monday.

There was at least one exception to his willingness to share information with his law clerks: *Brown v. Board of Education*. The justices were very secretive about this highly sensitive landmark case. Ellis Hughes and Ernest Bernstein were the law clerks in the spring of 1954, when the justices were deciding the case. They were not involved in writing the first draft, nor were they able to view the Conference Book. Consequently, they had no idea when the opinion would be handed down or how the vote would go. They shared the anticipation with the country as a whole as they awaited the decision. On the morning of May 17, 1954, my father walked through the room where the law clerks worked and said, "I think you boys should be in the courtroom this morning." The law clerks knew from his remark that *Brown* was about to be handed down, and the justice didn't want them to miss that historic event.[5]

My father was a workaholic, but never expected more of others than of himself and was invariably fair and considerate. Vester Hughes, who clerked briefly in 1952 before being called for service in the Korean War, provided an incident that illustrates these qualities: "One day before conference there was an unusually large number of cert petitions. Clerks would have to work through the night to finish them. The Justice divided the certs into three stacks—one for each clerk and one for himself so that no one had to stay up all night."[6]

He would also ask law clerks if there was any case that was of special interest to them and, if appropriate, would assign that case accordingly. Charles Reed (October term 1965) had a degree in chemical engineering as well as law—a background that was helpful in dealing with patent laws. He expressed an interest in a series of patent cases brought to the Court, known as the "Trilogy cases," involving the standard of patentability under the 1950 Patent Act. According to Reed, "there is not a more arcane and specialized area of law than patents. I wrote the first draft, the Justice rewrote it extensively, improving it greatly, turning it into a masterpiece of workable law. Although your father went around telling the patent bar that I did the real work, the fact was quite the opposite."[7] Reed's experience clearly shows my father's willingness to give credit to a law clerk for a job well done, even when doing so minimized his own credit.

Despite his easygoing manner and the familial atmosphere of the office, my father ran a tight ship. Larry Temple (October term 1969) described him as having "a gentle demeanor but iron-handed firmness."[8] Fred Rowe (October term 1952) recalled that "[Justice Clark] set firm deadlines and you had to deliver and produce in all things he expected."[9] At the same time, he was a good listener who sought and respected his clerks' views. If a law clerk discovered that the justice had made an error and pointed it out to him, my father had no problem admitting his mistake. Jim Knox (October term 1961) recalled receiving a typically self-effacing note from the justice after such an incident: "I am wrong, you are right—as always."[10]

Law clerks felt comfortable expressing—even debating—their viewpoints when they disagreed with him, but their arguments were to no avail if he felt strongly about the issues involved. The well-known obscenity case known as Fanny Hill[11] (a book whose real title was *John Cleland's Memoirs of A Woman of Pleasure*) provides a clear example. The law clerks felt strongly that the book was not obscene and argued their point with the justice. Despite their efforts, they failed to move him, and he issued a strongly worded dissent to the majority's 5–4 opinion. "Though I am not known to be a purist—or a shrinking violet—this book is too much even for me." In the dissent, he also objected to the standard followed by the Court at that time that materials defined as "obscene" must be "utterly without social value." That rule he regarded as allowing "the smut artist free rein to carry on his dirty business."[12]

No matter what the circumstances, my father never lost his sense of humor, much to the amusement and sometimes amazement of his law clerks. Charles Reed recalled the time an FBI memo was delivered to the office warning the chambers that a marine who had gone AWOL had been heard threatening to get that "blankety-blank Tom Clark." My father wasn't in his office when the memo arrived, so Miss Alice placed it on his desk where he would be certain to see it. A short time later, my father returned the memo to her with a note attached: "If this man asks for an appointment, don't give it to him!"[13]

On one occasion, his sense of humor had negative repercussions. My father and his last law clerk, Tom Marten (October term 1976), were traveling back to D.C. after a trip to the Eighth Circuit. Airport security was in its infancy at that time, and people were still adjusting to it. My father got through the security system with no problem, but when Marten went through he set off the alarm. "I told you not to bring that gun, Tom," my father joked. The woman at the checkpoint heard the comment and threatened to call the police. "You'd better call two," my father responded. The woman retaliated, and an FBI agent appeared. The matter was cleared up quickly, but, according to Marten, my father was uncharacteristically quiet on the flight home. Finally he said, "I should have kept my . . . mouth shut. It wasn't enough to make the first crack, I had to make a second one." Then, after a brief pause he added, "Let's not tell Mrs. Clark about this."[14]

In 1967, my father retired as an associate justice after President Lyndon Johnson appointed my brother Ramsey to be attorney general. He was a young sixty-seven, in fine health and still in his prime. Many legal scholars thought his retirement was unnecessary since the solicitor general, rather than the attorney general, is usually the one to argue cases before the Supreme Court. My father, however, revered the Court and feared that remaining on it would create a perception of a conflict of interest. He was also extremely proud of Ramsey and of his accomplishments. He did not want to create any problems for Ramsey and his appointment, so he happily retired.

My father kept in touch with most of his clerks throughout the years. He had a number of namesakes among their children. After his death, his law clerks looked for a way to commemorate him and in his honor established a Tom Clark Judicial Fellow as part of the Supreme Court Judicial Fellows Program. The program, established in 1973 by Chief Justice Warren Burger, offers mid-career professionals the opportunity to work for a year at one of the four agencies of the federal judiciary: the Supreme Court, the Federal Judicial Center, the Office of the U.S. Courts, or the U.S. Sentencing Commission. It continues today, and each year someone from one of the four agencies is selected as the Tom Clark Judicial Fellow. In an award ceremony he or she receives a framed bow tie from Tom Clark's voluminous bow tie collection. My father had a strong preference for bow ties and wore them almost exclusively. Although others may have a different perception of bow ties, I have always thought they fit my father's personality, reflecting his good nature, sense of humor, and unpretentiousness.

The Tom Clark Judicial Fellows award is a lasting tribute from my father's former law clerks and a symbol of the devotion and respect they felt for him. Many viewed him as a surrogate father during their year of service. I believe Larry Temple's words best express the sentiments of his fellow law clerks: "[Justice Clark] lived the kind of full, active and productive life that is the envy and model of all who aspire to make a lasting contribution to this world. . . . He was the sweetest and most thoughtful man I have ever known."[15]

Notes

1. The main source for this essay was the biography I wrote of my father. See Mimi Clark Gronlund, *Supreme Court Justice Tom C. Clark: A Life of Service* (Austin: University of Texas Press, 2010). Letters I received as the result of a questionnaire I sent to his law clerks in 1994 are another important source. A great deal is also based on personal knowledge and experience.

2. Gronlund, *Supreme Court Justice Tom C. Clark*, 150–51.

3. William D. Powell to author, June 20, 1995.

4. John E. Nolan Jr. to author, October 31, 1994.

5. Gronlund, *Supreme Court Justice Tom C. Clark*, 183.

6. Vester T. Hughes to author, May 23, 1995.

7. Gronlund, *Supreme Court Justice Tom C. Clark*, 212–13.

8. Larry E. Temple to author, December 22, 1994.

9. Fred Rowe to author, November 12, 1994.

10. James E. Knox to author, November 22, 1994.

11. *Memoirs v. Massachusetts,* 383 U.S. 413 (1966).

12. Gronlund, *Supreme Court Justice Tom C. Clark*, 193.

13. Ibid, 260–61.

14. Ibid., 261.

15. Larry E. Temple, dedicatory remarks at the Dedication of Tom C. Clark State Court Building, Austin, Texas, June 11, 1993.

NORMAN DORSEN

Learning Many Things as a Law Clerk to Justice John Marshall Harlan

One can best appreciate what it was like to be a law clerk to Justice John Marshall Harlan by recognizing that he was, deep down, a practicing lawyer. He came to the Supreme Court in early 1955 with very little background in constitutional law. His first three years of legal study were at Oxford University, where as a Rhodes Scholar he studied jurisprudence and English common law and obtained the benefits of sustained and critical analysis from dons who were erudite but not conversant with American judicial opinions and trends. He received a "First" in jurisprudence at Oxford, finishing seventh in a class of 120. Harlan's sole year of legal study in the United States, at New York Law School, was part-time because he simultaneously started his long career as a litigator for a leading Wall Street firm, almost entirely in commercial cases. During World War II, he served as chief of the Operational Analysis Section of the Eighth Air Force, which was based in London and comprised of mathematicians, physicists, architects, electricians, and lawyers who provided technical advice on bombing raids over Germany. He spent less than a year as a Second Circuit judge before President Dwight D. Eisenhower appointed him to the Supreme Court.[1]

Harlan worked with extraordinary effort and tenacity, but at the start he needed help. In his early years he relied on Justice Felix Frankfurter, with whom he shared an affinity for Oxford and friendships among leaders of the bar who had been Frankfurter's students at Harvard Law School. He also relied heavily on his law clerks—masterfully delegating, supervising, editing, and, above all, forging a product that was distinctively his despite the important contribution of the clerks.

By the time Harlan retired in September 1971, he was no longer merely a superlative lawyer; he was a Supreme Court justice with an unparalleled reputation. Judge Henry Friendly of the U.S. Court of Appeals for the Second Circuit, who first worked with Harlan as a young lawyer in the 1920s and 1930s, asserted that "there has never been a Justice of the Supreme Court who has so consistently maintained a high quality of performance or, despite differences in views, has enjoyed such nearly uniform respect from his colleagues, the inferior bench, the bar and the academy."[2] Paul Freund, a leading constitutional scholar during Harlan's time, expressed a similar accolade, writing that even students who disagreed with Harlan's position in a case "freely acknowledge that when he has written a concurring or dissenting opinion they turn to it first, for a full and candid exposition of the case and an intellectually rewarding analysis of the issues."[3]

More than half of Harlan's law clerks were from Harvard Law School, because of his admiration for the school and for Henry Hart, almost surely the leading legal thinker of his era and the Harvard professor who chose Frankfurter's clerks. The rest were from other top-drawer law schools: Columbia, Michigan, Stanford, Virginia, and Yale. Harlan interviewed the finalists—in my case, at his country house in Connecticut—but he relied heavily on the recommendations of those he trusted, perhaps more than on his own reaction to a candidate after a short conversation.

New clerks learned the ropes from reading the work product of their predecessors—their memoranda on all certiorari petitions (and the now vestigial notice of appeal) and bench memos on many argued cases. Harlan himself did not spend time, at least in my year, describing the duties of a law clerk to me and my co-clerk, Henry J. Steiner (October term 1957). In Harlan's later years several clerks stayed on for a second term with him, and they explained things to the new clerks.

In those days there was no cert pool in which one clerk selected in rotation from the chambers of the justices in the pool wrote a memorandum for all the pool justices. Nor was there the kind of active clerks' "network" that emerged in later years. Naturally, there were many discussions of cases among the clerks, particularly in our private lunchroom, but I do not recall a thriving exchange of serious one-to-one conversations over the year. Harlan never asked me to find out what another justice was thinking about a case from one of his clerks or to advocate a position, but William T. Lake (October term 1969) reports that Harlan occasionally sent him as an emissary (but only to Justice Hugo Black).

Harlan's chambers were a quiet place. I don't think I ever heard him raise his voice about anything, and while he was good-humored, there were no fun and games, as in some other chambers (Justice Byron R. White's golf putting, Justice William H. Rehnquist's contests of all kinds).[4] If I had to choose one word to describe Harlan, it would be "dignified," in carriage, style, and dress (black old-fashioned suits, waistcoat complete with his grandfather's pocket watch).[5] The other two descriptive words, often mentioned by law clerks, are "patrician" and "gentleman."

His longtime secretary, Ethel McCall, was able and hard-working. The clerks regarded her as "formidable," and there may have been a little tension at times when she asserted her prerogatives. These were prefeminist days, and, in hindsight, it would not surprise me if at some level McCall resented her clerical destiny while watching the all-male clerks move each year to prestigious legal positions upon leaving the Court. As a law clerk I had not thought that Ethel McCall had feminist inclinations, but John Rhinelander (October term 1961) reports that she initially refused to type Harlan's unanimous opinion in *Hoyt v. Florida,* which upheld Florida's statute permitting women to exclude themselves from jury duty solely because of their sex. Paul Burke, Harlan's chauffeur and messenger, was a capable and good-natured man who acted as a general assistant in the chambers.

Like other justices, Harlan forged relationships with his clerks and, when possible, with members of their families. Harlan attended at least one wedding— of Nathan Lewin (October term 1961)—and he played in his chambers with the clerks' children. Harlan was kind to me when, during a softball game that the law clerks in my year played against the Covington & Burling law firm, I was slightly hurt (in a way that I do not recall). Harlan was on hand because he had volunteered to pitch an inning for the clerks. After my injury, he insisted on joining one or two others in taking me to the hospital (from which I was promptly discharged).

Harlan was invariably warm and upbeat with his clerks, although most of us differed with him on particular cases, and a few of us, including myself, probably argued intemperately, which never seemed to bother him. Only rarely did Harlan discuss certiorari petitions after I submitted my memoranda to him, but when he was writing an opinion there was often close discussion of ideas, prior cases, and language. As Norbert Schlei (October term 1956) recalled, "The work of the Court was to Justice Harlan not just important but sacred. No amount of effort was too much to get the opinion just right—to make sure that each sentence hit the mark and contained nothing that was inadvertent."

Despite having strong positions on some issues—for example, favoring a strong version of federalism and enforcement of limitations on standing, ripeness, and other doctrines that could expand the Court's jurisdiction—Harlan was famously open-minded and was willing to listen to his clerks' views even when he began with a pretty fixed opinion. Thomas Stoel Jr. (October terms 1967 and 1968) summed up what most of us experienced: "[I talked] with him about the pros and cons of decisions, sometimes watching him change his mind two or three times as he weighed the merits and decided how to vote."

The most notable incident of this kind occurred in *Cohen v. California,*[6] one of Harlan's last cases. Cohen had been convicted of disturbing the peace "by offensive conduct" for walking around a Los Angeles courthouse with a sign saying "Fuck the draft" during the Vietnam War. The Supreme Court agreed to hear Cohen's claim that the conviction abridged his freedom of speech. After oral argument, Harlan was inclined to affirm the conviction, not treating it as a serious First Amendment claim. But Tom Krattenmaker (October term 1970) persuaded Harlan to hold off until Tom could write a memorandum. Harlan did so, and, after much reflection, decided that Cohen's protest was protected free speech. Indeed, he wrote the opinion of the Court to that effect—based on Tom's memorandum—that is now a First Amendment classic.[7]

Harlan often worked with clerks in the evening at his Georgetown home, and he was known from time to time to sip his favorite bourbon, Rebel Yell, to facilitate the writing of an opinion. He also invited law clerks to join his wife, Ethel Harlan, and him for dinner or at a cultural event.[8] Ethel Harlan was deeply interested in music and the arts, and she was a gracious hostess until she became ill during Harlan's later years on the Court. Several clerks report how considerate he was to her while simultaneously doubling down on his work as a partial escape from his domestic concerns.

Harlan's habits, in particular his relations with clerks, were not static. Like other justices, Harlan could not maintain exactly the same sort of relationship with clerks when their number increased from two to three in 1966, but in reading the remembrances of the clerks from Harlan's later years one cannot detect a reduction in their access to him or in their closeness. The increase in the number of law clerks allocated to the justices coincided with Harlan's rapidly failing eyesight, and indeed may have been part of the reason that the Court voted to allow each justice to hire a third clerk (there are now four). As his condition worsened, Harlan became dependent on having the clerks read cases and other materials to him. This deepened the relationships.

Marvin Gray Jr. (October term 1970) recalls reading to Harlan the record in Muhammad Ali's effort in the Supreme Court to obtain a reversal of his conviction for draft evasion; he observed how Harlan became convinced of Ali's sincerity in seeking a deferment from the military for conscientious objection, leading to a unanimous decision for Ali.[9] And several clerks have graphically described what Bert Rein (October term 1966) called "a singular movie-going experience" during a period when the Supreme Court, under the prevailing legal standard, was deciding case-by-case whether a censored film was constitutionally obscene. A clerk would sit with Harlan (and other justices) in a darkened room and narrate to him the gyrating sexual activity on the screen. From time to time Harlan would exclaim "extraordinary" or "remarkable" on hearing what was going on, but could not see. Charles Nesson (October term 1964) had a similar experience in another medium while reading Justice Harlan *The Housewife's Handbook on Selective Promiscuity*, the subject of *Ginzburg v. United States*.[10]

An imponderable variable in the interaction between Harlan and his clerks was where he stood ideologically on the Court. From 1955 to 1962 the Court had four liberal members (Earl Warren, Hugo L. Black, William O. Douglas, and William Brennan Jr.), who would prevail only if they could coax a vote from one of the other five—which included Harlan. But from 1962 to 1969 there was a liberal majority of five, and briefly six, which constituted the legendary "Warren Court" that dramatically changed constitutional law. (This was the only period in Supreme Court history when there was a stable liberal majority.) During this era Harlan was a restraining force, and his dissenting opinions were intelligent, determined, professionally skillful, and, above all, principled. When Earl Warren and Abe Fortas left the Court in 1969, they were replaced by two conservatives, Chief Justice Warren Burger and Justice Harry Blackmun (before his liberal conversion). Harlan then became the key justice because he was now in the center of the Court ideologically and enjoyed respect from his brethren of all persuasions.

The "imponderable variable" I refer to above is whether Harlan and, therefore, Harlan in relation to his clerks, had a different approach to his opinions in the three broad periods of his service on the Court. From 1955 to 1962, as I have mentioned, he was part of the Court's moderate to conservative majority, led by Justice Frankfurter, that struggled to hold its five votes in many cases. From 1962 to 1969, as the prime dissenter from the Court's liberal opinions, Harlan rarely was able to muster a majority in contested cases, and he may have written more freely in dissent to put down a marker for the future rather than shape his opinions in order to prevail in a current case. In 1969, when he became a swing vote and often wrote majority opinions, he lost the luxury of ignoring suggestions from justices who might be persuaded to join his opinion.

Harlan is well known for his opposition to many of the Warren Court's most important doctrinal innovations. He dissented from *Baker v. Carr*,[11] *Reynolds v. Sims*,[12] and other political apportionment cases, and from the prevailing view that selectively incorporated the Bill of Rights to the states through the Fourteenth Amendment.[13] He also dissented from the *Miranda* decision[14] and other interventions into state criminal procedure, from the Court's effort to protect poor people as a class,[15] from the Pentagon Papers case,[16] and from the invalidation of attempts to expatriate U.S. citizens for unlawful or objectionable conduct.[17]

But this is far from the whole story. Harlan often joined the liberal consensus of the Warren Court. Justice Potter Stewart said at Harlan's memorial event in New York after he died in 1971,[18] "I can assure you that a very interesting law review article could someday be written on 'The Liberal Opinions of Mr. Justice Harlan.'"[19] These opinions include unvarying adherence to *Brown v. Board of Education* as applied to state actors,[20] strong Fourth Amendment protection against unlawful searches and seizures,[21] leading free speech cases such as *New York Times v. Sullivan*,[22] and dedication to separation of church and state.[23] And he wrote influential concurring opinions in the *Bivens* case,[24] which first authorized private enforcement of Fourth Amendment rights, and in *Griswold v.*

Connecticut,[25] the contraception case that protected the sexual privacy of married couples.

Such was the justice that Harlan's clerks came to know. He was not a strong civil libertarian; there are too many cases to the contrary, and he did not view the world that way. But he had a deep, almost visceral desire to keep things in balance, to resist excess in any direction, as the body of his work shows. Or, as Charles Lister (October terms 1966 and 1967) summed it up, "[Harlan] was conservative, but by temperament not ideology. His conservatism came from what he was . . . not borrowed from someone's theory. Its roots were craftsmanship, honesty and intellectual modesty. He struggled to get it right, not Right."

My clerkship year attracted unusual public attention because at the end of the prior term, in May and June 1957, the Court (foreshadowing the glory days of the Warren Court) handed down a large number of liberal decisions, most of which Harlan joined. Several reflected the decline of the McCarthy era: the reversal of contempt citations against witnesses who refused to answer questions about possible Communist associations[26] and narrowing of the Smith Act, which punished conspiracies to "overthrow the government by force and violence."[27] The Court also permitted a criminal defendant to have access to his or her relevant FBI files[28] and used the antitrust laws to scotch a proposed merger of IBM and GM, a case that alarmed the business community.[29] The spotlight on the Court increased in December 1957 when William H. Rehnquist, a former law clerk to Justice Robert H. Jackson and a justice-to-be, published an article in a national news magazine attributing the May and June decisions largely to the influence of liberal law clerks.[30] Most of the clerks in my year doubted that they had that much sway over their justices, and some were envious of their predecessors because the magazine ran photographs of each of them.

The first case I remember working on was *Rowoldt v. Perfetto,*[31] in which a 5–4 majority, in an opinion by Frankfurter, held that an alien could not be deported under the Internal Security Act for having been a "member" of the Communist Party because he did not have a "meaningful association" with the party. Harlan dissented.[32] Despite my personal support for the majority view, I wrote a strongly worded draft dissent saying there was sufficient evidence that the alien was a "conscious member of the party as a political organization." Harlan, by then aware of my liberal proclivities, smilingly chided me for my heated language even on his behalf. Later in the term, I drafted other "conservative" opinions. One was a dissent from a ruling that denied gold mining companies the right to "just compensation" under the Fifth Amendment for World War II regulations that had effectively closed their mines.[33] A second was an opinion of the Court denying a due process claim of a man convicted of murder who was denied access to a lawyer he had already retained.[34]

I also assisted Harlan with liberal decisions, including two internal security cases in which the Court held that the government lacked sufficient evidence to strip naturalized Americans of their citizenship for "fraudulently" swearing that they were "attached to the principles of the Constitution" while they were members of the Communist Party.[35] And in the most important case of the 1957 term, *NAACP v. Alabama*, Harlan wrote for a unanimous Court to overturn, on a then novel freedom of association ground, an attempt by Alabama, for punitive purposes, to obtain the membership records of members of the NAACP within the state. My co-clerk Henry Steiner worked on the case, but two other principal actors were Justices Black and Frankfurter, who consulted closely with Harlan on the opinion and sparred at length over how to characterize the "incorporation" of the First Amendment by the Fourteenth as it applied to the states. In the end, of course, it was Harlan's opinion, but key passages were approved in advance by the two senior justices.

Two incidents from the year are worth relating. As I have intimated, Harlan was remarkably tolerant of other people. Notably, I did not hear him say a critical word about any of his brethren during the entire year. The closest came when Justice Charles Whittaker circulated a proposed opinion in a complex case involving the extent of the Court's jurisdiction over military discharges (honorable, general, bad conduct, dishonorable). Whittaker's opinion was badly flawed, and when Harlan read it with us he smiled and slightly raised one eyebrow, suggesting that Whittaker may not have fully grasped the issue in the case. That was the extent of Harlan's criticism; he did not say a word. The opinion was soon withdrawn.[36]

The second incident involved Frankfurter, who famously relished intellectual combat. One day, after the Court held a conference on pending cases, Frankfurter walked into his clerks' office when I was there. At the conference, at Frankfurter's initiative, the Court disposed of a pending case that presented a hard First Amendment question by vacating the judgment of the lower court with a brief opinion explaining its action.[37] Before the conference I had thought that a simpler route to the same result was to deny certiorari and thus leave the lower court to work out the problem, and I so advised Harlan. For a reason I never understood, Frankfurter exploded upon seeing me, first questioning the correctness of my suggestion (which Harlan had passed on at the conference), then complaining about "interfering" law clerks, and finally and irrelevantly challenging the views of anyone (such as myself) who disagreed with his dissent in the famous flag salute case,[38] which was a critical juncture in Frankfurter's status on the Court and the Court's general direction. He spoke sharply, eventually returning to his own office and slamming the door. I was alarmed, even fearing for my position at the Court since this event occurred early in the term.[39] But Frankfurter was as friendly to me after the incident as before, frequently inquiring about my postclerkship plans, and urging me in a letter to argue a case before the Court "while I am still here."

Each justice works in a distinct way with law clerks, who are able to offer a variety of services. The clerks make written recommendations on certiorari petitions and argued cases, prepare the justices for oral argument, review the opinions of other justices and discuss whether their justice should join them, draft some opinions for their justices, and proofread all of the draft opinions. In addition, they often bring to their chambers the latest constitutional theories from law schools. There is a notable example in Justice Harlan's case— legal process theory, which was developed in the late 1940s and the 1950s and brought to fruition by Henry Hart and Albert Sacks (later dean) of Harvard Law School in their landmark book, *The Legal Process: Basic Problems in the Making and Application of Law.*[40]

After its publication (in mimeograph form), law clerks from Harvard Law School and increasingly from other schools became familiar with the theory, which dominated legal analysis until the 1970s. Its moderate philosophy was tailor-made for Harlan. It emphasized the role that procedure plays in assuring judicial and legislative objectivity, and among other innovations developed a "principle of institutional settlement," which held that decisions properly arrived at by the executive, legislature, administrative agency, or court while operating within their appropriate sphere of authority should be accepted as binding on society until duly modified. This legal theory, which many of Harlan's law clerks championed, guided him for many years.[41]

The clerks in my year followed tradition by inviting every justice to talk with us off the record at lunch, and almost all did so. We also invited a series of prominent figures to meet with us. These included Senator John F. Kennedy, former secretary of state Dean Acheson, Senator Wayne Morse, Deputy Attorney General William Rogers, Solicitor General J. Lee Rankin, and Representative Patricia Schroeder. Many of my fellow clerks and I were athletic after a fashion, and we regularly played touch football, softball, and basketball among ourselves or with teams from the Justice Department or a law firm.

Harlan held annual reunions of his law clerks, unlike some justices who convened their clerks biannually or every five years. The black-tie Saturday dinners and the Sunday brunches were family affairs, with Mrs. Harlan attending and the married law clerks usually accompanied by their wives. With two notable exceptions, the conversations were general, pretty much what one would expect at an elegant New York dinner of the kind Harlan frequently attended. The first exception to the pattern took place in the spring of 1963, the first term of the Court in which Justice Arthur Goldberg, replacing Frankfurter, became the fifth liberal vote, enabling a majority to begin its renovation of much constitutional law. The clerks at the reunion (in April or early May) could not know what decisions the Court would announce at the end of the term.

At prior reunions, Harlan had made informal and unexciting after-dinner remarks, commenting, for example, on what Mrs. Harlan and he were planning for the summer, the health of the older justices, and any administrative changes at the Court, such as the length of oral argument. The former clerks were startled when Harlan on this occasion spoke about the "troubling" or "disquieting" situation at the Court, referring to unspecified decisions expected over the next month or two. He was plainly disturbed and, if I remember correctly, went so far as to express concern for the future of the Court. We sensed that a new and more liberal jurisprudential era was at hand. By then I was taking cases from the American Civil Liberties Union, and I supported the apparent new direction of the Court, but on a human level, knowing what Harlan had invested in a more conservative approach, my heart went out to him.

A coda to Harlan's after-dinner comments was a reference to Justice Black. He called Black the "savior" of the Court and "a man of the institution," unlike some other (unnamed) justices. This added new surprise to the occasion because, when most of us were law clerks, Black was our chambers leading adversary. While Harlan was speaking I looked across the table at Paul Bator (October term 1956), who was one of Harlan's more conservative clerks and among those closest to Harlan. I will never forget the expression on Paul's face. It was an indescribable mélange of anger at the Court's new majority and disbelief in Black's new virtue. Of course, the former law clerks did not know that Black had begun what many observers later described as a move to the center or even the right wing of the Court, but which Black maintained was simply an adherence to his longtime principles that his former liberal allies were abandoning. Howard Lesnick (October term 1959) recalls that in subsequent years Harlan continued to speak "more and more appreciatively, and even affectionately, about Justice Black . . . perhaps because [they] shared a level of rigorous intellectual integrity" and were, they learned, distant cousins.

The second notable exception at a dinner came a few years later, when the Warren Court was in full swing. At these dinners each new (that is, current) law clerk would briefly introduce himself and his wife (if he had one), say where he went to college and law school, what were his major legal and other interests, and what postclerkship plans he had made. On this occasion, one of the new clerks strongly criticized the liberal justices and their works. The clerk's comments were well prepared, but I was upset by the unprecedented substantive remarks, with which I disagreed. But now it seems to me that more comments by law clerks, from different perspectives, about the work of the Court would have made the annual reunions more interesting.

Although the thirty-nine law clerks to Harlan varied in views, we shared pride in our justice, and there was considerable camaraderie. Perhaps that explains the enthusiastic response of the clerks when I suggested after Harlan died that the clerks hold another reunion, in 1981, the tenth anniversary of Harlan's retirement. Two-thirds of the clerks attended the dinner to hear Justice

Stewart (Harlan's closest colleague after Frankfurter's retirement). At a second reunion five years later our guest was his former law partner, John E. F. Wood, who eventually succeeded Harlan as head of the litigation department at the firm that had morphed into Dewey Ballantine before expiring in 2012. The final reunion was in 2001, the thirtieth anniversary of Harlan's retirement, at which Justice Stephen Breyer spoke. Almost all the clerks attended, knowing it was to be our last time together as a group. The book of our remembrances was distributed at the dinner.[42]

The afterlife of his law clerks provided Harlan with much pleasure. More than a third became law professors, and the others worked in prestigious law firms or the higher reaches of government, or both. I am slighting the exceptional achievements of most former clerks when I mention the names only of those who made a mark in some additional way. Michael Boudin (October term 1965), after practicing law in Washington, D.C., became a judge and eventually chief judge of the U.S. Court of Appeals for the First Circuit. Paul Brest (October term 1968) was dean of Stanford Law School and president of the Hewlitt-Packard Foundation. Louis R. Cohen (October term 1967) and Kent Greenawalt (October term 1963) were deputy solicitors general. Charles Fried (October term 1960) was solicitor general and briefly sat on the Supreme Court of Massachusetts. Philip B. Heymann (October term 1960) was deputy attorney general. Thomas G. Krattenmaker (October term 1970) was dean of William and Mary Law School. Matthew Nimetz (October terms 1965 and 1966) was counselor to the State Department and undersecretary of state. Thomas B. Stoel Jr. (October terms 1967 and 1968) was a leading founder of the Natural Resources Defense Council.

A few years ago, when I described my clerkship with Justice Harlan to a friend, he wisely said that I had omitted the most important thing, the effect it had on me. The first consequence concerned my constitutional approach. I was a moderate liberal before attending Harvard Law School in the early 1950s. There I assimilated the prevailing legal philosophy, identified with Justice Frankfurter, of caution and judicial self-restraint in enforcing the Constitution, as opposed to the liberal activism then associated with Yale Law School and Justices Black and Douglas.

Immediately after law school I worked on the army legal staff against Senator Joseph McCarthy and his counsel, Roy Cohn, during the 1954 Army-McCarthy hearings. The hearings deepened my political liberalism and awakened civil liberties impulses, but I viewed these in the context of legislative hearings. The following year I clerked for Calvert Magruder, chief judge of the U.S. Court of Appeals for the First Circuit, who had been Justice Louis Brandeis's first law clerk and then a professor and vice-dean at Harvard Law School. I learned many things from the brilliant and fair-minded Magruder, but an activist approach to civil liberties was not one of them.

When I arrived in Harlan's chambers I was still (perhaps unknowingly) very much in the Harvard mold, which viewed justices such as Frankfurter and Jackson as objective constitutionalists while regarding Black and Douglas as "result-oriented" who imposed their personal views on the Constitution. During my clerkship year, as the cases were argued, discussed, and decided, I concluded that all the justices, especially in hard and contested cases, ruled in ways that were consistent with their life views and in accordance with their philosophical or political predilections. This eventually led me in a civil liberties direction, and I ended my year with Harlan differing sharply with his approach to constitutional law.

The other effects on me were long term. They included a more considered opinion of Harlan as a justice and deeper appreciation of his virtues as a person. During Harlan's service, I and most others viewed him as a strong and even right-wing conservative. But having seen the evolution of the Court over the decades, we have a better idea of what conservatives are and have learned that Harlan, as well as Frankfurter and Jackson, was not one of them. Instead, all these justices were centrists or, perhaps more accurately, sometimes liberal and sometimes conservative. In my opinion, Harlan tried as hard as a judge could to transcend his preconceptions, an observation reinforced by the many law clerks who have remarked on his extraordinary open-mindedness.

I have already commented on Harlan's sterling personal qualities. In closing, rather than try to recount how I came to appreciate these qualities more as time passed, I will relate how several of his clerks view him. Richard Hiegel (October term 1962) focuses on Harlan's "delightful sense of humor and inexhaustible patience." Leonard Leiman (October term 1955), one of Harlan's earliest clerks, has said that Harlan "dealt with him in a way that somehow made me bigger than I was, [thereby] earning respect, loyalty and affection." Lloyd Weinreb (October term 1963) says Harlan was "wise, firm, generous understanding; he rarely spoke philosophically, but his conduct bespoke his philosophy." And David Shapiro, who has edited an excellent book on Harlan's judicial philosophy, concludes that "[t]he Justice was loved by all who knew him because he really cared about others, because he respected their ideas and smiled benignly at their eccentricities."[43] We should all do as well.

Notes

Portions of this essay have been adapted from Norman Dorsen, "The Second Mr. Justice Harlan: A Constitutional Conservative," N.Y.U.L. Rev. 44 (1969): 248; Norman Dorsen, "John Marshall Harlan, Civil Liberties, and the Warren Court," N.Y.L.S.L. Rev. 36 (1991): 81. The quotations from Justice Harlan's law clerks are from Norman Dorsen and Amelia Ames Newcomb, eds., John Marshall Harlan, Associate Justice of the Supreme Court 1955–1971: Remembrances by His Law Clerks (Boston: privately printed, 2001).

1. The best biography of Justice Harlan remains Tinsley E. Yarbrough, *John Marshall Harlan: Great Dissenter of the Warren Court* (New York: Oxford University Press, 1992), which has been of great help to me in writing this essay.

2. Henry J. Friendly, "Mr. Justice Harlan, As Seen by a Friend and Judge of an Inferior Court," *Harvard Law Review* 85 (1971): 382, 384.

3. Paul A. Freund, foreword to *The Evolution of a Judicial Philosophy: Selected Opinions and Papers of Justice John M. Harlan*, edited by David L. Shapiro (Cambridge, Mass.: Harvard University Press, 1969), xiii.

4. See Kevin J. Worthen, "Short Takes: Clerking for Justice White," in *In Chambers: Stories of Supreme Court Law Clerks and Their Justices*, edited by Todd C. Peppers and Artemus Ward (Charlottesville: University of Virginia Press, 2012); Artemus Ward, "Making Work for Idle Hands: William H. Rehnquist and His Law Clerks," in Peppers and Ward, *In Chambers*, 350. The clerks during October term 1960, Charles Fried and Phil Heymann, apparently had a practice of shooting rubber bands at each other, and Phil reports that Harlan spent time in the clerks' office picking them up.

5. Harlan kept in his chambers an easy chair used by his grandfather when he was a Supreme Court justice. Other former clerks and I do not recall whether there were other memorabilia of the first Justice Harlan.

6. 403 U.S. 15 (1971).

7. For a fascinating firsthand discussion of how the case developed and its implications for the First Amendment, See Thomas G. Krattenmaker, "Looking Back at *Cohen v. California*: A 40-Year Retrospective View from Inside the Court," *William & Mary Bill of Rights Journal* 651 (2012). A film, *Muhammad Ali's Greatest Fight* (HBO, 2013), was made of the case, with Christopher Plummer playing Justice Harlan.

8. Several clerks, including Stephen Shulman (October term 1958), have related what has become part of the lore of clerking with Harlan, who preferred to attend the opera and symphonies in black tie. When he invited a clerk to join him and Mrs. Harlan, he recommended that the clerk do the same so he would be "more comfortable." At the performance, however, Harlan and the clerk were the only two people so attired.

9. *Clay, aka Ali v. United States*, 403 U.S. 698 (1971).

10. 383 U.S. 463 (1966).

11. 369 U.S. 186, 330 (1962) (Harlan, J., dissenting).

12. 377 U.S. 533, 589 (1964) (Harlan, J., dissenting).

13. See, for example, *In re Gault*, 387 U.S. 1 (1967) (Harlan, J., concurring in part and dissenting in part), 65.

14. *Miranda v. Arizona*, 384 U.S. 436, 504 (1966) (Harlan, J., dissenting).

15. For example, *Shapiro v. Thompson*, 394 U.S. 618, 655 (1969) (Harlan, J., dissenting).

16. *New York Times Co. v. United States*, 403 U.S. 713, 752 (1971) (Harlan, J., dissenting).

17. See *Perez v. Brownell*, 356 U.S. 44 (1958); overruled, *Afroyim v. Rusk*, 387 U.S. 253, 368 (1967) (Harlan, J., dissenting).

18. See *John Marshall Harlan, 1899–1971, Memorial Addresses Delivered at a Special Meeting of the Association of the Bar of the City of New York* by Justice Potter Stewart, former attorney general Herbert Brownell, and Paul M. Bator, April 5, 1972.

19. Proceedings were held in the normal course at the Supreme Court on October

24, 1972, in memory of Justice Harlan. Seven of Harlan's law clerks were members of the Committee on Resolutions.

20. See, for example, *Heart of Atlanta Motel, Inc. v. United States*, 379 U.S. 241 (1964) (public accommodations); *Goss v. Board of Educ.*, 373 U.S. 683 (1963) (public schools).

21. See, for example, *Giordenello v. United States*, 357 U.S. 480 (1958); *Jones v. United States*, 357 U.S. 493 (1958).

22. *New York Times Co. v. Sullivan*, 376 U.S. 254 (1964).

23. See, for example, *Lemon v. Kurtzman*, 403 U.S. 602 (1971).

24. *Bivens v. Six Unknown Agents of Federal Bureau of Narcotics*, 403 U.S. 388, 398 (1971).

25. 381 U.S. 479, 499 (1965). See also Harlan's masterful opinion in *Poe v. Ullman*, 367 U.S. 497, 522 (1961), which dissented from the Court's dismissal on jurisdictional grounds of a suit brought by a married couple that presented the constitutional question eventually decided in *Griswold*. Harlan's opinion maintained that for a state to deny married couples the use of contraceptives violated the Due Process Clause of the Fourteenth Amendment, disagreeing with Justice Douglas's opinion for the Court, which rested on a right of privacy.

26. *Watkins v. United States*, 354 U.S. 178 (1957); *Sweezy v. New Hampshire*, 354 U.S. 234 (1957).

27. *Yates v. United States*, 354 U.S. 298 (1957).

28. *Jencks v. United States*, 353 U.S. 657 (1957).

29. *United States v. du Pont & Co.*, 353 U.S. 586 (1957).

30. William H. Rehnquist, "Who Writes Decisions of the United States Supreme Court?," *U.S. News and World Report*, December 13, 1957, 74–75. Responses to Rehnquist kept the issue before the public. William D. Rogers, "Do Law Clerks Wield Power in Supreme Court Cases?," *U.S. News and World Report*, February 21, 1958, 14; Alexander M. Bickel, "The Court, An Indictment Analyzed," *New York Times*, April 27, 1958, 6.

31. 355 U.S. 115 (1957).

32. Ibid., 121.

33. *United States v. Central Eureka Mining Co.*, 357 U.S. 155 (1958).

34. *Cicenia v. Lagay*, 357 U.S. 504 (1958).

35. *Maisenberg v. United States*, 356 U.S. 670 (1958); *Nowak v. United States*, 356 U.S. 660 (1958).

36. The case was *Harmon v. Brucker*, 355 U.S. 579 (1958).

37. *Barr v. Mateo*, 355 U.S. 171 (1957).

38. *West Virginia Board of Educ. v. Barnette*, 319 U.S. 624 (1943).

39. I discuss this incident in Norman Dorsen, "Book Review," *Harvard Law Review* 95 (1981): 367, 369n7, and report on a similar occasion when Frankfurter had a "herculean debate" with one of his law clerks, Albert Sacks, and praised him lavishly afterward.

40. Henry Hart and Albert Sacks, *The Legal Process: Basic Problems in the Making and Application of Law* (tentative ed., 1958).

41. Many years later, two enterprising law professors arranged for the publication in hard covers and contributed a comprehensive introduction on the development of public law in the United States. William N. Eskridge Jr. and Philip B. Frickey, *Hart and*

Sacks, The Legal Process: Basic Problems in the Making and Application of Law (West-bury, N.Y.: Foundation Press, 1994). Earlier, I prepared *Supplementary Materials to The Legal Process* (1984) for teaching purposes.

42. Norman Dorsen and Amelia Ames Newcomb, eds., *John Marshall Harlan, Associate Justice of the Supreme Court 1955–1971: Remembrances by His Law Clerks* (Boston: privately printed, 2001).

43. The most poignant remembrances, by several law clerks, including Barrett Pretty-man (1955) (who served at the end of October term 1954, when Harlan arrived at the Court), Henry R. Sailer (October term 1958), and James R. Bieke (who served at the start of October term 1971 when Harlan was hospitalized), are those written about their visits to Harlan at the George Washington University Hospital, where he spent his last weeks with uncomplaining fortitude.

A Two-For Clerkship

Stanley F. Reed and Earl Warren

D uring October term 1967, I had the unusual, though not unique, experience of serving as law clerk to two Supreme Court justices at the same time, one retired and one active. This opportunity arose because a retired Supreme Court justice is authorized to hire a single law clerk. A retired justice remains a federal judge and is eligible to serve, at the designation of the chief justice, on any federal court in the country, except the Supreme Court. Thus, each retired justice is allotted a law clerk to assist with the justice's workload.

In 1957, Stanley F. Reed retired after nineteen years of service on the Court. In the early years of his retirement, Justice Reed, who left the Court at the relatively young age (as Supreme Court justices go) of seventy-two, sat with some frequency on various federal courts around the country. From the beginning, Chief Justice Earl Warren had an understanding with Justice Reed that when the latter was not using his clerk (Justice Reed did not sit on a full-time basis), the clerk would be available to the Chief. In those days it was the practice for the chief justice's clerks to prepare memoranda for circulation to the entire Court on each of the cases on the in forma pauperis docket, which consists of cases, mostly appeals of criminal convictions or of the denials of postconviction relief, in which the petitioner cannot afford the Court's filing fee.

Because of this extra workload, Congress had provided an extra clerk for the chief justice. He had three in those days, while the associate justices were allotted two apiece. But particularly as federal constitutional issues gained much greater importance in criminal cases, the size of the in forma pauperis docket burgeoned, and the one extra clerk was simply not enough to keep up with the workload.

Justice Reed was from Maysville, Kentucky, a tiny town on the Ohio River not far from Cincinnati, and he had been a lawyer for railroads, tobacco interests, and agricultural cooperatives in the 1920s. He took a job with the Federal Farm Board in 1929, arriving in Washington, D.C., just after the Wall Street crash that set off the Great Depression. Less than six years later, he found himself in the position of solicitor general of the United States. In that role, Reed earned President Franklin D. Roosevelt's gratitude for his stalwart defense of the New Deal before an often hostile Supreme Court, and in 1938 was appointed an associate justice on the Court.

During his service on the Court, he earned the genuine affection and respect of his colleagues, and particularly Chief Justice Warren, for his courage as a southerner in signing on to the Court's decision in *Brown v. Board of Education*.[1] He was the last justice to serve on the Supreme Court without a law degree, though he studied law at both Columbia and the University of Virginia.[2] At one point during his service on the Court, Justice Reed had suffered from serious hypertension. He had devoted one entire summer recess to the Duke University Medical Center's famous rice diet and had lost some twenty-four pounds.[3] Many years later, his daily lunch still consisted of a plate of rice and an apple, served to him in chambers by messenger Gerald Ross, who was one of the true characters of the Supreme Court.

By the time I arrived at the Court in the late summer of 1967, Justice Reed was eighty-two years old and no longer sitting on lower federal courts with any frequency. In fact, during my year at the Court, Justice Reed sat only one day, on the U.S. Court of Claims, and he was not assigned any opinion for the court and did not undertake to write any dissenting or concurring opinion. Thus I did almost no work for Justice Reed; however, my office was in his chambers, so I had the opportunity to get to know him; his secretary, Helen Gaylord; and his messenger, Gerald Ross. Helen Gaylord was a delightful person who, on the occasions when the work seemed overwhelming, made my life much more cheerful. All three of them were a major part of my experience at the Court.

Gerald was, like the justice, from Maysville, Kentucky. He had worked for a time as a caddy at the local golf course and had carried Reed's bag several times. Gerald went to Washington in the 1930s, and when Reed was appointed to the Court, Gerald applied for a job as his messenger and was hired.[4] By the time I came to the Court, Gerald was largely in charge of catering to the rather imperious whims of Mrs. Reed, taking her to the grocery store and the beauty parlor and running household errands for her. Gerald was perfectly capable of putting on the air of a longtime family retainer, calling the justice "the Boss" and speaking with an exaggerated air of deference. When he served Justice Reed's daily lunch of rice and apple quarters, Gerald donned a white waiter's jacket.

But things are not always as they seem. One day Gerald walked into my office with an air of nonchalance and pulled from behind his back a paperback book, which he handed to me, saying, "I thought you might want to read this." It was *The Autobiography of Malcolm X*, the firebrand Black Muslim who raised fear and outrage among whites by his fervent attacks on white racism, and who was assassinated after he broke with Elijah Muhammad, the founder and leader of the Black Muslims. It was a powerful book, in which Malcolm X detailed the outrages perpetrated on him and his family by whites when he was young and his struggle to come to terms with the racial divide in America as an adult. I read it and discussed it with Gerald. It was the first of many long conversations I had with this interesting man.

Gerald was very bright, but he had been handicapped all his life by the relatively poor education the South offered to its black citizens and by the absolute cap it put on their aspirations. Nonetheless, he had read a lot, and he was a close observer of the institution where he worked. He would occasionally slip into the courtroom to listen to an argument, and he had a list of his least favorite decisions of the Supreme Court. At the top of this list was the grisly case of *Louisiana ex rel. Francis v. Resweber*.[5] It involved the question whether it was a violation of the Constitution to electrocute a man twice. The state of Louisiana had tried to execute the defendant, who had been sentenced to die, and had sent vast currents of electricity surging through his body. The state had botched the job, however, and the defendant lived and recovered. After he was well, the state wanted to do it all over again. The Supreme Court held, 5–4, that there was no denial of due process of law in this. Though the case was decided twenty years earlier, and the prevailing opinion was written by Justice Reed, it still outraged Gerald in 1967, and he became agitated when he talked about it.

On a daily basis I served as an extra clerk for Chief Justice Warren, and he and the rest of his staff treated me as one of his own. I arrived at the Court sometime around Labor Day and dug into the work that had piled up over the summer recess. While the justices hear no cases, except in rare emergencies, between the end of June and the beginning of October, when the Court's new term begins, the cert petitions continue to pile up, and the briefs are filed in cases where the Court has granted cert. Thus my new co-clerks and I had a lot to do before the term began. The chief justice wanted a memorandum for his use on each cert petition on the paid or "appellate" docket and a "bench memo"—a much more detailed examination of the issues and arguments—in each case that the Court was going to hear. And we had to do the memos for the whole Court on the in forma pauperis petitions.

My co-clerks were an interesting and pleasant group, and we all got along very well throughout the year. One was designated the chief clerk, whom the chief justice held responsible for the mechanics of processing the work of the chambers. This was Charlie Wilson, a tall, taciturn man from Massachusetts who had just graduated from Boalt Hall, the law school at the University of California at Berkeley. Charlie and I later practiced law together for several years.

Tyrone ("Ty") Brown, a graduate of Cornell Law School, was only the second African American to serve as a Supreme Court law clerk. It had been almost twenty years since Justice Felix Frankfurter had hired Bill Coleman, later secretary of transportation in the Ford administration, as his clerk. Ty was an extraordinarily able and pleasant person. He went on to a distinguished career in private practice and served as commissioner of the Federal Communications Commission from 1977 to 1981.

Larry Simon had graduated from Yale Law School, and he was the only one of us to have clerked at a lower court before joining the chief justice's staff (it was only then becoming common for justices to choose clerks who had a year of "seasoning" at a lower court, though that practice swiftly became universal). Larry had clerked for Judge Irving Kaufman on the Second Circuit Court of Appeals in New York. Kaufman was notorious for his blatantly pro-prosecution, Red-baiting performance as the presiding judge in the trial of Soviet spies Julius and Ethel Rosenberg, and he and Larry had not gotten along. Larry later became a law professor at the University of Southern California.

Rounding out the chambers was Larry Nichols, who was Justice Tom C. Clark's clerk. Justice Clark had announced his retirement over the summer to remove potential conflicts arising from the appointment of his son Ramsey as attorney general. He was replaced by Thurgood Marshall, the great African American lawyer who had led the campaign to overthrow legally enforced segregation and had argued *Brown v. Board of Education.* After retiring, Justice Clark had made it clear to the chief justice that, at least initially, he did not want to sit on lower federal courts in retirement. Thus he had no use for a law clerk. The chief justice leaped at this chance for more help, and Larry, like me, was essentially an extra Warren clerk. Larry was from Oklahoma and had gone to the University of Michigan Law School. He became my best friend among the clerks and my golfing companion.

The work of the chambers was essentially distributed at random. When we arrived there was an enormous pile of unprocessed cert petitions that were ready for action by the Court. Each of us would go up to the pile and grab a handful of petitions off the top, as many as we thought we could process in a day or two. If the Court granted cert in a case, that case stayed with the clerk who had worked on the petition. Thus it was a matter of the luck of the draw how many of one's cases were ultimately decided on the merits by the Court and how interesting those cases were. There was, however, a payback. The more of one's cases the Court decided to hear, the more work one had to do. It was a fair tradeoff.

A cert memo was generally a fairly short document, though in a complicated case it could take a fair amount of time to prepare. We would check to make sure the Court had jurisdiction and that procedural formalities had been complied with; state the facts succinctly; outline the issues presented; and discuss those issues briefly, stating, for example, whether they were firmly resolved by existing precedent, or whether there was a conflict on them in the lower courts. In the final paragraph of the memo, the chief justice encouraged us to make a recommendation to him as to how he should vote on the petition and why. In a cert memo in an in forma pauperis case, our recommendation paragraph appeared only on the chief justice's copy. We said nothing to the other justices about what we thought should be done with the case.

A bench memo in a case where cert had been granted was a much more elaborate affair. We would outline the parties' arguments in considerable detail and offer our own analysis of those arguments and of the Court's precedents in the area. It was harder here to separate our legal analysis from our opinions, but we tried to confine the latter to a section at the end, longer than the final section of a cert memo, where we would spell out our views in somewhat greater detail.

Although some have argued that law clerks often exert great influence over their justices, I was never really sure that the chief justice paid much attention to the recommendations we made in either our cert memos or our bench memos. He had been on the Court for almost fifteen years, and he was pretty confident of his own mind on most matters. If he looked to others for guidance, it was, I believe, to his colleagues—and in particular to Justice William J. Brennan Jr., to whom he was very close—and not to his callow law clerks. I thought the recommendation sections of the memos were basically sops to our young egos, though we all took the responsibility to try to formulate a proposed course of action very seriously.

Chief Justice Warren arrived from California a few days before the term was scheduled to begin. I have never forgotten our first meeting with him. Earl Warren had been, and remained for all of his life, the golden California politician. When he entered a room, he lit it up. Not because he was a noisy, self-promoting glad-hander. He wasn't. He was instead quiet and dignified, someone people instinctively liked and respected and to whom they looked for leadership. He had the knack of all great politicians of making the person he was talking to at the moment feel like the most important person on earth. Whenever the chief justice called me into his office to discuss a matter of Court business, he began with unhurried inquiries about me and my family, and he gave the impression that he really cared and seemed to listen to my responses.

He was a great person to work for. In my experience, especially in the political world, there are two kinds of bosses: those who make their staff members feel useful and those who make them feel used. Earl Warren was supremely one of the former. Of all the public figures and officials I have met, he was the one with the least difference between his public and his private personas. He was the one really great man, in my estimation, that I have ever known. He sought the presidency in 1952 and would have made a formidable president, but maybe he was needed more where he went.

The chief justice welcomed us in that first meeting warmly, inquired of us individually about ourselves, and told us what he expected of us in our work. We were, he said, his lawyers, and our work for him was, in his view, covered by the attorney-client privilege. That meant that we were to maintain the confidentiality of our dealings with him. We were not to talk about cases to anyone outside the Court. He acknowledged that we would inevitably discuss the Court's work with clerks from other chambers, but even here, he cautioned, what was said in his chambers was to stay there. He told us that the Court was a friendly and collegial place, and that was borne out by the obvious affection and respect that all his colleagues had for the chief justice.

Presiding over the chief justice's chambers was his secretary, Margaret Mc-Hugh, known universally among the law clerks as "Mrs. Chief Justice Mc-Hugh." She had been Chief Justice Fred Vinson's secretary, and she stayed on to guide the new chief justice through the labyrinth of the Court, where the tiny staff and the traditions of secrecy and independence bore no resemblance to the governor's office in California. She viewed it as one of her tasks to keep the law clerks in a state of sufficient intimidation that they would give no trouble. Mrs. McHugh had a gruff demeanor when she needed it, but underneath it was a real fondness for us and a twinkle in her eye. She and I always got along very well.

A few months after I left the Court, when I was interviewing for a job in his law firm, Edward Bennett Williams, who was close to the chief justice, asked me if I would mind his calling the Chief for a reference. I said not at all. An amused smile then flickered across his face, and he said, "Would you mind if I called Peggy McHugh? You know that's a different question, don't you?" I acknowledged that it was indeed a very different question and said I had no qualms about his calling Mrs. McHugh. She must not have knocked me, for I got the job.

At that time, most chambers at the Court consisted of a suite of three large rooms. There was a central room, where the justice's secretary sat, which served also as a reception room for those waiting to meet with the justice. On one side was the justice's spacious and comfortable office, with a small law library, and fitted out with a working fireplace. On the other side of the secretary's office were the law clerks in a generous room of their own containing a similar array of law books.

The chief justice's arrangement was different. His reception room was larger, and it contained the desks of Mrs. McHugh and two or three others, who provided typing assistance and help with the chief justice's many administrative duties, which included overseeing the operation of the Supreme Court building, the clerk's office, the marshal's office, and the Supreme Court police; leading the Judicial Conference of the United States and its standing committees;

and serving as chancellor of the Smithsonian Institution. The Chief's own office was larger than those of the other justices, and his suite also contained the Court's conference room, where the justices met in secret to discuss and vote on argued cases, and its robing room, where the justices gathered each day the Court was sitting to don their robes before taking the bench. The Chief's suite of offices was directly across the hall from the back wall of the courtroom itself, so the justices could walk directly from the robing room to the courtroom as they were ushered in by the marshal's call to order.

Lacking in the chief justice's suite was any separate room for law clerks, so his clerks were housed in a large suite of offices on the second floor of the building. This had two major consequences. First, his clerks had less direct personal contact with him than the clerks for other justices had with their bosses. If an associate justice wanted to ask his clerk a question, or just sit and chat, he could walk to an almost adjoining room and sit down, or call the clerk into his office within the same suite. For the chief justice to confer with one of his clerks was much more of a project, which involved the clerk hiking for several minutes from the upstairs office. The second consequence, however, was that Larry Nichols and I did not feel deprived of contact with the chief justice by virtue of the fact that our offices were in the chambers of our retired justices. Indeed, Justice Reed's chambers were on the first floor, so I was physically closer to the Chief's chambers than his own clerks were. All of us saw the Chief on business only when summoned to his office by Mrs. McHugh, and then usually to discuss something specific, such as an opinion that one of us was working on.

The location of our offices, however, did not mean that we had no relaxed time with the chief justice. Whenever he was in town, he took us to lunch on Saturdays. We regularly worked Saturday mornings, and sometime after noon we would get a call from Mrs. McHugh telling us to meet the chief justice down in the Court's underground garage, where we would all pile into his Court limousine and head off for lunch, often at the University Club or the Federal City Club.

These were wonderful sessions that we clerks cherished. The chief justice liked to relax with a drink or two before lunch on Saturday (vodka gimlets on the rocks), and he was very open and freewheeling with us. He loved sports, and in the fall lunch would usually extend to at least halftime of whatever college football game was on ABC (the only network then broadcasting college football) that week. As the term wore on and we became more comfortable around him, we asked more pointed and interesting questions about his life experience and his views on a variety of topics, and the chief justice responded with candor and relish.

One day somewhere in the middle of the term, George Cochran, an earlier Reed/Warren clerk, stopped by the Reed chambers to pay his respects to the justice. He came into my office and introduced himself, and we had a very pleasant chat. In the course of our conversation, George asked if I had yet received "the invitation." I said I didn't know what he was talking about. He told me that I would receive an invitation to lunch with the Reeds on a Sunday at the Sulgrave Club, an exclusive women's club located in a beautiful old mansion near Dupont Circle in downtown Washington. George said that the lunch was a command performance. Sure enough, not long after George's visit, I did receive an invitation for my wife, Louise, and me to join the justice and Mrs. Reed for lunch on Sunday, which was only a couple of days away. Louise and I arrived at the appointed time, a little intimidated by the idea of making conversation all by ourselves with the Reeds. The justice I knew and was comfortable with, but I had not met Mrs. Reed, and her reputation as something of a grande dame was widespread.

As it turned out, we were not alone with the Reeds. Mrs. Reed had invited Justice Douglas and his then new and very attractive young wife to join the party. Justice Douglas was out of town, but his wife, Cathy, came. My principal memory of the occasion is how confident and graceful she was. She was several years younger than my wife and I, and there had been a lot of snickering when she became the much-older justice's fourth wife. But she carried off the lunch with great aplomb, calling the Reeds "Stanley" and "Winifred," and treating us with kindness and interest. It was one of the more odd but memorable occasions of my year at the Court.

Cert memos and bench memos are all well and good, and some are interesting and challenging, but a law clerk lives for working on opinions. It is by far the most exciting part of the job. At its best it offers an opportunity to express, perhaps even to help shape, the thinking of the judge or the Court on an issue, and it holds out the hope of a little bit of immortality, or at least what passes for immortality in the rather narrow world of the law—having one's own words printed in the official publication of the Court's opinions.

Just how much and what kind of work a law clerk gets to do on opinions is a function of the work habits of the judge and of the degree of trust the judge reposes in the judgment and writing skill of the individual clerk. At the Supreme Court in 1967, for example, Justices Hugo L. Black and William O. Douglas, both of whom had served roughly thirty years on the Court and were men of strong opinions and forceful expression, did almost all their own writing. Their clerks principally checked the citations in the justices' drafts to make sure there were no mistakes, found precedents to support positions the justices wanted to take, offered suggestions on various points, and got to draft an odd footnote here or there. Some justices asked their clerks for extensive, detailed memos on particular aspects of a proposed opinion, parts of which they might incorporate in the opinion itself. Some let the clerks write the statement of facts at the beginning of the opinion, but reserved the legal analysis for themselves. Others split the writing with their clerks, with the justice doing the first draft of some opinions and the clerks drafting others.

Chief Justice Warren, at least by the time I clerked for him, did none of the original drafting of opinions. I never asked him why, but none of his prior jobs had involved much writing. His success as a politician was not dependent on memorable rhetoric, but on performance. He outworked everyone else and did a first-rate job.

The fact that he did not put the words on paper, however, did not mean that the opinions were not ultimately the Chief's product. Before a law clerk began work on an opinion draft, the chief justice would have a lengthy conversation with the clerk, in which he made clear what he wanted the opinion to say and what arguments he found persuasive. Once the law clerk had produced a draft with which he was happy and that had passed the inspection of the other clerks in chambers, it would be submitted to the chief justice. After he had read it carefully, the Chief would call the law clerk into his office and go over the opinion literally word by word, reading it aloud to the clerk, including the footnotes. This could be an excruciating, and excruciatingly long, process.

If the chief justice encountered an argument he did not like, or a citation he thought did not support the assertion for which it was offered, or found a word or phrase that offended his sensibilities, he would stop, discuss the issue with the clerk, and tell him how to revise the draft. Once the dodgy parts had been rewritten to the Chief's satisfaction, he would send the draft to the printer for typesetting and circulation. Thus the final product was something he controlled intimately and carefully. The words might be mostly the words of the clerk, but the opinion was that of the chief justice.

One of the prerogatives of being chief justice is that you get to choose which opinions you and others write for the Court. At the end of each conference, the chief justice would call us into his office along with the clerk of the Court, to whom he would communicate the Court's rulings for publication. After the clerk left, he would tell us about the votes in argued cases and answer any questions we had about what had gone on.

Chief Justice Warren never discussed opinion assignments with us clerks, but it was easy to see that he made in the first instance a scrupulous effort to spread the work of the Court evenly among the justices. He also tried, I think, to spread around the more interesting and important majority opinions, but this is a tricky business. If a justice finds himself or herself in disagreement with the chief justice on most issues of constitutional law, he or she can hardly complain that the plums always go elsewhere. And in difficult or important cases, there is undoubtedly a temptation for the chief justice to keep the case or assign it to a close ally on whom he can count to write an opinion with which the chief justice will be comfortable. Despite Chief Justice Warren's best efforts, I recall Justice Potter Stewart at some point complaining that he got too many "dogs" to write, especially tax cases.

In the remainder of this essay, I will be writing in some detail about my efforts in connection with the preparation of a couple of opinions, which naturally raises the question whether that is consistent with the chief justice's emphasis on confidentiality. This is an important question, and to answer it, I must leap forward some thirty years. One of the cases I worked on, *Terry v. Ohio*,[6] was from the beginning famous and controversial. In 1998, John Q. Barrett, of St. John's Law School in New York, undertook to organize a conference of legal scholars to celebrate the case's thirtieth anniversary and to debate various aspects of the decision and its effects.

By this time I was on the faculty of the University of Virginia School of Law and was teaching criminal procedure regularly. John learned that I had been the Chief's law clerk on *Terry* and its companion cases, *Sibron v. New York* and *Peters v. New York*,[7] and he called and invited me to talk at the conference about the Court's decision-making process in the case. I initially declined, citing the Chief's strong feelings about confidentiality. I said I had no trouble acknowledging in a private conversation with a fellow academic that I had worked on a particular case for the chief justice, but that I had never spoken in public or even in any detail in private about my work for him. John thanked me and said he hoped I would at least attend the conference.

A couple of months later John called me back and said that he had been researching in the Court's archives at the Library of Congress, which contained Chief Justice Warren's papers, and that he had copies of all my memos to the Chief, all the opinion drafts in the cases, and memos sent to the Chief by other justices. He was, he said, preparing a detailed article on the Court's inner deliberations in *Terry* for publication in connection with the conference and that it would be based to no small degree on my writings.[8] In fact, he sent me copies of all the material I had written in connection with the case. I figured that the attorney-client privilege had been pretty solidly waived, and I agreed to speak at the conference.[9]

Terry v. Ohio and the two other cases that the Court had consolidated with it for argument and consideration dealt with the controversial police practice known as "stop and frisk," which the Supreme Court had never before considered. The 1960s were a tumultuous and violent time, marked by sometimes feisty political demonstrations in favor of civil rights and against the Vietnam War, by political assassinations and race riots, the latter venting the pent-up frustration of the black community with the slow pace of legal and social change, and by a rise in the general rate of violent crime. In this overheated and often dangerous context, police officers asserted the authority to stop people they suspected of engaging in or planning criminal activity and to frisk them by patting down their clothing to see if they were carrying weapons. The police argued, with some force, that they needed this authority to protect themselves and others from possible injury or death. A number of states gave sanction to these practices by statute or judicial decision.

The criminal defense bar and civil rights lawyers argued that the practice violated the Fourth Amendment to the Constitution, which prohibits "unreasonable searches and seizures" and bars the issuance of search or arrest warrants without "probable cause, supported by oath or affirmation." The term "probable cause" had been interpreted by the Court to mean that the magistrate—or the police officer acting without a warrant—must be possessed of sufficient evidence "to warrant a man of reasonable caution in the belief that an offense has been or is being committed" before a person could be arrested or a search of his or her person, house, papers, or effects could be undertaken.[10] The standard was a significant bar to police action. Essentially the officer had to demonstrate that the evidence in his or her possession made it more likely than not ("*probable* cause") that criminal activity was afoot and that the individual seized or searched was engaged in it.

The facts in *Terry* illustrated the problem clearly. Martin McFadden, an experienced plainclothes detective on patrol in downtown Cleveland, observed Terry and two other men pacing up and down the same block and alternately peering intensely into a store window and conferring with one another. This went on for some time. McFadden believed that the men were "casing" the store for a possible robbery or burglary. He went up to the men, identified himself as a police officer, and asked their names. When one of them "mumbled something" in response, McFadden grabbed Terry, placed him between himself and the other two, and frisked him, finding a revolver in his overcoat pocket.

Terry was prosecuted for illegal possession of a concealed firearm, and his lawyer objected to the introduction of the weapon in evidence on the ground that the prosecution's possession of it was the result of an unconstitutional search and seizure. It was clear that McFadden did not possess "probable cause" to arrest Terry or his companions for any crime before he found the gun. But as the finding of the revolver underscored, it was difficult to say that McFadden was wrong in suspecting that the men were armed and dangerous and up to no good (one of the other men was also found to possess a gun).

The initial question in the cases was whether the Fourth Amendment applied at all, whether a "stop" was a "seizure" of the person and whether a "frisk" was a "search." The police took the position that the Fourth Amendment did not come into play until a person was arrested and taken to the police station, at which point they concededly needed "probable cause." The lesser intrusion represented by a "stop and frisk," they urged, could be undertaken on a less-demanding evidentiary showing. The other side argued, with the force of considerable logic, that when a policeman grabs a person forcibly, spins the person around, and pats him or her down for weapons, the officer has undoubtedly physically "seized" the person and conducted a "search," acts for which the officer needs "probable cause," which, they asserted, was often lacking when the police acted quickly on the basis of their "hunches" about suspicious-looking persons. Civil rights advocates made the additional troubling point that this kind of police conduct was most often directed at members of minority groups who frequently lived in "ghettos" in major cities and were targeted by police sometimes without rational basis. (McFadden was white; Terry and his friends were black.)

These were very hard questions, and they arose in the context of the bitterly contested 1968 presidential campaign, in which former vice president Richard Nixon was leading an attack on the Court as siding too often with "the criminal forces" against "the peace forces" in its decisions holding police and prosecutors to the strictures of the Bill of Rights. In this context, some have argued, the Court blinked and pulled back from the confrontation.[11] Its initial vote at the conference after argument in the *Terry* cases was a unanimous one to uphold the "stop and frisk" practices. The chief justice assigned the opinions in all three cases to himself, and as I had been the clerk who did the cert and bench memos, the drafting fell to me.

The Court's initial unanimity in *Terry*, as I later learned, masked an almost complete lack of consensus about how to justify the police conduct under the Fourth Amendment. The chief justice told me that the opinion should say that stop and frisk practices were indeed searches and seizures subject to the constraints of the Fourth Amendment, and that the appropriate standard was "probable cause," but that in the context of potentially dangerous street encounters with suspicious persons, "probable cause to frisk" demanded less evidence than the traditional "probable cause" to make an arrest or a full-body search. I drafted an opinion along these lines, and the chief justice seemed pleased with it. We circulated it, and it sank like a stone to the bottom of a pool of water. No one joined it. The problem was that, while it might well be that Officer McFadden had acted reasonably in the circumstances, it was difficult to argue with a straight face that he had "probable cause" to do anything.

After several weeks of deafening silence, Justice Douglas gave the chief justice a memorandum with a suggested rewrite of portions of the opinion. The Chief was unimpressed and rejected the Douglas draft. Then Justice Brennan, the Chief's closest ally on the Court, offered his own suggested revisions of parts of the opinion. The essence of the Brennan suggestion was to uncouple the two clauses of the Fourth Amendment. The Court had said in the past that the only standard for a "reasonable" search under the first clause was "probable cause," for the simple and persuasive reason that a police officer should not have the authority to do something on his or her own that a magistrate could not authorize the officer to do if he or she applied for a warrant.[12] This made sense, Brennan argued, in situations where applying for a warrant was at least theoretically possible; however, in rapidly unfolding street encounters between police and citizens, where getting a warrant was completely out of the question, the standard for defining an "unreasonable search" could be separated from the "probable cause" standard of the Warrant Clause. Standing on its own, "reasonableness" could permit a sliding-scale approach that weighed the information possessed by the police officer against the risk involved in the situation and the intrusiveness of his actions. Measured against this standard, McFadden's pat-down of Terry was, according to Justice Brennan, reasonable.

It was an ingenious and typically Brennanesque move, and the chief justice decided to adopt it. He told me to prepare a new draft incorporating the Brennan suggestions. In the process of doing so, I had numerous conversations with Justice Brennan's clerk on the cases, Ray Fisher, later a judge on the U.S. Court of Appeals for the Ninth Circuit, with whom I was friendly and who also spoke at John Q. Barrett's conference thirty years later. The move led, however, to the defection of Justice Douglas, who adhered to the view that the clauses should be read *in pari materia* and thus that McFadden's actions could be justified only if he had "probable cause" of some sort.[13]

There then developed a sticking point that led to my scariest experience as a law clerk. Chief Justice Warren's instinct had been from the start to uncouple the "stop" and the "frisk" and to give the Court's explicit approval only to the latter, as a necessary protective device. He was much more troubled by the power to "stop," to detain a person possibly for investigative purposes on less than probable cause. He thought it was potentially subject to great abuse and could lead to what amounted to arrests in many cases on mere suspicion. Thus the initial draft of the opinion had said that, since McFadden had done nothing that could be construed as a "seizure" before he grabbed Terry and patted him down, the Court need not reach the issue of investigative stops at all. Justice Brennan suggested, however, that the Court reach and decide the "stop" issue in favor of the police.

I was very concerned and wrote the chief justice a long memo urging him not to accept this part of the Brennan position. Somewhat to my surprise, the chief justice shared my memo with Justice Brennan. He called me into his office one morning and said that Justice Brennan did not share my concerns and had assured him that there was no problem in reaching the "stop" issue. When I stuck to my guns in our conversation, the chief justice buzzed Mrs. McHugh and asked her to find out if Justice Brennan was in his office. When she buzzed back a couple of minutes later and said the justice was in, the chief justice stood up and said, "Come on." I was, to say the least, shell-shocked. Mrs. McHugh didn't help. As we passed her desk, she said under her breath so that only I could hear, in a little singsong, "He's gonna be sur*prised*."

As we entered Justice Brennan's office, Chief Justice Warren was in the lead. When Justice Brennan saw him, his face broke into a huge grin. When he saw me, it froze. The chief justice was obviously troubled and was, I think, looking to have a debate between Justice Brennan and me over the "stop" issue. I soon learned to my great relief that there was one person in the room who wanted such a debate even less than I did. Justice Brennan seized the floor and began telling jokes nonstop, as only a delightful Irishman could. After about five minutes, the chief justice got the point and we left.

In the end, Chief Justice Warren stuck with his own initial instinct and avoided the "stop" issue.[14] This led to concurring opinions from Justices John Marshall Harlan and Byron White urging that logic required the Court to reach the "stop" question.[15] But the chief justice's opinion with the Brennan modification, and without any approval of investigative stops, garnered a solid majority of six. And I like to think that it may have led the Court to approach the "stop" issue in future cases with great caution and to place serious limitations on the power to detain for investigation on less than probable cause.[16]

My final opinion-drafting exercise involved another case of great public interest and controversy, *Powell v. Texas*,[17] and my work on the case was truly an eye-opening experience. *Powell* raised the question whether it constituted "cruel and unusual punishment," prohibited by the Eighth Amendment, to convict a chronic alcoholic of the crime of being drunk in public. The state of California had in the 1950s made it a crime to be addicted to narcotics. In 1962, in the case of *Robinson v. California*,[18] the Supreme Court had struck down this law under the Eighth Amendment, holding that to penalize under the criminal law a "status"—being an addict, over which one might have no control—as opposed to an act, which one presumably undertook voluntarily, violated basic norms of a free society and constituted "cruel and unusual punishment."

In the wake of *Robinson*, defense lawyers around the country had sought to extend its reach to chronic alcoholics and to their punishment for public drunkenness. The argument was that being an alcoholic was a status, like being a narcotics addict, and that an alcoholic could not control his or her state of inebriation in a public place. It was thus, the argument ran, essentially the punishment of a mere status.

Some lower courts, most notably the federal court of appeals for the District of Columbia Circuit, had bought the argument and reversed the convictions of alcoholics for public drunkenness. Others had rejected it. The topic was hotly debated in the law reviews and among lawyers generally.

Leroy Powell, a Texan with a long history of arrests and convictions for public drunkenness, was arrested once again in public in a state of inebriation. His lawyer put on expert testimony that Powell was an alcoholic and that a chronic alcoholic, at least once he or she takes the first drink, has no power to control his or her further consumption of alcohol. Powell took the stand in his defense, and on cross-examination the prosecutor took a shot in the dark. He asked Powell if he had had anything to drink that morning before the trial. The shot hit home. Powell admitted that he had taken one drink that someone had given him, presumably to steady his nerves. The prosecutor pressed his advantage, getting Powell to admit that he had been able to stop at one drink that day because of the importance of his trial. Even in the face of this admission, the trial court found that Powell was a chronic alcoholic and that as an alcoholic he had no power to stop drinking once he had started, but ruled that this was no defense to the charge. The Texas Court of Criminal Appeals denied its version of cert, and the U.S. Supreme Court granted Powell's petition.

The stock liberal position favored Powell's argument. Lawyers for him and for people like him contended that the Constitution should be used to break the "revolving-door" cycle of arrest, conviction, brief incarceration, release, and rearrest that these unhappy people faced and force the states to replace it with some form of humane treatment. In my bench memo, I urged the chief justice to adopt this position.

The Chief was clearly troubled by the case, and at our Saturday lunch the weekend before the argument he took the unique step our term of asking the assembled clerks for their views of what he should do. He went around the table, and all five of us in turn expressed our support for Powell's position. The Chief chuckled and said, "Well, that's very interesting, because I think I am going to vote the other way." He explained that, while psychiatrists now generally agreed that alcoholism was a disease, there was no real consensus about what that meant; that there was no agreed-upon course of treatment for alcoholics; and that even if there had been, there weren't enough psychiatrists in the country to treat all the alcoholics, even if the latter could all afford treatment and the doctors dropped their treatment of all other patients.

He went on to say that no city would tolerate large numbers of unruly and often unsanitary drunks on its streets, and that the inevitable result of decriminalizing public drunkenness by alcoholics would be involuntary "civil commitment." The latter would carry with it indefinite incarceration until the patient was "cured," which in most cases would simply never happen, both because of the intractability of the condition and of the lack of resources to try to treat it. At least under the present system, despite its obviously ugly features, the chronic alcoholic convicted of public drunkenness got a few days in jail to sober up, some solid food, and, most important of all, his or her liberty back once he or she had served his or her brief sentence.

It was a powerful argument, and it was vintage Earl Warren. It cut through, if indeed it did not ignore, nuances of constitutional theory and focused on the practical impact of legal rules on human beings. The chief justice was deeply schooled in the craft of government, and he had spent a lot of time thinking about how the actions of government actually affect people. And the argument was at bottom intensely empathetic and humane.

At the conference after the argument, the Court voted 5–4 to reverse Leroy Powell's conviction. The split defied conventional liberal-conservative distinctions. The majority consisted of Justices Douglas, Brennan, Stewart, White, and Fortas. Stewart and White were on many issues among the more conservative members of the Court. The dissenters were the chief justice and Justices Black, Harlan, and Marshall. Warren, Black, and Marshall were thought of as stalwart liberals. Justice Douglas, as the senior associate justice in the majority, assigned the opinion to Justice Fortas. The chief justice made it known that he was contemplating writing a dissent.

Once the proposed majority opinion by Justice Fortas had circulated, the chief justice called me in and instructed me to prepare a dissent. Its outline was to be essentially the argument he had presented to his clerks over lunch several weeks earlier. I got to work, and I found as my research delved more deeply into alcoholism and its treatment that the chief justice had spoken from solid knowledge throughout. I also made use of Powell's admission on cross-examination that he could limit himself to one drink if the incentive were powerful enough, in an effort to undercut the defense bar's implicit assertion that the "disease concept" of alcoholism had a clear meaning. While I was still working on the draft, Justice White switched his vote, circulating a brief statement saying only that *Robinson* was distinguishable because it involved punishment of a mere status, while in this case the acts of getting drunk and going into public were the crux of the offense. Thus the status of the chief justice's emerging draft opinion was unclear, but on his instructions I continued to cast it as a dissent from the Fortas draft.

The Chief seemed pleased with my draft, and after a few revisions it was ready to circulate. Or so I thought. At the end of our last meeting he said, with an apparently musing air, "I think I'll show this to Thurgood." I assumed he meant that he would try to get Justice Marshall to sign on before he circulated the draft, in order to show that it already had some purchase among the erstwhile dissenters. As I learned, however, he was up to something deeper.

I soon began to get a lot of phone calls about the draft from Peter Lockwood, one of Justice Marshall's clerks, that seemed to go into more detail than would have been required to decide whether to sign on to a proposed dissent. Then one day, to my complete surprise, I received a printed version of the draft headed, "Mr. Justice Marshall, with whom the Chief Justice joins, dissenting."

Peter and his justice had made a few modifications, but it was for the most part the draft I had given the chief justice. Justices Black and Harlan also signed on, though Justice White stuck to his brief concurrence,[19] so the opinion ultimately spoke for a plurality of the Court. Peter Lockwood and I had a good laugh, and he proclaimed me an honorary Marshall law clerk.

I never took the opportunity to ask the chief justice why he had done what he did, but if I had studied his career on the Court with a little more care, I might have seen it coming. Chief Justice Warren disagreed from time to time with the majority of the Court, as all justices do. He joined dissenting opinions. But he relatively rarely wrote them himself. I think I know why. A dissenting opinion inevitably is a frontal attack on the work of a colleague, and while most judges develop fairly thick skins, they are not immune to the sting of criticism. I believe the chief justice thought that such attacks were divisive and could, if undertaken often enough, undermine his relationships with other justices and his ability to build consensus in the large run of cases, as he believed it was his responsibility as the Chief to do. So he put Justice Marshall out front, at one and the same time avoiding the need to take on Justice Fortas directly and giving the spotlight in a major case to a newly minted justice. I learned a tremendous amount from the chief justice in the *Powell* case, both about the sometimes tenuous relationship between legal doctrine and the practicalities of decision making, and about leadership in a group of equals. It was a bravura performance.

In May 1968, my co-clerks and I attended our first reunion of the chief justice's law clerks. It was an annual gala event. Former clerks came from around the country to pay their respects to the Chief and to renew acquaintances or friendships with each other. It was a weekend-long affair. The former clerks wandered in and out of chambers on Friday afternoon, chatting with Mrs. McHugh and the others. On Saturday night there was a black-tie dinner for the chief justice and the clerks, and on Sunday morning the Chief and Mrs. Warren hosted a brunch for the clerks and their wives and significant others. It was a very pleasant ritual, and it went on until the chief justice died in 1974.

In 1968, one of Chief Justice Warren's former clerks, Jim Gaither, was working as an aide to President Lyndon B. Johnson. It was the Chief's fifteenth anniversary on the Court, and Jim arranged for President Johnson to come to the Saturday evening dinner as a surprise to the Chief. It was the height of the Vietnam War and only two months after deep opposition to the war in the Democratic Party had led Johnson to withdraw from the presidential race. When the president entered the room during the cocktail hour, a hushed silence fell over the crowd. It was very odd. I sensed no hostility to Johnson, despite the fact that many of us strongly opposed his handling of the war. We all thought it was a very nice gesture on his part to come to honor the Chief. It was just, I think, that we had no idea what to say at a cocktail party to the president of the United States—this despite the fact that the group was full of sophisticated lawyers, many of them already well launched on what would be very distinguished careers, who had been chatting away quite comfortably with the highest judicial officer in the land.

The president slid over to the bar, took pains to shake hands with the wait staff, ordered a Scotch, and chug-a-lugged it. After about fifteen minutes of really awkward small talk, he said some very nice things about the chief justice, handed him a gift-wrapped present, and departed. We learned from Jim Gaither that Johnson had originally planned to stay for dinner but decided to leave when things seemed so uncomfortable.

In retrospect, I felt sorry for President Johnson. He must have been very lonely. The chief justice did not open his gift from the president while the latter was still there. There was a tradition of the clerks collectively giving the Chief a gift, and he did not open that until after-dinner remarks were under way, so the president's gift was set aside and opened after dinner as well. When the Chief opened the president's gift, it turned out to be a bronze bust of President Johnson himself. The Chief said, a bit ruefully, "I guess I should have opened that while the president was here."

As the Supreme Court term wore down toward its end, Chief Justice Warren continued his kindly interest in us and our families. He insisted that we pick out a morning when my wife, Louise, and one-year-old son, Will, could come to the Court to see him. He had met Louise at the reunion festivities, but he wanted to chat with her more personally and to see Will. He had a politician's gusto for babies. We still have the picture of Will, roughly a year old, in the Chief's arms. Two years later, on Valentine's Day, Will, remembering the Chief's kindly manner, decided to send him a Valentine card. The chief justice wrote back a thoughtful thank-you note, complimenting Will on how well he made his letters.

Our last day at the Court was both a pleasant and a bittersweet one. The chief justice called us all into his office, gave us autographed pictures of himself, and told us what a pleasure it had been working with us. He also told us that he had sent his retirement letter to President Johnson that morning. The news came as a shock to us law clerks. None of us could really remember a chief justice before him, and we all admired him enormously. We knew that he deserved retirement—he was almost eighty and had been in public service all his adult life—and that he had some health issues. But we also knew that his leadership would be sorely missed. The world of the Court was about to change, and not, I thought, for the better. As it turned out, Chief Justice Warren served another term when President Johnson's choice as his successor, Justice Fortas, withdrew his name after a bruising confirmation fight in the Senate.

During the years following my clerkship, I continued to have occasional and very warm contact with Chief Justice Warren. Of course, I attended the annual law clerks' reunions. I have mentioned that the Chief was a big sports fan and personally close to Ed Williams, the senior partner at Williams and Connolly, where I practiced law beginning in 1969. Williams was president of the Washington Redskins, and the Chief was a regular guest in the Redskins' president's box at RFK Stadium when the team was playing at home. At halftime the team served food and drinks to the guests, and members of the law firm were welcomed. I often had a chance to chat briefly with the Chief while warming up between halves. One day my friend Dennis Flannery, another former Warren clerk from Wilmer, Cutler, and Pickering, and I took the Chief out for a memorable lunch at a fancy downtown restaurant.

I did not see a lot of the chief justice in the six years after my clerkship ended, but I saw enough to realize that despite his cheerful and upbeat demeanor, his health was beginning to fail. The end came on July 9, 1974. It was decided that his body would lie in state in the Great Hall of the Supreme Court. Mrs. McHugh quickly organized an honor guard of former law clerks to stand by the casket. Mostly because we were close at hand, Charlie Wilson and I were among the first group to serve in this capacity. It was taking Mrs. McHugh a while to find a second shift, so we stood for more than two hours, as thousands of people walked by the flag-draped bier in a remarkable outpouring of emotion to pay their respects to this great man. I felt sad but honored to be able to take part in this tribute.

Notes

1. 347 U.S. 483 (1954).

2. John D. Fassett, *New Deal Justice: The Life of Stanley Reed of Kentucky* (New York: Vantage Press, 1994), 12, 14–15.

3. Ibid., 470–72.

4. Ibid., 211.

5. 329 U.S. 459 (1947).

6. 392 U.S. 1 (1968).

7. Both decided under the rubric of *Sibron v. New York,* 392 U.S. 40 (1968).

8. See John Q. Barrett, "Deciding the Stop and Frisk Cases: A Look Inside the Supreme Court's Conference," *St. John's Law Review* 72 (1998): 749. For a discussion of my writings in the cases, see ibid., 793–830.

9. For an edited and expanded version of my talk, see Earl C. Dudley Jr., "*Terry v. Ohio,* the Warren Court, and the Fourth Amendment: A Law Clerk's Perspective," *St. John's Law Review* 72 (1998): 891.

10. *Brinegar v. United States,* 338 U.S. 160, 175–76 (1949).

11. For an argument that the Warren Court's reputation for innovation and courage

in the sphere of constitutional criminal procedure is overrated, not only in *Terry* but more broadly, see the fine article of my former student Corinna Barrett Lain, "Counter-majoritarian Hero or Zero? Rethinking the Warren Court's Role in the Criminal Procedure Revolution," *University of Pennsylvania Law Review* 152 (2004): 1361.

12. See, for example, *Wong Sun v. United States,* 371 U.S. 471, 479 (1963).

13. See *Terry,* 392 U.S. at 35 (Douglas, J., dissenting).

14. Ibid., 19n16.

15. Ibid., 31 (Harlan, J., concurring); 34 (White, J., concurring).

16. See Dudley, "Law Clerk's Perspective," 895–98.

17. 392 U.S. 514 (1968).

18. 370 U.S. 660 (1962).

19. 392 U.S. at 548 (White, J., concurring).

III Modern Clerks

Memories of Clerking for Potter Stewart

Unlike other justices in this collection of essays, few clerkship accounts have been written by the law clerks of Justice Potter Stewart, who served on the Court from 1958 to 1981. When we contacted former clerk Monroe Price, he not only agreed to write an essay but also reached out to his fellow law clerks to solicit their memories as well. What follows is a collection of eight different essays solicited and edited by Price. Collectively, they provide a rare glimpse into the lives of Justice Stewart and his clerks.

Thomas Kauper, October Terms 1960–1962

When I reported to the Court in July 1960, Washington was a small southern city. My wife could drive downtown, park on the street, and shop in the major department stores. Tysons Corner was nothing but fruit stands and orchards. There were trolley cars on Pennsylvania Avenue and elsewhere. The structure of the city was simple.

The same can be said of Justice Stewart's chambers. I was fortunate to clerk at a time when the justice took his clerks for two-year staggered terms, hiring only one new clerk per year. So the chambers housed the justice, two clerks, two secretaries, and one messenger. It was an intimate setting, far more so than is the case today. The justice's door was generally open, as he himself was. He took interest in our families. There were regular inquiries about my wife's pregnancy. The night before the inauguration of John F. Kennedy, Washington was hit with one of the heaviest snowfalls in its history. By late afternoon, traffic was at a standstill. Cars were abandoned by the thousands as they ran out of gas. I managed to get home to Alexandria by 9:00 p.m. At about 11:00 we were awakened by a call. It was Justice Stewart, concerned about whether I got home safely (he did not—having left his car on the street, he stayed with friends in Georgetown).

This essay's contributing authors include Thomas Kauper, Alan R. Novak, Steven M. Umin, Thomas D. Rowe Jr., David M. Schulte, Frederick T. Davis, and Daniel R. Fischel.

It was a simpler time. Clerks typed their memos on certiorari petitions. Volumes of carbon copies of my memos sit on my bookshelves today. We were generally not trained typists, and our memos looked awful, but Justice Stewart was a tolerant man and put up with it (although there was probably little else he could do). Interchambers communications were generally handwritten and delivered by messengers.

We all have memories of particular moments with the justice. Saturday lunches at the Methodist Building, away from the Court, were relaxed and seldom focused on the Court's work. Meetings with the justice prior to Friday Court conferences when we discussed the cases scheduled for a vote were open and sometimes argumentative. Justice Stewart used these sessions to test his ideas and to make sure we had touched all the bases. He always heard us out, although there were surely times when he thought we were a little foolish and perhaps a bit too idealistic.

When opinions were assigned, the justice seldom asked us for opinion drafts. He generally wrote his own opinions, using briefs and memos we prepared. He wrote quickly and extremely well, with a flair for using a turn of the phrase to highlight a point, or sometimes to obscure an issue. His pornography line in *Jacobellis v. Ohio* is well known: "I know it when I see it."[1] In *Silverman v. United States*,[2] a case with which I was involved, the Court held that evidence obtained through use of a so-called spike mike (a device driven into a wall to make contact with heating ducts) was inadmissible. In a narrow opinion Justice Stewart found that because driving into the wall was "an authorized physical invasion," the case could be distinguished from *Goldman v. United States*.[3] The Court had been asked to overrule *Goldman*. Justice Stewart's response—"[w]e find no occasion to re-examine *Goldman* here, but we decline to go beyond it, by even a fraction of an inch"—was a classic. And so the issue was disposed of. Other members of the Court seldom proposed purely editorial changes to his opinions.

Every clerk recalls particular cases on which he or she worked. They are usually the significant cases of the day. In my two terms we had our share. In the long run, the case with the greatest impact was *Baker v. Carr*,[4] opening the federal courts to review of state legislative appointment schemes. The case was argued twice, and Justice Stewart's vote was critical to the outcome. In *Engel v. Vitale*,[5] the Court turned to school prayers. *Mapp v. Ohio*,[6] applying the exclusionary rule to the states, was another case with a lasting impact.

In a series of cases charging individuals who refused to testify before congressional committees about Communist Party membership, Justice Stewart held that indictments in each of a significant number of cases was insufficient,[7] a holding that disposed of the whole group of cases on narrow grounds, avoided the difficult constitutional issues they presented, and led, I fear, to a wholesale rewriting of the law concerning indictments. There was even an antitrust case—*Brown Shoe v. United States*[8]—with, unfortunately, a long-lasting, pernicious impact. Justice Stewart could not be talked out of joining the Court's opinion. In my career in antitrust, I could never get away from *Brown Shoe*. I believe to this day that it was wrong.

Of significant cases there were many. But I will focus instead on a case that can fairly be said to be of no significance whatsoever, a case without precedential impact of any kind, but a case that caught the justice's interest and resulted in the expenditure of research effort, analysis, and discussion that in hindsight may seem unwarranted. Justice Stewart was a navy man who served on oil tankers during World War II. His naval experience led the chief justice, impressed with the justice's use of "bow" and "stern" rather than "front" and "rear," to assign him admiralty cases. It also helps to explain his interest in *Bell v. United States*.[9] In *Bell*, petitioners were American soldiers who were captured during the Korean War and imprisoned in Korea. Within the camp they "behaved with utter disloyalty to their comrades and to their country." They made anti-American recordings for broadcast in China, and took a variety of other actions that directly harmed others in the camp. At war's end they refused to return to the United States and went instead to China. They were dishonorably discharged.

They had a change of heart and returned to the United States, where they filed a claim with the Department of the Army for back pay covering their time in captivity. Their claim was rejected by the army and the court of claims. The Court granted certiorari for reasons that are hard to discern, except, perhaps, out of some need to show that the justice system worked even for these turncoats. The briefs and arguments of the parties passed like ships in the night. Petitioners relied on an 1814 statute, reenacted several times, that seemed to give captured military personnel an absolute right to pay during captivity. Knowing that it had virtually no case under the 1814 act, the government basically ignored it, relying instead on the Missing Persons Act of 1942. It provided for payment to persons "in active service" who were "officially determined to have been captured." Petitioners dealt with the 1942 statute as the government had done with the earlier statute: they virtually ignored it. In sum, the parties were of little help.

Hours of research were expended on the relationship between the two statutes and on such esoteric questions as whether disregard of orders of the senior American officer in the camp, or direct collaboration with the enemy, supported a finding that the collaborators could be deemed absent without leave or not "in active" service while still within the camp. Cartloads of materials arrived from the Library of Congress. We had many hours of discussion over a number of weeks as the research progressed. In the end, the decision rested on a simple proposition. While the army had determined that petitioners had been captured during the war, it had never made any other findings relating to "active service" under the 1942 act. It had actually denied the claims based on a determination that the petitioners were members of the Communist Party, which did not seem relevant to much of anything. And so it turned out. The appropriation act provision on which the finding relied was repealed before the claim was presented. There were simply no findings in support of any part of the government's argument. A very brief opinion should have been sufficient. But the opinion, in which the justice held that the soldiers were due back pay, is long by Stewart standards.

Given the actual holding, why was so much time expended? The subject was inherently interesting, particularly to those with a historical bent. The Korean War and the events that followed were still fresh in American minds, as the final paragraph in the opinion notes. Strangely, the case at the outset was complex, in part because the parties did not present it well. In the end, however, the explanation rests in the justice's own fascination with the case, and with the meeting of two naval vessels in 1807. He was simply enjoying the exercise.

The opinion begins with a discussion of military pay generally. It then recites a brief history, beginning in 1333, of collaboration by prisoners of war with their captors. This is followed by the treatment of pay claims by returning captured soldiers and sailors. Then comes an analysis of the 1814 and 1942 statutes. It is no accident that the centerpiece of the opinion is the confrontation in 1807 between HMS *Leopard* and the U.S. frigate *Chesapeake* off the coast of Virginia. An American seaman taken off the *Chesapeake* was impressed into British service. Following his return and death, his widow successfully claimed his pay during the period of imprisonment.

The incident between the *Chesapeake* and the *Leopard* is a major element in American naval history. Justice Stewart was a navy man. Given the chance to give the navy a prominent role in an opinion, he did not want to give it up even though, in the end, it was completely irrelevant. So all of the history, developed through weeks of research, remained. Perhaps better lawyering would have pointed to the deficiency of findings earlier, and the opinion would have said little else. Or perhaps the *Chesapeake* and *Leopard* would not have found each other, and a different opinion might have appeared. From my point of view, that would have been too bad. The case gave me a relationship with Justice Stewart we might not otherwise have had. We were simply having a good time together.

Perhaps because the case had little meaning except to the parties—and the justice did believe the outcome was very much in the country's interest—he was free to do pretty much as he wished with the opinion. He had a virtual carte blanche from the rest of the Court, which had split 4–4 without him (although the decision was ultimately unanimous). He took advantage to be a little bit of a navy man again. I worked on cases of far greater significance than *Bell.* None was as much fun. For that I thank the *Chesapeake* and the *Leopard.*

Alan R. Novak, October Term 1963

Justice Stewart and I, and our families, shared a warm friendship that extended for years beyond 1963. Sadly, time and circumstances caused the relation to fade in his later years. But I still feel I know this man, this justice pretty well. Personally, he was gentle, decent, and unpretentious. He and his wife, Mary Ann ("Andy"), were committed to each other and to their three children, Harriet, Patsy, and David, in that "Greatest Generation" way. David needed developmental help as a child, which brought them even more closely together, and it turned out well. Professionally, the justice was hardworking, jurisprudentially principled, apolitical, and nonpartisan, albeit a Scranton Republican. He did not fancy himself a brilliant jurist, but he was proud of his writing skills, and insisted on doing the first draft of every opinion.

Stewart's modesty, which extended to his view of the role of a justice, played out in various ways. Office activity was very easygoing and unpretentious. Internal case deliberations were straightforward and even-handed. His modesty, coupled with a genial and friendly manner, enabled him to relate well to the other justices, particularly John Marshall Harlan and Byron R. White, but also Hugo L. Black and William J. Brennan. Cutting the other way, respect for Stewart made him clearly a candidate for chief justice, but his inclination was to decline (too bad really; he would have been effective and collegial). I view his early retirement also in part driven by his modesty—in retrospect, a loss to the Court and bearing some relation to his untimely passing.

The Warren Court in 1963 had, it was generally thought, two "conservative" justices, Stewart and Harlan, and White, the new guy, who seemed to be leaning that way. Stewart's clerks came mostly from Yale, that bastion of liberalism, yet most Stewart clerks, I believe, were not uncomfortable with his jurisprudence. My co-clerk, Jan Deutsch, a second-year clerk and, according to many, the smartest guy to graduate Yale Law School, was comfortable with Stewart, because the justice was invariably reasonable and unwilling to rule just on the basis of an outcome. Less disciplined that Jan and more liberal, even I never thought of Stewart as "conservative" but more a down-the-middle guy, progressive particularly about race, with a good feel for the institutional role of the Court vis-à-vis Congress, the executive, the agencies, states, and the protected rights of the individual.

Turning eighty, and looking back over almost sixty years since college, my year with the justice ranks right at the top of my memories. And in that year,

1963, Justice Arthur Goldberg passing clerks on the stairs between the lunch-room and chambers, shouting the president had been shot.

Monroe E. Price, October Terms 1964 and 1965

In trying to re-create, even slightly, the experience of clerking for Justice Stew-art, I have relied on memory, mostly, and a bit on the little red volume each clerk got (at least my year) of cases in which his or her justice wrote opinions. Justice Stewart's volume in 1964–65 was relatively thin—a product of his style of writing and the extent to which the major hitters (Chief Justice Earl Warren and Associate Justices William J. Brennan, Hugo L. Black, William O. Douglas, and Arthur Goldberg) got the big cases. I also had another source to refresh my memory: letters that I sent to my fiancée, Aimée Brown, then in Paris, typed at my sheltered desk in Stewart's chambers at the Court. These were love letters, after a fashion, but they also gave some insights into my thoughts and activities at the time.

In those letters, I gave brief accounts of playing basketball up above the Court's library with Justice White and other clerks, and returning, at times, in a sweat, to meet with the justice before a sweltering fire in his fireplace. I wrote about the distinguished bow-tied and crew-cut Archibald Cox and the respect he commanded as solicitor general and "Tenth Justice." I wrote about my meticulous co-clerk, Paul Dodyk, and our relationships with clerks in other chambers. The letters reflect my hopes and apprehensions about the tasks at hand and about the future. They tell the story, too, of observing Potter Stewart as a decent man, an elegant product of his generation and class, conscientiously performing a high national civic duty.

In an early letter, for example, I wrote about the close, almost intimate na-ture of the chambers: "the Court is a sealed-off enterprise where everyone inside feels special and is constantly on guard to protect against an invasion from outside. . . . The Court is one big family. Our office, for example, con-tains a very sweet, efficient and devoted secretary (Helene Dwyer), Justice Stewart, who is also sweet, efficient and devoted, and us, the two clerks, who are sweet, devoted and learning to be efficient." I wrote of "[Westley J.] Pitt-man, the chauffeur, delivery man and Man Friday," who for me was symbolic of the Court as a nineteenth-century institution, caste-fixed, still reflecting mild remnants of racial segregation. Pittman was a preacher and had a con-gregation he served on weekends, and his devotion and faith were part of the office routine.

Not only the chambers, but the Court, was a privileged place, a temple de-voted to the texts produced by its own gods. "At the Court, every whim is ca-tered to. If any book is needed or any paper or furniture to be fixed, all you do is call and you are deluged by devoted hangers-on from the staff offices below." The guards knew each clerk well and greeted them in the mornings.

In my imagination, the Court was a more intimate place with only two clerks per justice (Douglas only asked for one), compared to the approximately four that current justices have. In this environment, the justice was not only our boss but also sometimes our friend or father figure, always of human interest. My letters reveal one of my first initial encounters: "Justice Stewart was here yesterday afternoon; he came in around 3 in a madras sport coat and khakis, having played golf and swum all morning. I felt slightly like a teen-ager swooning over her movie god." He invited us for tea. He wanted to talk about cases. He asked us, at least once, to the Alibi Club, a privileged retreat where he met a small group of friends with whom he felt comfortable. We learned who his pals were, whom he looked forward to seeing each summer at the Bohemian Grove, a place of social legend in the redwood forests of Northern California.

I wrote my fiancée about poring through Justice Stewart's opinions for the previous five years. "It is very helpful in figuring what he wants and it will help disguise ignorance when he makes obscure references." In those early days of clerking, I wrote that "I am steadily becoming indoctrinated and noticing a tendency on the part of all clerks including me and my co-clerk to think like the office, which is actually okay."

> The term is starting with a bang on October 5 when the constitutionality of the Civil Rights Act will be argued. Most of the Justices have been away for the summer so there hasn't been a lot of discussion about the War with Congress. But there was resentment when the salaries for the Justices weren't increased for the reason that some guys across the street (on the Hill) didn't like the opinions that were coming down.

That summer, before the term began, I wrote about being loaned for a few weeks (along with other clerks) to the Warren Commission on John F. Kennedy's assassination. I was assigned to check footnotes in the section on Lee Harvey Oswald's period in the Soviet Union. It was a heady way to start.

Part of my general assignment was reading the *Congressional Record* daily and also the *Wall Street Journal,* marking articles that might interest the justice. The *New York Times* was prominent on his impressive picture-filled desk. Journalism fascinated him. He had been at the *Yale Daily News,* and its chairman, and worked one summer for the *Times-Star* in Cincinnati. The clarity and brevity of his writing reflected this background (as did his admiration for and friendship with journalists). He loved keeping up with White House and Hill gossip. And there was a tremulous thrill through the chambers during a few precious weeks when he was mooted as a potential moderate Republican future presidential or vice-presidential candidate.

For all the clerks, Washington and its extraordinary social life was part of the bargain. I wrote of my introduction to greater D.C.:

> Everybody is an assistant to somebody or attached someplace. Everyone manifests a peculiar sort of ambition here too: they are attempting to struggle from one place to another, or one category to another. For an outsider it is extremely difficult to figure out why one place is more desirable or whose ear it is wise to get. It is clear, though, that the Court enjoys a place above the battle, and the clerks are viewed as temporarily removed from all the grasping, but only temporarily.

I went horseback riding with some of my fellow clerks and played tennis with others.

By custom, one of the justice's law clerks was to house-sit in his beautiful house on Palisade Lane while the justice and his family summered in New England. I was the lucky one. One of the duties was maintaining the pool and using it, and another was feeding and maintaining the cat. I did reasonably well at the first, but failed at the second. The cat disappeared, it seemed, shortly before the justice's return. Fortunately, the family found the cat, half-starved, hidden in a closet. At the beginning, in a letter I described my introduction to the house. "There is a beautiful screened terrace at the justice's where we will have breakfast after swimming fifteen laps in his pool. The justice was extremely cordial and said I could have anyone there and as many people as I want, and his wife, Andy, showed me where all the party serving plates were and I said I didn't plan any balls, and she said why not?"

There are mildly interesting comments on cases in my fervent letters. For example, I wrote about the argument in *Griswold v. Connecticut,* dealing with Connecticut birth-control legislation. "The Court has been fairly exciting the last two days.... The Kennedy women were there (at the oral argument): Mrs. Bobby and Mrs. Teddy looking very glamorous with white leather coats and pretty hairdos." I described the mood and the tendency of the justice:

> Though the legislation is distasteful, there is no clear reason why the Court should say Connecticut can't pass it. The danger is that the judges will say what laws are good and what laws are bad and strike down the latter. Justice Black, in particular, from his questions, seemed loathe to substitute his judgment for that of the Connecticut legislature, no matter how neanderthal that collection is.

> In the end, Justice Stewart dissented from Justice Douglas' landmark privacy opinion, with Justice Black at his side. Stewart called the law "uncommonly silly," but not unconstitutional.[10]

One of my favorite cases was *Estes v. Texas*,[11] in which a criminal defendant alleged that his due process rights were violated when his pretrial hearing was televised. I think the case engaged Stewart because of its relationship to journalism and public involvement in the provision of justice. Tom Clark, writing for the Court majority, held that television coverage interfered with Estes's rights. Stewart disagreed, and, in a dissent engaged in his characteristically detailed factual analysis, narrowed the case. "I think the introduction of television into a courtroom is, at least, in the present state of the art, an unwise policy. It invites many constitutional risks, and it detracts from the inherent dignity of the courtroom ... [but] I am unable to find, on the specific record of this case, that the circumstances attending the limited televising of the petitioner's trial resulted in the denial of any right guaranteed to him by the United States Constitution."

I saw and loved what might be called the sometimes radical Justice Stewart. One case our term that exhibited this side of him was *McLaughlin v. Florida*,[12] a case involving the criminalization of interracial cohabitation. Justice White, for the Court, struck down the offending statute, but did so leaving some wiggle room for the states if they could show some future "overriding statutory purpose." Justice Stewart concurred, with a characteristically brief and terse opinion (nicely joined by Justice Douglas). "I cannot conceive of a valid legislative purpose under our Constitution for a State law which makes the color of a person's skin the test of whether his conduct is a criminal offense."

That term, too, Justice Stewart wrote the opinion in *Carrington v. Rash*,[13] a milestone in Court history. Texas had prevented soldiers who moved to Texas during their service years from then registering to vote. This was a way, of course, to protect the Texas electorate from pollution by outsiders, and the Court struck it down. In a nice conclusion, a rhetorical flourish, Justice Stewart quoted former Georgia governor Ellis Arnall: "The uniform of our country ... [must not] be the badge of disfranchisement for the man or woman who wears it."

One of the proudest moments of the chamber was after *Stanford v. Texas*[14] was handed down. *Stanford* was a significant search and seizure case, and Justice Stewart had the privilege of writing the opinion for the Court. "Two centuries," he wrote, "have passed since the historic decision in *Entick v. Carrington* almost to the very day. The world has greatly changed, and the voice of nonconformity now sometimes speaks a tongue which Lord Camden might find it hard to understand. But the Fourth and Fourteenth Amendments guarantee to John Stanford that no official of the State shall ransack his home and seize his books and papers under the unbridled authority of a general warrant—no less than the law 200 years ago shielded Entick from the messengers of the King." The afternoon the judgment came down, the messenger from Justice Black's office came with a note. My recollection is that it said, "Your opinion today makes me proud to be a member of this Court." Justice Stewart, properly beaming, shared this note with us.

Justice Stewart was a creature of habit, and that was reflected in his selection of clerks. He generally—at least at the time I was selected—chose one of his law clerks from Yale Law School (largely on the basis of academic standing). But there were additional factors that may have helped me. I was from Cincinnati, Stewart's hometown and where his father had been mayor (and he had been a councilman). When I was in high school and a reporter for the *Chatterbox*, the school newspaper, I had been given the assignment of writing about Stewart's appointment to the High Court. I hadn't remembered this, but when I came in for the interview, Stewart's devoted secretary brought out the clipping. Also, another prior Stewart clerk, Jan Deutsch, was, like me, born in Vienna and had come to the United States as a refugee. I think the justice had a soft spot for these stories of achievement and the American dream.

I did not clerk for Justice Stewart when he wrote the opinion in *Jacobellis v. Ohio*,[15] and included his famous phrase about pornography. Commenting on the difficult and inconsistent Court approaches, he said he would not attempt further to define the kinds of material that constitute hard-core pornography. Famously, he admitted a limit on judicial capacity. But even if he could never "intelligibly" further such a definition, he could fulfill his responsibility and cast a vote: "I know it when I see it, and the motion picture involved in this case is not that."

A collection about those who clerked for Justice Stewart might properly conclude with the origin of this phrase. My predecessor as clerk was the extraordinary Alan Novak (who undoubtedly had recommended me to Stewart at that significant moment when clerks cabined with the justice to consider their successors). Novak was and is a man of many extraordinary parts. His role as clerk in the *Jacobellis* quote is recounted in a blog written by Peter Lattman.[16] Lattman used Fred Shapiro as a source, the great Yale Law School librarian who collected and published books on legal quotations. Novak, in a letter to Fred Shapiro, wrote:

> After several days reviewing with the other court members the materials related to the '63 Term pornographic materials, Justice Stewart came to the office for a Saturday stint of opinion writing. I was there alone when he arrived, and we visited together to discuss his reaction to the case. . . . I had been a Marine officer; he a Navy officer. We discussed our experiences with material we had seen during our military careers, and discovered we had both seen materials we considered at the time to be pornographic, but this conclusion was arrived at somewhat intuitively.

We agreed that "we know it when we see it," but that further analysis was difficult. The justice went back to his office, and shortly thereafter produced a draft concurring opinion, which has by now become somewhat famous. I am sure he never expected, intended, or desired notoriety for this element of his work.

Novak's comment about the circumstances of this close Saturday-morning conversation captures the spirit of Justice Stewart's chambers.[17]

By May, I was writing my fiancée about the closing down of activities at the Court and vigorously anticipating her return. Clerks were thinking of their next assignments in life, off to jobs in the administration, at law firms, and in teaching. The even-tempered justice was turning to summer, to Vermont, and, obliquely, to our esteemed successors.

Steven M. Umin, October Term 1965

The phone rang in San Francisco, where I was working in 1965, my first year out of Yale Law School.[18] "Hello, Steve. This is Potter Stewart. I am calling to see whether you'd like to come to Washington for a year to be my law clerk." Would I like to come? I would have crawled over miles of broken glass to get there. That invitation made me one of the luckiest young lawyers in America: I was welcomed into that small company of recent graduates who each year get to serve one term as a Supreme Court law clerk. I knew, of course, that the job would be wonderful in the literal sense of that word. What I did not know was that I would begin a friendship with a man who remains a model for us all.

Come to think of it, the kind of man he is was there in the very first call. Unlike the way I received the news of my first job, by mail, this offer came personally, and not from "Justice" but from "Potter" Stewart. And from a man who, even after seven years on the Court, would not assume the obvious answer to his question. I know now that it was important for him to share in the pleasure of giving a gift and hearing the recipient's joy.

One year later, I watched him pace around his chamber, complaining that it was, as always, impossible to choose the next clerks from the résumés in front of him. Even after struggling to winnow the list to a final six, he continued to labor, to find the slim distinctions that would help him choose among the leading law graduates who had applied. He wouldn't take my suggestion that if he left the final choice to fortune, he could still be confident of having two high-quality assistants in the next term. I think his reply was: "Yes, but this is very important to them. So it just has to be this important to me."

These personal qualities marked Potter Stewart's work as a justice as well. The law clerks do not participate in the discussions that the justices have among themselves or in their official and highly secret daylong conference, when cases are decided. But we learned of Justice Stewart's reputation for lowering the temperature of the Warren Court's often tempestuous battles. It was no surprise to me. He got the best out of us as well with his easy personal style in dealing with his legal whippersnappers. Much of our work had to be written, but we were always welcome in his chambers to talk out an issue or make a suggestion, and he took special care right after each court conference to come into his clerks' office and tell us what had just happened.

Some people have cynically suggested that Potter Stewart has announced his retirement now because as a strong Republican he could be assured that President Reagan would name an equally conservative successor. No one who knows him would imagine that that is the reason. He chose to leave, I am sure, for the most important reason of all: he knew that he wanted to go. For although there is no room in judicial decision-making for personal values, Potter Stewart taught his law clerks, by example, that there is hardly room in the good life for anything else.

No clerk who was present at one of our annual reunion dinners will forget how he explained why he chose not to be considered by President Nixon as chief justice. It was well known that Justice Stewart was Nixon's likely choice. But unlike the other justices, the chief justice is provided with a chauffeured limousine. For Potter Stewart, that car was the symbol of the multitude of ceremonial and administrative duties that come with the office. Some people would say that such duties do not fit easily with his perceptible shyness. Justice Stewart acknowledged, of course, that it would be prestigious to occupy the nation's highest judicial office as one of John Marshall's successors. "But I have always kept my own hand on my own wheel. And I wanted to keep it that way."

Such a man is the justice who never omitted a courtesy, no matter how torrid the Court's pace, who always found time to chat with a law clerk or a secretary about a personal problem. And he even thought to thrill forever a former law clerk's mother by writing a note to her while her son was giving his first oral argument in the Court, years after her son's clerkship was over. Alas, he voted against me in that case, for that was a matter of principle. But if your hand is firmly on the wheel, there is time, even on the job, to make someone feel happy, as I do today—happy to have made that trip to Washington.

What sort of successor should President Reagan find? Find one like him, Mr. President. If you can.

Thomas D. Rowe Jr., October Term 1970

In fall 1970, Justice Stewart's beloved Cincinnati Reds were in the World Series against the Baltimore Orioles. When our justice was on the bench, he wanted reports every half inning; we clerks (Duncan Kennedy, Evan Davis, and I) rotated in that duty. One afternoon when I was on watch, I had reported that Cincinnati had fallen behind 4–1. In Baltimore's turn at the plate, the pitcher hit a grand-slam home run. Bad news though it was, I thought it deserved a special bulletin and so passed a note to the messenger behind the bench: "Baltimore pitcher hits first grand-slam home run by a pitcher in World Series history. Baltimore 8, Cincinnati 1." I then watched from the side as the note reached Justice Stewart, who looked down gravely and passed the note to his neighbor Justice Thurgood Marshall, who had spent a good deal of his career in Baltimore. Marshall smiled and beckoned for the messenger to take the note to junior Justice Blackmun, who hadn't yet judicially shown the baseball enthusiasm he soon afterward displayed in *Flood v. Kuhn*,[19] at the far end of the bench. Blackmun passed the note to his neighbor Justice Brennan, who was immersed in books and seemed to pay it no attention, perhaps because he had no dog in that fight (and may have been concentrating on the argument).

In spring 1981, when Justice Stewart announced his intention to retire from the Supreme Court, I was on academic leave from Duke Law School in a Justice Department think tank, the Office of Legal Policy. I had started under the Democrats, but after the election of President Reagan, the new Republican assistant attorney general for the office happened to be an old college friend; he mercifully kept me on until it was time for me to go back to Duke. One morning he appeared in my office and told me that Justice Stewart was retiring; I told him that it was a good thing I didn't believe in shooting messengers. He agreed and asked me if I could draft a statement for the president on the justice's retirement. I came up with a series of liberal-conservative antinomies, such as putting in the president's mouth the words that the justice had "reflected concern for striking appropriate balances between . . . preservation of our timeless values and the need to allow for reform and change." To my amazement, the draft made it through many levels of review in the Justice Department and the White House almost unscathed. I wondered if, as a liberal, I should have pressed any further but thought that I had probably gone as far as I could get the Reagan administration to sign on to.

Justice Stewart was personally cordial with many other justices, but he observed that the Court operated pretty much as nine separate law offices and not as the collegial body he had expected when he was appointed after serving on the Sixth Circuit. He was a very fine stylist, perhaps the best on the Court in his time, and when I did drafts I was very impressed at how good his editing was. His approaches to getting opinions written varied greatly depending on various factors, such as his knowledge of an area (say, when he'd written opinions before) and the importance of the fine line drawing (say, when he was the swing justice in related cases while going one way in one and the other way in another). He would sometimes write a draft and ask for checking and editing; or he would give detailed guidance orally and ask for a clerk draft based on his guidance; or he would give pretty free rein for the clerk to do a first draft, which he would review carefully and thoughtfully.

I believe he was the last justice ever put on the Court initially as a recess appointment; he was confirmed later. Such an appointment would be unthinkable today.

David M. Schulte, October Term 1972

Justice Stewart was a superb judge because he was a superb man. I was privileged to work as one of his law clerks during October term 1972, when *Roe v. Wade*[20] came down after having been argued the prior year. We were sandwiched between *Roe* and the Nixon tapes case, but actually it was a pretty quiet year.

Justice Stewart was a midwestern patrician, born to a powerful father and married to an elegant and wealthy wife. While a graduate of Hotchkiss, a Yalie, and a member of Skull and Bones, he was far from elitist. He had that wonderful blend of common sense, high intelligence, and a grace that enabled him to go anywhere, anytime, and engage anyone. He had been a college journalist, editor of the *Yale Daily News,* and he loved reporters. Dave Beckwith and Nina Totenberg were regulars in our chambers. Because he understood and loved journalists, he was comfortable that he learned more from them than he gave. I don't believe he ever leaked anything that had not been made public, but I am sure he took delight in educating reporters and debating with them. That said, he was oddly shy and taken to nibbling at the corner of his neckties.

Stewart was gentle in dealing with his clerks and with his colleagues as well. He thought Chief Justice Burger was a horse's ass, but did not show it. When he was newly on the Court, Felix Frankfurter used to visit him and push hard to move Stewart to whichever position he was then peddling. Stewart always resented that, and never did it with colleagues whether they were newly appointed or not. He liked most of them, and respected their ability and obligation to make up their own minds.

In our year, Senator Sam Ervin opened the Watergate hearings, and the justice's secretary, Helene Dwyer, had a TV on her desk that was always turned on to the proceedings. Thurgood Marshall regularly came and hung out, glued as most of us were to the TV. Not Justice Stewart. He'd come out every hour or so, interested only in whether anything bad had come out about two of his friends: George H. W. Bush and Elliot Richardson. I don't think the justice cared much for or about Nixon, but he loved Bush and Richardson and was willing them to be clear of taint, as they were. President Bush (41) gave a warm and appreciative eulogy at Justice Stewart's funeral service. The two Yalies were neighbors and played bridge together.

The work of us clerks was mostly to sift through mountains of cert petitions that arrived each week. With the justice having already served on the Court for fourteen years, most of the issues that came up had already been before him in one way or another, and he'd already thought through them at least generally. He had a pretty good idea what was an important question and what he'd vote to hear, and we figured him out on that fairly quickly. So the cert petition part of the job was fairly routine. In our day there was no pool, no sharing of cert memos. Justice Stewart hired his own clerks and wanted to hear from *them*. He was only mildly interested in what we thought, and not at all interested in what clerks in other chambers thought.

Stewart was comfortable in his own skin, and very much his own man. Some of his clerks may think they moved the justice in important ways on major issues. I doubt that they did. Our compensation for digging through all those petitions was a meeting on each Thursday night, before the Friday conference, in which we talked about the cert "discuss list" and cases that had been argued that week. The justice never cut those sessions short. He heard us out, his way of thanking us for all we saved him from having to do.

When it came to opinions, the job of clerk got better. Our task was to do a first, sometimes a second, third, or fourth, draft of opinions. Then the justice would take over and make it his own. In doing this, one tried to understand the justice's view of relevant doctrine and make everything consistent. I was assigned a Fourteenth Amendment case, *San Antonio v. Rodriguez*,[21] in which a three-judge federal court had held that financing public education through the property tax was unconstitutional under the Equal Protection Clause. The California Supreme Court had already decided the same way in *James v. Valtierra*.[22] Well, Stewart was having none of it. He had been on the Board of Education in Cincinnati, and knew more about financing public schools than the litigants did. He knew, for example, that poor people sometimes live in tax-rich districts where there are factories and other commercial uses that increase the per capita tax base. So not only did he not subscribe to novel extensions of the Fourteenth Amendment into economic rights, he also thought the argument was just plain wrong.

At that time almost every state financed public education through the property tax, and affirmance would have turned school finance throughout the country upside down. I, however, as his law clerk, believed the liberal line and saw this as my chance to move the justice and change the world. I wrote draft after draft, memo after memo, and he put each into his desk drawer. He never really wanted to discuss the case. I tried in vain to make sense out of the justice's prior Fourteenth Amendment opinions. On matters of race and police conduct, Stewart was steadfast for the little guy. On matters of economic rights, he wasn't. Terms like "strict scrutiny," "suspect classification," and the like were, for him, window dressing. So in novel cases one was a little lost.

One day I walked into his office. There he was, chewing on his tie and reading his favorite periodical—the L. L. Bean catalog. "Mr. Justice," I volunteered, "I have figured out your theory of the Fourteenth Amendment." He looked up and smiled. "Oh?" he wondered. "Yes," I answered, "yours is the good fucking reason test." He looked puzzled. "You believe a state statute is valid unless there's a good fucking reason for it not to be." He grinned, then laughed, "That's about it," he agreed. Then, in the spring, I took a long weekend off to drive to the Kentucky Derby. Justice Stewart went into the conference, cast his vote, and said, "Now's the time, my clerk's out of town." The case came down on Monday. The man simply didn't want to hurt my feelings.

Potter Stewart was a smart and well-educated midwesterner who had politics in his genes and a bit of it in his direct experience. He saw action in the navy in World War II, and compared allegedly obscene pictures to what his men brought back on board in Casablanca. His generation literally saved the world, and, while he adored gossip, he had no patience for trivial bickering. He sat on a Court rich in diverse backgrounds—White, a professional football player, lawyer, and Kennedy politico; Brennan, a New Jersey politician; Warren, a California governor; Marshall, a civil liberties litigator; Harlan, the embodiment of the New York white shoe lawyer; and Douglas, the uncontrollable New Dealer from the West. Today the Court is less diverse in the experiential sense. They are all former appellate judges, and may think they have little to learn from one another. What's left is endless doctrinal quibbling. We lose something in that, and each of us would benefit from having more justices like Potter Stewart. The Court would have more guts and relevance, and a clearer sense of what it's there to do.

Frederick T. Davis, October Term 1973

Being chosen by Potter Stewart followed an oddly aggressive step I took. Somewhat late in the recruiting season, when I had applied to Potter Stewart but also other justices, I was invited down to interview with Justice White. The interview went fine, but of course it was still at best a roll of the dice whether I would be chosen. Also, I preferred Stewart. Against everything my parents told me about "politeness" and circumspection around important people, I screwed up my courage (or chutzpah), scrounged in my pocket for a quarter or two, and from a dial phone in the basement of the Court building I called Potter Stewart's chambers, noting that I was in Washington and would be glad to meet with the justice right that minute if he were free. To my amazement, the secretary put me on hold for a few minutes, came back, and said, "Yes, he would be glad to see you." I got an offer by phone a week later.

The two adjectives that always come to my mind about Potter Stewart are "decent" and "patriotic," the latter before the term took on partisan connotations. He really believed in "doing the right thing" and really did not have a political agenda. He was very proud of his country and proud that he came from its heartland.

He had a playful, and respectful, relationship with White, whom he knew at Yale. He seemed scared of Rehnquist, who would try to talk Stewart into joining him. He hated Chief Justice Burger—just hated him. Oddly, two years ago or so I ran into Bob Woodward in Paris. He had interviewed me for *The Brethren*[23] (about the Watergate tapes decision, our year), and a number of people thought I was his source, which I wasn't. A few years ago Jeffrey Toobin's book *The Nine*[24] noted that Potter Stewart talked with Woodward. So when I saw Woodward, I reminded him of our interview and said that the Toobin book was a sort of belated relief to me. Woodward roared with laughter, and said that Potter Stewart "sang like a canary," meeting several times and in detail, out of his dislike for Burger.

Stewart deeply respected Powell, and viewed him as something of an heir to Harlan. But overall I was surprised by how little he and the other justices socialized. He was a pretty private guy. He would invite all of us clerks into his office the night before decision conferences with the other justices; we called this the "Thursday Night Fights" because we often disagreed with him. He was great because he really encouraged disagreement, and in fact we thought he sometimes feigned a position to elicit ours.

He wrote the majority opinion in *Milliken v. Bradley*,[25] the first modern school busing case lost by the plaintiffs. I worked hard on the opinion, and I recall some specific inputs he had on it. It was emotionally traumatic for him to rule against black plaintiffs, and he felt bad about it. The day it came out, word went around the Court that White went to Marshall's office and said, "Let's you and me go out and get a drink and get this behind us."

Daniel R. Fischel, October Term 1978

Being selected as a clerk by Justice Stewart and serving in that capacity was a great privilege, one of the things to this day I'm most proud of in my career. I felt Justice Stewart both personally and professionally was a model of what a Supreme Court Justice should be. Because of my profound respect and affection for the justice, I named my oldest son after him—his name is Joseph Stewart Fischel.

Notes

1. 378 U.S. 184 (1964).
2. 365 U.S. 505 (1961).
3. 316 U.S. 129 (1942).
4. 369 U.S. 186 (1962).
5. 370 U.S. 421 (1962).
6. 367 U.S. 463 (1961).
7. *Russell v. United States,* 369 U.S. 749 (1962).
8. 370 U.S. 294 (1962).
9. 366 U.S. 393 (1961).
10. 381 U.S. 479, 527 (1965).
11. 381 U.S. 582 (1965).
12. 379 U.S. 184 (1964).
13. 380 U.S. 80 (1965).
14. 379 U.S. 476 (1965).
15. 378 U.S. 184 (1964).
16. http://blogs.wsj.com/law/2007/09/27/the-origins-of-justice-stewarts-i-know-it -when-i-see-it/.
17. Novak was already celebrated for writing the over-the-top, subversively witty "Man, His Dog and Birth Control: A Study in Comparative Rights," *Yale Law Journal* (June 1961): 70.
18. Editors' note: This essay was originally published in the *New York Times* on June 24, 1981—one week after Justice Stewart announced his retirement. Umin died in 2012.
19. 407 U.S. 258 (1972).
20. 410 U.S. 113 (1973).
21. 411 U.S. 1 (1973).
22. 402 U.S. 137 (1971).
23. Bob Woodward and Scott Armstrong, *The Brethren* (New York: Simon & Schuster, 1979).
24. Jeffrey Toobin, *The Nine: Inside the Secret World of the Supreme Court* (New York: Random House, 2007).
25. 418 U.S. 717 (1974).

TODD C. PEPPERS, CHAD OLDFATHER,
AND BRIDGET TAINER-PARKINS

Of Cert Petitions and LBJ

Clerking for Justice Abe Fortas

Many of the essays featured in this book draw upon the extensive public writings of a specific justice's former law clerks. In a sense, one could argue that the number of pages written by these former clerks, whether the essays are "in memoriam" pieces or defenses of the justice's jurisprudence, serve as a proxy measure of the strength of the relationship between the justice and his or her clerks; the tighter the bonds between justice and clerk, the greater the number of articles written by the former clerks about their justice. Prime examples are the writings of law clerks for Oliver Wendell Holmes Jr., Louis D. Brandeis, Hugo Black, or Earl Warren, whose devoted clerks have spilled gallons of ink serving as guardians of their justices' legacies.

As a group, the law clerks of Justice Abe Fortas have remained relatively silent. This is partially explained by the fact that Justice Fortas served on the Supreme Court for approximately four years, and, in that time, hired only six law clerks (two of whom he inherited from the outgoing Justice Arthur Goldberg). Simply put, there aren't many former clerks to write articles or give lectures about Fortas. Other factors, however, may also explain the silence. As discussed below, the Fortas law clerks did not typically enjoy a warm personal relationship with the justice, and he, in turn, was not interested in serving as a mentor. Moreover, the professional ties between the justice and at least some of his clerks were strained by their perceptions of the justice's results-oriented jurisprudence, together with his unprecedented involvement with the Johnson White House and its prosecution of the Vietnam War.

We were fortunate enough to interview four of the justice's former law clerks: Daniel Levitt (October terms 1965 and 1966), John Griffiths (October terms 1965 and 1966), David Rosenbloom (October term 1967), and Walter Slocombe (October term 1968). Former clerks Peter Zimroth (October term 1967) and Martha Field (October term 1968) declined our repeated interview requests. What emerges is a unique picture of a clerkship model subject to the strains of Justice Fortas's political activities, ethical lapses, and nascent constitutional philosophy.

Selection Practices

Fortas's first two law clerks, Daniel Levitt and John Griffiths, were selected to clerk for Justice Arthur Goldberg and had started their clerkships when Justice Goldberg resigned in July 1965 to take the position of United Nations ambassador. The former Goldberg clerks maintained their normal work schedule in the weeks following Justice Goldberg's resignation, reviewing cert petitions and "assuming" that they would be hired by the justice's successor. When Justice Fortas joined the Court, he agreed to hire the two young men on the condition that they would clerk for two years so Fortas would not have to immediately start interviewing clerks for the next term. According to Daniel Levitt, Justice Fortas did not seem to care that the two young men had diametrically opposed political ideologies from one another.[1]

Looking back at his clerkship, John Griffiths suggested that Fortas may have regretted asking the clerks to stay for two years.

> I have often wondered whether Fortas was happy with his decision to ask us to stay for a second year. His law clerks had more seniority on the Court than he did, and, especially in the second year, I think that he would have liked law clerks who were more deferential. We [Levitt and Griffiths] were both sometimes rather resistant to his way of doing things. When Fortas let me know that he was dissatisfied with something, I often gave him some feedback if I disagreed—I didn't take his comments as words from heaven.[2]

Subsequent law clerks were vetted by an informal screening committee (the membership of which included Levitt), finalists were interviewed by Justice Fortas, and the clerks served one-year terms. Besides Levitt and Griffiths, former justice Goldberg made one further contribution to the Fortas law clerk corps when he called Fortas and persuaded him to hire Goldberg's assistant at the United Nations, a young Harvard Law School graduate named David Rosenbloom.

When Fortas selected Martha Alschuler (now Field) to clerk during October term 1968, he became one of the first Supreme Court justices to hire a female law clerk. William O. Douglas had hired Lucile Lomen when male applicants were scarce during World War II, and Hugo Black had been strong-armed by Washington insider and friend Tommy "the Cork" Corcoran to hire Corcoran's daughter, Margaret (a decision that proved to be a disaster). "It didn't strike me as remarkable that the Justice was hiring a female law clerk," explained Levitt.

"She was very smart. She was clearly an outstanding candidate. The fact that she was a woman wouldn't have bothered Fortas—he practiced law with his wife."[3] Field's co-clerk, Walter Slocombe, added that Field was treated "as an absolute equal. For someone from his [Fortas's] era, that was a big deal."[4]

Nevertheless, Fortas's decision to hire Field may have been partially due to paternalism. "I remember that Martha came down for her interview," said Levitt. "William O. Douglas walked in during the interview, and he later told Fortas 'if you don't hire her, I will.' So Fortas hired her to protect her from Douglas"[5]—a justice who was difficult to work for and whose wandering eye and philandering was an open secret at the Court.

As laudable as Fortas's gender-neutral hiring practices may have been, the justice proved less tolerant of candidates with medical disabilities. Sometime after arriving at the Supreme Court, Justice Fortas and Judge David Bazelon, of the D.C. Court of Appeals, agreed that Judge Bazelon would hire a Yale Law School graduate each year; the graduate would first clerk for Bazelon and then for Fortas. The clerks were to be selected by Yale Law School professors Joseph Goldstein and Abraham Goldstein. The two Yale Law School professors subsequently tapped Thomas Grey for this honor—only to have the offer rescinded when the justice learned about Grey's epilepsy.[6]

"I must have mentioned at the interview [with the professors] that I was a grand mal epileptic, though the disorder was controlled by medication," recalled Grey. Justice Fortas subsequently learned of Grey's epilepsy, and he bluntly told the selection committee that he did not want to hire an epileptic. "It was some time later that I was told . . . that when Justice Fortas heard about the epilepsy, he decided he didn't want to deal with it. Apparently he had grown up with an aunt who frequently had seizures around the house, and the memory filled him with horror."[7] Yale Law School classmate William Iverson replaced Grey as the Bazelon/Fortas law clerk. It was Grey, however, and not Iverson, who made it to the Supreme Court. While Grey subsequently clerked for D.C. Court of Appeals judge J. Skelly Wright and Justice Thurgood Marshall, Iverson completed the Bazelon clerkship, but was left without the coveted Supreme Court clerkship when Justice Fortas abruptly resigned in the face of a political firestorm.

This would not be the only time that Justice Fortas would be involved in rescinding a clerkship offer. He also pressured fellow justice William J. Brennan Jr. to withdraw a job offer to clerkship candidate Michael Tigar, this time over concerns about the young man's political activities. As an undergraduate student at University of California at Berkeley, Tigar had been involved in political protests and was a member of several radical political groups—facts that Justice Brennan's hiring committee believed should not disqualify Tigar for consideration. After Justice Brennan hired Tigar, news of the appointment upset political conservatives. Justice Fortas met with FBI director J. Edgar Hoover's personal assistant, Clyde Tolson, about the matter, before privately meeting with Justice Brennan. "Fortas came in to see me to tell me that if I went through with this there might well be an inquiry [conducted by Congress], which would be most embarrassing to Tigar and to me—and to the Court," Justice Brennan recalled years later.[8] Despite the fact that Tigar and his young family had already driven from California to Washington, D.C., to begin the clerkship, Justice Brennan rescinded the job offer.[9]

The Job Duties of the Fortas Clerks

Historically, new Supreme Court justices are often forced to lean heavily on their law clerks as the new jurists learn the proverbial ropes, but Justice Fortas needed no such assistance. "He virtually took no time to get up to speed. You would have assumed from the first day that he had been there for years," explained Levitt. The former clerk attributed the lack of a learning curve to the fact that Fortas had personal or professional relationships with many of the justices. "He knew most of the Justices very well. It was almost as if the Solicitor General had come to the Court."[10]

Once on the Supreme Court, Fortas continued his role as informal adviser and confidante to Lyndon B. Johnson. "Depending on the occasion, [Justice] Fortas served as political adviser, speechwriter, crisis manager, administration headhunter, legal expert, war counselor, or just plain cheerleader," wrote Fortas biographer Bruce Allen Murphy.[11] The justice often talked on a daily basis with the president, using a private line installed in his office (a red light outside his office warned his staff that he was talking to President Johnson and was not to be disturbed). Moreover, in subsequent terms Fortas's energies were devoted to Senate hearings regarding his nomination to replace Chief Justice Warren as well as damage control regarding his financial relationship with businessman Louis Wolfson and the Wolfson Family Foundation.[12]

Given the sheer number of outside distractions, one might hypothesize that Fortas could not help but overly rely on his law clerks. The evidence in support of this hypothesis is mixed. Rosenbloom flatly rejected the suggestion that Fortas's extrajudicial commitments forced him to delegate unusual responsibility to his law clerks. "Fortas believed that in most matters he knew far more about the law than the clerks. He was probably right on many subjects. Those subjects that bored him . . . he left to the clerks."[13] Griffiths also dismissed the idea that excessive outside obligations forced Fortas to depend on his clerks. "He [Fortas] was a very good and fast lawyer (especially in his own estimation)," stated Griffiths, "and if I may be immodest, we were damned good clerks."

While Fortas's outside commitments may not have forced him to delegate excessive responsibilities to his law clerks, his late night meetings at the White House did have consequences. Levitt believes that Fortas did not make a greater impact during his short time on the Court because he was stretched too thin. Some days Fortas repeatedly spoke by telephone with President Johnson, and after work he went to the White House to provide advice and counsel on policy matters. Fortas often did not get home until the early hours of the morning. "When he came to the Court every morning, Fortas was tired because of his evening visits to the White House," stated Levitt. "They took away his ability to make a mark on the Court. I don't think his White House work colored his views on cases, but when you come to the Court tired because you were up to 2:00 a.m. picking out bombing targets—that sapped a lot of his talent and energy."[14]

The role of the Supreme Court law clerk was changing when Justice Fortas came to the Court, and he adopted the "modern" model in which clerks were involved in all aspects of chambers work. A set of office procedures prepared by John Griffiths outlines a detailed routine for day-to-day life in chambers.[15] The first responsibility of the Fortas clerks was to review the mountains of cert petitions and prepare short memoranda for the justice. Although the law clerks prepared cert memoranda, Griffiths explained that the law clerks did not routinely meet with Justice Fortas to discuss their work product. "While the cert petitions required an enormous amount of work, they didn't produce expressions of either satisfaction or dissatisfaction from the Justice," stated Griffiths. He recalled a cert petition originating from North Dakota that did not present a federal question. "My memo read: 'This petition raises fascinating questions of North Dakota law. Cert. should be denied.'" Griffiths had half expected a reaction from the justice—preferably a laugh—but none was forthcoming.

While Justice Fortas did not routinely discuss the cert petitions with his clerks, the clerks themselves believe that their recommendations closely aligned with the justice's subsequent voting behavior. "Fortas relied a lot on his clerks in the review of cert petitions," recounted Slocombe. "That was one place where he was very interested and attentive to law clerk recommendations."[16] In the opinion of Griffiths, the agreement between justice and clerk was especially strong when appeals presented rather pedestrian issues. "I do believe that his judgment was in concert with ours on almost all the cert petitions whose disposition was fairly cut and dried," stated Griffiths. "For those cases, I would guess he looked at our memos briefly and didn't look at the petitions himself."[17]

While the October term 1965 clerks prepared bench memoranda in all cases,[18] Justice Fortas abandoned this practice by October term 1967.[19] Instead, Fortas would sit down and talk with the clerks prior to oral argument, using the previously drafted cert memoranda as a jumping-off point. After oral argument, the Fortas clerks would meet with the justice, learn what cases had been assigned to him, and receive their marching orders for preparing opinion drafts.

In his "Office Procedure," law clerk John Griffiths set forth the justice's expectations for the writing of opinions. When the justice was assigned an opinion, or decided to write a dissent, he "frame[d] the procedure to be used within [c]hambers on that case to fit the particular situation."[20] One clerk would be responsible for each case, and the clerk was usually to write a memo or draft opinion.[21] Sometimes, however, the justice would pen the first draft and pass it along to the law clerk to edit.[22] According to Griffith's explanation of the procedure, the justice directed the law clerks to listen to the oral argument prior to proceeding with any opinion writing.[23] The remaining tasks set forth regarding the drafting of opinions was administrative in nature—directing the clerks to maintain all cited materials, to check cites to make sure they were still "good law," and to maintain all working papers, such as memoranda, drafts, and circulations, in the case file.[24]

Justice Fortas's contribution to the first draft of an opinion varied by term and by the legal issues raised in the appeal. Writes Slocombe: "Most opinions were first drafted by one of us. The Justice would tell us the result and basic line of analysis. Sometimes (especially on dissents [and] concurrences, but also on opinions) he did the first draft. He always reviewed our drafts carefully."[25] Often times, Justice Fortas would divide up the drafts based on the clerks' interests or areas of expertise; during Levitt's and Griffiths's clerkship, for example, Levitt was given the business and antitrust cases, while Griffiths was assigned the civil rights/liberties and juvenile cases.[26] Once the drafts were completed, they were submitted to the justice for an exacting review. Slocombe described Fortas as a "magnificent editor," adding that "the Justice operated best if he had a first draft in front of him."[27] There were times, however, when Justice Fortas edited with a very light hand; Rosenbloom stated that the justice "didn't change as much as a comma in the opinion" that the clerk drafted early in his term.[28]

Biographer Laura Kalman suggests that Fortas's lack of a coherent judicial philosophy shaped the function of the law clerks in opinion drafting. "Fortas's approach to a case instead reflected the opportunistic outlook of a good lawyer. . . . Griffiths suggested that Fortas regarded them [legal principles] as 'a necessary form of packaging that had to provide for things he wanted to do.'"[29] Therefore, law clerks "decorated" opinions:

> Griffiths remembered giving a draft of a particular memorandum to Fortas. After telling his clerk that the draft was unsatisfactory, Fortas "took it off and wrote it himself with the very strong emphasis on the factual part." On his return, Fortas threw the memorandum on Griffiths's desk. "Decorate it," he ordered. The "decorations" consisted of legal cases that

would justify a decision Fortas had already reached. . . . Observers have commented that Fortas's opinions contained more than the requisite number of legal citations. But they were there to a large extent because his clerks insisted upon them.[30]

Regarding the "decorate it" quotation that appears in Kalman's book, Griffiths stated that the comment was made in connection with the *In Re Gault*[31] case. "I had done my best to produce a legal argument that supported the result. Justice Fortas took one look at it and said 'that's not how to do it.' Fortas re-wrote my draft and then handed it back (he didn't throw it at Griffiths in anger) and told him to 'decorate it'"—which meant provide the footnotes. "His strength was in presenting facts in a way that more or less compelled the result he had decided upon. . . . He was never explicit about a legal or judicial philosophy. He would just say 'no, that is not how I want it' [concerning a draft opinion by one of his law clerks]. And he would bring it back with a beautiful fact section and almost no legal analysis."[32]

The materials relating to *Gault* in Justice Fortas's papers are broadly consistent with this depiction of what transpired. The files contain a page of oral argument notes in Fortas's handwriting, along with twenty-four pages of handwritten notes—which also appear to be entirely or almost entirely in Fortas's hand—which formed the basis for the initial draft of the opinion. The first printed version of the opinion includes the fact section only, and is accompanied by a typewritten version that bears a handwritten notation (in what appears to be Griffiths's hand): "AF's draft #1 (preceded by several prior drafts)." There are several typewritten, preliminary drafts of the other sections of the opinion that include editing by both Fortas and Griffiths. In general, Fortas's comments are relatively sparse and relate to the text, while Griffiths's are extensive and relate both to the revision of the text and the addition of authority in footnotes. The opinion went through six printed drafts. Editing by Fortas is apparent only on two—the second, which are not insubstantial but which reflect the perspective of someone doing top-level review rather than more technical editing, and the sixth, which contains marginal notes that appear to be part of a final review of the overall structure and content of the opinion.

A copy of the third printed draft bears the initials "DL" and has comments in what appears to be a third set of handwriting, presumably Levitt's. These comments are almost entirely of a technical nature, suggesting that someone asked Levitt to proofread the draft. Overall, then, what appears in the justice's papers comports with the story of Fortas drafting an opinion and then largely relinquishing it to Griffiths for "decoration" and editing.

Fortas's papers contain two other items related to *Gault* that shed some light on the role of his clerks. The first is a typewritten note that Griffiths prepared as a recommended response to Justice White's concurring opinion. The draft includes heavy editing by Fortas. The second is a draft of Justice Harlan's opinion concurring in part and dissenting in part, which bears on its first page a note that reads "I think this is weak & lousy, & requires no change at all in your opinion. JG." The draft appears to have comments from Fortas, too, and so it is not entirely clear which of them wrote "bull" in the margin next to Harlan's assertion that Fortas's opinion does not address a certain category of cases. A later draft of Harlan's opinion includes this note: "There is nothing new in this. JG." In sum, the *Gault* materials show a justice who was delegating the detail work, at a minimum, and clerks who were willing to assert themselves even in the context of a case in which Justice Fortas took a substantial interest.

The materials relating to Justice Fortas's earlier majority opinion in *Kent v. United States,* in which the Supreme Court held that juvenile court systems must provide minors with the full panoply of constitutional rights, provide further support for this assessment.[33] The *Kent* opinion appears to have been drafted according to the procedure that was customary in Justice Fortas's chambers. John Griffiths was the law clerk assigned to the case. The file includes a draft of the opinion entitled "Draft 1 by AF,"[34] which includes a direction to the law clerk to fill in certain areas.[35] It also appears that the law clerk inserted the footnotes into the opinion.[36]

Based on the case file materials, it appears that the primary responsibility of the law clerk in this instance was to fill in details and citations regarding the statutes and case precedents that Justice Fortas had relied upon in reaching his conclusion. The file contains a second draft of the opinion, which has many handwritten notes; while some appear clearly to be by Fortas and others by Griffiths, their handwriting is similar enough that it is difficult to discern the authorship of all of the notes.[37] Overall, the drafts suggest that Justice Fortas devised the holding and an outline of the legal reasoning for his result. Griffiths's role in assisting with the opinion was not solely limited to cite-checking, as he was also tasked with elaborating on the outline provided by the justice and expanding on the legal reasoning that supported the Court's holding.

Griffiths also recalled the case of *United States v. Price,*[38] in which Mississippi police officers were prosecuted for the murders of three civil rights workers. The dispositive issue in the case was whether the defendants had acted "under color of state law."

> Justice Fortas thought that my draft opinion read like a law review article in that it extensively reviewed the precedents to show how they lead to the conclusion that the defendants acted under color of law. The Justice crossed out that whole section of the draft, more or less ignoring the difficulties in the preceding decisions of the Court. When I protested, he told me that I could put the analysis in a footnote.

Added Griffiths: "The Justice found [the] extended legal analysis a distraction even though it got the Justice where he wanted to go, namely, that the federal statute covered what the defendants had done."[39]

The conclusion that Justice Fortas lacked a discernable judicial philosophy rested, in part, on Griffiths's brief clerkship with Justice Goldberg, "who was very interested in having a consistent legal philosophy." Griffiths recalled that he and Levitt were charged with selecting law review articles for Justice Goldberg to read during the summer vacation of 1965. "He asked us to collect what we thought were the most interesting law review articles for him to read over his summer break. Stuff like legal theory and conflicts of law. Goldberg wanted to know about new legal theories that were being discussed in the law schools, and he liked to have serious discussions with his clerks." In contrast, Justice Fortas did not use his clerks as sounding boards. "We were, however, never intellectual 'sparring partners' for Justice Fortas. He was not really interested in that sort of thing."

Levitt takes a more charitable view toward Fortas's nascent jurisprudence. Levitt argues that most practicing lawyers don't have a judicial philosophy, and that Abe Fortas arrived on the bench as a practicing lawyer who was used to solving problems for his clients. "I don't think that Fortas had time to formulate a judicial philosophy during his time on the Court. He was the smartest man on the bench, although he did not have the jurisprudential clarity of a William O. Douglas or Bill Brennan yet."[40] Levitt added, however, that "Fortas was a legal genius . . . [who] could look at a problem and see it in a way that no one else had seen it before. . . . [I]f Fortas had stayed on the Supreme Court, he would have been one of the greatest Justices in history because of his extraordinary mind and writing skills."

As for law clerk influence over the judicial process, at least one law clerk believes that the clerks wielded substantive influences in those cases in which the justice was disinterested. Rosenbloom commented that the clerks "definitely had influence over the issues that Fortas did not care about." He pointed to the example of a state tax case that "Fortas could not have given a damn about. How the opinion came out would be left to us."[41]

The Nonjudicial Duties of the Fortas Clerks

Given Justice Fortas's ongoing role as the consummate Washington insider, it is not surprising that his law clerks had nonjudicial duties as well. Levitt recalled making written recommendations on how Justice Fortas might diffuse the public backlash to the Warren Commission's report (Levitt's suggestions included releasing the Kennedy autopsy photographs). Moreover, at the end of the week Levitt would drive Fortas to the White House, where Fortas helped President Johnson select bombing targets. Levitt also recalled overhearing telephone conversations between Justice Fortas and President Johnson, during which Fortas sought to bolster Johnson's spirits.[42]

The most important advice that Levitt provided Justice Fortas, however, was unsolicited. Shortly before his nomination to the Supreme Court, Justice Fortas's law firm (now Arnold & Porter) began representing Louis Wolfson, a businessman whose stock trading habits had attracted the attention of the Securities and Exchange Commission (SEC). After Justice Fortas took his seat on the Court, he entered into a written agreement to be a consultant for the Wolfson Family Foundation at an annual salary of $20,000. In January 1966, the first of what the two men agreed would be a series of annual lifetime payments was mailed to Fortas.[43]

It was during the summer of 1966 that Levitt stumbled onto the financial relationship between the justice and the Wolfson Family Foundation. "I knew that Fortas had a relationship with Louis Wolfson, that Wolfson was close to being indicted [by the SEC], that Wolfson was still a client of Arnold and Porter, that Fortas had been appointed to sit on the board of the Wolfson Foundation, and that Fortas traveled to Florida to attend Foundation meetings," stated Levitt. "And I [also] knew that Wolfson was still sending Fortas letters, asking him about the legal advice that he was receiving from Arnold and Porter. That didn't bother me because Fortas did not sit on any Arnold and Porter cases, so there was no conflict of interest."[44]

One night Levitt was contacted by the White House operator, who was looking for Fortas (who happened to be in Florida at a Wolfson Family Foundation meeting). On the following Monday morning Levitt mentioned the call to Fortas's secretary, adding that it was very likely that Wolfson was going to be indicted. "I wondered out loud why Justice Fortas and Wolfson were so close, and the secretary replied that the Justice was being paid $20,000 a year to be on the Board." A surprised Levitt replied that a federal criminal statute made it a "high misdemeanor" for a justice to practice law. "I told the secretary that if the Justice was getting paid to be on the Foundation, and if he is getting $20,000 a year from Wolfson and giving him legal advice, then that is an impeachable offense."[45]

The secretary suggested that Levitt tell Justice Fortas, but Levitt refused. Instead, Levitt took a copy of the federal statute, circled the applicable provision, and left it on the justice's desk. When Justice Fortas returned to his chambers, the secretary told him that "Dan thinks that you should look at this [statute]." Justice Fortas promptly told the secretary to tell the young clerk "to mind [his] own business," but one hour later Fortas dictated a letter in which he resigned from the foundation. Fortas did return the money, but delayed writing a check until December 15, 1966, so he did not have to report the salary on his 1966 tax return.[46] Justice Fortas never spoke to Levitt about the matter. But years later, after hearing a colleague praise Levitt's work at Arnold & Porter, Fortas replied that Levitt "actually did something more valuable for me a year or so ago"—alluding to the Wolfson affair and Levitt's implicit recommendation that the justice resign from the foundation.

Fortas's October term 1968 law clerks, Martha Field and Walter Slocombe, were also given extrajudicial job duties upon President's Johnson's nomination of Abe Fortas to replace retiring Chief Justice Earl Warren. Before the confirmation hearings, the clerks were instructed to review the judicial opinions of Senate Judiciary Committee member Sam J. Ervin, who had been a justice on the North Carolina Supreme Court, and determine if they could find any information in the opinions that might be useful to Justice Fortas during the upcoming hearings (Justice Fortas anticipated attacks from the southern senators on the Judiciary Committee). During his research, Slocombe found an opinion in which then-justice Ervin had commented that precedent should not be followed if a prior opinion was not decided correctly. The information was subsequently used by Fortas in the confirmation hearing.

> Fortas's inability to resist making debaters' points [during the confirmation hearings] grated. On his first day before the committee, he attempted to prove that as a Justice of his state supreme court Senator Ervin, a Judiciary Committee member, had been more of a judicial activist than Abe Fortas. He quoted from one of Ervin's opinions, which said that courts need not observe precedent when to do so would perpetuate wrongs. "Senator, I would not go that far myself," Fortas sanctimoniously noted.[47]

Throughout the confirmation hearings, the law clerks sat behind Fortas and would occasionally get materials for the justice. Asked to characterize the hearings themselves, Slocombe described them as "theater" in which members of the Judiciary Committee "were playing to the crowd. Justice Fortas was not born yesterday. He understood that it was theater."[48]

Justice Fortas's failure to be confirmed marked the beginning of a chain of events that ended in his resignation from the Court. In May 1969, *Life* magazine published a story on Justice Fortas and his relationship with Louis Wolfson (now convicted and serving a prison sentence) and the Wolfson Family Foundation. The article contained troubling allegations that Fortas had been more than a mere consultant to the Wolfson Family Foundation, arguing instead that the justice had worked behind the scenes to protect Wolfson from criminal prosecution and conviction. The article quickly led to cries for Justice Fortas's impeachment.

As the political storm raged outside the walls of the Marble Palace, the Fortas law clerks tried to focus on the work at hand. The charges against the justice did impact their daily lives, however, when Fortas turned to them for legal advice and tasks related to the allegations against him—for example, asking Field to research the question of whether his nonjudicial behavior could result in criminal prosecution.

After Justice Fortas resigned in May 1969, Field and Slocombe spent the remainder of their clerkships working on cert petitions for Chief Justice Warren. Slocombe would have one final encounter at the Court with Fortas. He was working in the clerk's office in the former Fortas chambers when he was startled to see Fortas appear in the doorway. When asked what he was doing, Slocombe replied that he was studying for the bar exam. "You have my sympathy," replied Fortas. "Taking the bar was the worst experience of my life." Fortas then explained that he himself did not take the bar exam until he was preparing to leave government service for private practice, and at the time Fortas was terrified that he would fail and see newspaper headlines trumpeting the fall of a prominent New Dealer.[49]

Interactions with Other Chambers

Not only did the Fortas law clerks come in contact with other justices, but they also observed how their own employer interacted with his peers. "I thought that Douglas was a bit of a jerk. He was an impossible human being," stated Rosenbloom. He recalled an occasion when a French-speaking dignitary from North Africa came to visit Douglas, and a call went out for a translator. Rosenbloom was pressed into service, much to Douglas's dismay. "If Douglas could have lasered me with his eyes, he would have. He hated the idea that I was there." Rosenbloom added that "Douglas was a truly horrible person, and during my term he drove his sole clerk into the hospital."

As for Slocombe, his most memorable encounter came with Justice Hugo Black. Slocombe recalled talking to Justice Black's law clerk, Walter Dellinger, when the justice walked into the office. This was shortly after Justice Fortas had written the opinion in *Tinker v. Des Moines,* an opinion that expanded the free speech rights of schoolchildren (and an opinion that had angered Justice Black). Looking at Slocombe, Black commented: "You look awfully old to be Abe's law clerk. He is awfully fond of young people."[50]

Two other former Fortas clerks witnessed the tension between Justice Black and Justice Fortas. Rosenbloom simply remarked that "Black was in his southern gentlemen phase, and Fortas had had a bellyful of Black [and was] impatient with him." For Levitt, the source of friction stemmed from Black's unsuccessful efforts to control the newest member of the Court. "Every time a new Justice came to the Supreme Court in the 1950s and 1960s, Black assumed that he would make him a follower of his constitutional views," explained Levitt. "And Black was very angry when Fortas did not become a follower."

According to Levitt, the tensions between the two justices erupted during the Court's review of *Time v. Hill*[51] (another free speech case). After Justice Fortas circulated a draft opinion, Justice Black circulated a memo characterizing Fortas's draft as the worst First Amendment decision he had read since *West Virginia State Board of Education v. Barnette*[52] (a case that upheld the state's rights to require students to salute the American flag). Black stated that he would work all summer on his dissent and would publish it in the fall—despite the fact that the majority was prepared to issue their majority opinion.

Levitt believes that Justice Black's delaying tactics were a shrewd political move, since it forced the Court to schedule the case for reargument. Black then circulated a dissent that "was very hostile to Fortas, and it included a parody of Fortas's writing style. Fortas was a very good writer, and he demanded an apology from Black—which he received." After reargument, the majority opinion was assigned to Justice Brennan, and Justice Fortas found himself in the minority.

The Personal Bonds between the Justice and the Clerks

For many law clerks, the long hours at the Court are mitigated by their youthful devotion to their specific justice. While the adoration may fade over time, it is replaced by a respect for their former employer and gratitude for the rare opportunity to clerk at the Supreme Court. The feelings of the Fortas law clerks, both during and after their clerkships, are more decidedly mixed. The conventional view of the relationship between Justice Fortas and his clerks can be found in a biography by Bruce Allen Murphy, who writes:

> "Fortas law clerks absolutely despised him," explained Benno Schmidt [a law clerk to Earl Warren]. "They said the most awful things about him, which really surprised me since most clerks tend to revere their Justice. They said that he was not a man of principle on a principled court, what with the finished jurisprudential philosophies of men like Black, Douglas, and Harlan. . . . In time, the clerks came to see Fortas as totally unprincipled, and intellectually dishonest."[53]

There is little evidence, however, that the Fortas clerks "despised" their justice. Rosenbloom called Schmidt's observation "foolish," adding that Schmidt likely talked to a single Fortas clerk who was unhappy with the justice's involvement in the Vietnam War. "I had no problem with the Justice. He was an odd guy to work for after Goldberg because Fortas played things very close to the vest and was not communicative (unlike Goldberg)." He did add, however, that he thought that the justice "did play one clerk off the other."[54] Slocombe echoed this observation, explaining that the justice followed the pattern of "having one clerk who he liked and one clerk he didn't like."[55]

For Griffiths, his relationship with Fortas—which he characterized as "distant"—was colored by the justice's close ties with the Johnson White House. "I was very unhappy that a sitting Justice was helping run the Vietnam War. I knew at the time that he was very close to LBJ . . . but we did not know of his heavy involvement in the War."[56]

Griffith became engaged to be married during his clerkship, but even the wedding present that he received from Fortas came with a twist. While in chambers one day, Griffiths overheard a conversation in which the justice told his secretary that he was disposing of some unwanted items during a home renovation. When Griffiths heard that Justice Fortas was arranging to have the brass bed he had admired when visiting Fortas's house carted off as junk, he asked Fortas if he could have it. The justice responded, "Sure, John—I will give it to you as a wedding present."[57]

Griffiths quickly added, however, that he greatly benefited from the clerkship itself. "I had two wonderful years at the Supreme Court," stated Griffiths. "The fact that I had, at the end, a low opinion of Fortas did not affect my clerkship experience. And despite all my reservations about him as a person and as a judge, I certainly learned a lot during those two years." Griffiths did not have a postclerkship relationship with the justice. "Fortas never evidenced any interest in what happened to me after the clerkship."[58]

Of all the former clerks, Levitt has the fondest memories of a justice whom he believed was destined for greatness. At a memorial proceeding before the Court, Levitt observed that "anyone who came into contact with Abe Fortas was greatly touched by him" and spoke of the "kind, even tender personality" that Fortas occasionally displayed toward his clerks and their families.[59]

After his clerkship, Levitt went to work at the justice's former firm. He was immediately recruited to work on Fortas's nomination to be chief justice. "I knew Fortas' opinions, so I was brought in." Levitt's job duties included writing speeches of support for senators to read on the Senate floor (Levitt asserts that every speech given by a senator on the floor of the Senate was written by him) as well as the Judiciary Committee's report in support of the nomination. Levitt also wrote editorials for various newspapers to run in support of Fortas and drafted an article that a senator wrote in support of Fortas, an op-ed piece that claimed that the justice was "an apostle of judicial restraint."

Conclusion

The story of Justice Abe Fortas and his law clerks is a cautionary tale that reminds students of Supreme Court history that not all clerkships result in strong professional or personal relationships between a justice and his or her clerks. While certainly the Fortas law clerks were not subjected to the pressures associated with clerking for a James C. McReynolds or William O. Douglas (whose clerkship practices included mental abuse of their clerks), the morale of the Fortas clerks was affected by their disdain for both Justice Fortas's political activities as well as his results-oriented jurisprudence. In recent years, some Court scholars have questioned whether the justices should use an ideological litmus test to select law clerks. A case study of Justice Fortas and his clerks, however, suggests that perhaps too much ideological distance between a justice and his or her clerks can produce a clerkship that is disquieting and unsatisfactory for the young men and women who strive to clerk in the Marble Palace.

Notes

1. Daniel Levitt interview by Todd C. Peppers, January 4, 2011.

2. John Griffiths interview by Todd C. Peppers, March 10, 2011.

3. Levitt interview.

4. Walter Slocombe interview by Todd C. Peppers, February 10, 2011.

5. Levitt interview.

6. Todd C. Peppers correspondence with Thomas Grey, 2011.

7. Ibid.

8. Laura Kalman, *Abe Fortas: A Biography* (New Haven, Conn.: Yale University Press, 1990), 314 (quoting from Nat Hentoff, "The Constitutionalist," *New Yorker,* March 12, 1990, 61–62).

9. See generally Michael E. Tigar, *Fighting Injustice* (Chicago: American Bar Association, 2002); Andrew Kopkind, "Brennan v. Tigar," *New Republic,* August 27, 1966.

10. Levitt interview.

11. Bruce Allen Murphy, *Fortas: The Rise and Ruin of a Supreme Court Justice* (New York: William Morrow, 1988), 235. Griffiths summarizes Fortas's outside interests succinctly: "He was practically running the [Vietnam] War at some point." Todd C. Peppers correspondence with John Griffiths.

12. See generally Murphy, *Fortas;* Kalman, *Abe Fortas.*

13. Todd C. Peppers correspondence with David Rosenbloom.

14. Levitt interview.

15. See generally John Griffiths, "Office Procedure," June 15, 1967.

16. Slocombe interview.

17. Griffiths interview.

18. Ibid.

19. While in subsequent terms Justice Fortas occasionally asked for a formal bench memorandum, the norm evolved into oral discussions between justice and clerk. Rosenbloom correspondence; Todd C. Peppers correspondence with Walter B. Slocombe, February 10, 2011.

20. Griffiths, "Office Procedure," 13.

21. Ibid.

22. Ibid.

23. Ibid., 13–14.

24. Ibid.

25. Slocombe correspondence. Rosenbloom also writes that the law clerks "drafted many, but not all, opinions." Rosenbloom correspondence.

26. Griffiths interview.

27. Slocombe interview.

28. David Rosenbloom interview by Todd C. Peppers, January 6, 2011.

29. Kalman, *Abe Fortas*, 271.

30. Ibid., 271–72. Of course, some judicial scholars would argue that Fortas's approach was no different in kind (if not in style) from that of any other Supreme Court justice.

31. 387 U.S. 1 (1967).

32. Griffiths interview.

33. *Kent v. U.S.,* 383 U.S. 541 (1966).

34. Kent Case File, Collection MS 858, Series 1, Box 16, Folder 331, 17, Fortas Papers, Yale University.

35. Ibid., 17–51.

36. Ibid.

37. Ibid., 52.

38. 383 U.S. 787 (1966).

39. Griffith interview.

40. Levitt interview.

41. Rosenbloom interview.

42. Levitt interview.

43. Kalman, *Abe Fortas,* 322–24.

44. Levitt interview.

45. Ibid.

46. Kalman, *Abe Fortas,* 325; Levitt interview.

47. Kalman, *Abe Fortas,* 338.

48. Slocombe interview.

49. Ibid.

50. Ibid.

51. 385 U.S. 374 (1967).

52. 319 U.S. 624 (1943).

53. Murphy, *Fortas,* 219. Benno Schmidt served as Chief Justice Earl Warren's law clerk during October term 1966.

54. Rosenbloom interview.

55. Slocombe interview.

56. Griffiths interview.

57. Ibid.

58. Ibid.

59. Daniel Levitt, *Proceedings of the Bar and Officers of the Supreme Court of the United States: In Memoriam Honorable Abe Fortas* (Washington, D.C.: 1982).

REBECCA HURLEY

In the Chief's Chambers

Life as a Law Clerk for Warren Earl Burger

For thirteen months during the years 1983 and 1984, I had the privilege of serving as a law clerk in the chambers of Warren Earl Burger, the fifteenth chief justice of the United States.[1] At that time, "the Chief"—as he delighted in being called by virtually everyone, at his own request—had been "first among equals" on the Supreme Court for fourteen years and, although unknown to us at the time, was reaching the end of his seventeen-year tenure. Many life lessons were taught, and learned, in the Chief's chambers over those years: lessons not only about jurisprudence, legal reasoning, and the workings of the court system but also about history, the arts, work ethic, tradition, and character. The Chief's lessons have been passed along many times in the years since, frequently in the form of war stories and work anecdotes shared by his law clerks with their friends and colleagues, and not infrequently with the accompaniment of a glass of the wine that the Chief himself so much enjoyed.

For most of us, the journey to the Chief's chambers began with a phone call: specifically, a phone call from one of the Chief's former law clerks that constituted an invitation to an interview. Unique among the justices at that time, the Chief had created a committee of his former law clerks to facilitate the process of reviewing the enormous volume of clerkship applications that arrived each year, determining which applicants should be interviewed, conducting the interviews, comparing notes and impressions of the leading candidates, and then recommending to the Chief a team of four individuals who would serve in his chambers for the upcoming term. As is well known, the Chief attended law school at St. Paul College of Law, now William Mitchell College of Law, in St. Paul, Minnesota. Based upon his experiences there and throughout his career, he was aware that not all of the most talented and capable law students in the country were to be found at Ivy League and other "top-ranked" law schools. In the Chief's view, deploying his large, nationwide network of former law clerks to screen and interview clerkship applicants increased the likelihood that he would find exceptional candidates who might otherwise have escaped notice. Moreover, because former law clerks also had firsthand knowledge of the importance of teamwork and collegiality among those inside and outside the Chief's chambers, they were uniquely qualified to evaluate candidates for those attributes and to recommend for hiring a slate of individuals representing an optimal balance of talents, temperaments, and experiences.

My phone call came from the Honorable Kenneth F. Ripple, now a member of the U.S. Courts of Appeals for the Seventh Circuit and then professor of law at Notre Dame Law School. Judge Ripple had served as special assistant to the chief justice in the 1970s and was the member of the Chief's clerkship selection committee responsible for interviewing candidates from the central region of the United States. Because I had attended law school in Texas and was then clerking for the late Honorable Irving L. Goldberg, U.S. Court of Appeals for the Fifth Circuit, my application had landed in Judge Ripple's stack, and within days I found myself sitting in his office in snowy South Bend, Indiana. The interview that followed was challenging and heavily substantive. From a well-prepared list of topics, Judge Ripple drew all manner of questions, including hypothetical questions about complex issues recently decided by and still pending before the Court. He delved deeply into my prior background, inquiring as to how my previous career in teaching might inform my views on cases related to education and child welfare. And he pressed me to describe in detail just how I would react and respond if the Chief and I had divergent views about the outcome of a case. I learned later that Judge Ripple had performed significant outside due diligence as well, calling several members of my law school faculty to measure my intellectual capabilities as well as my ability to work well with others.

Five weeks later, Judge Goldberg received a telephone call from the Chief. After a few pleasantries, the Chief asked Judge Goldberg what sort of law clerk I had turned out to be. Whatever the judge's response, it was obviously found sufficient, because the Chief then asked the judge to extend to me an offer to serve as his law clerk during the 1983 term. Shortly after their conversation, I received a letter on official Supreme Court stationery confirming that the call was not some sort of prank and that a clerkship in the Chief's chambers lay ahead. The Chief later explained that, as a matter of protocol, he thought it appropriate to contact personally the judges for whom his prospective law clerks were then working to advise them of his selections, and from that grew his practice of having those judges actually extend the offers of clerkship.

As a result of this process, most of the Chief's clerks of that era faced the daunting prospect of arriving at the Court for the first day of work never having met, or even spoken with, their new boss, who just happened to be the chief justice of the Supreme Court of the United States. Moreover, new law clerks then began their clerkships during July, just after the conclusion of the Court's prior term, when most of the justices had already left for a summer break. For this reason, it was not unusual for several weeks to pass before new law clerks met or had a chance to interact with the Chief. The Chief more than made up for this artifact of scheduling, however, by making a real ceremony out of his clerks' initiation into life at the Court. At the earliest available opportunity after arrival, each of us was treated to an official "swearing in" as a law clerk in one of the beautiful conference rooms on the first floor of the Supreme Court building, an occasion that included an oath delivered personally by the Chief, the presence of witnesses, the services of an official Court photographer, and a postceremony tea with the Chief. The "swearing in" served as his law clerks' introduction to the Chief's love of rituals and traditions, particularly those associated with life at the Court. More important, although no legal requirement existed compelling the administration of an oath of office to Supreme Court law clerks, the Chief did so to impress upon his clerks the seriousness and gravity with which he viewed the duties that he, and we, would undertake in serving the judicial system.

The most basic of those duties involved the review of the hundreds of petitions for writ of certiorari that came before the Court each term. The Chief was an original participant in, and active proponent of, the cert pool arrangement that had been put in place in the 1970s, under which this responsibility was divided among the law clerks serving multiple justices; during the 1983 term, there were six justices who participated. Each week, the Chief's share of the aggregate cert petitions to be processed would be delivered and allocated among his four law clerks. Within a matter of days, we would review each cert petition, prepare a memorandum containing our analysis of the petition and a recommended disposition thereof, and circulate the memorandum among the other participants in the cert pool. Initially, the magnitude of this task seemed somewhat overwhelming; no matter how many cert petitions were received and dispatched, dozens and dozens more were sure to appear the following week, and each cert memorandum that went out the door contained a recommendation that could influence the thinking of not only the Chief but also the other five justices in the cert pool. With time, however, the efficient review of cert petitions and timely production of cert memoranda became part of the rhythm of life at the Court.

The Chief's membership in the cert pool also meant that we reviewed the cert memoranda prepared by law clerks serving in the chambers of the other participating justices.[2] This gave us our initial opportunity to begin developing relationships outside our own chambers, as we would regularly call the author of a cert memorandum to discuss his or her views as to the particulars of a case. The Chief requested that his own law clerks annotate the cert memoranda from other chambers to indicate whether we agreed or disagreed with the analysis and recommendation contained therein; if we disagreed, he would frequently ask us to visit with the author of the memorandum to discuss our differing conclusions and/or prepare a supplement to the cert memorandum setting forth our own thoughts and conclusions.

As the beginning of the term approached, and the calendar for oral argument was finalized, the law clerks' attention turned to the preparation of bench memoranda regarding the cases slated to come before the Court. The bench memoranda prepared by each justice's law clerks were exclusively for the benefit of his or her own personal preparation; stated differently, no analog to the cert pool existed with respect to cases that warranted oral argument. In the Chief's chambers, we law clerks divided the cases equally among ourselves based in part upon our particular substantive interests[3] and, later in the term when opinion assignments had begun being made, our respective workloads. Some effort was also made to assure that the anticipated "marquee" cases were assigned fairly among us.

Our bench memoranda were structured in a very particular fashion prescribed by the Chief to assist in his review. He wanted to see first a statement of the question presented, followed by the procedural history of the case, the disposition thereof by the court below, a succinct summary of only those facts necessary to an understanding of the question presented, and then the pertinent legal analysis, together with a recommended holding. As this was also the structure utilized by the Chief in writing his opinions, a well-drafted bench memorandum could prove invaluable to a law clerk whose case was assigned to the Chief in the Court's postargument Friday conference. The Chief also had a strong preference for lots of white space on the page; he asked that we use wide margins and multiple line-spacing in our documents so that he could interlineate his editorial thoughts and comments throughout our memos with ease.

Once one of us took on a case that was scheduled for oral argument and prepared the related bench memorandum, that clerk was responsible for the work on that case until its final disposition. This might involve assisting the Chief with the drafting of an opinion for the Court, commenting upon a draft opinion from one of the other justices, or assisting the Chief with the drafting of a concurring or dissenting opinion. Accordingly, we waited with anticipation for news of the results of the Court's conference on the Friday following oral arguments, for it was in conference that the writing assignments were ordinarily made. This news was typically delivered to us by Jan Horbaly, who occupied a unique position within the chambers as the Chief's special assistant for judicial affairs.[4] Jan, who served the Chief for a number of years, functioned as his chief of staff on all matters that were judicial in nature.[5] Jan's presence provided a welcome sense of continuity from term to term, and his deep familiarity with the Chief's habits, thought processes, and other proclivities was of tremendous value to the law clerks, whose tenure was much briefer.

One of the most helpful pieces of knowledge imparted by Jan concerned the Chief's somewhat infamous "Thoughts While Shaving." "Thoughts While Shaving," generally referred to by us as "TWSes," were exactly that: the thoughts and ideas regarding a particular case that came to the Chief's mind as he went about his regular grooming ritual. When questioned about the origin of TWSes, the Chief explained that he found shaving to present the best possible opportunity for reflection and rumination, because while doing so it was impossible to look at anything other than the mirror, speak to anyone other than oneself, or hear anything other than one's own thoughts. For this reason, the Chief developed the habit of dictating his TWSes immediately following his morning shave and bringing the dictation tape straight to his office at the Court for transcription. Not long thereafter, the law clerk responsible for the case would receive a typed copy of the TWSes, which usually began with a statement of the question presented, continued with page after page of the Chief's legal reasoning and analysis, and included references to the Supreme Court precedents (including other opinions authored by the Chief) that informed his views. From these beginnings, together with material gathered from our bench memoranda and legal research, we would assemble initial drafts of opinions for the Chief's review and comment.

The Chief was naturally blessed with a direct and straightforward writing style reflective of his Minnesota roots, and he placed a premium upon the clarity of our drafting. The law clerk whose prose was deemed by the Chief to be particularly dense was sure to find large puffy question marks or the annotation "DGI" scribbled in the wide margins of the page, both signals that the Chief "didn't get it." Neither was the Chief a fan of overlong opinions, as demonstrated when he returned one of my drafts with the following note: "Good, but ⅓ to ½ too, *too*, TOO LONG!"

The Chief always had a clear vision of the direction he wished to take in his opinions, and the TWSes were his roadmap. There was never any question in our chambers as to who made decisions about the result to be reached in a case or what legal principles informed that outcome: the Chief was, in every substantive respect, the Chief. His law clerks provided research and drafting assistance that enabled him to leverage his time, resources, expertise, and experience, in much the same way that associates in a law firm assist senior partners. The clerks' opinion-writing responsibilities entailed the weaving together of various threads into one coherent whole. And, of course, the Chief himself enjoyed wielding the pen. The distinctive ring of the dedicated phone line between the Chief's desk and ours was often harbinger of a summons to the Chief's chambers to work through the language of an opinion in progress. He was a consummate editor, and frequently spent hours reviewing and revising each passage until he had crafted precisely the message that he wished to convey.

The Chief imposed no "litmus test" upon candidates for positions as his law clerks; he welcomed, and indeed seemed to enjoy, having his chambers populated with intelligent and articulate men and women having different political persuasions as well as varying views on legal issues. A list of the Chief's law clerks who considered themselves more "liberal" than he—at least during their tenure at the Court—would be long. He was always respectful when we disagreed with his position and was open to listening to an opposing view, but, as noted, at the end of the day it was the Chief's opinion that prevailed.

No account of Warren Burger could fail to include a description of his physical appearance and the almost uncanny way in which it befitted his position. Tall and handsome,[6] with a full mane of white hair, he truly personified the conventional mental image of a high-ranking officer of court,[7] and his commanding baritone furthered that impression. The Chief occasionally chose to use these native gifts to great effect, as when *Keeton v. Hustler Magazine*[8] was set for oral argument and *Hustler* magazine publisher Larry Flynt attempted to disrupt the Court's proceedings with a profanity-laden outburst in the courtroom. As if on cue, the Chief's stentorian voice echoed through the courtroom and out into the Great Hall as he ordered the bailiffs to "take [this man] into custody!" Neither Flynt—nor any other person within earshot that day—had any doubt that the imposing presence wielding the gavel embodied the full force and authority of the U.S. judicial system.

For all that, however, the Chief was not terribly interested in or concerned about outward appearances. There was an inherent modesty to him that was reflected in his preference for practicality over style or fashion. Due to issues with his back and feet,[9] he favored black suede Wallabees for their comfort and slip-on ease, an affinity he shared with his colleague Justice Rehnquist, and frequently had to be reminded to change into "dress shoes" for visits outside the Court building. He favored the warmth of a cardigan when working in chambers, particularly on weekends, and the tradition of a plain black robe on the bench.

A year in the Chief's chambers also afforded his law clerks many meaningful opportunities to observe and interact with the man on a personal level. When his schedule and the press of business permitted, the Chief enjoyed lunching with his law clerks, whether in the justices' private dining room at the Court or at other venues around the city. The City Tavern Club in Georgetown was a favorite dining spot, in no small part because it had been a gathering place for many figures of historical significance, including Founding Fathers George Washington, Thomas Jefferson, and John Adams. Having the opportunity to leave the building, if only for a little while, seemed to please him greatly. He could frequently be found taking a walk around the block during fine weather, accompanied by one or more of us and holding forth on topics ranging from a recently published biography of Dwight D. Eisenhower[10] to the origin of the Japanese maples planted on the grounds of the Supreme Court building. Because his role as chief justice carried with it such other responsibilities as chancellor of the Smithsonian Institution, his calendar was crowded with official events and appointments external to the Court, and he regularly invited his clerks to come along. In this manner, we were treated to "field trips" such as a program commemorating the thirtieth anniversary of the Department of Justice Honors Program and a celebration of the investiture of Kenneth W. Starr, another former Burger clerk, as a judge on the U.S. Court of Appeals for the District of Columbia Circuit. In addition, each of us was deputized as the Chief's traveling companion on at least one occasion during the clerkship year, accompanying him to, for instance, the annual convention of the American Bar Association[11] and a conference on prison reform held at the Johnson Foundation at Wingspread near Racine, Wisconsin.[12]

Of all our personal interactions with the Chief, Saturday workdays at the Court were among the most memorable. Due to the volume of work at hand and the technology available at the time,[13] Saturday office hours were essential, but the attire on those days was decidedly more informal and the atmosphere more relaxed than during the regular work week. Among our Saturday rituals was an "in chambers" lunch that was always prepared by the Chief himself in a small kitchen adjacent to his private office. The menu usually included the Chief's renowned homemade bean soup, which he served alongside cold cuts, cheese, good bread, and various condiments, including his orange marmalade (likewise homemade). On one such Saturday, shortly after the Christmas holidays, the Chief closed out our repast by passing around a plate piled high with slices of fruitcake, which he had soaked in spirits prior to serving. Each of us politely took a piece and began nibbling away as our table talk continued; the Chief, however, did not. After quite a few moments had passed without incident, the Chief at last reached for the plate of fruitcake and served himself. Chuckling, and with a twinkle in his eye, he confided that the fruitcake had been a holiday gift from an unknown admirer and that only after it had been screened by the Court's security officers and taste-tested by his law clerks was he confident it was safe to eat!

Our Saturday lunch conversations were lively and wide-ranging in scope. In those private hours we had the opportunity to ask the Chief about all manner of things, and he the opportunity to respond openly and expansively. We learned that although the Chief initially disagreed with the decision in *Miranda v. Arizona*,[14] he had come to believe that its holding ultimately added stability and certainty to the criminal justice system and thus should not be revisited or overturned. Conversely, we listened as the Chief bemoaned the Court's holding in *Bates v. State Bar of Arizona*,[15] expressing dismay at the way in which attorney advertising had—as predicted in his separate opinion concurring in part and dissenting in part[16]—already contributed to a demise in the professionalism of law practice. We debated the then-pending bill to make Martin Luther King Jr.'s birthday a national holiday and commiserated about the disruption caused by the protests held outside the building on the anniversary of the Court's decision in *Roe v. Wade*.[17]

Our discussions also reflected the Chief's many and varied interests beyond the law. Art and antiques were an avocation, and he regularly had several painting, sculpture, and/or woodworking projects in progress. He was quite gifted in this area, as can be seen from the bas-relief sculpture of Chief Justice John Marshall displayed in the aptly named John Marshall Dining Room at the Supreme Court.[18] Both this artistic streak and his deep love of history were in evidence from an early age. As a boy, the Chief was fascinated by the tale of William the Conqueror's victory at the Battle of Hastings in 1066. After having read and committed to memory numerous accounts of the story, he created a drawing of the event extraordinary in its detail. This sketch was a treasured possession, taking pride of place in his bookcase and providing entertaining conversational fodder for his law clerks as well as his many guests.

Given the Chief's position, he received a steady stream of visitors hailing from all over the country and around the world, many of whom wanted to offer him a gift of some kind. And given the Chief's position and inherent frugality, finding an appropriate present for him—for any occasion—could be somewhat challenging. Fortunately, the Chief's well-known enjoyment of a glass of good wine provided a ready solution for those in need of a suggestion. He received many bottles over the years—German whites were particular favorites—and was generous in sharing them with others. It became his custom to ask the bearer of a gift of wine to sign and date the label, and he enjoyed reminiscing about both the benefactor and the occasion when he uncorked each one.

The Chief's public reputation has grown to be that of a private and formal man, and he did exhibit a reserve that some may have interpreted as aloofness. Those who had the opportunity to work closely with him, however, saw this as an outgrowth of his upbringing—those Minnesota roots again—and were fortunate to have experienced a more intimate side of him. The Chief was extremely hospitable to his clerks' spouses, significant others,[19] children, and parents, and went to great lengths to include all of them in his life, both during the clerkship year and thereafter. During the period that I served in his chambers, the Chief and his beloved wife, Vera, hosted the law clerks at a brunch at Washington, D.C.'s Alibi Club early in the term to welcome us into the fold; the following spring, we were invited to their home in Arlington, Virginia, one Saturday to participate in the Chief's annual spring gardening ritual and join

him for a postplanting lunch.[20] Toward the end of the term, at a farewell dinner held again at his Arlington home, the Chief presented us with various inscribed photographs that he had framed personally at the carpentry shop at the
Supreme Court. He was equally warm and hospitable to our families, always
finding time for tea, conversation, and a tour of the chambers with each set of
our parents as they paid visits to us throughout the course of the year. Even
after his clerks departed his chambers to embark upon their own legal careers,
he remained regularly in touch, forwarding along copies of his speeches and
articles that he thought would be of interest. Shortly after the Philippine Bar
Association published a volume of the opinions he deemed his "most significant," each of us received a copy inscribed "[t]o insure sound repose, read for
ten minutes at bedtime."[21]

Nowhere were the Chief's abiding connections to his law clerks—and theirs
to him—more in evidence than at the reunion dinners for the group, which
was (and continues to be) dubbed the "WEB Fete Society."[22] Traditionally
held annually at the Supreme Court building on a Saturday evening in the fall,
the dinners were formal catered affairs at which the men dressed in tuxedoes
and the women in cocktail attire. The gatherings served as a way for the members to reunite with one another and the Chief and were well attended by clerks
from throughout the Chief's tenure. Naturally, these occasions lent themselves
to much telling of tales, and at the end of each evening the Chief always spoke
a few words and took questions from the assembled group. This tradition has
continued, although with less frequency, since the Chief's death in 1995 thanks
to the sponsorship of sitting justices of the Court and is now the principal occasion at which the members of the WEB Fete Society have the collective opportunity to reminisce about their common experiences.

Of course, life at the Court involved interaction without, as well as within,
the Chief's chambers, principally with other law clerks[23] but also with their
justices as well. From a substantive standpoint, and as is to be expected, the
Chief's clerks worked most closely with the law clerks of justices who were
joining the Chief in an opinion or hoping to secure his joinder in one of theirs,
as the language of such opinions was carefully crafted and refined to accommodate the nuances of each of their views. For that reason, we naturally saw
a great deal of our colleagues in the chambers of Justices O'Connor, Powell,
and Rehnquist. More informally, the law clerks for all of the justices generally
took a common lunch break, either in the law clerks' lunchroom[24] or outside in
one of the building's courtyards, where spirited but friendly debates about the
matters on our desks were the norm.[25]

By tradition, the law clerks in each chambers invited each of the other justices out for lunch at some point during the Court's term; dining with Justice
O'Connor at The Monocle (said by her clerks to be one of her favorite places)

and with Justice Rehnquist at the Hawk 'n' Dove (where he ordered a draft beer along with his cheeseburger) provided us with rare and precious opportunities to spend time with the Chief's colleagues. The annual Christmas party for the Supreme Court "household," of which the Chief had formally designated Justice Rehnquist chairman in the 1970s,[26] disclosed other hidden interests and talents of the latter. Attended by everyone who worked in the Supreme Court building as well as their spouses and numerous other guests, the party ended with a rousing sing-along conducted by Justice Rehnquist to the piano accompaniment of the husband of Justice Blackmun's secretary. After having exhausted every religious and secular Christmas carol and holiday song known to him, Justice Rehnquist proceeded to lead the group through the fight songs of all of the colleges attended by the assembled law clerks, beginning with "On Wisconsin" in a nod to his home state. It was, to say the least, a highlight of the term.

In September 1986, the Chief retired from his position as chief justice in order to devote himself full time to the role of chairman of the Bicentennial Commission formed to commemorate the 200th anniversary of the Constitution that would occur in 1987. This transition, which was unexpected and sparked much speculation about the reasons therefor, was an entirely natural path for him to take. While serendipitous, it was altogether fitting that the Chief and the Constitution shared the same birthday—September 17—and he quietly but genuinely enjoyed the coincidence. The Chief revered the Constitution: it was quite literally his lodestar. I have no doubt that he felt an enormous responsibility to assure that the anniversary of a document so significant to his life, and to the life of our nation, was celebrated with all due reverence and that he considered it his personal duty to take whatever steps were necessary to that outcome.

A year after the Chief's death at age eighty-seven, his son Wade announced that the Chief's lifetime personal and professional papers and memorabilia would be donated to the College of William & Mary, of which the Chief had served as chancellor from 1986 until 1993. Plans were made to renovate and expand the college's Swem Library to house the collection[27] and to create a space closely resembling the Chief's chambers at the Supreme Court building. When the formal acceptance of the gift was made and fund-raising for the project began, several events were held in Williamsburg to mark the occasion, and many of the Chief's former law clerks attended. Margaret Thatcher, who succeeded the Chief as the school's chancellor, was a special guest at these events and gave a moving tribute to the Chief, expressing her great admiration for him and his work, both on the bench and behind the scenes in promoting the administration of justice. At a private luncheon attended by the Chief's law clerks and close friends, she reached into her purse and pulled out a "pocket copy" of the U.S. Constitution. In her lilting British accent, Lady Thatcher explained that the small volume had been a gift to her from the Chief on the occasion of her investiture as chancellor, intended to symbolize the many similarities between the British and American systems of justice. She closed by remarking that she carried that copy of the Constitution with her at all times as a constant reminder of the Chief and the principles they held in common.

Those of us fortunate enough to have served as law clerks to Warren Burger also carry with us constant reminders of him and the principles by which he conducted himself. Having sold life insurance during the day to finance the college education he pursued at night, he had a firsthand appreciation for the value of hard work, and throughout his career he demonstrated a prodigious work ethic that exhausted law clerks many decades his junior. Although he was a Republican and always labeled a "conservative," his body of work reveals an even-handed and less absolutist approach[28] that by today's lights might well be deemed middle of the road. Also unusual in today's world, he had genuine friendships with political figures on both sides of the aisle, including not only fellow Minnesotans and U.S. senators Hubert H. Humphrey Jr. and Walter F. Mondale but also U.S. senator Henry M. ("Scoop") Jackson, all of whom were Democrats but with all of whom he shared similar values and beliefs.[29] And throughout his life and career he relied upon a powerful and personal moral compass to guide his every action and decision. As the years pass, these and the many other lessons we learned simply by observing the Chief in action resonate more and more deeply, as does our gratitude for the opportunity.

Notes

1. Mark B. Helm, Peter M. Lieb, and J. Michael Luttig were my esteemed "clerk brethren" in the chief justice's chambers during that term.

2. This was common practice in the chambers of those justices who participated in the cert pool and addressed concerns that the cert pool process might give undue weight to the views and analysis of a single law clerk. See, for example, Randall P. Bezanson, "Harry Blackman and His Clerks," in *In Chambers: Stories of Supreme Court Law Clerks and Their Justices,* edited by Todd C. Peppers and Artemus Ward (Charlottesville: University of Virginia Press, 2012), 329–30.

3. As the only one of the Chief's law clerks that term who was more interested in a transactional law practice than litigation, I was pleased to take on two tax-related cases that were of far less interest to my colleagues than to me, especially so when the Chief ultimately assigned himself responsibility for writing the Court's opinions in both. See *United States v. Arthur Young & Co.,* 465 U.S. 805 (1984); *Dickman v. Commissioner,* 465 U.S. 330 (1984).

4. Jan later served as circuit executive and clerk of court of the U.S. Court of Appeals for the Federal Circuit, a position from which he retired in 2013.

5. The responsibilities of the chief justice included not only his role as a sitting justice of the Supreme Court but also the task of administering the entire judicial branch of the government. For support in connection with those administrative responsibilities, the Chief had assembled a separate team of nonlegal advisers and assistants then headed by Mark Cannon, special assistant for administrative affairs. For more on this aspect of the chief justice's duties, and in particular Chief Justice Burger's leadership in working to improve the administration of the federal courts, see Warren E. Burger, *Delivery of Justice* (St. Paul, Minn.: West Publishing, 1990).

6. John Paul Stevens, *Five Chiefs* (New York: Little, Brown, 2011), 136 (referring to "our handsome leading man").

7. Ronald L. Trowbridge, *With Sweet Majesty, Warren E. Burger* (Washington, D.C.: Trust for the Bicentennial of the United States Constitution, 2000), 148 (interview with Judge J. Michael Luttig).

8. 465 U.S. 770 (1984).

9. Trowbridge, *With Sweet Majesty*, 119–20 (interview with Burnett Anderson).

10. Stephen E. Ambrose, *Eisenhower the President* (New York: Simon and Schuster, 1984). Ambrose apparently shared with the Chief in a private conversation information suggesting that President Eisenhower had considered the Chief as a candidate for chief justice prior to Eisenhower's eventual nomination of Earl Warren to the post in 1953. The Chief expressed genuine surprise at this revelation when confiding it to his law clerks.

11. That year's convention happened to be held in Las Vegas, and those in charge of the Chief's travel arrangements were careful to assure that his hotel accommodations were appropriate for a man of his station.

12. The Chief's advocacy for prison reform, and his support for the concept of prisons as "factories with fences," is well documented. See, for example, "Factories with Fences: 75 Years of Changing Lives" (Unicor, 2009).

13. During the 1983 term, the Court had in place the same centralized word-processing system then in use at the *Washington Post*, which was "state of the art" at the time. Because the system was operational only between 8:00 a.m. each morning and midnight each night, it had a material impact upon the office hours observed by most of the law clerks.

14. 384 U.S. 436 (1966).

15. 433 U.S. 350 (1977).

16. Ibid., 386 (Burger, C.J., concurring in part and dissenting in part).

17. 410 U.S. 113 (1973).

18. Trowbridge, *With Sweet Majesty*, 99.

19. The Chief would have abhorred the use of this term, as he did most of the modern linguistic conventions that we would now ascribe to "political correctness." He once took me to task for using the word "foreperson" to refer to the individual chosen to lead jury deliberations, going so far as to count the number of times the word appeared in my draft opinion before instructing me, in the clearest possible terms, to "change it back to foreman."

20. The Chief had two green thumbs and derived great pleasure from working in his yard, where he seemed able to relax fully. He also enjoyed sharing this love of gardening with his law clerks and friends. See Trowbridge, *With Sweet Majesty,* 110–11, 146.

21. *Significant Supreme Court Opinions of the Honorable Warren E. Burger: Chief Justice of the United States* (Manila: Philippine Bar Association, 1984).

22. The intentional play on words reflected in the name bestowed upon his law clerk alumni (that is, "webbed feet") appealed greatly to the Chief's wry sense of humor.

23. In addition to the eight sitting justices, retired Justice Potter Stewart maintained offices in the Supreme Court building and was assisted by one law clerk at that time.

24. A separate lunchroom had been set aside for the law clerks in the early 1980s after members of the press accurately predicted the holding in a pending case based upon the lunch-table conversations of law clerks overheard while dining in the building's public cafeteria.

25. Although it is generally presumed that the justices select law clerks whose views on legal issues are aligned with their own, that is certainly not always the case, and it was not at all uncommon for a law clerk's position during our informal conversations to diverge widely from that held by his or her justice.

26. Artemus Ward, "William H. Rehnquist and His Clerks," in Peppers and Ward, *In Chambers,* 375.

27. In accordance with the donor agreement, the Chief's papers will be opened to researchers in 2026.

28. Alex Kozinski, "A Tribute to Chief Justice Warren E. Burger," 100 *Harvard Law Review* (1987): 975.

29. The Chief was known to comment that he and "Scoop" Jackson agreed on so many issues that he was uncertain why the senator called himself a Democrat.

NANCY S. MARDER

Justice Stevens and His Clerks

To the public, Justice John Paul Stevens's identifying feature is his bow tie. To his law clerks, however, the identifying feature and fondest association is his well-worn leather armchair in the law clerks' office, where he sat each morning with a cup of coffee and talked with us. The conversations were far-ranging, from the headlines in the newspaper to how his sports teams were faring to the cases before the Court and how our work was progressing. It was a daily ritual—except when he had an early morning tennis game—and it was a ritual that we truly appreciated.

I had the privilege of serving as Justice Stevens's law clerk from 1990 to 1992, which was almost midway in his thirty-four-year career as a U.S. Supreme Court justice, spanning from 1975 to 2010. I am confident that the law clerks who preceded me and the law clerks who followed me valued these early morning conversations as much as I did.

These conversations, which typically took place around 7:45 a.m., were the perfect way to start the day, even for those of us who were night owls. They provided a peaceful interlude before the start of the workday, and they allowed for a perfect blend of the professional and personal. We were able to talk to Justice Stevens about the cases—an argument that was in need of support or a line of reasoning that was not proving persuasive—but he also took an interest in our personal lives—how our spouses were doing and what they were doing—while we were engaged in this year (or two in my case) of intense work.

The Nature of the Work

Justice Stevens had a very well run chambers. He did his work quickly, deftly, and with great attention to detail. We, his law clerks, tried not to slow Justice Stevens down too much, but we were definitely the weak link in the chain. He always looked so pleased when we had finished reading the briefs and were ready to discuss a case with him or had completed work on a draft opinion he had given us to review and were ready to give him our suggested changes. Some of the ways Justice Stevens organized the work in his chambers probably stemmed from his own Supreme Court clerkship with Justice Wiley Rutledge in 1947–48,[1] but they suited Justice Stevens well.

CERT PETITIONS

Although the public is most familiar with the Court's judicial opinions, an important part of the Court's work involves the behind-the-scenes decisions about which cases to review. Most of the Court's docket, with a few exceptions, consists of cases that the Court, in its discretion, has decided to review. The Court makes this decision by reviewing petitions for writs of certiorari, or "cert petitions" as they are familiarly called. These petitions are written by parties who have lost in the court below and who would like the Court to review their case.

The justices meet at a conference, to which nobody else is privy, including the law clerks, to decide which cert petitions to grant. In preparation for this meeting, the cert petitions have to be reviewed. Different justices handle the cert petitions in different ways. For example, Justice William J. Brennan Jr. used to review all of the cert petitions on his own. However, when I clerked, and even today, most of the justices belonged to the cert pool, which means just one law clerk will review the petition and write an extensive memo about it that will be shared with all of the chambers that belong to the cert pool. As a result, rather than each chambers doing its own review of the cert petition, the justices who belong to the cert pool depend on the one memo prepared by the one cert pool writer, though the clerks in some chambers, like those of Justice Harry Blackmun, added their own notes and commentary to the cert pool writer's memo.

The practice of the cert pool originated with Justice Lewis F. Powell, who thought it would be a more efficient means for handling the ever-growing number of cert petitions.[2] When Justice Powell proposed a cert pool, which was before Justice Stevens joined the Court, Chief Justice Warren Burger and Justices Byron R. White, Harry Blackmun, and William H. Rehnquist agreed with the suggestion, and became part of the cert pool.[3]

Justice Stevens never belonged to the cert pool. Perhaps this was one of the practices he took from his own clerkship with Justice Wiley Rutledge, who also depended on his own law clerks to review all of the cert petitions.[4] Justice Stevens thought that it was important for some chambers not to belong to the cert pool so that each petition was reviewed by more than just the cert pool writer. In his memoir, *Five Chiefs*, Justice Stevens recalled that Justice Potter Stewart thought that no more than five justices should ever belong to the cert pool.[5] Justice Stevens joined Justices Brennan and Stewart in "abstaining" from the cert pool when he joined the Court.[6] He attributed his decision to abstain from the cert pool in part to his work as general counsel to a special commission that had investigated whether there had been improprieties at the Illinois Supreme Court.[7] From that experience, he was wary of relying on a single memo prepared for a "pool" of justices.[8]

Consistent with his view that some justices should work independently of the cert pool, Justice Stevens had his law clerks (of which there were only two in the early years, typically three when I clerked, and four in later years) review all of the cert petitions. The huge stacks of cert petitions, consisting of paid petitions and in forma pauperis petitions, arrived every week and were divided evenly among Justice Stevens's law clerks. However, we did not need to write lengthy memos for each cert petition, like the cert pool writer. Rather, we reviewed each cert petition and wrote short memos of a page or two in length for those cert petitions where we recommended that some action should be taken or where we thought that the cert petition was likely to be discussed at the justices' conference. We could also ask Justice Stevens to look over cert petitions about which we were uncertain.

As Justice Stevens explained in his memoir, he did not need a detailed memo, like the one provided by the cert pool writer, because "in most cases [he] could make an accurate judgment about whether to grant or deny the petition more easily by glancing at the original papers than by reading an unnecessarily detailed description of the arguments favoring and opposing review."[9] When we began our clerkship over the summer, we spent a lot of time reviewing cert petitions. By the time the term began on the first Monday in October, we thought that we could handle the cert petitions along with the other work we had to do.

ORAL ARGUMENT

In preparing for oral argument, as with reviewing cert petitions, Justice Stevens made sure that his law clerks did only work that was truly needed. Unlike law clerks in other chambers, we did not prepare bench memos, nor did we suggest questions for oral arguments. Rather, we read the briefs on the cases that we assisted with, and we discussed them with Justice Stevens prior to and after oral argument. Typically, Justice Stevens's law clerks would meet with the justice as a group to discuss the cases. The clerk who had read the briefs for that case would take the lead in discussing the case with Justice Stevens, but the other law clerks always felt free to add their views.

After oral argument, we would also talk with Justice Stevens about the case and would discuss whether we had heard anything during oral argument that had surprised us or that led us to view the case in a different light. Although many advocates think that the justices make up their minds before oral argument, this is not the case with Justice Stevens. As he explained in one speech: "[L]awyers are capable of persuading judges to change their minds. I cannot tell you how often a case seemed perfectly clear when I finished reading the [petitioner's] blue brief, equally clear the other way after reading the [respondent's] red brief, and back again to the petitioner's side after the yellow brief and the advocates' oral arguments were digested."[10] Although both justice and law clerk would discuss the case after reading the briefs, those early views were still tentative, and could change after oral argument or even after reading a particularly persuasive draft of an opinion.

The questions that Justice Stevens asked during oral argument were always of his own devising, and of course the manner in which he asked them was in his own distinctive style. He would typically wait until the other justices had asked most of their questions, and then he would politely ask the advocate: "Counselor, may I ask you a question?" Although the question was always posed in the most polite manner possible, it was inevitably the toughest question of the oral argument and always went to the crux of the issue.

Today's Supreme Court justices seem to ask far more questions than the justices did back in the 1990 and 1991 terms. Although this is just impressionistic, and is not based on an empirical analysis, it seems to me that today's bench barely gives the advocate a chance to respond before another question has been interjected. Other Court-watchers have noted this trend.[11] For example, Stephen Wermiel, who covered the Supreme Court for the *Wall Street Journal* in the 1980s, observed: "A lawyer arguing a case may be only a few words into answering a multipart question from one justice before another justice interrupts to take the argument in a different direction entirely. . . . Some arguments now more closely resemble a Ping-Pong match than a dialogue or conversation."[12] When I clerked, there were some justices who rarely spoke, such as Justice Marshall in the 1990 term, Justice Clarence Thomas who replaced Justice Marshall in the 1991 term, and others, such as Justice Blackmun, who spoke only occasionally. The main constraint on an advocate's time came from Chief Justice Rehnquist, who was a strict taskmaster when it came to keeping time. He was known for cutting off an advocate mid-sentence when the red light came on, indicating the end of the advocate's allotted half-hour.[13]

The law clerks had their own special section in the courtroom from which to listen to oral argument. We sat near the pillars on the right side of the courtroom if one were facing the justices. We were unobtrusive, so it was easy for us to come and go, though most of us liked to hear as much of the oral argument as possible. Unlike members of the public, we were allowed to take notes during oral argument. On days when a particularly controversial case was being argued or a particularly well known advocate was appearing, all of the law clerks from all of the chambers would attend. For some of the lesser known cases or advocates, however, mainly those clerks who had been assigned to the case attended the oral argument. Although the dress code for law clerks was fairly casual in Justice Stevens's chambers, on days when we attended oral argument, we wore business attire as a sign of respect.

OPINIONS

Justice Stevens was the only justice when I was clerking who wrote his own first drafts of opinions. He continued to write his own first drafts until the day he retired. Justice Stevens explained that he wrote his own first drafts because he believed that the writing process helped him to understand the case. If an opinion was proving difficult to write, it might signal that he should reexamine his view of the case.[14] Thus, the writing process was integral to the thinking process. In writing his own first drafts of opinions, Justice Stevens also continued a practice he had seen firsthand when he had clerked for Justice Rutledge, who also wrote his own first drafts of opinions.[15]

Once Justice Stevens had completed a draft of his opinion, he would give it to the law clerk who was working on that case. (The law clerks would have divided up the cases according to their interests; the law clerk who chose first one time would choose last the next time.) It was the law clerk's job to make editing suggestions, check citations, and add footnotes to strengthen an argument. It was a collaborative process in that the draft would go back and forth between justice and law clerk until both were satisfied with the opinion. Justice Stevens was generous in his praise and made the law clerk feel that he or she had helped to improve the opinion, but it was always Justice Stevens's opinion.

By writing his own first draft, Justice Stevens ensured that the opinion reflected his understanding of the case, his organizational structure, and, of course, his inimitable turns of phrase. After all, his law clerks would be hardpressed to come up with phrases like the Court putting on its "thick grammarian's spectacles"[16] or an allusion to "propaganda broadcasts to our troops by Tokyo Rose."[17] These were phrases that reflected Justice Stevens's life and times. Also by writing his own first drafts, he ensured that opinions were completed in a timely fashion and that he was always available for additional writing assignments. Because he wrote his own first drafts, he did not take the full allotment of law clerks. He did not think there would be enough work for them to do.[18] Although we, his law clerks, probably differed on this point, we appreciated the close-knit nature of a small chambers.

Once the opinion was circulated to the other justices, they would decide whether they could join the opinion, would join it only after changes had been made, or would write separately. Justice Stevens and the law clerk would continue to work together to see if the requested changes could be made, and if they could be, then they would be. After all, even if a justice had been assigned to write the majority opinion, it would be the majority opinion only if at least five justices signed on to it.

If another justice chose to dissent, then there would be a back-and-forth of drafts as majority and dissent responded to each other's arguments. Much of this back-and-forth took place in the footnotes; all of this back-and-forth took place in writing. Justice Stevens and the law clerk would continue to work together to respond to the dissent's arguments; thus, the collaboration of justice and law clerk continued even at the level of the footnotes.

In addition to writing the majority opinions assigned to him, Justice Stevens often wrote separate opinions in other cases to explain his views. He did so out of a strong sense that judges and justices should give reasons for their decisions. At the very least, they had an obligation to the parties and the public to explain their vote. Justice Stevens had seen what happened in his home state of Illinois when state court judges failed to give reasons and acquiesced to decisions even though they disagreed with them.

When Justice Stevens was in private practice in Illinois, he had been asked to serve as general counsel to a special commission charged with looking into alleged wrongdoing at the Illinois Supreme Court. As a result of the special commission's investigation and findings, two Illinois Supreme Court justices resigned.[19] One lesson that Justice Stevens drew from this experience was the importance of judges and justices giving reasons for their decisions.[20] He adhered to this practice both as a judge on the Seventh Circuit[21] and as a justice at the U.S. Supreme Court.[22]

EMERGENCY STAYS

Another type of work that law clerks assisted their justices with were the emergency matters that came before the Court from time to time. Sometimes a party sought an emergency stay from the Supreme Court so that a lower court order would not go into effect until the party could seek review from the Supreme Court (in other words, the party wanted to preserve the status quo until the Court could decide whether to grant the cert petition and to hear the case). The party would apply to the Supreme Court justice who had responsibility for matters that arose from that circuit. For example, Justice Stevens had responsibility for matters that arose from the Seventh Circuit, where he had once served as a federal appellate court judge. The matter, though it went first to the justice with responsibility for that circuit, usually ended up being turned over to all of the justices. However, the justice from that circuit could take the lead and circulate a memo to the other justices recommending a course of action.

When such matters arose, Justice Stevens and one of his law clerks would read the accompanying papers, discuss the case, and consider the repercussions of possible responses. Oftentimes, these matters arose from interesting disputes having to do with labor law, election law, or even sports events. However, the defining feature of these disputes was that a decision had to be made right away. This meant that whatever Justice Stevens and the law clerk were working on, they had to put it aside so that the emergency matter could be addressed.

Another area of law that required immediate attention was a death penalty case on the day or night that an execution was scheduled. During the time that I was clerking, a number of states were executing prisoners who had been sentenced to death. After death-row prisoners had exhausted their appeals, and sometimes even before, the state would schedule their execution. Sometimes the state court or lower federal court would grant them a stay of execution, particularly if they had not yet exhausted all of their appeals. However, if the state and lower federal courts had denied a stay, then the prisoner would typically seek a stay of execution from the Supreme Court. These applications for stays to the Supreme Court might be made at the last minute, when it became clear that no other court was going to grant a stay. Sometimes these stay applications reached the Supreme Court during the day, and other times they reached the Supreme Court in the middle of the night.

Justice Stevens believed that the prisoners were always entitled to exhaust their state and federal appeals. He would vote to grant a stay application if they had not yet exhausted all of their appeals. Once they had exhausted their appeals, then the issue was whether the prisoner had raised a cert-worthy issue (an issue on which the Supreme Court would grant a cert petition). Whether the stay application arrived during the day or whether it arrived in the middle of the night, each justice had to vote in writing on whether to grant or deny it. This meant that in each chambers, a law clerk had to inform the justice that a stay application had been filed and had to find out how the justice wanted to vote.

Sometimes these conversations took place at 3:00 a.m. This was the hardest part of the job for me and for many other law clerks. It brought to mind the words of one of my law professors, Robert Cover, who had written about the difficulties of judging and who had recognized that "judges deal pain and death."[23]

At the time that I clerked for Justice Stevens, he adhered to the Court's view that the death penalty was constitutional. He had been one of the authors, along with Justices Stewart and Powell, of a jointly written Court opinion early in his tenure on the Court in which the Court upheld the constitutionality of the death penalty.[24] Toward the end of his tenure on the Court, however, he concluded that the death penalty no longer served the purposes of incapacitation or deterrence, leaving it serving only the function of retribution. In *Baze v.*

Rees,[25] he explained why he had come to the conclusion that the death penalty violated the Eighth Amendment. Justice Stevens was not the only justice to have reached this conclusion.[26]

Life Lessons Learned

Although the clerkship enabled us to learn about cutting-edge constitutional and statutory issues, the clerkship was far more than just the work. The highlight was learning from Justice Stevens. There were many life lessons that we, his law clerks, took away from the clerkship and that remain with us no matter how many years ago we clerked for him. Although not all law clerks took away precisely the same lessons, I have no doubt that if all 114 of Justice Stevens's Supreme Court law clerks were polled,[27] there would be many lessons in common.

One lesson from my clerkship years was the importance of optimism, and a corollary was the need to take a long-term perspective. During October terms 1990 and 1991, Justice Stevens was often in dissent. He would return from a conference in which the justices had discussed the cases and voted on them, and he would report that the initial vote in a case (or cases) was 8–1, and that he was the one.

Nevertheless, Justice Stevens remained upbeat, even though we, his law clerks, often felt despair. He was not deterred. He was willing to write dissents even if no one else joined him. Plus, there was always the possibility that he might sway another justice to his view. Even if he did not, he was content to write for the future. A dissent spoke not only to the present but also to the future. It provided future litigants with arguments to use when the issue arose again. Then, when the Court revisited the issue, it might reach a different result and embrace the reasons given in the earlier dissents, as it did in several dissents written by Justice Stevens.[28] A dissent also signaled to future litigants that the issue was not so clear-cut that all of the justices saw it in the same way. A dissent provided hope for the future.

It was not until years later, when Justice Stevens published his memoir, *Five Chiefs,* that I realized the toll that dissenting takes on the dissenter—even on one as optimistic as Justice Stevens. One sentence, in particular, sheds light on how the dissenting judge feels: "[a] dissenting judge is never happy, because it is obvious that either the majority has come to the wrong conclusion or his own reasoning is flawed."[29] Of course, it is hard to know whether Justice Stevens always felt that way about dissenting or whether he grew to feel that way over time. After all, he had another eighteen years of dissenting ahead of him, and perhaps the additional years took a toll. Or perhaps I am reading too much into that one sentence.

Along with his optimism, Justice Stevens imparted to his law clerks the need to treat people with respect and to think the best of them. This attitude extended to the lawyers who appeared before the Court, and whom Justice Stevens always questioned thoroughly, but respectfully, during oral argument. He taught us that courteousness and civility had an important role to play even when lawyers were engaged in the rigorous give-and-take that often characterized oral argument at the Supreme Court.

Another example that is passed down from law clerk to law clerk is when a lawyer once referred to the "justices" as "judges" during oral argument. Chief Justice Rehnquist corrected the "mistake." He believed that it was important for lawyers to address the justices as "justices" and not as "judges."[30] However, when another lawyer made the same mistake several days later at another oral argument, and the chief justice issued the same correction, Justice Stevens came to the lawyer's aid: "Excuse me, but if I am not mistaken, Article III refers to us as judges."[31]

Justice Stevens also treated lower court judges with respect. In his opinions, he acknowledged the fine work they were doing, particularly when they were being criticized by other justices. If lower court judges did not seem to be following the Court's strictures, he assumed it was because the Court had been unclear in the tests it had developed or inconsistent in how they were to be applied and not because the lower court judges were unable or unwilling to perform their role properly.[32] He praised their reasoning and often relied on it in his own opinions.

Of course, we, Justice Stevens's law clerks, benefitted from his willingness to see the best in people. Justice Stevens was always appreciative of the work we did. The justice thought we added to his opinions, and he thanked us for having done so. He had an open door policy, and we were free to interrupt him throughout the day. He was willing to consider new arguments and new ways of looking at a case. Sometimes our arguments persuaded him and sometimes they did not, but he was always willing to listen. I learned from Justice Stevens that the way to inspire people to work their hardest and to produce their best work was to make sure that they felt appreciated. It is a practice that too few bosses follow and a lesson that I took to heart.

Another lesson that Justice Stevens has passed on to his law clerks is his deep and abiding respect for the institution of the Supreme Court. During our clerkship, he shared with us many of its traditions. Some of these traditions are designed to foster collegiality. For example, before the justices go on to the bench to hear oral argument, they shake hands with each other. No matter how much they might disagree with each other during oral argument, the handshake is a reminder that they are part of a collegial body. The disagreements about cases do not interfere with their personal relationships.

On days when only a few justices have lunch together in one of the smaller dining rooms adjacent to the justices' dining room, they do not discuss the cases.[33] Again, this is a way of preserving their collegiality. Chief Justice Burger started the tradition of the justices celebrating each other's birthdays with a glass of wine, a toast, and a rendition of "Happy Birthday."[34] As Justice Stevens remarked in his memoir, the custom played "an important role in maintaining the cordial relations among the nine individuals" who could end up in strong disagreement when it came time to decide cases.[35]

The justices, however, do not shy away from disagreement. In fact, one of the other traditions of the Court is that at least once each term a justice should deliver an oral dissent from the bench. This is usually reserved for a case about which a justice feels strongly. During my first year of clerking, *Payne v. Tennessee* was such a case.[36] In *Payne,* the Court held, in a 6–3 decision, that the prosecution could use "victim impact" statements to support its request for the death penalty. Justice Stevens felt strongly that the use of victim impact statements in this manner violated the Eighth Amendment's command that the death penalty not be imposed arbitrarily or capriciously; thus, he wrote a dissent (joined by Justice Blackmun).

He also read an oral dissent from the bench on June 27, 1991,[37] which was the last day of the 1990 term and the day on which Justice Marshall announced his retirement from the Supreme Court.[38] Justice Stevens later explained the Court's tradition of oral dissents, as it had been explained to him: "[Justice] Potter Stewart told me that [Justice] John Harlan had more than once expressed the view that in every term, at least one dissenter should announce his opinion from the bench. He thought that such announcements revealed qualities of some of our disagreements that could not be adequately expressed in writing."[39] Although the justices' disagreements could run deep, the Court traditions allowed them to disagree with each other "without being disagreeable."[40]

One other lesson that we could not help but learn from Justice Stevens was the importance of enjoying one's work. Justice Stevens clearly loved his job. It brought him great satisfaction. As soon as he was assigned an opinion to write, he would go and write it. There was no procrastination. He relished the task. He loved thinking about the law. When we talked about a case late in the day, he might come in the next day with additional thoughts about the case. He had been mulling it over all evening. The law was an all-consuming endeavor. The law was also a great teacher. As Justice Stevens described it, "learning on the job is essential to the process of judging."[41]

In January 2009, I traveled to D.C. for the inauguration of President Barack Obama, at which Justice Stevens administered the oath of office to Vice President Joseph Biden. The next day I stopped by the Supreme Court to visit with

Justice Stevens. He mentioned how much he loved his job and wanted to continue doing it. I told him that I hoped he would keep doing it for a long time.

On April 9, 2010, however, Justice Stevens sent a letter to President Obama, in which he wrote that he would be retiring from active service,[42] and, by stepping down at the end of October term 2009, he hoped to give the president time to name his successor before the start of the next term. Justice Stevens was about to turn ninety[43] and had served as a justice for over thirty-four years.[44] Many of us believed that Justice Stevens had retired too soon. After all, even in his last term he was issuing major opinions. For example, his written dissent in *Citizens United*,[45] which was over ninety pages long and joined by Justices Ruth Bader Ginsburg, Stephen Breyer, and Sonia Sotomayor, was a tour de force of powerful reasoning as to why Congress's campaign financing statute regulating corporations' electoral expenditures should have been upheld.

To most onlookers, though, Justice Stevens does not seem to have retired at all; rather, "he is forging a new model of what to expect from Supreme Court justices after they leave the bench."[46] Thus far, Justice Stevens has had a very busy "retirement." He has received numerous awards, including the Presidential Medal of Freedom, the highest award that can be bestowed upon a civilian.[47] He has appeared on popular television programs, such as *60 Minutes*[48] and the *Colbert Report;*[49] appeared in documentaries, such as Ken Burns's two-part series on Prohibition;[50] and has been interviewed by Brian Lamb as part of a series on Supreme Court justices[51] as well as by Ken Manaster for a documentary about the special commission he served on in Illinois. He has given public speeches[52] and academic lectures[53] and has published academic articles,[54] book reviews in the *New York Review of Books*,[55] and a memoir, *Five Chiefs*, which recently appeared in paperback.[56]

In some ways, Justice Stevens's retirement appears to have been liberating. It has allowed him to do things that he otherwise would not have done, such as make television and movie appearances and give interviews. Yet, in other ways, he continues to pursue the same interests he did as a justice. He continues to speak and write about cases. Of course, he still has chambers at the Supreme Court—the one he occupied when he first became a justice. And, of course, the large, leather armchair is still there—the one that is so beloved by his law clerks.

Notes

1. Bill Barnhart and Gene Schlickman, *John Paul Stevens: An Independent Life* (DeKalb: Northern Illinois University Press, 2010), 65.

2. John Paul Stevens, *Five Chiefs: A Supreme Court Memoir* (New York: Little, Brown, 2011), 139.

3. Ibid.

4. John M. Ferren, "Wiley Blount Rutledge Jr. and His Law Clerks," in *In Chambers: Stories of Supreme Court Law Clerks and Their Justices*, edited by Todd C. Peppers and Artemus Ward (Charlottesville: University of Virginia Press, 2012), 233.

5. Stevens, *Five Chiefs*, 139.

6. Ibid., 140

7. Justice John Paul Stevens, "Foreword," in Kenneth A. Manaster, *Illinois Justice: The Scandal of 1969 and the Rise of John Paul Stevens* (Chicago: University of Chicago Press, 2001), ix, xi.

8. Ibid.

9. Stevens, *Five Chiefs*, 139.

10. *Almanac of the Federal Judiciary* (2009) 2:25 (quoting Justice Stevens in his speech to the American Bar Association, August 1996).

11. Adam Liptak, "Nice Argument, Counselor, but I'd Rather Hear Mine," *New York Times*, April 10, 2010, A1.

12. Ibid.

13. Justice Stevens had observed this about Chief Justice William Rehnquist in his memoir. See Stevens, *Five Chiefs*, 172.

14. Adam Liptak, "From Age of Independence to Age of Ideology," *New York Times*, April 10, 2010, A1.

15. Ferren, "Wiley Blount Rutledge Jr.," 233; Stevens, *Five Chiefs*, 188.

16. *West Virginia University Hospitals, Inc. v. Casey*, 499 U.S. 83, 113 (1991) (Stevens, J., dissenting).

17. *Citizens United v. Federal Election Commission*, 558 U.S. 310, 424 (2010) (Stevens, J., dissenting).

18. It was finally the law clerks who assisted Justice Stevens during the 2000 term, when *Bush v. Gore*, 531 U.S. 98 (2000) occupied center-stage, who persuaded him that there really was enough work for four law clerks and that he should hire four clerks going forward, as the other justices, with the exception of the chief justice, had long done. This case, with its importance to the country and its need for immediate resolution, persuaded the law clerks, and ultimately Justice Stevens, that it would be useful to have four law clerks in the future.

19. For a detailed account of the investigation, see Manaster, *Illinois Justice*.

20. Stevens, "Foreword," xii.

21. In 1970, President Richard M. Nixon appointed John Paul Stevens to the U.S. Court of Appeals for the Seventh Circuit, where he served for five years. *The Supreme Court of the United States: Its Beginnings & Its Justices 1790–1991* (Washington, D.C.: Commission on the Bicentennial of the United States Constitution, 1992), 228.

22. President Gerald R. Ford nominated then judge Stevens to the U.S. Supreme Court on December 1, 1975, and the Senate confirmed his appointment on December 17, 1975. Ibid.

23. Robert M. Cover, "Violence and the Word," *Yale Law Journal* 95 (1986): 1601, 1609.

24. *Gregg v. Georgia*, 428 U.S. 153, 169, 187 (1976).

25. *Baze v. Rees*, 553 U.S. 35, 71 (2008) (Stevens, J., concurring in the judgment).

26. Justices Brennan, Marshall, and Blackmun had reached similar views. *Furman v. Georgia*, 408 U.S. 238, 257 (1972) (Brennan, J., concurring); id. at 314 (Marshall, J., concurring); *Callins v. Collins*, 510 U.S. 1141 (Blackmun, J., dissenting from denial of certiorari).

27. I have included in this number all of the law clerks who assisted Justice Stevens at the U.S. Supreme Court. These included those he hired as a justice and retired justice, as well as those hired by retired justices White and Powell, who also assisted Justice Stevens (consistent with the Court practice that a retired justice's law clerk also can assist one of the nine justices). See Justice Stevens's Law Clerks Supreme Court of the United States, dated May 2012 (list on file with author).

28. For example, Justice Stevens dissented in *Bowers v. Hardwick*, 478 U.S. 186 (1986), but his dissenting view became the majority's view in *Lawrence v. Texas*, 539 U.S. 558 (2003).

29. Stevens, *Five Chiefs*, 235.

30. Ibid., 173.

31. Diane Marie Amann, "John Paul Stevens, Human Rights Judge," *Fordham Law Review* 74 (2006): 1569.

32. Stevens, *Five Chiefs*, 152.

33. Ibid.

34. Ibid.

35. Ibid.

36. *Payne v. Tennessee*, 501 U.S. 808, 856 (1991) (Stevens, J., dissenting).

37. *Payne v. Tennessee*, No. 90–5721, opinion announced June 27, 1991, The Oyez Project at IIT Chicago-Kent College of Law, http://www.oyez.org/cases/10990–1999/1990/1990_90_5721.

38. See, for example, Andrew Rosenthal, "Marshall Retires from High Court; Blow to Liberals," *New York Times*, June 28, 1991, A1; "Justice Marshall Resigns," *Washington Post*, June 28, 1991, A22.

39. Stevens, *Five Chiefs*, 158.

40. Ibid., 244.

41. John Paul Stevens, "Learning on the Job," *Fordham Law Review* 74 (2006): 1561, 1567.

42. James Oliphant, "Court's Lead Liberal Resigns; Stevens Leaving Supreme Court after 34 Years," *Chicago Tribune*, April 10, 2010, 7.

43. Justice Stevens was born on April 20, 1920. *Supreme Court of the United States*, 228.

44. He was appointed by President Gerald Ford on December 1, 1975. Thirty years later, former president Ford wrote a letter in which he said that the decision he was most proud of during his presidency was his decision to appoint Judge Stevens to the U.S. Supreme Court: "For I am prepared to allow history's judgment of my term in office to rest (if necessary, exclusively) on my nomination thirty years ago of Justice John Paul Stevens to the U.S. Supreme Court." William Michael Treanor, "Introduction: The Jurisprudence of Justice Stevens," *Fordham Law Review* 74 (2005): 1557, 1559.

45. *Citizens United v. Federal Election Commission,* 558 U.S. 310, 393 (2010) (Stevens, J., dissenting).

46. Adam Liptak, "Stevens Settles Legal Mystery in Frank Essay," *New York Times,* November 28, 2010, A1.

47. "An Honor from the President," *New York Times,* May 30, 2012, A15.

48. *60 Minutes* (aired on CBS on November 20, 2010).

49. *The Colbert Report* (aired on Comedy Central on January 19, 2012).

50. Ken Burns and Lynn Novick, "Prohibition" (aired on PBS on October 2, 3, and 4, 2011).

51. "Supreme Court Week" (interviews with the justices aired on C-SPAN on October 9, 10, and 11, 2009).

52. For example, Justice Stevens gave a public lecture on April 18, 2013, when he received the 2013 Brandeis Medal, awarded by the Louis D. Brandeis School of Law, at the University of Louisville, in Kentucky. "Retired Justice to Speak, Get Medal," *Louisville Courier-Journal,* March 14, 2013, B3.

53. Justice Stevens gave the Albritton Lecture, "*Kelo,* Popularity, and Substantive Due Process," at the University of Alabama on November 16, 2011, and gave a lecture, "The Ninth Vote in the 'Stop the Beach' Case," at IIT Chicago-Kent College of Law on October 3, 2012.

54. See, for example, Justice John Paul Stevens (Ret.), "The Ninth Vote in the 'Stop the Beach' Case," *Chicago-Kent Law Review* 88 (2013): 553.

55. John Paul Stevens, "Should We Have a New Constitutional Convention?," *New York Review of Books,* October 11, 2012 (book review); John Paul Stevens, "Should Hate Speech Be Outlawed?," *New York Review of Books,* June 7, 2012 (book review); John Paul Stevens, "A Struggle with the Police & the Law," *New York Review of Books,* April 5, 2012 (book review); John Paul Stevens, "Our 'Broken System' of Criminal Justice," *New York Review of Books,* November 10, 2011 (book review); John Paul Stevens, "On the Death Sentence," *New York Review of Books,* December 23, 2010 (book review).

56. Stevens, *Five Chiefs.*

CRAIG M. BRADLEY

Clerking for Mr. Right

Late in 1974, when I was an assistant U.S. attorney in Washington, D.C., I brashly sent a letter to all the Supreme Court justices suggesting that since criminal procedure cases were a major part of their docket, and since neither they nor their clerks had any experience in the field, they should hire me as a law clerk. I expected to get the brush-off from them since I wasn't applying in the normal course of events as a recent law school graduate who was currently working for a U.S. Court of Appeals judge.

I did indeed get the expected brush-off from all but one of the justices. That one was William H. Rehnquist, who had only been on the Court since January 1972. As it happened, I had met Justice Rehnquist very briefly when I was a newly minted attorney in the Justice Department four years earlier. He was the assistant attorney general for the Office of Legal Counsel and was in charge of the "College Visitation Program" (a program where a group of Justice Department volunteers went out to college campuses to promote good relations between the government and college students, which were at a low ebb at the time because of the war in Vietnam). I was one of thirty or so volunteers who met with Justice Rehnquist and Attorney General John Mitchell. I wasn't very impressed with Justice Rehnquist, who wore hush puppies and long sideburns and seemed to go out of his way to suck up to Mitchell, even holding his chair for him at the meeting. I did later go out to several colleges, but didn't encounter Justice Rehnquist again. Nevertheless, I mentioned my participation in this program in my letter to him.

When Justice Rehnquist invited me for an interview, I mentioned the interview to Mike Buxton, whom I knew at the U.S. Attorney's Office and who had clerked for Justice Rehnquist. He assured me that the justice was a great guy to work for and offered to put in a good word on my behalf. I gratefully accepted. Justice Rehnquist and I hit it off at the interview. I think the most telling part was when I pointed out to him that, unlike other applicants who were applying because it was the natural course to follow if you had done well in law school and gotten a court of appeals clerkship, I was applying because I really wanted the job and was willing to take a pay cut to do it. He told me that

Justice Byron R. White also had a clerk, John Nields, who had been an assistant U.S. attorney and that seemed to be working out well. Whatever his reasons, he offered me the job. The salary was $18,500.

I was to start the following July. On the appointed day I showed up at the Court. It was really a thrill to walk into that Marble Palace, though I had been there a number of times before to see oral arguments. Justice Rehnquist's chambers, in common with most of the others, consisted of a huge reception room with a thirty-foot-high ceiling and contained two lonely-looking secretaries and a small desk off to the side for the "messenger." To the left was Justice Rehnquist's office—a generous space, but not huge, with room for some furniture, a conference table, and a private full bathroom. It was decorated with paintings borrowed from the National Gallery of Art. To the right was the clerk's office—an office of maybe fifteen by fifteen feet into which the three clerks were crowded, plus a staff bathroom. It had been designed in the 1930s when each justice had one clerk.

I was struck by how modest the "perks" of a Supreme Court justice were. The six of us were his entire staff. Justice Rehnquist commuted to work on his own, though the chief justice had his own limousine. Meals were not provided, nor were any other special privileges a part of the job. Justice Rehnquist's social life did not include going to parties with Washington bigwigs, though I believe it could have if he'd been interested. He did have a regular poker game with some well-known people, including future justice Antonin Scalia, but I don't know if it was going on when I clerked.

The justices also didn't socialize much with each other—Justice Rehnquist pointed to the large age gap among them as one of the reasons why. He was fifty at the beginning of my clerkship. After he became chief justice, Justice Rehnquist did organize social events for the Court, like chamber music performances, but that was not happening in October term 1975. As far as I could tell, his social life centered around the Lutheran church and other families with children the age of his three.

A word about the "messenger": in the days before the late 1930s, when the justices' offices were at their homes rather than in a Supreme Court building, it was necessary for each justice to have a messenger to take drafts of opinions, as well as other communications, around to the other justices. The messenger still performed this function in 1975, but with everybody being in the same building it was hardly a full-time job. He also performed as a general aide to the justice: picking up his dry cleaning, taking his car to be repaired, and so forth. What else he did, I'm not sure, but he didn't spend much time sitting at his desk in the reception area, or interacting with the law clerks. Justice Rehnquist's messenger was a pleasant man named Harry Fenwick, who told me at a future reunion that he had become head of food services at the Court.

When I arrived in July, Justice Rehnquist, in common with the other justices, was not there. He spent his summers in Vermont and communicated with us by mail. I don't recall any phone conversations from Vermont, but there may have been. I arrived the same day as one of my co-clerks, Jack Mason. The third clerk, Bill Jacobs, was a leftover from the previous term who would stay on one more week to orient us. He explained what we were supposed to do and instructed us to call Justice Rehnquist "Boss," which is how all the clerks subsequently referred to him until he became chief justice, when they started calling him "Chief." His original clerks had worked for him at the Justice Department, and they called him "Bill," so one could get an idea of when someone had clerked by how they referred to the justice.

For the first two months the job consisted of screening incoming petitions for certiorari—that is, petitions asking that a case be heard by the Court. Justice Rehnquist, along with the three other Nixon appointees (Burger, Powell, and Blackmun) plus White belonged to the cert pool. This meant that instead of Justice Rehnquist's clerks reading every petition that came in, the incoming petitions would be divided among clerks in the chambers of these five justices. Thus, instead of reading a third of the petitions, I was expected to read about one-seventh of them, since some of the other justices in the pool had four clerks. I would then write a memo about my petitions to be shared among the five participating chambers.

A substantial percentage of the cases were called pro se, which meant that they were written by prisoners acting on their own, not by a lawyer. These petitions generally had no merit and could be dispensed with in a memo of a few lines. Other cases were much more substantial, required careful reading of the briefs and opinions below, as well as other cases. The memo was longer, though we tried to keep them as short as possible. I would then make a brief handwritten annotation at the top of a third of the memos from the other chambers, as well as my own, as to whether I thought the case would be of interest to Justice Rehnquist, grading them A to D. Of particular interest was whether there was a conflict among the lower federal courts on the issue presented. Each week we would bundle up the memos that had been done that week and mail them off to Justice Rehnquist.

Once the third clerk, Bill Eggeling, arrived, we fell into a comfortable routine doing what felt like a full-time job. There were about a hundred petitions a week, so I was writing about six cert memos and commenting on about thirty-three for Justice Rehnquist. I noted in the diary that I kept for the first couple of months that I had rejected the conclusion of the memo writer in a couple of cases and that Justice Rehnquist had agreed with me, so we were scrutinizing the other memos carefully.

One day an old man came into the chambers, asking for Justice Rehnquist.

This was odd because security wouldn't allow people to just wander into the chambers. If they wanted to see a justice, they would have to go to the clerk's office and be escorted to the chambers, assuming the justice wanted to see them. It turned out the man was retired justice Stanley F. Reed, who had an office just down the hall. He had retired from the Court in 1957 at the relatively young age of seventy-two. Justice Reed explained that he was trying to set a longevity record for retired justices, a modest goal. We told him that Justice Rehnquist was in Vermont. Retired justice Tom Clark was also in the building at that time. He was active hearing cases argued in the court of appeals. In fact, I had argued before him in the D.C. Circuit and was impressed by his acuity.

We played basketball every day about 4:30 p.m. Since the three Justice Rehnquist clerks were the three best players, we had to divide up. Later, after the justices came back, Justice White joined us occasionally. He played basketball like the football player he was. He usually guarded me, and even though I had three inches on him, I could not get off a shot without being pushed or grabbed. I didn't feel I could call fouls on him, so I suffered in silence. Sometime after Justice Rehnquist came back he told us we could not all be gone from the chambers at once, so one of us had to forego playing every day.

So it went until early September, when Justice Rehnquist arrived back in Washington. The term of the Supreme Court started the first Monday in October, but, before that, the Court had to decide whether to grant the petitions that had come in over the summer. In the fall they would hear and decide cases where certiorari had been granted the previous term. The cases granted from the summer petitions would be heard the following year beginning in January. So everything changed in September. There was still a constant flow of incoming petitions that had to be reviewed, but now we had to go over the petitions that had come in over the summer to prepare for the late September megaconference in which some of these petitions would be granted and scheduled for oral argument. And we had to begin to prepare for oral arguments in the cases where cert had previously been granted.

For every conference, Chief Justice Burger would issue a "discuss list," proposing that certain cases should be discussed in the conference. Any justice was free to add to this list. Justice Rehnquist estimated that between 15 to 30 percent of all petitions were discussed; the others were denied without discussion.[1] Since hundreds of cases had accumulated over the summer, we had to spend time going through the "discuss list" to decide whether there were any cases the justice wanted to add. Frequently his annotation to the cert memo would be "J3." This meant that he was willing to join three others if they wanted to grant a petition for certiorari—it took four justices for certiorari to be granted. Thus he had to make sure that cases that he had denominated "grant" or "J3" were on the discuss list. Of course, the majority of the cases discussed were not granted. Sometimes a justice will write a dissent from the denial of cert in a case, though the justice didn't do this during my term.

The September conference took several days and didn't involve deciding any cases since the Court, admirably, finishes its work from the previous term before the end of that term (sometimes a case that can't be decided the previous term, often because of a vacancy having occurred, leaving the remaining eight justices divided 4–4, will be set for reargument the following term). This conference produced a number of cert grants. These, plus the cases already set for argument in the fall, then had to be divided up among the clerks as being one clerk's primary responsibility. This meant that if it fell to Justice Rehnquist to write the opinion or the dissent in the case, that clerk would write the first draft. We used an "NFL draft" system, choosing the most desirable cases first and the less desirable (for example, tax cases) last. In keeping with my implied promise to Justice Rehnquist, as well as my interest, I tended to choose criminal cases. As it happened, the most significant cases in which Justice Rehnquist wrote opinions that year were *not* criminal cases, so I inadvertently reduced my role in history.

In keeping with what I had gleaned from my interview, as well as from former clerks Mike Buxton and Bill Jacobs, Justice Rehnquist was a fairly demanding but very pleasant boss. He wanted us to get our work out promptly and to keep it short, which was in keeping with my inclinations. In our early discussions about the summer cert petitions, I was very impressed with his keen mind and legal reasoning ability. He also had the uncanny ability to remember the volume number, and sometimes the actual page number, of prior Supreme Court cases. So if we had a question about what had been said in a previous case, he would tell us where to find it on the shelf in his office. Justice Rehnquist was dismissive of this ability, which obviously just came to him without any special effort, but we were impressed.

During the first week in October, oral arguments began. The other clerks eagerly attended these, but I realized (based on past experience) that they were not usually very interesting or insightful. In particular, state attorneys general, eager to make a public appearance on behalf of their states, but usually with no experience and little ability, would make embarrassingly bad arguments. Nowadays many states have solicitors general who are experienced appellate advocates and represent their states well before their state supreme courts, as well as federal appellate courts, and, when called upon, the U.S. Supreme Court. The solicitor general's office, consisting of really top-flight lawyers, could be depended upon for good arguments, and was often solicited by the Court to participate in an advisory capacity when it was not directly involved in the litigation.

I did, however, attend arguments in the death penalty cases—perhaps the most important cases of the term. In 1972, the Supreme Court had struck down the death penalty provisions of all the states as "cruel and unusual punishment" because they were too arbitrary and unguided. The Court invited the states to draft new statutes.[2] In my term they heard arguments in five cases from five different states and decided, in a series of split decisions, what the requisites of an acceptable death penalty system were. Civil rights attorney Anthony Amsterdam argued effectively against the death penalty, but in the end, it was upheld with certain limitations.[3]

The system established by those cases, with considerable tinkering, remains in place today. While these cases generated a lot of discussion among the clerks, Justice Rehnquist voted to uphold the death penalty in all five cases, and, though he did write a dissent in one case,[4] it wasn't "my" case, and I don't recall much discussion of them with him.

When I interviewed, Justice Rehnquist didn't ask about my politics, which were quite a bit more liberal than his. He did ask if I was aware of his political beliefs and felt that I could work with him. I assured him that I could, and that proved to be the case. I considered clerking for the justice to be similar to an attorney representing a client—I represented him as best I could regardless of my politics.

In general, I didn't argue with him about outcomes in criminal cases, but I can remember two occasions when I did. *Goldberg v. United States*[5] involved a complex issue of whether the prosecutor had to hand over to the defense notes of his interview with a witness after the witness testified. The trial court had denied the defendant's request, but Justice Brennan had circulated a majority opinion requiring that the case be remanded to the trial court for reconsideration of this decision.

Justice Powell had circulated a draft concurrence in the judgment, basically disagreeing with this decision. Justice Rehnquist was prepared to join Powell, but I convinced him that the prosecutor was wrong. His response was telling: "I usually like to go with Lewis [Powell]." In other words, in a case in which he had no particular interest or expertise, he would go along with Powell, usually his political ally, rather than Brennan. Nevertheless, he deferred to my experience and joined the Brennan opinion. I later rewarded him for this by citing this case as an example of his flexibility, against a charge of "extremism" by Senator Edward Kennedy, in a law review article and a submission to Congress,[6] when he was nominated for chief justice.[7]

The other case involved an issue that was not decided by the Court until 1978 in *Franks v. Delaware*.[8] For some reason, this issue was already before the Court in 1976. The appeal raised the issue of whether the defendant should be able to challenge the truth of a search warrant affidavit. Since this had been written by police early in the investigation, it seemed obvious that the defendant ought to be able to challenge it the first time he got a chance—at the hearing on his motion to suppress evidence. But Justice Rehnquist insisted not, and ultimately wrote the dissenting opinion in *Franks* when seven of the justices took my point of view. This was the one time I thought he was insisting on a position that was not supported by a reasonable-sounding argument. Otherwise, he had a remarkable ability to make his conservative views sound reasonable, even if I didn't agree with him.

I guess there must have been other occasions when my liberal views came out because he dubbed me his "most liberal clerk ever" (but did not mean it as an insult). In fact, the justice told me that he didn't like it when people recommended clerkship candidates by saying, "You'll really like him, he's very conservative." Justice Rehnquist liked having someone to argue with. Nevertheless, many of his subsequent clerks were, in fact, very conservative.

As I said, I rarely argued with Justice Rehnquist about results—if it was a criminal case, you basically knew that he was coming out against the defendant. Where we did most of our good-natured arguing was about the contents of opinions, and on this I felt perfectly free to express my views. As noted, the clerks wrote the first drafts of all opinions. According to a book collecting his opinions for the term, in which I marked my cases, I wrote the first drafts of five of seventeen majority opinions, five of thirteen dissents, none of three concurrences, and four of eight per curiam opinions. Justice Rehnquist wrote a majority of the per curiam opinions because he was the justice most likely to be up to date on his current work.

In those days before computers, I would type my draft and give it to him. Depending on how well he liked it, he would either mark up my draft slightly, cross out some part of my draft and insert his own sentences, or produce a new draft (I think by dictation). He would pass it back to me, and then, after I considered his changes, we would get together to try to hammer out an agreed-upon version. While I'm sure I must have shown deference to him in these discussions, I remember them as being completely freewheeling, in which I would argue strongly if I thought that something that had been in my draft should not have been eliminated or that something he added should be. And I often prevailed.

I did not save most of my papers from the clerkship so I can't, in general, say which opinions were mostly my work and which mostly his (even if I had the papers it would be difficult since the final decision was hammered out in oral discussion). I do still have a note from him about one dissent saying, "An excellent job. Very minor changes indicated and one deletion which I'm sure you expected." The deletion was "Because I would rather be right than precedent, I dissent." Too bad he wouldn't use it.

In addition to my regular duties I also helped him write speeches, including one at the University of Texas, published in the *Texas Law Review,* which has often been cited, called "The Notion of a Living Constitution."[9] In this he spelled out his judicial philosophy:

> It is almost impossible . . . to conclude that the [Founding Fathers] intended the Constitution itself to suggest answers to the manifold problems that they knew would confront succeeding generations. The Constitution that they drafted was intended to endure indefinitely, but the reason for this well-founded hope was the general language by which national authority was granted to Congress and the presidency. These two branches were to furnish the motive power within the federal system, which was in turn to coexist with the state governments; the elements of government having popular constituency were looked to for the solution of the numerous and varied problems that the future would bring.

In other words, as he elaborated in a dissenting opinion in *Trimble v. Gordon* in 1977,[10] nothing in the Constitution made "this Court (or the federal courts generally) into a council of revision, and they did not confer on this court any authority to nullify state laws which they merely felt to be inimical to the court's notion of the public interest." These words sound like quintessential Justice Rehnquist with no help from me.[11] I did suggest that he add a subtitle to *The Notion of a Living Constitution:* "Better Dead Than Red," a joke he shared with the Texas audience but didn't actually include in the manuscript.

He also asked my opinion of a novel he was writing. It was about the arcane subject of a federal district judge on a three-judge court who would do anything, including murder, to get on the court of appeals. I told him gingerly that I didn't think that this was a plot that would capture the imagination of the general reading public. Maybe if his aspiration were the Supreme Court? But he didn't want to make that change, and, as far as I know, the novel was never completed. Instead, Justice Rehnquist turned his extracurricular writing attention to the Supreme Court, producing three very good books on Supreme Court history, including one that discussed his own experiences as both a law clerk (to Justice Robert H. Jackson) and a justice.[12]

I almost got into trouble over the novel. Shortly after I read it a Powell clerk asked me how the novel was coming. I said something noncommittal, and told Justice Rehnquist what the clerk had asked me. He acted irritated and implied that I had improperly disclosed this information to the clerk. I hadn't been aware it was a secret, but as it happened, I hadn't mentioned it to anybody. I asked the clerk how he knew about it, and he replied that Justice Powell had told him. I told this to Justice Rehnquist, who sheepishly admitted that he had told Powell.

Several times during the term we were invited to Justice Rehnquist's home for dinner. Once again I was surprised by the modesty of his lifestyle. I had expected a grand house, in keeping with his high position. It was, in fact, a very ordinary house in the then-rather distant and not fancy (at least where he lived) suburb of McLean, Virginia. Justice Rehnquist drove a beat-up old BMW to work every day and, like everybody else, often complained about the traffic. It is not surprising that he lived modestly since his salary at the time was $63,000 a year, and his wife was not employed outside the home. His three children all still lived at home.

Mrs. Rehnquist was very nice, and we enjoyed our dinner. The other two clerks brought their wives, and I brought my girlfriend (subsequently my wife), Cindy. After dinner, we were forced to play charades, which everyone groaned about but Cindy and I enjoyed. I have subsequently used this tactic to force charades when I've had students over, something you can't do when you're entertaining your peers.

Justice Rehnquist was a ruthless charades player and was widely criticized by the rest of us by giving the line "other women cloy the appetites they feed" as the clue to be acted out. None of us was familiar with this line, which Antony says of Cleopatra, but I have remembered it ever since. Justice Rehnquist acted surprised that we didn't know it, so mastery of Shakespeare was evidently among his achievements.

Usually I had lunch in the Supreme Court cafeteria with other clerks. We started eating in the public area, but then the chief justice had a special room set aside for us so that our conversations could not be overheard. We, of course, discussed the justices as well as the pending cases. The consensus was that Chief Justice Burger and Justices Blackmun and Marshall were not really up to the job intellectually. In fact, Marshall's clerks complained that they could not get him away from his afternoon television programs to read and comment on their draft opinions. Blackmun's clerks had a different complaint. They felt like they inserted their opinion drafts through a slot in the door, and three weeks later the opinions came back out with no opportunity for discussion of any changes he might have made. Thus, unlike later clerks discussed in Linda Greenhouse's book, *Becoming Justice Blackmun,* these early clerks had very little influence on his opinions, much less his outcomes.

Chief Justice Burger was the subject of particular dislike by the clerks because he frequently issued memos referring to the "eager beaver law clerks" and other demeaning terms. And his chief clerk would send memos to other justices when their cert memos were not up to date. Justice Rehnquist frequently called or visited the Chief and, very deferentially, tried to straighten out flaws in the Chief's draft opinions. Once, some other clerks and I were hanging out in the courtroom, and I noticed that the Chief's chair had a three-inch cushion on it to make him appear bigger than the surrounding justices when he was presiding. I was sorely tempted to put a whoopee cushion under this pillow, but managed to restrain myself.

One of the perks of being a law clerk was that you were entitled to take each of the justices out to lunch. We foolishly didn't take advantage of this with Blackmun and Marshall, and Brennan couldn't fit us in because our invitation was rather late in the term. Somewhat to our surprise, our lunch with Burger, held in a fancy dining room in the Court called the "Ladies' Dining Room" (I don't remember a "Men's Dining Room"), was very pleasant. He was very nice to us, even supplying the food, and proved to know a great deal about Supreme Court history, with which he regaled us.

Our lunch with Justice Potter Stewart, who was also very nice, produced a fascinating story. He was asked how he came to be the youngest judge on the court of appeals, which he was prior to joining the Supreme Court. He told us that after his graduation from Yale Law School, he had returned to his hometown of Cincinnati to practice law. One afternoon he was sitting in the kitchen of the home of Robert Taft, then Republican leader of the Senate (and the son of President Taft). Stewart was socializing with Robert's son, a contemporary of his. Robert Taft walked in and began complaining that he was having difficulty filling a vacant seat on the Sixth Circuit, which, as the senior senator from Ohio, it was within his power to fill. Suddenly he looked at Stewart. "What about you?" he asked. After Stewart got over his shock, he agreed, and in a few years he was named by Eisenhower, presumably at Taft's suggestion, to the Supreme Court.

The lunch with White was mostly about football. White, known as "Whizzer," was an all-American at the University of Colorado. He was then drafted by the Pittsburgh Steelers. His description of what it was like in the NFL in his day was very interesting.

Justice Douglas, who had been on the Court since 1939, had a stroke in November 1975 and retired. I never had the opportunity to meet him beyond shaking his hand at an early reception of the clerks. He, of course, had a huge reputation as a great liberal but not a nice person, especially to women and law clerks.[13] Douglas's retirement meant that President Ford had to find a replacement as soon as possible because in the meantime there were eight justices on the closely divided Court, with the four Nixon appointees being considered conservatives and the other four liberals, though they didn't always fulfill these stereotypes.

Around this time, it fell to Justice Rehnquist, as the junior justice, to plan the Supreme Court Christmas show, and he in turn appointed me to collaborate. We decided to base the show around various interest groups singing, to the tune of Christmas carols, songs to a guy in a Michigan football uniform, who represented Ford. The songs expressed the views of their various groups. Thus, one was,

> I heard from Bella[14] on Christmas Day,
> Her old familiar grating bray,
> "Please be a pal,
> Appoint a gal,
> Peace on a Court that's not just men."

Another was to the tune of "Angels from the Realms of Glory":

> Liberals from the realms of theory
> Should adorn our highest bench
> Though to crooks they're always cheery,
> At police misdeeds they blench.[15]

At this point the chorus fell to their knees: "Save Miranda, Save Miranda, Save it from the Nixon four!"

The audience laughed hard at this performance, with one exception. Chief Justice Burger did not crack a smile, evidently not considering the subject of Supreme Court nominees to be an appropriate matter for jollity. He showed his pique in the next round of opinion assignments by only assigning Justice Rehnquist one case: an American Indian tax case.

After Ford appointed Justice John Paul Stevens to the Court, Justice Douglas, who had evidently become increasingly senile, tried to attend the conference as if he were still on the Court. He had to be talked out of it by the chief justice. I remember Justice Rehnquist becoming very upset and having to leave the room when he tried to describe this incident to us. Evidently, he and Douglas had become friendly, despite the difference in age and politics, because they were both westerners. Justice Douglas would not give up his chambers, and instead consigned Justice Stevens to Chief Justice Warren's retirement chambers—two rooms instead of three.[16] Burger could have thrown him out, but, presumably with Stevens's agreement, didn't have the stomach for it. Douglas lived until January 1980. Fortunately, Stevens only had two clerks.

I remember Justice Rehnquist grousing a good deal about Stevens, even in his first months. I think he was disappointed that Stevens was not a new, reliable conservative vote to replace the liberal Douglas. Stevens was a moderate at first who became a liberal in frequent opposition to Justice Rehnquist. However, they were friendly, both being nice guys. I played Ping-Pong with Justices Rehnquist and Stevens and one of Stevens's clerks on several occasions. Justice Rehnquist commented that it was only because of legal training that the justices could argue as vociferously as they did and still get along with each other.

An interesting issue arose with the Ping-Pong table. It was originally in the basement, but Justice Rehnquist got the Chief to move it into a vacant upstairs room next to the gym. One day Justice Rehnquist and I went to play and noticed one of the young janitors coming out of the room. When we went in, the room reeked of marijuana smoke. "What's that?" asked Justice Rehnquist. I explained. He didn't comment, and, as far as I know, he didn't contact the Chief to get the janitor fired, which surely would have happened had the Chief found out.

In general, it seemed to me that Justice Rehnquist acted much more like a moderate in his daily life than he did a staunch conservative. He didn't give religious pronouncements or talk like conservatives I have known who make me uncomfortable. He never hinted that he was pro-life. He just really believed that the federal government was one of limited powers, as set forth in the Constitution, and the right to abortion was not there.[17]

We frequently walked the square block around the Court to discuss cases or personal matters. He took a real interest in my life and, at one point, without my asking, advised me to marry my then girlfriend, Cindy. He also advised me to go to work for a big law firm, but after my good experience teaching at Indiana, I think he came to realize that teaching was a good life. He later recommended another clerk, Joe Hoffmann, to come to Indiana, and he did. I shared my work with Justice Rehnquist, which was mostly about Supreme Court criminal procedure cases, at his insistence, but, not surprisingly, he didn't offer substantive critiques.

In the years after my clerkship, I saw Justice Rehnquist quite frequently— first when I worked for the Public Integrity Section in Washington, and then, after I moved to Indiana, whenever I was in Washington. We would often have lunch, usually at The Monocle restaurant, and go to a museum afterward. He came out to Bloomington, at the law school's invitation, on two occasions as well.

I was also a regular attender of the clerks' reunion, which was held every summer at the end of the term. This involved a formal dinner at the Court on Saturday and then a picnic, at first at Justice Rehnquist's, and then at an ex-clerk's house, on Sunday. This was widely attended since Justice Rehnquist had made it clear that he liked former clerks to attend. He would read off a list of clerks from particular years who had all made it back. There were some hilarious skits performed by the current year's clerks at these reunions. It was nice to see the older clerks every year, but as a new set of three was added each year, it became a large group (about 100) to keep up with. Nevertheless, I usually attended, including one of several hosted by Chief Justice Roberts after Justice Rehnquist's death.

When Chief Justice Rehnquist died of thyroid cancer on September 3, 2005 (the weekend of Hurricane Katrina), I went to the funeral—held at the Catholic Cathedral of St. Matthew the Apostle though it was a Lutheran service. It was a very big deal; everyone from the president on down was there. Rehnquist was the first justice to die in office since Justice Robert H. Jackson. Rehnquist's children and grandchildren attended, as did Justice O'Connor, who had known him since Stanford.

The law clerks served as pallbearers at various stages of the event—I did it from the church to the hearse. The casket was quite heavy, and, as it happened, I was in the front. I was very worried that I would trip going down the steps of the Cathedral, creating a national embarrassment. Fortunately, I didn't.

Notes

1. See William H. Justice Rehnquist, *The Supreme Court* (New York: Vintage Books, 2001), 234.

2. *Furman v. Georgia*, 408 U.S. 238 (1972).

3. See, for example, *Gregg v. Georgia*, 428 U.S. 153 (1976).

4. 428 U.S. 280 (1976).

5. 425 U.S. 94 (1976).

6. I actually testified on his behalf, but didn't use my prepared text, which was this article.

7. Craig Bradley, "Criminal Procedure in the Justice Rehnquist Court: Has the Rehnquisition Begun?," *Indiana Law Journal* 62 (1987): 273, 282.

8. 438 U.S. 154 (1978).

9. *Texas Law Review* 54 (1976): 693.

10. 430 U.S. 762.

11. Obviously I had no part in the *Trimble* dissent since it was written the year after I left.

12. Rehnquist, *Supreme Court*.

13. See Bruce Allen Murphy, *Wild Bill: The Legend and Life of William O. Douglas* (New York: Random House, 2003), for a very interesting and detailed account of his various exploits.

14. This referred to Bella Abzug, a leading feminist spokesperson and member of Congress at the time.

15. This is an alternative spelling of "blanch," which Justice Rehnquist knew about.

16. Since then, the Thurgood Marshall Building, about three blocks from the Court near Union Station, has been built and is where retired justices now have their offices.

17. Although we spoke quite freely about many matters, I think that if he were pro-life he probably wouldn't have shared it with me.

JULIA C. AMBROSE

Clerking for the FWOTSC

Recollections of a Former O'Connor Clerk

S pending a year as a law clerk for a justice of the U.S. Supreme Court is an exceptional experience under any circumstances, but I feel particularly lucky to have clerked for Justice Sandra Day O'Connor—the First Woman on the Supreme Court, or "FWOTSC," as she has called herself. To a young woman about to enter the legal profession, Justice O'Connor was an icon, a door-opener, a fearless role model. I knew her background and the remarkable trajectory of her career, I recalled the buzz and excitement of her nomination and confirmation, and I had studied her opinions with special care for nearly three years as I worked toward my law degree. I never imagined that I would become a part of her law clerk family.

I first met Justice O'Connor in the spring of 1994, toward the end of my third year of law school at Vanderbilt University. I had already been offered a position for the first year following my graduation, as a law clerk to Judge J. Harvie Wilkinson III on the U.S. Court of Appeals for the Fourth Circuit in Charlottesville, Virginia. I expected that, after that clerkship ended, I would join one of the firms at which I would spend time as a summer associate. In my final year of law school, Anne Coughlin, my law school professor and mentor who had clerked for Justice Lewis F. Powell, suggested that I consider a different plan: applying for a Supreme Court clerkship. I understood the odds—the number of supremely qualified applicants, the few available positions, the fact that my law degree would not come from an Ivy League law school—but decided to give it a whirl, reasoning that I had nothing to lose, but stood to gain something remarkable. That "something remarkable" was the chance to meet a Supreme Court justice, because even securing an interview, a chance to talk one-on-one with a sitting justice, would be an extraordinary experience for a young lawyer. With that as my goal, I mailed my application package to Justice O'Connor at once. If I was going to hope for an interview, I wished it to be with her.

At that time, the justice relied on her clerks to help screen applications and narrow down those candidates she wanted to interview. She did not have a formal committee of former clerks, professors, or the like that she relied upon; she did, however, always place special weight on a recommendation from a former clerk, who of course would be able to identify candidates that would be a good fit for the justice and whose records exhibited the characteristics she valued.

When the invitation to come to Washington, D.C., for that hoped-for interview arrived weeks later, I was equal parts awestruck and terrified. I prepared for the interview much like I studied for my law school finals and the bar exam, methodically reviewing Justice O'Connor's most noteworthy opinions and reading every O'Connor biography, article, and interview I could get my hands on. I had the impression that the justice would be dignified and serious and would quiz me on my understanding of her background, opinions, and judicial philosophy. Let's just say I was off the mark.

The justice (SO'C to her clerks and others at the Court) is matter-of-fact, sharp, warm, and engaging. Her office at the Court reflects her personality: it is colorful, bright, and welcoming, filled with books and papers, tidy but not sterile, decorated with nods to her southwestern upbringing. Our interview wasn't a rapid-fire quiz on matters of legal substance. It was a friendly chat about my upbringing, the source of my interest in the law, my plans for my career and my future. We sat facing each other in her office—the justice welcomes all visitors to her chambers with an enthusiastic "Come sit down!"—while she talked about herself and her role on the Court as openly and casually as if I had just dropped by for a visit.

Later in the day, her current clerks were given the opportunity to grill applicants—a task they attacked with gusto. I sat in a chair in the room beside the administrative area of the justice's chambers, where two of the four clerks worked (the other two had desks on the upper floor of the Court building, and the four clerks rotated office space halfway through the year). The four clerks gathered their chairs in a semicircle facing me, and what began as a friendly chat about my background and law school experience quickly turned into a substantive legal "discussion," with questions coming at a rapid pace from the four clerks.

I was terribly nervous and confess to having a rather dim memory of the particulars at this point (and a very vivid memory of my feeling of relief when the questioning ended!), but I do recall a series of questions about the justice's First Amendment jurisprudence, which fortunately was an area of interest to me and a topic I had studied fairly closely. Every one of my answers prompted several follow-up questions from the clerks, and the questions did much more than test my memory or knowledge about Supreme Court cases. The clerks wanted to hear my theories, my criticisms of particular decisions or legal rules, and so forth. What they were looking for, I understand, was not simply academic knowledge, but a deeper, more thoughtful consideration of the pertinent legal rules and issues. I left the interview thrilled beyond words that I had just had exactly what I had not dared to hope for, the chance to sit and talk with the first woman to serve on the U.S. Supreme Court. Still mindful of the odds, and completely delighted that I had come this far, I figured that would be it.

Many weeks later, I was sitting at my kitchen table studying for the last of my third-year law school final exams when my telephone rang. The voice on the other end of the line asked me to "please hold for Justice O'Connor," and before I could process the notion that I was about to be on the telephone with *a sitting justice of the U.S. Supreme Court,* the justice herself came on the line to offer me a job as one of her four law clerks the year following my Fourth Circuit clerkship. Our telephone exchange was every bit as warm and matter-of-fact as our meeting had been, although it was several days before my sense of disbelief faded.

To this day, I am not certain how I made the cut. I suppose it helped that Professor Coughlin, who recommended me, had clerked for Justice Powell, with whom Justice O'Connor had a particularly close relationship at the Court: she has credited him publicly with helping her and her husband, John, find a home in Washington, with allowing her to poach one of his secretaries to ease her transition when she joined the Court, and with offering her, as a new justice, an always open door to answer questions and discuss cases. Perhaps it helped that I came from a non–Ivy League school and had made my way through both college and law school with scholarships, grants, loans, and part-time jobs. The justice does not, in my experience, choose her clerks based on ideology or for their propensity to agree with her, and she does not shy away from lively debate with clerks who do not share her view of a case or an issue. Instead, she values a strong work ethic, self-reliance, determination, and a history of overcoming obstacles or adversity—surely a by-product of her no-nonsense upbringing, with its emphasis on hard work and self-sufficiency, and her determination to forge a career in the male-dominated legal world.

I clerked for Justice O'Connor during October term 1995. The cases the Court heard and decided that term were important and interesting (as the business of the Court almost always is): *United States v. Virginia*[1] (the Virginia Military Institute case), *Roemer v. Evans,*[2] and two significant Voting Rights Act cases (which produced some of the aforementioned lively debate with one of my co-clerks). Research, writing, analyzing, debating, and discussing cases with the justice and each other were the heart of the work the law clerks did from day to day. The clerks' workload was a full one, and our workdays at the Court were long and busy. Playing a role, however small, in the Court's decision-making process was heady (and demanding) stuff, but it was only a part of what made the clerkship experience truly extraordinary. In between cert pool memos, bench briefs, and research projects, we spent time with Justice O'Connor, and that time made up the heart and richness of my clerkship experience.

The clerks also regularly interacted with John O'Connor. He was a frequent visitor to the Court and would spend time in the justice's chambers, where we all had the opportunity to talk with him. They seemed to have a busy and rich social life in Washington, so many of his appearances at the Court were in anticipation of their nights out at the theater or something similar. We all recognized the mutual affection, respect, and pride they felt for one another.

Justice O'Connor's relationship with her law clerks was far from all business. She expected from her clerks what she demanded of herself: hard work, careful preparation, attention to detail, thorough and thoughtful evaluation. But she also insisted that our clerkship year be a rich experience, that we have the opportunity to know the Court, its personnel and its history, the justice herself, and the District of Columbia. The justice, in her characteristically thoughtful and orderly way, made certain that that happened. What follows are a few of my favorite memories.

The clerks typically arrived at the Court in the summer months, when the Court's fall term had not yet begun and the justices were traveling, lecturing, and attending to other business away from Washington. We had time to settle in and learn (at least a few of) the ropes before the new term got under way. With the justice's arrival in advance of the October term, the pace and energy in chambers intensified. And my days became even longer and more action-filled, because it was time to resume Justice O'Connor's long-standing early morning aerobics class.

The class met almost every weekday morning in "the highest Court in the land," the basketball gym on the top floor of the Court building (the justice spent one or two mornings engaged in tennis and other pursuits, and she spent her vacations away from the Court skiing and golfing; her physical energy was limitless). The justice's female law clerks were encouraged to join the class, women clerks for the other justices were invited, and a small group of "regulars" from the District who'd been aerobicizing with the justice for years made up the rest of the gang—the justice's "Aerobics Club." The early 1990s marked the heyday of the step aerobics trend, and Justice O'Connor's aerobics class followed along. In place of the iconic molded-plastic Reebok step, though, we stepped up and down on solid wood steps built by the Supreme Court's woodshop at the justice's request. The steps were undeniably sturdy and *incredibly heavy*; the act of dragging one into the middle of the gym floor was a workout in itself.

It was also a bonding experience. By the term's end, our little gang of step-aerobicizers had become a close-knit group. It was the justice's practice to celebrate the end of the term by asking the club to create a slogan to represent our year together and design shirts that incorporated the slogan, which were handed out over a celebratory lunch at the Court (a funny experience—it was the first time that I had seen many of my fellow aerobicizers in ordinary street clothes and not athletic gear). My "Supreme Court Aerobics Club" shirt still hangs in my closet. It's a collared shirt, golf-shirt style, a dark maroon, with a graphic of the Court on the front and our term's Aerobics Club slogan imprinted on the back: *"Justice Never Rests."* Truer words were never spoken.

The aerobics class kicked off our mornings with the justice, and the days that followed were long and full. The work done by Supreme Court law clerks is well documented: we worked with the justice to prepare for upcoming arguments, to draft opinions in argued cases, and to evaluate cert petitions, and in between she tasked us with a series of special projects. On the special project front, I won the lottery. Nineteen ninety-five marked the seventy-fifth anniversary of the ratification of the Nineteenth Amendment, which gave women the right to vote in 1920. The justice had been invited to deliver a speech in Arizona in September to mark the occasion, and she asked me to work with her to research and prepare her remarks. I could not have imagined a more inspiring project as a newly minted lawyer than working with the FWOTSC to craft a presentation about the efforts and sacrifices made by the women who fought at the turn of the century for the right to vote regardless of gender.

I still marvel that I spent hours talking with Sandra Day O'Connor about where women in this country might be today if Representative Harry Burns, of Tennessee, had not heeded his mother's advice—she wrote him a letter saying, "Son, I hope you will support this women's suffrage amendment," a story the justice delights in recounting—and voted in favor of ratification. The justice deeply values the study of the history of the women's suffrage movement; she has said that young women often do not have a sufficient appreciation of the struggles that led to the opportunities we enjoy today. Thanks to Justice O'Connor, I certainly do.

There was much buzz in Justice O'Connor's chambers about the women's suffrage movement as the date for her speech drew near, all of which opened the door to other, more personal conversations about the justice's own experience growing up as a self-proclaimed cowgirl on the Lazy B Ranch, earning her law degree as one of only six women in her law school class, entering a profession that was inarguably dominated by men, and forging a professional path for herself in circumstances that were less than hospitable. She told us about her search for a job after graduating from law school and the offer she received of a secretarial position (conditioned upon a showing that she could type "well enough"). The story has been repeated often in articles written about the justice, but it has a most different tenor when it she tells herself, in her usual matter-of-fact fashion, and not without her characteristic humor.

The suffrage movement speech had another consequence in chambers that year. It was one of Justice O'Connor's many traditions that her law clerks decorated a chambers pumpkin every Halloween. Prior O'Connor pumpkins often had reflected some bit of business before the Court or some legal theme. It seemed only fitting that our chambers pumpkin in October 1995 was dressed as a suffragette. We researched the dress of the day and constructed a suitable outfit for the suffragette squash: she wore a bonnet and carried a placard demanding equal voting rights for women. The justice was tickled.

The pumpkin-decorating event was just one of the many traditions and events that the justice arranged during the term. She loved outings with her law clerks around the District, often on the spur of the moment (or at least it seemed that way to a busy clerk with a mountain of work planned for the day ahead). And the trips we took with the justice speak volumes about the things she enjoys and values. Among the mementos of my clerkship year are brochures for the Hiroshi Teshigahara exhibit at the Kennedy Center, the exhibit of Treasures from the Bibliothèque Nationale de France at the Library of Congress, the Winslow Homer and Johannes Vermeer exhibits at the National Gallery of Art, and the U.S. Botanic Garden.

When the justice decided it was time for one of these field trips, we'd pile into her car, the justice behind the wheel, and make our way around the District. At every destination, the justice led us through the exhibits and spaces at a brisk pace and spoke energetically about things that caught her eye. We clerks had long since grown accustomed to her characteristically robust approach to every case, issue, outing, and event.

I recall these trips outside the Court building as both fun-filled and educational. I learned a tremendous amount about art and culture, of course, and I learned how easily and often the justice was recognized in public. The National Gallery was closed briefly to allow our small group to see the Vermeer exhibit, for example; the justice wandering freely through the exhibit likely would have caused an uproar and certainly would have disrupted the normally orderly operations of the museum, something the justice would have wanted to avoid. When we visited the less-crowded Botanic Garden in the middle of a weekday, we were able to wander around mostly—but not entirely—unrecognized, but even there, her presence could cause a stir. She took it all in stride and was unfailingly gracious when approached in public.

I remember one other "field trip" from my clerkship particularly vividly: a January outing to see a production of *Henry V* at the Shakespeare Theater, starring Harry Hamlin (then) of *L.A. Law* fame. The group of clerks sat in the audience, but the justice did more than watch the play: she had been invited to make a surprise (to the rest of the audience) appearance as Isabel, queen of France. She had one line, and oh, how fitting it was: *"Hap'ly a woman's voice may do some good."* The playwright could not have designed a more perfect role for her. And she nailed it, of course.

The zenith of the clerk field trips came toward the end of the term. It was the justice's long-standing tradition to arrange a chambers "field trip" for the clerks at the end of every year—a trip of greater magnitude and complexity than our other impromptu outings. Planning began months in advance, and the justice solicited input from all of us to come up with a destination and an agenda. As it happened, one of my co-clerks was an avid fisherman, a passion the justice shared, so it was decided that our year-end outing would be a fishing excursion, with expert guides to increase the odds of us actually catching something, on the Potomac River. The plans came together, the weather cooperated, and on the appointed day, we set sail on the Potomac in two fishing boats, each staffed with a very capable guide. We spent a delightful day soaking up the sun, taking in the D.C. vistas (particularly spectacular when viewed from the river), and enjoying the relaxed time talking with the justice, who was in her element, being a very capable fisherwoman among her many other skills and talents. As it turned out, though, the fishing component of the outing was only moderately successful, producing something less than an abundance of fish, most of which were not edible (the justice, as I recall, caught several; the group of clerks significantly fewer). But the day ended on a high note with dinner at the justice's home that evening, prepared by her. Her home, like her office, was a perfect reflection of the justice herself: warm, inviting, filled with books and personal mementos—and a spectacular kitchen. The justice is, unsurprisingly, a talented and inventive cook. Although I do not recall precisely what was on the menu that evening, I do recall that it was delicious, that plates were cleaned, and that many compliments were paid to the chef.

The "year-end field trip" was not the only occasion when the justice cooked a meal for us. When we were required from time to time to meet in chambers on a weekend to prepare for upcoming oral arguments, the justice would make an elaborate lunch in her own kitchen, pack the food, bring it to the Court, and reward our work with an exceptionally good home-cooked meal. I would have welcomed any opportunity to spend a Saturday discussing, analyzing, and debating with the FWOTSC the gravely important issues that were to be addressed and resolved by our nation's highest Court. Having lunch prepared and served by her—and an indescribably delicious meal at that—was icing on the cake.

The year I spent as a law clerk for Justice O'Connor was chock-full of these sorts of moments, outings, and experiences, and I look back on them fondly and with a sort of wonder that they happened to me at all. Happily, we all have a regular opportunity to reminisce: the group of O'Connor clerks reunites with the justice once every few years for clerk reunions. Reunions don't happen on any predictable schedule but only when the justice's still extremely full schedule allows. Getting word that a reunion is in the works is thrilling, because we have too few opportunities to catch up with the justice and each other—

although her door is always open at the Court, and she always welcomes her former clerks with enthusiasm. The closing paragraph of her farewell letter to me at the end of my clerkship reflects the genuine affection she feels for all of her former clerks and her eagerness to maintain contact with them: "I shall miss you greatly in the months and years ahead. I will follow your life and career with great interest. Please stay in touch with me in the years ahead. You will always be a cherished member of my law clerk family."

I have accepted her invitation to stay in touch, and I have visited her at the Court whenever an opportunity arose. Still, those opportunities are too infrequent, especially in the years since the justice's retirement (when commitments outside Washington began to fill her schedule), so clerk reunions are treasured.

Reunions are not built on any sort of strict agenda or unwavering tradition, although every reunion incorporates key elements: some casual time for clerks to visit with the justice and introduce our families to her and to each other, some event or outing that celebrates the place or the setting where we've gathered, and a more formal dinner gathering for the clerks and their guests that almost always incorporates some mixture of clerk reminiscing and remarks by the justice. Here I cannot help but pause to mention that the justice's remarks in recent years, both at clerk reunions and in other settings, focus less on her years on the Court and her role as the FWOTSC and more on the issues that have come to be most meaningful to her—most important, civics education in our public schools.

I had the privilege of sitting in the audience several weeks ago while the justice addressed a gathering of the Federal Bar Association in Richmond, Virginia. She answered a series of questions about the Court, its business, and her years as a justice with her usual good humor, but when the topic of civics education came up, she grew noticeably more animated. Alarmed by the notion that many graduates of our public schools cannot name the three branches of government, in 2009 the justice founded iCivics, Inc., a 501(c)(3) nonprofit organization, to increase young Americans' civic knowledge and participation. She was determined to reinvigorate civics education, and she attacked the issue with her usual vigor and commitment (it comes as no surprise, then, that iCivics.org has become "the nation's most comprehensive, standards-aligned civics curriculum that is available freely on the Web," per the iCivics website). When the justice sets her mind to something, she does not stop until she's met her goal. *Justice never rests.*

The only other time in recent memory that I have seen the justice so animated is when she is surrounded by her clerks at a reunion. Law clerk reunions are relaxed gatherings, incorporating spouses and children, built around places and events that are particularly meaningful to the justice. Recent O'Connor clerk reunions have been held in Arizona rather than in Washington, where the group of clerks toured and celebrated the Sandra Day O'Connor United States Courthouse in Phoenix and, most recently, the relocation of the historic Sandra Day O'Connor House to Tempe Papago Park. An upcoming reunion is planned for Washington, D.C., with time to be spent at the American History Museum and the Court.

I have the sense that the justice enjoys our reunions even more than the clerks do. She's in her element, surrounded by a group that she considers a family. She's particularly fond of the children of her former clerks, her "grand-clerks"—so designated by the justice herself—and confirmed by the specially prepared T-shirts that bear the Court insignia and the "grandclerk" label.

I leave every reunion utterly in awe that I am a member of such a group (the members of which are incredibly accomplished—state and federal judges, es-teemed law professors, best-selling authors, to name just a few), that I worked in such a capacity, that I had a chance to meet, know, work beside, and form a relationship with such a truly extraordinary woman.

Notes

1. 518 U.S. 515 (1996).
2. 517 U.S. 620 (1996).

Justice Souter and His Law Clerks

During my third year of law school, as was the schedule at the time, I applied for Supreme Court clerkships. During the next year, while clerking on the District of Columbia Circuit, I interviewed with three justices, Souter among them. None offered me a job. I applied again the next year, and got only one interview, with Justice Souter. This time around he hired me, for October term 1999. He had been concerned, he explained, that I would not be sufficiently willing to disagree with him, but subsequent conversations with my recommenders had convinced him I would. That second interview clarified for me why the first had taken a slightly awkward tack: the justice had offered progressively more unusual views in an attempt to provoke disagreement, while I had focused on remaining polite. It also displayed two of Justice Souter's traits as a judge: he wanted clerks who would disagree with him, and he was willing to change his mind.

There was a connection between these two traits, though not the obvious one. I have no doubt that Justice Souter would have changed his position had a clerk convinced him that his initial views were wrong, but I am also quite sure that such a thing never happened. Justice Souter listened to clerks with gracious attention, but we learned a lot more from the conversations than he did. One theme of the relationship Souter had with his clerks—and I suspect with other people as well—was that a structure that was supposed to allow us to help him ended up working the other way. Looking back, I believe that a lot of what we did in the job was for our benefit, not his. Justice Souter gave us work we would enjoy and learn from, even if, I suspect, he often did not need our work product.

When I talked about cases with Justice Souter, he encouraged me to go first, and in our first few conversations, he said little more than "I agree." I was not foolish enough to think that my exposition was winning him over, but it was still a surprise when, for the first time, he told me he saw things differently. I spent several hours over the next days honing arguments and presenting them to him, and finally he said, "Thank you. You've done your job; now I must do mine." Looking back on that case with a bit more experience, I can see that his position, which was based on institutional realities rather than abstract theories, was the sounder one.

The reason that Justice Souter wanted clerks who would disagree with him was that he wanted to be exposed to the widest possible range of viewpoints, and the reason he was willing to change his mind was that he had no ideological commitment to particular outcomes. He cared only about the soundness of reasoning and justification. He believed that a judge's task in writing an opinion was not to win a battle with the dissenters, but rather to come as close as possible to the truth. For this reason he was willing, in a way many judges are not, to acknowledge the strengths of the other side's position and the difficulty of reaching a decision; he was able to put aside any sense of partisan identification with a position in favor of reason and dispassion.[1] He had the open-minded equanimity of a good academic, and, in this sense, Souter was a very academic justice who brought a scholar's perspective to the work of judging.

Justice Souter was able to maintain this perspective even in the face of harsh criticism. I remember the experience of reading a colorful dissent circulated in response to a Souter majority opinion. My reaction was a mix of mortification and rage, but Souter seemed mildly amused and concerned primarily with deciding whether the dissent made any valid points that would justify alterations in his opinion. The term that I clerked included some high-profile and divisive cases, including the invalidation of the Violence Against Women Act in *United States v. Morrison*,[2] and of Nebraska's "partial birth" abortion ban in *Stenberg v. Carhart*.[3] Even when not in the majority, Souter retained his equanimity. The most pointed remark I can remember from him, in response to a doctrinal innovation I viewed as an outrage, was that "the crazier it gets, the sooner it will be swept away."

What we could call Justice Souter's academic temperament (though I cheerfully admit that it is one many academics lack) is probably the reason that so many of his clerks went on to become law professors. About half are in academia, the highest percentage of any justice's clerks. It was not that Justice Souter had any particular enthusiasm for legal scholarship. He cared about doctrine and would read scholarship that illuminated it, but he was certainly not a follower of the sort of esoteric high theory that is typically most valued by academics. He was far more interested in history, which is appropriate. When, for example, the Court confronted the limits of executive power in cases about the detention of terrorism suspects, the history of the Japanese American internment in World War II, and the executive's handling of those cases, it offered him more significant insight than any professor's theoretical musings.[4]

Nor, so far as I know, did Justice Souter actively encourage any clerks to go into academia. When I spoke to him about my own plans to do so, he said that I must make sure to spend at least some time in private practice first so that I could experience the real world. (It was good advice, and I took it.) But he had the scholar's temperament; he sought out clerks with similar traits, and, I think, the process of working with him showed many clerks a sort of ideal of what the academic life could be like: measured, thoughtful analysis of vitally important issues. We couldn't be Justice Souter, but in scholarship we could come close.

Life in Chambers

Justice Souter's clerks, as best I could tell from my limited sample of comparisons, enjoyed a relatively low-key and unpressured year. The workload varied, but we seldom put in the extreme hours that some other chambers seemed to clock as a routine matter. The work we did was typically distilled to a high degree of concentration: Justice Souter was so self-sufficient that he required very little of the labor-intensive groundwork that some other justices' clerks performed. He placed no restrictions on our contacts with other chambers, knowing, I expect, that talking about cases with fellow clerks was one of the most fun parts of the job and also one of the parts least likely to have any effect on the Court's actual decisions.

The justice reviewed our work with a keen but gentle eye—he might disagree, but he would never disparage—and he was not an authoritarian presence in chambers. Typically, we wished that we saw him more than we did, and the two clerks who worked upstairs would always rush down in the afternoon when alerted that the justice had come out from chambers for his daily coffee break. For half an hour or so, the five of us would talk about nonlegal matters, and usually Justice Souter would regale us with some amusing anecdotes about his time in New Hampshire or at Oxford University. Once he accompanied us to the National Gallery of Art and during the visit instructed us each to pick out the one piece we wanted to take home. He was a much warmer and more charming man than media portrayals suggested.

Personal Traits

The media tended to focus on Justice Souter's quirks, of which there were certainly a few. He was presented as a throwback to the nineteenth century, and it is true that he did not use a computer or even a typewriter. I vividly remember trying to decipher his ornate longhand script. He was viewed as reclusive, and it is true that he shunned Washington society and decamped with great relief to New Hampshire as soon as the Court's term concluded. He was considered unnaturally thrifty, and it is true that he would read by daylight rather than waste electricity, even if this left him standing by the window in a darkened room (this habit could be disconcerting to clerks who would come into his office and wander blindly until their eyes adjusted). He even once left me a note written on a napkin found on my desk, rather than waste a sheet of paper.

But, as is not uncommon with media portrayals, the stories about Souter tended to miss the forest for the trees. The storied quirks actually are important, not because they define Souter but because they point to deeper underlying themes of his character: modesty, respect, and lack of pretention. His thriftiness, for instance, seemed odd largely because he refused to waste taxpayers' money as well as his own—their electricity to read by, their paper to write on. It is hard to imagine that a Supreme Court justice would not feel important enough to waste a little electricity, but self-importance is something Justice Souter lacked entirely.

Likewise, his avoidance of Washington social events and end-of-term dash to New Hampshire would seem odd in most justices. Who would not want to enjoy the social status conveyed by such a lofty rank? Someone who insisted on seeing others as persons rather than positions, and who defined himself the same way. The social hierarchy of D.C., which rests on excruciatingly precise calculations of power and status, went fundamentally against Souter's nature. As a person, he was intensely nonhierarchical.

Just as Souter saw people rather than positions, he was very careful to evaluate ideas independent of their source. Most people think of Souter as one of the more distinctively regional justices—a New England Yankee—and that is certainly true in terms of his personal traits, to say nothing of his accent. But in a very important sense, he was deeply cosmopolitan, and the rejection of parochialism is one of the themes that has stuck with me from our conversations. You cannot trust people just because they seem to be the right sort, he believed. That kind of thinking, that presumes the correctness and probity of those who went to the right schools, or those who resemble us, has led the government to some of its most serious mistakes.

LEGAL PHILOSOPHY

Each year, Justice Souter stayed in Washington as long as needed to fulfill his duties and left as soon as the work was done. In my mind, that end-of-term escape to New Hampshire serves as a microcosm for his relationship with the Court. Souter loved the law, and he loved judging, and for most such people, sitting on the Supreme Court would have been the ultimate achievement, a delight to be savored as long as possible. But Souter retired at sixty-nine, an unusually young age for a justice; he does not seem to have felt that way.

My guess is that he found the Supreme Court an uncomfortable fit for the same reasons that make it so enticing to other people. Clerking first at a federal court of appeals and then at the Supreme Court, I was able to see firsthand the differences between the caseload at those levels. At the federal appeals level, most questions are technical and nonpartisan; right answers exist, and judges generally come to agreement. At the Supreme Court, many questions are inescapably moral or political and consequently partisan; right answers frequently do not exist in any obvious sense, and disagreements prove intractable. That makes the Court's work attractive for those who want to wield power and make policy, those who have agendas to advance.

Justice Souter had no agenda, and I think that the court of appeals model fits his ideal of the law much more closely than the Supreme Court model. The justice believed in law as a moderating force and courts as a refuge from the tumult of partisanship. At the court of appeals level, such a philosophy can find an easy expression in right answers unaffected by politics. At the Supreme Court level, it manifests as a cautious incrementalism that resists extremes. Resisting extremism is certainly a theme of his jurisprudence, and there were some hugely important cases where his presence made all the difference. But fighting partisans is not fully satisfying for those who think the real foe is partisanship: your side may win or it may lose, but something is still wrong as long as there are sides at all.[5]

RELATIONSHIP WITH CLERKS

Justice Souter's relationship with his clerks did not stop with the job's end. He liked his clerks. He cared about our welfare. And because he refused to consider himself more important than other people, he was quite generous with his time. He spent an hour having lunch with my parents when they visited chambers, even though, characteristically, he consumed only a cup of yogurt and an apple. Former clerks regularly stopped by and were always granted some time with the justice. He read their articles; he discussed their careers and their families. Once, while I was clerking, he took his mentoring efforts to the next level, or at least the next generation: a former clerk brought his wife and new baby to visit, and when I poked my head into Souter's office to ask a question, I saw him teaching the baby to crawl.

After my clerkship was over, I visited the Court several times while Justice Souter was there, and he was always extremely welcoming. Once, when I was working on a television pilot based on a novel I had written, I took an actor and the producer on a tour of Washington to scout possible locations. The show had a legal theme, so they were interested in seeing the Supreme Court, and I brought them to the side entrance that the clerks use. "It's a Saturday," the security guard said when I asked him to call chambers to see if anyone was in who could show us around. "So you know who's there." Only the justice, he meant, working by himself (Justice Souter regularly worked Saturdays; endearingly, he would "dress down" from his usual suit to a jacket and tie). I felt a little bad for interrupting, but I asked the guard to make the call anyway. Justice Souter came out and talked with great cordiality for ten or fifteen minutes, only then revealing that he had been in the middle of writing an opinion and wanted to return to it while the fire still burned. I was horrified, of course, but Justice Souter didn't seem the least put out. That kind of selfless generosity was the norm for him.

After his retirement, the justice began scheduling reunions less frequently, saying he doubted that many of us would want to make a trip just for him. When some clerks finally browbeat him into it, he reserved a small room in Boston. Of course it proved quite unable to contain everyone who showed up. As far as the clerks are concerned, I think, that also is Souter in microcosm: a man who is much larger in our lives than he lets himself admit.

Notes

1. See, for example, *Printz v. United States,* 521 U.S. 898, 970–76 (1997) (Souter, J., dissenting) (acknowledging that he finds the cases "closer than I expected" and mentioning strengths of the other side's argument). The Souter dissent in *Printz* also shows Justice Souter admitting that an earlier view no longer persuades him. Ibid., 976. See also *City of Erie v. Pap's AM,* 529 U.S. 277, 316–17 (2000) (opinion of Souter, J.) (acknowledging a change in his view of the First Amendment).

2. 529 U.S. 598 (2000).

3. 530 U.S. 914 (2000).

4. See, for example, Peter Irons, *Justice at War* (New York: Oxford University Press, 2004), describing the executive branch's lack of candor with the Supreme Court during the litigation over internment of Japanese Americans. Indeed, Fred Korematsu filed an amicus brief in the *Hamdi* case, attempting to draw the justices' attention to just that parallel.

5. In this respect, Souter resembles the nineteenth-century justice Joseph Story, a fellow New Englander, who also believed that partisanship had diminished the Supreme Court.

A Family Tradition

Clerking at the U.S. Supreme Court

Without question, former Supreme Court law clerks are members of one of the most elite legal fraternities in the country. There is, however, an ever more exclusive club whose membership is comprised of former law clerks whose children have also gone on to clerk at the High Court.[1] Since 1882, approximately 2,000 men and women have clerked at the Supreme Court, but we believe that only thirteen pairs of fathers and their children can lay claim to having multigenerational clerkships.[2] (There has yet to be a mother-daughter or mother-son duo.)

This unique club was founded by former New Dealer Tommy "the Cork" Corcoran and his daughter, Margaret. The elder Corcoran clerked for Oliver Wendell Holmes Jr. during October term 1926, while the younger Corcoran clerked for Hugo L. Black during October term 1966. Their clerkship experiences could not have been more different. The Holmes law clerks were as much social companions as they were law clerks. While Justice Holmes did assign some legal work (mainly reviewing cert petitions), the clerks (called "private secretaries") were also expected to manage the justice's bank accounts, accompany him on jaunts around the District, debate the justice on a variety of philosophical and social issues, and listen to his tales about the Civil War. "Being with this man was an incredible personal experience and his ideas were burned into me so deeply that I have made evaluations by his standards ever since," observed Tommy Corcoran years after his clerkship.[3] In turn, Holmes, who described Corcoran as "quite noisy, quite adequate, and quite noisy," came to rely heavily on the young man.[4]

Margaret Corcoran never spoke publicly about her clerkship during Octo-

This essay's contributing authors include Victor and James Brudney; Newton and Martha Minow; Abner J. and Mary L. Mikva; Robert M. and David O'Neil; Louis R. Cohen and Amanda Cohen Leiter; Charles F. Lettow, Renée Lettow Lerner, and Kristen Silverberg; Carter G. and Jessica Phillips; and J. Harvie III and Porter Wilkinson.

ber term 1966, likely because of the disastrous year she spent at the Court as well as her premature death. An average-at-best law student at Harvard, whose studies were impacted by her drinking and mood swings, Justice Black nevertheless extended Margaret a clerkship offer because of his friendship with her father. The hiring of Margaret Corcoran was a noteworthy event, with the *Washington Post* reporting on the selection of the "petite and attractive" Corcoran as only the second woman to clerk at the Supreme Court.[5]

> Initially, the Blacks had high hopes for Margaret. In a December 28, 1966 letter to Tommy Corcoran, Elizabeth Black wrote: You were nice to thank me for my kindness to Margaret. Really, though, having Margaret is its own reward. It is our pleasure! I have great faith that she will do a great deal to perpetuate the things that Hugo believes in. She is a daughter of whom you may be justly proud. Hugo and I both worry that she pushes herself too hard, but he is as exacting with her as he would want you to be with one of his children. He is eager to have her excel, as he thinks that she has fine capabilities. Margaret is a smart girl, but, better than that, she is pretty, feminine and generous hearted. We both hope that she will consider her year with Hugo a very outstanding one in her life.[6]

Yet the early promise that Margaret demonstrated faded as the term progressed, and soon Elizabeth Black was making references in her diary to Margaret's travails. In one entry, Mrs. Black recorded that Justice Black was "still upset because Margaret flew off the handle and said she could not do thirty-five *certs.* on the weekend. She had to go to parties with her daddy."[7]

Margaret's co-clerk during October term 1966, Stephen Susman, also remembers Margaret's failures as a law clerk. "I did all of her work that year, and I didn't complain one iota because Margaret provided my wife and I with a wonderful social life in Washington," recalled Susman.[8] He added that Margaret often arrived late to Black's chambers and "slept all day" in an upstairs office. As for how Black handled the situation, Susman stated "very well. He understood as soon as he appointed Margaret that it was a mistake and that he wasn't going to change Margaret."[9]

Thomas Corcoran biographer McKean writes that Corcoran himself knew that his daughter was floundering in the clerkship, and he tried to mitigate the damage by apologizing to the Blacks and "assisting her in writing legal briefs for the Justice."[10] Margaret's downward spiral continued after the clerkship, and on January 9, 1970, she took a fatal overdose of sleeping pills. Despite Margaret's mediocre performance as a law clerk, the Blacks were fond of the young woman and grieved her death. In a March 31, 1970, letter to Tommy Corcoran, Elizabeth Black writes: "I think of our lovely girl so often, and it is comforting to contemplate the lessons of Easter."[11]

There have been more fruitful parent/child clerkship combinations in the history of the Court, and many of those familial combinations have graciously agreed to share their experiences. Their recollections below offer a rare glimpse not only into the chambers of the justices but also the institutional evolution of the Supreme Court and the "clerkship institution," that is, the rules and norms surrounding the hiring and utilization of law clerks.

Victor Brudney (Rutledge, October terms 1942, 1943) and James Brudney (Blackmun, October term 1980)

I (Victor) clerked for Justice Rutledge from early 1943 when the justice was appointed through the summer of 1944, which spanned two Court terms. In 1943–44, each justice had one law clerk, and some of us had been friends before clerking or we grew to be close. While it may not have been the norm in that era, several other clerks served for multiterm periods during my tenure. By contrast, I (Jim) was one of four law clerks working for Justice Blackmun during October term 1980. Seven of the nine chambers had four law clerks, and all but one of the thirty-three clerks served for that single term.

Probably because of the small number of clerks and my extended tenure, I (Victor) had some interaction with justices from other chambers, as did a few of the other clerks. Relationships with Justices Hugo L. Black, Felix Frankfurter, and Frank Murphy grew initially from my friendship with their clerks and the fact that I would therefore often visit their chambers—which led over time to talking with their justices and getting to know them. Eventually, situations arose when there were serious, and occasionally humorous, exchanges with those justices regarding work being done on opinions. On one occasion, Justice Black came to me with a draft of an opinion on the permissible procedure for challenging a person's draft classification. Saying that he understood that I thought he (the justice) was something of a jingo, he handed the draft to me and asked me to take out any jingo language I might find in it—but not to touch anything else.

My sense, which I doubt I could have articulated at the time, was being part of a single community of the justices and their law clerks. There was plenty of tough and even angry disagreement among the justices, and the dialogue was something of which we as clerks were often aware.

I (Jim) did not have the same sense of a unitary justice–law clerk community when I clerked in October term 1980. Exchanges with other justices were almost exclusively through lunches where the four clerks from our chambers invited a justice to a local restaurant for what was primarily a social interaction. From my vantage point, the Court seemed to operate at times as separate law firms, each with a "partner" assisted by a team of loyal associates. I was friends with a number of clerks from outside the Blackmun chambers, but, given the size of the law clerk group, relations were not prevalently all that close. In addition, the very long hours spent working for Justice Blackmun left little or no time for visiting with other clerks in their justices' chambers. My one face-to-face exchange with another justice (John Paul Stevens) on a substantive matter came about through a draft opinion on which I had worked, but to my knowledge that kind of interaction was unusual.

Another difference between the early 1940s and early 1980s relates to the clerks' pre-Court legal experiences. In 1980–81, I (Jim) and virtually all other clerks had gone straight from law school to clerk for a federal appellate judge or occasionally, as in my case, a federal district court judge for the one or two years immediately preceding service at the Court. A lower court clerkship was viewed as the orthodox training or seasoning experience. I and my co-clerks therefore arrived at the Supreme Court with a judicially shaped perspective on what our work would be like. This preparatory orientation paralleled in some respects the pre-Court backgrounds of our justices: five of the nine had served as federal appellate judges and a sixth as a state supreme court justice.

In 1943–44, I (Victor) and some of my colleagues came to the Court with a very different set of legal exposures. As I recall, only the clerks for Justices Harlan Fiske Stone and Frankfurter had prior judicial clerkships. I had been an attorney at the Securities Exchange Commission (SEC) and in the solicitor general's office before clerking for Justice Rutledge. Others in my cohort had worked for a range of federal agencies prior to arriving at the Court: the SEC, the NLRB, the FCC, the DOJ Claims Division, and the Board of Economic Welfare. (A couple of clerks came straight from law school.) The clerks' modest experiences with how law applies in a political setting were more than matched by the backgrounds of the justices for whom we clerked. Justices Black and Murphy had extensive elected office experience, while Justices William O. Douglas, Stanley Reed, Robert H. Jackson, and Frankfurter had been influential figures in and around the Roosevelt administration. Only Justice Rutledge had served on a federal appellate court.

Looking backward (a risky endeavor, to be sure), it may be that my legal approach and intellectual orientation as a law clerk were influenced by these preclerkship experiences. Decision making at the Court often involves a blend of legal and policy judgments. The 1943–44 Court, functioning in an exigent wartime setting, included both justices and law clerks with some understanding of, and a lively interest in, how the political branches operated. This understanding and interest inevitably informed, if it did not infuse, the nature of legal analyses. I don't mean to suggest that the clerks amounted to much as contributors—we tended to take ourselves seriously and at times pompously, which may well have further limited our influence. But we approached our po-

sition with some firsthand appreciation for how policy as well as legal judgments were integral to the Court's work, and for such import as our views had
they were offered.

Law clerks during October term 1980 probably took ourselves just as seriously, but I (Jim) believe we spent most of our energies focused on judging as
a professional craft. By that I mean we were dedicated to producing and per-
fecting cert memos, bench memos, and draft opinions in a way that required
critical attention to the precise rhythms of legal argumentation before a court
and to a careful if at times colorless prose style. We were hardly unaware of
political realities: President Ronald Reagan was elected early in our term, and
no one doubted the significance of his election for the Court's future docket
and its membership. Yet I did not have firsthand experience with or any special
interest in how the executive branch, much less Congress, functioned.

Despite these differences, the clerkship experience was not without its moments of humor for both of us. An enjoyable feature of the Blackmun clerkship was having breakfast with the justice in the Court cafeteria on weekday
mornings. In the fall of 1980, as the workload ratcheted up and two co-clerks
had contracted colds or coughs, the justice said one morning, which happened
to be the day before Thanksgiving, that he was concerned about our health.
He then added, in his characteristically somber tone, "I want to make one
thing perfectly clear; I don't want any of you to be anywhere near this Court
on Christmas day." As we walked back up to chambers after breakfast, one of
my co-clerks pulled me aside and said, "You know what that means, right—we
had better be in here tomorrow." I scoffed at this implication, responding that
the justice was simply making clear his feelings about Christmas (this was well
before *expressio unius* had become a favored Court canon). The next morning,
Thanksgiving morning, I was in the shower at my apartment when I received a
phone call from that co-clerk. The message was "The Justice is looking for you;
he wants to go over the draft concurrence you worked on." I was dressed and at
the Court in reasonably short order.

Justice Frankfurter and I became sufficiently friendly during my Rutledge
clerkship so that one time when we encountered each other in the corridor, the
justice asked me whether I would know what was meant by the statements that
a young lady was "pretty" or "lovely" or "intelligent" or "smart" or "interesting."
I had earlier been tilting with the justice on the meaning of language in statutes,
and I replied that it might depend on whether the young lady was his sister or
relative or girlfriend or a stranger. The justice responded by telling me not to
be so uptight, that he was simply referring to the young lady he had heard was
to be married to John Frank (Justice Black's law clerk). I relaxed on realizing
that this was simply small talk, and told the justice that he might have seen her
yesterday because she had lunch with me at the Court. The justice said, "Oh,

I'm so sorry"—apparently thinking that I had been a competing suitor. A few weeks later, when the justice was chiding his own law clerk for working too late and his clerk said that he and his wife were waiting to go to dinner with me and a different young lady, the justice remarked on what he characterized as "Vic's amatory resilience."

Newton Minow (Vinson, October term 1951) and Martha Minow (Marshall, October term 1980)

Newton: When I was a law clerk for Chief Justice Vinson in the early 1950s, it never occurred to me that one day I would have a daughter serving as a Supreme Court law clerk. It turned out that my wife and I have three daughters who all became lawyers (the last thing we anticipated!) and that one daughter would serve as a Supreme Court law clerk twenty-nine years after I did. Martha told us that when she arrived to fill out her papers in the Supreme Court's clerk's office, she was asked if she was related to me, and she said, "Yes, he is my dad." Martha was surprised that someone at the Court remembered me. But when she next went to the Supreme Court library to get a library card, she was also asked if she was related to me. She said, "Yes, he's my dad," to which the librarian responded, "Please tell your father to return the books he still has out." The librarian was kidding, but it did demonstrate that there is not much staff turnover at the Supreme Court!

There is no greater honor for a young lawyer to serve as a law clerk in our country's Supreme Court. My generation of law clerks included my law partner Howard Trienens, future chief justice Bill Rehnquist, future secretary of state Warren Christopher, and future chief judge of the Court of Appeals for the District of Columbia Circuit Abner Mikva. It did not include any women—despite the Court's role as the defender and champion of equality. Fortunately, things have changed, and thankfully, for the better.

Martha: One family photograph we cherish shows my dad as a law clerk for Chief Justice Vinson standing next to the seated chief justice—who held my baby sister Nell on his lap. Growing up, I never thought I would be a lawyer, much less have the chance to be a law clerk myself. Very few women were lawyers when I was a child, but I did have a woman cousin—also named Martha—who was a lawyer, and I had parents who believed that their daughters could do anything. Discussions at the dinner table may have been the best preparation for law school and clerking.

When I was a law clerk for Justice Thurgood Marshall, I was one of three women clerks among some thirty-four of us. Several people working at the Court connected me with my dad. It was a thrill to bring my parents to visit the Court. Dad tells a story about once driving Chief Justice Vinson home (that being one of the clerk's jobs then), and the chief justice was unusually silent. Dad asked if something was wrong; the Chief reported that he'd been asked that day to consider becoming the commissioner of Major League Baseball. Dad replied that this was wonderful but surely the chief justice could not step down to take that job. A great fan of the game, Chief Justice Vinson replied, "I know, and it is killing me!"

Dad also recalls when he and his fellow clerks talked with Justice Felix Frankfurter about postponing the Court's consideration of *Brown v. Board of Education*. Apparently the justice made note that without the reargument, the case would be resolved in an election year. How amazing that nearly thirty years later, the lead lawyer in that case was a distinguished justice, who gave me the privilege of serving as a clerk.

Abner J. Mikva (Minton, October term 1951) and Mary L. Mikva (Brennan, October term 1981)

Both Abner Mikva and his eldest daughter, Mary, who cowrote this recollection, spent much of their legal careers as judges. Abner was on the Federal Court of Appeals for the District of Columbia Circuit from 1979 until 1994; Mary has been a state court judge in the Circuit Court of Cook County since 2004. At the outset of their legal careers, they also each clerked for justices of the U.S. Supreme Court. Abner clerked for Justice Sherman Minton from August 1951 until July 1952. In August 1981, Mary began clerking for Justice William J. Brennan Jr., who had been appointed by President Eisenhower to replace Justice Minton, working in the same offices her father had worked in thirty years earlier.

As they discussed their clerkships, Abner and Mary recognized that, in many respects, Justices Minton and Brennan used their clerks quite differently. Justice Minton had only two clerks, Abner and his co-clerk, Ray Gray. Justice Minton primarily used his clerks to analyze the petitions for certiorari and write short memos with recommendations on each petition that was going to be discussed in conference. He also used them to prepare bench memos on cases to be argued.

Most often, Justice Minton would dictate the opinions that he had been assigned to write to his secretary. His law clerks would proof the opinions and check cites and could comment on use of case law and grammar, but generally not on the substance or the analysis. However, on rare occasions, law clerks would do a first draft. Abner was particularly proud of one opinion, *United States v. Wunderlich*,[12] which Justice Minton approved without changing a word. Unfortunately, soon thereafter Congress effectively overruled the Supreme Court opinion in *Wunderlich* with a statutory change.

Justice Brennan had four clerks, and they all spent most of their time drafting, editing, and discussing the opinions that Justice Brennan had been assigned or the dissents that he had decided to write. Clerks wrote short bench memos on each case that was to be argued, but most of the analysis occurred when the justice discussed all of the cases that were set for argument with all four of his clerks, the day before argument. The justice would then come back from the Court's postargument conference with his assignments, and the clerks would meet again with the justice to discuss those opinions that he was going to write. An opinion would then be assigned to one of the clerks to do a first draft, but all four law clerks had to read and sign off on every draft opinion before it went to the justice for him to review.

The way that the Court dealt with petitions for certiorari was one of the bigger changes between 1951 and 1981. When Abner clerked for Justice Minton, each of the justices had his own law clerks review the petitions and write memos regarding whether the justice wanted to be one of the four votes in favor of hearing the case. In order to lessen the burden of reviewing thousands of petitions, the chief justice circulated a "dead list" of petitions for certiorari, and those cases were not discussed or voted on at conference unless a justice specifically asked that the case be discussed.

By the time Mary clerked for Justice Brennan, Chief Justice Warren Burger had started the "cert pool" including himself and Justices Lewis F. Powell, Byron White, Harry Blackmun, and William H. Rehnquist. The clerks for the justices who were in the cert pool shared the burden of writing memos on each of the cases, and the memo and recommendation went to all members of the pool, who tended to vote as a bloc. The cert pool was started over the strong objection of Justice Brennan, who continued to review his own petitions for certiorari. He did not even use his clerks in this review. He told them he could quickly "smell" whether a petition had merit.

The relationship between clerks in different chambers changed quite a bit during the thirty years between Abner's clerkship and Mary's. When Abner clerked there were a total of eighteen clerks, and the clerks were all very friendly, except for Bill Rehnquist, who clerked for Justice Robert H. Jackson and kept to himself. Abner believes that law clerk Rehnquist kept to himself both because he viewed most of the other clerks as quite liberal and because he was, by nature, a bit of a loner. Rehnquist, however, was never unfriendly. The clerks would all eat together in the clerks' private dining room. They would all play basketball in the late afternoon, often against other Court personnel who would routinely beat them.

By the time Mary joined the Court, most of the justices had four clerks, and the group, which now constituted more than thirty law clerks, had begun to polarize along the political lines of their justices. Thus, as a Brennan clerk,

Mary socialized regularly with Justice Thurgood Marshall's clerks and Justice Harry Blackmun's clerks, but did not socialize very much with the clerks from other chambers (except for the small number of women clerks, who sought each other out, regardless of whom they clerked for). The male clerks did still play basketball every afternoon. However, the practice of all the clerks eating together was over.

The hours at the Supreme Court changed a lot over the thirty years. When Abner worked for Justice Minton, the justice came in about ten, and the clerks usually arrived at work only about a half an hour before that. The justice left around five, and the clerks a half an hour later. The clerks generally worked Saturday but seldom Sunday and seldom in the evenings. Justice Minton's clerks had time enough, once or twice a week, to play golf before work, come back to chambers, use the justice's shower, and be at their desks before the justice arrived. While some of the other chambers worked longer hours, overall the year of the clerkship was viewed by the clerks as a great time to get to know Washington, to socialize with each other, and as a break before they started their legal careers in earnest.

By the time that Mary began her clerkship, almost all of the clerks worked extraordinarily long hours. The computer system at the Court shut down on Sunday evening. However, other than that forced night off, clerks generally worked most nights and weekends.

The role for women had also changed. When Abner was a law clerk, all the justices and all of the law clerks were male and had always been. The year that Mary clerked was the year that Justice Sandra Day O'Connor joined the Court as the first female justice. Mary's recollection is that there were five female law clerks that term. Justice O'Connor started an early morning exercise class for the female clerks and the secretaries, and was a great symbol to all the women at the Court that their role was changing.

Mary was only Justice Brennan's second female law clerk, and she felt a burden to perform well so as to open the door for more female clerks. Mary had heard that Justice Brennan had some concerns about female clerks. His four clerks had to work very closely together, and he may have worried about how that dynamic would be impacted by having a female. His first female clerk was Marsha Berzon, in 1974. After that, it was seven terms before Mary was hired in 1981. Then it was four terms until the next female was hired for 1985. After that, he pretty much had a female clerk every term until his retirement. Although Mary worried about the justice's hesitation to hire female law clerks, the justice never expressed any concerns to her directly or made her feel uncomfortable in any way.

In Abner's day, a Supreme Court clerkship did not open the kind of doors it did by the time that Mary was a Supreme Court law clerk. Abner did not really think about the long-term job prospects when he applied for a Supreme

Court clerkship. He was encouraged to apply by Edward Levi, who was dean of University of Chicago Law School, and Bernard Meltzer, who was one of his favorite professors.

In Washington, D.C., a Supreme Court clerkship was an excellent credential. However, back in Chicago, it was less appreciated at that time. In fact, Abner, who returned to Chicago after his clerkship, was frequently asked why he had "wasted" a year. Abner wanted to be an assistant United States attorney, and Justice Minton wrote a handwritten letter, recommending him to Otto Kerner Jr., who was then the United States Attorney for the Northern District of Illinois. However, Kerner was not impressed, and, when Abner could not provide the endorsement of his ward committeeman, he was not hired. However, Abner did find a job at a small law firm at which Arthur Goldberg was the senior partner, and he later served in all branches of government, including time in the Illinois state legislature, the U.S. Congress, and the D.C. Court of Appeals, and as White House counsel for President Clinton. As time went on, the clerkship's value grew. In fact, every time Abner was introduced, throughout a long career and a number of other achievements, the fact that he had clerked on the Supreme Court was mentioned.

By the time that Mary finished her clerkship, law firms throughout the country and numerous government agencies aggressively recruited the Supreme Court law clerks. She ended up at a small boutique firm in Washington, D.C., for a short time and then returned to Chicago, where she practiced as a criminal defense lawyer, as a lawyer for the city, and as a plaintiffs' employment lawyer, before she was elected to the circuit court. She credits her credential as a Supreme Court law clerk with allowing her to change directions several times throughout her career and then get elected to the bench.

Both Abner and Mary have looked back on their clerkships from their later role as judges. They have treasured their relationships with their clerks as they did their relationships with their justices. They both appreciate the important role for the clerks in bringing youth and new ideas to an institution that tends to get stale and to justices and judges who are often removed from new ideas and cutting-edge thinking. At its best, the judicial branch, with its clerkship tradition, manages to fuse the energy and new ideas of youth with the experience and wisdom of legal elders, all in the pursuit of what one hopes are just and fair outcomes.

Robert M. O'Neil (Brennan, October term 1962) and David O'Neil (Ginsburg, October term 2001)

While the two generations of O'Neils (Robert and David) share certain experiences—both majored in American history, both spent three years at the Harvard Law School and served on the *Law Review,* and each took two years out between college and graduate school—the paths by which they traveled to the Court are strikingly different. One, for example, followed many of his class-mates in clerking for a federal appellate judge, which had become all but man-datory by the twenty-first century for those seeking a Supreme Court clerk-ship, while the other found no occasion to clerk elsewhere, as relatively few of his contemporaries had done. The main difference in Robert's and David's paths to the Court, however, lies in our respective previous knowledge of the Supreme Court and in our shared inspiration pursuing a clerkship there.

PATHS TO THE COURT

After a stint in graduate school studying and teaching history, Robert trans-ferred to law school and on the side taught speech courses at Tufts University. He then spent a year as research assistant to Paul Freund, perhaps the preemi-nent constitutional scholar of his generation. The task on which they collabo-rated was the volume on the Hughes Court for the *Oliver Wendell Holmes De-vise,* which was to be Freund's magnum opus along with several shorter works (the Hughes volume was never finished despite the efforts of several other able researchers, who were also Brennan clerks, including Daniel Rezneck and Roy Schotland. G. Edward White eventually completed it as a splendid tribute to Freund).[13]

One day in the fall of 1961, Freund stopped by for coffee, an informal touch we treasured as his junior associates. Fairly directly, he asked whether Robert might enjoy a year clerking for Justice William J. Brennan Jr., who had joined the Court five years earlier but had already established a reputation for protec-tion of civil liberties and especially First Amendment interests. Indeed, what was already striking to O'Neil (as he prepared to teach his initial course on free speech and press at San Francisco State University) was how ingeniously Jus-tice Brennan had managed to cobble together a tenuous majority. Sometimes he managed to enlist Justice Felix Frankfurter, though more often relied upon other unlikely free expression adherents.

Given these constraints, Robert and his co-clerk (future judge) Richard Pos-ner naturally assumed that our Brennan apprenticeship would be a comparably perilous process. But late in the summer, after surviving a stroke, Frankfurter retired. He noted quite publicly that his successor would almost certainly be Jewish, but hoped it would not be "that damned traffic cop from Connecticut" (Governor Abraham Ribicoff).

Justice Arthur Goldberg immediately became an unshakeable Brennan ally the day he joined the Court, visibly welcomed by President John F. Ken-nedy, who strode up the Court's center aisle while extending a hand across the bench. Indeed, during Brennan's final years, we were struck by the presence of photos of only two colleagues; where one would have expected to see pictures of Earl Warren, William O. Douglas, or Hugo Black on the credenza, there were pictures only of Justices Goldberg and Thurgood Marshall—his two revered protégés. Needless to note, the ensuing 1962 term differed dramatically from our expectations only months earlier; when asked right after the Court rose for the summer how many times he had dissented—we assumed that number would be at least a dozen—he held up four fingers.

Unlike Robert, but thanks in large part to Robert's experience with Justice Brennan, David grew up with a keen understanding of what a special and unique opportunity it is to work closely with a Supreme Court justice. Regaled since a young age with Robert's stories of Justice Brennan's wisdom, grace, and kindness, David was thrilled when, one spring day in 1996, Robert invited him to lunch with Justice Brennan in the retired justice's chambers. Although the justice was somewhat frail by that point, David saw firsthand the qualities that had left such a lasting impact on Robert.

Two events from that lunch stand out in David's mind. The first was the moment that Justice Brennan looked at David and, with a firm gaze, raised his hand—this time holding out two fingers, not four. "Your father and I," the justice said, "were like this." The second was after lunch, when Robert and David were discussing with the justice's clerk a decision that David was then mulling about which of two paralegal job offers to accept for the next year—one focusing on corporate real estate transactions and the other in support of a litigation practice. To the surprise of the participants in the conversation, Justice Brennan, who appeared to be immersed in the newspaper, perked up and with a boyish grin enthusiastically interjected "litigation!"—the choice that he believed would be more fun, exciting, and rewarding. David not only took that advice, but he also resolved at that point to do whatever he could to earn the opportunity to return to the Supreme Court as a law clerk.

That opportunity came four years later, when, after sending résumés and applications to every justice—a practice unknown in Robert's time but now standard protocol—David received a call to interview with Justice Ginsburg on the Tuesday before Thanksgiving in 1999. Justice Ginsburg offered David the job at the end of that interview, and it was fitting that David's first stop after receiving the good news was to his family for a particularly joyous Thanksgiving celebration.

EXPERIENCES ON THE COURT

A major element in Justice Brennan's genius as a Court observer, or even manager, was his uncanny capacity to invoke majorities for consistently liberal precepts. Conversely, he skillfully eschewed cases he could not win. One afternoon, after conference, Brennan and Goldberg were chatting in the corridor. Goldberg was puzzled that his senior colleague had not joined in granting cert in a Texas case in which an indigent defendant was compelled to waive his privilege against incrimination as a condition of being represented by court-appointed counsel. Brennan turned to him, asking with a touch of classic Brennan humor, "And where, Arthur, were you going to get the fifth vote?" The senior justice knew, as his junior colleague did not but soon learned, that California's former governor (and tough-minded Bay Area prosecutor) would not join his otherwise liberal colleagues on that issue. Brennan's four 1962 term dissents, however, were in no sense mistakes, but rather were rare cases in which he genuinely disagreed, usually with Warren. But the near unanimity of that first post-Frankfurter term was truly extraordinary.

In September 2013, the surviving clerks (seventeen out of nineteen) from the 1962 term joined Justice Ruth Bader Ginsburg in a fiftieth reunion at the Court. Even in the best of times, there are many fewer former clerks from Robert's day than from David's. The chief always recruited three clerks, reflecting his greater workload. For years Justice William O. Douglas traded one clerkship slot for an additional editorial assistant, and Justice Potter Stewart used a rotational process to create two-year stints for his clerks. But the entire group was small enough to arrange monthly luncheons with such remarkable guests as Dean Acheson, Robert Kennedy, and Dean Rusk, as well as informal visits with most of the other justices. Sadly, along with the annual White House dinner that members of the Court and their spouses regularly attended, that tradition seems to have atrophied. Those of us who recall those events regret the demise of such opportunities as a casualty of the times.

One further facet of the Brennan experience also bears mention. To the best of Robert's knowledge, all of the 115 earlier and later Brennan clerks seem to have been fully involved in both discussion of pending cases before conference and in drafting opinions after votes were recorded and shared within chambers. However, clearly some of us were more deeply involved than others over the years.

After we received our initial assignments in early October, Richard Posner and I spent most of the ensuing week drafting a first effort. The justice took the drafts home, anticipating a Monday morning coffee hour review of both drafts. With feigned anger, he strode into our office and slammed both drafts down upon our respective desks. "I've spent all weekend, and I can't make more than a few cosmetic changes. I don't want to see them again. Take them both to the printer." The simple fact was that we were both shameless mimics, having had substantial journalistic experience. We unconscionably overused terms like "plainly," one of Brennan's favorites. But a vital caveat follows: during our long-scheduled luncheon with the justice, one of our less deferential colleagues asked about a relatively obscure footnote in a utility regulation case. Robert panicked, doubting very much that the justice had read the footnote.

How wrong could I have been? The justice smiled, and replied to the impertinent inquiry, "Dick, if you'd read the next sentence you have a better sense of just what we meant." Such questions never recurred.

It was a bit like Brennan's incredible expertise in labor law, spawned both by his father's union roots and his extensive practice in the only law firm ever to feature in its title the names of two justices (Mahlon Pitney and Brennan). One day Justice Byron R. White, still new to the Court, sought out the Chief, puzzled by the nonassignment of two arbitration cases in his second term. "Chief," lamented White (whom Warren always called "Whizzer," despite his clear preference for "Byron"), "I thought I was the Court's labor law expert." Warren responded with a classic smile, "We have no experts here." In fact, it was apparent that there was one other labor law expert, named Brennan, who ended up with all the arbitration cases he could possibly handle.

By the time David began his clerkship for Justice Ginsburg in July 2001, much had changed about the Court and its inhabitants. In the nearly forty years between Robert's and David's clerkships, the Court had been thrust into the middle of increasingly contentious disputes. While protests outside the Court were a rare event in Robert's time, in David's they were a routine, even expected, part of life as a clerk. The term before David's had been a particularly searing one, and among the outgoing clerks there remained a sense of lingering animosity from the battles of the previous year. Perhaps as a result, the clerks of David's year were intent on maintaining close and collegial relationships that endured through the inevitable disagreements about ideology or cases. The clerks of October term 2001 have been remarkably successful in that effort: twelve years later, they remain in frequent contact and go out of their way to support one another in their lives and careers.

For David, the year with Justice Ginsburg was intensely rewarding. Justice Ginsburg is many things—a skilled lawyer, advocate, judge, and manager—but she is perhaps above all else an excellent teacher. Like any good teacher, she began the year by making clear to her new pupils the unwavering and exacting standards she expected in her chambers, and her demeanor was that of a teacher at the start of a fall semester: welcoming but firm, cordial but not overly familiar. David and his fellow clerks recognized immediately that the justice's respect needed to be earned, and that the only way to do so was to strive constantly to meet the very high bar she set for herself and those around her. Each clerk surely has memories of instances in which they fell short—failed to capture the factual background in the most precise way, obscured a key distinction, or used five words where one would suffice—but each clerk also has the pride of recalling moments in which he or she met the justice's expectations and merited her praise, which was all the more satisfying because it was offered only when genuinely deserved.

David's fondest memory of the year was the steady evolution of his relationship with the justice from professional to familial. Over time, as David worked closely with the justice and earned her confidence, her first-day professorial demeanor gave way to that of a warm and generous mentor and ultimately, by the end of the term, to something very close to a family member. Justice Ginsburg speaks often of her family of law clerks, and for her that phrase is more than just an analogy; it is a genuine expression of her deep affection for those who have had the intense experience of spending a year in her chambers. That affection is borne out in the keen interest she takes in all aspects of her clerk's lives, from career developments to the birth of children, who invariably receive their own "RBG Grandclerk" T-shirt accompanied by a personal note from the justice. For David, whose interest in the Court was inspired by one member of his family, leaving the Court with this new familial bond was particularly meaningful.

Louis R. Cohen (Harlan, October term 1967) and Amanda Cohen Leiter (Stevens, October term 2003)

Louis: Law clerks generally treasure their experience, but working for Justice John Marshall Harlan during October term 1967 was a special prize. He was, first of all, a wonderful "senior partner," a born manager who knew how to get the very best work out of his subordinates. He has a well-deserved reputation for craftsmanship, and at least a small part of that came from his skill in making craftsmen out of the junior members of the team. It was also the height of the Warren Court, and he was a frequent dissenter, fighting battles (now long since lost) against reapportionment, "incorporation" of Bill of Rights provisions into the Fourteenth Amendment, and various new principles of criminal procedure; this meant a lot of separate opinions to draft and, whatever one's own beliefs, the heady adventure of fighting for lost causes. And by that point in his life, Justice Harlan had lost most of his eyesight, which made our experience all the more intimate: there was a lot of reading drafts aloud and editing them in conversation; there were a lot of chambers meetings to discuss the decisions that had been reached in conference, which he needed to tell us from memory rather than notes. We were also a larger part of his social life, routinely joining him at lunch and at home, than were clerks to justices who didn't have this limitation.

Justice Harlan, an Eisenhower appointee, was in many ways a conservative, but he was not a "textualist" or an "originalist" (terms not then in use). Although I don't remember him putting it this way, he thought of constitutional interpretation as a common law process, in which the text and what can be gleaned of the framing generation's intentions often don't get you very far in resolving current issues, and you have to rely heavily on the wisdom of your predecessors on the Court and, inevitably, on your own judgment, exercised with as much care and restraint as possible. That approach—apart from its theoretical merits—was another spur to intimacy between justice and law clerk. There was no doubt about whose views counted in the end, but he was constantly trying out theories and readings of past cases and listening carefully to ours, often with a wonderful chuckle when a clerk had either scored a point or, more frequently, missed one.

I enjoyed an especially close personal relationship because my wife and I lived around the corner from the Harlans until the birth of our daughter (my present coauthor). He instructed me to come by for coffee every morning and ride to the Court with him and ride back with him each evening. This meant that my day in the office ended when his did, something today's clerks can only envy, but it also meant that work with him on the Court's cases often took place before and after the time in the office.

The mechanics of the Court's work have changed a lot since 1967–68. Back then, most justices had two clerks; Justice Harlan had three, ostensibly because of his blindness, but I think in fact the arrangement was partly the result—and partly the cause—of the large number of opinions he wrote. We worked on manual typewriters, constantly changing ribbons and pressing very hard to produce dark typescripts that he could, with great effort, read (it was almost literally an example of working one's fingers to the bone). There were of course no computers in the Court, and there were also no copying machines; the latter had been invented, but the Court thought they would compromise security, so the only way of getting any copy of anything, other than using carbon paper in one's own typewriter, was to take it to the printer (a term that then meant a person) in the basement. There was also no cert pool. Each justice had his (no need, back then, to say "or her"; in fact, they were still called "Mr. Justice . . .") own way of reviewing cert petitions. Justice Harlan's way was to have us deal them out like playing cards and type a memo on every one; for better or worse, his very limited reading ability and our callused fingers made for economical memos.

During my term, I had lots of contact with clerks from other chambers. We ate lunch together and chatted in hallways. We also debated cases among ourselves fairly extensively. That may have been helped by the fact that there were fewer clerks, generally two per justice, and almost all were on the first floor. We also had contact with other justices. William J. Brennan Jr., Potter Stewart, Byron R. White, Hugo Black, and Thurgood Marshall all knew who I was and would engage in casual conversations. None of them came to chambers to talk to law clerks, for Justice Harlan would (properly) have regarded that as an intrusion. Justice Harlan had annual reunions that were very jolly affairs, in large part because the clerks all felt great loyalty to him. Some of my lasting personal friendships are with Harlan clerks from other years. I also remember taking baby Amanda over to meet the justice and Mrs. Harlan. He was delighted; her reaction is not recorded. Justice Harlan died in 1971, so the postclerkship relationship with him was not lengthy.

I once described Justice Harlan as the man I would send to Mars to show the Martians what human beings could be like. I don't know what percentage of clerks would say that they would not trade their clerkships for anything else in their professional lives, but I'm in that group.

Amanda: I had the opportunity to clerk thirty-six years later, in "OT03." My experience was similar to my father's in many ways, but there were also important differences. Like Justice Harlan, Justice John Paul Stevens is a terrific manager—I couldn't have hoped for better. He treated my three co-clerks and me with respect and knew just how hard to push to prompt our very best work. At the same time, he trusted us to produce that work and kept the perfect distance—never micromanaging but always making himself available if we had questions or concerns. He actively solicited our opinions but did not hesitate to remind us of key precedents that he invariably remembered (with chapter and verse) but we sometimes did not, to debate us when he disagreed, and to insist (gently and properly) on his own view if we still had doubts.

Justice Stevens's willingness to press his view in the face of disagreement underlies one of his best-known habits: he often wrote separately about cases, whether in concurrence, concurrence in judgment, or dissent. For his clerks, this trait necessarily meant more work, but we willingly rose to the occasion once we understood the rationale. He is a firm believer in the common law tradition: (in my words) law as a wall, ever under construction, growing upward toward some more perfect justice, past opinions—even those that failed to persuade at the time they were drafted—serving as the foundation for future legal trends. The only views that are lost to time, he patiently explained, are those that are never committed to writing.

My fondest memories of learning from the justice concern our location and his attire. On cold days, we sat around a low table in chambers, Stevens at the head, sometimes hastily tying his bow tie before argument, sometimes informally dressed in tennis shorts and athletic socks pulled up to his knees. In spring, we chatted over lunch around a patio table in one of the Court's four hidden courtyards, discussing that day's arguments or votes while the justice ate a peanut butter sandwich brought from home.

Because of moments like those, I will always associate true wisdom with humility (and peanut butter sandwiches). The justice's memory is legendary and his intellect formidable, but he never chided us for forgetting some fact or pressing a faulty argument. His only boasts concerned his tennis game. Further, although he regularly disagreed with his colleagues, sometimes vehemently, I cannot recall his ever suggesting that their views resulted from anything other than a reasoned analysis that led them in a different direction than his own.

During that year, Justice Stevens was not alone in his attitude of collegiality and respect. I have certainly heard that in some years prior and post, divisive cases have created serious divisions within and among chambers. But even though we had our fair share of tough issues—from campaign finance, to the detention of foreign nationals, to the addition of the phrase "under God" to the Pledge of Allegiance—our nine bosses for the most part seemed truly to enjoy each other, and I was lucky to have thirty-four co-clerks who could disagree during the workday and then chat happily at weekly evening gatherings.

There was a tradition that the justices would each go out to lunch (or tea) with the clerks from the other chambers. We did that with six of the nine—tea with Ruth Bader Ginsburg in her chambers, a big communal brownbag lunch with David Souter, lunch in chambers with Sandra Day O'Connor, out to lunch with William H. Rehnquist and Clarence Thomas. I don't recall that we did anything with the others. These are the memories I treasure, but other aspects of that year also bear mention. As my dad notes, the Court has changed a lot since his day. Most important, the weekly clerk happy hours now involve not just wives but husbands and partners, and we represented a variety of races, ethnicities, and sexual orientations. Also, more than a few clerks were juggling the responsibilities of the job with care for young children—my own son learned to crawl up stairs by practicing on the Court's marble staircases.

There were more mundane differences, too. We had not one but two computer networks, one for internal emails and opinion drafts, and a separate one for external emails and research. To ensure this separation, each clerk had two computers at his or her desk, with only a monitor and a switch to connect them. Further, the advent of the Internet meant we could do much of our research online and on our own.

Yet some things remained wonderfully the same. The fabulous Court library and librarians still proved invaluable, particularly if we needed to refute a historical argument by one of the justice's originalist colleagues. The stacks of cert petitions and briefs that arrived each week still sported covers in precisely specified shades of gray, blue, red, tan, orange, or green. And the Court still declined to broadcast its arguments out of concern that arguing for a panel of nine is and should remain a very different exercise than arguing for a television (or radio) audience.

Finally, I can't resist closing by saying that while Justices Harlan and Stevens exemplify innumerable outstanding traits, if I were given the opportunity to send a stellar example of humanity to Mars, I would pick my dad.

Charles F. Lettow (Burger, October term 1969),
Renée Lettow Lerner (daughter; Kennedy, October term 1996),
and Kristen Silverberg (daughter-in-law; Thomas, October term 1999)

We have a few things in common respecting our clerkships for justices, but only a few. Each of us clerked for a circuit judge before clerking at the Court, and each of those circuit judges had previously sent, and continued to send, other clerks to the Court to serve clerkships for justices. The similarities end there. We went to different undergraduate colleges and different law schools and, after the clerkships, have taken different professional paths. For each of us, however, the year clerking for a justice was demanding, instructive, and memorable.

A historian who looked at the Court with a long perspective would almost certainly consider that each of us clerked for a justice during the "modern" era, even though one of us clerked there over forty years ago. The number of clerks to justices has been roughly the same throughout those years, as have the clerks' functions (the exception forty-plus years ago was that Justice William O. Douglas had only one clerk).

A few changes are, nonetheless, notable. First, no woman served as a law clerk during the year Charles clerked for Chief Justice Warren Burger. Second, from a law clerk's perspective, an aspect of the work that has changed markedly is the resources that were available. Charles clerked at a time when the chief justice's clerks had great familiarity with petitions for certiorari on the nonpaid docket because they prepared memoranda for the entire Court on those cases. That was just prior to the advent of copying machines at the Court, and those memoranda were circulated on "flimsies," that is, carbon copies on thin paper.

The Court had a small typing pool that received typewritten drafts from the chief justice's law clerks, usually with handwritten annotations and corrections, and then prepared a "fair" final version for circulation. The more junior justices received relatively faint carbon copies, but nonetheless seemed to cope. For paid cases, each justice's chambers separately handled the petitions. This was just prior to the initiation of the cert pool. In the chief justice's chambers at the time, the memoranda on paid petitions were folded around the petitions, responses, replies, and any amicus briefs, secured by a rubber band, and put in the chief justice's hands well before the weekly conference. After review, he would then prepare and circulate an "X-Deny" list of petitions that were not set for discussion at the conference. Any justice could, and did, take petitions off that list and include them in the petitions to be discussed.

Other facilities at the Court at that time would similarly be viewed as archaic today. The Court had nothing akin to a computer. Legal precedents were available in books, not via online, computer-based resources. Electronic correcting typewriters were the current innovation in use at the Court. The typewriters used by the clerks were purchased by the clerks themselves. Drafts of opinions would be typewritten and reviewed and revised with interlineations until a draft was sufficiently polished to be sent downstairs to the Court's print shop, which was located on the lower level. At that point, further revisions could be made until the draft was ready to be circulated. Proper use of printers' marks was a necessary skill. The law clerks invariably had previously acquired that training through work on law reviews and law journals, which at that time were all put in final form by print shops using the same system.

By the time Renée and Kristen clerked in the late 1990s (for Justices Kennedy and Thomas, respectively), petitions for certiorari filed with the Court were distributed evenly—and apparently randomly—among all the chambers participating in the cert pool. All chambers were part of the cert pool at that time, except those of Justice John Paul Stevens. The chambers then further divided the petitions for certiorari among the clerks. A clerk receiving a petition for certiorari read it, the response, the reply, any submissions by amici, and the view of the government if applicable. The clerk then wrote a cert memo, discussing the facts, the law, and whether the petition met the criteria for granting a writ of certiorari. The memo could vary in length from a paragraph to several pages, depending on the complexity and "cert worthiness" of the issue. At the end, the clerk made a recommendation: "deny," "grant," "call for the views of the solicitor general," and so forth. Justice Antonin Scalia always told any clerk he talked to about the subject—which he made sure was all of them—"You can never go wrong recommending 'deny.'"

There were many barriers to obtaining a grant of certiorari, including procedural requirements, such as whether the issue had been properly raised below. An eager clerk might overlook these restrictions. In addition, justices often liked an issue to "percolate" for some time in other courts to get opinions from different judges before deciding an issue themselves. Justice Scalia said that almost all cert-worthy issues would come before the Court repeatedly. Most clerks took Justice Scalia's advice seriously, and recommended "grant" sparingly, at most once or twice during a term. There were ways a clerk could flag a case for a closer look by other chambers without recommending "grant." One clerk wrote a long cert memo in a case on a widespread and contested issue, ending with the recommendation: "Close case, deny." The Court ultimately granted certiorari. The cert pool system had worked.

It was, Renée believes, a good thing that Justice Stevens's clerks did not participate in the cert pool, although Justice Stevens's clerks might not have seen it that way. Justice Stevens had three clerks (every other chambers had four), and those three clerks had to address every petition that was filed. The extra check could prove valuable in flagging issues for the Court. Certainly Justice Stevens seemingly had a different approach to cert petitions than other justices, and appeared more likely to vote in favor of granting certiorari.

The Court had developed technologically by the time Renée and Kristen clerked, and research was conducted primarily online. Clerks had access to email when Renée arrived in the summer of 1996, although only to send communications within the Court, not to addresses outside the building. The Court had adopted a number of additional measures to try to protect the privacy of the Court's deliberations. For example, clerks ate in a separate area of the cafeteria, with a wall of glass dividing the clerks from tourists, members of the press, and others. Clerks from all chambers regularly had lunch there. Free from worries about being overheard, clerks discussed topics ranging from pending cases to politics to sports and anything else of interest. The clerks were of different legal and political views, and could express opinions strongly, although not rudely, as Renée recalls.

For clerks in both the late 1960s and 1990s, the working day and week tended to be a relatively long one. Saturdays were virtually a regular workday, except that clerks typically left in the late afternoon. Chief Justice Warren Burger would fairly often lunch with his clerks on Saturdays, having brought in soup or something light to eat and having stored it in the chambers' refrigerator.

The pace of work was sufficiently demanding that a clerk did not have very many occasions to reflect on the significance of the Court's role and the clerk's very minor and temporary contribution to the Court's work. Once in a great while, an event would occur that caused a bit of reflection, however. At the time Charles clerked, three of the chief justice's clerks had their desks in a small office to the north of the Court's conference room. A thick wall covered by a bookcase plus a heavy red velvet curtain on the doorway from that office to the conference room separated the two rooms and ensured that the conference room was well screened from the clerks' office. A set of *U.S. Reports* was shelved on the bookcase.

When working on an opinion citing a very early decision, Charles checked the relevant report of the decision and happened to glance at the flyleaf of the volume. That book, and a number of others, bore Chief Justice John Marshall's distinctive signature. Chief Justice Marshall had obviously used those volumes, and over the years they had remained with the chief justice's chambers. The Court's antiquarians soon had those volumes transferred elsewhere for better preservation.

For Renée and Kristen several decades later, a feature of clerking on the Court was the all-night vigils in death penalty cases. At that time, executions were often scheduled for the middle of the night or very early morning. As the time of execution approached, counsel might file a flurry of last-minute petitions for certiorari and stays of execution (the petitioner had nearly always previously filed a petition for certiorari within the ordinary time, which had been denied). A clerk for the justice assigned to the circuit in which the execution was to take place typically stayed in chambers, awaiting these petitions and helping the justice write a memo or memos to the other justices. This process sometimes meant that the clerk had to spend almost the entire night in chambers (many states have since moved executions to the middle of the day, so these vigils are generally no longer necessary). A considerable amount of administrative coordination was needed to handle these petitions, which was ably done by the Court's staff attorney who handled emergency filings. The clerks appreciated her calmness, clear-headedness, and organizational skills.

For Kristen, one important and memorable aspect of the year was the "clerk conferences" in Justice Thomas's chambers prior to oral argument. The four clerks and Justice Thomas would debate at length the merits of each case. If the clerks found themselves in agreement, one clerk would often play "devil's advocate" to test the group's assumptions, a role Justice Thomas enjoyed as well. A clerk conference might take several hours, although the group usually found time at the end of the session to talk about sports (and especially Nebraska Cornhuskers football). Renée recalls discussions about particular cases with Justice Anthony Kennedy and the clerks at which each person had his or her say. Justice Kennedy, who likes to teach and has a visual streak, often used a white board and different colored markers to diagram ideas.

Outside events and circumstances can have an effect on the Court wholly apart from its caseload. When Charles clerked, protestors against the Vietnam War would occasionally clash with police on the streets of Washington. At those times, the chief justice would try to travel as inconspicuously as possible. The law clerks who commuted to the Court by car then had parking spaces in the garage beneath the Court building. Because Charles had a very unremarkable American-made car, not too old and not too new, and lived within a few miles of the chief justice, on several occasions he had the responsibility of driving the chief justice home.

Justice Thomas developed his own strategy for traveling incognito. The year Kristen clerked, Justice Thomas and his wife, Ginny, bought a forty-foot renovated bus. Beginning that year, the justice and Ginny would spend part of each summer recess on the road, frequently visiting friends and former clerks along the way, and would always come back with wonderful stories of their road trips across America. They would typically park the bus at night at a rest stop and sometimes have long conversations with other travelers, many of whom never realized that the person next door served as a justice on the Supreme Court. Once when Justice Thomas was getting gas for the bus, he chatted with another customer at the station. The person told him, "You look just like Clarence Thomas!" Justice Thomas smiled and said that "[he had] been told that before."

Any personal interaction with a justice for whom the clerk was not working was rare at the time Charles clerked. From the clerk's perspective, each justice's chambers necessarily operated as a self-contained unit. Confidentiality within chambers was preeminent. By custom, each justice would make an annual visit to the clerks' dining room, which was off a hall closed to the public near the Court's cafeteria. Justice Byron White was an exception to this general rule because he would occasionally join the clerks in a basketball game in the basketball court on the upper floor of the building. He was a fierce competitor who gave no quarter and made his physical presence very well known, especially in rebounding.

Any other interaction with another justice was haphazard. On one Saturday, Charles had Renée, then barely two years old, with him at the Court (Renée had just acquired a baby brother), and they went to see one of Charles's classmates who was clerking for Justice Marshall, intending to visit very briefly. As they were conversing, Justice Marshall came out of his office, and Charles introduced Renée to him. Renée acknowledged the introduction by saying hello to "Justice Marshmallow," which the justice considered to be hilarious. Gregarious storyteller that he was, Justice Marshall then related a few anecdotes suitable for the occasion. The visit took a bit longer than expected.

By the 1990s, it was more common to interact with other justices. Each of the justices went to lunch with the clerks of every other chambers (in the case of Justice Ruth Bader Ginsburg, it was tea in her chambers with tasty baked goods made by her husband). One of the Kennedy clerks' favorite lunches was with Chief Justice William H. Rehnquist at the Monocle restaurant on Capitol Hill. After he had finished his cheeseburger, the chief justice leaned back, smoked a cigarette, and answered questions about serving in the army as an eighteen-year-old enlisted man at the end of World War II. He was assigned to a unit in Casablanca, after the Allies had recovered it. He said his unit's schedule included a trip to the airfield for an hour in the morning to check on the weather and the French. They spent the rest of the day playing touch football and swimming. At night, there were plenty of places just like "Rick's Café," but sans Humphrey Bogart.

Chief Justice Rehnquist's down-to-earth but organized style strongly influenced the atmosphere of the Court at the time Renée and Kristen clerked. Both Renée and Kristen were surprised to discover that, notwithstanding the media attention surrounding the Court, the chief justice took a quiet, solitary walk around the grounds of the Court each day. Tourists sometimes asked him for directions, having no idea who he was. Chief Justice Rehnquist also loved to sing, and had a resonant baritone voice. Each term, he organized two sing-alongs for the justices, clerks, and other staff, one at Christmas and the other at the end of the term. For both, he had songbooks compiled and distributed. The Christmas book contained the standard carols and hymns. Justice Stephen Breyer never missed these occasions, and had a good voice himself. Once when the chief justice had to step out of the room, Justice Breyer gamely led the group in singing about little Lord Jesus asleep on the hay. The end-of-term songbook was full of American favorites, including "Ballad of Casey Jones," "On Top of Old Smoky," and Stephen Foster songs.

The end-of-term festivities included a trivia contest that the chief justice designed and over which he presided. Knowing his interest in history and the West, the Kennedy clerks targeted their studies a bit. The preparation paid off when they recalled the Treaty of Guadalupe-Hidalgo, earning an approving nod from the chief justice. At the end of each term, the clerks would write and perform skits. One memorable skit was based on a case during Renée's term. Justice Scalia, played by one of the clerks, drove a virtual bus (holding the other justices) that was pulled over for speeding. The officer, played by another clerk, gave him a ticket and said, "Just one more question before you get gone."

Chief Justice Rehnquist liked to gamble for de minimis stakes. He organized a pool among the clerks for the college football bowl games, with different clerks making the book for each bowl. He also organized a pool on the length of the president's State of the Union address. President Bill Clinton taxed the justices' predictive powers with the length of his addresses.

In the late 1990s, the clerks played basketball games on the "highest court in the land," just as clerks had done for many years. One notable game occurred when Renée was clerking for Judge Stephen Williams on the D.C. Circuit. The female Supreme Court clerks during October term 1995, calling themselves the "Supreme Women," challenged the women clerking for judges on the D.C. Circuit to a basketball game at the Court. Everyone played hard, but at the end no one could remember the score!

The justices maintained cordial and sometimes warm relations with each other, despite jurisprudential differences. Likewise, relations among the clerks in the late 1990s were good, with little friction and plenty of fellowship. Chambers took turns hosting happy hour in the courtyards for the other clerks, and several generous clerks organized parties for all clerks, at their respective homes.

For Charles, Renée, and Kristen, one of the rewards of clerking was a longstanding friendship with the justice. Kristen continues to see Justice Thomas regularly at monthly get-togethers for former clerks. Renée helps organize periodic events involving Justice Kennedy and his prior clerks. Charles served for many years on Chief Justice Burger's clerkship screening committee.

Carter G. Phillips (Burger, October term 1978)
and Jessica Phillips (Souter, October term 2007)

Carter: My first contact with Chief Justice Warren Burger's chambers was an interview I had with one of his former law clerks, Charlie Hobbs. It was during

December 1977, while I was clerking for Judge Robert Sprecher on the U.S. Court of Appeals for the Seventh Circuit. The chief justice did not interview law clerk candidates. Instead, he asked four of his former law clerks each to interview ten law clerk candidates, and then the chief justice selected four based on the recommendations of the interviewers and his own assessment of the candidates. I did not actually meet "the Chief" until I had been clerking for him for a few weeks.

The interview itself was not as memorable as the turmoil in getting from Chicago to Washington, D.C. On the day I was scheduled to be interviewed, a huge snow and ice storm hit Chicago, which crippled most transportation in the city. My car was frozen, as were all forms of public transportation. My wife told me I should just forget the interview because my odds of getting a clerkship were pretty remote, and it was not safe to travel. I decided to take matters into my own hands by setting out on foot toward O'Hare Airport (we lived on the far east side next to Lake Michigan, so the distance was probably twenty miles), hoping that some form of divine intervention would get me to my appointed interview. The strategy worked because within two blocks of our apartment I was greeted by a cab driver who had just started work for the day. I hailed him; he stopped and took me to the airport about four hours early.

The interview was not memorable, although I do recall being asked what I would do if I just completely disagreed with a legal position the chief justice proposed to take in a case. I told Charlie that I would express my disagreement politely but firmly and, if I did not succeed in persuading him, to recognize that he is the boss and get on board with his view. I guess the answer satisfied Charlie (and the Chief), although it suggested that perhaps the Chief had had a bad experience with a former law clerk.

The hiring process made that first day of the clerkship in early July somewhat disembodied because I still had never met my employer. I did arrive about ninety minutes too early to get into the Court, and so I walked around the building several times, soaking it in and trying to convince myself that I really was about to become one the chief justice's law clerks for October term 1978.

I was the first of the Chief's law clerks to arrive that term, which had two very positive consequences. First, I was allowed to choose my office, which was on the same level as the Chief's office—and, in fact, was only about twenty-five feet from his back office, where he did all of legal work. His chambers were divided by the justices' conference room. The chief did all of his work on the administration of justice in his role as the chief justice of the United States in his "front office," and he did his legal work in the back one. That proximity gave me great access to the Chief. It also was the nicest office I will ever occupy. It had a twenty-foot-high ceiling, walls lined with all of the U.S. Reports and lower federal court opinions and statutes, a huge easy chair, and an even bigger desk.

Second, I had a chance to meet all four of his law clerks from the 1977 term, and they were very helpful in orienting me. They teased me about how hard the first few weeks would be, trying to master the art of writing cert pool memos, and how I would look back on those days at the end of the term and realize that they would be the easiest of the year. They were right about that. The clerkship workload was purely additive. First, you write pool memos, then you add preparing bench memos for the Chief, then you start working on opinions for the Court and then concurring and dissenting opinions. The Court heard almost 140 cases that term compared to about 75 cases that are decided after oral argument these days. So the pace of work began to build to a crescendo from October when the oral arguments began and peaked in April as the final arguments took place and as the number of opinions to be circulated increased. During March and early April, the job was certainly seven days a week and tended to be twelve to fifteen hours a day.

The law clerks also spared me substantial embarrassment later in the term when the Chief called me into his office and invited me to stay on as one of his law clerks for another year. This was his routine practice, and fortunately the outgoing law clerks were tasked with telling the incoming ones that it was just fine for the new law clerk to decline the Chief's gracious offer (of course with deep appreciation). It was great that I had this warning because otherwise there would be enormous personal pressure to say yes because obviously I owed him so much by allowing me to clerk for him. On the other hand, given the workload, my wife told me that if I had agreed to stay on for twenty-four hours beyond the year of the clerkship, she would have divorced me. So when the time came, I was able to avoid both divorce and embarrassment by following my predecessors' advice and simply thank the Chief, but politely decline. That was clearly the answer he was expecting.

There are a number of events or circumstances that I can discuss consistent with my obligation not to reveal confidences that are some of my strongest and fondest memories of my year with the chief justice.

1. *Going to Court and meeting the Chief.* The first day I met the chief justice is obviously memorable. And during that meeting he gave me a piece of advice that has served me well during thirty years of practicing before that Court. His advice was to read every Supreme Court opinion with a very skeptical eye because it is not the case that "the Court always says what it means or means what it says." What he meant was that many Court opinions contain language that even the justices who signed on to the opinion did not necessarily embrace. Thus, even if an opinion suggested how a particular case should be decided, I should never assume that such "dicta" would command a majority. Over the years I cannot count the number of opinions I have read (even in my own cases) where the Court has said that certain language might be read to require

a particular result, but the Court refuses to read it that way or to be a slave to dicta.

2. *The cert pool.* A few years prior to my clerkship, five members of the Court had joined together to pool their law clerks for purposes of sharing memoranda concerning each petition for certiorari. The chief justice (four clerks), Justices Byron White (four clerks), Harry A. Blackmun (four clerks), Lewis F. Powell (four clerks), and William H. Rehnquist (three clerks). So each week the petitions were divided among the nineteen clerks, which meant that in general each law clerk had between four and six memoranda to write recommending that the Court either grant or deny the petition or perhaps take some other action.

But what made the pool particularly interesting was the fact that four justices—the number needed to grant a petition for certiorari under the long-standing tradition of the Court—were not in the pool. I always thought those outside the pool imposed a real restraint on the pool writer because it was difficult to think of anything more embarrassing than to recommend that certiorari be denied and have it granted by the four justices not in the pool. That never happened my year, and I firmly believe it is because of the dynamic of limiting the pool to five members of the Court. The arrangement clearly pushed each law clerk to write memoranda without any tilt.

3. *The workload.* I was all but overwhelmed by the workload at times because the Chief wanted memoranda written in so many situations. In addition to writing pool memos, we also wrote extensive bench memos about how each case should be decided based on our reading of the briefs and independent research. For the 135-plus cases, that meant that each clerk would write between thirty and forty memos. We also wrote memos for every case that the Chief put on the "discuss list," which was the mechanism for putting before the conference the cases that each justice believes should be discussed and voted on individually by all of the justices in deciding whether to hear a particular case on the merits.

The chief justice would initiate the list, and then each justice would add any case or cases that he thought merited discussion. For all of the cases the Chief put on the list, he wanted us to draft a one-page (and only one page) memorandum that outlined our view of how the Chief should vote and what the case was about to assist him in the conference presentation. Once opinions were circulated, the Chief wanted a memorandum about each draft opinion. Thus, if the majority opinion in a case was in circulation, and the Chief had voted to decide the case in the same way as the draft opinion, we were tasked with drafting a memorandum that would indicate to the Chief whether he should join the opinion and whether there was any language that we thought the Chief should urge the opinion writer to change or delete.

If he had voted the other way in the case, we were supposed to write a memorandum indicating whether we thought the Chief should stay the course and dissent or whether we thought that it might be possible for the Chief to join the majority opinion. Usually, if the Chief voted to dissent from the majority, he assigned the opinion to someone else, and our recommendation would be for him to wait until that dissenting opinion was circulated before deciding what to do.

The Chief then wanted us to write a memorandum about every concurring and separate dissenting opinion and each revised draft of all of the opinions. Often these revisions were trivial, and our memos were correspondingly short. But sometimes they would trigger the need for a longer explanatory memorandum.

Of course, the most fun was working on opinions. The advantage of clerking for the chief justice is that he can assign opinions to an individual justice in every case. Thus, when he is in the majority, he assigns the majority opinion, but when he is in the dissent, he still gets to assign the dissent if there is another justice with him in dissent. Thus, the Chief tended to take for himself the most interesting cases of the term. I got to work closely with the Chief on five opinions for the Court, which was both a lot of work and exhilarating.

At the end of the term, consistent with Chief's clear mandate, I dutifully placed all of the memoranda and draft opinions I had prepared or worked on for the Chief in huge burn bags. There were more than 800 such memos or drafts. Some were longer than twenty-five pages; many were just a paragraph or two. But the single most striking characteristic of each of those memos was their fidelity to the Chief's command (communicated during the law clerk orientation) that each memo begin with a clear statement of what I recommended that the Chief should do in response to whatever the issue was. So for a pool memorandum, I would recommend either grant or a deny (95 percent were to deny) or, for a case on the merits, I would recommend affirm, reverse, or some other disposition. While it was a bit daunting to abandon the law student's or academic's penchant for suggesting on every question that "it could be argued X or it could be argued Y," the cumulative effect of making 800-plus recommendations in a year that were accepted by the Chief almost always was to build real confidence in my judgment. That confidence has served me well over the years.

I can complain about the volume of work, but I have to confess two points. First, I loved every minute of it. Second, the Chief worked six days a week and put in extremely long hours. So whenever I felt a bit stretched, I walked next door to my office and saw the Chief in his chambers working away and realized that given our age differences, I had nothing to complain about.

4. *No page limits.* One of the most memorable aspects of my year was the

fact that the Court had no page limits for briefs. I candidly do not remember whether there were any limits on briefs in the Seventh Circuit, but I was still stunned by briefs that were 400 and 500 pages long. I worked on more than a few cases that year in which the briefs by the parties and amici were thousands of pages.

What struck me was that the solicitor general's briefs in those cases were fewer than fifty pages. It was hard not to focus on a brief that made extremely cogent arguments in a digestible format. While every clerk no doubt felt an obligation to read each party's brief from cover to cover, at some point during argument fifteen I would be lying if I did not confess that my mind wandered.

Between the time I clerked and the time I joined the solicitor general's office as an assistant to the solicitor general, the Court adopted the rule limiting merits briefs to fifty pages and amicus briefs to thirty, which happened to be the length of the United States's briefs under informal guidelines set up by the solicitor general before the rule change. I have to say I am much happier under the page-limitation regime. I know how hard it is to restrain clients and co-counsel from making arguments, and having the leverage of saying that a new argument can go in only if it replaces one that is already in the draft is powerful stuff. I know exactly how briefs without fixed limits drift into hundreds of pages, and no one benefits, particularly not the justices and certainly not the law clerks.

5. *Death penalty.* My term was the first one in which a death row inmate was executed over the defendant's vigorous objection and defense after the death penalty was reinstituted in the wake of *Furman v. Georgia.*[14] The defendant was John Spinkelink, who was accused of shooting his gay lover. Of all of the death penalty cases I worked on that year, this was one of the least shocking. All of the others seemed to involve horrible facts that made me all but nauseous. On the other hand, Florida was quite set on executing Spinkelink, which led to a series of execution warrants being issued, which were stayed by Justice Thurgood Marshall. Eventually, the full Court voted to deprive Justice Marshall of authority to issue a stay of execution in that case without the approval of the full Court. The case caused enormous strains within the Court—between law clerks, between justices—it was a very emotional situation. Fortunately, we had only one such event, but it was clear to me that the Court would face a tidal wave of these crises and would be in for some hard times in the years after Spinkelink's execution.

6. *Oral arguments.* I loved watching oral arguments at the Court and would have watched all of them if I could have, but I never had enough time to sit in on all of them. So I went to all of the arguments in the cases I was assigned to work on, and a few of the "big ticket" cases of the term. What made going to arguments particularly uninviting were the seats. They were without question the most uncomfortable chairs I have ever spent any time sitting on. Plus, they

were off on the side, and it was impossible to see the justices' facial expressions or the advocate's demeanor.

In 1978, there was no specialized "Supreme Court bar." There was no "buzz" among the law clerks to watch an advocate who was particularly skilled at oral arguments. To be sure, there were some lawyers in the solicitor general's office who appeared more than once, but no one in private practice. And the quality of advocacy for the states and most businesses was so much less impressive than for the United States that it was striking. One argument that I personally remember was Joel Klein arguing as amicus in a case involving the standard of proof in a civil commitment hearing. He represented a private organization as amicus, which never happens now if the amicus is not the United States or one of its agencies, but his argument for a heightened burden of proof in the civil commitment setting was strikingly persuasive. It made me believe in the importance of amicus efforts, and has affected my legal practice over the past thirty years.

7. *Basketball.* In some ways I always thought that playing basketball on "the highest court of the land" on the top floor of the court kept the law clerks who played regularly sane. We pretty much played religiously three times a week. That year none of the women clerks played (of the twenty-eight clerks, five were women). The absence of a locker room for women near the court probably had something to do with their lack of interest in playing hoops. But all the men played at least a few times, and there were quite a few of us who played whenever we could squeeze in the time.

Without question, the most exciting part of basketball was the appearance of Justice White almost every week. He did insist on three-on-three half-court games when he came up to play, and of course he usually had his own clerks play with him. But he always needed at least one of the other clerks, and often more, to get to six players. Given that Justice White was sixty-one that term, it was amazing how well he played. He had quite a nifty hook shot that was extremely hard to stop, and he played with stunning intensity.

Of course, he was a former Hall of Fame football player, and he had amazing strength and was not unwilling to grab a player who thought he could go past the justice for an easy layup. With Justice White, there were no easy baskets. Moreover, when he grabbed you, you stayed grabbed. When it was just the law clerks playing, we often called fouls both on ourselves and the person who committed the foul. Sometimes there was disagreement, but generally no real controversy. But Justice White never called a foul on himself, and none of us was willing to do that. Given the thirty-plus year gap between our ages, it seemed only fair to let him foul with impunity. I did take a memorable elbow in my chest, which proved that he took every game seriously and that he was once an NFL superstar.

8. *Technology.* When I interviewed with Charlie Hobbs, he asked me if I

could type because the Chief's secretaries were fully occupied and probably would not be available to type our memos, particularly if our work was time sensitive, as much of it was. Fortunately, I was an adequate typist, but the good news was that October term 1978 was first time that the Court experimented with computers for use as word processors. We had one Wang computer terminal in each justice's chambers, except for Justice Blackmun (who for some reason declined). Of course, having one computer and four law clerks, we had to share it among the four of us. But my co-clerks—Walter (Jack) Pratt, Chris Walsh, and Rob Lacy—were easy to work with, and so we managed to share the same machine with a minimum of stress.

I have two particularly vivid memories of the Wang. The first was when I thought I was by myself at the Court on a Saturday afternoon and was working on some document on the Wang and was sitting at the machine. I had taken my shoes off to relax and had my feet up on a table as I was editing on the computer. Out of the blue, the Chief walks in on me. I jumped to my feet and we had a conversation, but the whole time his eyes were drifting toward my bare feet, which no doubt horrified him, but he was far too nice and dignified to say anything. I never went barefoot at the Court again.

The second memory was when the Chief called and asked me to come see him in his office. He handed me a revised version of an opinion with his handwritten edits on it. He asked me to review his changes and get the opinion back to him when the edits had been implemented and the draft retyped. Since our meeting was on a Saturday, he said I should give his edits to his secretary on Monday and get the changes made. I suggested offhandedly that I might have the opinion revised before Monday, but he paid no attention.

I returned to the Chief's office less than an hour later with all of his edits inputted because the opinion was on the Wang and edits were easy to make. The Chief looked genuinely shocked and asked whether I had made any of his changes. So I brought him his handwritten edits and showed them in the revised clean version. He knew immediately that this was the kind of technology that would improve the administration of justice, and I knew that courts would have Wangs or similar computers in short order because the Chief clearly was sold on the value of the technology. The Chief had brought copier machines to the Court soon after he was confirmed as the chief justice, and one of his greatest strengths was his willingness to promote technology throughout the federal court system.

9. *Relationship with the Chief.* As I have already indicated, the Chief liked to receive very clear memoranda that explained plainly the recommendations of the clerks on each issue that triggered the need for a memorandum. On the other hand, the Chief would ask us into his office the day before oral argument and explain his views of the case and discuss with us individually our views

about how he should vote. Sometimes the conversations were quite brief because we were in "violent agreement." Sometimes we disagreed, and I remember vividly blurting out: "What's your theory, Chief?" Then I realized it was not really my place to ask that question or his to answer it.

But every one of the Chief's clerks will agree that our lunches on Saturdays with the Chief were the highlight of the clerkship. He did not invite us every week, but it was a pretty routine event. Of course, it meant that we had to be in our offices at the Court by 9 a.m. to be sure to receive the invitation, but we were going to be working anyway, and the prospect of sharing the Chief's homemade bean soup made the trip to the Court early on a Saturday easy to justify.

The menu was pretty much always the same: bean soup, which the Chief cooked in the kitchen next to the justices' conference room inside the Chief's chambers. My impression was that the Chief had a huge vat of bean soup stock to which he added whatever was in the refrigerator or the kitchen that day. He always had some bread with the soup, and he would offer us wine from his cellar in the basement of the Court. We never drank wine with him because we had work to do after lunch.

But the best part of the lunches was the Chief telling us stories about his life as a lawyer in Minneapolis and his time as the assistant attorney general of the Civil Division of the Justice Department. It was very special to listen to him tell stories about meeting President Eisenhower when there was an emergency that required an injunction. I looked forward to every one of those lunches, and I still treasure the memories of those stories because they were the times when the Chief was completely relaxed and happy to talk with his "boys."

I owe Warren Burger almost every success in my legal career. He recommended me for my job in the Justice Department, and he was the kind of mentor that any young lawyer would want to help him or her succeed. I wish I could discuss our relationship in working on specific cases because that experience had so much to do with the lawyer I became, but the bottom line is that with thirty-plus years after my year at the Court, I still owe Warren Burger a debt I can never repay.

Jessica: During the summer of 2005, after my second year of law school, I applied to be a law clerk for then judge Samuel Alito on the Third Circuit. He interviewed me later that summer, and in early September he extended me an offer to clerk for him beginning in the fall of 2006. I was thrilled at the opportunity and spent not an insubstantial amount of time trying to determine where I should live when I clerked in New Jersey.

The summer and fall of 2005 were, of course, notable for Supreme Court–watchers because Justice Sandra Day O'Connor announced her resignation on July 1, 2005, and Chief Justice Rehnquist passed away on September 3, 2005, leaving two vacancies on the Supreme Court for the first time in over a decade. Being a Court-watcher myself, I followed the nominations of John G. Roberts Jr. and Harriet Miers with much interest but did not realize how much those events would impact me directly.

After Miers asked President George Bush to withdraw her nomination—and almost two full months after I had accepted Judge Alito's offer to clerk for him on the Third Circuit—I woke up the morning of October 21, 2005, to watch President Bush announce that he was nominating Judge Alito to the Supreme Court to replace Justice O'Connor. And just like that I was without a clerkship. I figured that obtaining another clerkship for the fall of 2006 was a real long shot because most of the judges around the country began hiring in early September, but I got very lucky. Judge Joel Flaum was at the time the chief judge of the Seventh Circuit and had not yet hired any law clerks for 2006 because he had been busy with his administrative responsibilities for the Judicial Conference. And, critically, he was a Northwestern University Law School graduate with a strong relationship to the school. I dropped off my application, and he asked me to interview with him a few weeks later. After the interview, Judge Flaum called me and told me that he wanted to offer me a clerkship with him. But he told me that I needed to call Judge Alito first and tell him about the offer. If Judge Alito did not get confirmed and become Justice Alito, he would have to hire a new law clerk.

I spent the day fretting about making the call to Judge Alito. I knew he was busy meeting with senators and preparing for his confirmation hearings. He certainly did not need to be bothered by me, but I also did not want to lose out on the opportunity to clerk for Judge Flaum. I called Judge Alito, who told me that he was thrilled that I had the opportunity to clerk for Judge Flaum. He told me to take the clerkship, which I did.

Of course, Justice Alito ultimately was confirmed and took his seat on the Supreme Court on January 31, 2006. That summer he invited me to apply to him for a clerkship at the Supreme Court. I sent him my application materials, he interviewed me over the phone, and a few weeks later he offered me the job.

1. *Arrival to the Court.* I started my clerkship with Justice Alito on July 23, 2007. Our orientation was scheduled to begin at 9 a.m. I arrived at the Court a bit after 7:30 in the morning. I spent the next hour walking around the outside of the building trying to prepare myself for the year ahead in awe and disbelief that this was my new place of employment. I never lost that sense of awe in entering the building—even on early Saturday mornings.

The Court was in the middle of a rather extensive renovation project, and Justice Alito's chambers had just been moved so that the construction could begin on a new section of the building. This meant that unlike our predecessor clerks, none of the four Alito clerks would have an office in his chambers. Two of the clerks shared an office on the second floor of the building, where numerous other law clerks also had offices (and where Justice Ginsburg's chambers were located). The other two law clerks had offices outside of the Court's library on the third floor. We were told that this was the first time in the Court's history that law clerks were located on the third floor.

Initially, I was concerned that being two floors away from the justice would impact my ability to interact with him. As it turned out, my concerns were unfounded. The justice always made himself available for meetings and was more than happy to have any of us drop by for an impromptu discussion. Those one-on-one discussions that I had with the justice were some of the most memorable moments of my clerkship experience.

2. *The cert pool.* During October term 2007, Justice John Paul Stevens was the only justice who did not participate in the cert pool. The other seven associate justices and the Chief all participated in the cert pool, which meant that the cert petitions were divided equally among those eight chambers and further divided equally among the law clerks for each of those chambers.

Each week like clockwork a new stack of paid petitions and a new stack of in forma pauperis (IFP) petitions would arrive on my desk. I was responsible for drafting a cert pool memo for each of those petitions that would be circulated to the eight justices participating in the cert pool. The memo contained my analysis of the petition and the brief in opposition and an ultimate recommendation to the justices about how to dispose of the petition. Justice John Paul Stevens's position outside of the cert pool meant that his four law clerks had to review a substantially larger pile of petitions each week. This outside review was a good check, and those of us drafting cert pool memos would often consult with the Justice Stevens clerk who had been assigned the same petition. In addition, the Court keeps an electronic database of all of the cert pool memos written by previous law clerks. That technological resource was also a good check to see how the Court had handled previous petitions that dealt with certain questions presented. Reviewing cert pool memos from previous terms was helpful in identifying legal and factual nuances in petitions that could explain why the Court granted or denied a particular petition.

During the first few weeks of the cert pool, I was overwhelmed by how long it took me to write each cert pool memo. It seemed to me that there was not sufficient time in the day to add preparation for merits cases and opinion drafting to my workload. As it turns out, there is a steep learning curve for writing cert pool memos. By the end of our clerkships, my colleagues and I marveled at how much more efficiently we were able to get through our respective stacks.

At the end of my term, Justice Alito held a meeting with his four law clerks and asked our opinions about whether he should remain in the cert pool. We provided our thoughts, and Justice Alito made the decision to opt out of the cert pool at the end of the 2007 term. After Justice Stevens retired, Justice Alito became the sole justice not participating in the cert pool.

3. *The workload.* In addition to writing our cert pool memos each week, the Alito law clerks divided up the merits cases for each oral argument session. We were responsible for writing bench memos to the justice analyzing the case and giving the justice a recommendation on how the case should be resolved. We would write the bench memos and email them to the justice a week or so in advance of the oral argument. The justice would read through the briefs and our bench memos, and then schedule a meeting with all four of his law clerks to discuss the upcoming session.

Just like my impromptu one-on-one discussions with the justice, those meetings held between the five of us were some of the most intellectually stimulating conversations I have ever had. We always gathered for those meetings in the justice's office in his chambers. The law clerk assigned to a given case had primary responsibility for leading the discussion with the justice and for answering his questions about the case, but we were all encouraged to speak up if we had thoughts on cases for which we were not primarily responsible. The first meeting we held lasted over three hours, and while it was a productive meeting, I nonetheless struggled through it because I was freezing throughout the whole meeting. The justice usually kept his office at around sixty-five degrees, which is far too cold for my taste.

I planned ahead for our next meeting and made sure to have a couple of sweaters with me. As it turns out they were unnecessary because the justice had noticed how cold I had been in the previous meeting and had lit a fire in the fireplace so that I would be more comfortable. It was an extremely thoughtful gesture that was much appreciated. The only meeting we held to discuss merits cases that did not take place in his chambers' office was when the justice forgot to open the flue before he started a fire. We were smoked out of his office within two minutes.

In addition to meeting with the justice to discuss merits cases, we also met with him before the justices' conferences to decide on pending cert petitions. We would review the petitions that had been listed by the Chief on the discuss list. The Chief would first circulate a list of the petitions that he believed the Court should consider granting. The next most senior justice, Justice Stevens, would then add any petitions that he believed should be considered that had been left off the list by the Chief. The process continued down the line of seniority. Because Justice Alito was the most junior justice during the 2007 term, by the time the discuss list had been circulated to us, it was almost always the case that the petitions that we had deemed worthy of being discussed by the Court had already been listed by the eight other justices. But we did discuss our recommendations as to how the justice should vote on each of the petitions listed on the discuss list every week.

After the justices voted on merits cases and opinions were assigned, the justice would return to chambers and fill us in on the opinion for which we were responsible. If the justice had been assigned an opinion (either majority or dissent) in a case for which I was primarily responsible, I would write the first draft of the opinion.

4. *Death penalty.* In late September 2007, the Court granted cert in *Baze v. Rees,*[15] which was an Eighth Amendment challenge to the three-drug protocol used to execute capital prisoners by lethal injection. After the cert grant, there was an effective moratorium on executions across the country. This had a very real impact on the clerkship responsibilities for my term. As a result of the moratorium, my colleagues and I only had to handle a handful of last-minute requests for stays of execution. I firmly believe that the fact that we did not have to work on those cases (which are usually highly stressful and laced with high emotions) directly impacted how well the law clerks got along during my term. We avoided what could have been a major source of tension and strife between chambers because of the death penalty moratorium.

5. *Oral arguments.* I thoroughly loved watching oral arguments. I did not get to watch every one that was argued my term, but I went to many more than just the cases that I worked on for the justice. We had a number of high-profile cases my term, including *D.C. v. Heller* (Second Amendment), *Kennedy v. Louisiana* (the death penalty for child rape), *Boumediene v. Bush* (Guantanamo Bay), and *Medellin v. Texas* (presidential authority to enforce international treaties). I attended each of the oral arguments in those cases. The late senator Edward Kennedy attended the argument in *Boumediene v. Bush* and squeezed past me to use the restroom during the oral argument.

My father argued five cases in front of the Court the year that I clerked for Justice Alito. They were *CSX Transportation v. GA State BD. of Equalization, Hall Street Associates, L.L.C. v. Mattel, Inc., Quanta Computer v. LG Electronics, Warner-Lambert Co. v. Kent,* and *Sprint Communications v. APCC Services.* I had seen my father argue a number of cases before the Court during my childhood, but I had not seen him argue since I had attended law school. I had every intention of watching each of his arguments during the year I clerked. He argued two cases in one week during the November session, and I managed to sit through about five minutes of each case before my nerves got the better of me. I left the courtroom and sat in the Lawyers' Lounge and listened to the streaming audio of the arguments.

I should also note here that the Court and Justice Alito had very strict rules ensuring that I was never permitted to work on any of the cases that my father's law firm handled in any capacity at any stage before the Court. Moreover, the justice prohibited me from being present in chambers (even if I was outside of his office) when the justice was discussing the cases that my father handled personally. The justice called it the "Cone of Silence." I was not permitted to see any of the drafts of opinions, votes, or communications about any of his cases. I did not know the outcome of any of those five cases until the days the opinions were read from the bench.

6. *Basketball.* Playing basketball at the Court was definitely one of the highlights of my time clerking for Justice Alito. It served as a wonderful outlet both socially and athletically. We had a solid group of between five and eight clerks who played every Monday, Wednesday, and Friday almost without fail the entire year. Occasionally, a few of the Court staffers would also join us. Depending on how many people came to play ball, we would run games of three-on-three or four-on-four. The basketball court that sits above the courtroom is not regulation size, so playing five-on-five gets a bit crowded.

When I started my clerkship, I was told by our predecessor law clerks that each year there is a single clerk who injures himself or herself while playing basketball. I had the dubious honor of being that individual during the 2007–8 term. We were playing a four-on-four game, and I ran out to put a hand in the face of a fellow law clerk and landed on his shoe, which caused my ankle to twist and break. My mother had to drive to the Court, pick me up, and take me to the emergency room. My ankle eventually healed, and I began playing basketball again around February.

7. *Relationship with Justice Alito.* One of the things that surprised me most about Justice Alito was his sense of humor. He has a quiet, low-key demeanor—almost shy. But he has a wicked sense of humor that provides levity and relief at the perfect moment.

One afternoon a few months into my clerkship with the justice, we had planned a birthday lunch for the justice's conference secretary. The justice, his wife, his personal assistant, his conference secretary, and the four clerks gathered in one of the rooms in chambers. As I explained above, the justice's chambers were always a little colder than I like, so I planned ahead and wore my coat down to lunch. It was a traditional khaki trench coat, and I had it buttoned all the way up. We were getting lunch laid out, and everyone was sitting down around the long table when a lull came over the group. Justice Alito broke the silence. He looked at me with a twinkle in his eye and asked me, "Have you solved any good mysteries today, Jessica?" Everyone at the table roared.

Having clerked on the Court himself, my father gave me some advice before I started the job. He told me that "it only lasts for a year and it's the best legal job you will ever have so be present and truly appreciate the experience." It was great advice that I tried always to follow.

J. Harvie Wilkinson III (Powell, October terms 1971, 1972) and Porter Wilkinson (Roberts, October term 2008)

Dad: Porter was obstreperous at the dinner table long before she went to law school and got a Supreme Court clerkship. A warning to parents: children with clerkships advance their arguments with even more than the usual authority.

Porter: We frequently have to remind Dad that Article III jurisdiction doesn't extend into the home front and that he doesn't get to preside over family arguments.

And so it goes. Dad (who clerked for Justice Lewis F. Powell Jr.) tells Porter (who clerked for Chief Justice John G. Roberts Jr.) that he clerked in the tough old days. The Court today hears only about half the number of cases that it did in the early 1970s. And there were only three clerks (not the present four) in most chambers to do the job. All this took place in a technologically primitive era: clerks in the tough times had no computers, only Coronas, Dictaphones, and yellow legal pads. Communications were quaint, with carts clattering down the corridors of the Court carrying the mail and the internal correspondence of the justices. And by the way, there was no cert pool. During Dad's first term as a clerk, each chambers had to prepare all its own cert memos. His second term, the pool kicked in and eased the workload.

Now we both think it's altogether good that the present Court concentrates its finite energies on fewer cases. Moreover, the cert pool serves a useful function, because the pool memos can be more thorough and because individual chambers in the prepool days tended to let the certiorari function slide a bit at the end of a term. But from the standpoint of the clerks themselves, let's be honest: Dad thinks Porter had it soft.

Porter thinks Dad speaks with more than a whiff of hypocrisy, because those who worked in the days of one- or two-clerk chambers probably thought, with some justification, that the clerks of Dad's three-clerk era had it soft, too. The whole debate about who had it soft is bogus, Porter says, because the justices of every era have exacting standards, and their expectations mean clerks have more than enough to do. And with fewer cases on the docket, the number and complexity of separate opinions have increased, giving the justices more to write and respond to. Still, Dad thinks one of the enduring joys and prerogatives of fatherhood is to tell the kids we had it tough back then.

One big difference between today and yesteryear: the clerks of Dad's day got no law-firm signing bonus. The $280,000 (and upward) bonus for today's "Supremes" makes Dad feel like he played baseball in the days before free agency. One law firm did offer Dad a $17,000 yearly salary, but even adjusting for inflation, that still makes Dad a piker. Of course, the absence of a tempting law-firm bonus made it easier for Dad to go into teaching immediately, which was what he always wanted to do. But Dad still gets wistful when he realizes Porter and his own law clerks are out-earning him and the justices for whom they clerked in their first years in private practice.

The bonus babies have transformed Supreme Court clerkships in another way. Both Dad and Porter think there's more pressure on getting prestigious clerkships up and down the line: from feeder professor to feeder circuit judge and now, with the trend toward clerks with a year or two of practice, from feeder law firms. In Dad's day, law clerk placement had not become quite the present cottage industry. It isn't just the money. It's that people are increasingly known and identified, especially in Washington legal practice, by their clerkships—they are becoming the indispensable cachet. Blogs track the developments. Not just for individuals but for institutions. Recruitment and placement of law clerks have taken on the most competitive aspects of athletic culture, where the best high schools are the top law schools, the colleges are circuit judges, and the Supreme Court justices sit atop the whole structure as the pros.

There's a danger, to put it mildly, of misplaced priorities: the wonderful thing about a clerkship truly is the opportunity for service, not the label or the bonus bucks. All part of law's change from a profession to a business, we guess. There's a risk that the lionizing of contemporary law clerks can make them forget they are serving the institution.

Leaks before a decision comes down or revelations of internal discussions afterward have no place. But Dad, as an incorrigible old journalist, thinks inside reporting on any institution, including the Court, serves a useful purpose. Still, he remembers when *The Brethren* came out in 1979 and reported unflattering remarks some justices had made about their colleagues. To say a pall was cast over exchange within the Court is an understatement. Both Dad and Porter think clerking will cease being clerking if the relationship between clerk and justice becomes increasingly guarded and on-edge.

There are several big developments from the day of Dad's clerkship to Porter's that merit comment. The demographics of clerking have changed dramatically, along with those of legal education and practice. When Dad clerked, there were fewer female law clerks than there are now female Supreme Court justices. Dad thinks most guys of his day now feel a bit shortchanged in that regard. Men and women do each other a whole lot of good in the workforce. At least that has been Dad's experience for many years in his own chambers. Of course, with a daughter having held two clerkships, Dad could hardly get away with holding any other opinion! But it's the truth.

The clerks of Dad's day were almost uniformly of a liberal persuasion. That did not prevent them from faithfully executing in every particular the views of the justices for whom they served. Then, too, a liberal approach to politics often coexisted with a more traditional approach to legal methodology. Dad was always thankful that Justices Powell, Potter Stewart, and Byron R. White, like Hugo Black and John Marshall Harlan before them, were among those who seemed committed to neutral principles of law that transcended political outcomes.

Still, it was an odd thing in a presidential year for Dad to be one of only two or three clerks at the Court not to vote for George McGovern. That changed dramatically by Porter's time. Law clerks are more diverse ideologically and thus less likely to exert a philosophical pull in a single direction. If there is a problem now, it is that justices may be too reluctant to hire a counter-clerk or two to stir crosswinds within their chambers.

The Ivy League cast of the Supreme Court clerkship is still running strong. Harvard and Yale dominate the clerkship ranks in Porter's time just as they did in Dad's. Perhaps that is because so many of the justices attended those two institutions. Recently there has been a bit of a thaw. When Dad clerked, there were few southerners among his peers, or at least few who had been to southern law schools. Now, however, the University of Virginia, which both Porter and Dad attended, does quite well in the clerkship derby, though there has been nothing close to a general democratization of clerkships among the nation's law schools. This is not at all a comment on the quality of the many superlative law schools around the country, so much as a testament to the powers of habit and, frankly, to the level of confidence that the very top graduates of the very top law schools have instilled in the members of the Supreme Court year after year.

Are the justices "grade snobs" or "school snobs"? That seems too simplistic an antimeritocratic swipe. The problem is significantly one of scarcity, not snobbery. The justices receive hundreds of wonderful applicants each year, but they have only three or four spots to fill.

A final change is that more Supreme Court clerks are hired after not only a circuit court clerkship but a year or two of practice or government service as well. This seems okay up to a point. Along with several others, Dad came to clerk for the Supreme Court immediately after graduating from law school. The experience was a bit overwhelming at first, and Dad is certain that a clerkship at the circuit level would have done him good. Whether it is desirable to hire clerks after a year or two of practice or government service seems to us a closer question.

We think a brief stint in the "real world" may well be beneficial, and some of the very finest Supreme Court clerks have come to their justices after just such an experience. But among the great values of a clerkship is that it is not just another job or rung on the career ladder. The affection that many feel for their clerkships comes from the fact that it was their very first professional experience of any duration. The intergenerational exchange between those near the end of a long and distinguished career and those at the very beginning of a promising path in law is a special thing. It is true that this traditional model requires the justices to educate clerks for legal practice rather than vice versa. But the distinctive value of a clerkship is that of an apprenticeship. And if we clerks arrive at the Court in a pristine state, that only enhances our eagerness to perform at the highest level, and it only deepens our affections for our first mentors over the years.

There is physical change at the Supreme Court as well. Construction is all about. Security has tightened; few people walk through those great bronze doors anymore. Not all change is bad, though. The curatorial displays and the gift shop are much livelier. And for all the changes between Dad's day and Porter's, the continuity is even more evident. The clerks still sit to the side in that same beautiful courtroom. They still roam the Great Hall and corridors with the busts and portraits of bygone justices to inspire them. They still play basketball on the Court's top floor. They still spar in the cafeteria. They still lunch, more than in Dad's day, with justices from other chambers. Their chatter and curiosity and creativity and, yes, immodesty still keep the Court humming and alive.

Dad and Porter are grateful to have served this remarkable institution, even in a small way. It's really quite a special father-daughter bond. The justices for whom we worked also shared many traits: Chief Justice Roberts and Justice Powell brought the gifts of great private practitioners to the Court. Their standards were high; their manner unfailingly kind. Their country should be immensely proud of them both; we can state as an abiding fact that their law clerks surely are.

Notes

1. A smaller club still consists of siblings who have clerked at the Supreme Court. It includes Alger and Donald Hiss (who both clerked for Justice Oliver Wendell Holmes Jr.), Benjamin and Edwin Hanna (who both clerked for the first Justice John Marshall Harlan), and Luther, Stephen, and Rufus Day (who all clerked for their father, Justice William R. Day).

2. In addition to the parent/child clerks featured in this recollection are the following four families: Walter Gellhorn (Stone, October term 1931) and Gay Gellhorn (Marshall, October term 1983); Rex Lee (White, October term 1963) and Thomas Rex Lee (Thomas, October term 1994); Mark Tushnet (Marshall, October term 1972) and Rebecca Tushnet (Souter, October term 1999); Jack B. Owens (Powell, October term 1973) and John B. Owens (Ginsburg, October term 1997)

3. John S. Monagan, *The Grand Panjandrum: Mellow Years of Justice Holmes* (New York: University Press of America, 1988), 120.

4. David McKean, *Tommy the Cork: Washington's Ultimate Insider from Roosevelt to Reagan* (South Royalton: Steerforth Press, 2004), 21.

5. Dorothy McCardle, "She'll Clerk at Supreme Court," *Washington Post,* February 9, 1966.

6. Elizabeth Black to Tommy Corcoran, December 28, 1966, Personal Papers of Thomas Corcoran, Library of Congress.

7. Hugo L. Black and Elizabeth Black, *Mr. Justice and Mrs. Black: The Memoirs of Hugo L. Black and Elizabeth Black* (New York: Random House, 1986), 168.

8. Stephen Susman, interview by Todd Peppers, 2014.

9. Ibid.

10. McKean, *Tommy the Cork,* 296–97.

11. Elizabeth Black to Tommy Corcoran, March 31, 1970, Personal Papers of Thomas Corcoran, Library of Congress.

12. 342 U.S. 98 (1951).

13. Paul A. Freund, *The Oliver Wendell Holmes Devise: History of the Supreme Court of the United States* (New York: Macmillan, 1971).

14. 408 U.S. 238 (1972).

15. 553 U.S. 35 (2008).

LAURA KRUGMAN RAY

From Clerk to Justice, From Justice to Clerk

Judicial Influence in Supreme Court Chambers

I t is generally recognized that a clerkship with a Supreme Court justice is one of the greatest honors and career enhancements that a recent law school graduate can hope to attain. Six of those fortunate law clerks—William H. Rehnquist, Byron White, John Paul Stevens, Stephen Breyer, John G. Roberts Jr., and Elena Kagan—eventually returned to the Court as justices, and three of the six currently constitute a third of the Court. Some of those former clerks have discovered, however, that the honor and enhancement may come with strings attached. In later life, but particularly on the occasion of their nominations to the Court, former clerks may find that the bond with their justices can provoke criticism as well as admiration. Justice Elena Kagan's 2010 confirmation hearing offers a vivid illustration of that consequence. Coming before the Senate Judiciary Committee as the nominee and solicitor general of a Democratic president, Kagan found that the Republican members of the committee seemed more interested in her clerkship twenty-three years earlier with Justice Thurgood Marshall than in her current ties with President Barack Obama.

As the Republican senators made their opening statements, Kagan's clerkship emerged as a potential obstacle to her confirmation. Senator Jeff Sessions set the tone by noting that "[i]mportantly, throughout her career, Ms. Kagan has associated herself with well-known activist judges who have used their power to redefine the meaning of the words of our Constitution and laws in ways that, not surprisingly, have the result of advancing that judge's preferred social policies and agendas."[1] Noting specifically her clerkship with Justice Marshall, he insisted that "[f]ew would dispute this record tells us much about the nominee."[2] Senator Jon Kyl continued that theme, conceding that "it is not surprising that as one of his clerks, she held him in the highest regard," but worried that she "appears to enthusiastically embrace Justice Marshall's judicial philosophy, calling it, among other things, 'a thing of glory.'"[3] More specifically, he found that her work as Marshall's clerk "contains evidence that she shares his vision of the Constitution."[4] He brushed aside Kagan's explanation that in her clerkship role she was "channeling" Marshall rather than acting on her own beliefs.[5] The clerkship bond, in Kyl's view, was a reliable predictor of the nominee's own judicial philosophy.

Rehnquist experienced a harsher variant of Kagan's experience during his confirmation hearing for his elevation to chief justice in 1986. As law clerk to Justice Robert H. Jackson when the Court was deciding *Brown v. Board of Education*,[6] Rehnquist had written a memo to Jackson arguing that the separate but equal rationale of *Plessy v. Ferguson*[7] should lead the Court to deny relief in *Brown*. In its most controversial language, the memo spoke in the first person to endorse *Plessy:* "I realize that it is an unpopular and unhumanitarian position, for which I have been excoriated by 'liberal' colleagues, but I think *Plessy v. Ferguson* was right and should be re-affirmed."[8] Questioned about the memo's embrace of *Plessy,* Rehnquist disassociated himself from its substance, insisting that it "was intended as a rough draft of *his* [Jackson's] views at the conference of the justices, rather than as a statement of my views."[9] Since he was, Rehnquist insisted, merely performing his assigned role of drafting language to express Jackson's position, the clerk as scribe should not be held accountable for the justice's position.

Scholars have questioned the accuracy of Rehnquist's explanation, one that relies on the complete identification of the clerk with the justice, in light of the particulars of the episode.[10] Nonetheless, despite their rather different circumstances, both Kagan and Rehnquist defended themselves by arguing that the loyal and cooperative law clerk may, in Kagan's word, channel without absorbing the jurisprudence of the justice. The clerk, they suggested, becomes for a year the justice's alter ego, adopting viewpoints and arguments that should not be attributed directly to the clerk once the clerkship ends. The influence, in short, is a temporary and functional aspect of the year spent in the justice's chambers.

It is worth noting in connection with Rehnquist's defense that long before his appointment to the Court he identified what he considered a very different and sinister form of influence running in the opposite direction, from law clerk to justice. In an article written for *U.S. News and World Report* shortly after his clerkship ended, Rehnquist suggested that the largely left-leaning clerks of that era might be influencing their justices' selection of cases for the Court's docket.[11] He argued, based on his own experience at the Court, that there was "the possibility of the bias of the clerks affecting the Court's certiorari work."[12] More recently, Edward Lazarus, himself a former clerk to Justice Blackmun and the author of a controversial insider book about his year on the Court, described what he considered deliberate attempts by conservative law clerks to influence the opinions of their centrist justices.[13] In these scenarios, law clerks, far from falling under the sway of their justices, may instead be deliberately attempting to influence their decisions.

With three clerks turned justice now serving on the Court, the more intriguing question to ask is not whether clerks can influence the judicial performance of their justices during a single term but instead whether justices may, long after a clerkship has ended, influence the judicial performance of their former clerks. That proposition may be tested by exploring the records of two of those clerks who, decades later, returned to the Court to shape their own judicial identities, John Paul Stevens and Stephen Breyer.

Clerk and Justice: John Paul Stevens and Wiley Rutledge

In recent decades, the selection process for Supreme Court law clerks has involved a rigorous search for a capable and congenial addition to a justice's chambers. For John Paul Stevens, however, it was a literally the flip of a coin that won him his position with Justice Wiley Rutledge. Two professors at Northwestern University School of Law were asked to hire two law clerks, one to work for Chief Justice Fred Vinson in the 1948 term and the other for Justice Rutledge in the 1947 term. As Stevens himself has told the story, the professors selected Stevens and Art Seder, coeditors in chief of the law review and veterans enrolled in an accelerated two-year program, leaving it up to them to match clerk with justice:

> While more prestige would attach to a clerkship with the Chief Justice, given our advanced age, we both wanted the earlier opportunity. To resolve the conflict, we resorted to a tie-breaking method, one that I have often been tempted to use during my years on the bench: We flipped a coin. Needless to say, I won the toss and have had nothing but fond memories of the Law Review and of my good friend Art ever since.[14]

Stevens's account makes clear that his decision wasn't based on any perceived jurisprudential differences between Vinson and Rutledge. Luck and timing determined what turned out to be a successful match.

Yet, on paper, Rutledge and Stevens would not have seemed to have much in common. Rutledge followed a difficult and unconventional path to the Court.[15] Born into the Kentucky family of a Baptist minister, he was nine years old when his mother died of tuberculosis, a disease that would later strike him as well. And the law was by no means his first choice of profession. After studying Latin and Greek at a small Tennessee college, he transferred to the University of Wisconsin in his senior year to study chemistry in the hope of pursuing a scientific career. It was only after he did poorly in his new major that Rutledge focused his ambition on the law, enrolling in Indiana University's law school while teaching high school to cover his expenses. Unable to manage his dual responsibilities, Rutledge had left law school when he contracted tuberculosis, requiring a lengthy convalescence at a North Carolina sanatorium. He completed his legal education at the University of Colorado, practiced briefly, and became a legal academic, eventually serving as dean of the University of Iowa law school. President Roosevelt appointed him to the Supreme Court in 1943, reportedly commenting, "Wiley, you have a lot of geography."[16]

Stevens's background could scarcely have differed more from Rutledge's. Born into a wealthy Chicago family, he grew up in the luxurious Stevens Hotel, built by his father and uncle, where he crossed paths with such celebrities as Amelia Earhart and Charles Lindbergh. In contrast to Rutledge's rocky educational history, Stevens moved easily from the University of Chicago's laboratory school to the university itself; he graduated Phi Beta Kappa before joining the navy in 1941, serving as a cryptographer in the Pacific and receiving a bronze star. His law school career was equally illustrious; in addition to his law review editorship, Stevens graduated with the highest grades on record and won his Supreme Court clerkship.

After working as an antitrust attorney in Chicago and teaching as an adjunct faculty member at local law schools, he was appointed to the Court of Appeals for the Seventh Circuit in 1970 and then to the Supreme Court by President Ford in 1975. Yet, despite their biographical differences, Stevens's clerkship year with Rutledge was apparently a successful one that served in several ways, both positive and cautionary, to influence Stevens's own approach to his Supreme Court role.

Although Stevens himself has not written specifically about the details of his clerkship duties, two other Rutledge clerks, Victor Brudney and Richard F. Wolfson, have provided a vivid account of the way in which the chambers operated during their clerkships.[17] They describe what they call "an intimate association" of justice and clerk in which "the clerk was constantly made to feel equal."[18] Clerks were encouraged to speak freely to provide Rutledge with "the ideas of a different generation," which they were then challenged to defend in what sometimes became vigorous debates.[19] In preparing for conference, "[i]t was his custom—until forbidden to do so by his doctor—to sit with his law clerk, into the following morning if necessary, and go over in detail the cases to be decided and the petitions for certiorari."[20] The clerk was also given the draft opinions from other chambers to read and comment on: "Indeed, he was at liberty, one half hour before a decision was to be announced, to go into the justice's office and plead again that he change his vote."[21]

As John M. Ferren, Rutledge's biographer, has noted, that model was no longer squarely in place by the time of Stevens's clerkship. According to Ferren's interviews with some of Rutledge's later clerks, their relationships with the justice were "somewhat more hierarchical, more businesslike, and thus less intimate than those spelled out by Brudney and Wolfson."[22] The change, Ferren believes, may in part have been the result of the addition of a second clerk in 1947, Stevens's clerkship year, altering the dynamic of the justice–single clerk relationship.[23] Stevens himself has noted that although Rutledge "welcomed disagreement," he did not continue to ask his clerks for their views on his draft opinions as he had with Brudney and Wolfson.[24]

Even the earlier active partnership model did not, however, assign his clerks the task of drafting Rutledge's opinions. Instead, the clerk would research the case and discuss it with the justice, who then did the writing himself. On rare occasions Rutledge might make use of a clerk's research memorandum as a basis for "interlineating, cutting, and adding."[25] And the clerk was usually allowed to draft one opinion during his term of service; Stevens reported preparing the first draft of both a majority opinion and a concurrence during his term.[26]

When Stevens returned to the Court more than two decades after his clerkship ended, he brought with him not just the memories but also some of the customs of the Rutledge chambers. Todd Peppers has described Stevens as the only member of his Court who had not "fully adopted the rules and norms of the modern clerkship model," preferring instead to rely on the practices that had shaped his own clerkship experience.[27] Stevens chose to hire only three law clerks rather than the four provided by Congress. And he decided not to join the cert pool, an arrangement put in place three years earlier in which a single clerk prepares a cert memo for circulation to all of the participating justices. Stevens explained that in light of his earlier experience with the cert process, "I thought I could get through the certs faster without joining the pool."[28] At a time when the docket was considerably smaller, Rutledge himself read all of the cert petitions and discussed them with his clerks. Faced twenty-eight years later with an overwhelming number of petitions, Stevens compromised, relying on his clerks to screen the docket and flag the potentially cert-worthy cases for his personal review.

If Stevens preserved the collaborative spirit of Rutledge's approach to the cert process while adjusting its form to meet the new reality, he followed more precisely Rutledge's opinion-writing practice. Departing from his colleagues' preference for delegating the preparation of first drafts to their clerks, Stevens consistently wrote his own drafts, which he then gave to his clerks for their review of both substance and style.[29] He offered two reasons, one theoretical and one pragmatic, for his approach. He summarized his theory succinctly: "I'm the one hired to do the job."[30] His practical explanation offered two advantages. First, he explained that he wrote the first draft "for self-discipline. I don't really understand a case until I write it out."[31] And second, he found that his "draft is typically much shorter than a law clerk's draft, and the justice is less likely to showboat with long cites and flowery language."[32] While writing his own first drafts, Stevens did preserve the Rutledge custom of no-holds-barred discussions of cases. As one appreciative Stevens clerk has observed, "I can imagine few bosses so interested in the views of their employees, so prepared to engage in free-flowing debate, and so enthusiastic to be proven wrong."[33]

Stevens's preference for short, simply written opinions suggests another departure from Rutledge's model. In an admiring though not uncritical essay written several years after Rutledge's death, Stevens assessed the strengths and weaknesses of Rutledge's opinions.[34] Chief among the weaknesses was Rutledge's preference for long, sometimes "redundant" opinions in which "[h]e habitually used a pair of words where one would have served almost as well."[35] Those weaknesses, Stevens argued, were the consequence of his virtues: his determination to explain fully the bases for his opinion and his willingness to examine an issue from several angles before resolving it. "To me," Stevens concluded, "Rutledge's long opinions are evidence of two virtues of a great judge—tolerance and judgment."[36] Those long opinions also reflected Rutledge's insistence on responding to all the arguments raised by counsel, regardless of whether those arguments were relevant to his own position. As Rutledge explained, "however foolish or trivial his arguments, I want them to know that I heard him."[37]

Stevens also saw Rutledge's frequent separate opinions as evidence of another virtue, his integrity. Far from viewing Rutledge's use of concurrences to clarify his own position as unnecessary, Stevens—himself a frequent practitioner of the form—saw them as essential because Rutledge's "conscience literally *forced* him to add the statement of the real basis for his vote."[38] For Stevens as well, the separate opinion was not an indulgence but rather an important form in which to express his independent views. In his thirty-five terms he authored 399 opinions for the Court, 340 concurrences, and 708 dissents, with his majority opinions less than half the number of his separate opinions.

Finally, Stevens admired another quality in Rutledge's opinions that readers have found in his own, their unpredictability. Although known as a strong supporter of individual liberties, Rutledge did not, in Stevens's words, "automatically champion a claimed liberty interest," instead providing "a painstaking review of every aspect" of the cases before him and at times reaching surprising resolutions.[39] In one of his best-known opinions, his dissent in *In re Yamashita*, Rutledge found a denial of due process in the procedures of the trial by military commission that convicted the commanding general of the Japanese army in the Philippines of violations of the law of war; the harshness of the plaintiff's behavior did not neutralize the claims of due process.[40] Yet Rutledge also voted with the majority in *Hirabayashi v. United States,* upholding the curfew for Japanese Americans,[41] and two years later also joined in *Korematsu v. United States,* upholding the government's internment policy, apparently feeling constrained by his earlier vote.[42]

That quality of unpredictability has also been one of the hallmarks of Stevens's jurisprudence. The term appears in a scholar's list of words describing Stevens's approach to his decision making, a list that also includes "maverick" and "wild card."[43] Like Rutledge, Stevens approached each case as a discrete legal package whose resolution should be based on its own distinctive features rather than on a comprehensive legal philosophy. Thus, Stevens, usually a strong First Amendment voice, surprised observers by dissenting from the Court's decision in *Texas v. Johnson* striking down a state flag-burning statute, basing his opinion on the distinctive nature of the American flag.[44] Six years later, Stevens again dissented from a First Amendment decision, this time from the opposite side, insisting that the Court erred in allowing the Ku Klux Klan to place a Latin cross on state property in *Capitol Square Review and Advisory Board v. Pinette.*[45] His opinion relied on the particularities of the case, focusing on whether an ordinary person would perceive state endorsement in the placement of the cross. And, in an unusual pragmatic stroke, he appended a photograph of the cross and its label, allowing the reader to make an independent judgment.[46]

Returning to the Court after decades of practice and five years of experience as an appellate judge on the Seventh Circuit, Justice Stevens brought with him as well the experience of his own clerkship with an admired justice. In some of the qualities that have defined Stevens's tenure on the Court—the role assigned his clerks, his hands-on approach to opinion writing, and his use of separate opinions to fine-tune his positions—it is possible to glimpse the influence on a novice lawyer of an experience given to only a handful of the Court's members, a year spent inside the chambers of another justice on the other side of the justice-clerk relationship.

Clerk and Justice: Stephen Breyer and Arthur Goldberg

Where Justices Rutledge and Stevens emerged from vastly different backgrounds, Justices Arthur Goldberg and Stephen Breyer had considerably more in common. Born exactly one generation apart—Goldberg in 1908, Breyer in 1938—they illustrate two phases of the American Jewish experience. And their paths to the Court represent two versions of the legal career open to talent in the twentieth century.

Goldberg was born in Chicago, the eleventh child of Jewish immigrants from Russia, where his father had been a town clerk. In America, however, he supported his family by selling produce from a horse-drawn wagon, with his young son often accompanying him. Goldberg was eight when his father died, and the older children in the family went to work to provide the family's income. Goldberg worked too, from the age of twelve throughout his school years, at a variety of jobs, "wrapping fish, selling shoes, and working as a page in a library"; his favorite job was selling coffee at Wrigley Field from the urn he carried on his back.[47] The only member of his family to finish high school, he attended Crane Junior College and De Paul University before graduating from Northwestern University Law School in 1929 at twenty-one with, according to his biographer, then the highest grade point average in its history.[48] Goldberg was editor in chief of the *Illinois Law Review* and worked with Dean John Henry Wigmore on the third edition of his celebrated evidence treatise.[49]

Graduating into the Depression in 1929, he took a job with a Jewish law firm, handling foreclosures and bankruptcies, before leaving four years later to start his own firm, where his practice grew to include union clients. During World War II, he was recruited by William J. Donovan of the Office of Strategic Services to create an international intelligence network of labor leaders. After returning to his own labor practice shortly before the end of the war, he became chief counsel for the Congress of Industrial Organizations (CIO) and helped to engineer the merger of the CIO with the American Federation of Labor (AFL). He was named secretary of labor by President Kennedy, who subsequently appointed him to Felix Frankfurter's seat—then known as the Jewish seat—on the Supreme Court in 1962.

In contrast to Goldberg's challenging Horatio Alger rise to distinction, Breyer was born into a solidly middle-class family in San Francisco, where his father, who had attended Stanford University, was an attorney for the city's board of education and his mother volunteered for the Democratic Party and the League of Women Voters.[50] Breyer attended public schools, including the "academically prestigious" Lowell High School, where he was voted the most likely to succeed in his class.[51] During his student years, he worked as a ditch digger and waiter, though the job he recalled most fondly was at a camp in the Sierras.[52]

After graduating from Stanford with highest honors in 1959, he won a Marshall Fellowship to Oxford's Magdalen College, where he received a B.A. in philosophy, politics, and economics with first class honors in 1961. He then went on to Harvard Law School, graduating magna cum laude in 1964 and serving as articles editor of the *Harvard Law Review*. Where, despite his outstanding academic record, Goldberg had found limited employment opportunities, Breyer moved from Harvard directly to his Supreme Court clerkship. From the Court, he went to the Justice Department's Antitrust Division for two years before joining the Harvard Law School faculty, where he remained, with a few breaks for government positions, until his 1980 appointment to the Court of Appeals for the First Circuit and his subsequent elevation by President Clinton, in 1994, to the Supreme Court.

A comparison of Justices Goldberg and Breyer is complicated by the huge difference in their terms of service. While Breyer has served on the Court for nineteen years, Goldberg served for only three years before resigning to accept President Lyndon Johnson's appointment as the U.S. ambassador to the United Nations in an episode that has produced more speculation than clarity.[53] After later running unsuccessfully for governor of New York, Goldberg returned to private practice in Washington, apparently regretting his decision to relinquish what his wife called the job that he had "wanted, wanted, *wanted.*"[54] Breyer clerked for Goldberg in the third and final year of his judicial tenure, serving as one of his six clerks and one of the even smaller number to offer a firsthand account of life in the justice's chambers. And even the few clerks who have written or spoken about Goldberg focus less on his procedures in chambers and more on his broader role as adviser and friend. It is in that continuing relationship that his former clerks locate the influence that Goldberg had on their professional and personal lives.

Writing on the occasion of Goldberg's death in 1990, Breyer asked a rhetorical question: "What was it like clerking for this active, practical, humane man during one of the three years he served as an Associate Justice of the United States Supreme Court?"[55] Breyer does not, however, answer his own question with the kind of specifics that other clerks writing about their justices on less solemn occasions have provided. He tells the reader that Goldberg had "a strong and imaginative legal mind," "a strong social conscience," "a highly practical view of the Constitution," and an attitude toward government that "was respectful but not necessarily reverential."[56] And he notes that Goldberg was "in his element"[57] on the Court and that working for him was "great fun."[58] The remainder of the brief memorial mentions the personal relationship that developed between justice and clerk, including Saturday lunches and an ecumenical Seder at the Goldberg home. The clerkship, he concludes, was the first phase of a lifelong friendship in which the justice "followed our lives and those of our families with interest" and "called us with help and advice."[59]

Another clerk has been more expansive in drawing the contours of that lifelong friendship. Peter Edelman, a clerk during Goldberg's first term on the Court, has described a more personal relationship in which the justice served as "the all purpose attendant" at his wedding and offered important career guidance by advising Edelman to work for the Kennedy administration after his clerkship ended.[60] Alan Dershowitz, a third Goldberg clerk who, like Breyer, joined the Harvard Law School faculty, recalls Goldberg as a justice who "loved having intense discussions with his law clerks about jurisprudence and the role of the Supreme Court."[61] Dershowitz also offers the most concrete example of the way in which Goldberg used his law clerks, once dispatching him to ask Justice Brennan if he would be interested in supporting the goal of, in Goldberg's words, "end[ing] capital punishment in the United States."[62]

If Breyer's memorial essay offers nothing so revealing about his experience in Goldberg's chambers, neither does his testimony at his own confirmation hearing. In his opening remarks, Breyer first said that Goldberg "became a wonderful lifelong friend" and then described an important lesson learned from the justice, "that judges can become isolated from the people whose lives their decisions affect" and should remain engaged in their communities.[63] But in his responses to the senators' questions, he never followed Edelman in describing Goldberg as a mentor or echoed Dershowitz's account of helping Goldberg to pursue a jurisprudential goal that he later shared with the justice.[64]

When asked about his role in drafting Goldberg's concurrence in *Griswold v. Connecticut*,[65] an opinion relying on the Ninth Amendment to support an unenumerated right to privacy, Breyer disclaimed any independent role in shaping the opinion:

> If you had worked for Justice Goldberg as I did, you would be fully aware that Justice Goldberg's drafts are Justice Goldberg's drafts. It was Justice Goldberg who absolutely had the thought, that his clerks implemented, and both my coclerk Stephen Goldstein and I did—there were two at that time—and we worked on that draft. I might have worked on it a little more than he. But it is Justice Goldberg's draft.[66]

And when asked directly by Senator Leahy about his own views on the source of unenumerated rights, Breyer made clear the difference between his views and Goldberg's, replying that "I do not think it is in the Ninth Amendment, but it is true that Justice Goldberg wrote an opinion about the Ninth Amendment."[67] His clerkship and his work on *Griswold* did not, he indicated, automatically mark him as Goldberg's loyal disciple.

Almost a decade after joining the Court, Breyer was still resisting questions about the effect of his clerkship with Goldberg. In a 2003 interview at the John F. Kennedy Library, he was asked: "How did he influence you? What did you learn from him, and who influenced him?"[68] His first response was to challenge the questions ("Now, I'm not sure we're influenced."), and his second was to reaffirm his personal affection for Goldberg ("I loved Arthur Goldberg. I thought he was a great man. I was his clerk. He kept up with his clerks in the years.").[69] But Breyer then reframed the issue to describe the particular judicial lesson he had learned from Goldberg, how to respond to a failure to win a majority for his position:

And I think, my goodness, stop complaining. You have a lot more to decide and a lot more cases in which to write opinions that may start as a dissent and may end up as a majority. You start feeling sorry for yourself because you lost that case? Go somewhere else. There's a lot to do. And I say, who would have told me that? Arthur Goldberg.[70]

Breyer offered a more polished version of that response two years later in an interview with Jeffrey Toobin:

"Your opinions are not your children," Breyer told me. "What they are is your best effort in one case. The next one will come along, and you'll do your best. You'll learn from the past. [Justice] Goldberg taught me never to look backward. People ask all the time whether I was sorry that I was in the minority in Bush v. Gore. I say, 'Of course I was sorry!' I'm always sorry when I don't have a majority. But, if I started moping about it, I can hear Goldberg saying, 'What are you talking about, feeling sorry for yourself? There's no basis for feeling sorry for yourself. Get down and do it. Keep going. Maybe they didn't agree yesterday. Maybe they'll agree tomorrow.'"[71]

Rather than personal mentor or jurisprudential model, Goldberg seems to have served Breyer instead as a source of practical judicial wisdom about dealing with the inevitable conflicts and disappointments that accompany the work of a collegial court.

Although his tenure on the Court was considerably briefer than Breyer's, Goldberg was not slow to hit his stride. From his arrival he assumed an activist stance, what Stephen J. Friedman has described as a willingness "to set out a wholly new constitutional ground with a verve not ordinarily characteristic of a new Justice."[72] Goldberg's senior colleague, Justice Sherman Minton, was blunter in making the same point, calling Goldberg "a walking Constitutional convention!"[73] Goldberg himself later defended the Warren Court's approach on the ground that "proper respect for the democratic process—the philosophy that 'underlies judicial restraint'—is perfectly compatible with 'activism' in some areas, particularly where the rights of *minorities or the health of the democratic process itself are at issue.*"[74] That willingness to stake out new doctrine is less apparent in his opinions for the Court and his dissents; it is in his concurrences that Goldberg apparently felt freer to argue for new constitutional rights.

Goldberg's reliance on the Ninth Amendment in *Griswold,* as noted earlier, is one prominent example, but it was no anomaly. In *New York Times v. Sullivan,*[75] where the Court announced its new actual malice standard for libel, Goldberg in concurrence noted that his colleagues had not gone far enough.

He proposed an even more speech protective standard, "an absolute, unconditional privilege to criticize official conduct despite the harm that may flow from excesses and abuses."[76] And when the Court in *Bell v. State of Maryland*[77] remanded a criminal trespass conviction of restaurant sit-in demonstrators to the lower court for review in light of state law changes, Goldberg joined the majority but appended his own thirty-two-page concurrence. Though based in part on the history of the Fourteenth Amendment, the concurrence also relied on "the logic of *Brown v. Board of Education*" to support "the right of all Americans to be treated as equal members of the community with respect to public accommodations."[78]

Goldberg's most strenuous effort to change the Court's jurisprudence came not in an opinion but in a memorandum to his fellow justices. When the petitions for certiorari in *Rudolph v. Alabama*[79] and five other cases raised the issue of capital punishment, Goldberg decided to use the occasion to challenge the Court's established jurisprudence. In a highly unusual step, he circulated a memorandum to his fellow justices urging them to consider "[w]hether, and under what circumstances, the imposition of the death penalty is proscribed by the Eighth and Fourteenth Amendments to the Constitution."[80] His approach to that issue was an aggressive one, viewing the issue "in light of the world-wide trend toward abolition" and insisting that "in certain matters—especially those relating to fair procedures in criminal trials—this Court traditionally has guided rather than followed public opinion in the process of articulating and establishing progressively civilized standards of decency."[81] The effort was unsuccessful, with only two justices, Douglas and Brennan, joining Goldberg's eventual dissent from denial of cert in all six cases. Nonetheless, Goldberg later claimed credit for authoring what he called "the first decision where a Justice expressed doubts about the death penalty."[82]

Although Breyer, like Goldberg, is generally identified as a member of the Court's liberal bloc, he has never been an activist justice in the Goldberg manner. Rather than trying, as Goldberg did, to fit cases into his own jurisprudential design, Breyer prefers to treat each case individually with an eye to its particular facts. Where Goldberg saw a case as an opportunity to extend the boundaries of individual rights, Breyer sees each case in terms of its likely practical consequences. His characteristic concern is one of proportionality, and he is likely to ask whether, on the given facts, there is a fit between the identified harm and the proposed remedy. This perspective surfaced in his *Bush v. Gore* dissent, where he insisted that "[b]y halting the manual recount, and thus ensuring that the uncounted legal votes will not be counted under any standard, this Court crafts a remedy out of proportion to the asserted harm."[83] Where Goldberg attempted to use *Rudolph* as a vehicle for a desired change in the law, Breyer has observed that "[j]udges cannot change the world,"[84] and he is therefore more inclined to defer to legislatures. When, for example, he voted with the majority to uphold the constitutionality of specific legislative caps on political contributions, he accused the dissent of "mak[ing] the Court absolute arbiter of a difficult question best left, in the main, to the political branches."[85] Where Goldberg staked out new territory in First Amendment law, Breyer has taken a more tempered view. Dissenting in a case involving the statutory protection of children from sexually explicit television programming, he has argued that a judge should be asked "not to apply First Amendment rules mechanically, but to decide whether, in light of the benefits and potential alternatives, the statute works speech-related harm (here to adult speech) out of proportion to the benefits that the statute seeks to provide (here, child protection)."[86]

This emphasis on proportionality is central to his view that "[l]aw is not an exercise in mathematical logic" but rather is rooted in practical reality.[87] That approach can sometimes produce unexpected outcomes, like his dissent from the Court's decision striking down the Child Online Protection Act. "In the real world," he argued, "where the obscene and the nonobscene do not come tied neatly into separate, easily distinguishable packages," what he called a "middle way" was a better approach to "tempering the prosecutorial instinct in borderline cases."[88]

As an empiricist engaged in real-world analysis, Breyer frequently cites data to support his positions. At times he may rely on material provided by the parties, as he did in noting that "29 million children are potentially exposed to radio and audio bleed from adult programming,"[89] or praise a party for providing such data rather than relying "upon 'mere speculation.'"[90] He may even provide his own data, as he did in rejecting the majority's assertion in *Clinton v. Jones* that civil suits against sitting presidents would happen only rarely.[91] Or, more dramatically, he may attach an appendix containing supporting materials. Dissenting from the Court's decision upholding a copyright extension, he provided two appendixes: the first supplied a statistical analysis supporting his position that the extension would be of little financial benefit to copyright holders, while the second described circumstances supporting his argument that the extension would do little to create uniformity.[92] The former academic in Breyer surfaces in his use of empirical data to drive home his positions, often those offered in dissent.

In spite of the occasional cases in which his real-world approach separates him from his usual colleagues, Breyer is considered a solid member of his Court's liberal bloc, just as Goldberg was considered a solid member of the Warren Court's liberal majority. In light of that connection, it is curious that Breyer has seldom affirmed it by mentioning Goldberg in his opinions. Aside from a few obligatory parenthetical cites to Goldberg as the author of relevant labor law decisions, his name rarely appears. There are, however, two Goldberg opinions that Breyer has quoted with approval. The first is *Swain v. Alabama,* a case decided during Breyer's clerkship, where Goldberg's dissent addressed the issue of peremptory challenges. Breyer has twice quoted this key passage: "Were it necessary to make an absolute choice between the right of a defendant to have a jury chosen in conformity with the requirements of the Fourteenth Amendment and the right to challenge peremptorily, the Constitution compels a choice of the former."[93] Referencing that language, Breyer noted that, for him, "a jury system without peremptories is no longer unthinkable."[94]

A second Goldberg opinion, written before Breyer's clerkship, seems to have had even greater resonance for him. In *School District of Abington Township v. Schempp,* the Court struck down the required reading of Bible verses or the Lord's Prayer in a public school classroom.[95] Goldberg joined the majority opinion but added his own concurrence to point out the difficult nature of the issue. "There is for me," he found, "no simple and clear measure which by precise application can readily and invariably demark the permissible from the impermissible."[96]

Breyer quotes that passage in his own concurrence in *Van Orden v. Perry,* where he surprised observers by supplying the fifth vote to hold a Ten Commandments monument on public land constitutionally acceptable.[97] Breyer's position characteristically relied on the facts of *Van Orden,* including the absence of any complaint about the monument for the forty years preceding the challenge before the Court, to support his view that the presence of the monument did not provoke any religious divisiveness. In the course of his opinion, he mentioned Goldberg's name four times, most prominently in the conclusion, where he again quoted Goldberg's *Schempp* opinion by observing that "where the Establishment Clause is at issue, we must 'distinguish between real threat and mere shadow.' . . . Here we have only the shadow."[98] It is hard not to see in this passage an acknowledgment of the common ground inhabited by justice and clerk on the delicate nature of Establishment Clause issues.

A generation apart, Goldberg and Breyer share their urban Jewish heritage and membership in their Courts' liberal blocs. Yet they also differ significantly in the approach to their work. Where Goldberg was committed to expanding individual rights and eager to seize an opportunity, like the *Rudolph* memorandum, for pursuing his judicial agenda, Breyer has shaped a more nuanced role. He prefers to weigh each case on its own merits, relying on its particular facts to guide his response and remaining a less predictable justice. Thus, though Goldberg and Breyer have often ended up in the same jurisprudential place, their routes have been markedly different. Where they do, however, find a closer kinship is in their judicial temperament. Both have recognized the challenges of a collegial Court, where the opponent in one case may become the ally in another, and through the civility of their discourse have kept open channels for future cooperation. The lesson that Breyer has acknowledged learning from his clerkship with Goldberg is that of patient persistence, accepting defeat philosophically and looking forward to the next opportunity for success in shaping the law in accord with his own sense of justice.

Conclusion

The careers of two clerks turned justices, Stevens and Breyer, illustrate the subtle ways in which a clerkship experience decades in the past may influence judicial performance. For Stevens, his year with Rutledge is reflected most directly in his candid case discussions with his law clerks and his practice of writing his own first opinion drafts; for Breyer, his year with Goldberg is reflected more broadly in his attitude toward the vicissitudes of life on a collegial Court. For both, however, the year spent as a clerk in Supreme Court chambers served as more than simply a résumé enhancement. It provided an early introduction to the Court's decision-making process and a resource for defining the way in which each would shape his role of Supreme Court justice.

In the past decade, another two justices have brought their clerkship experiences to the Court—John G. Roberts, who served in the chambers of then–associate justice Rehnquist, and Elena Kagan, who served in the chambers of Justice Marshall. As they continue to write their opinions and define their roles on a collegial body, Roberts and Kagan may well provide Court-watchers with intriguing further variations on the ways in which a single clerkship year may help to shape a lengthy Supreme Court career.

Notes

Portions of this essay incorporate two previously published articles, Laura Krugman Ray, "Clerk and Justice: The Ties That Bind John Paul Stevens and Wiley B. Rutledge," *Connecticut Law Review* 41, no. 1 (2008): 211; and Laura Krugman Ray, "The Legacy of a Supreme Court Clerkship: Stephen Breyer and Arthur Goldberg," *Penn State Law Review* 115, no. 1 (2010): 83.

1. Tobe Liebert, ed., *Hearings and Reports on Successful and Unsuccessful Nominations of Supreme Court Justices by the Senate Judiciary Committee 1916–2010* (William S. Hein, 2012), 23:6.
2. Ibid.
3. Ibid., 19.
4. Ibid., 20.
5. Ibid.
6. 347 U.S. 483 (1954).
7. 163 U.S. 537 (1896).

8. Roy M. Mersky and J. Myron Jacobstein, eds., *Hearings and Reports on Successful and Unsuccessful Nominations of Supreme Court Justices by the Senate Judiciary Committee 1916–1975* (William S. Hein, 1977), 8:624.

9. Ibid., 1505.

10. See, for example, Laura K. Ray, "A Law Clerk and His Justice: What William Rehnquist Did Not Learn from Robert Jackson," *Indiana Law Review* 29 (1995): 535; Mark Tushnet and Katya Levin, "What Really Happened in *Brown v. Board of Education*," Columbia Law Review 91 (1991): 1867.

11. William H. Rehnquist, "Who Writes Decisions of the Supreme Court?," *U.S. News & World Report,* December 13, 1957, 74–75.

12. Ibid., 75.

13. Edward Lazarus, *Closed Chambers: The First Eyewitness Account of the Epic Struggles Inside the Supreme Court* (New York: Penguin Books, 1998), 274. Lazarus singled out Justices O'Connor and Kennedy as the most susceptible to clerk influence.

14. John Paul Stevens, "A Personal History of the Law Review," *Northwestern University Law Review* 100 (2006): 25, 26.

15. The following account draws heavily on John Ferren's excellent biography of Rutledge. John M. Ferren, *Salt of the Earth, Conscience of the Court: The Story of Justice Wiley Rutledge* (Chapel Hill: University of North Carolina Press, 2004).

16. Ibid., 219.

17. Victor Brudney and Richard F. Wolfson, "Mr. Justice Rutledge—Law Clerks' Reflections," *Indiana Law Review* 25 (1950): 455.

18. Ibid., 460.

19. Ibid.

20. Ibid., 456.

21. Ibid., 460.

22. John M. Ferren, "Wiley Blount Rutledge Jr. and His Law Clerks," in *In Chambers: Stories of Supreme Court Law Clerks and Their Justices,* edited by Todd C. Peppers and Artemus Ward (Charlottesville: University Of Virginia Press, 2012), 237.

23. Ibid.

24. Ibid., 239.

25. Brudney and Wolfson, "Mr. Justice Rutledge," 457.

26. Todd C. Peppers, *Courtiers of the Marble Palace: The Rise and Influence of the Supreme Court Law Clerk* (Charlottesville: University Of Virginia Press, 2006), 130, 266n293.

27. Ibid., 195.

28. "An Interview with Supreme Court Justice John Paul Stevens," *Third Branch* (April 2007), http://www.uscourts.gov/news/TheThirdBranch/07-04-01/An_Interview_with_Supreme_Court_Justice_John_Paul_Stevens.asx.

29. Peppers, *Courtiers,* 195.

30. Ibid.

31. Artemus Ward and David K. Weiden, *Sorcerers' Apprentices: 100 Years of Law Clerks at the Supreme Court* (New York: New York University Press, 2006), 223.

32. Peppers, *Courtiers,* 195.

33. Ibid., 197.

34. John Paul Stevens, "Mr. Justice Rutledge," *Mr. Justice,* edited by Alison Dunham and Philip B. Kurland (Chicago: University of Chicago Press, 1956), 177.

35. Ibid., 181.

36. Ibid., 182.

37. Ferren, *Salt of the Earth,* 10.

38. Stevens, "Mr. Justice Rutledge," 193.

39. Ibid., 178–79.

40. 327 U.S. 1 (1946).

41. 320 U.S. 81 (1943).

42. 323 U.S. 214 (1944); Ferren, *Salt of the Earth,* 249.

43. William D. Popkin, "A Common Law Lawyer on the Supreme Court: The Opinions of Justice Stevens," *Duke Law Journal* (1989): 1087, 1088.

44. 491 U.S. 397, 436–37 (1989) (Stevens, J., dissenting).

45. 515 U.S. 753, 769–70 (1995) (Stevens, J., dissenting).

46. Ibid., 816.

47. Robert Shaplen, "Peacemaker—I," *New Yorker,* April 7, 1962, 58.

48. David L. Stebenne, *Arthur J. Goldberg: New Deal Liberal* (New York: Oxford University Press, 1996), 5.

49. Ibid., 5–6. Subsequent biographical information is drawn from Shaplen, "Peacemaker"; Stebenne, *Arthur J. Goldberg.*

50. Stephen G. Breyer—Biography, http://www.oyez.org/justices/stephen_g_breyer.

51. Ibid.

52. Roy M. Mersky, J. Myron Jacobstein, and Bonnie L. Koneski-White, eds., *Stephen G. Breyer, Hearings and Reports on Successful and Unsuccessful Nominations of Supreme Court Justices by the Senate Judiciary Committee 1916–1994* (William S. Hein, 1996), 19:167.

53. For accounts of the decision, with diverse theories of both Goldberg's and Johnson's motivations, see, for example, Laura Kalman, *Abe Fortas: A Biography* (New Haven, Conn.: Yale University Press, 1990), 241; Lyndon Baines Johnson, *The Vantage Point: Perspectives of the Presidency 1963–69* (New York: Holt, Rinehart, Winston, 1971), 544; Bruce Murphy, *Fortas: The Rise and Ruin of a Supreme Court Justice* (New York: William Morrow, 1988), 163–72; and Peter Edelman's comments in Symposium, "Arthur Goldberg's Legacies to American Labor Relations," *John Marshall Law Review* 32 (1999): 667, 678.

54. Dorothy Goldberg, *A Private View of a Public Life* (New York: Charterhouse, 1975), 134.

55. Stephen Breyer, "Clerking for Justice Goldberg," *Journal of Supreme Court History* (1990): 4.

56. Ibid.

57. Ibid., 4, 5.

58. Ibid., 6.

59. Ibid.

60. "Arthur Goldberg's Legacies," 676–77.

61. Alan M. Dershowitz, "Justice Arthur Goldberg and His Law Clerks," in Peppers and Artemus Ward, *In Chambers,* 295.

62. Ibid., 296.

63. Breyer, "Clerking for Justice Goldberg," 168.

64. Goldberg and Dershowitz later coauthored a law review article calling for the Court to strike down the death penalty. Arthur J. Goldberg and Alan M. Dershowitz, "Declaring the Death Penalty Unconstitutional," *Harvard Law Review* 83 (1970): 1773.

65. 381 U.S. 479 (1965).

66. Mersky, Jacobstein, and Koneski-White, *Breyer, Hearings,* 19:348–49.

67. Ibid., 314.

68. *A Conversation with Justice Stephen Breyer,* September 21, 2003, John F. Kennedy Library, 38.

69. Ibid., 39.

70. Ibid.

71. Jeffrey Toobin, "Breyer's Big Idea," *New Yorker,* October 31, 2005, 36.

72. Stephen J. Friedman, "Arthur J. Goldberg," in *The Justices of the United States Supreme Court 1789–1969: Their Lives and Major Opinions,* edited by Leon Friedman and Fred L. Israel (New York: R. R. Bowker, 1969), 4:2980.

73. Bernard Schwartz, *Super Chief: Earl Warren and His Supreme Court—A Judicial Biography* (New York: New York University Press, 1983), 446.

74. Arthur J. Goldberg, *Equal Justice: The Warren Era of the Supreme Court* (Evanston, Ill.: Northwestern University Press, 1971), 52.

75. 376 U.S. 254 (1964).

76. Ibid., 298 (Goldberg, J., concurring).

77. 378 U.S. 226 (1964).

78. Ibid., 316–17 (Goldberg, J., concurring).

79. 375 U.S. 889 (1963).

80. Arthur J. Goldberg, "Memorandum to the Conference Re: Capital Punishment, October Term, 1963," *South Texas Law Review* 27 (1986): 493.

81. Ibid., 500.

82. "Stripping Away the Fictions: Interview with Mr. Justice Goldberg," *Nova Law Journal* 6 (1982): 553, 558.

83. 531 U.S. 98, 147 (2000) (Breyer, J., dissenting).

84. *United States v. Morrison,* 529 U.S. 598, 660 (2000) (Breyer, J., dissenting).

85. *Nixon v. Shrink Missouri Government PAC,* 528 U.S. 377, 399 (2000) (Breyer, J., concurring).

86. *United States v. Playboy Entertainment Group,* 529 U.S. 803, 841 (2000) (Breyer, J., dissenting).

87. *Parents Involved in Community Schools,* 551 U.S. 701, 831 (2007) (Breyer, J., dissenting).

88. *Ashcroft v. ACLU,* 542 U.S. 656, 676 (2003) (Breyer, J., dissenting).

89. 529 U.S. 839 (Breyer, J., dissenting).

90. *United States v. United Foods Inc.,* 533 U.S. 405, 430 (2002) (Breyer, J., dissenting).

91. *Clinton v. Jones,* 520 U.S. 681, 722 (1997) (Breyer, J., dissenting).

92. *Eldred v. Ashcroft,* 537 U.S. 186, 267–69 (2003) (Breyer, J., dissenting).

93. *Swain v. Alabama,* 380 U.S. 202, 244 (1965) (Goldberg, J., concurring).

94. *Miller-El v. Dretke,* 545 U.S. 231, 272 (2005) (Breyer, J., concurring). The second cite occurs in *Rice v. Collins,* 546 U.S. 333, 344 (2006) (Breyer, J., concurring).

95. 374 U.S. 203 (1963).

96. Ibid., 306 (Goldberg, J., concurring).

97. 545 U.S. 677, 698 (Breyer, J., concurring in the judgment). Two other mentions of Goldberg in the opinion are parenthetical citations to Goldberg's authorship of *Schempp.* Ibid., 700, 702.

98. Ibid., 704, quoting 378 U.S. at 304 (Goldberg, J., concurring).

CONTRIBUTORS

JULIA C. AMBROSE served as a law clerk for Judge J. Harvie Wilkinson III of the U.S. Court of Appeals for the Fourth Circuit and then for Associate Justice Sandra Day O'Connor of the Supreme Court of the United States during October term 1995. She is presently a partner at Brooks, Pierce, McLendon, Humphrey & Leonard, LLP, in Raleigh, North Carolina.

JOHN Q. BARRETT is a Professor of Law at St. John's University and the Elizabeth S. Lenna Fellow at the Robert H. Jackson Center in Jamestown, New York. Barrett is the editor of *That Man: An Insider's Portrait of Franklin Delano Roosevelt* by Robert H. Jackson (2003).

CRAIG M. BRADLEY was a law clerk for Associate Justice William H. Rehnquist of the Supreme Court of the United States during October term 1975. Prior to his death in 2013, Bradley was the Robert A. Lucas Professor of Law at Indiana University Maurer School of Law.

JAMES BRUDNEY served as a law clerk for Judge Gerhard A. Gesell of the U.S. District Court in Washington, D.C., and then for Associate Justice Harry A. Blackmun of the Supreme Court of the United States during October term 1980. He presently teaches at the Fordham University School of Law.

VICTOR BRUDNEY clerked for Associate Justice Wiley Rutledge of the Supreme Court of the United States. Brudney is the Robert B. and Candice J. Hass Professor Emeritus in Corporate Finance Law at Harvard Law School.

LOUIS R. COHEN clerked for Associate Justice John Marshall Harlan of the Supreme Court of the United States. A member of the law firm of Wilmer Hale since 1967, Cohen also served as the Deputy Solicitor General in the U.S. Department of Justice from 1986 to 1988.

BARRY CUSHMAN is the John P. Murphy Foundation Professor of Law at the University of Notre Dame Law School. He is the author of *Rethinking the New Deal Court: The Structure of a Constitutional Revolution* (1998).

CLARE CUSHMAN is the Director of Publications at the Supreme Court Historical Society. She is the editor of *Supreme Court Justices: Illustrated Biographies* (2012) and author of *Courtwatchers: Eyewitness Accounts in Supreme Court History* (2011). Cushman served as editor and contributing writer for *Supreme Court Decisions and Women's Rights* (2000).

FREDERICK T. DAVIS served as a law clerk for Chief Judge Henry J. Friendly of the United States Court of Appeals for the Second Circuit and then for Associate Justice Potter Stewart of the Supreme Court of the United States. He is now counsel with Debevoise and Plimpton.

NORMAN DORSEN clerked for Chief Judge Calvert Magruder of the U.S. Court of Appeals for the First Circuit and for Associate Justice John Marshall Harlan of the Supreme Court of the United States. Since 1961, he has taught at the New York University School of Law. Dorsen also served as President of the American Civil Liberties Union from 1976 to 1991.

EARL C. DUDLEY JR. clerked for retired Associate Justice Stanley Reed of the Supreme Court of the United States and for Chief Justice Earl Warren of the Supreme Court of the United States. Dudley's subsequent career included working as a lawyer in Washington, D.C., and then as a law professor at the University of Virginia School of Law. He is the author of *An Interested Life* (2009).

JOHN D. FASSETT clerked for Associate Justice Stanley Reed of the Supreme Court of the United States. He is the author of *New Deal Justice: The Life of Stanley Reed of Kentucky* (1994).

DANIEL R. FISCHEL clerked for Chief Justice Thomas E. Fairchild of the United States Court of Appeals for the Seventh Circuit and then for Associate Justice Potter Stewart of the Supreme Court of the United States. He is currently the Lee and Brena Freeman Professor Emeritus of Law and Business at the University of Chicago Law School.

MIMI CLARK GRONLUND is the daughter of Associate Justice Tom C. Clark of the Supreme Court of the United States and the author of *Supreme Court Justice Tom C. Clark: A Life of Service* (2010).

THOMAS KAUPER is a former law clerk for Associate Justice Potter Stewart of the Supreme Court of the United States and is now the Henry M. Butzel Professor of Law Emeritus at the University of Michigan Law School.

REBECCA HURLEY served as law clerk to Judge Irving L. Goldberg of the U.S. Court of Appeals for the Fifth Circuit and then for Chief Justice Warren Burger of the Supreme Court of the United States during October term 1983. Hurley is now the Executive Vice President and General Counsel of the LHP Hospital Group.

AMANDA COHEN LEITER clerked for Judge Nancy Gertner of the U.S. District Court for the District of Massachusetts, for Judge David Tatel of the U.S. Court of Appeals for the District of Columbia Circuit, and for Associate Justice John Paul Stevens of the Supreme Court of the United States. She currently is a member of the faculty of American University Washington College of Law.

RENÉE LETTOW LERNER served as a law clerk for Judge Stephen F. Williams of the U.S. Court of Appeals for the District of Columbia Circuit and then for Associate Justice Anthony Kennedy of the Supreme Court of the United States during October term 1996. She is currently Professor of Law at the George Washington University Law School.

CHARLES F. LETTOW clerked for Judge Ben C. Duniway of the U.S. Court of Appeals for the Ninth Circuit and then for Chief Justice Warren Burger of the Supreme Court of the United States during October term 1969. He practiced with Cleary Gottlieb for over thirty years and presently sits on the U.S. Court of Federal Claims.

NANCY S. MARDER clerked for Associate Justice John Paul Stevens of the Supreme Court of the United States during October terms 1990 and 1991. She is a law professor and the Director of the John Paul Stevens Jury Center at the Chicago-Kent College of Law.

ABNER J. MIKVA was a law clerk to Associate Justice Sherman Minton of the Supreme Court of the United States. Mikva subsequently served in the U.S. House of Representatives, on the District of Columbia Circuit Court of Appeals, as a law professor at Northwestern University Law School and Chicago Law School, and as White House Counsel to President Bill Clinton. In November 2014, he was awarded the Presidential Medal of Freedom by President Barack Obama.

MARY L. MIKVA clerked for Judge Prentice Marshall of the U.S. District Court for the Northern District of Illinois and then for Associate Justice William J. Brennan Jr. of the Supreme Court of the United States. She currently serves as a judge of the Circuit Court of Cook County, Chancery Division (Chicago).

MARTHA MINOW served as a law clerk for Judge David Bazelon of the U.S. Court of Appeals for the District of Columbia Circuit and then for Associate Justice Thurgood Marshall of the Supreme Court of the United States. Minow presently holds the position of Dean of the Harvard Law School.

NEWTON MINOW clerked for Chief Justice Fred Vinson of the Supreme Court of the United States. The former Head of the Federal Communications Commission, Minow is now Senior Counsel with the law firm of Sidley Austin.

ALAN R. NOVAK is a former law clerk for Associate Justice Potter Stewart of the Supreme Court of the United States. Since his clerkship, Novak has primarily worked in the fields of investment banking and real estate development.

CHAD OLDFATHER served as a law clerk to Judge Jane R. Roth of the U.S. Court of Appeals for the Third Circuit and worked at the law firm of Faegre & Benson before returning to the legal academy. He is currently a law professor at Marquette University Law School, where his research focuses on judging and the judicial process.

DAVID O'NEIL was a law clerk for Judge Robert D. Sack of the U.S. Court of Appeals for the Second Circuit and for Associate Justice Ruth Bader Ginsburg of the Supreme Court of the United States. A longtime employee of the U.S. Department of Justice, O'Neil has worked in the Office of the Solicitor General and served as the Acting Head of the Department of Justice's Criminal Division.

ROBERT M. O'NEIL clerked for Associate Justice William J. Brennan Jr. of the Supreme Court of the United States during October term 1962. The former Director of the Thomas Jefferson Center for the Protection of Free Expression as well as the former President of the University of Virginia, he currently holds the position of Professor of Law Emeritus at the University of Virginia School of Law.

TODD C. PEPPERS holds the Henry H. & Trudye H. Fowler Chair of Public Affairs at Roanoke College, and he is also a Visiting Professor of Law at the Washington and Lee University School of Law. He is the author of *Courtiers of the Marble Palace: The Rise and Influence of the Supreme Court Law Clerk* (2005) and the coeditor (with Artemus Ward) of *In Chambers: Stories of Supreme Court Law Clerks and Their Justices* (2012).

CARTER G. PHILLIPS clerked for Judge Robert Sprecher of the U.S. Court of Appeals for the Seventh Circuit and then for Chief Justice Warren Burger of the Supreme Court of the United States. Phillips practices with the law firm of Sidley Austin, and as a member of that firm he has argued seventy cases before the Supreme Court of the United States.

JESSICA PHILLIPS was a law clerk for Judge Joel Flaum of the U.S. Court of Appeals for the Seventh Circuit and for Associate Justice Samuel Alito of the Supreme Court of the United States during October term 2007. She is presently an associate at the law firm of Latham & Watkins, LLP.

MONROE E. PRICE clerked for Associate Justice Potter Stewart of the Supreme Court of the United States during October term 1964. A former Dean of the Benjamin N. Cardozo School of Law, he currently serves as the Director of the Center for Global Communication Studies at the Annenberg School for Communication at the University of Pennsylvania.

LAURA KRUGMAN RAY is a Professor of Law at Widener University Law School. A former law clerk to Associate Justice Ellen Peters of the Connecticut Supreme Court, Ray is the author of "The Legacy of a Supreme Court Clerkship: Stephen Breyer and Arthur Goldberg," *Penn State Law Review* 115, no. 1 (2010), and "Clerk and Justice: The Ties That Bind John Paul Stevens and Wiley B. Rutledge," *Connecticut Law Review* 41, no. 1 (2008).

KERMIT ROOSEVELT III clerked for Judge Stephen F. Williams of the U.S. Court of Appeals for the District of Columbia Circuit and then Associate Justice David Souter of the Supreme Court of the United States during October term 1999 before joining the law faculty at the University of Pennsylvania. He is the author of *The Myth of Judicial Activism: Making Sense of Supreme Court Decisions* (2006) and two novels, *In the Shadow of the Law* (2005) and *Allegiance* (2015).

THOMAS D. ROWE JR. served as a law clerk for Associate Justice Potter Stewart of the Supreme Court of the United States during October term 1970. Rowe is now the Elvin R. Latty Professor Emeritus of Law at Duke Law School.

DAVID M. SCHULTE is a former law clerk for Associate Justice Potter Stewart of the Supreme Court of the United States. He is the founder of the investment firm Chilmark Partners.

ARTHUR R. SEDER JR. clerked for Chief Justice Fred Vinson of the Supreme Court of the United States during October term 1948. Seder subsequently worked as an attorney for the American Natural Gas Company in Detroit, before becoming the company's president.

KRISTEN SILVERBERG clerked for Judge David Sentelle of the U.S. Court of Appeals for the District of Columbia Circuit and then for Associate Justice Clarence Thomas of the Supreme Court of the United States during October term 1999. Silverberg presently holds the position of General Counsel of the Institute of International Finance. She previously served as an Assistant Secretary of State and also as the U.S. Ambassador to the European Union.

JOHN PAUL STEVENS was a law clerk for Associate Justice Wiley Rutledge of the Supreme Court of the United States during October term 1947. Stevens is one of only six Supreme Court law clerks to subsequently sit on the Supreme Court, serving as an Associate Justice from 1975 to 2010. He is the author of *Five Chiefs: A Supreme Court Memoir* (2011).

BRIDGET TAINER-PARKINS clerked for Judge James C. Turk of the U.S. District Court for the Western District of Virginia before entering private practice. She is currently an adjunct professor at Roanoke College.

RAYMOND S. TROUBH clerked for Associate Justice Harold Burton of the Supreme Court of the United States. A New York City financial services consultant, Troubh has also served as a Governor of the American Stock Exchange.

STEVEN M. UMIN clerked for Chief Justice Roger Traynor of the California Supreme Court and then Associate Justice Potter Stewart of the Supreme Court of the United States during October term 1965. He practiced law with the firm of Williams & Connolly from 1966 to 2004.

J. HARVIE WILKINSON III was a law clerk for Associate Justice Lewis F. Powell Jr. of the Supreme Court of the United States during October terms 1971 and 1972, an experience that he wrote about in *Serving Justice: A Supreme Court Clerk's View* (1974). Wilkinson presently sits on the U.S. Court of Appeals for the Fourth Circuit.

PORTER WILKINSON served as a law clerk for Judge Brett M. Kavanaugh of the U.S. Court of Appeals for the District of Columbia Circuit and then for Chief Justice John G. Roberts Jr. of the Supreme Court of the United States during October term 2008. A former associate at the law firm of Gibson, Dunn & Crutcher, LLP, she is presently the Chief of Staff to the Regents at the Smithsonian Institution.

INDEX

Note: The justices for whom the law clerks worked are indicated in parentheses after each clerk's name—for example, Acheson, Dean (Brandeis). Photographs in the unfolioed illustration gallery are indexed according to sequence (e.g., *gallery page 1*).